Reframing Health Behavior Change With Behavioral Economics

Reframing Health Behavior Change With Behavioral Economics

Edited by

Warren K. Bickel
University of Vermont

Rudy E. Vuchinich
Auburn University

 LAWRENCE ERLBAUM ASSOCIATES, PUBLISHERS
2000   Mahwah, New Jersey   London

Lawrence Erlbaum Associates, Inc., Publishers
10 Industrial Avenue
Mahwah, NJ 07430

Cover design by Kathryn Houghtaling Lacey

Library of Congress Cataloging-in-Publication Data

    Reframing health behavior change with behavioral
economics / edited by Warren K. Bickel, Rudy E. Vuchinich
        p. cm.
    Includes bibliographical references and index.
    ISBN 0-8058-2733-1 (cloth : alk. paper)
    1. Health behavior—Economic aspects. 2. Medicine and
psychology. I. Bickel, Warren K. II. Vuchinich, Rudy, E.
(Rudy Eugene), 1949-
    RA776.9 .R433   1999
    338.4'33621—dc21   99-015327
                                            CIP

Books published by Lawrence Erlbaum Associates are printed
on acid-free paper, and their bindings are chosen for strength
and durability.

Printed in the United States of America
10 9 8 7 6 5 4 3 2 1

To Rebecca, Keefer, and Corena, my raison d'être,
for making every day better and every experience richer.

—Warren K. Bickel

Contents

Foreword

My first exposure to behavioral economic theory occurred when I was writing on the topic of relapse prevention in the early 1980s. At that time, I was consulting with Professor Lee Beach, a colleague in my department whose expertise is in the area of decision-making research and theory. Together, we were trying to understand if the process of relapse in people who were trying to give up a bad habit such as smoking could be considered a rational or irrational decision or choice. It appeared to us that the process of relapse often involved a series of choices or "minidecisions" that successively increased the probability that an individual eventually would experience a lapse, despite the original commitment to abstinence. Together, we coined the term *apparently irrelevant decisions* to describe the rationalizations that many people use to "explain" a decision that otherwise appeared to increase the risk of relapse. As an example, one recent ex-smoker told his spouse that he was going out for a long walk to get some exercise, and then walked across town to a store that sold his favorite brand of cigarettes at discount rates; he ended up buying a pack and smoking several cigarettes on his way back home. Another client of mine who had made a commitment to stop drinking decided after 3 months of abstinence that it was now OK for him to purchase a bottle of sherry to keep in his home, "just in case guests drop by for a visit." He ended up drinking the bottle himself several days later after an argument with his wife. In both cases, the apparently irrelevant decision (to take a long walk, or to purchase the sherry for guests) appeared to us to be rationalized rather than irrational in content. However, we were still puzzled by the sudden shift in goals as these individuals suddenly "changed their minds" and succumbed to temptation when faced with the immediate temptation of cigarettes or alcohol, despite their long-term prior commitment to abstinence.

On one day during this period, I came to my office to find a reprint of a journal article Lee Beach had left for me to read. On the cover page, he had written in bold red ink this message: "The truth is in Ainslie!" The article, written by George Ainslie, was entitled "Specious reward: A behavioral theory of impulsiveness and impulse control" (published in 1975 in the *Psychological Bulletin*). This was, indeed, a breakthrough in our understanding of the sudden shifts in intentions many individuals seemed to experience in the relapse process, from a long-term commitment to abstinence to the short-term "choice" of resuming drug use. Here, at last, was a paradigm that could help us understand the difference between *self-control* (defined as the choice of a more delayed but highly valued outcome, such as maintaining abstinence and experiencing improved health and well-being) and *impulsiveness* (choosing a more immediate but less valued outcome, such as taking that first cigarette or drink). As stated by Logue (chap. 7, this volume), "For example, if someone chooses to smoke, that person is choosing the immediate positive stimuli associated with smoking instead of a long, healthy life. Therefore, smoking can be defined as impulsiveness and not smoking can be defined as self-control." (p. 168)

The material in this book provides a wealth of information of great value to professionals working in the area of health psychology and behavioral medicine, both at the level of individual behavior change and at the policy-making level. A wide variety of health behaviors are covered by various authors, including smoking, excessive drinking and eating, illicit drug use, and compulsive gambling. Many new theoretical models and constructs are introduced as well, reflecting the considerable growth of the behavioral economic literature since my first exposure to this approach. This book will have a wide appeal to those who are actively involved in working with those who are attempting to make positive health and lifestyle changes, including therapists, researchers, educators, and policymakers. As is evident in the chapters that follow, the introduction of behavioral economics into behavioral psychology has been a very productive merger of disciplines. The implications for the prevention and treatment of health problems are likely to have a profound influence on this field.

To further whet your appetite for consuming the rich diet of ideas presented in this volume, I would like to provide a sampling of some of the ideas that stimulated my thinking as I read through the various chapters. My choice of what to highlight in this brief preview is largely dictated by my own interests as a therapist, researcher, and clinical theoretician who specializes in addictive behavior problems. My background and theoretical orientation is primarily associated with social learning theory and its application to cognitive–behavioral therapy (e.g., relapse prevention) and to a broader, public-health approach to changing addictive behavior (harm reduction). My comments to follow are selectively biased by my theoretical orientation and are geared to those readers who may be new to behavioral economics or who are otherwise reluctant to embrace a theory of choice based largely on economic theory and often based on research studies with animals. My goal is to show how bridges can be forged between the behavioral economic approach and more traditional approaches to health behavior for those who reside on the other side of the Skinnerian tracks.

I learned from reading Madden's overview of behavioral economics (chap. 1, this volume) that the process of suddenly "changing one's mind" (e.g., from a prior commitment to abstinence to an initial smoking episode) can be defined as a *preference reversal*. A basic principle of behavioral economics that is referred to in almost every chapter is that delayed consequences (reinforcers, punishers) are less effective in maintaining behavior than are consequences that are delivered immediately after the specified behavioral response. The value of a delayed outcome or reinforcer is "discounted" (i.e., rendered less valuable as a commodity) as a function of the delay in its delivery. In short, the longer the delay of a future desired outcome (e.g., prolonged life expectancy for remaining abstinent), the more the outcome is discounted, or less preferred. Thus, when outcomes are more immediate, the "present value" of the immediately available reinforcer often outweighs the value of the delayed, future outcome. When this is the case, a preference reversal is highly likely. The following example provided by Madden clearly illustrates this process:

> The obese patient may indicate a preference for dieting and commit to better eating habits and attendance at overeaters anonymous meetings. Leaving the office, however, puts the dieter in closer temporal proximity to high-fat foods. If a box of double-chocolate doughnuts greets the obese patient when he or she returns to the office ... , preference for the healthy diet reverses as the high-fat doughnut is consumed. (p. 19)

Among the many key concepts in behavioral economic theory reviewed by Hursh (chap. 2), I found his analysis of "demand curve elasticity" to be particularly useful. The relationship between the cost of a given reinforcer (the money or effort required to obtain it) and consumption of that reinforcer is termed a demand curve. As the cost of a commodity (reinforcer) increases, consumption usually decreases, particularly when the demand is elastic (i.e., sensitive to price changes). For example, if the price of peas continues to increase, proportionally fewer people will buy and consume peas, turning to other vegetable substitutes that are less expensive (elastic demand for peas). On the other hand, if the commodity is highly desired and other alternatives are scarce, the demand is more likely to be inelastic (i.e., less sensitive to price changes). Hursh gives the example of gasoline consumption during the price increases in the 1970s—even though gas prices increased threefold during that period, gas consumption decreased by only 10% (inelastic demand). Applying this concept to the problem of drug abuse, Hursh notes: "In the context of drug abuse therapy, an alternative drug reinforcer such as methadone may be used as a medical intervention designed to reduce demand or increase elasticity of demand for the drug of abuse" (p. 41). Extending this notion, Hursh compares the relative attractiveness of heroin and methadone for the opiate addict. He concludes that although methadone has many advantages over heroin (e.g., reduced criminal liability; less chance of HIV injection by needle-sharing, because methadone can be administered orally; etc.), it is an "imperfect substitute" for heroin. Although methadone is effective in preventing opiate withdrawal, it is a weak substitute for the immediately reinforcing euphoria associated with heroin use. This analysis helps in our understanding of why many methadone users still occasionally purchase heroin for its unique euphorogenic properties. The same analysis can be used to show why many smokers who attempt to quit using nicotine replacement therapies (e.g., nicotine gum) often "cheat" on their program by smoking cigarettes even while trying to stick to the nicotine gum. In short, they are looking for a bigger bang for their buck.

The material presented by Carroll and Campbell (chap. 3, this volume) illustrates the important role that animal research plays in understanding behaviors such as acquisition of drug-taking behavior and the reinforcing properties of various substances. Here, I found their analysis of the relapse process based on animal studies particularly illuminating. They describe showing that the reinstatement of previously extinguished drug self-administration provides a parallel to the relapse process shown by human drug users. Animals are first trained to self-administer a drug such as cocaine by a bar-pressing response. After being trained to a criterion level, the extinction phase begins, in which bar-pressing is no longer reinforced by cocaine—gradually the animal slows down and eventually gives up on responding in the absence of any reinforcing consequences. Later, however, if the animal is administered a single "priming dose" of the target drug, bar-pressing for additional injections of the drug is rapidly reinstated. Although this does appear to provide an analogue of human drug relapse, the ecological validity of this model suffers from the fact that the priming dose that triggers the ensuing relapse behavior is externally administered by the experimenter in the form of an imposed drug injection, rather than sought out on a "voluntary" basis as is the usual case with human drug relapse episodes. The chapter also features a review of studies showing the impact of substituting nondrug reinforcers (such as access to food) for drug self-administration in animals.

The economic analysis of substance use and abuse is the primary subject discussed by Chaloupka and Pacula (chap. 4, this volume). Here, I found support for the hypothesis that drug-taking behavior can be considered a rational behavior. As stated by the authors,

> Indeed, in the past, many researchers have viewed addictive consumption as an irrational behaviors and therefore presumed it fell outside the realm of the standard economic analysis....The findings [reviewed in this chapter] clearly demonstrate that even in the case of addictive commodities, the law of demand still applies. (p. 90)

They provide ample empirical evidence showing that the "law of demand" (which implies that individuals will consume less of a good as its price rises) does apply to the consumption of tobacco, alcohol, and illicit drugs. Two frameworks for modeling addictive behaviors are described in behavioral economic terms: myopic models and rational models. In contrast to myopic models, which assume that drug users behave shortsightedly and ignore future consequences associated with the current drug use level, the rational addiction model presumes that the individual's desire for a drug does not necessarily change over time, but the demand for that drug may change due to the addictive nature of the drug (e.g., influence of increased drug tolerance over time). The authors emphasize that

> Rationality, in these models, implies that the future consequences of past and current consumption are considered when making current consumption choices. This contrasts with the myopic models that assume that the future implications of addictive consumption are ignored when making current consumption decisions. (p. 92)

One of the important clinical applications of the rational addiction model is that it is congruent with treatment approaches that foster an image of the drug user as an "informed consumer," and that interventions that focus on the immediate and delayed consequences of either drug use or drug abstinence can be a helpful aid in the decision-making process (e.g., use of a decision matrix in which clients are asked to anticipate both the positive and negative outcomes for both the short-term and long-term futures for using or not using drugs).

Another topic that has captured the attention of cognitive–behavioral researchers is the role of outcome expectancies for alcohol or other drug use. Studies have shown that youth who harbor unrealistic positive outcome expectancies about drinking ("more is better" or seeing alcohol as a "magic elixir" with no negative costs involved) appear to be at greatest risk of alcohol abuse and dependency. Although not described in this book, the topic of outcome expectancies seems a good match for behavioral economists interested in determinants of choice behavior.

In chapter 5, I learned a great deal about the concept of economic substitutability, or the extent to which other commodities are available for alternatives for the one whose price is increased, and that substitutable reinforcers are those that are functionally similar. A case in point is the extent to which social support or interpersonal influence can serve as a substitute reinforcement for addictive behaviors such as smoking. Complementary reinforcers, on the other hand, are generally used jointly and are consumed in close proportion to each other (e.g., bagels and cream cheese, smoking and drinking). Green and Fisher (chap. 5, this volume) draw an important distinction between social support as a potential commodity or as a resource. Viewing social support as a reinforcer in its own right suggests that it may offer a substitute to unhealthy personal behavior patterns, or as stated by the authors, "'Having more to live for' in satisfying social relationships may provide incentives for quitting smoking, managing diabetes, or other kinds of positive behavior changes to which social support has been linked" (p. 129). In contrast, the resource model sees social support as facilitating behavior change through the skills and assistance it provides (e.g., recruiting friends and others' cooperation in not smoking in the presence of the recent ex-smoker). If the commodity model applies, then the influence of social support would be limited to the time when social support is available to facilitate successful quitting.

The resource model, on the other hand, predicts that socially facilitated changes in skills should persist, once learned, and continue to promote abstinence from smoking. This distinction is a useful one in that it helps us understand how social support can either be protective against relapse (as a substitute for smoking) or actually may increase relapse risk (if social contact serves as a complementary reinforcer, going out to a restaurant or to a bar may be associated with increased risk of a smoking relapse).

Howard Rachlin (chap. 6, this volume) takes the position that social support and its lack are at the center of the addiction process. The main point of his relative addiction theory is that "addicts are addicts *because* they are lonely" (p. 145). A major assumption of this approach is that obtaining social support by means of social activity is a learned skill. Rachlin points to research that shows that decreases in social support are often linked with increases in addiction, and that programs to treat addiction problems often work better when social support is available (e.g., continued access to 12-step recovery groups facilitates treatment outcome). Rachlin concludes that drugs supercede social support, unless the substance being consumed is more available through contact with fellow users: "The opium addict does not go to the opium den for the social support (if any) to be found there" (p. 156). One apparent contradiction to this proposition can be observed among groups of smokers in contemporary antismoking American society. At a recent stopover at the Denver airport, I observed the behavior of a large group of smokers in the smoking room located in one of the main (otherwise smoke-free) terminals. These smokers, usually ostracized by their nonsmoking counterparts, were a jolly lot, everyone smoking to the max, lighting each others' cigarettes and mutually lamenting their plight as minority citizens. They appeared to prove the old adage that misery loves company.

Logue's (chap. 7, this volume) discussion of self-control and health behaviors provides a rich resource of material for those interested in modifying high-risk health behaviors. In contrast to vague constructs such as "will power," Logue defines *self-control* as an intertemporal choice of a more delayed (but ultimately more valued) outcome over a less delayed (but less valued) outcome. Logue correctly points out that "Although research on self-control can help us to understand how and why humans do and do not show self-control, this research does not by itself tell us when humans *should* show self-control" (p. 170). Congruent with a harm-reduction, pragmatic perspective, she concludes that "it is more useful to try to understand self-control and impulsiveness with regard to their causes and consequences than to label them as inherently good and bad behaviors." Among the strategies described to enhance self-control, Logue states that people may be less impulsive (i.e., show greater self-control) if their attention is directed in such a way that they are distracted and do not think about the tempting situation. Logue cites the work of social learning theorists, such as Walter Mischel, who have developed cognitive imagery strategies to help individuals resist the lure of immediate gratification (e.g., training people to engage in "cool thoughts" about outcomes). Similar strategies have been advocated by members of Alcoholics Anonymous, who urge members on the verge of relapse to "think through the drink"—to imagine taking the drink and the consequences it may have on the self, family, and community to the point that the individual foresees the long-term negative consequences and decides not to take the first drink. An inventor friend of mine suggested manufacturing a "will power box" as yet another self-control device: The box can be used to contain materials (e.g., addictive substances) in a locked foolproof container, but can only be opened at preset time delays (e.g., set to open only on Saturday nights). But would the owner have the self-control to set the lock far enough ahead to make a difference?

In Chapter 8, Simpson and Vuchinich provide a model for why people often behave paradoxically: "They do things they later wish they had not done, and they fail to do things they later wish they had" (p. 193) As the authors point out, behaviors with negative health consequences often are tied to the tangible rewards of the "temporally circumscribed present" and its alternative reinforcers (e.g., "I don't want to exercise and miss that TV program"). It follows that behavior patterns that promote long-term health frequently lose the competition with more immediately rewarding choice options. As a result, health promotion activities targeted toward reducing behaviors with negative health consequences such as substance abuse should attempt to minimize the cost of treatment or other nondrug activities. As the authors correctly point out, "Interventions that focus relatively less attention on increasing 'health' and relatively more attention toward increasing access to the immediately valuable, tangible activities and rewards to which optimal health allows access potentially will provide the most powerful and lasting interventions" (p. 211). To take a case in point, I recently attended an alcohol and drug prevention program for Native American adolescents. One very attractive program for these youth was the potential participation in a special "Canoe Family" programming, in which native elders taught adolescents how to construct a traditional wooden canoe that would hold groups of people as they paddled from tribe to tribe in the waters of Puget Sound. To gain entry into this and other highly desirable "alternative activity" programs, prospective participants only had to show up in a "clean and sober" state. Access to these rewarded activities was denied to those who were under the influence at the time. This program appears to be very successful in its recruitment of adolescents who are alcohol and drug-free and may represent a low-cost alternative to traditional drug treatment programs (high cost, high threshold).

Tucker and Davison (chap. 9, this volume) explore the importance of time constraints in health care utilization. The authors point to the fact that "When monetary costs to consumers are minimal or nonexistent, time costs function to reduce and regulate demand" (p. 220). As research reviewed in this chapter clearly documents, delays in access to health care can have serious health consequences. Substance abuse is a critical example, in that less than 25% of persons with substance abuse problems seek help or treatment (this percentage also holds for those with mental health problems). Results from a major literature review show that an inverse relation exists between delay of receiving a medical appointment and the subsequent probability of keeping the appointment: The longer the wait, the greater chance of drop out. Travel time to reach the help provider, along with office waiting time, are also critical to successful health care access. Adopting a consumer orientation to prospective health care seekers may help reduce attrition and drop-out rates. Examples here would include establishing low-threshold treatment-on-demand programs (a goal now embraced by the providers of substance abuse services in San Francisco), offering consumers samples of different treatment options from which to choose ("treatment sampling"), and other consumer-friendly alternatives.

The topic of tobacco and the behavioral economics of smoking are covered in chapter 10 by Perkins, Hickcox, and Grobe. These authors provide a unique and comprehensive interpretation of factors that promote both smoking and interventions designed for smoking cessation, each from a behavioral economic perspective. All smoking intervention programs 'can be seen as increasing the response cost of smoking or reducing the cost of abstaining from smoking" (p. 265). The relation between the "unit price of tobacco" and smoking is described; unit price reflects the behavioral, social, and economic costs of smoking, often expressed as a cost–benefit ratio for acquiring a given amount of the reinforcer. Research is reviewed showing that when price is low, tobacco consumption changes very little after an increase in unit price (inelastic demand). When prices increase to a high level, however, further increases in unit price result in rapid decreases in smoking. The recent settlement made by state attorneys general with tobacco companies already has produced a marked increase in the price of cigarettes, hopefully leading to a decrease in smoking among adolescents and young adults. Smoking, the most lethal bad habit in terms of health consequences (upwards of 400,000 tobacco-related deaths per year in the United States), has perhaps the lowest unit price of any other drug, both licit and illicit. As noted by the authors, nicotine replacement therapy (e.g., gums, patches, sprays) costs at least $3 per day, more than the cost of a pack of cigarettes. Clearly, less expensive alternatives are needed to compete with the allure of a single cigarette.

After reading the chapter on the behavioral economics of obesity by Epstein and Saelens (chap. 11, this volume), I was reminded of the recent changes in per capita alcohol consumption and the prevalence of smoking in American society: Both have decreased considerably over the past several decades. Rates of obesity, on the other hand, have increased dramatically even in the past 10 years. As the authors state, "Behavioral economics provides a comprehensive methodological and conceptual approach to studying choices of what to eat, when to eat, and how much to eat, as well as whether to be active, what type of activity, at what intensity, and for what duration" (p. 293). A tall order, indeed, but the research reviewed in this chapter provides a solid base for a behavioral economic approach. I found particularly noteworthy the material on preferences for high-calorie foods and sedentary behaviors compared to exercise choices among obese children. Results show, for example, that reinforcing these children to decrease sedentary behaviors (TV and video watching) is associated with increased physical activity. In a novel twist on this approach, the authors report that access to highly preferred sedentary activities can serve as an effective reinforcer for physical exercise. These findings show how these two behaviors can be considered an interactive reinforcement process. Prevention of obesity is a critical and challenging task for health providers. The material in this chapter provides important markers to guide us on this path.

Besides the problem of obesity, the other behavioral problem that also seems to be on the rise is gambling. This is clearly documented by Ghezzi, Lyons, and Dixon (chap. 12, this volume) in their comprehensive socioeconomic perspective on gambling rates and problems in the United States. In many ways, gambling is a behavior that is shared across many addictive behaviors. Every time a smoker lights up, he or she is placing a bet that this cigarette will not be the one that triggers lung cancer. A recent cartoon illustrates the gambling state of mind. In the first panel, a middle-aged man is being confronted by his physician, who tells his patient that the chances he will develop a terminal illness as a result of his long-term smoking habit are one in two. "It won't happen to me," the smoker replies. In the second panel, the same man is shown at a lottery sales desk. "The odds of winning the lottery are about 1 in 500 million," the clerk tells him. "This could be my lucky day!" he replies, eagerly buying his ticket. The material in this chapter shows how various factors can enhance gambling problems, such as the "illusion of control" provided by video poker games. Interventions for problem gamblers are still in the early developmental stage; this chapter should be "must reading" for therapists working with these clients.

The title of the final chapter by Bickel and Marsch (chap. 13, this volume) captures the essence of the topic of this book: the tyranny of small decisions. In this fascinating essay, the authors provide a global account of how people so often engage in a behavior that is desirable in the present moment, even if they know it is harmful in the long run. Each small decision can pave the way to some big problems down the road. We all have known this since we read of the first big temptation that occurred in the Garden of Eden: How was Adam to know that the Apple was a forbidden fruit and that consumption would be followed by the Big Fall? In this chapter, we are provided with an historical overview of how many cultural and environmental factors have contributed to a shortening of our "temporal horizon" since we have evolved from a hunter-gatherer society to one based on longer-term goals (agricultural societies), and on to the present day where our sense of time has been dramatically shortened by the advent of television, computers, and the doctrine of the "instant fix." Data are presented showing that many health problems, including addictive behaviors, depression and suicide, obesity and bulimia, and crime rates have increased in tandem with this cultural evolution of a short-sighted, myopic focus on immediate gratification. The heroin addict who longs for the next fix is unable to accept the way things are in the present moment. Craving for drug reinforcers locks the addict into a fixation on the immediate future, and long-term costs often are discounted. Data reviewed in this chapter support the hypothesis that alcohol-dependent individuals show a significantly shorter awareness of the future, or "future time perspective." Intervention and treatment programs need to integrate time perspective into their programs, because individual differences in future time perspective may be a factor that affects treatment outcome. Promising new techniques, such as mindfulness meditation, may be able to shift future time perspectives back into the present moment. All in all, a provocative final chapter—one to look foreword to as a reward for reading through this important and exciting book.

I take this opportunity to thank the authors for educating me on the basics of behavioral economics and how it applies to the understanding of health behaviors. It is truly a tour de force, and I feel honored to be asked to provide this Foreword by the editors, Warren Bickel and Rudy Vuchinich. For readers who are just beginning to read this "baker's dozen" of chapters (adding one more to the dozen always makes good economic sense), bon Appétite!

—G. Alan Marlatt,
University of Washington

REFERENCES

Ainslie, G. (1975). Special reward: A behavioral theory of impulsiveness and control. *Psychology Bulletin, 82,* 463–496.

Preface

Our society is preoccupied with health. Health care is the biggest industry in the United States (Kaplan, Sallis, & Patterson, 1993), and the media routinely inundate us with messages about what is good and bad for our health and the latest medical treatments for a variety of health problems. This concern with health is amply justified, because some modicum of physical health is a necessary precondition for virtually everything that we do.

What compromises our health has changed dramatically over the last 100 years. Infectious diseases were the primary threats to health at the beginning of the 20th century. Since that time, technological innovations in vaccinations, medications, sewage disposal, water treatment, and food preservation have reduced significantly mortality and morbidity that is due to infectious disease. With the exception of AIDS, the main threats to health in the contemporary United States are chronic diseases, such as cardiopulmonary disease, cancer, diabetes, and stroke. These health problems typically develop slowly over long periods of time, are persistent, and have important relations with lifestyle and individuals' behavior. That is, these chronic diseases are at least partly attributable to substance abuse (especially cigarettes and alcohol), poor diet, and lack of exercise. As succinctly stated by Knowles (1977), "Over 90 percent of us are born healthy and suffer premature death and disability only as a result of personal misbehavior and environmental conditions" (p. 1104). Diseases attributable in part to health behavior cause inestimable human suffering and staggering economic costs. Manning, Keeler, Newhouse, Sloss, and Wasserman, (1991) have estimated that each pack of cigarettes smoked, each alcoholic drink consumed, and each mile not traveled on foot costs our society 15 cents, 22 cents, and 24 cents, respectively, for a total annual bill of hundreds of billions of dollars.

Health behavior obviously deserves the extensive attention it has received from the relevant scientific disciplines. Psychological science has played a major role in studying health behavior, and health psychology is a thriving arena of applications. It therefore is fair to ask what yet another edited volume could possibly add to this already vast literature. We believe behavioral economics offers a perspective for studying and understanding health behavior that has little precedent in the existing literature and that research guided by behavioral economics will make important positive contributions to the field. That is why the word "reframing" appears in the title of the book.

The orienting assumptions and analytic concepts of behavioral economics depart significantly in important ways from the contemporary psychological "normal science" of health behavior. That normal science paradigm ascended during the "cognitive revolution" in psychology during the 1960s and 1970s. Those who fomented that revolution believed that the concepts offered by then-prominent frameworks (e.g., respondent and instrumental conditioning) were too limited to extend from the laboratory to understand complex human behavior. It was clear that the environmental events (i.e., stimuli and reinforcers) present when a particular behavior occurred were insufficient to explain why the behavior occurred; some context more general than the immediate environment alone was needed. The more general context specified by the cognitive revolution was the various internal psychological mechanisms and processes that can mediate between past and present environmental events and present behavior. Mainstream psychological science thus proceeded to articulate how the internal workings of the now-opened "black box" relate to health behavior.

The behavioral scientists who laid the foundation for behavioral economics also recognized both the problems with concepts limited to the immediate environment alone and the need for a more general context. However, the context they specified was the manner in which temporally extended patterns of behavior—of which present behavior is a part—entrain with temporally extended patterns of commodity availability. Those scientists thus proceeded to articulate how the "black box," as a whole, moves about in its constrained world. The conceptual and empirical issues raised by this type of psychological analysis dovetailed with issues faced by microeconomics, and behavioral economics was born.

We (the editors) met at a convention in 1988 and immediately realized that both of us perceived potentially important implications of extending behavioral economics, which was then about a decade old, to studying substance abuse and other health behaviors. While pursuing our individual career trajectories after that meeting, we occasionally talked over the phone or got together at other conventions. The idea for this book was hatched at one of those conventions in 1995. We have learned that behavioral economics provides a forum for interactions between individuals who too often have little to say to each other. One of us is an experimental psychologist (Bickel) and the other is a clinical psychologist (Vuchinich). The chapter authors are experimental psychologists, clinical psychologists, and economists. Thus, the book represents a confluence of extensions from basic behavioral science, clinical psychology, and economic theory to the applied arena of health behavior. To date, the behavioral economic literature has consisted mostly of primary journal articles and a few book chapters. This book is in part an effort to bring this literature to the attention of a broader audience. Thus, we hope the book will be of interest to a broad range of students and professionals concerned with health behavior, including researchers, clinicians, and policymakers. This book is our only collaborative project, but we have shared the intellectual excitement of exploring the implications of some new ideas for understanding some old problems. We hope that at least some of that excitement is conveyed in this book, and, if so, that it is contagious. Most of all, we hope that the material contained in this book will lead to improved clinical interventions and public policies that will alleviate some of the suffering that results from poor health behavior.

—*Rudy E. Vuchinich*
Warren K. Bickel

REFERENCES

Kaplan, R. M., Sallis, J. F., Jr., & Patterson, T. L. (1993). *Health and human behavior.* New York: McGraw-Hill.
Knowles, J. H. (1977). Editorial. *Science, 198*, 1104.
Manning, W. G., Keeler, E. B., Newhouse, J. P., Sloss, E. M., & Wasserman, J. (1991). *The costs of poor health habits.* Cambridge, MA: Harvard University Press.

BEHAVIORAL ECONOMIC CONCEPTS AND METHODS

CHAPTER ONE

A Behavioral Economics Primer

Gregory J. Madden
University of Wisconsin—Eau Claire

This chapter is designed to serve as an introduction to the major concepts, measures, and methods of behavioral economics. As such, the target audience is composed of readers who are relatively unfamiliar with behavioral economics. For this subset of readers, this chapter allows a better understanding of the remainder of the book. This chapter also is intended for those readers who are somewhat familiar with the behavioral economics literature but have yet to see the utility of the analyses. This chapter contains several examples illustrating the practical relevance of behavioral economics. This chapter glosses over the quantitative complexities of behavioral economics, focusing instead on an overview of some of the more important findings and concepts emanating from this literature. Readers with greater experience in behavioral economics or who are interested in the quantitative details of behavioral economics can safely proceed to Hursh (chap. 2, this volume), which examines these more advanced concepts.

This chapter begins with a brief history of the origin and development of behavioral economics within behavioral psychology (behavior analysis) and experimental economics. From these roots, we can begin to define the field of behavioral economics, recognizing its evolving status. In the sections that follow, two measures of consumer behavior frequently examined in behavioral economic experiments (consumption and spending) are outlined, followed by an overview of some of the important economic variables known to affect consumer behavior (price, alternative sources of reinforcement, discounting delayed consequences, and income). Throughout these sections,

3

behavioral economic methods, principles, concepts, and measures are introduced and their relevance to a more thorough understanding of health behaviors is discussed.

A BRIEF HISTORY OF THE DEVELOPMENT
OF MODERN BEHAVIORAL ECONOMICS

The term *behavioral economics,* as it is used throughout this book, was apparently first coined by Kagel and Winkler (1972) in an article published in the *Journal of Applied Behavior Analysis.* According to these authors, behavioral economics referred to the area of economic research concerned with predicting and controlling human behavior, a task that had been identified explicitly by Skinner (1956) as the goal of the experimental analysis of behavior (i.e., behavior analysis). The behavioral economic research summarized by Kagel and Winkler primarily was composed of large-scale mathematical–statistical analyses and models used to predict the behavior of large populations interacting with the natural economy. These models were largely based on untested economic axioms (Kagel & Winkler, 1972) and, as it turned out, these models yielded few predictions that performed better than chance ("Economists Play the Numbers Game," 1971; Leontief, 1971). Given these shortcomings of economic approaches to human behavior, Kagel and Winkler argued for a synthesis of economic principles with procedures and preparations pioneered within the experimental analysis of behavior (e.g., token-economic systems, use of animal subjects, and use of schedules of reinforcement). This synthesis, they argued, may yield better predictive models of human behavior and better technologies with which to control economic systems.

Shortly after the publication of the Kagel and Winkler (1972) article, empirical work representing their "synthesis" began to appear in the published literature (e.g., Battalio et al., 1973a, 1973b; Hursh, 1978; Kagel et al., 1975; Kagel, Battalio, Winkler, & Fisher, 1977). Hursh (1978), for example, presented an empirical argument that animal subjects working for food and water in "Skinner boxes" provided a useful model of behavior affected by economic variables. The behavior of the monkeys in Hursh's experiments, for example, was affected by the price at which each commodity could be obtained (i.e., the number of responses the monkeys were required to make in order to earn a fixed amount of food or water), and this effect was altered by the availability of free feedings occurring between sessions. By the end of the 1970s, behavioral economic researchers were using animal and human laboratories to observe directly the interplay between economic variables, such as price and alternative sources of reinforcement, on the behavior of individuals. The results of these early experiments laid the foundation for subsequent research illustrating the generality of behavioral economic findings and subsequent conceptual analyses that would help us to better understand clinically relevant behavior, such as substance abuse.

The beginning of the 1980s saw the publication of two important articles in behavioral economics. In the first, Hursh (1980) argued more completely that animal experiments were modeling components of the economic contexts in which human behavior typically occurs and that conceptual and quantitative analyses of behavior that failed to integrate economic concepts would be too simplistic to yield accurate and meaningful predictions of human behavior. In the second article, Kagel and Battalio (1980) illustrated that several components of economic theory (e.g., downward-sloping demand curves) proved accurate in predicting the behavior of animal subjects under appropriate economic conditions. Together, these articles laid the empirical and conceptual groundwork for subsequent work in behavioral economics. For example, in the years that followed, topics as varied as labor supply (e.g., Green, Kagel, & Battalio, 1982; Hursh & Natelson, 1981) and choice involving delayed or uncertain outcomes (e.g., Battalio, Kagel & MacDonald, 1985; Mazur, 1987) were investigated in the behavioral economics laboratory with animal subjects (see also Green & Kagel, 1987).

Application of behavioral economic concepts to human behavior, in general, and substance abuse, specifically, was argued for cogently by Vuchinich and Tucker (1988). Specifically, these authors used quantitative models of choice (e.g., Herrnstein, 1970) to show that when the price (broadly defined) of an array of nonalcohol reinforcers increased (e.g., when access to a social support network becomes constrained), behavior would be increasingly allocated to alcohol-related reinforcers (whose price remains unchanged). Vuchinich and Tucker's conceptual analysis would be followed by laboratory research demonstrating that, indeed, when nondrug reinforcers are plentiful (i.e., available at a low price), initiation of drug use, drug dependence, and relapse to drug use are far less likely than when these alternative reinforcers are either unavailable or significantly constrained (see Carroll, 1987, for a summary of this research). Vuchinich and Tucker's analysis was instrumental in expanding behavioral economics into the laboratory study of human drug dependence (e.g., Bickel, DeGrandpre, Higgins, & Hughes, 1990; Bickel, DeGrandpre, Hughes, & Higgins, 1991) and continued behavioral economic conceptual analyses of problems of drug dependence (Bickel, DeGrandpre, & Higgins, 1993; Hursh, 1991). This volume speaks to the continued expansion of behavioral economics into the socially important arena of health-related behaviors.

Given the evolving and expanding nature of behavioral economics, it is difficult to provide a concise definition of the field to which all behavioral economists would subscribe. At a minimum, behavioral economics is the study of variables (primarily economic, but noneconomic as well) affecting the behavior of consumers. More specifically, behavioral economics is the combination of microeconomic concepts, principles, and measures along with concepts, principles, and experimental methods developed by behavior analysts (e.g., focus on the behavior of individual subjects and extensive use of animal subjects). Together, these techniques and principles are employed to gain a more complete understanding of the interaction between behavior and the economic context in which it occurs.

Before moving on to an overview of the measures of consumer behavior employed within behavioral economic research, a note about technical vocabulary. Economists speak of *goods* and *services*, whereas psychologists speak of *reinforcers*. The economist's good refers to tangible possessions or merchandise, and service refers to labor supplied by another. Some of these goods and services will motivate the consumer to work in order to earn them; others will not. Within behavior analysis, those goods and services that do motivate behavior (i.e., those consequences that increase the future probability of the behavior or behaviors that led to their delivery) are referred to as reinforcers. Because behavioral economists are interested in those consequences that affect individual behavior, I use the term *reinforcer* throughout this chapter.

MEASURES OF CONSUMER BEHAVIOR

Consumption

The first primary measure of consumer behavior within behavioral economics is consumption. *Consumption* may be defined broadly to include a variety of activities, such as eating, drinking, using the services of another, or using light or durable goods. Consumption is a particularly appropriate measure of several problem behaviors commonly seen in clinical populations. For example, drug consumption over time is an important measure of the success of a drug- or alcohol-abuse treatment program or a program designed to produce smoking cessation. Likewise, measures of caloric or fat consumption or medication compliance are important measures in the treatment of obesity or in the treatment of patients at risk for a number of health deficits (e.g., heart attack, stroke, high blood pressure, etc.). Other medical or psychiatric disorders with important consumption components that require monitoring include feeding disorders in infants, pica, and kleptomania. The interested reader will find behavioral economic analyses of factors affecting cigarette smoking and eating disorders in chapters of this book (see chap. 10 and 11, respectively).

Within behavioral economics, consumption of any reinforcer (be it an item that benefits or damages the organism) is conceptualized as an instance of consumer demand for that reinforcer (for purposes here, *demand* may be viewed as synonymous with *consumption*). Conceptualizing psychiatric disorders as consumer demand for a particular reinforcer allows an analysis of that disorder using economic principles and knowledge about economic variables known to affect consumer demand.

Spending (Response Output)

A second important measure of consumer behavior is *spending*, which may be defined broadly as the amount of money, work, or time that an individual will allocate toward obtaining a particular reinforcer. Tracking treatment-produced changes in spending (as previously defined) may be important in assessing the efficacy of treatments for psychiatric disorders such as gambling or obsessive–compulsive disorders. The amount of time, effort, and money spent in drug-seeking, drug-related, and nondrug-related activities is also an important component to monitor and target for change in a substance-abuse treatment program. Several researchers have demonstrated reductions in substance use and abuse when a central component of treatment is patient participation in enjoyable nondrug-related activities that compete with drug-related activities (e.g., Higgins et al., 1993). Other researchers (e.g., Carroll, 1996) demonstrated under laboratory conditions that allowing animals to allocate their time and effort to alternative reinforcing activities (e.g., working to obtain a sweetened liquid) can effectively compete with drug reinforcers. Together, this evidence suggests that activities that compete with drug use may be important in the successful treatment of substance abuse (and perhaps other disorders as well), and, thus, monitoring these components of spending may be important in treating and assessing the efficacy of treating these disorders.

Although the examples discussed thus far suggest a direct relation between consumption and spending, this is not always the case. Increasing the price of a gallon of gasoline, for example, is likely to produce a modest decrease in per capita gasoline consumption, modest because most drivers have limited nonessential automobile trips that they could cut from their daily activities. While gasoline consumption is declining, per capita spending on gasoline likely will increase in an effort to maintain consumption at a level approximating that consumed before the price increase. Because consumption and spending are sometimes affected in opposite ways by changing economic variables, measures of both consumption and spending are important to obtain a complete picture of a consumer's reaction to these changes.

ECONOMIC VARIABLES AFFECTING
CONSUMER BEHAVIOR

Price

Price Effects on Consumption. When we think of economic variables that affect our decisions to purchase and eventually consume a reinforcer, we immediately think of price. If the price of broiled lobster and melted butter were lower most people would probably eat more of it (cholesterol be damned). If Mercedes-Benz would substantially lower the price of its line of luxury automobiles, we would all probably increase our level of consumption (above zero). At the time of this writing, the U.S. Congress is debating imposing a larger tax on the price of a pack of cigarettes, with the belief that this will decrease per capita cigarette consumption, especially in teenage smokers (see Chaloupka & Wechsler, 1995).

These observations regarding the effects of a price change on consumption have been formalized in the economic demand law. The demand law states that, all else being equal, consumption of a reinforcer will decrease as its price is increased. Examples of this law abound in the natural human economy. Lea (1978) reported on the effects of increases in the price of a number of different consumer products (e.g., tea, aspirin, and pork sausages). With very few exceptions, as the price of these reinforcers increased, per capita consumption of these products decreased. These examples illustrate predictions of the demand law in the large populations that are typically the subject of economic analyses (i.e., all tea drinkers and sausage eaters), but does the demand law also describe individual consumers' reactions to price increases?

Although there are individual differences in the extent to which price increases decrease consumption, laboratory experiments with individual participants support the demand law. In these experiments, price is usually defined in terms of the number of discrete responses that must be emitted in order to obtain one unit of the reinforcer. This ratio of responses emitted per reinforcer consumed defines the reinforcer's *unit price*.[1] Several early experiments demonstrated that increasing the unit price at which food could be obtained decreased individual animal subjects' daily food intake (e.g., Collier, Hirsch, & Hamlin, 1972). More recently, several studies have found that individual human participants' cigarette (Bickel & Madden, in press) and coffee (Bickel, Hughes, DeGrandpre, Higgins, & Rizzuto, 1992) consumption decreased when the unit prices of these reinforcers were increased. Thus, consumption of three reinforcers that many would find difficult to do without (food, coffee, and cigarettes) decreases in the face of unit price increases.

---

[1]When considering the effects of price on consumption, it is important to measure price as unit price (i.e., spending or response-output divided by the reinforcer amount). Doubling the price of a pack of cigarettes is likely to have little effect on smoking if the number of cigarettes sold per pack is also doubled, because the unit price is unaffected by the price increase. Because unit price is, in essence, a cost–benefit ratio, unit price may be increased either by increasing costs associated with the reinforcer (e.g., increasing the amount of work required to earn the reinforcer) or by decreasing the benefits of the reinforcer (e.g., decreasing the magnitude of the reinforcer).

Elasticity of Demand: Sensitivity of Consumption to Price Changes.
For any individual consumer, consumption of some reinforcers may be highly
sensitive to price changes, whereas consumption of others may be relatively
insensitive to these changes. For example, if the prices of imported chocolate
and heating fuel (e.g., heating oil, natural gas, etc.) were to double, it is a
safe bet that most people who consume both products would cut back on
their chocolate consumption more than on their use of heating fuel. The
extent to which price increases produce decreases in consumption is referred
to as *price elasticity of demand.* Demand for a reinforcer is defined as *elastic*
if a 1% change in price produces greater than a 1% change in consumption.
Conversely, when demand for a reinforcer is *inelastic*, a 1% price change
produces less than a 1% change in consumption.

The discussion of price increases thus far has been limited to a single
increase from Price A to Price B. A complete understanding of the effects
of price changes on consumption, however, requires that we examine a
price range like that shown in Fig. 1.1 (note the logarithmic coordinates).
The function in the left panel of Fig. 1.1 illustrates the typical effects of price
increases on consumption and is referred to as a *demand curve.* The data
shown here were derived from 74 cigarette smokers who participated in 17
experiments conducted by Bickel and his colleagues (Bickel & Madden, in
press). In these studies, smokers earned cigarette puffs during 3-hr sessions
by making an effortful response (i.e., pulling a plunger). Unit price was

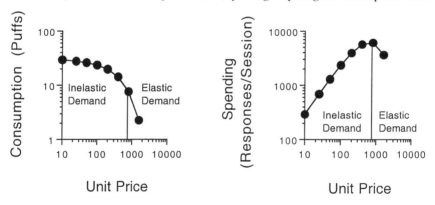

FIG. 1.1.   The left panel illustrates the relation between cigarette puffs smoked
in a three-hour session and the unit price at which cigarette puffs could be
obtained in that session. The right panel shows the effects of unit price on the
number of responses made during the session in order to earn cigarette puffs.
The vertical line in each panel separates the elastic and inelastic portions of
the demand and response-output curves. From *The Economic Analysis of
Substance Use and Abuse: An Integration of Economic and Behavioral Economic Research*, edited by F. J. Chaloupka, W. K. Bickel, M. Grossman, and
H. Saffer, in press, Chicago, IL: University of Chicago Press. Copyright © by
University of Chicago Press. Reprinted with permission.

manipulated by either changing the number of pulls required per puff or the number of puffs per work requirement completed. The fact that these data were collected with cigarette smokers working for puffs is relatively unimportant; similar curves could have been given for human demand for a variety of food products (Lea, 1978); or animal subjects' demand for food, water, or electrical brain stimulation (Hursh, 1980). What is important is that as unit price increases, cigarette smoking decreases along a positively decelerating demand curve. At unit price 10 (i.e., 10 responses per puff), smokers consumed an average of 30 puffs per session. However, when each puff cost 1,600 pulls, consumption fell to about two puffs in 3 hr.

The next thing to notice is that up until about unit price 750, demand for cigarettes is inelastic. This may be deduced by examining the slope of the demand curve. When consumption is plotted on double logarithmic coordinates, the slope of the demand curve provides a quantitative measure of elasticity. Demand is considered inelastic when slope is greater than −1 (see Fig. 1.1). At unit price 750, the slope of the demand curve is equal to −1, indicating unit elasticity (i.e., consumption changes proportionally with price changes). As is evident, unit elasticity does not last long. The final effect illustrated in the left panel of Fig. 1.1 occurs as prices increase above 750. Here, the slope of the demand curve becomes more negative with subsequent price increases. When slope is less than −1, demand is elastic, indicating that a 1% price increase yields greater than a 1% decrease in consumption.

As you have probably already deduced, consumption and spending (response output) are, under many conditions, intimately linked. That is, the more money you spend, or the more work you allocate toward earning reinforcers, the more you may consume. Therefore, to consider the treatment implications of price manipulations properly requires that we first examine the effects of price on spending.

Price Effects on Spending. Let us return to the previous examples in which the price of imported chocolate and heating fuel simultaneously doubled. Imagine that chocolate costs $3 per ounce before the price increase, and the consumer spent $15 per month on 5 ounces. After the price increase (up to $6 per ounce), consumption fell to 1 ounce per month, and the monthly expenditure for imported chocolate decreased to $6. Thus, the price increase simultaneously decreased spending and consumption. As we have seen already, there is not always a direct relation between price effects on consumption and spending. For example, imagine that the price of heating fuel increases from 50 cents to $1 per gallon, and the same hypothetical consumer adjusts the thermostat a few degrees lower and decreases fuel consumption by 5%. In order to maintain this reduced level of consumption, the consumer will have to pay about 90% more per month in heating bills. So, in this case, the price increase decreased consumption and simultaneously increased spending.

These examples illustrate an important feature of elastic and inelastic demand. When demand for a good is elastic (e.g., imported chocolate), a price increase decreases both consumption and spending. When demand for a good is inelastic (e.g., heating fuel), however, price increases decrease consumption and increase the amount of money, effort, or both allocated toward obtaining the good. The relation between elastic and inelastic demand for a reinforcer and spending are illustrated in the right panel of Fig. 1.1. Just like the demand curve in the left panel, the supply curve in the right panel of Fig. 1.1 illustrates the effects of a range of unit prices (i.e., the number of responses required per cigarette puff) on spending (i.e., the amount of labor supplied). Across the range of unit price increases where demand is inelastic, consumption is decreasing (left panel), but spending is increasing (right panel). Thus, across this range of prices, the consumer's reaction to a price increase is to increase expenditures in an attempt to defend a prior level of consumption. Across the elastic portion of the demand curve, however, price increases decrease both consumption and expenditures.

Treatment Implications of Price and Price Elasticity of Demand.
Knowledge about the effects of price manipulations and the price elasticity of demand for a particular reinforcer may have important treatment implications. Consider the effects of an increase in the price of heroin if it is currently available at a unit price of 10, as shown in Fig. 1.1. At this price, consumption is relatively unconstrained; therefore, small amounts of spending (i.e., drug-seeking activities) yield large amounts of heroin consumption. Because demand for heroin at this price is inelastic, law-enforcement efforts that moderately increase the price of heroin (e.g., supply reduction) are likely to yield two results. First, we should see a reduction in heroin consumption that is proportionally smaller than the price increase and, second, we should see an increase in drug-seeking activities (e.g., burglary and muggings) in an attempt to defend prior amounts of heroin consumption (Bickel & DeGrandpre, 1995; Hursh, 1991). At the same time, as the unit price of heroin increases, greater profits are now available to those willing to take the risk of selling heroin. According to labor supply theory, an unintentioned effect of such drug-interdiction initiatives is to increase the number of individuals who choose to make a living as a drug dealer (Hursh, 1991). If these increases in drug-seeking and drug-selling are more costly to the society than slightly higher levels of heroin consumption, then the merits of this intervention are questionable.

If, on the other hand, the current price of heroin were 1,000, as shown in Fig. 1.1, a price increase would decrease both consumption and drug-seeking activities. If spending and consumption are declining, the number of drug dealers who can be economically supported is reduced. Note, however, that these predicted effects of a price increase occur only when the price change occurs in the elastic portion of the demand curve. In Fig. 1.1, this portion of the demand curve falls in the unit price range to the right of the vertical line. Behavioral economists have termed this price at which demand shifts from inelastic to elastic as P_{max}. In an optimal economic environment, the price of heroin would be greater than P_{max}, such that supply-side law-enforcement efforts to increase the street price of heroin would decrease both consumption and spending. Realistically, however, demand for drugs, like heroin, tends to fall along the inelastic portion of the demand curve, and increasing street prices of these drugs toward the elastic portion of the curve is frequently impractical.

Behavioral economists are interested in identifying variables that affect price elasticity of demand. If we better understood how to make demand for problematic reinforcers more elastic, then we would render demand more sensitive to the host of variables that can affect the price of these reinforcers. Likewise, if we could make demand for beneficial reinforcers (e.g., fruits and vegetables, whole grains, exercise, attending alcoholic support group meetings, etc.) more inelastic, then we could make their consumption less sensitive to disruption by price fluctuations. For example, if demand for attending a weekly Alcoholics Anonymous meeting were made more inelastic, then the participant is more likely to drive an additional distance if the meeting is temporarily moved (an increase in the cost of attending a meeting) and may thereby be less likely to relapse to alcohol use.

Alternative Sources of Reinforcement

The previous discussion of price effects on consumption and spending presents a picture of consumer behavior as though behavior were controlled by only a single reinforcer, and the price of that reinforcer exclusively determines consumption and spending patterns. What this analysis thus far has omitted is an explicit recognition that behavior occurs in a context in which multiple sources of reinforcement are concurrently available (Herrnstein, 1970). That is, if you continue to read this chapter, there must be some reinforcing consequences for doing so, and at this moment they apparently outweigh a number of alternative reinforcers that are concurrently available (e.g., those reinforcers that maintain going for a walk, talking to a colleague, or taking a nap). As this analysis suggests, some types of concurrently available reinforcers compete for the resources of the individual (e.g., time and labor). The reinforcing consequences that maintain television watching, for example, compete for an individual's time with a host of other reinforcers, some of which maintain behaviors beneficial to the individual (e.g., the reinforcing consequences of exercising) or beneficial to the society (e.g., the gratitude of others that helps to maintain voluntary public service activities). However, not all concurrently available reinforcers are in competition with one another; some are independent of one another, and other reinforcers tend to be purchased and consumed together. The sections that follow examine these three different types of alternative sources of reinforcement: substitutes, independents, and complements.

Substitutes. Within economics, reinforcers that share important structural or functional properties are termed *substitutes*. Most readers already will be familiar with some economic substitutes. For example, artificial sweeteners (e.g., saccharine or Aspartame) compete for the money consumers spend on sugar products. Likewise, nicotine replacement products (e.g., nicotine gum or patch) are designed to substitute for the nicotine obtained by smoking tobacco. Generally speaking, if a new source of reinforcement is introduced (e.g., saccharin is introduced to the market), and consumption of and the resources allocated to obtaining the old reinforcer are reduced (e.g., consumption of and money spent on sugar decline), then we may classify the new reinforcer as a substitute for the old. Alternatively, if two reinforcers are concurrently available (e.g., both sugar and saccharine have been on the market for some time), and the price of one increases (the price of sugar doubles), then if we observe an increase in consumption of and resources allocated to obtaining the other reinforcer (saccharine), then we again can classify the latter as a substitute for the reinforcer whose price increased.

Petry and Bickel (1998) demonstrated that some drugs of abuse can substitute for one another. In their study, heroin addicts were given $30 with which to make hypothetical choices about which of several drugs they would purchase on a given day. In one condition, the price of heroin was increased while the price of several other drugs was unchanged. This represents a test to determine if the other drugs could substitute for heroin. The left panel of Fig. 1.2 shows that increasing the price of heroin decreased heroin consumption (as predicted by the demand law) and increased valium consumption, thereby establishing valium as a substitute for heroin.

There is a good deal of variability in the extent to which a reinforcer that is classified as a substitute can compete for the time and resources of the consumer. Obviously, if two reinforcers are identical (e.g., heroin vs. heroin), then the two reinforcers will, all else being equal, function as perfect substitutes. Accordingly, if two drug dealers sell heroin of identical quality at different prices, addicts are likely to purchase heroin exclusively from the dealer offering it at a lower price. Some reinforcers, however, may only partially substitute for another reinforcer. For example, when the price of coffee increased substantially in the 1970s, U.S. per capita consumption of tea increased to some extent. Tea contains some of the important reinforcing components of coffee (e.g., tea is a hot beverage containing caffeine), but not others (the taste of tea does not closely resemble coffee). Tea, therefore, can be classified as a partial substitute for coffee. Other partial substitutes (for most consumers) include nicotine-replacement products (partial substitute for cigarettes), powdered milk (for liquid milk), generic medications

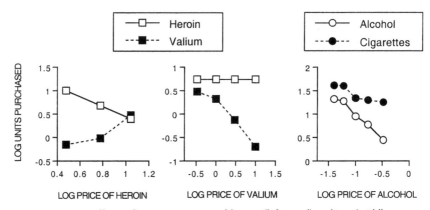

FIG. 1.2. Effects of increasing prices of heroin (left panel), valium (middle panel), and alcohol (right panel) on projected levels of spending on heroin and valium (left and middle panels), and alcohol and cigarettes (right panel). The left panel illustrates that valium will substitute for heroin while the middle panel illustrates heroin does not substitute for valium. The right panel reveals a complementary relation between cigarettes and alcohol. From "Polydrug Abuse in Heroin Addicts: A Behavioral Economic Analysis" by N. M. Petry & W. K. Bickel, 1998, *Addiction,* Vol. 93, pp. 321–335. Copyright © 1998 by Carfax Publishing Limited. Reprinted with permission.

(for name-brand pharmaceuticals), and replacement therapists (when the primary therapist raises his or her hourly fees or moves to an office inconvenient to the client).

Independents. As noted previously, not all alternative reinforcers compete with each other for the time and resources of the consumer. Sometimes introducing an alternative reinforcer will have no effect on consumption of and the resources allocated toward obtaining the first reinforcer. In a second component of the Petry and Bickel (1998) study in which heroin addicts made hypothetical decisions about how to spend their money on drugs, the price of valium was increased while the price of heroin was unchanged (the reverse of what they did previously). The results of these price changes are shown in the center panel of Fig. 1.2. Although increasing the price of valium decreased valium consumption, heroin intake was unaffected. When the slope of the heroin demand function approximates zero across the range of valium prices examined, we can conclude that heroin is an independent, with respect to valium. These data raise an important point: Reinforcer A (valium) may substitute for Reinforcer B (heroin), but Reinforcer B may not substitute for Reinforcer A.

Complements. When the introduction of an alternative reinforcer increases consumption of and resources allocated to obtaining another reinforcer, the new reinforcer may be classified as a complement. For example, several studies have demonstrated a complementary relation between cigarettes and alcohol: Drinking alcohol increases the frequency of cigarette smoking over levels maintained when alcohol is not consumed (e.g., Griffiths, Bigelow, & Liebson, 1976). A complementary relation between reinforcers may also be demonstrated when the price of Reinforcer A (e.g., soup) increases, and consumption of both Reinforcers A and B (e.g., soup and soup crackers) decreases. The results of an experiment conducted by Mello, Mendelson, Sellars, and Kuehnle (1980) are shown in the right panel of Fig. 1.2 (as these data were reanalyzed by Bickel et al., 1995). When the price of alcohol was decreased and cigarettes were available at a fixed price, consumption of both alcohol and cigarettes increased, indicating that cigarettes functioned as a complementary reinforcer for alcohol. No assessment of the symmetry of this relation was examined by Mello et al. That is, the price of cigarettes was not decreased while alcohol was available at a constant price. If both cigarette and alcohol consumption were to increase under the latter conditions, then a symmetric complementary relation would have been observed. However, decreasing the price of cigarettes possibly could have had no effect on (independent) or decreased alcohol consumption (substitute).

Treatment Implications of Substitutes, Independents, and Complements. Together, these behavioral economic findings and concepts suggest that clinicians must carefully consider the context in which problem behaviors occur or from which healthy behaviors are absent. In decreasing the probability of problem behaviors, a therapeutic strategy suggested by behavioral economics is to remove as many complementary reinforcers from the environment as possible and replace these with reinforcers that may substitute for the problematic reinforcers. For example, in treating cigarette smoking, patients may benefit from concurrently abstaining from alcohol (which appears to function as a complement for cigarettes; Mello et al., 1980) while using a nicotine-replacement product (which functions as a partial substitute for cigarettes). Conversely, when attempting to increase the frequency of healthy behaviors, the clinician must remove reinforcers that may substitute for the reinforcers that maintain these activities (e.g., for most humans, television probably substitutes for exercise) while concurrently increasing the availability of complementary reinforcers (e.g., for many, music serves as a complement for exercise).

Because consumption of a reinforcer and the amount of resources allocated toward obtaining that reinforcer covary, agonist pharmacotherapies that act as effective substitutes for illicit drugs are very appealing. Knowledge of the type and characteristics of effective substitutes for illicit drugs may be useful in developing substitute pharmacotherapies that may prove beneficial in treating substance dependence. Methadone, for example, has been used for decades in the treatment of heroin dependence. This practice is widespread not because methadone by itself is effective in breaking an addiction to opioids but, in part, because heroin addicts maintained on methadone are less likely to engage in criminal behavior in order to support an expensive heroin habit (Marsch, 1998). In behavioral economic terms, methadone substitutes for heroin to the extent that opioid withdrawal symptoms are avoided (although at the doses commonly employed in therapy, it does not produce a substitute for the euphoria produced by heroin). Similarly, by providing free needles to heroin addicts, we make readily available a substitute for used needles and reduce the spread of AIDS.

Knowledge of the illicit drugs that substance abusers are likely to begin using if the price of their primary drug of abuse is increased also may be useful during treatment and in managing this disorder. For example, if the potential side effects of the substitute drug(s) are found to pose a health threat to the addicted population (e.g., intravenous administration of a substitute drug may put the user at risk of contracting HIV), then treatment efforts can focus on warning addicts about the risks of using and misusing the substitute drug or on providing a safer alternative.

A particularly successful substance abuse treatment, based in part on making available substitute and complement reinforcers, has been developed by Higgins, Stitzer, and their colleagues (e.g., Higgins et al., 1994; Stitzer, Bigelow, & Liebson, 1979). In these treatment programs, patients earn vouchers by continuously abstaining from drug use. Vouchers may be exchanged for a range of goods and services available in the community, as long as these are consistent with treatment goals (Budney & Higgins, 1998). Vouchers, and the goods and services purchased with them, appear to function as substitutes for the reinforcers that maintain drug use. In addition to vouchers, patients receive skills training designed to increase the efficacy of social reinforcers (e.g., family relationships) that may either substitute for drug reinforcers or complement nondrug reinforcers that addicts are sampling with increased frequency after entering treatment. A host of other treatment and prevention strategies emanating from this behavioral economic analysis of substitutes and complements are discussed by Carroll and Campbell (chap. 3, this volume) and Simpson and Vuchinich (chap. 8, this volume).

Consumers Discount the Value of Delayed Consequences

A well-established principle within behavior analysis is that delayed consequences (e.g., reinforcers, punishers) are less effective in changing behavior than are consequences delivered immediately after the target response (e.g., Ainslie, 1974; Lattal & Gleeson, 1990; Mazur, 1987; Rachlin, 1974). Economically speaking, the value of a consequence is discounted as a function of the delay to its delivery. For example, the value of a canned drink from a vending machine would diminish if it were not delivered immediately. There can be little doubt that the frequency of using a particular vending machine would decrease if drinks were not released for 15 minutes after the button was pressed (especially if a machine delivering drinks immediately was located nearby). Said another way, a cold drink delivered 15 minutes from now is just not worth as much to us as a drink delivered immediately. Similarly, money scheduled to be delivered in the future is not worth as much to us as money in our pockets. This is illustrated when individuals who win a lottery and are scheduled to receive payments over several decades forfeit some percentage of their winnings to obtain a lump sum of money delivered now. As this example illustrates, "less is more" if the lesser amount is delivered now and the larger amount is delivered later.

Treatment Implications of Discounting Delayed Consequences. The diminished ability of delayed consequences to control behavior may be an important problem in the etiology and treatment of a number of health-affecting disorders. Consider, for example, the problem of cigarette smoking. Smoking a cigarette is relatively immediately followed by such reinforcing consequences as a nicotine rush, a taste smokers rate as favorable, improved concentration, and a calming sensation. Although these reinforcers are small when compared with the reinforcing consequences of cigarette abstinence (e.g., decreased probability of premature wrinkling, smoker's cough, emphysema, chronic bronchitis, stroke, heart disease, and lung cancer), "less is more" when the larger reinforcer is delivered later. The high rate of relapse in smokers attempting to quit suggests that the more immediate reinforcers associated with smoking are more effective in controlling behavior than are the delayed heath benefits of a successful quit attempt.

Relapse to cigarette smoking, alcohol or drug abuse, or quitting one's diet are all instances of what behavior analysts and behavioral economists call *preference reversals* (e.g., Rachlin & Green, 1972), or what we might refer to in everyday vocabulary as "changing one's mind." Understanding how we discount the value of delayed reinforcers may help us to better understand why we "change our minds" frequently in our everyday lives and why relapse to food and drug addictions are so common.

Much empirical research has focused on mapping the shape of the function describing how consequences are discounted over a range of delays. For these purposes, I confine my discussion to the discounting function describing the value of delayed reinforcers (as opposed to delayed aversive consequences). Figure 1.3 illustrates the diet choices faced by an obese individual. The height of the solid bars show the objective value of the reinforcers obtained by either eating a food item high in saturated fats (smaller bar) or by sticking to a low-fat diet (e.g., weight loss, improved appearance, increased frequency of compliments from others, decreased probability of health problems, etc.). Said another way, the height of the solid bars represents the undiscounted value of the respective reinforcers if we were to

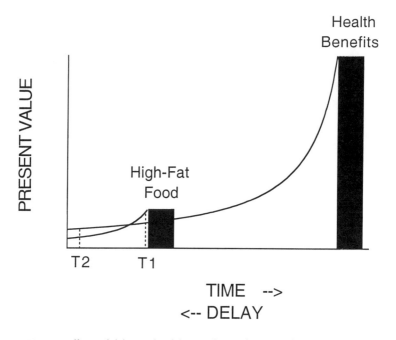

FIG. 1.3. Effects of delay to the delivery of a reinforcer on the present (subjective) value of that reinforcer. Points T1 and T2 represent times at which an individual might choose between the smaller sooner benefits of eating high-fat foods and the larger later health benefits of dieting. Preferences reverse across time points T1 and T2 because of the shape of the discounting functions.

assume that both were available immediately. Clearly, the objective value of the health benefits of dieting outweigh the objective value of eating a double-chocolate doughnut. The x-axis of the figure illustrates the passage of time (from left to right) and, conversely, the delays associated with the delivery of each reinforcer (from right to left).

At Time T1, the delay to the reinforcing consequences of a fattening food is brief (the distance from the left edge of the high-fat food value bar to the dashed line at T1), whereas the health benefits of dieting are delivered only after a lengthy delay (distance from T1 to the left edge of the health-benefits value bar). The curvilinear functions sweeping down and to the left of each reinforcer illustrate the present value of each reward.[2] Said another way, the

---

[2]The curvilinear functions in Fig. 1.3 were drawn using the hyperbolic discounting equation suggested by Mazur (1987). Substantial empirical evidence suggests that the shape of the discounting function is hyperbolic in nonhumans working for food reinforcers (e.g., Mazur, 1987); humans working for monetary rewards (e.g., Kirby & Marakovic, 1995); and humans choosing between delayed and immediate alcohol or heroin rewards (Madden, Petry, Badger, & Bickel, 1997; Vuchinich & Simpson, 1998). The degree of discounting used to draw the hyperbolic functions in Fig. 1.3 was reported as typical of human subjects (see review by Kirby, 1997).

functions illustrate how much each of the delayed reinforcers are worth to the consumer at the present time. At Time T1, we can see that the present value of the fattening food item is higher than the present value of the health benefits of dieting (the point at T1 along the high-fat food discounting function is greater than the comparable point on the weight-loss discounting function at T1).

If fattening foods are always immediately available, or if no other variables play a role in the decision to diet (e.g., physicians or loved ones pressuring the individual to consider losing weight), then it is unlikely that our obese individual ever will begin dieting. If, however, we increase the delays to both reinforcers by a constant amount by moving to Time T2, then the present value of both reinforcers are further discounted along their respective functions, and the present value of the high-fat food item is discounted below the present value of the reinforcing consequences of dieting.[3] This shift in time from T1 to T2 illustrates a preference reversal between choosing to consume a high-fat food item and choosing to diet. When the smaller–sooner reinforcer is no longer immediately available (at T2), resisting the allure of fattening foods is much easier.

Preference reversals also may occur from T2 to T1 (in Fig. 1.3). In the physician's office, for example, high-fat foods are unavailable and only can be obtained following some period of time (e.g., the time required to drive to a nearby fast-food outlet). Under these conditions (T2), the obese patient may indicate a preference for dieting and commit to better eating habits and attendance at overeaters anonymous meetings. Leaving the office, however, puts the dieter in closer temporal proximity to high-fat foods. If a box of double-chocolate doughnuts greets the obese patient when he or she returns to the office (a situation depicted at T1 of Fig. 1.3), preference for the healthy diet reverses as the high-fat doughnut is consumed. Similar preference reversals occur when the substance abuser commits to abstinence in the presence of his or her drug counselor (T2) only to relapse to drug use when drugs are immediately available from a drug-using friend (T1; see, e.g., Milby, 1988, and Unnithan, Gossop, & Strang, 1992, for descriptions of this pattern of behavior in the clinical treatment of opioid-dependence). Furthermore, countless smokers vow to quit each year (citing the delayed health benefits of abstinence), but later relapse when they experience nicotine withdrawal from which they can immediately escape by smoking a cigarette.

An implicit knowledge of preference reversals is evident in the common suggestion that dieters make decisions about what to eat well in advance

---

[3]The preference reversal from T1 to T2 occurs because of the hyperbolic shape of both discounting functions, a shape that enjoys considerable empirical support in both human and animal subjects (Kirby & Marakovic, 1995; Mazur, 1987). Readers interested in the quantitative details of the hyperbolic discounting function should see Logue (chap. 7, this volume) and Simpson and Vuchinich (chap. 8, this volume).

of eating. Thus, dieters are encouraged to buy all of their food at grocery stores and eat at home. Purchasing low-fat meals and snacks at T2 in Fig. 1.3 (i.e., at the store well in advance of eating) is not difficult because the present value of the reinforcing consequences of dieting exceed the discounted value of high-fat foods that are not immediately available. Later, at T1 (i.e., at home), high-fat foods are unavailable to tempt the dieter into a relapse to unhealthy eating habits. Similar advice is given to substance abusers when they are encouraged to stay away from their drug-using friends. Logue (chap. 7, this volume) and Simpson and Vuchinich (chap. 8, this volume) address some of the variables that can reduce the probability of preference reversals.

Income

When we think of all the changes that could possibly occur that would greatly impact personal behavior, a change in personal income must rank high on the list. If any of us had significantly more income, there are probably several products and services that we either would stop purchasing or would purchase at a reduced rate (e.g., used vehicles, whatever beer is on sale, and cleaning products), and several on which we would begin spending our newfound wealth (e.g., new cars, craft-brewed beers, and a maid). Likewise, a large reduction in personal income would cause a decrease in use of relatively expensive products such as airline tickets and restaurant meals and an increase in use of cheaper substitutes such as bus tickets and home-cooked meals.

When examining the effects of income changes on choices between concurrently available reinforcers, behavioral economists classify the reinforcers either as normal goods, inferior goods, or superior goods. The example illustrated in Fig. 1.4 helps to clarify each of these categories: If the personal income of a college graduate doubles when he or she lands a job in his or her chosen field, not only would there be a change in his or her daily activities due to new responsibilities but a change in the reinforcers he or she consumes would also occur. Some of these changes are likely to be healthy (e.g., consuming more fish and less hamburger), whereas others may not be in the individual's best interests (e.g., consuming more cocaine and spending less time with family; see Elsmore, Fletcher, Conrad, & Sodetz, 1980).

When these changes in income and consumption are plotted on logarithmic axes (as in Fig. 1.4), the direction and slope of the lines connecting consumption levels before and after the income change can be used to classify these reinforcers as normal, inferior, or superior. Fish consumption increased following the income change, but the increase was proportionally smaller than the change in income (this may be deduced by noting that the slope of the line connecting fish consumption before and after the income

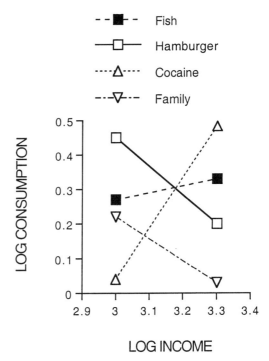

FIG. 1.4. Effects of an income change on consumption of a variety of reinforcers. Consumption of inferior goods decline as income increases while consumption of normal (fish) and superior (cocaine) goods increase.

change is less than 1.0). Because the increase in consumption was proportionally smaller than the change in income, fish is classified as a normal good. We may contrast this with the increase in cocaine consumption. The slope of this line is greater than 1.0, indicating that the increase in cocaine use is proportionally larger than the income increase. Cocaine, therefore, is classified as a superior good. Finally, hamburger consumption and the amount of time spent "consuming" family interactions decreased after the income hike, and therefore these can be classified as inferior goods.

Treatment Implications of Income Effects. Classifying changes in consumption relative to changes in income is not particularly useful unless insights may be derived or treatments inspired from this classification scheme. One of the benefits of studying income changes is that we can model the effects of an across-the-board increase in the price of one or more reinforcers and examine how this change will affect consumption of health-impacting reinforcers. That is, an across-the-board increase in the price of any product that an individual continues to purchase and consume following the price hike (e.g., gasoline or cigarettes) represents a decrease in personal income, as a larger proportion of one's income is allocated to purchasing the necessary item. The ability to predict the effects of such across-the-board price increases would be useful to public policymakers, who periodically consider the costs and benefits of imposing a larger tax on products having deleterious effects on public health (e.g., cigarettes and alcohol) or the environment (e.g., gasoline and electricity).

An experiment conducted by DeGrandpre, Bickel, Rizvi, and Hughes (1994) illustrates the potential utility of investigating the effects of income manipulations, in terms of informing public policy decisions. In this study, smokers were given varying amounts of money each day (i.e., different income levels) and were to choose between spending this money on their preferred or a less-preferred brand of cigarettes (subjects were free to spend as much or as little as they wanted on each brand). Because the preferred brand of cigarettes was more expensive than the less-preferred brand, the latter resembled generic cigarettes (which typically possess inferior smoking qualities and are available in the United States at a lower price than name-brand cigarettes). Manipulating smokers' income allowed an assessment of the likely effects of a cigarette-tax increase on consumption of generic and name-brand cigarettes.

The results of these income manipulations, averaged across subjects, are plotted in Fig. 1.5 (note the logarithmic axes). When within-session income

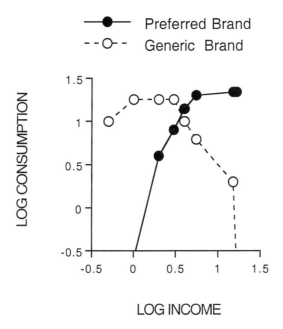

FIG. 1.5. Effects of an income change on consumption of a preferred and generic-like brand of cigarettes. From "Effects of Income on Drug Choice in Humans," by R. J. DeGrandpre, W. K. Bickel, S. A. T. Rizvi, & J. R. Hughes, 1993, *Journal of Experimental Analysis of Behavior, 59,* 483–500. Copyright © 1993 by *Journal of Experimental Analysis of Behavior.* Reprinted with permission.

was high (functionally similar to a situation in which no tax is imposed on cigarette purchases), smokers spend their money exclusively on the more expensive, preferred brand of cigarettes. However, as income levels decline (functionally similar to imposing increasingly larger taxes on the price of all cigarettes), the number of generic cigarettes purchased and consumed increases and eventually exceeds the rate at which the preferred brand of cigarettes was smoked. To the extent that the laboratory conditions provide a good model of the behavior of smokers in the natural economy, the public policy implications of these findings are clear and important: Price-initiated declines in smokers' incomes (via price increases) will not lead to significant reductions in cigarette smoking because generics will be used as an inexpensive substitute for one's preferred brand. These findings predict that the cigarette-taxation proposals recently debated by the U.S. Congress will have limited public health benefits for current cigarette smokers (a cigarette price increase, however, may reduce the number of consumers who become new smokers each year).

SUMMARY AND CONCLUSIONS

This chapter has provided an introduction to behavioral economics by first examining the historical development of the field as an outgrowth of behavior analysis and microeconomics. The remainder of the chapter outlined the major effects of four economic variables (price, alternative sources of reinforcement, delay, and income) on consumer behavior. Each of these variables was found to have important implications for understanding the etiology and treatment of a number of health behaviors, including eating disorders and drug addictions.

The benefits of a behavioral economic analysis, many of which have been outlined here, stem from the fundamental assertion that all behavior occurs in an economic context in which concurrent reinforcers vie for the resources of the consumer. Important to this analysis is that this assumption applies to all behaviors, whether they are beneficial or harmful to the individual. Thus, the treatment of problematic health behaviors, whether they are thought to have a genetic component or not, may benefit from examining the controlling economic context in which these behaviors are manifest. The findings outlined in this chapter and the remainder of this book illustrate the potential of such an approach to treatment of health behaviors. The relatively recent emergence of behavioral economics as a field, and the even more recent development of an applied branch of behavioral economics, suggests the limitations of this approach for understanding and treating a range of disorders are presently unknown.

ACKNOWLEDGMENTS

This research was supported by National Institute on Drug Abuse Grants DA06969, DA06526, and T32 DA07242.

REFERENCES

Ainslie, G. W. (1974). Impulse control in pigeons. *Journal of the Experimental Analysis of Behavior, 21,* 485–489.

Battalio, R. C., Kagel, J. H., & MacDonald, D. N. (1985). Animals' choices over uncertain outcomes: Some initial experimental results. *American Economic Review, 75,* 597–613.

Battalio, R. C., Kagel, J. H., Winkler, R. C., Fisher, E. B., Jr., Basmann, R. L., & Krasner, L. (1973a). An experimental investigation of consumer behavior in a controlled environment. *Journal of Consumer Research Policy Board, 1,* 52–60.

Battalio, R. C., Kagel, J. H., Winkler, R. C., Fisher, E. B., Jr., Basmann, R. L., & Krasner, L. (1973b). A test of consumer demand theory using observations of individual consumer purchases. *Western Economic Journal, 11,* 411–428.

Bickel, W. K., & DeGrandpre, R. J. (1995). Price and alternatives: Suggestions for drug policy from psychology. *International Journal of Drug Policy, 6,* 93–105.

Bickel, W. K., DeGrandpre, R. J., & Higgins, S. T. (1993). Behavioral economics: A novel experimental approach to the study of drug dependence. *Drug and Alcohol Dependence, 33,* 173–192.

Bickel, W. K., DeGrandpre, R. J., & Higgins, S. T. (1995). The behavioral economics of concurrent drug reinforcers: A review and reanalysis of drug self-administration research. *Psychopharmacology, 118,* 250–259.

Bickel, W. K., DeGrandpre, R. J., Higgins, S. T., & Hughes, J. R. (1990). Behavioral economics of drug self-administration. I. Functional equivalence of response requirement and drug dose. *Life Sciences, 47,* 1501–1510.

Bickel, W. K., DeGrandpre, R. J., Hughes, J. R., & Higgins, S. T. (1991). Behavioral economics of drug self administration. II. A unit price analysis of cigarette smoking. *Journal of the Experimental Analysis of Behavior, 55,* 145–154.

Bickel, W. K., Hughes, J. R., DeGrandpre, R. J., Higgins, S. T., & Rizzuto, P. (1992). Behavioral economics of drug self-administration: IV. The effects of response requirement on consumption of and interaction between concurrently available coffee and cigarettes. *Psychopharmacology, 107,* 211–216.

Bickel, W. K., & Madden, G. J. (in press). The behavioral economics of smoking. In F. J. Chaloupka, W. K. Bickel, M. Grossman, & H. Saffer (Eds.), *The economic analysis of substance use and abuse: An integration of economic and behavioral economic research.* Chicago: University of Chicago Press.

Budney, A. J., & Higgins, S. T. (1998). *Therapy manuals for drug addiction. Manual 2. A community reinforcement plus vouchers approach: Treating cocaine addiction.* Rockville, MD: National Institute on Drug Abuse.

Carroll, M. E. (1987). A quantitative assessment of phencyclidine dependence produced by oral self-administration in rhesus monkeys. *Journal of Pharmacology and Experimental Therapeutics, 242,* 405–412.

Carroll, M. E. (1996). Reducing drug abuse by enriching the environment with alternative nondrug reinforcers. In L. Green & J. H. Kagel (Eds.), *Advances in behavioral economics* (Vol. 3; pp. 37–68). Norwood, NJ: Ablex.

Chaloupka, F. J., & Wechsler, H. (1995). *Price, tobacco control policies, and smoking among young adults* (Working Paper Series No. 5012). Cambridge, MA: National Bureau of Economic Research.

Collier, G. H., Hirsch, E., & Hamlin, P. H. (1972). The ecological determinants of reinforcement in the rat. *Physiology and Behavior, 9,* 705–716.

DeGrandpre, R. J., Bickel, W. K., Rizvi, S. A. T., & Hughes, J. R. (1994). Effects of income on drug choice in humans. *Journal of the Experimental Analysis of Behavior, 59,* 483–500.

Economists play the numbers game. (1971, June 5). *Business Week, 2179,* 125–126.

Elsmore, T. F., Fletcher, G. V., Conrad, D. G., & Sodetz, F. J. (1980). Reduction of heroin intake in baboons by an economic constraint. *Pharmacology Biochemistry, & Behavior, 13,* 729–731.

Green, L., & Kagel, J. H. (1987). *Advances in behavioral economics* (Vol. 1). Norwood, NJ: Ablex.

Green, L., Kagel, H., & Battalio, R. C. (1982). Ratio schedules of reinforcement and their relationship to economic theories of labor supply. In M. Commons, R. J. Herrnstein, & H. Rachlin (Eds.), *Quantitative analyses of behavior: Vol. 2. Matching and maximizing accounts* (pp. 395–429). Cambridge, MA: Ballinger.

Griffiths, R. R., Bigelow, G. E., & Liebson, I. (1976). Facilitation of human tobacco self-administration by ethanol: A behavioral analysis. *Journal of the Experimental Analysis of Behavior, 25,* 279–292.

Herrnstein, R. J. (1970). On the law of effect. *Journal of the Experimental Analysis of Behavior, 13,* 243–266.

Higgins, S. T., Budney, A. J., Bickel, W. K., Foerg, F., Donham, R., & Badger, G. J. (1994). Incentives improve outcome in outpatient behavioral treatment of cocaine dependence. *Archives of General Psychiatry, 51,* 568–576.

Higgins, S. T., Budney, A. J., Bickel, W. K., Hughes, J. R., Foerg, F., & Badger, G. (1993). Achieving cocaine abstinence with a behavioral approach. *American Journal of Psychiatry, 150,* 763–769.

Hursh, S. R. (1978). The economics of daily consumption controlling food- and water-reinforced responding. *Journal of the Experimental Analysis of Behavior, 29,* 475–491.

Hursh, S. R. (1980). Economic concepts for the analysis of behavior. *Journal of the Experimental Analysis of Behavior, 34,* 219–238.

Hursh, S. R. (1991). Behavioral economics of drug self-administration and drug abuse policy. *Journal of the Experimental Analysis of Behavior, 56,* 377–393.

Hursh, S. R., & Natelson, B. H. (1981). Electrical brain stimulation and food reinforcement dissociated by demand elasticity. *Physiology and Behavior, 26,* 509–515.

Kagel, J. H., & Battalio, H. (1980). Token economy and animal models for the experimental analysis of behavior. In J. Kmenta & J. B. Ramsey (Eds.), *Evaluation of economic models* (pp. 379–402). New York: Academic Press.

Kagel, J. H., Battalio, H., Rachlin, H., Green, L., Basmann, R. L., & Klemm, W. R. (1975). Experimental studies of consumer demand behavior using laboratory animals. *Economic Inquiry, 13,* 22–38.

Kagel, J. H., Battalio, H., Winkler, R. C., & Fisher, E. B., Jr. (1977). Job choice and total labor supply: An experimental analysis. *Southern Economic Journal, 44,* 13–24.

Kagel, J. H., & Winkler, R. C. (1972). Behavioral economics: Areas of cooperative research between economics and applied behavior analysis. *Journal of Applied Behavior Analysis, 5,* 335–342.

Kirby, K. N. (1997). Bidding on the future: Evidence against normative discounting of delayed rewards. *Journal of Experimental Psychology: General, 126,* 54–70.

Kirby, K. N., & Marakovic, N. N. (1995). Modeling myopic decisions: Evidence for hyperbolic delay-discounting within subjects and amounts. *Organizational Behavior and Human Decision Processes, 64,* 22–30.

Lattal, K. A., & Gleeson, S. (1990). Response acquisition with delayed reinforcement. *Journal of Experimental Psychology: Animal Behavior Processes, 16,* 27–39.

Lea, S. E. G. (1978). The psychology and economics of demand. *Psychological Bulletin, 85,* 441–466.

Leontief, W. (1971). Theoretical assumptions and non-observed facts. *American Economic Review, 61,* 1–7.

Madden, G. J., Petry, N., Badger, G. J., & Bickel, W. K. (1997). Impulsive and self-control choices in opiate-dependent patients and non-drug-using control participants: Drug and monetary rewards. *Experimental and Clinical Psychopharmacology, 5,* 256–262.

Marsch, L. A. (1998). The efficacy of methadone maintenance interventions in reducing illicit opiate use, HIV risk behavior and criminality; A meta analysis. *Addiction, 93,* 515–532.

Mazur, J. E. (1987). An adjusting procedure for studying delayed reinforcement. In M. L. Commons, J. E. Mazur, J. A. Nevin, & H. Rachlin (Eds.), *Quantitative analysis of behavior: Vol. 5. The effect of delay and of intervening events on reinforcement value* (pp. 55–73). Hillsdale, NJ: Lawrence Erlbaum Associates.

Mello, N. K., Mendelson, J. H., Sellars, M. L., Kuehnle, J. C. (1980). Effects of alcohol and marijuana on tobacco smoking. *Clinical Pharmacology and Therapy, 27,* 202–209.

Milby, J. B. (1988). Methadone maintenance to abstinence. How many make it? *Journal of Nervous and Mental Diseases, 176,* 409–422.

Petry, N. M., & Bickel, W. K. (1998). Polydrug abuse in heroin addicts: A behavioral economic analysis. *Addiction, 93,* 321–335.

Rachlin, H. (1974). Self-control. *Behaviorism, 2,* 94–107.

Rachlin, H., & Green, L. (1972). Commitment, choice, and self-control. *Journal of the Experimental Analysis of Behavior, 17,* 15–22.

Skinner, B. F. (1956). A debate with Carl Rogers. *Science, 124,* 1057–1066.

Stitzer, M. L., Bigelow, G. E., & Liebson, I. (1979). Reinforcement of drug abstinence: A behavioral approach to drug abuse treatment. In N. K. Krasnegor (Ed.), *Behavioral analysis and treatment of drug abuse* (pp. 65–90). (DHEW Publication No. ADM 79–839). Washington, DC: U.S. Government Printing Office.

Unnithan, S., Gossop, M., & Strang, J. (1992). Factors associated with relapse among opiate addicts in an out-patient detoxification programme. *British Journal of Psychiatry, 161,* 654–657.

Vuchinich, R. E., & Simpson, C. A. (1998). Hyperbolic temporal discounting in social drinkers and problem drinkers. *Experimental and Clinical Psychopharmacology, 6,* 292–305.

Vuchinich, R. E., & Tucker, J. A. (1988). Contributions from behavioral theories of choice as a framework to an analysis of alcohol abuse. *Journal of Abnormal Psychology, 92,* 408–416.

CHAPTER TWO

Behavioral Economic Concepts and Methods for Studying Health Behavior[1]

Steven R. Hursh
Johns Hopkins University Medical School
and
Science Applications International Corporation

Concepts of behavioral economics have proven useful for understanding the environmental control of overall levels of behavior for a variety of commodities in closed systems (Bickel, DeGrandpre, Higgins, & Hughes, 1990; Bickel, DeGrandpre, Hughes, & Higgins, 1991; Bickel & Madden, 1997; Foltin, 1992; Hursh, 1984; Lea, 1978; Lea & Roper, 1977; Rashotte & Henderson, 1988) and the factors that control the allocation of behavioral resources among available reinforcers (Hursh, 1980, 1984; Hursh & Bauman, 1987). As a practical matter, this approach has borrowed terms from microeconomics, especially consumer demand theory and labor supply theory (Allison, 1983; Allison, Miller, & Wozny, 1979; Lea, 1978; Rachlin, Green, Kagel, & Battalio, 1976; Staddon, 1979; see Watson & Holman, 1977, for a review of relevant microeconomic theory); however, these terms often take on a special meaning when applied within behavior analysis and are not simple replacements for common behavioral processes, such as reinforcement, discrimination, differentiation, and the like. Indeed, behavioral economics has garnered interest because it has directed our attention to new phenomena previously ignored and new functional relations previously un-

---

[1]Reprints may be obtained by writing Steven R. Hursh, Science Applications International Corporation, 626 Towne Center Drive, Suite 301, Joppa, Maryland, 21085. The research described in this report was conducted in compliance with the Animal Welfare Act and other Federal statutes and regulations relating to animals and experiments involving animals and adheres to the principles stated in the *Guide for the Care and Use of Laboratory Animals*, NIH publication 86–23, 1985 edition.

27

named. In this chapter, behavioral economics is applied to the analysis of consumption of various reinforcers and the responding that produces that consumption. This chapter provides some basic groundwork that serves as a primer for understanding behavioral economic concepts as used in other chapters of this book.

BEHAVIORAL ECONOMIC CONCEPTS

One of the most important contributions of behavioral economics has been to redirect attention to total daily consumption as a primary dependent measure of behavior. In this context, responding is regarded as a secondary dependent variable that is important because it is instrumental in controlling consumption. Consideration of consumption as a primary factor required a major methodological shift. In most behavioral experiments, the practice has been to control "drive" by imposing some deprivation schedule. For example, animals reinforced by food are held to 80% of free feeding weight by limiting daily consumption and supplementing the amount of food earned in the test session with just enough food to hold body weight within a restricted range. This strategy was designed to hold drive constant and eliminate a confounding factor. Inadvertently, the practice also eliminated one of the major factors controlling behavior in the natural environment, defense of consumption. Under conditions of controlled drive, responding is not instrumental in determining daily consumption. This strategy of controlling deprivation or consumption, independent of behavioral changes, is what Hursh (1980, 1984) defined as an *open economy*. In more recent experiments, control of deprivation has been eliminated and participants have been allowed to control their own level of consumption, what Hursh termed a *closed economy*. The finding is that radically different sorts of behavioral adjustments occur in these two types of economies, especially when the reinforcer is a necessary commodity like food or water (see Bauman, 1991; Collier, 1983; Collier, Johnson, Hill, & Kaufman, 1986; Hursh, 1978, 1984; Hursh & Natelson, 1981; Hursh, Raslear, Bauman, & Black, 1989; Hursh, Raslear, Shurtleff, Bauman, & Simmons, 1988; Lucas, 1981; Raslear, Bauman, Hursh, Shurtleff, & Simmons, 1988). For those interested in understanding the control of food consumption and obesity, this is a fundamental distinction and must be considered when evaluating the extensive literature on food reinforcement and the control of food-reinforced behavior. Most studies of food reinforcement have been conducted in open economies and suggest that food consumption is reduced easily by changes in effort or rate of reinforcement. However, studies of food reinforcement in closed economies provide a striking contrast of persistent behavior that is very resistant to the effects of reinforcer cost (see Bauman, 1991; Foltin, 1992; Hursh, 1978). On the other hand, for those interested in drugs as reinforcers, most experiments involving drug self-administration have arranged a closed economy for the drug reinforcer; all drug administrations are response-dependent during the period of experimentation (Griffiths, Bigelow, & Henningfield, 1980; Johanson, 1978). When comparing drug-reinforced behavior to behavior reinforced by another reinforcer, such as food, a closed economy should be arranged for that other reinforcer as well. The behavioral difference between open and closed economies is best understood in terms of demand for the reinforcer, discussed in the next section.

Demand Curve Analysis

The relation between reinforcer cost and reinforcer consumption is termed a *demand curve*. As the cost of a commodity increases, consumption decreases, as illustrated in Fig. 2.1, for two commodities, food and saccharin-sweetened water. In this study with monkeys, the price of each commodity (food or saccharin) was increased gradually from 10 responses per reinforcer to more than 372 responses per reinforcer in a closed economy. The rate of decrease in consumption (sensitivity to price) relative to the initial level of consumption is called *elasticity of demand. Inelastic demand* occurs

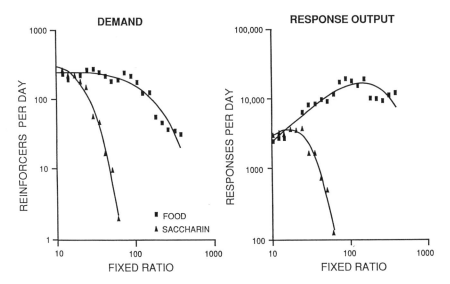

FIG. 2.1. Left panel: Two demand curves by a rhesus monkey working for either food (squares) or saccharin-sweetened water (triangles). The functions show the total number of reinforcers earned each day under a series of fixed-ratio (FR) schedules that ranged from FR 10 to FR 372. Right panel: Daily output of responding that accompanied the levels of consumption shown in the left panel.

when consumption declines slowly with proportionately large increases in price, as seen for food in Fig. 2.1. For this to occur, total responding must increase with increases in cost, as seen in the right-hand panel of Fig. 2.1 for food. To use a familiar human example, when the price of gasoline increased threefold during the 1970s, from 33 cents a gallon to more than $1 a gallon, consumption decreased by only 10%. This was an example of inelastic demand, and the result was that a larger share of household budgets was allocated to gasoline than was before.

Not all demand curves are inelastic; consumption of saccharin-sweetened water by these monkeys with an alternative source of water was elastic (Fig. 2.1, left panel). Consumption declined slowly for food but declined steeply for saccharin. As a corollary, total responding for food increased over a broad range, whereas responding for saccharin generally decreased over the same range (Fig. 2.1, right panel). The distinction between elastic and inelastic demand defines a continuum. Consumption of all reinforcers becomes elastic if the price is elevated sufficiently; the difference between reinforcers can be specified in terms of the price at the point of transition between inelastic and elastic demand (P_{max}) and coincides with the peak of the response rate functions, as shown in the right panel of Fig. 2.1. If that transition occurs at relatively low prices, then demand for that reinforcer is generally more elastic than is demand for a reinforcer that sustains response increases over a broad range of prices.

Carroll (1993) used demand curves to demonstrate that the addition of a saccharin reinforcer concurrent with a phencyclidine (PCP) reinforcer had the effect of increasing the elasticity of demand for PCP, increasing the slope of the demand curve and decreasing the price at which responding reached its peak. In general, demand curves for drug reinforcers conform to the same nonlinear, decreasing function typified by those in Fig. 2.1, and responding is an inverted U-shaped function of price (see subsequent discussion for details; also see review by Bickel, DeGrandpre, Higgins, & Hughes, 1990). Later in this chapter, I describe methods for using demand curves to assess abuse liability of drugs and the efficacy of interventions to reduce demand and drug-seeking behavior.

Measuring Demand

In order to use elasticity of demand as a basic yardstick for evaluating "motivation" for reinforcers, the conditions for measuring demand must be precisely specified. This includes clear definitions of the two primary variables, consumption and price. Hursh (1980, 1984, 1991; Hursh et al., 1988) proposed that consumption be measured in terms of total daily intake, which, for food reinforcement, would be the weight of food per day, and for drug reinforcers, the weight of drug per day adjusted for the weight of the subject (mg/kg/day). Many prior studies have measured consumption as "injections per hour" or some other measure of reinforcement rate. This measure obscures the assessment of consumption because total intake is the product of number of reinforcers (r, e.g., infusions per day) and the size of the reinforcer (d, e.g., dose per infusion); for a drug reinforcer, then, daily consumption (Q) is: $Q = r \cdot d$. The behavioral economic focus is on total consumption as a controlling factor and requires an appropriate measure of consumption that considers dose or reinforcer magnitude as a constituent factor. This factor extends to nondrug reinforcers as well. Rats given an opportunity to work for food reinforcers are sensitive to the amount of food in each reinforcer. Rats given a reinforcer that consisted of two food pellets consume about half as many reinforcers as do rats given a reinforcer that consists of one food pellet (Hursh et al., 1988). When consumption was plotted in terms of grams of food per day (not reinforcers per day), the demand curves of the two groups were nearly identical.

One useful way to define reinforcer "price" is as the ratio of response cost to reinforcer gain, termed *unit price* (Bickel et al., 1990; Bickel et al., 1991; Hursh, 1984; Hursh et al., 1988). For example, the unit price (P) of a drug reinforcer would be defined as the number of responses per reinforcer set by the fixed-ratio (FR) schedule divided by the dose (d): $P = FR/d$. The most important implication of unit price for the understanding of reinforcement is that it specifies that consumption is similarly controlled by increases in cost and decreases in reinforcer magnitude. In other words, responses per reinforcer and magnitude of each reinforcer can both be thought of as cost factors and have a monotonic relation to consumption. A stricter interpretation of unit price assumes that the constituents of unit price—response cost and reinforcer magnitude—have scalar equivalence, as well. In other words, a doubling of response cost is precisely equal to a halving of reinforcer magnitude. An example is shown in Fig. 2.2 from a study by Lemaire and Meisch (1985). Monkeys were given opportunities to consume a pentobarbital/ethanol mixture that varied in size from 2 to 16 deliveries per reinforcer. When consumption was measured as total drug consumed, and price was scaled as number of responses per milligram of drug, the demand curves across the range of reinforcer sizes coincided.

Some studies (Bickel, DeGrandpre, & Higgins, 1993; Hursh & Winger, 1995; Nader, Hedeker, & Woolverton, 1993) indicate that scalar equivalence may not be true in all cases, especially for the lowest reinforcing dose of a drug. A more recent approach defines demand curves in normalized units to avoid some of the scalar assumptions of unit price (Hursh & Winger, 1995), although this approach does not necessarily eliminate the deviations from unitary demand seen with low-dose drug reinforcers.

Demand for Pentobarbital/ Ethanol Mixture

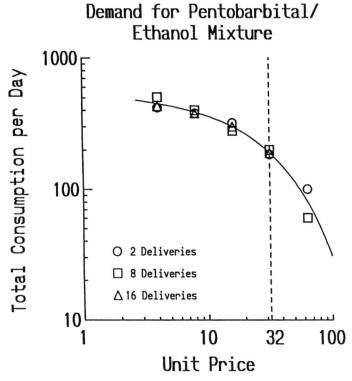

FIG. 2.2.   For a rhesus monkey, total daily consumption of pentobarbital/etha-nol mixture as a function of unit price, in log-log coordinates. P_{max} is indicated by a vertical grid line at a unit price of 32. The data are from "Oral drug self-administration in rhesus monkeys: Interactions between drug amount and fixed-ratio size," by G. A. Lemaire and R. A. Meisch, 1985, *Journal of the Experimental Analysis of Behavior, 44,* p. 377.

Normalized Demand

In a previous article (Hursh et al., 1988), reinforcer magnitude was shown to be an important factor determining measured demand. Reinforcer mag-nitude participates in both the determination of total daily consumption (i.e., number of reinforcers × magnitude) and unit price, expressed as a cost–benefit ratio (i.e., [responses × effort]/[reinforcers × magnitude]). *Reinforcer magnitude* is a general term that, in the context of drug reinforcers, includes both differences in dose and differences in potency. In order to compare two demand curves from different drugs accurately, it would be necessary to account for differences in both dose and potency. Having accounted for these differences, any residual differences in elasticity between the two drugs could then be fairly attributed to the inherent properties of the drug. Unit price is usually effective in accounting for differences in dose but does not accommodate differences in potency. For example, when comparing demand for two opiate agonists, nalbuphine and alfentanil, Winger, Woods, and Hursh (1996) showed that nearly 10 times as much nalbuphine was consumed at the lowest unit price as alfentanil but that nalbuphine ceased to support responding at much lower unit prices compared to alfentanil. This pattern of results would be expected if nalbuphine has lower potency and reinforcer magnitude compared to alfentanil (Hursh et al., 1988; see Woods, Winger, & France, 1992). A difference in magnitude does not necessarily indicate a basic difference in elasticity. For example, Hursh et al. (1988) showed that one food pellet has lower "magnitude" than two food pellets, but that demand curves adjusted for this difference in size have identical elasticity of demand.

An alternative method for computing demand corrects for any differences in reinforcer magnitude. With drug reinforcers, this includes differences in the arranged dose per reinforcer and differences in intrinsic potency. The method is essentially a normalization procedure. The maximum daily consumption observed at the lowest price is taken as a reference level. This is the amount of the reinforcer that has maximum total utility per day. This level is "defended" under the challenge of increasing prices or effort per reinforcer. The normalization procedure defines the demand curve in terms of percentage decreases from this reference level with increases in price. Elasticity of demand is the slope of this function in log-log coordinates and reflects the degree to which the subject emits increasing numbers of responses under increasing effort or response requirements (e.g., FR schedules) to prevent decreases from the normal daily level of consumption.

The specifics of the normalization procedure are described in Hursh and Winger (1995). For drug reinforcers, each dose is converted to a normalized unit that is the dose expressed as a percent of the total daily dose at the lowest price. For example, a drug that is consumed at an average baseline level of 100 mg/kg/day and is dispensed at the rate of 1 mg/kg per reinforcer would have a normalized value, q, of 1%. Normalized consumption and price under each FR schedule are computed in terms of the q value for each dose. Daily consumption is the product of total number of reinforcers per day (r) at each FR and the q value of each reinforcer: $Q = r \cdot q$. Normalized price (P) is the number of responses or dollars expended for each reinforcer (FR) divided by its q value: $P = FR/q$. Because q is in percentage units, dose and potency are no longer factors in determining the demand function. Note that at the baseline FR value, normalized consumption (Q) always will equal 100; hence, all normalized demand curves have a starting level of 100. Note also that normalized demand is formally very similar to unit price demand; the only difference computationally is that the normalization constant, q, is used everywhere that dose, d, would appear (see previous discussion). In

34 HURSH

fact, normalized price is a kind of unit price based on relative rather than absolute units of reinforcement.

In a comparison of drug self-administration with four drugs that varied by three orders of magnitude in potency, shown in Fig. 2.3, normalization permitted a direct comparison of elasticity of demand (Hursh & Winger, 1995). The chart compares best-fit demand curves for alfentanil, cocaine, nalbuphine, and methohexital. Elasticity was independent of potency; although nalbuphine was reinforcing at unit doses 10 times higher than the lowest dose of alfentanil and 2 orders of magnitude lower than the lowest dose of cocaine, it had a P_{max} of only 156, compared to 486 and 331 for alfentanil and cocaine, respectively.

The normalization procedure for computing demand curves permits comparisons of demand across different doses of individual drugs, across reinforcers of differing sizes and concentrations, across different reinforcers, across different conditions of availability of alternative drugs, and across nonhuman and human subjects.

One shortcoming of normalized demand is that it eliminates any differences in level of demand that may be inherent between the two comparison conditions, because all demand curves are normalized to 100%. Hence, if

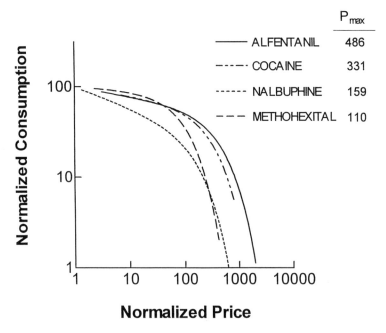

FIG. 2.3. Demand curves (see Equation 1) fit to average consumption of four drugs self-administered by rhesus monkeys. The drugs were alfentanil, cocaine, nalbuphine, and methohexital. Also shown are the P_{max} values for each drug.

some treatment alters level of demand but not elasticity of demand, this effect may be obscured. This problem can be resolved by noting that the most important implication of changes in level of demand relates to the overall level of performance involved in maintaining that level of consumption, not the specific measure of consumption, which largely is determined by the potency of the reinforcer. Recall that overall responding is generally an inverted U-shaped function of price, and the maximum level of performance for any commodity occurs at a single price, called P_{max}. Therefore, even when demand is measured in normalized units of consumption and price, the overall level of performance at P_{max} is a very useful measure of the overall level of demand and is mathematically similar to the area under the demand curve to the left of P_{max} (Hursh & Winger, 1995). This maximum level of performance maintained by the commodity is called O_{max} and has been shown to be a useful metric for comparison of overall level of demand across different drugs (Hursh & Winger, 1995). This measure has practical implications, as well. The overall level of performance expended to consume a commodity, such as a drug, is equivalent to what has been called "drug seeking." Drug seeking often refers to that constellation of behaviors to obtain the drug that dominates the participant's repertoire of behavior, interferes with normal functioning, and sometimes motivates criminal activity. Apart from the direct adverse health effects of the drug, drug seeking is the behavior that is most destructive for the drug user, and O_{max} is a quantitative measure of the capacity of a drug to motivate drug seeking. In the next section, methods are described for quantifying the shape of the demand curve and for defining precise measures of elasticity, P_{max}, and O_{max}.

Quantifying the Shape of the Demand Curves

As indicated in Fig. 2.1 and Fig. 2.2, demand curves in log-log coordinates are usually nonlinear, and the slope or elasticity changes as a function of price. The smooth curves drawn through the points in Fig. 2.1 and Fig. 2.2 are from an equation for demand that was fit to the data sets (see Hursh et al., 1988, 1989). This equation is based on the observation that elasticity generally increases as a linear function of price. This equation has three parameters: *L* for initial level of demand at minimal price, *b* for initial slope of the demand curve at minimal price, and *a* for the acceleration or increase in slope of the demand curve with increases in price. The equation is as follows, stated in the usual logarithmic units of price (*P*) and consumption (*Q*):[2]

---

[2]Equation (1) is derived from an exponential expression so that natural logs are required for accurate parameter estimates. The equation may be fit to demand curve data on any IBM compatible computer using GraphPAD Prism (GraphPAD Software, 10855 Sorrento Valley Road, #9, San Diego, CA 92121). The program fits Equation (1) to the data, estimates the three parameters (+/− standard errors), the value of r², and graphs the results (see Fig. 2.4). Consult the author for details.

$$\ln(Q) = \ln(L) + b(\ln P) - a(P) \qquad (1)$$

Elasticity of demand is the point slope (first derivative) of this function and, according to the model used here, is a linear function of price:

$$\text{Elasticity} = b - a(P)$$

Price yielding maximal output, P_{max}, can be precisely computed as:

$$P_{max} = (b + 1)/a$$

The overall output of performance, O, is defined by an equation very similar to that for overall consumption:

$$\ln(O) = \ln(L) + (b + 1)(\ln P) - a(P) \qquad (2)$$

The maximum output of performance, O_{max}, is the solution of Equation 2 at P_{max}.

In most cases, the b parameter is negative and close to zero so that elasticity differences are manifest in changes in a. Level shifts are seen as changes in the L parameter. The equation accounts for from 90% to 99% of the variance in consumption in studies conducted to date (Bickel, DeGrandpre, Higgins, Hughes, & Badger, 1995; Foltin, 1992; Hursh, 1991; Hursh et al., 1988, 1989; Hursh & Winger, 1995). When normalized demand curves are analyzed with the demand Equation 1 as shown in Fig. 2.3, the level parameter (L) is set to a constant of 100%, and only two parameters are free to vary, b and a. This method of analysis may have applications for assessing the abuse liability (likelihood of human acquisition and maintenance of drug taking) of new drugs prior to use in humans. Drug self-administration studies with nonhuman primates are commonly used to establish the reinforcing properties of drugs and to provide a qualitative assessment of the strength of performance maintained by them (Brady & Lukas, 1984; Johanson, 1978). Demand curve analysis based on an application of Equation 1 under standardized testing conditions could provide a quantitative assessment of abuse liability. The parameters of the demand equation provide an estimate of the expected level of consumption (L) and the sensitivity of consumption to increases in price (a). If other aspects of the experiment are held constant—for example, effort of the response, unit of consumption, and the length of daily test sessions—then abuse liability of different drugs could be compared based on the values of the parameters of the demand equation.

Demand curve analysis is not time-consuming. Once stable consumption is established at a low FR (e.g., FR 2), a demand curve can be estimated by increasing the *FR* in 20% to 40% steps each test day up to a maximum *FR* that reduces consumption to about 10% of baseline, a procedure that takes about 20 to 30 days. The demand curves in Figs. 2.1, 2.4, and 2.8 were obtained using this method. Several repetitions of this procedure may be used to establish the stability of the parameter estimates in time. Other studies have used test sequences with even larger step size each day that allow exploration of the range of consumptions in as few as 7 test days (Bickel, DeGrandpre, Higgins, Hughes, et al., 1995; see Fig. 2.8, see also Hursh et al., 1988; Raslear et al., 1988). Given the speed of the assessment, studies are feasible, in the same test subjects, to examine the modification of demand by competing reinforcers or substitution by other reinforcers, and these effects can be quantified in terms of changes in the parameters of Equation 1.

FACTORS THAT ALTER DEMAND

Elasticity of demand is not simply determined by inherent properties of the reinforcer. For example, one of the primary differences between open and closed economies is elasticity of demand. Although demand for food is inelastic in a closed economy (see Fig. 2.1), where the subject controls its own intake and no supplemental food is provided, demand for food in an open economy can be quite elastic. To illustrate this point, we provided a monkey access to low-cost food requiring only one response per pellet (*FR* 1) for 20 min after a 12-hr work period for food at higher prices. The price of food in the work period was increased to assess demand (Fig. 2.4). The subject could work for food in the work period at the prevailing price or wait and obtain food at a lower price later, analogous to obtaining low-cost food in the home cage within an open economy. Compared to demand for food when no low-cost food was available, demand when an alternative source was available was much more elastic, and responding reached a peak at a much lower price, indicated as P_{max}. Comparing Fig. 2.4 with Fig. 2.1, one can conclude that the addition of a substitute food source functioned to convert food in the work period into an elastic commodity, very similar to the nonnutritive saccharin solution shown in Fig. 2.1 and discussed previously. In general, elastic demand is typical for all reinforcers studied in an open economy.

One way to understand the difference between open and closed economies is to observe that the reinforcers provided outside the work period can substitute for reinforcers obtained during the work period. This is just one example of a more general set of interactions that can occur among commodities available simultaneously or sequentially in the course of the subject's interaction with the environment. Within a behavioral economic framework, reinforcer interactions are classified into several categories, illustrated in Fig. 2.5. Most studies of choice with animals have arranged for

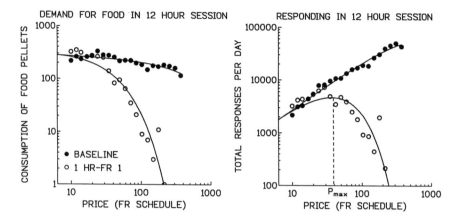

FIG. 2.4. Left panel: Two demand curves by a rhesus monkey for food during a 12-hr work period, either with no other source of food (closed circles) or with a 1-hr period of *FR* 1 food reinforcement immediately following the work period. Consumption is shown as a function of the *FR* schedule that ranged from *FR* 10 to *FR* 372. Right panel: The total number of responses emitted per day that produced the levels of food consumption during the work period shown in the left panel.

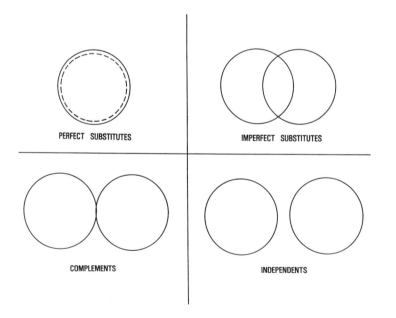

FIG. 2.5. Diagram of four hypothetical forms of reinforcer interactions.

the alternative behaviors to provide the same, perfectly substitutable reinforcer, usually food. This yields a specific kind of interaction in which the
amount of behavior to each roughly matches the amount of reinforcement
received from each (the *matching law*; see Davison & McCarthy, 1988).
When the two alternatives require a specific number of responses per reinforcer delivery, the subjects generally show exclusive preference for the
least costly of the alternatives (Herrnstein, 1958; Herrnstein & Loveland,
1975). This situation is much like comparison shopping for identical items
from different stores; all else being equal, one will go to the store with the
lowest price.

Most choices are between commodities that are not perfect substitutes.
The other interactions depicted in Fig. 2.5 are imperfect substitutes, complements, and independent reinforcers. Figure 2.6 illustrates the difference between imperfect substitutes and complements. Along the *x*-axis is the price of

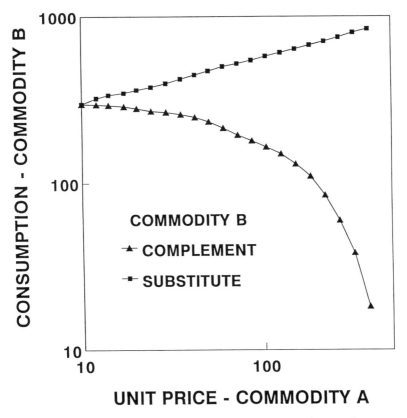

UNIT PRICE - COMMODITY A

FIG. 2.6.   Diagram of hypothetical changes in consumption of Commodity B
as a function of the unit price of Commodity A. Triangles indicate a complementary relation; squares indicate a substitutable relation.

commodity A; along the *y*-axis is the quantity of consumption of the alternative commodity B with fixed price. As the price of A increases, consumption of A decreases, the usual demand relation. If, at the same time, the consumption of B increases in response to these increases in the price of A, then B is defined as a substitute for A. If the consumption of B decreases, then B is defined as a complement of A.

Substitution

Choice between two imperfect substitutes is illustrated in Fig. 2.7 (Bauman et al., 1996). One alternative was a nutritive food pellet available after pressing a lever; the other alternative was pellets of sucrose freely available in a cup. The food pellet was a balanced diet, but less sweet; the sucrose was sweet and caloric but lacked many essential nutrients. The price of the food pellets was increased across conditions of the experiment; daily consumption of sucrose was measured at each price of food. Even at the lowest price of

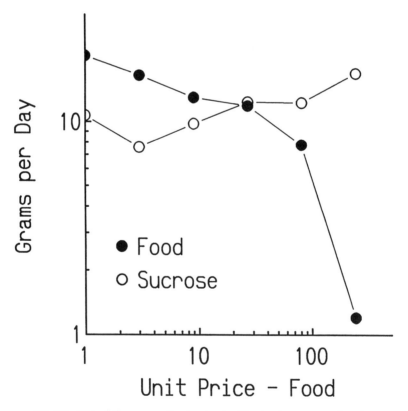

FIG. 2.7. Mean daily consumption by six rats of food and sucrose as a function of the unit price (*FR* schedule) for food, in log-log coordinates.

food (*FR* 1), some sucrose was consumed; as the price of food increased and food consumption decreased, consumption of sucrose increased as a partial substitute. The decline in food consumption was greater with sucrose available than when food was offered alone. However, even at the highest price of food (*FR* 243), some food was consumed despite the free availability of sucrose. This reciprocal trade-off between consumption of two reinforcers is typical of imperfect substitutes (Foltin, 1997).

In a parallel study (Bauman, Raslear, Hursh, & Shurtleff, 1996), monkeys were given access to a sweet nonnutritive saccharin solution concurrently with food reinforcement. As the price of food was increased, total amount of food consumed per day declined and saccharin consumption increased. However, in contrast to the sucrose experiment, the availability of nonnutritive saccharin did not alter the basic demand curve for food. The saccharin did not reduce the requirement to consume food, although reduced food consumption enhanced the reinforcing value of sweet saccharin solution.

In the context of drug abuse therapy, an alternative drug reinforcer such as methadone may be used as a medical intervention designed to reduce demand or increase elasticity of demand for the drug of abuse. Behavioral economics provides an approach to evaluation of the behavioral efficacy of this sort of drug therapy. In a manner parallel to that shown in Fig. 2.4 and discussed previously, the participant would be required to work for the target drug during "work periods"; varying amounts of the therapy drug would be given at other times, either independently or as a consequence of an operant response, during a "medication period." The efficacy of different therapies would be measured in terms of their effects on the elasticity of demand for the target drug measured during the work periods. As described previously, fitting the demand equation to the observed demand curves provides a quantitative tool for specifying these changes in terms of the parameters of the demand Equation 1 (see Hursh, 1991; Hursh et al., 1988, 1989).

Complementarity

Choice between two complements is illustrated in Fig. 2.8. One alternative provided pellets of food; the other alternative provided squirts of water. As the price of food increased, decreasing food consumption, daily consumption of water decreased. The value of water as a reinforcer declined as the consumption of food declined.

Determining Own-Price and Cross-Price Elasticity

Own-price elasticity of demand refers to the slope of the demand curve for a commodity when plotted in the usual log-log coordinates and reflects proportional changes in consumption of the commodity with proportional

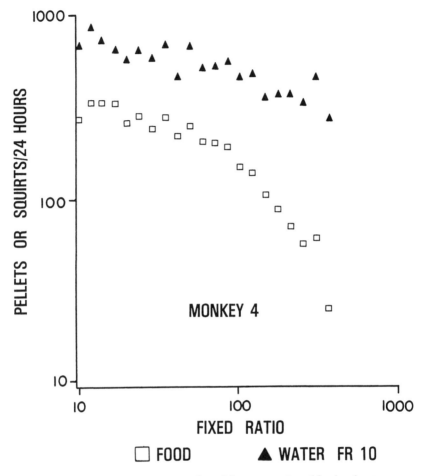

FIG. 2.8. For a representative monkey, daily consumption of food and water as a function of the fixed ratio for food, in log-log coordinates. Water was constantly available under an *FR* 10 schedule.

changes in its own price. As previously noted, demand curves are usually nonlinear, and elasticity increases with price. No single number can be used to represent elasticity of demand for comparison across experiments. The demand Equation 1 provides two methods for comparing elasticities. The first is to compare the rate of change in elasticity with price. The faster elasticity increases with price, the greater the elasticity is at any given price. The *a* parameter of the demand equation represents the rate of change in elasticity of demand and is a convenient parameter for comparison across conditions and experiments. The second method uses the demand equation to compute the price that produces maximum responding, P_{max}. This is the price at which the demand curve has a slope of −1 and represents a convenient common point of reference across conditions and studies. Generally, if demand becomes more elastic, then one will observe a decrease in the price associated with an elasticity of −1 and maximum responding (P_{max}).

Cross-price elasticity of demand is the slope of the function relating the consumption of a second commodity at fixed price to the changes in price of an alternative commodity (see Fig. 2.6). As noted previously, if this function has positive slope, then the second commodity is termed a substitute for the first; if the slope is negative, then the second is termed a complement of the first; if the slope is zero, they are considered independent. Insufficient research has been done to indicate if, in general, these cross-price curves are linear or nonlinear. If they are linear, then simple linear regression may be used to compute the slope of the cross-price demand curve and cross-price elasticity. If the functions are nonlinear, the demand Equation 1 may be applied to these data. An elasticity function can be plotted using the *a* and *b* parameters of the demand equation and would indicate if the cross-price elasticity was generally positive, negative, or close to zero, corresponding to substitution, complementarity, and independence, respectively.

Drug Interactions

Drug reinforcers may, by their neurochemical nature, reflect different forms of interaction that parallel the interactions seen with consumable reinforcers. Bickel, DeGrandpre, and Higgins (1995) conducted an extensive review of drug reinforcer interactions with other drug and nondrug reinforcers within a behavioral economic framework. They cited cases to illustrate a range of interactions: substitution, complementarity, and independence. An excellent illustration of different drug interactions emerged from a study by Carroll (1987). In this study, participants were given two drug alternatives, PCP or ethanol (ETOH). The price of each commodity was varied by altering the concentration of drug in each delivery; lower concentrations represented higher unit prices of the drug. In the first experiment, the unit price of PCP was varied, once without ETOH available and later with ETOH available. As the unit price of PCP was increased, consumption of PCP declined, and the decline was greater when ETOH was available as a substitute. At the same time, ETOH consumption increased at the highest unit prices of PCP. Thus, ETOH functioned as a substitute for PCP as the price of PCP was increased. In a second experiment, the unit price of ETOH was varied, once without PCP available and later with PCP available. As the unit price of ETOH was increased, consumption of ETOH declined, but the rate of decline was independent of the availability of PCP. Furthermore, there was little change in the consumption of PCP as the consumption of ETOH was driven down by increasing price. Thus, although ETOH served as a substitute for PCP in Experiment 1, in Experiment 2 PCP did not serve as a substitute for

NON-RECIPROCAL INTERACTION

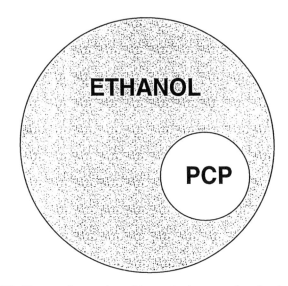

FIG. 2.9. Diagram of nonreciprocal interaction between ethanol and phencyclidine (PCP). Features of ethanol may substitute for PCP, but features of PCP
may not substitute for those of ethanol that are outside its domain of stimulation (shaded area).

ETOH. This study illustrates a nonreciprocal interaction between two commodities.

Figure 2.9 depicts diagrammatically how such an asymmetry might come
about. Conceive of each drug reinforcer as consisting of a group of stimulus
features, perhaps coinciding with areas of central nervous system stimulation.
If we think of ETOH as a drug with a relatively large set of stimulus features
(it has nonspecific action throughout the brain) and PCP as a drug that
stimulates only a subset of those same features (it activates specific neural
receptors), we can see that ETOH stimulation would substitute for PCP
stimulation of the subset, but that PCP stimulation could not substitute for
those stimulus features of ETOH that were outside the PCP domain of stimulation. Thus, observations of reciprocal and nonreciprocal reinforcer interactions may give some clue to the underlying neural mechanism of action
of the two alternative drug reinforcers.

Polydrug Abuse

Drug abuse is often not limited to the exclusive consumption of one drug
but involves either simultaneous or sequential use of multiple drugs. *Polydrug abuse,* as it is called, is frequently observed in the clinical population

and has been identified as a distinct and common pattern of drug use. The economics of consumer choice, discussed previously, provide a useful perspective for characterizing the behavioral interactions among drugs of abuse (see Petry & Bickel, 1998). The drug user may be thought of as a consumer making choices in an illicit market that offers the opportunity to consume multiple drugs at competing prices. The level of consumption of a single drug is not strictly determined by its own utility and market price but is partly determined by the utility and price of available alternatives. Changes in patterns of abuse can only be understood if this entire context of competing prices is understood. In addition, the administration of clinically prescribed medications, such as methadone, adds another dimension to what, in many cases, is already a complicated picture of multiple drug use. The result of such medications and compliance with medication schedules will depend, in part, on the various elasticities of demand in the entire polydrug market place. Ironically, interventions that inhibit reinforcement by one drug and reduce demand may, at the time, increase consumption of other drugs that serve as substitutes.

Demand Elasticity in Open and Closed Economies

The literature on demand curves contains examples of situations that span a range of research paradigms, from nonhuman primates working in an environment with restricted access to alternative drug and nondrug reinforcers, to humans in a laboratory setting with limited access to alternative reinforcers during the period of the experimental session, to humans in a more clinical setting with unrestricted access to alternative reinforcers. As pointed out previously (Hursh, 1980, 1984, 1993), conditions that permit the reinforcer under study to be consumed outside the experimental setting are called open economies and demand curves are generally more elastic compared to conditions that restrict access to the experimental setting, closed economies. For this reason, one would expect that the demand curves obtained in nonhuman primate studies using closed economies would be generally less elastic than those found in human studies with less restricted access or open economies. Nevertheless, relative changes in elasticity with changes in the availability of alternative reinforcers or resulting from pharmacotherapy should generalize across these research paradigms. However, this prediction has never been tested in a systematic comparative study.

The difference between inpatient and outpatient treatment for addictive behavior is an obvious parallel to the distinction between closed and open economies, respectively. Patients who undergo drug detoxification in an inpatient clinic, for example, frequently fail to maintain abstinence when they return to their community and undergo outpatient treatment (Wikler, 1977, 1980). It is safe to say that detoxification does not "cure" addiction.

In part, this may be due to long-lasting psychological conditioning: Cues in the client's neighborhood elicit conditioned drug effects. This explains the subjective sensations reported by the participant and, perhaps, the initial attraction to the prior drug-taking pattern. However, the ultimate breakdown in abstinence that often occurs during outpatient treatment is, fundamentally, a reflection of the unfavorable economic conditions that skew preference toward the illicit commodity: higher reinforcing value, greater convenience of use (economies of time and distance), and strong collateral social reinforcement. Yet, outpatient treatment is a necessary step in the treatment or rehabilitation process; successful progress will depend on a realization that outpatient treatment is an open economy in which the benefits of treatment are economic goods evaluated in a competitive market. Innovations that improve the economic utility and reduce the psychological costs of therapy will serve to swing more clients toward compliance with the outpatient protocol. This generalization is applicable for a range of outpatient programs, including treatment for drug and alcohol abuse, smoking, and obesity.

IMPLICATIONS FOR THERAPY INTERVENTIONS

The concepts of substitution and complementarity provide some insights into important limitations of individual therapy programs for the control or elimination of behaviors in excess in individual clients. Within a behavioral framework, one can conceptualize the therapeutic situation as one in which the therapist or the clinic attempts to shape new behavior under the control of acceptable reinforcers that compete with and reduce the occurrence of behavior to obtain unhealthy commodities, be they illicit drugs, alcohol, cigarettes, or excessive amounts of food. Thus, the reinforcers arranged by the therapeutic process interact with those from the target commodity (see Carroll, 1993; Thompson, Koerner, & Grabowski, 1984). For example, when monkeys were allowed to work for a sweet saccharin solution concurrently with consumption of PCP, elasticity of demand for PCP is increased and P_{max} moved to the left; however, considerable amounts of PCP still were consumed despite the presence of a competing reinforcer (Carroll, 1993). The effectiveness of the competition between a drug reinforcer, for example, and other reinforcers will depend, at least in part, on several economic factors: the amount of direct substitution between the two sources of reinforcement; the availability of desirable complements to the therapeutic reinforcers that will maximize their effectiveness; and the amount of direct competition that exists between the two sources of reinforcement, that is, does performance for one preclude or prevent reinforcement from the other.

These factors can be illustrated by considering the effectiveness of methadone therapy for users of heroin.

Agonist Therapy

Methadone is an imperfect substitute for heroin; it is an opiate agonist and has many of the psychoactive properties of heroin and morphine. It is explicitly formulated so that an oral dose will prevent opiate withdrawal but will not produce a pronounced euphoria or "high." It substitutes for heroin to prevent withdrawal symptoms, the aversive consequences of nondrug use, but does not substitute for the immediate positive reinforcing consequences of euphoria. One could predict, then, that even if a large price differential existed between the two commodities, some heroin would still be purchased from illicit sources for its unique reinforcing features (see Stitzer, Grabowski, & Henningfield, 1984).

In addition, heroin often is consumed as part of a social ritual, and these social events serve as complements to the primary reinforcing consequences of the drug. To the extent that the substitute, methadone, must be consumed in a clinical, nonsocial environment, its value will be diminished as an adequate substitute for heroin because it is not accompanied by important complementary social reinforcers (see Hunt, Lipton, Goldsmith, & Strug, 1984).

In general, agonist therapies must be understood as economic competitors for illicit goods. Factors that will control the success of agonist therapy are those that modulate the demand for any commodity in an open economy: the reinforcer magnitude of agonist drug (i.e., the quality of the "high" following administration); the relative price and convenience of obtaining it; the timing of opportunities to consume it in relation to opportunities to obtain the illicit good; and the availability of a complementary social environment in which to experience the agonist therapy. Compliance with a methadone treatment protocol, for example, may vary parametrically with the street price of heroin, the dose of methadone available at the clinic, and the proximity of the clinic to where the client lives. Given these competing economic factors, the long-term success of methadone treatment would seem to have a dismal forecast, were it not for the many additional positive reinforcers that are made possible by heroin abstinence, such as employment opportunities, avoidance of the violent and legal consequences of criminal activity, and positive social and family affiliations. However, many of these advantages emerge only after an established period of abstinence, and it is during these initial stages that the immediate economic conditions must be maximized to support compliance with the methadone program. For this reason, voucher programs that provide monetary incentives for methadone compliance offer a powerful adjunct to the traditional approach (Silverman,

Chutuape, Bigelow, & Stitzer, 1996; Silverman, Wong, et al., 1996). This is discussed subsequently at greater length.

Antagonist Therapy

The use of methadone as a treatment for heroin is an example of the use of an agonist to substitute for the drug of abuse and drive up elasticity of demand. An alternative approach is to provide a drug therapy that is a specific antagonist for the drug of abuse; the antagonist binds to the neurochemical receptor and blocks the action of the drug without itself producing a psychoactive effect. A common antagonist for opiate drugs is naltrexone or naloxone; it is used in emergency rooms to rapidly block the action of opiates in patients that have taken an overdose. As a therapy, the antagonist partially or completely blocks the action of the target drug and presumably would reduce demand.

This presumption has been tested in a study reported by Harrigan and Downs (1978). Monkeys worked for morphine under a series of increasing unit prices for morphine, arranged by decreasing the morphine dose per reinforcer. Morphine self-administration was studied either alone or when combined with one of three doses of intravenous doses of naltrexone. This yielded four separate consumption curves. Generally, the level of consumption of morphine at the lowest unit price increased in direct relation to the dose of naltrexone, and sensitivity to the effects of increasing the unit price also increased with the dose of naltrexone. This apparently complicated effect of naltrexone can be resolved by normalizing consumption and price to yield normalized demand curves, as shown in Fig. 2.10. Normalization compensates for any change in reinforcer potency of morphine produced by the naltrexone. Normalized demand for morphine, combined with naltrexone at all doses, was virtually identical to demand for morphine alone; naltrexone reduced the functional potency of morphine reflected in the decreases in the normalization constant, q, but did not alter the fundamental elasticity of demand for morphine.

At first, one might conclude that this indicates that antagonist therapy has no utility for the treatment of opiate drug seeking because it does not alter sensitivity to environmental price variables. In fact, this is not precisely true. The effect of naltrexone was to reduce the functional potency of the morphine. This had the effect of increasing the functional cost of morphine under each environmental cost, that is, the unit dose of morphine. Hence, increases in naltrexone moved consumption to the right on the demand curve and to lower daily levels. This effect is indicated by the dashed lines in Fig. 2.10. The smaller dashes indicate the highest environmental price for morphine when naltrexone was not infused, and the larger dashed lines indicate the functional price of that same environmental price of morphine

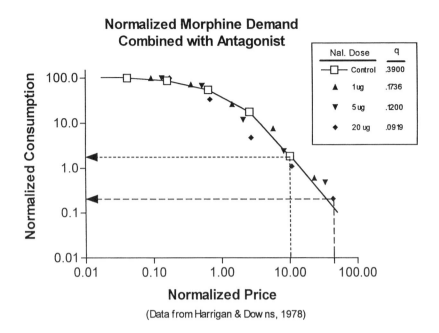

Normalized Morphine Demand Combined with Antagonist

Nal. Dose	q
⬜ Control	.3900
▲ 1 ug	.1736
▼ 5 ug	.1200
◆ 20 ug	.0919

Normalized Price

(Data from Harrigan & Downs, 1978)

FIG. 2.10. Normalized demand for morphine self-administration by monkeys receiving intravenous infusions of vehicle or one of three doses of naltrexone. The data are from "Continuous intravenous naltrexone effects on morphine self-administration in rhesus monkeys," by S. E. Harrigan and D. A. Downs, 1978, *Journal of Pharmacology & Experimental Therapeutics, 204*, p. 481.

when the highest dose of naltrexone was added. Price was increased from a normalized value of about 10 to a value of 45; consequently, consumption moved down the demand curve and was reduced by about one order of magnitude (see arrows along the y-axis). A sufficiently high dose of naltrexone would virtually eliminate any reinforcing value of morphine and, consequently, would move the functional price sufficiently far to the right that all consumption would cease under all levels of environmental cost. In effect, the morphine would be rendered ineffective as a reinforcer, and the cost–benefit ratio for expending any effort to obtain it would approach infinity. This would occur not because the fundamental demand for morphine was changed but because the functional potency of morphine as a reinforcer was changed.

The primary challenge for any antagonist therapy is that it requires that the subject voluntarily administer a drug that will drive up the functional cost of another reinforcer. Ordinarily, consumers choose to minimize cost, so such a choice would have to be compensated by a correlated increase in benefit from other sources of reinforcement, such as the retention of a well-paying job by a physician addicted to morphine. For many drug users, however, such alternative reinforcers are not present and are not provided by the therapeutic process itself. Consequently, Rawson and Tennant (1984) reported that patients receiving naltrexone treatment for 6 months showed a readdiction rate of more than 90% at a 5-year follow-up.

Interdependent Choice

Therapy for opiate addiction may include provision for other reinforcers along with methadone, such as a job and participation in a therapy group. The effectiveness of these alternative reinforcers as deterrents to further illicit drug use will depend, in part, on the existence of procedures to force a trade-off between drug use and these competing reinforcers, what is called *interdependent choice*. A study by Elsmore, Fletcher, Conrad, and Sodetz (1980) illustrated the importance of interdependent choice in reducing drug consumption by a nondrug reinforcer. In this experiment, baboons were intermittently presented with two key lights that signaled the availability of a choice between an intravenous infusion of heroin (0.1 mg/kg) or delivery of 3 gr of food (four 750 mg Noyes pellets). Only one reinforcer could be taken on each trial, and there was a limited number of trials. Hence, the number of possible choices for heroin depended on the number of choices for food, and vice versa. Trials were separated by an interval that was varied across conditions from 2 min to 12 min. By increasing the interval between trials, the number of total trials per day was decreased. Subjects lived in their test cages and received all their food under the test conditions. The results are shown in Fig. 2.11. When trials were plentiful (every 2 min), frequent choices of both food and heroin occurred; the mere presence of the alternative food reinforcement did not eliminate heroin consumption. However, as the frequency of trials decreased with longer intervals between choices, heroin choices were placed in competition with maintenance of food consumption. Under these conditions of reduced "income" of trials, the subjects allocated proportionately more of the available trials for food and less for heroin. Under the conditions with most infrequent trials (every 12 min), this competition imposed by the interdependent choice procedure reduced consumption of heroin an average of 83% compared to conditions with frequent trials. This finding of an income effect on choice behavior has been confirmed in several other studies with primates, mice, rats, and pigeons (Carroll, Rodefer, & Rawleigh, 1995; Hastjarjo, Silbergerg, & Hursh, 1990; Sakagami, Hursh, Christensen, & Silberberg, 1989; Shurtleff & Silberg, 1990; Silberberg, Warren-Boulton, & Asano, 1987). An analogous effect of income on drug choice by human test participants has been demonstrated by De-Grandpre, Bickel, Rizvi, and Hughes (1993). They manipulated the amount of money available to subjects who purchased puffs on cigarettes in a labo-

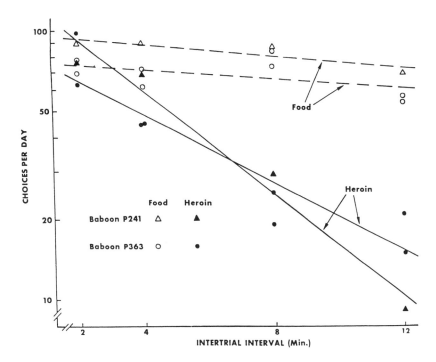

FIG. 2.11. For two baboons, choices per day for food and heroin as a function of the intertrial interval. Best-fitting straight lines are drawn through the points. The data are from "Reduction of heroin intake in baboons by an economic constraint," by T. F. Elsmore, D. G. Fletcher, D. G. Conrad, and F. J. Sodetz, 1980, *Pharmacology, Biochemistry, & Behavior, 13*, p. 729.

ratory experiment. They were given the choice of purchasing their preferred brand or a nonpreferred brand at a lower price. For most subjects, as the level on income was decreased, the frequency of choice for the nonpreferred cigarette increased.

These results suggest that procedures that require heroin abstinence as a prerequisite for retention of a job or admittance to the therapy group might be expected to enhance the direct competition between the drug and non-drug reinforcers. Of course, unlike the previously described study with food pitted against heroin, the winner of that competition may not be therapeutic alternatives given the other limitations of therapy. However, given sufficiently attractive therapeutic alternatives, such competition may be critical to elimi-nation of further illicit drug use. This may be especially true for early drug users prior to the development of tolerance and dependence as a conse-quence of repeated drug exposure, and prior to isolation from the nondrug-using community and integration into the social network of drug users

(Hubbard, Rachal, Craddock, & Cavanaugh, 1984; see Grilly, 1989, for a review).

Opportunity Cost

An important concept that is useful for understanding the control of drug and nondrug choice is the notion of *opportunity cost*. As defined by economists and applied within behavioral economics, "opportunity cost of a choice between two alternatives is the forgone value of the next best alternative (Baumol & Blinder, 1991)" (Bickel, DeGrandpre, & Higgins, 1993). If a person is given the choice between a drug and $100 and chooses the drug, then the opportunity cost of that drug choice would be $100.

A powerful clinical application of interdependent choice with methadone maintenance patients has been developed using voucher-based opiate abstinence reinforcement (Higgins et al., 1991; Higgins et al., 1994). In the clinical setting, the schedule of reinforcement for the illicit behavior is established by the natural environment and is not directly observed or controlled by the researcher or clinician. The interdependent voucher schedule provides an indirect but effective way to alter the price of drug consumption. In general, the procedure arranges for clients to receive vouchers exchangeable for money whenever they attend the drug treatment clinic as scheduled and provide a urine sample that verifies that they have abstained from illicit drug use. The longer the client remains drug-free, the larger the amount of money earned for each drug-free day (Silverman, Chutuape, et al., 1996; Silverman, Higgins, et al., 1996; Silverman, Wong, et al., 1996). In some examples of this system, clients can earn in excess of $3,000 for remaining drug-free. However, if the client consumes a detectable amount of drug, then the voucher is forfeit and the value of vouchers is reset to the initial value. In essence, the client can choose to consume the drug or to take money, but not both. Such procedures have proven very effective in increasing abstinence from both opiates and cocaine.

The cost of drug consumption in a voucher program is the opportunity cost of the loss of money that results from taking the drug. Studies using the voucher system indicate that probability of drug abstinence is directly correlated to the size of the monetary cost for drug consumption, as predicted by the demand law. In a laboratory analog of the voucher system, Spiga and Hursh (personal communication) provided human participants a simultaneous choice between a small dose of methadone and money that varied from zero to 20 cents per choice. Choices were registered by pressing one of two buttons, and 100 deliveries of any combination of methadone and money could be obtained. Figure 2.12 (solid line) displays demand for methadone as a function of opportunity cost, that is, the amount of money that was forfeited each time a methadone choice was made. For all four

Demand for Methadone

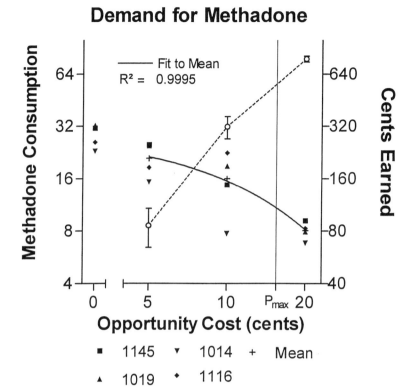

FIG. 2.12. Methadone consumption by human participants as a function of the amount of concurrently available choices of money. Solid line is the best-fit line for the demand Equation 1, and the dashed line is monetary earnings.

subjects, consumption of methadone was an inverse function of opportunity cost. At the same time, "consumption" of the alternative, money, increased as a direct function of its magnitude.

BEHAVIORAL ECONOMICS AND THE PROBLEM
OF DRUG ABUSE

Behavioral economic approaches to the problem of drug abuse can make contributions in several important domains. First, as pointed out by Bickel et al. (1993), the analysis of demand curves for drug reinforcers can serve as a convenient metric for comparing the "motivation" to procure and consume a drug. As explained previously, quantitative methods are available that could provide a standardized system for evaluating new pharmaceuticals for abuse liability (Hursh, 1991; Hursh et al., 1988, 1989).

Second, behavioral economic methods may be used to model therapeutic interventions to reduce drug use. Bickel, Madden, and DeGrandpre (1997) described a series of studies in which three different interventions to reduce smoking were explored within an economic framework: increasing cost of each response-dependent cigarette puff, availability of response-independent (substitutable) cigarette puffs, and concurrently available monetary reinforc-ers. The greatest decreases in smoking occurred when earned puffs were at the highest price and there were available both concurrent response-independent puffs and monetary reinforcers. The authors concluded that this model behavioral economic study illustrates the power of combining both pharmacological and behavioral interventions to produce reductions in smoking behavior. A similar study demonstrated reductions in smoking by simulated employment and recreational activities (Bickel, DeGrandpre, Higgins, et al., 1995).

Economic models of drug abuse interventions can be used to quantify the effects of drug therapies on the occurrence of behavior to obtain illicit drugs. I would suggest that an acceptable therapy drug must have three essential characteristics. First, the therapy must be *behaviorally efficacious* in substantially reducing demand for the illicit drug. Behavioral efficacy could be evaluated as described previously in terms of the effects of the therapy drug administered during medication periods or concurrently (e.g., a nicotine patch) on the elasticity of demand for the illicit drug. Second, the therapy drug must be *behaviorally safe.* The behavioral economic evaluation will indicate the dose and schedule of medication necessary to reduce drug demand. Behavioral economic and performance assessment methods then can be used to evaluate the behavioral effects of that therapy dose on cognitive and physical performance, as well as on general motivation for other activities. An acceptable therapy should have minimal effects on performance and general motivation. Third, to ensure compliance with the medication regimen, the therapy drug must be shown to be *nonaversive* or even mildly reinforcing. Although many techniques are available for evaluating the aversive properties of a stimulus, an economical method would evaluate the properties of the medication within the context of efficacy testing. As described previously, the medication would be given during designated "medication periods"; rather than dispensing the medication automatically, the drug could be offered to the participant according to a response-dependent schedule. If the beneficial properties of the drug support drug self-administration in test animals or attendance to a clinic and voluntary use of the medication by human patients, then we can be reasonably assured that the medication is not aversive and that compliance with a clinical medication schedule would occur. Therefore, by applying behavioral techniques, a program of testing would insure that these three evaluation criteria are satisfied and that the proposed medication would be effective, safe, and practical.

Finally, the behavioral economic model offers a framework for formulating a systematic, empirically based national policy for the control of drug abuse. This approach has been explained in Hursh (1991) and can be summarized in a diagram (see Fig. 2.13). Laboratory data are needed on any proposed medication or policy strategy. Behavioral economic methods permit researchers to model with human participants or nonhuman primates the essential economic features of the proposed policy. An artificial environment can be established using tokens to compensate for work and to serve as money to purchase alternative commodities including the illicit drug. Any policy can be modeled in terms of the simulated wage rates and consumption prices. The probable outcomes of the policy can be tested in terms of its effects on illicit drug consumption, work to obtain the illicit drug, sensitivity to therapy interventions, and sensitivity to supply-side restrictions. Bickel and DeGrandpre (1996) described this empirical approach with examples from their studies of cigarette smoking.

Results from laboratory and clinical experiments then can be combined with knowledge about the actual demand elasticities of the illicit marketplace to define more precisely the policy parameters. This refined policy proposal then can be tested in model projects to insure that unanticipated dynamics

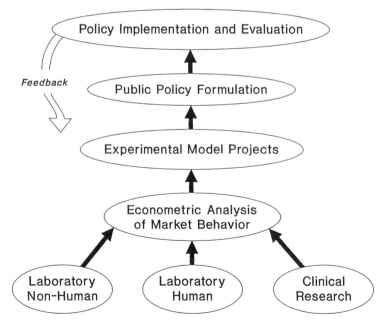

FIG. 2.13. Flow chart illustration of behavioral economic strategy for public policy formulation and implementation based on data and analysis from laboratory, clinical, and econometric studies and from practical applications in experimental model projects.

of the market do not overwhelm the expected effects of the policy. Based on further refinements from model projects, a rational national policy can be formulated that has minimal risk, maximal chances of success, and long-term benefit to society.

EXTENSIONS OF BEHAVIORAL ECONOMIC ANALYSIS TO OTHER HEALTH BEHAVIORS

The application of the general model in Fig. 2.13 is not limited to the problem of drug abuse, although this application is, perhaps, the most comprehensive and compelling. Take, for example, the problem of dietary selection and the specific problem of obesity. Food selection is a classic consumer choice problem, and there is an extensive literature on food choice in both humans and animals. The behavioral economic model provides a framework for combining the effects of the immediate reinforcing properties of the food selection with economic factors of cost, availability, and discounting of future gains. Shaping healthy dietary selections must consider all these factors. The most effective program to improve diet would combine attractive taste, convenience, and low overall cost with educational programs that promote the long-term benefits of the program. Appreciation of the demand law and commodity substitution leads to the obvious prediction that a dietary program that charges a premium for healthy foods that are bland tasting and require shopping at inconvenient specialty stores will not, in general, sustain healthy dietary choices in competition with substitutable, more appetizing, but less healthy foods from convenience stores and the local supermarket. The accompanying chapters of this book illustrate the application of behavioral economic concepts to a variety of health behavior problems and point to a comprehensive conceptual framework for the development of more effective preventative and therapeutic approaches.

REFERENCES

Allison, J. (1983). *Behavioral economics.* New York: Praeger.
Allison, J., Miller, M., & Wozny, M. (1979). Conservation in behavior. *Journal of Experimental Psychology: General, 108,* 4–34.
Bauman, R. A. (1991). The experimental analysis of the cost of food in a closed economy. *Journal of the Experimental Analysis of Behavior, 56,* 33–50.
Bauman, R. A., Raslear, T. G., Hursh, S. R., & Shurtleff, D. (1996). Substitution and caloric regulation in a closed economy. *Journal of the Experimental Analysis of Behavior, 65,* 401–422.
Baumol, W. J., & Blinder, A. S. (1991). *Microeconomics: principles and policy.* New York: Harcourt Brace Jovanovich.

Bickel, W. K., & DeGrandpre, R. J. (1996). Modeling drug abuse policy in the behavioral economics laboratory. In L. Green & J. Kagel (Eds.), *Advances in behavioral economics* (Vol. 3, pp. 69–95). Norwood, NJ: Ablex.

Bickel, W. K., DeGrandpre, R. J., & Higgins, S. T. (1993). Behavioral economics: A novel experimental approach to the study of drug dependence. *Drug and Alcohol Dependence, 33*, 173–192.

Bickel, W. K., DeGrandpre, R. J., & Higgins, S. T. (1995). The behavioral economics of concurrent drug reinforcers: A review and reanalysis of drug self-administration research. *Psychopharmacology, 118*, 250–259.

Bickel, W. K., DeGrandpre, R. J., Higgins, S. T., & Hughes, J. R. (1990). Behavioral economics of drug self-administration. I. Functional equivalence of response requirement and drug dose. *Life Sciences, 47*, 1501–1510.

Bickel, W. K., DeGrandpre, R. J., Hughes, J. R., & Higgins, S. T. (1991). Behavioral economics of drug self-administration. II. A unit-price analysis of cigarette smoking. *Journal of the Experimental Analysis of Behavior, 55*, 145–154.

Bickel, W. K., DeGrandpre, R. J., Higgins, S. T., Hughes, J. R., & Badger, G. J. (1995). Effects of simulated employment and recreation on cigarette smoking: A behavioral economic analysis. *Experimental and Clinical Psychopharmacology, 3*, 467–476.

Bickel, W. K., & Madden, G. J. (1997). *The behavioral economics of smoking.* Paper presented at The Economic Analysis of Substance Use and Abuse: An Integration of Econometric and Behavioral Economic Research (conference sponsored by the National Bureau of Economic Research).

Bickel, W. K., Madden, G. J., & DeGrandpre, R. J. (1997) Modeling the effects of combined behavioral–pharmacological treatment on cigarette smoking: Behavioral–economic analysis. *Experimental and Clinical Psychopharmacology, 5*, 334–343.

Brady, J. V., & Lukas, S. E. (Eds.). (1984). *Testing drugs for physical dependence potential and abuse liability* (DHHS Publication No. ADM 84–1332). Washington, DC: U.S. Government Printing Office.

Carroll, M. E. (1987). Self-administration of orally-delivered phencyclidine and ethanol under concurrent fixed-ratio schedules in rhesus monkeys. *Psychopharmacology, 93*, 1–7.

Carroll, M. E. (1993). The economic context of drug and non-drug reinforcers affects acquisition and maintenance of drug-reinforced behavior and withdrawal effects. *Drug and Alcohol Dependence, 33*, 201–210.

Carroll, M. E., Rodefer, J. S., & Rawleigh, J. M. (1995). Concurrent self-administration of ethanol and an alternative nondrug reinforcer in monkeys: Effects of income (session length) on demand for drug. *Psychopharmacology, 120*, 1–9.

Collier, G. H. (1983). Life in a closed economy: The ecology of learning and motivation. In M. D. Zeiler & P. Harzem (Eds.), *Advances in analysis of behavior: Vol 3. Biological factors in learning* (pp. 223–274). New York: Wiley.

Collier, G. H., Johnson, D. F., Hill, W. L., & Kaufman, L. W. (1986). The economics of the law of effect. *Journal of the Experimental Analysis of Behavior, 46*, 113–136.

Davison, M., & McCarthy, D. (1988). *The matching law: A research review.* Hillsdale, NJ: Lawrence Erlbaum Associates.

DeGrandpre, R. J., Bickel, W. K., Rizvi, S. A. T., & Hughes, J. R. (1993). Effects of income on drug choice in humans. *Journal of the Experimental Analysis of Behavior, 59*, 483–500.

Elsmore, T. F., Fletcher, D. G., Conrad, D. G., & Sodetz, F. J. (1980). Reduction of heroin intake in baboons by an economic constraint. *Pharmacology, Biochemistry & Behavior, 13*, 729–731.

Foltin, R. W. (1992). Economic analysis of the effects of caloric alterations and reinforcer magnitude on "demand" for food in baboons. *Appetite, 19*, 255–271.

Foltin, R. W. (1997). Food and amphetamine self-adminstration by baboons: Effects of alternatives. *Journal of the Experimental Analysis of Behavior, 68*, 47–66.

Griffiths, R. R., Bigelow, G. E., & Henningfield, J. E. (1980). Similarities in animal and human drug-taking behavior. In N. K. Mello (Ed.), *Advances in substance abuse* (Vol. 1, pp. 1–90). Greenwich, CT: JAI.

Grilly, D. M. (1989). *Drugs and human behavior.* Boston: Allyn & Bacon.

Harrigan, S. E., & Downs, D. A. (1978). Continuous intravenous naltrexone effects on morphine self-administation in rhesus monkeys. *Journal of Pharmacology & Experimental Therapeutics, 204,* 481–486.

Hastjarjo, T., Silberberg, A., & Hursh, S. R. (1990). Quinine pellets as an inferior good and a Giffen good in rats. *Journal of the Experimental Analysis of Behavior, 53,* 263–271.

Herrnstein, R. J. (1958). Some factors influencing behavior in a two-response situation. *Transactions of the New York Academy of Sciences, 21,* 35–45.

Herrnstein, R. J., & Loveland, D. H. (1975). Maximizing and matching on concurrent ration schedules. *Journal of the Experimental Analysis of Behavior, 24,* 107–116.

Higgins, S. T., Budney, A. J., Bickel, W. K., Feorg, F., Donham, R., & Badger, G. J. (1994). Incentives improve outcome in outpatient behavioral treatement of cocaine dependence. *Archives of General Psychiatry, 51,* 568–576.

Higgins, S. T., Delaney, D. D., Budney, A. J., Bickel, W. K., Hughes, J. R., Foerg, F., & Fenwick, J. W. (1991). A behavioral approach to achieving initial cocaine abstinence. *American Journal of Psychiatry, 148,* 1218–1224.

Hubbard, R. L., Rachal, J. V., Craddock, S. G., & Cavanaugh, E. R. (1984). Treatment outcome prospective study (TOPS): Client characteristics and behaviors before, during, and after treatment. In F. M. Tims & J. P. Ludford (Eds.), *Drug abuse treatment evaluation: Strategies, progress, and prospects* (DHHS Publication No. ADM 84–1329, pp. 42–68). Washington, DC: U.S. Government Printing Office.

Hunt, D. E., Lipton, D. S., Goldsmith, D. S., & Strug, D. L. (1984). Problems in methadone treatment: The influence of reference groups. In J. Grabowski, M. L. Stitzer, & J. E. Henningfield (Eds.), *Behavioral intervention techniques in drug abuse treatment* (DHHS Publication No. ADM 84–1282, pp. 8–22). Washington, DC: U.S. Government Printing Office.

Hursh, S. R. (1978). The economics of daily consumption controlling food- and water-reinforced responding. *Journal of the Experimental Analysis of Behavior, 29,* 475–491.

Hursh, S. R. (1980). Economic concepts for the analysis of behavior. *Journal of the Experimental Analysis of Behavior, 34,* 219–238.

Hursh, S. R. (1984). Behavioral economics. *Journal of the Experimental Analysis of Behavior, 42,* 435–452.

Hursh, S. R. (1991). Behavioral economics of drug self-administration and drug abuse policy. *Journal of the Experimental Analysis of Behavior, 56,* 377–393.

Hursh, S. R. (1993). Behavioral economics of drug self-administration: An introduction. *Drug and Alcohol Dependence, 33,* 165–172.

Hursh, S. R., & Bauman, R. A. (1987). The behavioral analysis of demand. In L. Green & J. H. Kagel (Eds.), *Advances in behavioral economics* (Vol. 1, pp. 117–165). Norwood, NJ: Ablex.

Hursh, S. R., & Natelson, B. H. (1981). Electrical brain stimulation and food reinforcement dissociated by demand elasticity. *Physiology & Behavior, 26,* 509–515.

Hursh, S. R., Raslear, T. G., Bauman, R., & Black, H. (1989). The quantitative analysis of economic behavior with laboratory animals. In K. G. Grunert & F. Olander (Eds.), *Understanding economic behaviour* (Theory and Decision Library, Series A, Vol. II, pp. 393–407). Boston: Kluwer Academic.

Hursh, S. R., Raslear, T. G., Shurtleff, D., Bauman, R., & Simmons, L. (1988). A cost–benefit analysis of demand for food. *Journal of the Experimental Analysis of Behavior, 50,* 419–440.

Hursh, S. R., & Winger, G. (1995). Normalized demand for drugs and other reinforcers. *Journal of the Experimental Analysis of Behavior, 64,* 419–440.

Johanson, C. E. (1978). Drugs as reinforcers. In D. E. Blackman & D. J. Sanger (Eds.), *Contemporary research in behavioral pharmacology* (pp. 325–390). New York: Plenum.

Lea, S. E. G. (1978). The psychology and economics of demand. *Psychological Bulletin, 85*, 441–466.

Lea, S. E. G., & Roper, T. J. (1977). Demand for food on fixed-ratio schedules as a function of the quality of concurrently available reinforcement. *Journal of the Experimental Analysis of Behavior, 27*, 371–380.

Lemaire, G. A., & Meisch, R. A. (1985). Oral drug self-administration in rhesus monkeys: Interactions between drug amount and fixed-ratio size. *Journal of the Experimental Analysis of Behavior, 44*, 377–389.

Lucas, G. A. (1981). Some effects of reinforcer availability on the pigeon's responding in 24-hour sessions. *Animal Learning & Behavior, 9*, 411–424.

Nader, M. A., Hedeker, D., & Woolverton, W. L. (1993). Behavioral economics and drug choice: Effects of unit price on cocaine self-administration by monkeys. *Drug and Alcohol Dependence, 33*, 193–199.

Petry, N., & Bickel, W. K. (1998). Polydrug abuse in heroin addicts: A behavioral economic analysis. *Addiction, 93*, 321–335.

Rachlin, H., Green, L., Kagel, J. H., & Battalio, R. C. (1976). Economic demand theory and psychological studies of choice. In G. Bower (Ed.), *The psychology of learning and motivation* (Vol. 10, pp. 129–154). New York: Academic Press.

Rashotte, M. E., & Henderson, D. (1988). Coping with rising food costs in a closed economy: Feeding behavior and nocturnal hypothermia in pigeons. *Journal of the Experimental Analysis of Behavior, 50*, 441–456.

Raslear, T. G., Bauman, R. A., Hursh, S. R., Shurtleff, D., & Simmons, L. (1988). Rapid demand curves for behavioral economics. *Animal Learning & Behavior, 16*, 330–339.

Rawson, R. A., & Tennant, F. S. (1984). Five-year follow-up of opiate addicts with naltrexone and behavior therapy. In L. S. Harris (Ed.), *Problems of drug dependence, 1983* (NIDA Research Monograph Series No. 49, pp. 289–295). Rockville, MD: National Institute of Drug Abuse.

Sakagami, T., Hursh, S. R., Christensen, J., & Silberberg, A. (1989). Income maximizing in concurrent interval-ratio schedules. *Journal of the Experimental Analysis of Behavior, 52*, 41–46.

Shurtleff, D., & Silberberg, A. (1990). Income maximizing on concurrent ratio-interval schedules of reinforcement. *Journal of the Experimental Analysis of Behavior, 53*, 273–284.

Silberberg, A., Warren-Boulton, F. R., & Asano, T. (1987). Inferior-good and Giffin-good effects in monkeys' choice behavior. *Journal of Experimental Psychology: Animal Behavior Processes, 13*, 292–301.

Silverman, K., Chutuape, M. A. D., Bigelow, G. E., & Stitzer, M. L. (1996). Voucher-based reinforcement of attendance by unemployed methadone patients in a job skills training program. *Drug and Alcohol Dependence, 41*, 197–207.

Silverman, K., Higgins, S. T., Brooner, R. K., Montoya, I. D., Cone, E. J., Schuster, C. R., & Preston, K. L. (1996). Sustained cocaine abstinence in methadone maintenance patients through voucher-based reinforcement therapy. *Archives of General Psychiatry, 53*, 409–415.

Silverman, K., Wong, C. J., Higgins, S. T., Brooner, R. K., Montoya, I. D., Contoreggi, C., Umbricht-Schneiter, A., Schuster, C. R., & Preston, K. L. (1996). Increasing opiate abstinence through voucher-based reinforcement therapy. *Drug and Alcohol Dependence, 41*, 157–165.

Staddon, J. E. R. (1979). Operant behavior as adaptation to constraint. *Journal of Experimental Psychology: General, 108*, 48–67.

Stitzer, M. L., Grabowski, J., & Henningfield, J. E. (1984). Behavioral intervention techniques in drug abuse treatment: Summary of discussion. In J. Grabowski, M. L. Stitzer, & J. E. Henningfield (Eds.), *Behavioral intervention techniques in drug abuse treatment* (DHHS Publication No. ADM 84–1282, pp. 147–156). Washington, DC: U.S. Government Printing Office.

Thompson, T., Koerner, J., & Grabowski, J. (1984). Brokerage model rehabilitation system for opiate dependence: A behavioral analysis. In J. Grabowski, M. L. Stitzer, & J. E. Henningfield (Eds.), *Behavioral intervention techniques in drug abuse treatment* (DHHS Publication No. ADM 84–1282, pp. 131–146). Washington, DC: U.S. Government Printing Office.

Watson, D. S., & Holman, M. A. (1977). *Price theory and its uses* (4th ed.). Boston: Houghton Mifflin.

Wikler, A. (1977). The search for the psyche in drug dependence. *Journal of Nervous & Mental Diseases, 165,* 29–40.

Wikler, A. (1980). *Opioid dependence.* New York: Plenum.

Winger, G., Woods, J. H., & Hursh, S. R. (1996). Behavior maintained by alfentanil or nalbuphine in rhesus monkeys: Fixed-ratio and time-out changes to establish demand curves and relative reinforcing effectiveness. *Experimental and Clinical Psychopharmacology, 4,* 131–140.

Woods, J. H., Winger, G., & France, C. P. (1992). Use of in vivo pA2 analysis in assessment of opioid abuse liability. *Trends in Pharmacological Sciences, 13,* 282–286.

PART TWO

PRICE AND CONSUMPTION

A Behavioral Economic Analysis of the Reinforcing Effects of Drugs: Transition States of Addiction

Marilyn E. Carroll
Una C. Campbell
University of Minnesota

Behavioral economic analyses have been applied to drug-reinforced behavior, and these methods have identified the optimal economic conditions under which prevention or treatment of drug abuse should occur (e.g., see reviews by Bickel & DeGrandpre, 1995, 1996; Bickel, DeGrandpre, & Higgins, 1993, 1995; Carroll, 1996; Hursh, 1991; Vuchinich & Tucker, 1988). Most of these studies involve paradigms in which there are ongoing, steady-state rates of drug self-administration in drug-experienced animals or humans. The purpose of this chapter is to consider using a behavioral economic framework to study the transition phases of the addiction process, such as acquisition in the naive animal and reinstatement of drug-seeking behavior (i.e., relapse) during a period of abstinence. Two economic concepts that are applied to studies of acquisition and reinstatement are *unit price* and *substitution*. In addition to these topics, a number of new findings are discussed that have emerged since acquisition and reinstatement were last reviewed (Carroll, 1996; Carroll & Comer, 1996; de Wit, 1996; Ramsey, 1991).

ACQUISITION OF DRUG SELF-ADMINISTRATION

The initial acquisition of drug-reinforced behavior has been described as a transition state. At this phase of the drug addiction process, there is a shift from little or no drug-maintained responding to high rates of drug-seeking behavior. Because it is unethical to study the acquisition process in drug-naive human volunteers, animal models have been of great benefit for identifying variables that affect acquisition. These animal models are essential for the development of methods that may prevent or reduce drug-taking behavior.

Methods for Studying Acquisition of Self-Administration Behavior

Acquisition of drug self-administration frequently has been evaluated by giving animals access to a drug during daily experimental sessions. Drug delivery is dependent on an operant response (e.g., lever press), and acquisition typically is measured as the number of days or drug sessions required for responding to stabilize. In some studies, food-restricted subjects are first trained to respond on the lever for food, and then food is replaced by drug. In other studies, food is taped to the lever to encourage lever pressing, or hand-shaping methods of successive approximations are used. Drug self-administration sometimes is initiated by the experimenter delivering one or two priming injections of the drug at the beginning of daily sessions.

In addition to these methods, an autoshaping procedure has been used to standardize and quantify acquisition of IV drug self-administration in rats (Carroll & Lac, 1993, 1997, 1998). This procedure originally was developed to train animals to acquire food-reinforced behavior (Brown & Jenkins, 1968). It was applied to the drug self-administration paradigm, because with food the acquisition curve could be controlled (e.g., slower acquisition and less intersubject variability) by manipulating the interval between lever retraction and onset of reinforcement (Messing, Kleven, & Sparber, 1986). Daily sessions include a 6-hr autoshaping component that is followed by a 6-hr self-administration component. The autoshaping component consists of six 1-hour periods. At the start of each hour, a retractable lever is extended into the operant chamber. After 15 seconds, or if the animal presses the lever, the lever is retracted immediately. One second after lever retraction, a drug infusion is delivered to the subject. During each of these 1-hour intervals, 10 drug infusions are automatically delivered under a random-interval (90-second) schedule. When all 10 infusions have occurred, there is a time-out period until the beginning of the next hour. Methods such as this that use experimenter-administered infusions or "primes" that are not contingent upon the animal's behavior have some face validity in the real-life setting. An individual's first drug exposure is often free and involuntary in the sense that it is propelled by peer pressure.

During the self-administration component, the lever remains extended, and every lever press is followed by a drug infusion. In these autoshaping studies, the acquisition process is evaluated for up to 30 days. Furthermore, the acquisition criteria are standardized across subjects and adjusted depending on the dose and type of drug available. The main dependent measures that can be used to assess acquisition are number of sessions to a criterion, number of self-administered infusions, and percentage of animals meeting the criterion.

Variables Affecting Acquisition of Self-Administration Behavior

Using these animal models, researchers have manipulated behavioral economic variables, such as unit price of drug and the ability of nondrug alternative reinforcers to substitute for the reinforcing effects of the drug. In behavioral economic terms, *unit price* is defined as the ratio of the response requirement to the magnitude of the reinforcer. In terms of drug self-administration, unit price usually is referred to as responses/mg of drug. Thus, unit price can be increased by increasing the response requirement or by decreasing the dose. The unit price model of drug consumption makes two basic assumptions for drug doses that serve as a reinforcer: (a) consumption of a drug decreases as unit price increases, and (b) consumption will be constant at a given unit price regardless of how the constituents of unit price (response requirement, dose) are varied (Bickel, DeGrandpre, Higgins, & Hughes, 1990). In the acquisition studies that are reviewed in this chapter, dose was the main variable that was changed. This is consistent with a change in unit price, but a direct test of the unit price hypothesis (by changing dose and response requirement in the same experiment and testing for equivalent levels of consumption) has not been done.

Drug Dose. In a recent study, Carroll and Lac (1997) examined the effects of drug dose on acquisition of amphetamine- and cocaine-reinforced behavior in rats. Both drugs were delivered under a fixed-ratio (FR) 1 schedule (using the autoshaping procedure), and three doses of amphetamine (0.03, 0.06, and 0.12 mg/kg) and cocaine (0.05, 0.2, and 0.8 mg/kg) were tested in six separate groups of rats. Thus, in that study, unit price (responses/mg) was varied by changing dose. As dose increases, unit price decreases, although the term *unit price* does not apply to the autoshaping component when infusions are not contingent on responding. Based on acquisition patterns in pilot rats, the acquisition criteria differed across doses of both drugs so that total intake during the 6-hour self-administration component of the procedure was at least 3 mg/kg for amphetamine and 20 mg/kg for cocaine. Thus, the criterion average number of infusions over 5 days was at least 100, 50, or 25 for the three doses of amphetamine and 400, 100, or 25 for the three doses of cocaine, respectively. Table 3.1 shows that as dose increased, both a greater percentage of rats per group acquired and the mean number of days to meet the acquisition criterion (in those

TABLE 3.1
Mean Number of Days to Meet Autoshaping Criterion
and Percent of Group Meeting Criterion

	Amphetamine (mg/kg)			Cocaine (mg/kg)		
	(0.03)	(0.06)	(0.12)	(0.05)	(0.2)	(0.8)
Days	18.5	9.6	6.9	20.0	9.5	6.8
Percent	80%	90%	100%	7.7%	100%	100%

that acquired) decreased. These data demonstrate that acquisition of amphetamine and cocaine self-administration was slowed or prevented at higher unit prices (lower doses), and this may be an important factor for preventing drug abuse.

In an extension of that study, the dose of cocaine was varied independently during the 6-hour autoshaping component and the 6-hour self-administration component of the daily session. Three doses were tested, 0.05, 0.2, and 0.8 mg/kg, and the rats were maintained under slight food restriction, 20 g per day. Figure 3.1 shows the effect of the autoshaping dose and the self-administered dose on speed of acquisition. The higher the dose in either the autoshaping or the self-administration component, the more rapid was acquisition. The optimal conditions for acquisition were to have a high dose (low unit price) for the response-independent infusions during autoshaping and a high dose for the response-contingent self-administered infusions. In terms of proportional changes as a function of dose, it appeared that increasing the dose (decreasing unit price) during self-administration had a more marked effect on acquisition than did increasing the dose during the autoshaping component.

In an earlier study, van Ree, Slangen, and De Wied (1978) investigated the effects of several unit doses of various drugs (e.g., heroin and amphetamine) on acquisition of IV drug self-administration in rats. In subjects responding under a continuous reinforcement schedule, the acquisition criterion was a minimum of 60 drug infusions. Three doses of heroin were tested (0.082, 0.188, and 0.375 mg/kg). Results showed that 50%, 100%, and 100% of rats that received these doses acquired heroin self-administration, respectively. Thus, similar to the Carroll and Lac (1997) study, the percentage of rats that acquired increased as dose increased, or as unit price decreased. In contrast, when four doses of amphetamine were also tested (0.105, 0.24, 0.54, and 1.2 mg/kg), results showed that 17%, 100%, 57%, and 0% of rats acquired amphetamine self-administration, respectively. Therefore, an inverted U-shaped function was found for the percentage of rats acquiring drug self-administration as dose increased. The amphetamine doses used in that experiment were higher than the doses used in the Carroll and Lac

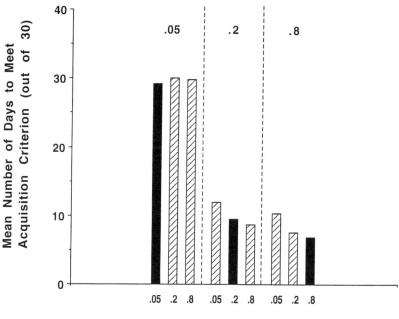

FIG. 3.1. Mean number of days to meet the acquisition criterion of a mean of
100 cocaine (0.2 mg/kg) infusions over a 5-day period is plotted as a function
of cocaine dose during the 6-hour autoshaping period in which cocaine infusions were administered automatically on a random-time 60-second schedule
(lower labels) and during a 6-hour self-administration component when infusions were contingent on a lever press response (upper labels). Each bar
represents a separate group of 5 to 13 rats. Filled bars indicate the conditions
in which the autoshaping dose and self-administered dose were the same.

(1997) study, which possibly explains the differences between studies. Taken
together, these results suggest that acquisition of drug-reinforced behavior
is a dose-related (unit price-related) phenomenon.

Recently, the effects of drug dose on acquisition of oral phencyclidine
(PCP) self-administration were studied in two groups of drug-naive rhesus
monkeys (Campbell, Thompson, & Carroll, 1998). During daily 3-hour sessions, one group had access to a low PCP dose (0.0375 mg/delivery), and
the other group had access to a high PCP dose (0.15 mg/delivery) from two
drinking spouts. The two groups went through an acquisition procedure
similar to one previously used to establish orally delivered PCP as a reinforcer
in monkeys (Carroll, 1982). Initially, subjects were fed ad libitum and had

access to water under an FR 1 schedule from both drinking spouts during daily 3-hour sessions. Each liquid delivery was contingent on one lip-contact response. Once behavior had stabilized, water was replaced by PCP. The monkeys were then food restricted, and after FR 1 behavior stabilized, the FR requirement was increased to 2 and then to 4 and 8. At FR 8, the limited food ration was given after the session and continued to be given at this time for the rest of the experiment. Subsequently, subjects had access to both water and PCP from the two spouts under concurrent FR 8 schedules to test for PCP-reinforcement. The criterion to demonstrate PCP reinforcement was if subjects consistently consumed more PCP than water.

Figure 3.2 (top panel) shows mean PCP and water intake for the two groups of monkeys under the condition that tested for a reinforcing effect of PCP. PCP intake was greater than water intake only in the high-PCP-dose group. The low-dose group consumed less than half the amount of PCP consumed by the high-dose group. Furthermore, in the low-dose group, PCP and water intake were similar. Within-group data showed that 85.7% of the high-dose group, but only 42.8% of the low-dose group, met the acquisition criterion of consistently consuming more PCP than water. Thus, compared to the group that was trained with a high PCP dose, acquisition was reduced in the low-dose group. It should be pointed out that at the end of the experiment, the four monkeys in the low-dose group that did not acquire were exposed to the acquisition procedure again with the high PCP dose. All but one of these animals acquired PCP-reinforced behavior. The data clearly demonstrate that high unit prices (low doses) of drug reduce acquisition of drug self-administration. Furthermore, the results from the low-dose group suggest that products containing smaller amounts of legal drug (e.g., alcoholic drinks, cigarettes, coffee, soft drinks) might be less likely to initiate drug-taking behavior in humans than do the high-dose brands.

Substitution of Alternative Nondrug Reinforcers

Another concept in behavioral economics that relates to the acquisition and reinstatement literature is substitution. *Substitution* is defined as an increase in consumption of Commodity A (that remains at a fixed price) as the consumption of Commodity B decreases (as unit price increases). A goal in drug treatment would be to have nondrug reinforcers (A) substitute for drug reinforcers (B), so as the unit price of drug increases, consumption would shift to a nondrug alternative commodity. It also should be noted that if drug reinforcers substitute for nondrug reinforcers when the price of the latter are increased, that situation may contribute to relapse.

Feeding Conditions. Feeding conditions have a large effect on drug self-administration. Food restriction has been shown to increase acquisition of IV, cocaine, etonitazene, and PCP self-administration in rats given con-

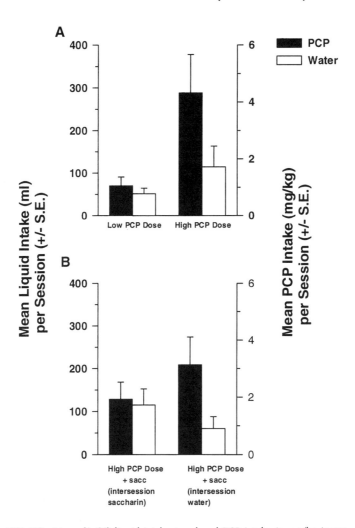

Test for PCP Reinforcement (PCP > water)

FIG. 3.2. Mean (± *SE*) liquid intake in ml and PCP intake in mg/kg is presented. Top panel shows liquid intake for the low- and high-PCP dose groups.
Lower panel shows liquid intake for the high PCP dose that had saccharin
available during intersession and after saccharin was replaced by water. Data
are for the test for reinforcement when PCP and water were concurrently
available under FR 8 schedules. Solid bars refer to PCP intake (ml or mg/kg),
and open bars refer to water intake (ml).

tinuous access to drug (Carroll, France, & Meisch, 1981). Recently, the effect of feeding conditions on acquisition of IV cocaine self-administration in rats has been examined extensively using an autoshaping procedure (Carroll & Lac, 1993, 1997, 1998). Both rate of acquisition and percentage of rats acquiring IV cocaine self-administration were compared in three groups of rats that had different amounts of food available per day. Food intake was restricted to 10 g in one group and 20 g in another group, and food was nonrestricted in a third group (Carroll & Lac, 1998). The criterion for acquisition was 5 consecutive days with at least an average of 100 infusions during the self-administration component of the procedure. Rats were given 30 days to reach this criterion. Figure 3.3 (open bars) shows that the mean number

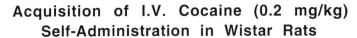

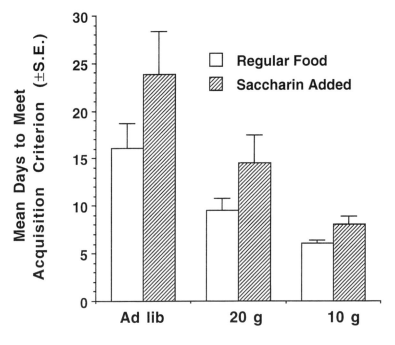

FIG. 3.3.   Mean (± *SE*) number of days to meet the acquisition criterion (average of 100 infusions over 5 consecutive days) as a function of the amount of food given (10 g, 20 g, or ad libitum) and whether saccharin (0.2% w/w) was added to the food. Open bars refer to ground food with no saccharin added, striped bars refer to the food that had saccharin added. Each bar represents a mean of 13 rats. A maximum of 30 days was allowed for acquisition to occur.

of days to reach the criterion increased as the amount of food increased. Furthermore, 100% of the rats in the two food-restricted groups acquired drug self-administration, whereas only 76.9% of the rats in the food-nonrestricted group acquired. Results from this study indicated that increased access to food (an alternative nondrug reinforcer) both reduces acquisition and slows the rate of acquisition of drug-reinforced behavior.

Acquisition of IV cocaine self-administration previously has been shown to vary as a function of body weight loss due to food restriction (De Vry, Donselaar, & van Ree, 1989). Three groups of rats were given either 5 g, 7.5 g, or 10 g of food each day. These levels of deprivation reduced body weights to 65%–75%, 75%–85%, and 85%–95% of their free-feeding weights, respectively, although body weights were not presented. During daily 6-hour sessions, rats were placed in operant chambers and could respond on a lever for IV infusions of either cocaine or saline under an FR 1 schedule. Acquisition of cocaine self-administration was defined as a significant difference between cocaine and saline infusions over 5 consecutive days. Rats that were reduced to 75%–85% of their free-feeding weight acquired cocaine self-administration. Rats that were reduced to 85%–95% or to 65%–75% of their free-feeding weight did not acquire. These findings indicated that it is the magnitude of body weight loss due to food-restriction that affects acquisition of drug self-administration.

Feeding conditions also have been reported to affect acquisition of oral PCP self-administration in rhesus monkeys (Carroll, 1982). In that experiment, two groups of monkeys that were maintained under different feeding conditions were exposed to an acquisition procedure to establish orally delivered PCP as a reinforcer. One group of monkeys was given a limited amount of food (food-restricted) and the other group was fed ad libitum (food-nonrestricted). The criterion for acquisition was if subjects consumed more PCP than water under the concurrent PCP and water choice step of the procedure. Both groups acquired PCP-reinforced behavior; however, compared to PCP consumption in the food-restricted group, PCP consumption was lower in the food-nonrestricted group. Furthermore, within-session patterns of responding differed among the two groups. The food-restricted group responded for PCP as soon as the 3-hour session started and responded steadily for 1 hour. The food-nonrestricted group often did not respond when the session began and responded intermittently throughout the 3-hour session.

Palatable Dietary Substances. In rats, Carroll, Lac, and Nygaard (1989) investigated the effects of concurrent access to a nondrug reinforcer, a glucose and saccharin (G + S) drinking solution, on IV cocaine self-administration. G + S previously had been shown to function as a reinforcer, because rats consume large amounts of this sweet solution (Carroll et al., 1989; Valenstein, Cox, & Kakolewski, 1967). In Carroll et al. (1989), some rats did not acquire either cocaine self-administration or G + S self-administration when both reinforcers were concurrently available. Interestingly, in the rats that had not yet acquired cocaine self-administration, removal of the G + S solution resulted in rapid acquisition of cocaine-reinforced responding. Similarly, replacing cocaine with saline led to rapid acquisition of G + S-reinforced responding in rats that had not yet acquired G + S self-administration. Thus, the presence of one reinforcing substance prevented acquisition of behavior reinforced by the other reinforcing substance (when both were available). The results can be explained in terms of reinforcer substitution: Drug and nondrug rewarding substances were substituting for one another as reinforcers. Other studies also have reported interactions between drug and nondrug substances (Gosnell & Krahn, 1992; Samson, Roehrs, & Tolliver, 1982; Samson, Tolliver, & Roehrs, 1983).

Carroll and Lac (1993) further examined the effects of nondrug alternative reinforcers (food and a G + S solution) on acquisition of IV cocaine self-administration in rats. Unlike the previous study, the acquisition process was quantified using the autoshaping procedure described previously. Both rate of acquisition and percentage of rats acquiring cocaine-reinforced responding were compared in five groups of rats. Groups 1 and 2 had concurrent access to a G + S solution and water in their home cages for 3 weeks prior to surgery (implantation of a jugular catheter). Groups 3, 4, and 5 had access to water only during this 3-week period (see Table 3.2). Following surgery, the animals in each group were moved to individual operant chambers to begin autoshaping. In these chambers, Groups 1 and 3 received both G + S and water, whereas Groups 2, 4, and 5 received only water. In addition, food availability was restricted to 20 g in Groups 1 through 4 but was

TABLE 3.2
Mean (± *SE*) Number of Days to Meet Acquisition Criterion
and Percent of Rats in Group Meeting Criterion

3 Weeks Before	*During Autoshaping*	
Autoshaping Began	*G + S*	*Water*
G + S, limited food	Group 1 22.8 (± 2.8) 50%	Group 2 9.1 (± 1.6) 100%
Water, limited food	Group 3 20.3 (± 2.2) 75%	Group 4 8.4 (± 1.2) 100%
Water, unlimited food		Group 5 17.3 (± 2.6) 71.4%

Note. G + S = glucose and saccharin.

nonrestricted in Group 5. Table 3.2 shows that all of the animals in Groups 2 and 4 acquired IV cocaine self-administration when no alternative reinforcers were available during autoshaping. However, the groups that had alternatives—such as G + S 3 weeks before and during autoshaping (Group 1), G + S during autoshaping (Group 3), or unlimited food (Group 5)—were slower in their rate of acquisition and lower in the percent of rats per group that acquired (50%, 75%, and 71.4%, respectively).

A subsequent experiment was designed to investigate whether the effect of the G + S solution on acquisition was due to the caloric content or palatability of the reinforcer (Carroll & Lac, 1998). In that study, acquisition of IV cocaine self-administration was examined in six groups of rats using the autoshaping procedure. Three groups received different amounts of ground food (10 g, 20 g, or ad libitum access). The acquisition data for these three food groups has been described previously (Fig. 3.3). Three other groups received the same amounts of ground food; however, palatability was increased by adding saccharin (0.2% weight/weight). Saccharin is a noncaloric reinforcer; thus palatability of the ground food was increased but not its nutritive content. The average number of days that it took for the different groups to acquire is displayed in Fig. 3.3. In the groups that had saccharin added to the food, acquisition of IV cocaine self-administration occurred at a slower rate. Furthermore, in the group that had nonrestricted access to food mixed with saccharin, only 38.4% of the rats acquired, compared to 76.9% in the nonrestricted group that had no saccharin added to the food. In the 10- and 20-g groups, there was 100% acquisition with regular food when saccharin was added. Taken together, these data demonstrated that in rats, both increased availability and palatability of food independently substituted for the reinforcing effects of IV cocaine self-administration. In addition, the results indicated that the combination of these factors has an additive effect in reducing acquisition.

The effect of a nondrug reinforcer on acquisition of drug self-administration recently has been extended to rhesus monkeys (Campbell et al., 1998). Acquisition of oral PCP self-administration was compared in two groups of monkeys. During daily 3-hour sessions, both groups had access to a high PCP dose (0.15 mg/delivery) from two drinking spouts. However, in one of these groups, a saccharin solution (0.03% w/v) and water were available during the intersession period. The other group had water only available during this time. Both groups were exposed to the acquisition procedure to establish orally delivered PCP as a reinforcer, described previously in the unit price section of the chapter. At the end of the experiment, the high-dose group (that had been trained with intersession saccharin) had saccharin replaced with water in order to determine whether responding for PCP would change. Figure 3.2 (lower panel) shows mean PCP and water consumption for the high-PCP-dose group that had saccharin available during intersession. In comparison to the high-PCP-dose group that received only water, PCP intake was lower in the intersession saccharin group. In fact, PCP and water consumption were similar in that group. However, when intersession saccharin was replaced with water, PCP intake increased to levels similar to the intersession water group. Only 42.8% of the monkeys in the intersession-saccharin group acquired, compared to 85.7% in the high-dose intersession-water group. The results from the intersession-saccharin group suggest that the initiation of drug-taking may depend on the environmental conditions occurring during initial drug exposure. These findings extend previous studies in rats and monkeys to a condition in which drug and the nondrug reinforcer were sequentially (rather than concurrently) available. The data also indicate that a history of saccharin access during the intersession period did not block acquisition, and this also was reported with rats (Carroll & Lac, 1993). In contrast, a previous study showed that a history of food restriction facilitated acquisition of IV cocaine self-administration in rats (Specker, Lac, & Carroll, 1994).

In summary, acquisition of drug self-administration is sensitive to economic variables such as unit price and substitution. The higher the dose or lower the unit price, the more rapid is acquisition, and a greater percentage of animals in each group acquire. Also, access to alternative nondrug reinforcers (e.g., food or a palatable substance) reduces the rate and success of acquisition. These factors may operate independently, interact or have an additive effect on acquisition. These variables should be taken into account when developing drug abuse prevention strategies.

REINSTATEMENT OF EXTINGUISHED DRUG
SELF-ADMINISTRATION

In the clinical setting, reinitiation of regular drug use after a period of abstinence (relapse) is one of the most challenging behaviors to treat or prevent in former drug users. This transition from nonuse to active drug seeking and eventual use has been discussed in recent reviews (e.g., Bickel & Kelly, 1988; Carroll & Comer, 1996; Stewart, 1983; Stewart & de Wit, 1987). Priming effects that induce reinstatement may result from exposure to external (lights, sounds) or internal (stress, brief exposures to drugs) stimuli or a combination of stimuli. The priming effects that reinstate drug-seeking behavior are similar to those that occur with traditional reinforcers such as food (de Wit, 1996). The priming effect is akin to the clinical setting in which an abstinent alcoholic takes one drink (a lapse) that leads to continued use (relapse).

3. THE REINFORCING EFFECTS OF DRUGS

Methods for Studying Reinstatement of Self-Administration Behavior

There are several approaches to studying reinstatement or relapse, such as animal and human laboratory models and using external and internal stimuli to produce reinstatement. External cues or stimuli play a prominent role in relapse to drug abuse in abstinent human addicts (Childress, McLellan, Ehrman, & O'Brien, 1988; Childress, McLellan, & O'Brien, 1986). In the laboratory, drug-related external stimuli trigger physiological responses and self-reports associated with drug craving (Childress et al., 1986). Treatment attempts have incorporated extinction of these external cues by repeatedly exposing subjects to places and equipment and the visual, tactile, and auditory characteristics of the drug-taking environment (Childress et al., 1986, 1988). An early study in animals also demonstrated that external stimuli generated substantial drug-seeking behavior that increased with drug (morphine) dose (Davis & Smith, 1976).

There has been more experimental attention directed toward interoceptive stimuli as priming agents. An early study by Pickens and Harris (1968) demonstrated that a single amphetamine injection reinstated responding in rats that were in a self-imposed period of abstinence. More recently, the priming injection has been used to initiate self-administration at the start of a session (e.g., Horger, Wellman, Morien, Davies, & Schenk, 1991). The use of the amphetamine prime also was extended to monkeys under extinction conditions in which the drug had been replaced with saline. After an amphetamine priming injection, saline self-administration resembled drug self-administration (Gerber & Stretch, 1975; Stretch & Gerber, 1973). A number of subsequent experiments employed this methodology, and several "standard" protocols for studying reinstatement were developed (e.g., de Wit & Stewart, 1981, 1983; Shaham, Rodaros, & Stewart, 1994; Wise, Murray, & Bozarth, 1990). Using the standard protocols, the priming effect has been applied to a wide variety of drugs and drug doses. This relapse phenomenon has been extended to different routes of administration such as oral (Chiamulera, Valiero, & Tessari, 1995) and intracranial–ventricular (Shaham et al., 1997; Stewart, 1984) and to other species such as humans (Chutuape, Mitchell, & de Wit, 1994; de Wit & Chutuape, 1993; Jaffe, Casalla, Kumor, & Sherer, 1989) and baboons (Kautz & Ator, 1995).

Several theories have been proposed to account for the priming effect, or the fact that motivationally significant stimuli increase the probability of behaviors directed toward the reinforcing stimulus. There are theories involving classical conditioning, instrumental learning (discriminative stimulus effects), memory reactivation, and loss of self-control (see review by de Wit, 1996). The incentive motivational theory (Bindra, 1974) has been applied to the reinstatement data in more recent literature (Stewart & de Wit, 1987; Stewart & Wise, 1992). A number of studies now exist that discuss the range of conditions under which the priming effect occurs. Many of the variables that have been tested are amenable to a behavioral economic analysis, and this section of the review focuses on the application of behavioral economic concepts to the laboratory study of priming effects. This review also summarizes recent additions to the literature on reinstatement that extend the range of priming conditions.

The basic priming procedure that was used in most of the work described here was developed by deWit and Stewart (1981, 1983) and modified by Wise et al. (1990), Comer, Lac, Curtis, and Carroll (1993) and Shaham et al. (1994). Rats are trained to press a lever that results in a drug-injection. Self-administration sessions last a short time (e.g., 2 hours), and then drug is replaced by saline or the vehicle for several hours. Responding is allowed to extinguish, which usually occurs within 30 minutes to 2 hours. During extinction, a priming dose of drug is administered by the experimenter, and responses are monitored for the next several hours. Under some variations of the procedure, several sessions are conducted each day (Shaham et al., 1994). When the number of responses that occur after a drug prime are significantly greater than those after a vehicle prime, per unit time, the increase in behavior is designated as reinstatement or relapse behavior.

Variables Affecting Reinstatement of Self-Administration Behavior

Unit Price Variables

The unit price hypothesis states that there is functional equivalence between the constituents of unit price—dose and response requirement—such that consumption will be constant at a given unit price regardless of how the consituents are varied. Although the unit price hypothesis has not been tested specifically using the reinstatement procedure, the following review discusses the effects of drug dose changes on reinstatement. In these studies, both constituents of unit price—drug dose and response requirement—have been manipulated during the self-administration phase; however, changes in the priming dose are not referred to as changes in unit price because the priming injection is not contingent on responding.

Drug Dose. Most of the dose effect studies have varied the dose of the priming drug rather than that of the self-administered drug. In two studies in which the maintenance dose was varied, the reinstatement effect was robust, and it did not vary significantly as a function of heroin (Shaham et al., 1994) or cocaine (Comer, Lac, Wyvell, Curtis, & Carroll, 1995) maintenance dose or unit price. However, there were dose-dependence increases in extinction responding prior to the priming injection.

The priming dose, on the other hand, appears to be an important factor in the magnitude of the reinstatement behavior. Reinstatement responding increased as priming dose increased or as unit price decreased, in rats that were maintained on cocaine (Comer et al., 1993; deWit & Stewart, 1981) or heroin (deWit & Stewart, 1983) and were primed with the same drug. The higher priming dose also maintained reinstatement responding longer, but there was a longer latency to reinitiate responding. Thus, the drug dose does not seem to be as important in the self-administration phase as it is during reinstatement. These findings also suggest that a higher unit price for drug during maintenance will be somewhat protective against reinstatement–relapse behavior. It should be noted, however, that in the animal priming studies, the priming doses that are most effective are generally much higher than the maintenance self-administration dose. For example, in a study by Comer et al. (1995), reinstatement effects were reported with a maintenance dose of cocaine as low as 0.2 mg/kg, but the effective priming dose had to be 3.2 mg/kg, a dose that is 16 times higher than the maintenance dose. As the maintenance dose increased, the discrepancy between the self-administration dose and the priming dose was less. Thus, the priming dose does not have to be higher than the maintenance dose to produce the reinstatement–relapse effect.

Response Cost. Another method by which unit price is varied is by changing the number of responses per dose of drug delivered. The FR typically has been changed by the same value across the drug and saline components, but it may be different for the drug and saline components. In the first case, the FR for cocaine delivery was varied from 1 to 2, 4, and 8 across the entire session (Carroll & Lac, 1996, unpublished data). Increasing the FR had no systematic effect on cocaine infusions during Hours 1 and 2, as the rats increased their responding proportionally; however, extinction responding and reinstatement responding decreased as the FR increased from 2 to 4 and 8 (Fig. 3.4).

In another study, the FR during the drug self-administration and saline extinction–reinstatement period was varied independently (Rawleigh, 1993, unpublished data). Two groups were under an FR 4 schedule of cocaine (0.4 mg/kg) delivery during the 2 hours of cocaine self-administration, but during the 5 hours of saline substitution, one group was on an FR 1 schedule and the other group was on an FR 4 schedule. The number of saline infusions during Hour 3 (extinction) was higher for the FR 1 group than for the FR 4 group (10.5 and 4.5 infusions, respectively). Likewise, the reinstatement responding after a 3.2 mg/kg cocaine priming injection was greater under the FR 1 versus the FR 4 condition (16 and 3.5 infusions, respectively). The same comparison was

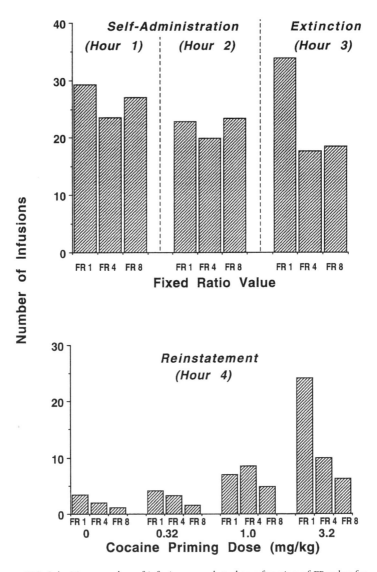

FIG. 3.4. Mean number of infusions are plotted as a function of FR value for the first four hours of the reinstatement model and for different priming doses (0-saline, 0.32, 1.0, and 3.2 mg/kg) that were given at the beginning of Hour 4 (lower frame). In the upper frames, data for Hours 1 to 3 were collapsed over the four different priming dose conditions because there were no systematic differences, and all behavior occurred before the experimental manipulation (priming injection).

made with two groups maintained on FR 8 for cocaine and either FR 1 or 8 for saline. The Hour 3 saline extinction infusions (49.25 and 25.33, respectively) and Hour 4 reinstatement infusions (32 and 7.33) were greater for the FR 1 versus the FR 8 group, respectively. It appeared that the higher maintenance FR generated greater extinction and reinstatement responding. These results also indicate that increasing the price of saline infusions reduces the effectiveness of a cocaine prime in reinstating behavior.

Substitution of Alternative Nondrug Reinforcers

In laboratory animals, alternative nondrug reinforcers mainly have consisted of increased amounts of food and other dietary enhancements. Addition of these substances to the environment markedly reduces acquisition of drug taking (Carroll & Lac, 1993, 1997, 1998) and ongoing drug self-administration (Carroll, 1985a; Nader & Woolverton, 1991). In humans, drug abuse and relapse rates have been reduced by nondrug alternative reinforcers that are contingent on drug abstinence (e.g., Higgins et al., 1994). Recent laboratory studies have extended the application of alternative reinforcement to the reinstatement–relapse model, and when access to alternative reinforcers was limited, reinstatement increased (Comer et al., 1995). This is consistent with the work of Vuchinich and Tucker (1996), showing that, in humans, alcoholic relapse becomes more probable when access to alternatives becomes more constrained.

Feeding Conditions. In a study with rats maintained on IV cocaine self-administration, the amount of daily food available was varied between 8 and 12 g, 20 g, or ad libitum postsession access in three groups (Comer et al., 1995). Another three groups of rats were fed the three different amounts before the 7-hour self-administration–extinction–reinstatement session. The different feeding conditions had no effect on the number of cocaine infusions during the 2 hours of cocaine self-administration; however, during saline extinction (Hour 3), there was a marked increase in the number of saline infusions in the low-food (8–12 g) group compared to the other feeding groups when food was given before the session. Several priming doses of cocaine (0, 0.32, 1.0, and 3.2 mg/kg) were tested at the start of Hour 4 at 4- to 5-day intervals. The higher priming doses (1.0 and 3.2 mg/kg) produced significantly higher increases in reinstatement responding during Hour 4 in the low-food group (8–12 g) compared to the groups fed 20 g or ad libitum before the session. In the three groups fed after the session, all cocaine priming doses (0.32–3.2 mg/kg) produced increases in saline infusions compared to the saline (0 mg/kg) prime, and the priming effect increased with greater food restriction.

Palatable Dietary Substances. As mentioned in the previous sections of this chapter, highly palatable sweetened foods or liquids prevent or slow the acquisition of drug self-administration by both IV (e.g., Carroll & Lac, 1993,

1998) and oral (Campbell et al., 1998) routes. Palatability and caloric content are factors that independently suppress drug intake (Carroll & Lac, 1998). A number of studies also have indicated that food and palatable dietary substances reduce ongoing, steady-state levels of drug self-administration, and the amount of suppression in drug intake increases with increased magnitude of the alternative reinforcer (Carroll, 1985a; Nader & Woolverton, 1991).

In one study conducted with rats and the relapse model, saccharin (0.2% weight/weight) was added to ground laboratory food, which was limited to 20 g per day and fed before or after the daily reinstatement session in different groups of rats (Carroll, 1985b). The cocaine maintenance dose was 0.4 mg/kg, and cocaine priming injections of 0 (saline), 0.32, 1.0, and 3.2 mg/kg were administered every 4 or 5 days. However, the results were no different than those of a group that was fed 20 g of standard ground food either before or after the session. Thus, under these limited conditions, enhancing the quality of food with a palatable additive did not suppress the reinstatement effect as it did with the acquisition and maintenance phases of the addiction process. Another attempt to manipulate reinstatement with alternative nondrug reinforcers was to use a food pellet as a priming agent in food-restricted rats. The food pellet did not reinstate responding that had been reinforced previously by 0.4 mg/kg cocaine during Hours 1 and 2.

Priming Drug

Whereas rats have been trained with only a few drugs that function as reinforcers (e.g., amphetamine, ethanol, cocaine, heroin, and morphine), a much wider range of drugs has served as priming stimuli. Table 3.3 indicates the priming drugs that were and were not effective when either cocaine or heroin served as the training or self-administered drug. Generally, drugs from the same pharmacological class or those that activate the same neuro-transmitter systems function as effective priming agents. Crossover effects also can be noted, such as cocaine-trained responding that is reinstated by a morphine prime and heroin-trained responding that is reinstated by a bromocriptine prime. This crossover effect is not always symmetrical; for example, heroin-trained behavior was not reinstated by cocaine, and co-caine-trained behavior was not reinstated by the opioid etonitazene. Further parametric work is needed to determine whether the asymmetry is due to the specific training and priming doses that were tested.

Priming With Treatment Drugs

One of the most clinically relevant questions regarding the priming effect is whether treatment drugs that reduce steady-state levels of self-administra-tion would elicit reinstatement of responding in abstinent individuals. There are examples in the human literature in which positive effects were found.

TABLE 3.3
Generality of Priming Effect

Variable	Self-Administered Drug	
	Cocaine	Heroin
Drugs that produced a priming effect	Amphetamine[c,d]	Amphetamine[c,d,e]
	Apomorphine[c,d]	Bromocriptine[h]
	Bromocriptine[h]	Heroin[c,d]
	Caffeine[i]	Morphine[c-g]
	Cocaine[b-e]	
	Codeine[e]	
	Morphine[c-g]	
Drugs that did not produce a priming effect	Buprenorphine[b]	Apomorphine[c,d]
	Chlorpromazine[e]	Cocaine[b-e]
	Clonidine[d,h]	Clonidine[h]
	Desipramine[a]	Nalorphine[g]
	Diazepam[c]	Naltrexone[b,g]
	Dimethyltryptamine[e]	Nicotine[b,g]
	Ethanol[c,h]	Saline[a-h]
	Etonitazene[b]	
	Heroin[c,d]	
	Methohexital[c,h]	
	Methylamphetamine[e]	
	Nalorphine[g]	
	Naloxone[e]	
	Naltrexone[b,g]	
	Nicotine[h]	
	Saline[a-h]	
	Secobarbital[e]	

[a]Comer (1992).
[b]Comer, Lac, Curtis, and Carroll (1993).
[c]de Wit & Stewart (1981).
[d]de Wit & Stewart (1983).
[e]Slikker, Brocco, and Killam (1983).
[f]Stewart (1984).
[g]Stewart & Wise (1992).
[h]Wise, Murray, and Bozarth (1990).
[i]Worley, Valadez, and Schenk (1994).

For example, the antidepressant desipramine is used in cocaine treatment (e.g., Gawin & Kleber, 1984; Kosten, Schumann, Wright, Carney, & Gawin, 1987), but Weiss (1988) suggested that the adverse reaction (jitteriness) produced by this drug might stimulate relapse to cocaine. Similarly, bromocriptine, a D_2 receptor agonist, has been used to treat cocaine craving (Dackis & Gold, 1985; Jaffe et al., 1989), but in the animal laboratory bromocriptine reinstated extinguished responding in cocaine-trained rats (Wise et al., 1990). Other potential treatment drugs (e.g., buprenorphine and naltrexone) have been tested as primes in the animal reinstatement model, but they did not increase responding for saline infusions. Self, Barnhart, Lehman, and Nestler (1996) reported that D_1-like and D_2-like dopamine receptor agonists have opposite effects on reinstatement and ongoing cocaine self-administration in rats. The priming effect was produced by D_2-like compounds (e.g., quinpirole) but not D_1-like (e.g., SKF 82958) dopamine receptor agonists. These results suggest that therapeutic efforts take into account the dissociation between different phases of addiction process and their potentially different underlying neurochemical processes.

Drug Pretreatment of Reinstatement

Another clinical application of the reinstatement model is that it can be used to screen potential treatment drugs. Few studies have been conducted in this area, and in the majority of them the treatment drug was given after the self-administration period, before the priming injection. For example, Comer et al. (1993) pretreated rats with buprenorphine, etonitazene, and naltrexone before a priming dose of cocaine. Buprenorphine and etonitazene, but not naltrexone, produced a dose-related suppression in reinstatement that suggested that the effect was due to opioid agonist actions. Others have shown that naltrexone, flupenthixol decanoate (a mixed dopamine antagonist), and raclopride (a D_2-like receptor antagonist) attenuated the effect of a heroin prime in heroin-trained rats (Shaham & Stewart, 1996; Stewart 1984). Recently, Lynch, LaBounty, and Carroll (1998) pretreated cocaine-trained rats with amphetamine, butorphanol, or morphine before the 2-hr cocaine self-administration session, which was $3\frac{1}{2}$ hours before the cocaine (or saline) priming injection. Amphetamine pretreatment produced a dose-dependent decrease in the number of cocaine infusions during Hour 1 but not Hour 2. In contrast, amphetamine produced a dose-dependent increase in the cocaine priming effect during Hour 4. Butorphanol decreased both cocaine self-administration and reinstatement elicited by a cocaine prime, as did morphine. Morphine produced a dose-dependent effect on cocaine self-administration but not on the priming effect. These findings suggest that treatment drugs may have the same or opposite effects on the maintenance and reinstatement phases of addiction.

Temporal Factors

The time between the end of the steady-state self-administration period and the first priming dose of drug during extinction is an important consideration for treatment, because it defines the period that an individual may be vulnerable to stimuli that could elicit relapse. In laboratory studies, this interval has been extended over long periods. Initially, de Wit and Stewart (1981) compared intervals of 10, 30, 60, 120, and 180 minutes between cocaine self-administration and the cocaine priming injection and found reinstatement at each. The peak responding occurred at about 10 minutes after the priming injection, and total number of infusions decreased as the interval increased. Shaham et al. (1994) recently showed that the reinstatement responding occurred in heroin-trained animals after a saline substitution period of 3 to 4 days. Later, they extended that interval to 8 days in heroin-trained animals (Shaham et al., 1994). Meil and See (1996) reported a delay of 43 days in cocaine-trained rats. Finally, Carroll and Lac (1996, unpublished observations) tested intervals of 1, 2, 4, 8, 32, and 64 days and found reinstatement responding after each with a 3.2 mg/kg priming dose of cocaine (compared to saline). Figure 3.5 compares reinstatement at the different delay intervals. It appeared that after the long delays (32 and 64 days), some of the rats showed reinstatement and some did not. However,

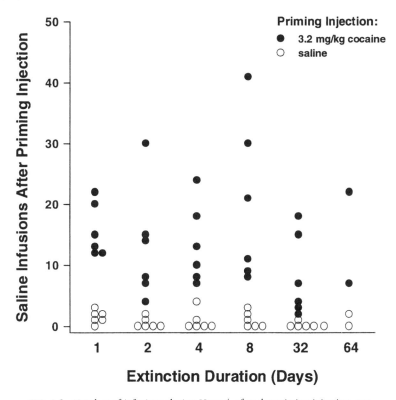

Extinction Duration (Days)

FIG. 3.5. Number of infusions during Hour 4, after the priming injection, are plotted for individual rats as a function of the delay interval (Days) between the last cocaine self-administration and the priming injection. Filled circles indicate saline infusions that occurred after a cocaine (3.2 mg/kg) injection, and open circles refer to the number of saline infusions earned after a priming injection of saline that was equal in volume to the cocaine injection. Saline primes were given first, and each animal received both a saline and cocaine prime. Different delay intervals were represented by different groups of rats.

the magnitude of the reinstatement response in those that showed the effect did not vary as a function of delay interval.

In summary, the stimuli that are important in the acquisition of drug self-administration are also key factors in reinstatement of extinguished responding during drug abstinence. These include the following: (a) a priming injection of the training drug, (b) access to a higher dose (or lower unit price), and (c) acute or chronic food restriction (Comer et al., 1995). The transition states of acquisition and reinstatement (relapse) are readily enhanced by these stimuli, and in some respects subjects are more sensitive to them in the transition states than during steady-state drug taking (Carroll & Comer, 1996). Another consistent finding in the acquisition and reinstatement phases was that alternative nondrug reinforcers, such as palatable dietary substances, or an increase amount of the standard diet reduces drug-seeking behavior possibly by functioning as an economic substitute for the reward value of drugs. Overall, a behavioral economic analysis of these transition states suggests that prevention of acquisition and reinstatement (reacquisition) may be accomplished by increasing the unit price of drugs and offering nondrug alternative reinforcers.

ACKNOWLEDGMENTS

Some of the research reviewed in this chapter was supported by National Institute of Drug Abuse (NIDA) grants R01 DA02486 and R37 DA03240 to M. E. Carroll. U. C. Campbell was supported by NIDA grant T32 DA07097 (Sheldon Sparber, Director).

REFERENCES

Bickel, W. K., & DeGrandpre, R. J. (1995). Price and alternatives: Suggestions for drug policy from psychology. *International Journal of Drug Policy, 6*, 93–105.
Bickel, W. K., & DeGrandpre, R. J. (1996). Modeling drug abuse policy in the behavioral economics laboratory. In L. Green & J. Kagel (Eds.), *Advances in behavioral economics* (Vol. 3, pp. 69–95). Norwood, NJ: Ablex.
Bickel, W. K., DeGrandpre, R. J., & Higgins, S. T. (1993). Behavioral economics: A novel experimental approach to the study of drug dependence. *Drug and Alcohol Dependence, 33*, 173–192.
Bickel, W. K., DeGrandpre, R. J., & Higgins, S. T. (1995). The behavioral economics of concurrent drug reinforcers: A review and reanalysis of drug self-administration research. *Psychopharmacology, 118*, 250–259.
Bickel, W. K., DeGrandpre, R. J., Higgins, S. T., & Hughes, J. R. (1990). Behavioral economics of drug self-administration. I. Functional equivalence of response requirement and drug dose. *Life Sciences, 47*, 1501–1510.

Bickel, W. K., & Kelly, T. H. (1988). The relationship of stimulus control to the treatment of substance abuse. In B. A. Ray (Ed.), *Learning factors in substance abuse* (pp. 122–140). Washington, DC: U.S. Government Printing Office.

Bindra, D. (1974). A motivational view of learning, performance, and behavior modification. *Psychological Review, 81,* 199–213.

Brown, P. L., & Jenkins, H. M. (1968). Autoshaping of the pigeon's keypeck. *Journal of the Experimental Analysis of Behavior, 11,* 1–8.

Campbell, U. C., Thompson, S. T., & Carroll, M. E. (1998). Acquisition of oral phencyclidine (PCP) self-administration in rhesus monkeys: Effects of dose and an alternative nondrug reinforcer. *Psychopharmacology, 137,* 132–138.

Carroll, M. E. (1982). Rapid acquisition of oral phencyclidine self-administration in food-deprived and food-satiated rhesus monkeys: Concurrent phencyclidine and water choice. *Pharmacology, Biochemistry & Behavior, 17,* 341–346.

Carroll, M. E. (1985a). Concurrent phencyclidine and saccharin access: Presentation of an alternative reinforcer reduces drug intake. *Journal of the Experimental Analysis of Behavior, 43,* 131–144.

Carroll, M. E. (1985b). The role of food deprivation in the maintenance and reinstatement of cocaine-seeking behavior in rats. *Drug and Alcohol Dependence, 16,* 95–109.

Carroll, M. E. (1996). Reducing drug abuse by enriching the environment with alternative nondrug reinforcers. In L. Green & J. Kagel (Eds.), *Advances in behavioral economics* (Vol. 3, pp. 37–68). Norwood, NJ: Ablex.

Carroll, M. E., & Comer, S. D. (1996). Animal models of relapse. *Experimental and Clinical Psychopharmacology, 4,* 11–18.

Carroll, M. E., France, C. P., & Meisch, R. A. (1981). Intravenous self-administration of etonitazene, cocaine and phencyclidine in rats during food deprivation and satiation. *Journal of Pharmacology and Experimental Therapeutics, 217,* 241–247.

Carroll, M. E., & Lac, S. T. (1993). Autoshaping i.v. cocaine self-administration in rats: Effects of nondrug alternative reinforcers on acquisition. *Psychopharmacology, 110,* 5–12.

Carroll, M. E., & Lac, S. T. (1996). Unpublished raw data.

Carroll, M. E., & Lac, S. T. (1997). Acquisition of i.v. amphetamine and cocaine self-administration in rats as a function of dose. *Psychopharmacology, 129,* 206–214.

Carroll, M. E., & Lac, S. T. (1998). Dietary additives and the acquisition of cocaine self-administration in rats. *Psychopharmacology, 137,* 81–89.

Carroll, M. E., Lac, S. T., & Nygaard, S. L. (1989). A concurrently available nondrug reinforcer prevents the acquisition or reduces the maintenance of cocaine-reinforced behavior. *Psychopharmacology, 97,* 23–29.

Chiamulera, C., Valiero, E., & Tessari, M. (1995). Resumption of ethanol-seeking behavior in rats. *Behavioural Pharmacology, 6,* 32–39.

Childress, A. R., McLellan, A. T., Ehrman, R., & O'Brien, C. P. (1988). Classically conditioned responses in opioid and cocaine dependence: A role in relapse? In B. A. Ray (Ed.), *Learning factors in substance abuse* (NIDA Research Monograph Series No. 84, pp. 44–61). Rockville, MD: National Institute of Drug Abuse.

Childress, A. R., McLellan, A. T., & O'Brien, C. P. (1986). Abstinent opiate abusers exhibit conditioned craving, conditioned withdrawal and reductions in both through extinction. *British Journal of Addictions, 81,* 655–660.

Chutuape, M-A. D., Mitchell, S. H., & de Wit, H. (1994). Ethanol preloads increase ethanol preference under concurrent random-ratio schedules in social drinkers. *Experimental and Clinical Psychopharmacology, 2,* 310–318.

Comer, S. D., Lac, S. T., Curtis, L. K., & Carroll, M. E. (1993). Effects of buprenorphine and naltrexone on reinstatement of cocaine-reinforced responding in rats. *Journal of Pharmacology and Experimental Therapeutics, 267,* 1470–1477.

Comer, S. D., Lac, S. T., Wyvell, C. L., Curtis, L. K., & Carroll, M. E. (1995). Food deprivation affects extinction and reinstatement of responding in rats. *Psychopharmacology, 121,* 150–157.

Dackis, C. A., & Gold, M. S. (1985). Bromocriptine as treatment of cocaine abuse. *Lancet, 1,* 1151–1152.

Davis, W. M., & Smith, S. G. (1976). Role of conditioned reinforcers in the initiation, maintenance and extinction of drug-seeking behavior. *Pavlovian Journal, 11,* 222–236.

De Vry, J., Donselaar, I., & van Ree, J. M. (1989). Food deprivation and acquisition of intravenous cocaine self-administration in rats: Effect of naltrexone and haloperidol. *Journal of Pharmacology and Experimental Therapeutics, 251,* 735–740.

de Wit, H. (1996). Priming effects with drugs and other reinforcers. *Experimental and Clinical Psychopharmacology, 4,* 5–10.

de Wit, H., & Stewart, J. (1981). Reinstatement of cocaine-reinforced responding in the rat. *Psychopharmacology, 75,* 134–143.

de Wit, H., & Stewart, J. (1983). Reinstatement of heroin-reinforced responding in the rat. *Psychopharmacology, 79,* 29–31.

Gawin, F. H., & Kleber, H. D. (1984). Open pilot trial with desipramine and lithium carbonate. *Archives of General Psychiatry, 41,* 903–910.

Gerber, G. J., & Stretch, R. (1975). Drug-induced reinstatement of extinguished self-administration behavior in squirrel monkeys. *Pharmacology, Biochemistry & Behavior, 3,* 1055–1061.

Higgins, S. T., Budney, A. J., Bickel, W. K., Foerg, F. E., Donham, R., & Badger, G. J. (1994). Incentives improve outcome in outpatient behavioral treatment of cocaine dependence. *Archives of General Psychiatry, 51,* 568–576.

Horger, B. A., Wellman, P. J., Morien, A., Davies, B. T., & Schenk, S. (1991). Caffeine exposure sensitizes rats to the reinforcing effects of cocaine. *NeuroReport, 2,* 53–56.

Hursh, S. R. (1991). Behavioral economics of drug self-administration and drug abuse policy. *Journal of the Experimental Analysis of Behavior, 56,* 377–393.

Jaffe, J. H., Cascella, N. G., Kumor, K. M., & Sherer, M. A. (1989). Cocaine-induced cocaine craving. *Psychopharmacology, 97,* 59–64.

Kautz, M. A., & Ator, N. A. (1995). Effects of triazolam on drinking in baboons with and without an oral self-administration history: A reinstatement phenomenon. *Psychopharmacology, 122,* 108–114.

Kosten, T. R., Schumann, B., Wright, D., Carney, M. K., & Gawin, F. H. (1987). A preliminary study of desipramine in the treatment of cocaine abuse in methadone maintenance petients. *Journal of Clinical Psychiatry, 48,* 442–444.

Lynch, W. J., La Bounty, L. P., & Carroll, M. E. (1998). A novel paradigm to investigate regulation of drug intake in rats self-administering i.v. cocaine or heroin. *Experimental and Clinical Psychopharmacology, 6,* 22–31.

Meil, W. M., & See, R. E. (1996). Conditioned cue recovery of responding following prolonged withdrawal from self-administered cocaine in rats: An animal model of relapse. *Behavioural Pharmacology, 7,* 754–763.

Messing, R. B., Kleven, M. S., & Sparber, S. B. (1986). Delaying reinforcement in an autoshaping task generates adjunctive and superstitious behaviors. *Behavioral Processes, 13,* 327–339.

Nader, M. A., & Woolverton, W. L. (1991). Effects of increasing the magnitude of an alternative reinforcer on drug choice in a discrete-trials choice procedure. *Psychopharmacology, 105,* 169–174.

Pickens, R. W., & Harris, W. C. (1968). Self-administration of d-amphetamine by rats. *Pscyopharmacology, 12,* 158–163.

Ramsey, N. F. (1991). *Cocaine dependence: Factors in the initiation of self-administration in rats.* (Doctoral Dissertation, University of Utrecht, 1991). The Netherlands.

Rawleigh, (1993). Unpublished raw data.

Samson, H. H., Roehrs, T. A., & Tolliver, G. A. (1982). Ethanol reinforced responding in the rat: A concurrent analysis using sucrose as the alternate choice. *Pharmacology, Biochemistry & Behavior, 17*, 333–339.

Samson, H. H., Tolliver, G. R., & Roehrs, T. A. (1983). Ethanol reinforced responding in the rat: Relation of ethanol introduction to later ethanol responding. *Pharmacology, Biochemistry & Behavior, 18*, 895–900.

Self, D. W., Barnhart, W. J., Lehman, D. A., & Nestler, E. J. (1996). Opposite modulation of cocaine-seeking behavior by D_1- and D_2-like dopamine receptor agonists. *Science, 271*, 1586–1589.

Shaham, Y., Funk, D., Erb, S., Brown, T. J., Walker, C.-D., & Stewart, J. (1997). Corticotropin-releasing-factor, but not corticosterone, is involved in stress-induced relapse to heroin-seeking in rats. *Journal of Neuroscience, 17*, 2605–2614.

Shaham, Y., Rodaros, D., & Stewart, J. (1994). Reinstatement of heroin-reinforced behavior following long-term extinction: Implications for the treatment of relapse to drug taking behavior. *Behavioural Pharmacology, 5*, 360–364.

Shaham, Y., & Stewart, J. (1996). Effects of opioid and dopamine receptor antagonists on relapse induced by stress and re-exposure to heroin in rats. *Psychopharmacology, 125*, 385–391.

Slikker, W., Brocco, M. J., & Killam, K. F. (1983). Reinstatement of responding maintained by cocaine or thiamylal. *Pharmacology, Biochemistry & Behavior, 41*, 615–619.

Specker, S. M., Lac, S. T., & Carroll, M. E. (1994). Food deprivation history and cocaine self-administration: An animal model of binge eating. *Pharmacology, Biochemistry & Behavior, 48*, 1025–1029.

Stewart, J. (1983). Conditioned and unconditioned drug effects in relapse to opiate and stimulant drug self-administration. *Progress in Neuro-Psychopharmacology and Biological Psychiatry, 7*, 591–597.

Stewart, J. (1984). Reinstatement of heroin and cocaine self-administration behavior in the rat by intracerebral application of morphine in the ventral tegmental area. *Pharmacology, Biochemistry, & Behavior, 20*, 917–923.

Stewart, J., & de Wit, H. (1987). Reinstatement of drug-taking behavior as a method of assessing incentive motivational properties of drugs. In M. A. Bozarth (Ed.), *Methods of assessing the reinforcing properties of abused drugs* (pp. 211–227). New York: Springer-Verlag.

Stewart, J., & Wise, R. A. (1992). Reinstatement of heroin self-administration habits: Morphine prompts and naltrexone discourages renewed responding after extinction. *Psychopharmacology, 108*, 79–84.

Stretch, R., & Gerber, G. J. (1973). Drug-induced reinstatement of amphetamine self-administration behavior in monkeys. *Canadian Journal of Psychology, 27*, 168–177.

Valenstein, E. S., Cox, V. C., & Kakolewski, J. W. (1967). Polydipsia elicited by the synergistic action of a saccharin and glucose solution. *Science, 157*, 552–554.

van Ree, J. M., Slangen, J. L., & De Wied, D. (1978). Intravenous self-administration of drugs in rats. *Journal of Pharmacology and Experimental Therapeutics, 204*, 547–557.

Vuchinich, R. E., & Tucker, J. A. (1988). Contributions from behavioral theories of choice to an analysis of alcohol abuse. *Journal of Abnormal Psychology, 97*, 181–195.

Vuchinich, R. E., & Tucker, J. A. (1996). Alcoholic relapse, life events, and behavioral theories of choice: A prospective analysis. *Experimental and Clinical Psychopharmacology, 4*, 19–28.

Weiss, R. D. (1988). Relapse to cocaine abuse after initiating desipramine treatment. *Journal of the American Medical Association, 260*, 2545–2546.

Wise, R. A., Murray, A., & Bozarth, M. A. (1990). Bromocriptine self-administration and bromocriptine-reinstatement of cocaine-trained and heroin-trained lever pressing in rats. *Psychopharmacology, 100*, 355–360.

Worley, C. M., Valadez, A., & Schenk, S. (1994). Reinstatement of extinguished cocaine-taking behavior by cocaine and caffeine. *Pharmacology, Biochemistry & Behavior, 48*, 217–221.

CHAPTER FOUR

Economics and Antihealth Behavior: The Economic Analysis of Substance Use and Abuse

Frank J. Chaloupka
University of Illinois at Chicago
and
National Bureau of Economic Research

Rosalie Liccardo Pacula
University of San Diego
and
National Bureau of Economic Research

Economists study the allocation of scarce resources among competing alternatives. One of the basic assumptions of economic theory is that individuals have limitless desires but limited budgets and therefore must make choices among the different alternatives, or *goods,* they desire. Markets facilitate these choices by determining the monetary price associated with each choice. Given these prices, individuals determine the best way to spend their limited budgets and still satisfy their most important desires. Economists refer to this process as *constrained utility maximization* and *rational choice.*

When individuals decide to buy a particular good at a specified price, they must be willing to pay the price that is being charged. Therefore, economists view price as a measure of a good's worth to the people who buy it. When the cost of a previously chosen alternative rises, individuals are faced with a new decision. They either can dedicate more of their limited budget to the more costly good, which requires that they reduce their purchase of the other alternatives, or they must reduce their purchase of the now more costly good so as to keep their consumption of the other goods the same (or some combination of the two). One of the fundamental principles of economic theory, known as the *law of demand,* implies that individuals will consume less of a good as its price rises. This means that an inverse relation will exist between the price of a good and the quantity demanded of that good, implying a downward-sloping demand curve.

Some have argued that the demands for tobacco, alcohol, and illicit substances of abuse differ from the demands for most other consumer goods because of the addictive nature of these products. The belief is that individuals do not choose to reduce their consumption of addictive substances when the price of these goods rises because doing so would force addicted individuals to experience withdrawal. Indeed, in the past, many researchers have viewed addictive consumption as an irrational behavior and therefore presumed it fell outside the realm of standard economic analysis (Elster, 1979; Friedman, 1962; Schelling, 1984; Winston, 1980).

This chapter reviews work that applies economic principles to the analysis of substance use and abuse. Specifically, we examine the impact of prices and public policies on the demands for tobacco, alcohol, and illicit drugs and on related outcomes. The findings from these studies clearly demonstrate that even in the case of addictive commodities, the law of demand still applies. Given the well-documented health and other consequences of substance use and abuse, policies lowering use, particularly by youth, are likely to result in significant long-run improvements in health.

THE ECONOMIC APPROACH
TO STUDYING HEALTH BEHAVIOR

Economic models of behavior detrimental to health, which have at their foundation the basic principles of consumer choice outlined previously, are not a relatively recent phenomenon. The fundamental ideas behind contemporary economic models of addiction, for example, were first outlined in Marshall's (1920) *Principles of Economics*. Despite the skepticism that quickly arose from both inside and outside the profession, economic models of antihealth behaviors continued to evolve from a series of pioneering works by Strotz (1956), Houthhakker and Taylor (1966, 1970), Pollack (1970, 1976, 1978), Hammond (1976), Stigler and Becker (1977) and Becker and Murphy (1988). Although these models almost exclusively have been used to describe addictions to particular substances developed over time, the framework is general enough to include more moderate health-related behaviors, such as healthy eating, exercise, and sleep.

A key to understanding how these basic models of consumer choice can be applied to health-related behaviors lies in how economists define price. To economists, *price* includes not only the monetary cost associated with purchasing a product, but also the time and other costs involved with buying and using that product. In the case of tobacco, for example, economists consider general public smoking restrictions as well as youth access restrictions as components of the price of tobacco because they raise the time, effort, and potential legal costs associated with smoking for adults and youths. Likewise, in the case of alcohol, the value of the time spent obtaining alcoholic beverages and the expected legal costs associated with underage drinking often are included as additional components of price when considering demand by youths. Conversely, policies that lower the penalties associated with possessing particular substances, such as marijuana decriminalization, lower the full cost of using these substances.

Just as the legal risks and penalties associated with use are considered to be components of price, so, too, are the perceived current and future health risks. For example, as consumers perceive greater health risks from cigarette smoking or drug use, perhaps due to warning labels on packaging or anticonsumption media campaigns, their demand for these products diminishes. Similarly, for those who are addicted to these products, the cost associated with cessation is also included. Thus, the *full price* of a good can be thought of as having four basic components: (1) monetary cost, (2) availability and time cost, (3) potential legal cost, and (4) potential health cost. When economists study the demand for alcohol, tobacco, and other substances, efforts are made to include not only the monetary price of these products, but also measures of the other costs associated with consuming them.

Although principally concerned with price effects, economists recognize that several other factors also influence the demand for particular products and try to incorporate these factors into their models. Disposable income is clearly an important factor influencing demand, because it is typically the main factor constraining the individual's choices. In general, consumption of most goods rises as income rises. Economists refer to these kinds of goods as *normal goods*. For some products, however, consumption falls as income rises. These are defined as *inferior goods*. An individual's tastes or preferences also will influence demand, but because these factors are difficult to measure, economists usually include sociodemographic characteristics as indicators of tastes. Examples of frequently utilized sociodemographic variables include gender, race and ethnicity, age, household structure, educational status and attainment, religious and family upbringing, marital status, and employment status.

Additionally, many recent economic studies of substance use have tried to account for the addictive nature of tobacco, alcohol, and other drug use. These models explicitly incorporate the intertemporal links in consumption by making current consumption decisions dependent on past choices, thus incorporating the tolerance, reinforcement, and withdrawal associated with addictive consumption. *Tolerance* is modeled by assuming that current satisfaction is lower when past consumption of an addictive substance is higher. *Reinforcement* refers to the positive effects of prior consumption on current consumption and is modeled by assuming that the additional satisfaction received from a unit of current consumption of the addictive substance is higher when past consumption is higher. *Withdrawal* refers to the negative effect on utility due to physical discomfort that occurs when the individual tries to quit use of the substance and is modeled by assuming current satisfaction is lower when addictive consumption is terminated. Two frameworks for modeling addictive behavior have been developed in the economics literature: myopic and rational models.

Myopic models assume that individuals behave shortsightedly and ignore all future consequences associated with current use of a substance. In these models, higher past consumption of the addictive substance leads to higher current consumption. Similarly, higher current consumption results in a stronger desire, or taste, for that good in the future, but the myopic individual ignores this effect because of an infinite discount rate on future consumption. Several of these models treat tastes as endogenous, implying that past and current consumption of an addictive substance change future preferences for that substance (e.g., Hammond, 1976; Houthhakker & Taylor, 1996, 1970; Pollack, 1970, 1976). Others treat tastes as fixed, or exogenous, capturing addiction through the assumption that an accumulation of past consumption affects current consumption because of a built-up tolerance for the drug.

The *rational addiction* framework models addictive behavior within the standard rational, utility-maximizing paradigm of economics (e.g., Becker & Murphy, 1988). In these models, an individual's taste for an addictive good does not change over time, but the demand in terms of quantity consumed for that good may change due to the addictive nature of that good. Rationality, in these models, implies that the future consequences of past and current consumption are considered when making current consumption choices. This contrasts with the myopic models, which assume that the future implications of addictive consumption are ignored when making current consumption decisions.

Generally, the demand functions that are derived by economists through constrained utility maximization are tested empirically with a variety of aggregate and individual-level data, using diverse econometric and other statistical methods. Many studies use aggregate, time-series data for the United States or for specific geographical units. Other studies employ pooled cross-sectional time-series data consisting of annual observations for countries, states, counties, cities, or other geographical units over time. Tax-paid sales and a variety of outcomes related to substance use and abuse are used in these studies. All of these measures are considered to be aggregate measures of use, because a particular individual's behavior cannot be identified. More recently, many economic studies of substance use employ self-reported measures of use and outcomes related to use taken from national survey data. These frequently are referred to as *individual-level* data. The use of these alternative data sets allows economists to capitalize on the substantial cross-sectional and intertemporal variations in price and control policies that exist for tobacco, alcohol, and other drugs.

EMPIRICAL EVIDENCE

Tobacco

There has been a surprisingly consistent finding in the relatively large economics literature that increases in cigarette prices are associated with reductions in cigarette smoking among the general population (National Cancer Institute, 1993; U.S. Department of Health and Human Services [USDHHS], 1989, 1992, in press). The consensus estimate of the price elasticity of demand for cigarettes that has emerged from these studies ranges from −0.3 to −0.5. Economists use the *price elasticity of demand* to explain how responsive consumption is to changes in the price of a good; it is defined as the percent change in consumption that results from a 1% increase in price. A price elasticity of demand ranging from −0.3 to −0.5, therefore, implies that a 10% increase in the price of cigarettes would reduce overall cigarette consumption in the general population by 3% to 5%.

Furthermore, economists found that the effects of increased cigarette prices are not limited to reductions in the number of cigarettes smoked by smokers. They also lead to significant reductions in smoking prevalence. These reductions in smoking prevalence reflect both increased smoking cessation among smokers and reduced smoking initiation among potential young smokers (Chaloupka & Grossman, 1996; Evans & Farrelly, 1996; National Cancer Institute, 1993). For example, Evans and Farrelly used 13 years of data from the National Health Interview Surveys (NHIS) and found that approximately one half of the impact of price on reducing adult smoking is on the decision not to smoke.

Early studies of youth and young adult smoking concluded that they were even more sensitive to changes in cigarette prices than were adults (Lewit & Coate, 1982; Lewit, Coate, & Grossman, 1981). Although this finding was contradicted by two later studies that used small samples from the Second National Health and Nutrition Examination (Chaloupka, 1991; Wasserman, Manning, Newhouse, & Winkler, 1991), more recent studies using larger samples confirmed the earlier result (Chaloupka & Wechsler, 1997; Chaloupka & Grossman, 1996; Evans & Farrelly, 1996). Evans and Farrelly, for example, pooled data from 13 surveys of the NHIS conducted from 1976 through 1992 and estimated an overall price elasticity of demand for young adults, ages 18 to 24, that was 50% larger than their estimate for adults ages 25 to 39 and nearly three times as large as their estimates for the full sample. Similarly, Chaloupka and Grossman estimated the price elasticity of demand for cigarettes by youths to be −1.31 using data on more than 110,000 eighth, tenth, and twelfth graders from the 1992–1994 Monitoring the Future Surveys (MTFS). They concluded that a 10% increase in cigarette prices would reduce youth smoking by 13.1%. Their estimates implied that the number of youth smokers would decline by nearly 7%, and that average cigarette consumption by young smokers would be reduced by more than 6% in response to a 10% price increase. Similarly, Chaloupka, Tauras, and Grossman (1997) found that both the prevalence and frequency of youth smokeless tobacco are inversely related to price. Given that nearly all smoking and other tobacco use initiation occurs by the time youths graduate from high school and that smoking habits become firmly established in young adulthood, these estimates suggest that substantial tax increases would be an effective way to achieve long-run reductions in smoking in all segments of the population.

Studies that applied economic theories of addictive behavior to the demand for cigarettes found that the long-run effects of price on cigarette demand is approximately double the short-run effects (Becker, Grossman, & Murphy, 1994; Chaloupka, 1991; Keeler, Hu, Barnett, & Manning, 1993). *Short-run*, in these models, refers to the relatively immediate effects of a price change on current consumption, whereas *long-run* refers to the cumulative impact of a permanent price change on use in all periods. These theoretical models, which attempt to capture the acquired tolerance, reinforcement, and withdrawal associated with consumption over time, predict that the long-run effect of a price change on demand will be larger than the more immediate effect because a permanent change in price will have a cumulative downward effect on consumption over time. Indeed, this is what is found. The long-run price elasticity of demand for cigarettes from these models ranges from −0.6 to −1.0, as compared to a range from −0.3 to −0.5 for short-run elasticities of demand.

Furthermore, relevant studies found that cigarette smoking is behaviorally addictive in the sense that past smoking decisions have a significant effect on current smoking. Some of the models (e.g., Becker & Murphy, 1988) assume that addicts are somewhat farsighted in their decisions, implying that future consequences of their addiction will lead to changes in the current decision. Empirical tests of these so-called rational addiction models find that cigarette smokers do take into account future effects of smoking in their current decision (Becker et al., 1994; Chaloupka, 1991, 1992; Chaloupka & Grossman, 1996).

As with changes in the monetary price of cigarettes, a number of studies provided evidence that tighter smoking restrictions, which increase the time cost and potential legal cost associated with tobacco use, reduce smoking among adults (Chaloupka, 1992; Chaloupka & Saffer, 1993; Evans, Farrelly, & Montgomery, 1996; Ohsfeldt, Boyle, & Capilouto, 1998; Wasserman et al., 1991). Relatively comprehensive restrictions on smoking in public places, particularly restrictions on smoking in workplaces, generally are found to be associated with both lower smoking prevalence and lower average daily cigarette consumption. Evans et al., for example, used survey data to examine the impact of workplace policies on smoking prevalence and intensity among workers. Their statistical model allowed for the possibility that workers self-select work sites based on their own smoking status and the workplace smoking policies. Their estimates suggested that workplace smoking bans reduce the probability of adult smoking by 5% and reduce average daily consumption among smokers by 10%. Chaloupka and Saffer (1993) used annual state-level data from 1975 through 1985 to examine the impact of smoking restrictions on aggregate cigarette sales. After controlling for the possibility that the state restrictions merely reflect general antismoking sentiment in the state (i.e., that smoking laws are endogenous), they found that relatively comprehensive restrictions on smoking in public places led to reductions in smoking.

There is a much smaller literature examining the impact of smoking restrictions on youth tobacco use, but it generally is found that public and school restrictions are effective at reducing smoking by youths (Chaloupka & Wechsler, 1997; Pentz et al., 1989; Wasserman et al., 1991). Using a sample of more than 16,000 students from 140 colleges and universities, Chaloupka and Wechsler (1997) found that stringent restrictions on smoking in public places significantly reduced the likelihood that college students smoke, and even weak restrictions were effective at reducing the quantity consumed by those who choose to smoke. Wasserman et al. used several waves of the NHIS from the 1970s through the 1980s to construct an index of antismoking regulations and found that increasing state restrictions on smoking from just a few public places to the most comprehensive restrictions would reduce overall teenage cigarette consumption by more than 40%.

Much less is known about the impact of youth access restrictions on the consumption of tobacco by youths, even though this has been the focus of recent antismoking campaigns. Chaloupka and Grossman (1996) examined the impact of a variety of state and local limits on youth access using data from the 1992 through 1994 MTFS. They found that minimum legal purchase ages for cigarettes, requirements that signs indicating the minimum purchase age be posted where tobacco products are sold, restrictions on vending machine cigarette sales, limits on the distribution of free samples of tobacco products, and vendor licensing provisions related to tobacco generally have no significant effect on youth smoking. Chaloupka and Grossman hypothesized that the lack of a significant finding was due to the relative weak enforcement of these restrictions in many states. This is consistent with what has been found by DiFranza, Norwood, Garner, and Tye (1987) and others that minimum purchase age laws have little success in reducing minors' access to tobacco because the laws are poorly enforced. Chaloupka and Pacula (1998), on the other hand, found that comprehensive and aggressive enforcement of and high compliance with the limits on youth access do lead to significant reductions in youth smoking.

Evans and Farrelly (1996) considered the compensating behavior of smokers in response to changes in price. In particular, using detailed data collected in the 1979 and 1987 NHIS regarding the brand of cigarette smoked, Evans and Farrelly developed several measures of smoking intensity, including total millimeters of cigarettes smoked and total tar and nicotine consumed daily. They found that smokers in higher tax states are more likely to smoke longer cigarettes and to smoke higher tar and nicotine cigarettes than smokers in lower tax states. They found that, for some groups, this compensating behavior is large enough to offset the health benefits of the reduced cigarette consumption that would result from a tax increase. Based on these findings, Evans and Farrelly argued that if higher cigarette taxes are being used to reduce the health consequences of smoking, then it would be more appropriate to tax cigarettes based on tar and nicotine content.

Moore (1996), however, presented some contrasting evidence that suggests that higher cigarette taxes and prices do have significant health benefits. Using annual state-level data on tobacco-related mortality rates for the period from 1954 to 1988, Moore concluded that increases in cigarette taxes lead to significant reductions in smoking-related deaths. His estimates imply that a 10% increase in the cigarette tax would lead to approximately 6,000 fewer deaths from smoking each year in the United States.

As these studies demonstrate, economists have been able to shed substantial light on smoking behavior. It is now firmly established that smokers are responsive to changes in the price of cigarettes. Moreover, it is widely accepted that smoking by youth and young adults is more responsive to price than is smoking by adults. Furthermore, models that account for the addictive nature of smoking find that the long-run effect of price on smoking is larger than the short-run impact. Stronger smoking restrictions, particularly restrictions on smoking in public and private workplaces, are found to be effective at decreasing smoking prevalence and average daily consumption among youth and adults. Smoking among youth, however, is generally not responsive to limits on youth access to tobacco products unless they are comprehensive, aggressively enforced, and complied with highly.

Alcohol

Considerable attention has been given to the effect of price on the demand for alcohol in the economics literature. Perhaps this is because of the increased awareness of alcohol-related problems, such as drunk driving and the consequent motor vehicle accident fatalities, domestic violence, and other crime. Numerous studies have been conducted employing aggregated state and national data as well as individual-level data. Although economists are in agreement that price clearly influences the quantity of alcohol consumed, estimates of the degree of responsiveness to price vary from study to study and from population to population. For example, Leung and Phelps' (1993) review of the economics literature that analyzed aggregate-level data for the general population found that the estimated price elasticity for beer ranges from −0.12 to −1.07. They concluded, based on these studies, that their best guess of the price elasticities for beer, wine, and distilled spirits are −0.3, −1.0, and −1.5, respectively. This suggests that beer consumption is far less sensitive to changes in price than wine and distilled spirits consumption. They noted that recent work using individual-level data suggests that alcohol demand may be even more responsive to price than their best guesses indicate. Recent studies by Grossman, Chaloupka, and Sirtalan (1998); Beard, Gant, and Saba (1997); Kenkel (1993, 1996); Manning, Blumberg, and Moulton (1995); Baltagi and Griffin (1995); and Moore and Cook (1995) used individual-level data and generally found price elasticities larger than those from aggregate studies.

Economists also have found that responsiveness to price varies by consumption level (Cook & Moore, 1993a; Kenkel, 1996; Manning et al., 1995; Mullahy & Sindelar, 1994). Manning et al., using data from the 1983 NHIS, found that moderate drinkers are the most responsive to changes in the price of alcohol, with an estimated price elasticity of −1.19, and both lighter and heavier drinkers have price elasticities that are closer to zero. Kenkel (1996) found somewhat different results using the 1985 wave of the survey. He estimated an average price elasticity of moderate drinking of −0.78. He further calculated separate elasticity estimates for heavy drinking by gender and found that heavy drinking among men is much less price sensitive than is heavy drinking among women, with the estimated price elasticities being −0.52 and −1.29, respectively.

Applications of the addiction models to alcohol consumption reveal generally similar findings to those that are found in the tobacco literature (Grossman et al., 1998; Moore & Cook, 1995). Grossman et al. (1998) applied the Becker and Murphy (1988) rational addiction model to the consumption of alcohol by young adults using longitudinal data from the MTFS. They found consistent evidence that increases in the full price of alcohol, resulting either from higher monetary prices or higher minimum legal drinking ages, significantly reduce drinking among young adults. Furthermore, they found strong evidence that drinking in this age group is addictive in the sense that there is a strong interdependency of past, current, and future alcohol consumption. They estimated an average long-run price elasticity of demand of −0.65, which is over twice as large as the estimate they got when addiction is ignored (−0.29). They also found that the long-run price elasticity of demand is approximately 60% larger than their estimate of the short-run elasticity.

Moore and Cook (1995) estimated both a myopic and rational model of addiction using data from the National Longitudinal Survey of Youth (NLSY) and found that, in both cases, consumption remains sensitive to changes in the full price of alcohol. They, too, found that the long-run elasticity of demand is significantly larger than that of the short-run elasticity of demand.

Studies focusing on drinking by youths and young adults consistently find that these populations are even more sensitive to changes in the price of alcohol than are adults (Chaloupka & Wechsler, 1996; Coate & Grossman, 1988; Cook & Moore, 1993a; Grossman, Coate, & Arluck, 1987; Laixuthai & Chaloupka, 1993). Grossman, Chaloupka, Saffer, and Laixuthai (1994) reviewed the literature on the effects of increased prices and minimum legal purchase ages for alcoholic beverages on youth drinking based on a number of nationally representative data sets. Their review indicated that youth drinking, including heavy drinking, is significantly related to alcoholic beverage prices, taxes, and minimum legal drinking ages. Grossman et al. (1987), for example, estimated the beer price elasticity for youth at −3.05 and spirits price elasticity at −3.83.

More recently, Chaloupka and Wechsler (1996) explored the relation between various measures of alcohol availability and youth drinking and binge drinking using data from the 1993 Harvard College Alcohol Survey. They found a strong positive relation between alcohol availability and drinking, particularly binge drinking. Furthermore, they found a strong negative relation between the strength of state-level policies related to drinking by youth and young adults and all measures of drinking. Their findings support those of others who have found that changes in the full price of alcohol lead to larger reductions in heavy or frequent drinking by youths and young adults.

In addition to examining the effects of price on alcohol consumption, a number of economists have studied the impact of the full price of alcohol on the negative consequences of alcohol use and abuse, including drinking and driving, alcohol-related accidents, liver cirrhosis mortality and other health consequences, and violence and other crime.

It is consistently found that raising the full price of alcohol is an effective way of reducing fatal and nonfatal motor vehicle accidents, many of which are related to driving under the influence of alcohol (Chaloupka & Laixuthai, 1997; Chaloupka, Saffer, & Grossman, 1993; Kenkel, 1993; Mullahy & Sindelar, 1994; Ruhm, 1996; Saffer & Grossman, 1987a, 1987b). Using annual state-level data for the period from 1975 through 1981, Saffer and Grossman (1987a), for example, predicted that a policy indexing the beer tax to the rate of inflation since 1951 would have reduced 18- to 20-year-old motor vehicle accident fatalities by 15%, and a uniform legal drinking age of 21 years would have lowered fatalities by 8%.

Chaloupka et al. (1993) considered the effects of beer taxes, legal drinking ages, alcohol availability, and all major state-level policies related to drinking and driving on youth and adult motor vehicle accident fatality rates (including alcohol-involved fatality rates) using state-level data for the period from 1982 through 1988. The drunk driving policies they examined reflect factors that influence the expected legal costs of drinking and driving by raising the probabilities of arrest and conviction for DUI, as well as the penalties imposed on conviction. They concluded that increases in many aspects of the full price of alcohol, including increased beer taxes; higher legal drinking ages; and swift, certain, and severe penalties for drinking and driving would lead to significant reductions in motor vehicle accident fatalities related to alcohol.

More recent research using individual-level data similarly has concluded that increases in beer taxes and drinking ages, as well as strong laws related to drinking and driving, are effective at reducing self-reported drinking and driving and involvement in nonfatal traffic accidents (Chaloupka & Laixuthai, 1997; Kenkel, 1993; Mullahy & Sindelar, 1994).

Similarly, several studies have examined the effects of the full price of alcohol on liver cirrhosis mortality and other health consequences related to alcohol (Chaloupka, Grossman, Becker, & Murphy, 1992; Cook & Tauchen, 1982; Sloan, Reilly, & Schenzler, 1994). Cook and Tauchen, for example, estimated that a $1 increase in the tax on a proof-gallon of distilled spirits would have reduced cirrhosis deaths by 5.4% to 10.8% during the period covered by their data, contradicting the then conventional wisdom that heavy alcohol consumption was unresponsive to price. This finding was confirmed by Chaloupka et al. (1992) in their application of the rational addiction model to heavy alcohol consumption that used cirrhosis mortality as a proxy for heavy consumption. Using state-level data from 1961 through 1984, they concluded that overall alcohol consumption does not reflect addictive behavior but that heavy alcohol consumption does reflect addiction. They estimated that a 10% increase in the price of alcoholic beverages would reduce cirrhosis mortality by 8.3% to 12.8% in the long run.

Similarly, Sloan et al. (1994) found that other deaths related to alcohol use and abuse, including deaths where alcohol is the primary cause or a contributing cause—suicides, and deaths from drownings, falls, and other accidents—fall as the full price of alcohol increases due to increases in monetary prices, reductions in the availability of alcoholic beverages, or both. Likewise, Ohsfeldt and Morrisey (1997) found that the probability of a nonfatal workplace accident is inversely related to the price of alcoholic beverages.

Finally, several recent economic studies considered the relation between alcohol control policies and violence and other crime (Chaloupka & Saffer, 1992; Cook & Moore, 1993b; Markowitz & Grossman, 1997; Sloan et al., 1994). Cook and Moore (1993b), for example, examined state-level data on violent crime rates for the period from 1979 through 1987. They concluded that higher beer taxes would lead to significant reductions in rapes and robberies but would have little impact on homicides and assaults. In a more detailed analysis for the period from 1975 through 1990, Chaloupka and Saffer (1992) concluded that increases in the full price of alcoholic beverages resulting from increased beer taxes or reduced availability of alcohol would lead to reductions in all measures of crime, including homicides, rapes, assaults, and various income-producing crimes. These findings generally are confirmed by the analysis of homicide rates by Sloan et al. (1994).

More recently, Markowitz and Grossman (1997) used individual-level data to examine the impact of the full price of alcoholic beverages on domestic violence directed at children. They found a strong inverse relation between the full price and both the probability of child abuse and overall violence toward children. For example, they estimated that a 10% increase in the beer tax would reduce the probability of child abuse by 2.2%, and reductions in the number of outlets licensed to sell alcoholic beverages would further reduce violence toward children.

Economic analysis, therefore, clearly demonstrates that drinking by adults, young adults, and youth is responsive to changes in the full price of alcohol. Generally, we find that young drinkers are more responsive than older drinkers. As with cigarettes, we find that long-term declines in drinking in response to price increases are larger than short-run declines due to the addictive nature of drinking. Contrary to popular opinion, economists find that heavy drinking and the health consequences associated with it, such as fatal and nonfatal motor vehicle accidents, cirrhosis mortality, suicides, drowning, and violent crime, are generally also responsive to increases in the full price of alcohol.

Illicit Drugs

Although considerable attention has been paid to the consumption of cigarettes and alcohol in the economics literature, there are significantly fewer empirical studies of the effect of illicit drug prices on drug use. This largely is attributed to two severe data limitations that make estimating demand equations for illicit drugs quite difficult. First, there are no aggregate data for illicit drugs comparable to the tax-paid sales data available for cigarettes and alcohol, and the few general population surveys that include questions pertaining to illicit drug use are plagued by validity and reliability concerns. As a result, many economists in the past have tried to estimate elasticities from either small, local samples of users or from annualized national crime or hospital data. Second, even less data are available on the prices people pay for the illicit drugs they consume and on the other aspects of the full price of these substances. Economists conducting the earliest research in this area, therefore, have been forced in many cases to use imperfect proxies for the prices of the drugs and to draw conclusions regarding actual price elasticities from these proxies. More recent research, however, has taken advantage of the more appropriate data that have become available on illicit drug use, drug prices, and control policies.

The majority of empirical studies on illicit drug use examine the effect of state decriminalization status on the demand for marijuana. States that have decriminalized marijuana have lower penalties associated with possession of small amounts of the drug (typically less than 1 ounce). These lower penalties reduce the expected legal cost associated with consuming marijuana and should therefore increase the demand for marijuana.

Studies that have examined the impact of decriminalization on the consumption of marijuana in the general population have found this to be the case (Model, 1993; Saffer & Chaloupka, 1997). Using the 1988, 1990, and 1991 waves of the National Household Survey on Drug Abuse (NHSDA), Saffer and Chaloupka (1997) estimated that decriminalization increases the probability of marijuana use in the past month by about 8.4% and in the past year by about 7.6%. Similarly, Model found that decriminalization significantly increased the number of marijuana-related emergency room visits.

Studies that focused on youth and young adult populations, however, generally have found that decriminalization status has little or no consistent impact on demand (Chaloupka, Grossman, & Tauras, 1998; DiNardo & Lemieux, 1992; Johnston, O'Malley, & Bachman, 1981; Pacula, in press; Thies & Register, 1993). This does not imply that youths are insensitive to changes in the price of marijuana, however. Nisbet and Vakil (1972) used data from interviews with students at the University of California, Los Angeles, to examine the demand for marijuana and estimated a price elasticity of marijuana at −0.40 to −1.51. Likewise, Pacula (in press) found that youth 30-day marijuana prevalence is sensitive to changes in the crime-per-officer ratio, a proxy for the price of marijuana, using data from the 1984 NLSY. Finally, Chaloupka et al. (1998), using data from the 1982 and 1989 waves of the MTFS, found that consumption of marijuana by high school seniors was reduced by increases in the associated fines for possession.

Several recent studies have taken advantage of new information on cocaine prices available from the Drug Enforcement Agency's System to Retrieve Information from Drug Evidence (STRIDE) data set and examined the sensitivity of cocaine use to changes in its price (Chaloupka et al., 1998; DiNardo, 1993; Grossman & Chaloupka, 1998; Saffer & Chaloupka, 1997, 1998). Using state-aggregated data from the 1977 through 1987 surveys of the MTFS of high school seniors, DiNardo found that price had no significant effect on cocaine use by youths. Grossman and Chaloupka (1998), however, found a significant effect using the individual-level longitudinal data from the 1976 through 1985 surveys of high school seniors. Within the context of the Becker and Murphy's (1988) rational addiction model, Grossman and Chaloupka (1998) estimated a short-run price elasticity of −0.96 and a long-run price elasticity of −1.35 for young adult cocaine demand. Furthermore, their estimates are consistent with the hypothesis of rational addictive behavior.

Likewise, Chaloupka et al. (1998) used data from the 1982 and 1989 waves of the MTFS and found that youth consumption of cocaine is sensitive to changes in price. They estimated an overall price elasticity of youth cocaine demand of −1.28 for use in the past year and −1.43 for use in the past month based on data from both survey years. Saffer and Chaloupka (1997) employed data that consisted mainly of adults and found that consumption of cocaine is still price-sensitive. Saffer and Chaloupka (1997) estimated an average participation elasticity for cocaine use in the past month of −0.28 and an average participation elasticity for use in the past year of −0.44 using data from the 1988, 1990, and 1991 waves of the NHSDA. Participation elasticities differ from overall price elasticities because they only examine the decision to use the drug, not the change in quantity consumed associated with the price change.

The empirical studies examining the influence of price on use of other illicit drugs is even sparser. Two early studies by Silverman and his colleagues suggested that the demand for heroin is inelastic (Brown & Silverman, 1974; Silverman & Spruill, 1977). Using a pooled cross-sectional time-series data set on 41 Detroit neighborhoods from November 1970 through July 1973, Silverman and Spruill found a price elasticity for heroin use of about −0.26. They also found that property crime rates were positively and significantly affected by the price of heroin, whereas nonproperty crime rates are not.

More recent studies using price data from the STRIDE data set and consumption data from the 1988, 1990, and 1991 NHSDA reveal that heroin consumption is much more price-sensitive than previously thought (Saffer & Chaloupka, 1998, 1997). Saffer and Chaloupka (1997) reported price elasticities for heroin participation in the past month ranging from −0.82 to −1.03 and price elasticities for participation in the past year from −0.60 to −1.02. These estimates are consistent with findings from Bretteville-Jensen and Sutton (1996), who estimated the price responsiveness of 500 Norwegian heroin users using self-reported price and consumption data. They reported a price elasticity of heroin of −1.23.

These estimates for the effects of price on illicit drug use are consistent with the evidence from the more extensive literatures on the demand for licit addictive substances. In particular, these studies found that illicit drug use is inversely related to price; that illicit drug demand by youth is more price-elastic than demand by adults; and, in the models accounting for the addictive aspects of consumption, that the long-run effect of price increases exceeds the short-run effect.

Polydrug Use and Cross-Price Effects

There is increasing evidence in the biomedical literature that the use of illicit drugs may heighten the effects of alcohol, just as drinking alcohol can heighten the effects of illicit drugs (National Institute on Alcohol Abuse and Alcoholism, 1993). These two behaviors, therefore, can reinforce each other. Indeed, recent statistics show that *polydrug use*, which is defined as the concurrent use of more than one substance, has become a fairly common practice, particularly among abusers (Grant & Harford, 1990; Martin, Clifford, Maisto, & Earleywine, 1996). In 1994, for example, more than 97% of young adults in the NHSDA who reported currently using marijuana also reported currently using alcohol. These findings suggest that a complementary relation exists between the demands for licit and illicit substances, particularly alcohol and marijuana. Economists examine how changes in the price of one good affect the consumption of a second good to determine the relation between these goods. If consumption of one good rises in response to an increase in the price of a second good, then economists consider the goods to be *substitutes*. Conversely, if an increase in the price of one good leads to a reduction in the consumption of a second good, then economics consider these goods *complements*.

Two recent econometric studies that examined the relation between alcohol and marijuana use by youth found evidence that the two were substitutes rather than complements (Chaloupka & Laixuthai, 1997; DiNardo & Lemieux, 1992). DiNardo and Lemieux employed state-aggregated data from the 1980 through 1989 MTFS to estimate prevalence equations for alcohol and marijuana that included the price of alcohol, the minimum drinking age, and marijuana decriminalization. They found that marijuana decriminalization had a significant negative effect on the prevalence of alcohol use by high school seniors, and the minimum legal drinking age had a significant positive effect on the prevalence of marijuana use. Both findings support the hypothesis that alcohol and marijuana are substitutes for youths. Many of the own-price effects were not significant, however.

Chaloupka and Laixuthai (1997) used individual-level data on youth drinking and nonfatal motor vehicle accidents from the 1982 and 1989 MTFS along with aggregate data on youth motor vehicle accident fatality rates from the Fatal Accident Reporting System to study the relation between alcohol and marijuana use. They included the beer tax, marijuana decriminalization, and, in some equations, the money price of marijuana in their estimation of a drinking frequency and heavy drinking equations. They found that both the frequency of drinking and the probability of heavy drinking were inversely related to beer prices, positively related to the price of marijuana, and negatively related to state decriminalization. These findings again suggested that alcohol and marijuana are substitutes for youths. Moreover, they found that, for youths, the probability of a nonfatal or fatal motor vehicle accident is inversely related to the full price of alcoholic beverages but positively related to the full price of marijuana. Given the evidence on the relative risks of driving under the influence of alcohol or marijuana, they concluded that this reflects substitution between the substances.

Other recent studies, however, found a complementary relation between alcohol and marijuana as well as other illicit drugs for young adults and adults (Pacula, 1997, in press; Saffer & Chaloupka, 1997, 1998; Thies & Register, 1993). All of these later studies employed individual-level data and estimated demand equations for alcohol and the other illicit substances, so it was possible in these studies to examine the cross-price effects in light of findings with respect to own-price effects. Thies and Register estimated the effect of marijuana decriminalization and minimum legal purchasing ages on the probabilities of alcohol, marijuana, and cocaine use with data taken from the NLSY. They found that state decriminalization status has a positive effect on alcohol and cocaine use, although it has no significant effect on heavy drinking or marijuana use. Using the same data, Pacula (in press) estimated the effects of changes in the full price of alcohol and marijuana on the probabilities of alcohol and marijuana use as well as the quantities consumed. She found that the tax on beer had a negative and significant effect on the decision to use both alcohol and marijuana, suggesting that the two substances are complements for her sample of young adults.

Saffer and Chaloupka (1997, 1998) conducted the most comprehensive analysis of cross-price effects among licit and illicit substances. Using a pooled sample of cross-sectional data from the 1988, 1990, and 1991 waves of the NHSDA, they estimated annual and monthly prevalence equations for alcohol, marijuana, cocaine, and heroin. A weighted average price of pure alcohol variable was included to capture the price of alcohol, state decriminalization status was included for the price of marijuana, and cocaine and heroin price information were added from the STRIDE data set. Saffer and Chaloupka (1997, 1998) found consistent evidence of a complementary relationship across all four drugs, with the exception of alcohol and marijuana, for which the evidence was mixed and depended on the population being examined.

To date, only one study has examined polydrug use while controlling for the addictive effects of consumption over time. Using a myopic model of multicommodity habit formation, Pacula (1997) estimated the youthful demands for alcohol and marijuana by gender. She included the tax on beer, minimum legal drinking age, decriminalization status, price of cigarettes, and a proxy for the monetary price of marijuana in all of her specifications. She found that for women, higher beer taxes reduce consumption of both alcohol and marijuana, implying a complementary relation. Similar evidence of a complementary relation was found in the demand equations for men. In addition to finding that the individual consumption of both substances was reinforced over time, Pacula (1997) also found for both men and women that previous use of marijuana significantly increased the current demand for alcohol, indicating that reinforcement can take place across substances.

The majority of studies to date have found a complementary relation between the demands for different substances. The mixed evidence with respect to alcohol and marijuana can be attributed to differences in the level of aggregation of the data as well as to differences in the populations being studied. When individual-level data are employed, and demand equations for marijuana also can be estimated, the findings are generally supportive of a complementary relationship between alcohol and marijuana. Until good measures of the money price of marijuana are obtained, however, this cannot be known with certainty.

IMPLICATIONS FOR PREVENTION POLICIES

As this literature review demonstrates, economists have made significant contributions to our understanding of the policy-manipulable determinants of the demands for tobacco, alcohol, and other drugs. Several clear conclusions emerge from this literature. First, the demands for addictive substances are not exceptions to the law of the downward-sloping demand curve, perhaps the most fundamental principle of economics, that is, significant increases in the monetary prices of cigarettes and other tobacco products; alcoholic beverages; and marijuana, cocaine, heroin, and other drugs will lead to significant reductions in the use of these substances. Similarly, increases in the other costs of substance use, which can be achieved by limiting availability, increasing the expected legal costs associated with use and abuse, and providing new and better information on the health consequences of use and abuse will lead to reductions in alcohol, tobacco, and other drug use. Moreover, these reductions in use will not be limited to reductions in the frequency of use or quantity consumed by users, but will be accompanied by reductions in the prevalence of use. This implies that large increases in taxes on cigarettes and other tobacco products and alcoholic beverages will lead to substantial reductions in cigarette smoking, alcohol use and abuse, and related outcomes. In contrast, these estimates imply that the legalization of currently illegal drugs, which would almost certainly lead to sharp reductions in the prices of these substances, would lead to sizable increases in the use and abuse of illicit drugs.

Second, the price sensitivity of demand for addictive substances is inversely related to age. Thus, youth and young adults are significantly more responsive to changes in price than are older adults. Given that most substance use is initiated during the teenage years and that patterns of use are firmly established during early adulthood, this implies that large permanent increases in prices, which will lead to disproportionately large reductions in substance use and abuse among youth and young adults, are likely to be the single most effective means of achieving long-run reductions in tobacco, alcohol, and other drug use in all segments of the population. This finding helps explain some of the recent trends in youth cigarette smoking.

After several years of decline, cigarette smoking and marijuana use among youth have been rising. The increase in youth smoking occurred at nearly the same time that cigarette prices were cut sharply by all major producers, beginning with Philip Morris' 40-cent price reduction for its Marlboro brand. Even with subsequent increases in state cigarette taxes, the real (inflation-adjusted) price of cigarettes is still below its level prior to the price cuts. The same applies to youth marijuana use, which has been rising at the same time as the real, purity-adjusted price of marijuana has been falling steadily. In contrast, youth alcohol use has changed little in recent years, and real alcohol prices have remained steady.

Third, in addition to affecting the use of tobacco, alcohol, and other drugs, price increases, strong and consistent evidence shows, will lead to reductions in the consequences of use, including morbidity and mortality, accidents, violence and other crime, and more. This implies that policies that raise the perceived probabilities of arrest and conviction and increase the swiftness and severity of the penalties imposed on conviction for underage drinking, drinking and driving, illicit drug possession, and other illegal activities will lead to significant reductions in these behaviors.

A fourth key finding from this research is that the long-run effects of changes in the monetary price or other costs associated with tobacco, alcohol, or other drug use will be larger than the short-run impacts because of the addictive nature of demand. This has important implications for the revenue-generating potential of large increases in cigarette and alcohol taxes. These increases will lead to significant reductions in use in the short run; they also will lead to sharp increases in tax revenues, given the relative inelasticity of demand in the short run. However, because of the addictive nature of consumption, the impact of tax increases on demand will grow over time, leading to smaller long-run increases in revenues than would be observed in the short run.

Furthermore, econometric studies of alcohol, tobacco, and other drug use done in the context of economic models of addiction find strong evidence of nonmyopic behavior. This implies that the future consequences of addictive consumption are considered to at least some extent when making current smoking, drinking, and illicit drug-use decisions. A key implication of this finding is that new and better information on the long-term health consequences of substance use and abuse will lead to immediate reductions in smoking, drinking, and other drug use. This clearly is supported by the sharp declines in cigarette smoking that were observed in the mid- to late-1960s after the release of the first U.S. surgeon general's report on the health consequences of smoking. The same was observed for cocaine use in the latter half of the 1980s after the death of college basketball star Len Bias from a cocaine overdose. This implies that school-based education programs, counteradvertising campaigns, and other efforts to improve the quantity and quality of information concerning the long-term consequences of substance use can lead to significant reductions in substance use and abuse.

Finally, the economic research on the demands for alcohol, tobacco, and other drugs suggests that there may be unintended consequences or benefits resulting from changes in control policies targeted at a single substance. For example, some studies concluded that stronger alcohol policies, although effective in reducing youth drinking and its consequences, may have led to increased marijuana use by teens. Several other studies, however, found evidence of a complementary relation between alcohol, marijuana, cocaine, and heroin use, implying that policies increasing the monetary price and other costs associated with the use of one of these substances would lead to reductions not only in the use of that substance but also in the use of the others. This is a relatively recent avenue of research by economists, and much more work clearly needs to be done before drawing definitive conclusions about the economic relations between various substances. Nevertheless, these findings do imply that the broader impact of policies directed at a particular substance must be considered before such policies are implemented.

REFERENCES

Baltagi, B. H., & Griffin, J. M. (1995). A dynamic model for liquor: The case for pooling. *The Review of Economics and Statistics, 75,* 545–554.

Beard, T. R., Gant, P. A., & Saba, R. P. (1997). Border-crossing sales, tax avoidance, and state policies: An application to alcohol. *Southern Economic Journal, 64,* 293–306.

Becker, G. S., Grossman, M., & Murphy, K. M. (1994). An empirical analysis of cigarette addiction. *American Economic Review, 84,* 396–418.

Becker, G. S., & Murphy, K. M. (1988). A theory of rational addiction. *Journal of Political Economy, 96,* 675–700.

Bretteville-Jensen, A. L., & Sutton, M. (1996). *Under the influence of the market: An applied study of illicitly selling and consuming heroin* (Discussion Paper No. 147). York, England: University of York, Centre for Health Economics.

Brown, G. F., & Silverman, L. P. (1974). The retail price of heroin: Estimation and applications. *Journal of the American Statistical Association, 347,* 595–606.

Chaloupka, F. J. (1991). Rational addictive behavior and cigarette smoking. *Journal of Political Economy, 99,* 722–742.

Chaloupka, F. J. (1992). Clean indoor air laws, addiction, and cigarette smoking. *Applied Economics, 24,* 193–205.

Chaloupka, F. J., & Grossman, M. (1996). *Price, tobacco control policies, and youth smoking* (Working Paper No. 5740). Cambridge, MA: National Bureau of Economic Research.

Chaloupka, F. J., Grossman, M., Becker, G. S., & Murphy, K. M. (1992, December). *Alcohol addiction: An econometric analysis.* Paper presented at the annual meeting of the Allied Social Science Associations, Anaheim, CA.

Chaloupka, F. J., Grossman, M., & Tauras, J. A. (1998). *The demand for cocaine and marijuana by youth* (Working Paper No. 6411). Cambridge, MA: National Bureau of Economic Research.

Chaloupka, F. J., & Laixuthai, A. (1997). Do youths substitute alcohol and marijuana? Some econometric evidence. *Eastern Economic Journal, 23,* 253–276.

Chaloupka, F. J., & Pacula, R. L. (1998, March). *Limiting youth access to tobacco: The early impact of the Synar amendment on youth smoking.* Paper presented at the second annual Health Services Research Symposium, University of Chicago.

Chaloupka, F. J., & Saffer, H. (1992, July). *Alcohol, illegal drugs, public policy, and crime.* Paper presented at the annual meeting of the Western Economic Association, San Francisco.

Chaloupka, F. J., & Saffer, H. (1993). Clean indoor air laws and the demand for cigarettes. *Contemporary Policy Issues, 10,* 72–83.

Chaloupka, F. J., Saffer, H., & Grossman, M. (1993). Alcohol-control policies and motor-vehicle fatalities. *Journal of Legal Studies, 22,* 161–186.

Chaloupka, F. J., Tauras, J. A., & Grossman, M. (1997). Public policy and youth smokeless tobacco use. *Southern Economic Journal, 64,* 503–516.

Chaloupka, F. J., & Wechsler, H. (1996). Binge drinking in college: The impact of price, availability, and alcohol control policies. *Contemporary Economic Policy, 14,* 112–124.

Chaloupka, F. J., & Wechsler, H. (1997). Price, tobacco control policies and smoking among young adults. *Journal of Health Economics, 16,* 359–374.

Coate, D., & Grossman, M. (1988). Effects of alcoholic beverage prices and legal drinking ages on youth alcohol use. *Journal of Law and Economics, 31,* 145–171.

Cook, P. J., & Moore, M. J. (1993a). Drinking and schooling. *Journal of Health Economics, 12,* 411–430.

Cook, P. J., & Moore, M. J. (1993b). Economic perspectives on reducing alcohol-related violence. In S. E. Martin (Ed.), *Alcohol and interpersonal violence: Fostering multidisciplinary perspectives* (Research Monograph No. 24, NIH Publication No. 93–3496, pp. 193–212). Rockville, MD: National Institute on Alcohol Abuse and Alcoholism.

Cook, P. J., & Tauchen, G. (1982). The effect of liquor taxes on heavy drinking. *Bell Journal of Economics, 13,* 91–96.

DiFranza, J. R., Norwood, B. D., Garner, D. W., & Tye, J. B. (1987). Legislative efforts to protect children from tobacco. *Journal of the American Medical Association, 257,* 3387–3389.

DiNardo, J. (1993). Law enforcement, the price of cocaine, and cocaine use. *Mathematical and Computer Modeling, 17,* 53–64.

DiNardo, J., & Lemieux, T. (1992). *Alcohol, marijuana, and American youth: The unintended effects of government regulation* (Working Paper No. 4212). Cambridge, MA: National Bureau of Economic Research.

Elster, J. (1979). *Ulysses and the Sirens: Studies in rationality and irrationality.* Cambridge, England: Cambridge University Press.

Evans, W. N., & Farrelly, M. C. (1998). The compensating behavior of smokers: Taxes, tar and nicotine. *RAND Journal of Economics, 29,* 578–595.

Evans W. N., Farrelly, M. C., & Montgomery, E. (1996). *Do workplace smoking bans reduce smoking?* (Working Paper No. 5567). Cambridge, MA: National Bureau of Economic Research.

Friedman, M. (1962). *Price theory: A provisional text.* Chicago: University of Chicago Press.

Grant, B. F., & Harford, T. C. (1990). Concurrent and simultaneous use of alcohol with sedatives and with tranquilizers: Results of a national survey. *Journal of Substance Abuse, 2,* 1–14.

Grossman, M., & Chaloupka, F. J. (1998). The demand for cocaine by young adults: A rational addiction approach. *Journal of Health Economics, 17,* 427–474.

Grossman, M., Chaloupka, F. J., Saffer, H., & Laixuthai, A. (1994). Alcohol price policy and youths: A summary of economic research. *Journal of Research on Adolescence, 4,* 347–364.

Grossman, M., Chaloupka, F. J., & Sirtalan, I. (1998). An empirical analysis of alcohol addiction: Results from the Monitoring the Future panels. *Economic Inquiry, 36,* 39–48.

Grossman, M., Coate, D., & Arluck, G. M. (1987). Price sensitivity of alcoholic beverages in the United States. In M. H. Moore & D. R. Gerstein (Eds.), *Control issues in alcohol abuse prevention: Strategies for states and communities* (pp. 169–198). Greenwich, CT: JAI.

Hammond, P. J. (1976). Endogenous tastes and stable long run choice. *Journal of Economic Theory, 13,* 329–340.

Houthhakker, H. S., & Taylor, L. D. (1966). *Consumer demand in the United States, 1929–1970: Analyses and projections.* Cambridge, MA: Harvard University Press.

Houthhakker, H. S., & Taylor, L. D. (1970). *Consumer demand in the United States, 1929–1970: Analyses and projections* (2nd ed.). Cambridge, MA: Harvard University Press.

Johnston, L. D., O'Malley, P. M., & Bachman, J. D. (1981). Marijuana decriminalization: The impact of youth, 1975–1980. *Monitoring the Future Occasional paper number 13.* Ann Arbor, MI: Institute for Social Research, University of Michigan.

Keeler, T. E., Hu, T. W., Barnett, P. G., & Manning, W. G. (1993). Taxation, regulation and addiction: A demand function for cigarettes based on time-series evidence. *Journal of Health Economics, 12,* 1–18.

Kenkel, D. S. (1993). Drinking, driving and deterrence: The effectiveness and social costs of alternative policies. *Journal of Law and Economics, 36,* 877–914.

Kenkel, D. S. (1996). New estimates of the optimal tax on alcohol. *Economic Inquiry, 34,* 296–319.

Laixuthai, A., & Chaloupka, F. J. (1993). Youth alcohol use and public policy. *Contemporary Policy Issues, 11,* 70–81.

Leung, S. F., & Phelps, C. E. (1993). My kingdom for a drink . . . ? A review of estimates of the price sensitivity of demand for alcohol beverages. In M. E. Hilton & G. Bloss (Eds.), *Economics and the prevention of alcohol-related problems* (Research Monograph No. 25, NIH Publication No. 93–513, pp. 1–32). Rockville, MD: National Institute on Alcohol Abuse and Alcoholism.

Lewit, E. M., & Coate, D. (1982). The potential for using excise taxes to reduce smoking. *Journal of Health Economics, 1,* 121–145.

Lewit, E. M., Coate, D., & Grossman, M. (1981). The effects of government regulation on teenage smoking. *Journal of Law and Economics, 24,* 545–569.

Manning, W. G., Blumberg, L., & Moulton, L. H. (1995). The demand for alcohol: The differential response to price. *Journal of Health Economics, 14,* 123–148.

Markowitz, S., & Grossman, M. (1997, July). *The demand for alcohol and child abuse.* Paper presented at the annual meeting of the Western Economic Association, Seattle, WA.

Marshall, A. (1920). *Principles of economics* (8th ed.). New York: Macmillan.

Martin, C. S., Clifford, P. R., Maisto, S. A., & Earleywine, M. (1996). Polydrug use in an inpatient treatment sample of problem drinkers. *Alcoholism: Clinical & Experimental Research, 20,* 413–417.

Model, K. E. (1993). The effect of marijuana decriminalization on hospital emergency room drug episodes: 1975–1978. *Journal of the American Statistical Association, 88,* 737–747.

Moore, M. J. (1996). Death by tobacco taxes. *Rand Journal of Economics, 27,* 415–428.

Moore, M. J., & Cook, P. J. (1995). *Habit and heterogeneity in the youthful demand for alcohol* (Working Paper No. 5152). Cambridge, MA: National Bureau of Economic Research.

Mullahy, J., & Sindelar, J. L. (1994). Do drinkers know when to say when? An empirical analysis of drunk driving. *Economic Inquiry, 32,* 383–394.

National Cancer Institute. (1993). *The impact of cigarette excise taxes on smoking among children and adults: Summary report of a national cancer institute expert panel.* Bethesda, MD: National Cancer Institute, Division of Cancer Prevention and Control, Cancer Control Science Program.

National Institute on Alcohol Abuse and Alcoholism. (1993). *Eighth special report to the U.S. Congress on alcohol and health.* Washington, DC: U.S. Department of Health and Human Services.

Nisbet, C. T., & Vakil, F. (1972). Some estimates of price and expenditure elasticities of demand for marijuana among U.C.L.A. students. *Review of Economics and Statistics, 54*, 473–475.

Ohsfeldt, R. L., Boyle, R. G., & Capilouto, E. I. (1998). *Tobacco taxes, smoking restrictions and tobacco use* (Working Paper No. 6486). Cambridge, MA: National Bureau of Economic Research.

Ohsfeldt, R. L., & Morrisey, M. A. (1997). Beer taxes, workers' compensation and industrial injury. *Review of Economics and Statistics, 79*, 155–160.

Pacula, R. L. (1997). Women and substance use: Are women less susceptible to addiction? *American Economic Review, 87*, 454–459.

Pacula, R. L. (in press). Does increasing the beer tax reduce marijuana consumption? *Journal of Health Economics.*

Pentz, M. A., Dwyer, J. H., MacKinnon, D. P., Flay, B. R., Hansen, W. B., & Wang, E. Y. I. (1989). A multi-community trial for primary prevention of adolescent drug use. *Journal of the American Medical Association, 261*, 3259–3266.

Pollack, R. A. (1970). Habit formation and dynamic demand functions. *Journal of Political Economy, 78*, 745–763.

Pollack, R. A. (1976). Habit formation and long run utility functions. *Journal of Economic Theory, 13*, 272–297.

Pollack, R. A. (1978). Endogenous tastes in demand and welfare analysis. *American Economic Review, 68*, 374–379.

Ruhm, C. J. (1996). Alcohol policies and highway vehicle fatalities. *Journal of Health Economics, 15*, 435–454.

Saffer, H., & Chaloupka, F. J. (1997). *The demand for illicit drugs* (Working Paper No. 5238, revised). Cambridge, MA: National Bureau of Economic Research.

Saffer, H., & Chaloupka, F. J. (1998). *Demographic differentials in the demand for alcohol and illicit drugs* (Working Paper No. 6432). Cambridge, MA: National Bureau of Economic Research.

Saffer, H., & Grossman, M. (1987a). Beer taxes, the legal drinking age, and youth motor vehicle fatalities. *Journal of Legal Studies, 16*, 351–374.

Saffer, H., & Grossman, M. (1987b). Drinking age laws and highway mortality rates: Cause and effect. *Economic Inquiry, 25*, 403–417.

Schelling, T. (1984). Self-command in practice, in policy, and in a theory of rational choice. *American Economic Review, 74*, 1–11.

Silverman, L. P., & Spruill, N. L. (1977). Urban crime and the price of heroin. *Journal of Urban Economics, 4*, 80–103.

Sloan, F. A., Reilly, B. A., & Schenzler, C. (1994). Effects of prices, civil and criminal sanctions, and law enforcement on alcohol-related mortality. *Journal of Studies on Alcohol, 55*, 454–465.

Stigler, G., & Becker, G. S. (1977). De gustibus non est disputandum. *American Economic Review, 67*, 76–90.

Strotz, R. H. (1956). Myopia and inconsistency in dynamic utility maximization. *Review of Economic Studies, 23*, 165–180.

Thies, C. F., & Register, C. A. (1993). Decriminalization of marijuana and the demand for alcohol, marijuana, and cocaine. *Social Science Journal, 30*, 385–399.

U.S. Department of Health and Human Services. (1989). *Reducing the health consequences of smoking: 25 years of progress. A report of the Surgeon General.* Rockville, MD: Author, Public Health Service, Centers for Disease Control, Center for Chronic Disease Prevention and Health Promotion, Office on Smoking and Health.

U.S. Department of Health and Human Services. (1992). *Smoking and health in the Americas: A 1992 report of the Surgeon General in collaboration with the Pan American Health Organization.* Atlanta, GA: Centers for Disease Control, Office on Smoking and Health.

U.S. Department of Health and Human Services. (in press). *The context for change: The efficacy of interventions for smoking prevention and control: A report of the Surgeon General.* Atlanta, GA: Author, Public Health Service, Centers for Disease Control, Center for Chronic Disease Prevention and Health Promotion, Office on Smoking and Health.

Wasserman, J., Manning, W., Newhouse, J., & Winkler, J. (1991). The effects of excise taxes and regulations on cigarette smoking. *Journal of Health Economics, 10,* 43–64.

Winston, G. (1980). Addiction and backsliding: A theory of compulsive consumption. *Journal of Economic Behavior and Organization, 1,* 295–324.

PART THREE

SUBSTITUTABILITY RELATIONS
BETWEEN ACTIVITIES

CHAPTER FIVE

Economic Substitutability: Some Implications for Health Behavior

Leonard Green
Edwin B. Fisher, Jr.
Washington University

Behavioral economics combines the experimental methodology of operant psychology with the theoretical constructs of economics. This conjoining of interests has enriched both disciplines: The methodological rigor of the psychological laboratory has been adapted in order to provide exacting experimental tests of economic models; the theoretical constructs of economics have broadened psychological theories of choice (e.g., Allison, 1983; Kagel, Battalio, & Green, 1995). Beyond its contributions to both disciplines, the experimental and conceptual richness of behavioral economics has led to its application to a variety of complex behaviors. One particular application is the study of behaviors that are considered risky because of their potential for long-term, deleterious health consequences to the individual.

Cigarette smoking clearly is a major health-risk behavior, and increasing evidence that diet contributes to major health problems such as obesity, diabetes, heart disease, and cancer (see, e.g., Drewnowski, 1992b) places food choice in the same category. Given the successes of behavioral economics in advancing our understanding of such risky behaviors as the self-administration of drugs of abuse (see, e.g., Green & Kagel, 1996; Hursh, 1991), we propose that concepts within behavioral economics, specifically the concept of *economic substitutability*, may provide intriguing new insights regarding diet, smoking, and nicotine consumption.

DEMAND AND SUBSTITUTABILITY

Elasticity of demand and *substitutability* are two central concepts of micro-economic theory that have been incorporated directly into psychological models of choice. Demand refers to the amount of a commodity that is purchased at a given price. The demand elasticity of a commodity is a measure of the degree to which consumption of a commodity varies with changes in its price. Demand for a commodity is said to be elastic when consumption decreases more than proportionately as its price increases, whereas demand for a commodity is said to be inelastic when consumption decreases less than proportionately as its price increases (see, e.g., Hursh & Bauman, 1987). For example, if the price of gasoline were to rise yet its consumption were to decrease very little, then demand for gasoline would be inelastic. On the other hand, if the price of movies were to rise and their consumption were to decrease substantially, then demand for movies would be elastic.

A behavioral economic concept central to understanding the degree to which consumption changes in response to changes in price (i.e., influences the demand elasticity of a particular commodity) is substitutability, that is, the extent to which other commodities are available as alternatives for the one whose price is increased. Consider the case of movies. The extent to which increases in the price of seeing a movie at a theater affect moviegoing will be markedly influenced by the substitutes available. As more first-run movies are shown on television, as videos are more accessible, and so on, individuals may reduce their attendance at movie theaters substantially. The videos, TV movies, larger TV screens, may all substitute for the theater movies. However, by improving the visual and auditory experience at the theater, the substitutability of home videos is reduced. Clearly, then, the extent to which price influences demand is strongly influenced by the substitutes in the situation: The same increase in price that has little impact on consumption of a commodity in one situation may, when substitutes are present, markedly influence consumption of that same commodity.

Importantly, substitutable reinforcers are those that are functionally similar. That is to say, substitutability is not a given property of a specific reinforcer. Rather, it is a characteristic of the relation between reinforcers. Although often qualitatively similar, the substitutability of reinforcers depends on their functional interdependence. Because of their functional similarity, substitutable reinforcers can be "traded" for each other. For example, Coke® and Pepsi® are functionally relatively similar—they are both sweet, refreshing, and so forth—and, therefore, likely to be substitutable for each other. Consequently, when the price of one of these reinforcers increases, its consumption likely will decrease and consumption of its substitute increase.

Complementary reinforcers, on the other hand, generally are used jointly and are consumed in fairly rigid proportion to each other (e.g., bagels and cream cheese; left shoes and right shoes). As the price of one of these reinforcers increases, consumption of it and of its complement both decrease. Reinforcers also may be independent, such that an increase in the price of one has no effect on consumption of the other (e.g., Coke® and left shoes). Clearly, then, demand for a commodity will be more elastic when there is an alternative, substitutable reinforcer in the situation than when the alternative is a complement or an independent (see Green & Freed, 1993, for an extensive discussion of substitutability).

BEHAVIORAL ECONOMIC ANALYSES OF FOOD CHOICE

Behavioral economic analyses of demand elasticity and substitutability have yielded some interesting results when applied to food choice. For example, Lappalainen and Epstein (1990) allowed normal-weight hungry adults to choose between making responses that earned points exchangeable for a moderately preferred food and making responses that earned points exchangeable for a highly preferred food. Points for the moderately rated food were earned for responses according to a fixed-ratio 1 (FR 1) schedule, whereas points for the highly rated food were earned for responses according to a ratio schedule that changed across conditions of the experiment from an FR 1 up to a variable-ratio 32 (VR 32). When points for both foods were easily earned (i.e., when each was on the FR 1 schedule—the baseline condition), the participants, not surprisingly, responded almost exclusively for the points associated with the highly rated food. However, as the response requirement for earning points for the highly rated food increased, responding for those points decreased and responding for points for the moderately rated food increased. Thus, because the moderately rated food substituted for the highly rated food, demand for the highly rated food proved to be elastic, even though that food was preferred nearly exclusively under baseline conditions.

A similar pattern of results was obtained by J. A. Smith and Epstein (1991), who studied obese children choosing between responding for points exchangeable for a highly preferred, high-calorie food and responding for points exchangeable for a less-preferred, low-calorie food. As might be expected, under the baseline condition (i.e., when both types of points were cheap and equally priced), the obese children responded exclusively for the points associated with the preferred, high-calorie food. However, when the price of the high-calorie food points was increased, consumption of the high-calorie food decreased markedly and consumption of the less-preferred, low-calorie food increased. The pattern of results indicates that even among children who are already obese, demand for the high-calorie food was elastic and consumption of the low-calorie food substituted for that of the high-calorie food. These results may be somewhat surprising because one reasonably might have predicted that the exclusive preferences obtained during baseline would be difficult to overcome, especially in the case of an obese person's presumably strong preference for a high-calorie food. Also, if constitutional factors play a role in such cases of obesity, then one might expect high-caloric preferences to be highly resistant to situational factors. Nevertheless, J. A. Smith and Epstein demonstrated that preference, even when extreme, does not necessarily predict how elastic the demand for that commodity might be.

Fat Consumption

Given the particular health risks associated with diets high in fat, an aspect of food choice particularly worthy of attention is that of fat consumption. For example, children with diets high in fat, when compared with children whose diets were much lower in fat, had significantly higher mean serum levels of total cholesterol and low-density lipoprotein cholesterol (LDL–C; Gonzalez-Requejo et al., 1995). Wiseman (1992) noted, "For more than two decades the evidence linking dietary fat to cardiovascular disease has developed to the extent that there is a degree of unanimity over the relationship unusual in the field of medicine" (p. 2). Dietary fat in adult women also has been linked to an increased risk of ovarian cancer (Cramer, Welch, Hutchison, Willett, & Scully, 1984; Risch, Jain, Marrett, & Howe, 1994) and has been shown to influence total cholesterol and LDL–C levels (Mata et al., 1992), which, in turn, are associated with an increased risk for ovarian cancer (Helzlsouer et al., 1996).

Much of the laboratory research on dietary fat consumption has been conducted with rats because of their extreme attraction both to the nutritional properties of fat and to its flavor (i.e., taste, smell, and texture). This attraction to fat, termed *fat appetite*, is apparent early in life and might even be innate. In one early study of fat appetite, Hamilton (1964) gave 120-day-old male rats access to powdered Purina chow mixed with 0%, 10%, 20%, and 30% lard, by weight. By the eighth day of testing, the rats were eating much more of the 30% lard mixture and consuming at least four times more calories from it than from the plain chow. A second group of rats given access to the same concentrations of a petrolatum-blended chow demonstrated a similar preference for the orosensory qualities of a noncaloric fat. By the end of testing, these rats were taking in approximately the same number of calories from the 30% petrolatum mixture as from the plain chow. Because petrolatum is noncaloric, the rats were consuming approximately 30% more of the petrolatum mixture (in grams) than the plain chow. These results suggest that even a nonnutritive fat such as petrolatum has orosensory qualities to which rats are attracted. Similarly, Carlisle and Stellar (1969) found that rats preferred greasy (Crisco® oil- or mineral oil-infused) chow over regular chow (as measured by grams consumed), regardless of the caloric value of the greasy diet.

More recently, Ackroff, Vigorito, and Sclafani (1990) measured 6-, 9-, 12-, and 15-day-old rat pups' ingestion of and mouthing responses to fluids delivered through an oral cannula over a 10-min test session. Among the fluids tested were 10% corn oil, 30% corn oil, 30% mineral oil, and tap water. By 12 to 15 days of age, the pups showed stronger mouthing responses to and ingested more of the oil emulsions than of the tap water. The pups displayed no significant differences between the type of oil (corn oil or mineral oil) or between the different concentrations of corn oil. Ackroff et al. suggested that their findings "raise the possibility that [the rat pups] also have an innate appetite for the flavor of oil" (p. 177). Moreover, adult rats showed equal acceptance of 30% mineral oil and 30% corn oil in brief (3-min and 30-min) one-bottle acceptance tests, and the amount consumed increased when the rats were food-deprived.

Results like those from Hamilton (1964), Carlisle and Stellar (1969), and Ackroff et al. (1990) indicate that when a source of fat is available, rats will consume it readily, consistent with the notion of a fat appetite. The strong if not innate predilection that rats show for fat might not be so different from that in humans, who also show excessive fat consumption, deriving approximately 37% of their total daily calories from fats (Drewnowski, 1992a). Such results imply that food choice involving fats would be extremely difficult to modify. The health implications are clear but unfortunately do not augur well for public health programs to modify fat consumption. However, the acceptance- and preference-test methodology used in these previously discussed experiments might not be an appropriate predictor of how readily modifiable a given preference is, that is, preference- and acceptance-tests are analogous to the baseline conditions studied by Lappalainen and Epstein (1990) and J. A. Smith and Epstein (1991), in which the consumables available in the situation were equally priced. Those conditions revealed extreme preferences; however, the changes in consumption produced by subsequent changes in the price of the preferred commodity were not predictable solely on the basis of the baseline preference. Despite degree of preference, it is the availability of substitutes that may influence the ease by which consumption of fats might be modified. If so, then health policy proposals would be significantly different from those derived from a non-behavioral economic framework that relates ease of modifiability with degree of preference (as determined from acceptance studies or from baseline choices). Thus, the behavioral economic perspective leads to a different methodology with which to study food choice and fat consumption and may offer suggestions for approaches to behavior change that might otherwise not have been apparent.

A Behavioral Economic Analysis of Fat Consumption

A behavioral economic analysis that considers demand elasticity and substitutability offers a means by which to evaluate the modifiability of preference. In behavioral economic terms, reinforcers are equivalent to commodities, the prices of which are specified by the schedule of reinforcement. Rachlin, Green, Kagel, and Battalio (1976) were the first to examine directly elasticity of demand and substitutability between reinforcers. Specifically, they compared rats' choices between root beer and Tom Collins mix, and between food and water. The price of each reinforcer was determined by an FR schedule associated with a particular response lever. When the root beer and Tom Collins mix were equally priced under the baseline condition, the rats strongly preferred the root beer. However, when the root beer was subsequently made more expensive and the Tom Collins cheaper, the rats showed strong substitution effects, that is, consumption of the more expensive root beer decreased and that of the made-cheaper Tom Collins mix increased markedly: Demand for root beer was elastic. These results stand in pointed contrast to those from the food and water comparison. In this case, increasing the price of food produced only a slight shift in consumption toward the relatively cheaper water, consistent with the complementary relation between food and water (Green & Rachlin, 1991; Hursh, 1978; Rachlin & Krasnoff, 1983).

The degree of substitutability between pairs of reinforcers is studied directly with an *income-compensated price change* paradigm, as illustrated in Fig. 5.1. An organism chooses between responding for Reinforcer *X* and responding for Reinforcer *Y*. The solid line represents a baseline condition in which the reinforcers are equally priced. The individual can purchase any combination of the two reinforcers that falls anywhere on (or below) this budget constraint but cannot purchase combinations exceeding the constraint, due to income limitations. The filled circle indicates the number of *X* and *Y* reinforcers obtained under baseline. In subsequent conditions, the prices of the reinforcers are changed, and total income is adjusted so that the original consumption amounts still can be obtained. The broken line drawn through the filled circle represents a price change condition in which Reinforcer *Y* is made more expensive and Reinforcer *X* is made cheaper. Importantly, income (total number of responses allocated per session) also is adjusted so that the individual's baseline consumption of *X* and *Y* still can be achieved. A change in consumption under this new condition reflects the degree to which the two reinforcers are substitutable. A change in consumption to that indicated by the square would indicate little substitutability between the reinforcers (as was observed with food and water), whereas a change in consumption to that indicated by the triangle would indicate a high degree of substitutability (as was the case with root beer and Tom Collins mix).

Consider a simplified situation in which an individual could purchase orange soda at \$2 a bottle and milk also at \$2 a bottle, and had a monthly

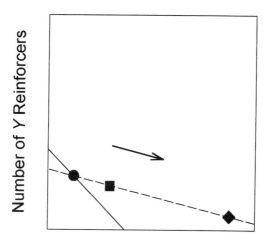

Number of X Reinforcers

FIG. 5.1. Commodity space in which Reinforcers X and Y are concurrently available. The solid line indicates a baseline budget condition in which both reinforcers are equally priced. The broken line represents an income-compensated price change through the obtained baseline consumption point (●). Under this income-compensated price change, the price of Reinforcer Y is increased, the price of Reinforcer X is decreased, and total responses are adjusted so that the organism can consume the same amounts of both reinforcers under the price change as it had under the original baseline condition. Changes in consumption in the direction of the arrow (to points ■ and ▲, respectively) indicate increasing degrees of substitution of the made-cheaper reinforcer for that of the made-more-expensive reinforcer.

income of $20 to spend. The individual could purchase 10 bottles of soda, 10 bottles of milk, or some combination within his or her income. The individual might choose 4 bottles of soda and 6 bottles of milk. If the price of milk were to be doubled and that of the soda halved but monthly income were to remain constant, a decrease in consumption of milk would occur. Such a decrease is not surprising; it might simply reflect the fact that the individual could not purchase the same amount of milk as before. But suppose the individual's income were increased to compensate for the increase in the price of the milk, that is, when prices are changed, total income is increased to $28. Under this income-compensated price change, the individual still could purchase the 6 bottles of milk (now at $4 a bottle) and 4 bottles of soda (now at $1 a bottle) as he or she purchased originally. But suppose that, even though the original 4 bottles of soda and 6 bottles of milk still could be purchased, the individual instead were to purchase 16 bottles of soda and 3 bottles of milk. Now the change in consumption can be attributed to the made-cheaper soda substituting for the more expensive milk.

This situation can be portrayed in Fig. 5.1 with orange soda designated as Reinforcer X, milk designated as Reinforcer Y, and the original income constraint and budget line represented by the solid line. The filled circle indicates the individual's purchases under this income and price constraint. The new budget line under the income-compensated price change is represented by the dashed line. The degree to which milk consumption decreases and soda consumption increases represents the degree of substitutability of the soda for the milk.

In a series of studies conducted with Debra Freed, we employed precisely this behavioral economic paradigm to determine the modifiability of rats' preferences for fats and carbohydrates. The results from these studies showed that as prices were manipulated, rats' choices of fats and carbohydrates depended significantly on whether an alternative, substitutable reinforcer was available.

In one experiment (Freed & Green, 1998, Experiment 1), we tested whether plain tap water or an isocaloric sucrose solution would substitute for a corn oil solution. In different conditions, rats were offered choices between a corn oil solution, an isocaloric sucrose solution, and plain tap water. Substitutability was assessed under three conditions: (a) when reinforcers were isocaloric and identical (i.e., corn oil vs. corn oil); (b) when reinforcers were isocaloric but nonidentical (i.e., corn oil vs. sucrose); and (c) when reinforcers were nonisocaloric and nonidentical (i.e., corn oil vs. water). Obviously, we expected a reinforcer to be most substitutable for one to which it is identical (corn oil vs. corn oil). With reinforcers that are qualitatively different in terms of taste–palatability, caloric content, or both, we were interested in determining their relative degree of substitutability.

We assessed the substitutability between pairs of reinforcers by using the income-compensated price change methodology shown in Fig. 5.1. Consumption of each reinforcer in the pair was studied under several budget conditions. Each budget condition specified a price (i.e., VR schedule) for each reinforcer and an income (i.e., allotment of daily responses to be "spent" on those reinforcers). Under baseline conditions, the reinforcers were available according to independent concurrent VR 20 VR 20 schedules, and 500 daily responses were allowed. Subsequent conditions were income-compensated price changes from the baseline budget. The VR schedule (and therefore price) of the initially more preferred reinforcer was doubled to VR 40, whereas that of the less-preferred reinforcer was halved to VR 10. Income also was adjusted so that, under the new schedule values, the baseline amount of each reinforcer still could be obtained (see Fig. 5.1). Under the income-compensated price change, then, changes in consumption from baseline reflect the degree to which the reinforcers are substitutable. Additional income-compensated price changes were performed in which the VR schedule associated with the initially less preferred reinforcer was doubled from baseline to VR 40 and that of the more preferred reinforcer was halved to VR 10. Income again was adjusted accordingly.

Representative results are presented in Fig. 5.2. The solid line indicates the baseline budget condition in which the rat responded under concurrent VR 20 VR 20 schedules and had an income of 500 responses. The broken lines show income-compensated price changes from the baseline condition. Filled circles indicate the mean number of earned reinforcers from the last 5 days of the baseline budget condition; squares represent mean number of earned reinforcers when the price of the reinforcer noted on the x axis was halved and that of the y-axis reinforcer was doubled; the upright triangle represents mean consumption when price of the x-axis reinforcer was doubled and that of the y-axis reinforcer was halved.

The leftmost panel presents the results for a condition in which corn oil was available for responding on the left and on the right levers. As expected, when identical reinforcers were available, income-compensated price changes produced drastic changes in the rat's consumption in favor of the made-cheaper commodity. At baseline, the rat earned an average of 14.4 corn oil reinforcers from the left dipper and 10.6 from the right. When the price of the left corn oil was doubled to VR 40 and that of the right corn oil was halved to VR 10 (and income was adjusted so that the new budget line passed through the baseline consumption), the rat's consumption shifted exclusively to the right corn oil. Similarly, when the price of the left corn oil was reduced to a VR 10 and that of the right corn oil increased to a VR 40 (and income changed accordingly), the rat's consumption now shifted almost exclusively to the left corn oil. These data represent the extreme end of substitutability, that is, a reinforcer is perfectly substitutable for the identical reinforcer.

The data presented in the middle panel show average number of reinforcers earned from conditions in which the same rat chose between isocaloric but different reinforcers, namely, corn oil and sucrose reinforcers. As is evident, consumption under the income-compensated price changes showed marked changes in consumption from that at baseline to near exclusive choice of whichever reinforcer was made cheaper. Thus, consumption under the new budgets was entirely a function of the relative price of the reinforcers, not the type of reinforcers.

What is noteworthy about the data is the remarkable similarity in the pattern of results between the identical reinforcer comparison (left panel) and the isocaloric but nonidentical reinforcer comparison (middle panel). Under each type of comparison, when the price of one reinforcer was doubled and the price of the other was halved, the rat's responding and consumption shifted almost entirely in favor of the made-cheaper reinforcer.

These results stand in marked contrast to those obtained when one reinforcer was corn oil and the alternative reinforcer was plain water. As is evident in the rightmost panel of Fig. 5.2, income-compensated price changes

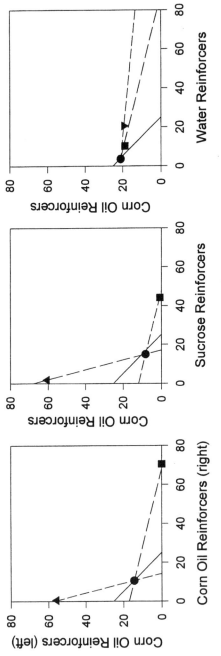

FIG. 5.2. Amounts consumed under income-compensated price changes. Near-complete substitutability is evident with identical, corn oil reinforcers (leftmost panel), as well as between isocaloric but nonidentical reinforcers (corn oil *vs.* sucrose; middle panel), that is, increases in the price of one of the solutions produced substantial substitution into the made-cheaper alternative. On the other hand, minimal substitution is evident with a caloric reinforcer (corn oil) and noncaloric plain water (rightmost panel), that is, comparable increases in the price of the caloric solution produced little substitution into the made-cheaper water. The symbols represent average consumption from the last 5 days of each condition for one representative rat. (Adapted from Freed & Green, 1998).

from baseline, in which water was the reinforcer made increasingly cheaper, produced only small increases in water consumption, a result quite different from that shown in the other panels. Water was not substitutable for corn oil. This result is even more notable when one considers that under a further income-compensated price change condition in which water was made even cheaper (i.e., available on a VR 5) and the corn oil solution was made even more expensive (i.e., available on a VR 50), the rat continued to respond overwhelmingly for the nonwater solution (shown as the inverted triangle).

Substitutability was clearly evident between two reinforcers when they were isocaloric and palatable. Substitutability was not found when one of the reinforcers was plain water, that is, when only one of the reinforcers was caloric or palatable. These results indicate that rats readily gave up the corn oil and the sucrose solutions when an isocaloric, palatable solution was available. However, the results do not indicate whether substitutability occurred on the basis of calories or on the basis of palatability. Thus, were sucrose and corn oil substitutable for each other because they were equivalent sources of calories or because they were both highly palatable? A second experiment (Freed & Green, 1998, Experiment 2) addressed this issue by examining rats' choices between reinforcers that were palatable but nonisocaloric, again using the income-compensated price change procedure.

In different conditions, rats were offered choices between pairs of reinforcers that were nonisocaloric: a corn oil solution and a sodium saccharin solution, and the corn oil solution and a mineral oil solution. Neither the saccharin nor mineral oil solutions contained calories.

Representative results are presented in Fig. 5.3. As the price of the noncaloric but sweet-tasting saccharin solution was decreased and the price of the caloric, greasy corn oil was increased, consumption shifted markedly in the direction of the made-cheaper saccharin (left panel). The same result was true when mineral oil served as the noncaloric alternative to corn oil (right panel). In spite of the exclusive preference for the corn oil over the noncaloric mineral oil under the baseline budget condition, consumption of the made-costlier corn oil decreased considerably and consumption of the made-cheaper mineral oil increased substantially under the income-compensated price change. Regardless of baseline preferences, responding and consumption under the income-compensated price changes were controlled almost exclusively by the relative prices of the reinforcers, even though one of the reinforcers in each pair was caloric and the other was noncaloric.

Noncaloric but palatable reinforcers (i.e., mineral oil and saccharin) substituted for reinforcers that were a source of calories (i.e., corn oil), just as a caloric, palatable reinforcer (sucrose) had. Substitution of an alternative reinforcer for one that was caloric and palatable occurred when the alternative was also palatable, even if it was not caloric. When the alternative was neither caloric nor palatable (i.e., plain water), substitution did not occur.

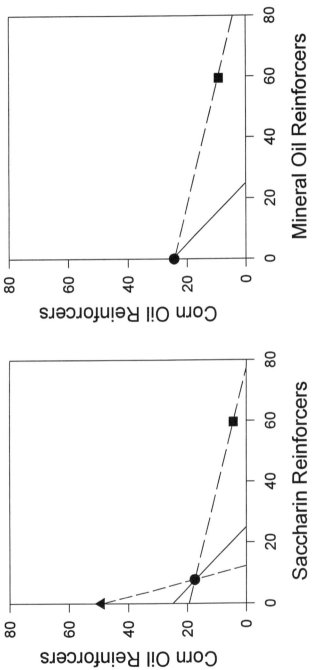

FIG. 5.3. Amounts consumed under income-compensated price changes with nonisocaloric, nonidentical reinforcers. Substantial degrees of substitutability are evident between corn oil and noncaloric saccharin (left panel) and between corn oil and noncaloric mineral oil (right panel) solutions. (Adapted from Freed & Green, 1998).

Conclusions Regarding Food Choice

Economic demand theory holds that the degree to which consumption of a commodity (reinforcer) is modified when its price changes depends, to a large extent, on the other commodities available in the situation. Indeed, we found that fat intake could be dramatically reduced when the price of the fat was increased, as long as there was a palatable alternative reinforcer available. On the other hand, fat intake was considerably less affected by comparable price changes when plain water was the alternative reinforcer available.

The results counter the supposition that extreme and possibly innate preferences are necessarily difficult to modify. Demand for the corn oil differed depending on whether a substitute was available, not on the degree of preference. Therefore, fat appetite appears to be mutable even when baseline preference for the fat solution is extreme. The implications from having used this behavioral economic approach are substantial. Preference–acceptance studies highlight the strength and apparent stability of fat preferences. However, behavioral economic studies highlight two critical features of strong fat preferences: (a) their mutability, and (b) aspects of the economic context of these preferences that influence their expression.

The importance of the provision of attractive alternatives in reducing preferences for fat makes clear that effective programs to reduce fat consumption need to go beyond "Just Say No" exhortations (Drewnowski, 1992a). Specifically, our results indicate that the ability to say no may depend not so much on factors within the organism but on the alternatives available to it. Economic substitutes may override even very strong preferences. Moreover, our results suggest that the introduction of nonnutritive fat "substitutes" in human foodstuffs may provide a means by which people can reduce their fat consumption. In fact, many food manufacturers are expanding their product lines with reduced-fat and low-fat foods, many of which contain fat substitutes.

However, our data also suggest that the mere introduction of such alternative foodstuffs may not be sufficient. Serious consideration must be paid to various characteristics of the alternative. An emphasis on pleasurable alternatives to high-fat foods is consistent with a key aspect of our findings, namely that a "fat substitute" must be palatable in order to substitute—in the economic sense—for fat. Merely introducing low-fat or fat-free alternatives without significant regard to their taste is unlikely to result in long-term, continued consumption (recall the introduction and then elimination of McDonald's® McLean™ burger). Similarly, low- and no-fat foodstuffs that taste like cardboard and sugary straw may not produce long-term reductions in fat consumption. Of course, we still need to determine the parameters of palatability. Clearly, texture and flavor play a significant role, but the interactions among factors must be understood if effective substitutes are to be developed (see Mela & Marshall, 1992, for a discussion of sensory properties of fats).

This set of studies has shown the applicability of the economic concepts of substitutability and elasticity of demand to a behavior pertinent to health, namely, food preferences. In the next section, we extend these concepts to an interesting and important dilemma regarding the role of social support in health behavior. A substantial literature indicates that social support is a very strong factor in risk reduction, management of chronic diseases, and emotional adjustment. Yet, research evaluation treatments that provide social support, such as to encourage maintained abstinence from smoking, have achieved disappointing results. Behavioral economics may provide a useful perspective for clarifying these apparently conflicting findings.

EXTENSION TO HEALTH PROMOTION APPLICATIONS: SUBSTITUTABILITY OF CIGARETTE SMOKING AND SOCIAL SUPPORT

Social support may be the most important poorly understood influence in health and health care. Epidemiological research and some intervention studies have shown impressive effects of social support (House, Landis, & Umberson, 1988), but other studies have reported marginal (C. E. Smith, Fernengel, Holcroft, Gerald, & Marien, 1994) or no effects of support (Villar et al., 1992). Reflecting the variability in findings in the social support literature in general, a paradoxical set of findings has emerged in research on smoking cessation. As early as 1971, research indicated the importance of social support in adult smoking and its cessation (Eisinger, 1971). Although the influence of others on adult smoking was relatively ignored amidst the popularity of self-control procedures in the 1970s' literature on behavior change (cf. Fisher, 1986), the 1980 and 1982 surgeon general's reports each identified social support as associated with cessation among adults. Additional studies found that ratings of support from spouses, living partners, other family members, or friends predicted abstinence among those trying to quit (e.g., Coppotelli & Orleans, 1985; Mermelstein, Cohen, Lichtenstein, Baer, & Kamarck, 1986; Morgan, Ashenberg, & Fisher, 1988).

Countering enthusiasm about social support, Lichtenstein, Glasgow, and Abrams (1986) noted that although social support had been correlated repeatedly with abstinence, social support interventions for smoking cessation had not been markedly successful in terms of long-term, sustained abstinence from cigarettes. Here, we consider how these negative effects may be better understood from the perspective of behavioral economics, viewing social support as a commodity and examining its substitutability with other commodities.

The Commodity Model of Social Support

Harlow (1958; Harlow & Harlow, 1965; Harlow & Zimmerman, 1959) pitted the need for comfort against the need for food in his famous comparison of affinity for a wire surrogate mother rigged to provide milk versus affinity for a terry cloth surrogate that provided warmth and comfort. Except when hungry, the infant monkeys preferred the terry cloth mother, suggesting that association with food was not the source of such attraction. From this perspective, social support may function as a good thing in and of itself, not merely as a means or resource to the achievement of some other end.

If social support is simply a good thing, then it may function by providing incentives for life-enhancing behavior as well as by offsetting the impacts of stressors that otherwise might lead to emotional upset. For instance, "having more to live for" in satisfying social relationships may provide incentives for quitting smoking, managing diabetes, or the other kinds of positive behavior changes to which social support has been linked. The presence of social contact and support also may guard against depression by offsetting depressed mood in the same way that other positively valued events may offset depression. In a similar vein, individuals may prefer to be in the company of others when placed in an anxiety-arousing situation. For example, Schachter (1959), in a classic study on affiliation, placed college students in a situation that was presented either as threatening or as nonanxiety-producing. When participants in both groups were given the choice of waiting alone or waiting together, a significantly greater proportion of the participants in the threatening situation chose to wait together.

From the conceptual framework of behavioral economics, viewing social support as a commodity leads to interest in the possibility that it is substitutable with other commodities. Perhaps, for example, the relation between social support and success in smoking cessation reflects social support's being substitutable for cigarettes when it is available and cheap (Fisher, 1996). But if social resources are limited, then the probability of choosing cigarettes may increase. In the remainder of this chapter, we refer to this as a *Commodity Model* of social support. Before exploring it further, we need to consider the alternative, and more common, *Resource Model* of social support.

The Resource Model of Social Support

Several features of social support have been identified as important. Support may include direct assistance or instrumental support and information about problems and help in coping with stress (Cohen & Syme, 1985; Cutrona,

Russell, & Rose, 1986). It may enhance immune function (e.g., Baron, Cutrona, Russell, Hicklin, & Lubaroff, 1990) and thereby reduce the risks even of the common cold (Cohen, Doyle, Skoner, Rabin, & Gwaltney, 1997). From work such as Bowlby's and Ainsworth's studies of attachment (Ainsworth & Bowlby, 1991; Bowlby, 1988), the support of a "secure base" appears to enhance both social and task performance. Similarly, the psychotherapy literature, including Rogers' (1957) characterization of essential ingredients in change, Kohut's (1977) articulation of the importance of a good "self-object," and Garfield's (1983) identification of general characteristics of effective therapies, has emphasized the benefits of empathy on client performance. Research on response to trauma shows the benefits that victims gain simply from describing their experiences (Pennebaker, 1989). Such descriptions of experience may enhance recovery from trauma or stress through a range of processes, such as by increasing "cognitive clarity," clarifying that one's own reactions are not aberrant, or increasing a sense of belonging to a group that can provide security (Harber & Pennebaker, 1992).

These several perspectives on key components of social support all view it as a group of resources (instrumental, emotional, informational, etc.) that facilitates goal-directed behavior, general emotional adjustment, or coping with stressors. In this Resource Model, support enhances an individual's efforts to cope with problems or achieve personal goals. Although not mutually exclusive, the Resource and Commodity Models of support emphasize different aspects of support and lead to somewhat different predictions about its impacts.

Comparison of the Commodity and Resource Models

The Resource Model emphasizes support as that of providing resources (e.g., information, material assistance, enhanced confidence) that enhance pursuit of personal goals and coping with stress or other problems. In the Commodity Model, social support is a valued commodity in an economic system, competing with other commodities for the choices of the individual. Application to smoking cessation of the Commodity and Resource Models may be depicted in terms of the paths shown in Fig. 5.4.

In the Resource Model, social support influences smoking through the skills and assistance it provides. These may include gaining others' cooperation in not smoking in their presence, agreeing to share activities that do not include temptations to smoke, avoiding tension-producing topics at times of the day such as after dinner when the would-be quitter is most likely to want to smoke, or praising the quitter's efforts and helping to develop plans for avoiding further temptations.

In the Commodity Model, social support's influence on smoking would be direct in the form of a commodity that competes with cigarettes for

Resource Model

Commodity Model

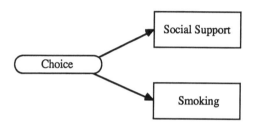

FIG. 5.4. Resource and Commodity Models of Social Support and Smoking.

consumption. To the extent that social support is attractive and available, choices for smoking would be less likely, that is, to the extent that the individual has ready access to enjoyable (i.e., substitutable) interactions with friends or family, the likelihood of choosing to smoke is reduced.

The Commodity Model explains why difficult life circumstances may raise the appeal of both social support and smoking. Such circumstances would increase the probability of choosing support, smoking, or both from among other activities and commodities available. Thus, stress at work might raise the probability of choosing to spend time with friends or to smoke, relative to the probability, for example, of choosing to work on household chores. But within this, the choice of friends versus smoking still would depend on their relative attractiveness and availability (i.e., their price).

Commodity Versus Resource Models:
Continued Availability of Social Support

If the Commodity Model is accurate, then social support's influence on smoking should be limited to the time when social support is available, that is, if social support ceases to be available, its ability to substitute for cigarettes should terminate. The Resource Model, by contrast, predicts that changes in skills or competencies that social support may have fostered should persist, once learned, and continue to facilitate abstinence from smoking. The failure of some social support interventions to improve long-term abstinence from smoking may be seen as reflecting the importance of the distinction between the two models, not the importance of social support, per se.

Descriptive Research Regarding the Continued Availability of Support. In a study of predictors of short- and long-term cessation (Mermelstein et al., 1986), ratings of spouses' or other partners' support for cessation completed 1 week after quitting predicted abstinence 3 but not 12 months later. On the other hand, the smoking status of members of the social network (e.g., being married to a smoker, number of friends who smoke) predicted smoking status at the 12-month follow-up. Similar effects of smoking among members of one's social network have been documented in large-scale epidemiological studies (Eisinger, 1971). Rather than ratings of satisfaction with support from others completed during the first weeks of abstinence, the actual smoking habits of family and friends may be better predictors of the long-term support they will provide. If this is the case, then the association between family and friends' smoking and long-term abstinence is consistent with the Commodity Model's emphasis on the enduring level of support. From a practical perspective, promoting enduring support for nonsmoking through influencing the norms and standards of the settings in which people live, for example, through worksite smoking policies, may be more effective than supplying short-term social support.

A "Natural Experiment": Widowhood and Removal of Support. According to the Commodity Model, reduction of social support should lead to increased likelihood of smoking or of return to smoking. Consistent with this, the 1988 surgeon general's report (U.S. Department of Health and Human Services, 1988) noted that divorced or separated men had the highest prevalence of smoking (48.2%) of any subgroup defined by sex and marital status (p. 571). But the link between divorce or separation and smoking is open to several interpretations. For example, extroversion or tendencies toward antisocial or rebellious behavior are associated with smoking (Eysenck, 1980; Fisher, Lichtenstein, & Haire-Joshu, 1993). Similar personality characteristics may incline to problems with divorce as well as smoking. Indeed, one study found divorce to be associated with a greater likelihood of having ever smoked and having begun smoking prior to age 18 (Waldron & Lye, 1989). Presumably, the deprivation of social support that may have followed divorce did not cause initiation of smoking earlier in life.

Widowhood, on the other hand, would appear to be relatively independent of the widowed individual's behavior or personality, but still constitute a major loss of social support. Accordingly, this model predicts that widowhood would be associated with increased incidence of smoking. Pertinent studies identified through Medline (June 1994; described in greater detail in Fisher, 1996) found an association of widowhood (and divorce, separation, and single marital status) with greater prevalence of, increases in, and return to smoking.

Manipulation of Duration of Support. That the benefits of social support are significant but decline when support is terminated was demonstrated in a study of enhanced group cohesion for smoking cessation (Etringer, Gregory, & Lando, 1984). As long as the cessation groups continued to meet, abstinence rates were greater in the group with enhanced cohesion than in a control group. However, after the group meetings ended, the advantages of the enhanced cohesion ebbed to nonsignificance.

This same pattern was reflected in a study using a social support treatment that minimized attention to self-management but emphasized social support, including unstructured small-group discussions to heighten support among participants, a buddy system with a nonsmoker outside the group, and recruitment of social support from friends and family (Fisher et al., 1991). The standard treatment condition emphasized self-management, required all participants to quit on the day of the third meeting, and minimized group interchange and social support among participants. The schedule and treatment times were the same in both conditions. Percent abstinence for the social support and the standard treatment groups at the end of the 3-month treatment, as well as follow-up at 6 and 12 months, are shown in Fig. 5.5.

Although abstinence at 12-month follow-up was comparable in the two groups (27% and 21% for the social support and standard treatments, respectively), the patterns of relapse were quite different. There was greater relapse in the standard treatment condition during treatment and greater relapse in the social support condition after treatment, that is, at the time treatment ended (3 months after quitting), 64% of the participants in the social support treatment were abstinent, whereas just 36% of the participants in the standard, self-management treatment were abstinent. After treatment ended, however, relapse was greater in the social support condition. From the Resource Model's expectation that social support somehow should engender skills that persist beyond treatment, the results of the social support treatment are disappointing. In contrast, the results are consistent with the Commodity Model's view that social support will reduce choices for cigarettes, but only as long as the support is available.

The benefits of sustaining even modest social support are suggested by a study of support-by-telephone for individuals quitting smoking. Orleans et al. (1991) provided telephone counseling at 6, 18, 34, and 60 weeks after participants had received a self-quitting guide and a support guide for family and friends. At the end of 16 months, 21.5% of those receiving telephone counseling reported abstinence of at least 1 month, in comparison to 12.3% to 15.2% of those in several control groups.

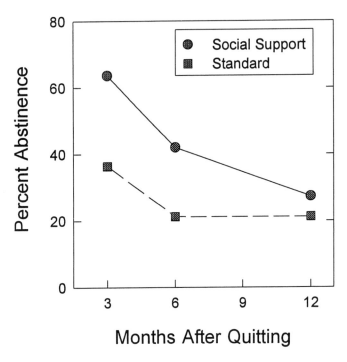

FIG. 5.5. Smoking abstinence following a Social Support Intervention Treatment (circles) and a Standard, Self-Management Intervention Treatment (squares). Treatment lasted 3 months; follow-up continued for 12 months after initiation of the treatment intervention.

Availability and Attractiveness of Support. According to the Commodity Model, the extent to which support may substitute for smoking depends not only on its continued availability but also on its attractiveness. This also was reflected in the protocol of Orleans and her colleagues that provided supportive phone calls 6, 18, 34, and 60 weeks after participants received smoking cessation manuals (Orleans et al., 1991): The "counselors sought to . . . provide positive, nonjudgmental feedback and reinforcement appropriate for the quitter's particular stage of change" (p. 441).

The Commodity Model's emphasis that support be enjoyable and easily available also is reflected in a distinction we have drawn between *nondirective* and *directive support* (Fisher, 1997; Fisher, La Greca, Greco, Arfken, & Schneiderman, 1997). Nondirective support is cooperative, entails working with the objectives chosen by the recipient, and entails accepting and validating the recipients' feelings (e.g., "Wow, no wonder you were upset"). In contrast, directive support is prescriptive, entails taking routine responsibility for key tasks, and entails encouraging the recipient to experience feelings that the provider judges to be correct or appropriate (e.g., "Look on the bright side"). Consistent with the Commodity Model, nondirective support is governed by the recipient's needs and preferences, whereas directive support is governed more by the provider's judgment. Thus, nondirective support comes closer to the high availability that should enhance substitution of support for smoking. Intuitively, also, nondirective support would appear more enjoyable to receive than would directive support. Bringing together these themes and the varied success of social support interventions for smoking cessation, those interventions that are more successful appear to provide more nondirective than directive support and, consistent with the Commodity Model, appear to provide more enjoyable and available support (Fisher, 1997).

Extensions and Implications

Substitutability Does Not Require Physical Equivalence. In many cases of economic substitutability, there is apparent physical resemblance between the two commodities that are substitutable. For example, most purchasers will choose among brands of gasoline on the basis of price or convenience, assuming near equivalence among the products. In animal studies of substitutability of different foods, a common feature such as taste or nutritive value is assumed to be the basis for the substitutability. In the case of smoking and social support, however, there is no apparent physical resemblance between the two commodities. Commodities may be substitutable, then, because of shared characteristics whose similarity may not be qualitatively or physically apparent.

Research on the nature of smoking indicates three important effects of nicotine: anxiety-reduction, mood-elevation, and arousal (Fisher et al., 1993; Henningfield & Nemeth-Coslett, 1988). The experienced smoker is able to adjust consumption so as to achieve these three effects throughout the day. This may include using nicotine as an energizer at the beginning of the day, using it for anxiety reduction and mood elevation during the day, and using it to relax prior to falling asleep. Interestingly, social support has been suggested to provide similar benefits. With regard to anxiety reduction, the literature indicates the value of social support in buffering the effects of stress (Cohen & Hoberman, 1983) and facilitating response to trauma (Harber & Pennebaker, 1992). In terms of impact on mood, the literature suggests a relation between lack of social support and depressed mood and, thus, by implication, the value of social support in reducing or avoiding depression (Brugha et al., 1990; Henderson, 1981). Thus, anxiety-reduction, mood-elevation, and arousal may be common, beneficial psychological effects of both social support and nicotine. These may account for the substitutability of smoking and support.

Regardless of whether the relation between support and smoking is based on shared physiological or psychological effects, the observed substitutability stands on its own as an objective relation between the behaviors of receiving support and smoking. Substitutability is definable and verifiable independent of the characteristics of the two commodities that may enter into it. Substitutability, then, is a characteristic of choices between two commodities, not necessarily a characteristic of the inherent nature of those two commodities.

Of course, the benefits of social support (e.g., arousal or enhanced performance) overlap with the Resource Model discussed above. However, it still may be worthwhile to distinguish between (a) the need for social support to continue to be available in order to enhance performance—the Commodity Model; and (b) the ability of social support to enhance skills that then persist past the time at which support is terminated—the Resource Model.

Complementarity of Smoking and Social Behavior. Anecdotal as well as systematic evidence (Marlatt & Gordon, 1985) indicates that social behavior often may facilitate smoking rather than reduce incentives for smoking. For instance, would-be quitters frequently relapse from quit attempts when they socialize. This might occur because other people supply relapse cigarettes rather than because the socializing, per se, raises the attractiveness of smoking. Nevertheless, reported increases in the rate of smoking associated with increased socializing raise the possibility of complementarity between smoking and support. If smoking and socializing can be complementary, then increasing smoking might increase socialization. Such a relation might be occurring with designated smoking areas in public facilities and businesses. Indeed, there are anecdotal reports of meetings in designated smoking areas increasing interdivisional communication and, thereby, innovation in workplaces.

That smoking and social behavior might be tied together by both complementarity and substitutability raises several interesting conceptual possibilities. First, these relationships might themselves be context-dependent. Thus, in the context of efforts to quit smoking, social support may be substitutable for smoking. As another example, trauma or stress may increase the attractiveness of both support and smoking but set an occasion in which the two are substitutable. So the availability of good social support in stressful circumstances or following trauma might be associated with reduced likelihood of smoking. As noted previously, loss of support through widowhood is associated with increased likelihood of smoking. In contrast to contexts that may increase substitutability of smoking and support, other aspects of the smoking context may be complementary with socializing. For example, going out to a restaurant or a bar with friends might be associated with increased cigarette consumption. Thus, substitutability versus complementarity might be dependent on several contexts, including the objectives of the individual, the occurrence of recent stress or trauma, a pleasant meal, or the atmosphere of a bar.

Another approach to understanding how support and smoking might be either complementary or substitutable entails the possibility that these relations are dependent on fine distinctions among the commodities involved. Thus, the empathy of a good friend, who listens patiently to the recounting of stressful interactions that one had with one's boss, may be substitutable for smoking. In contrast, the conviviality of a group of friends may be complementary to smoking. That such molecular characteristics of commodities should determine whether they are complementary to or substitutable for other commodities is surely congruent with the level of specification of other commodities explored in behavioral economics research.

The complementarity between a pair of commodities also might be influenced by characteristics of other commodities to which they are linked. Consider how coffee or alcohol might influence the substitutability or complementarity between smoking and socialization. There is evidence that, among alcoholic-dependent individuals, rate of cigarette smoking increases during sessions in which ethanol is provided (Griffiths, Bigelow, & Liebson, 1976). Marshall, Epstein, and Green (1980) reported that undergraduate smokers receiving coffee smoked more than those who were not provided coffee during 1-hour test sessions. Such results are consistent with the view that under certain situations, smoking may be complementary with coffee and with alcohol. Consider that coffee and alcohol are often consumed in social situations in our culture. Consequently, the apparent complementarity between socialization and smoking may reflect a masking of the substitutability between smoking and socialization by the complementarity of smoking and coffee or alcohol that is usually part of the social setting. Clearly, the interactions between coffee and cigarette smoking, or between alcohol consumption and cigarette smoking, are complex (see, e.g., Bickel, DeGrandpre, & Higgins, 1995; Bickel, Hughes, DeGrandpre, Higgins, & Rizzuto, 1992). A behavioral economic approach to understanding these interactions may provide new insights into understanding the determinants of and implications for changing the behaviors (see also Green & Kagel, 1996).

CONTEXTUAL APPROACH

The lack of any apparent physical similarity between social support and smoking argues for a contextual approach to understanding the economics of substitutability and complementarity. Choices among commodities take place in and are influenced by their broader contexts. In attempts to alter choices, greater focus might be placed on contexts and prices than on presumed but sometimes highly inferential shared characteristics of, for example, social support and nicotine, that is, greater effectiveness might derive were attention to be focused on providing more and cheaper social support to reduce choices for nicotine than on searching for inferred, shared characteristics of the two. Similarly, as noted in the first part of this chapter, providing attractive and inexpensive alternatives to high-fat foods may be more effective than merely encouraging overweight individuals to just say no.

That substitutable and complementary relationships among choices may change according to the context is of significance for efforts to change behavior. For instance, if elevated levels of stress are liable to cause smoking and social support to be substitutable, then efforts to promote nonsmoking should include easily accessible and cheap sources of support, especially for those experiencing heightened stress. On the other hand, if routine socializing or socializing in circumstances relatively free of stress is associated with increased smoking, then efforts to promote nonsmoking might do well to encourage more solitary recreational and relaxation experiences. For example, a community-based smoking cessation program might do better to offer quitters free tickets to a local movie theater than free admission to a nightclub.

EXTENSION TO OTHER BEHAVIOR RELATED TO HEALTH

Parallel to this analysis, Vuchinich and Tucker (1988, 1996) emphasized the substitutability of social support and social contact for alcohol consumption. In discussing models of alcoholism, they distinguished between "molecular" approaches that focus on biological or psychological processes within the individual and "molar" or economic approaches that evaluate choices for alcohol as determined by factors in the environment of the individual. Within the molar, economic model, the availability of social support and social contact in the individual's environment reduces the likelihood of alcohol consumption. Both their model of alcoholism and this analysis of smoking direct attention to the provision of attractive and inexpensive sources of support and socialization in efforts to promote healthier behavior.

In addition to approaches regarding smoking and drinking, this discussion of substitutability suggests approaches for efforts aimed at improving dietary patterns. Epstein and Saelens (chap. 11, this volume) provide a behavioral economic approach to understanding obesity and exercise. Additionally, viewing social support as a substitutable commodity might be especially pertinent to binge eating. Because binge eating is linked to emotional distress, and social isolation is linked to distress, it may be that social support or social contact might be substitutable for binges. Consistent with this suggestion, women who scored high on a measure of psychological characteristics associated with binge eating did better in a weight-loss program that emphasized small-group discussion and social support (along with cognitive–behavioral tactics for addressing anxiety and low mood) than did similar women in a program that emphasized standard behavioral procedures to reduce problem eating patterns (Krug-Porzelius, Houston, Smith, Arfken, & Fisher, 1994). In contrast, women without psychological characteristics associated with binge eating did better with the standard behavioral procedures.

Chronic Disease Management

Beyond its importance for understanding and modifying cigarette and food consumption, the substitutability of social support also may have implications for other health behaviors. As more people live longer, they are more likely to develop chronic diseases such as diabetes or arthritis. With the advances in medical treatment for these diseases has come an increased burden on the individual. For example, rather than taking one injection of insulin a day and avoiding sweets, diabetic adults may be asked to take insulin three or four times a day, to measure their blood sugar before each dose and adjust the dose accordingly, and to follow a complicated diet that balances complex carbohydrates, fats, and proteins. Social support may be critical in encouraging sustained performance of such complicated, effortful chronic-disease management.

The Diabetes Control and Complications Trial (DCCT) achieved substantial reductions in long-term complications of diabetes through persistent, intensive management of insulin to approximate normal blood sugars (Diabetes Control and Complications Trial Research Group, 1993). The benefits of this regimen were dependent on the adherence of participants to a regimen of frequent insulin injections, frequent monitoring of blood sugar, and careful adjustment of insulin according to blood-sugar levels and intercurrent events. Anecdotal reports of both DCCT participants and staff indicated the importance of staff support for adherence. Accordingly, colleagues at Washington University conducted interviews with DCCT participants to obtain their characterizations of those key aspects of staff support that they considered important for adherence during the trial (Davis, Heins, & Fisher, 1997). Strikingly, the majority of support the participants reported from the professional staff for adherence to a complicated and demanding regimen of the DCCT was nondirective. If, as discussed previously, the Commodity Model and nondirective support share recipient control over the receipt of support and, perhaps, the enjoyableness of that support, then the Commodity Model also may be helpful in understanding support for chronic-disease management. Importantly, the Commodity Model suggests that support for such complicated regimens may not need to be provided by highly trained— and expensive—professionals, but may be sufficient when provided by nonprofessionals with, perhaps, access to professionals for authoritative answers to occasional questions that arise.

A key feature of the DCCT was that it required and achieved adherence to a demanding regimen over 6 to 8 years. This suggests that nondirective support and the Commodity Model may be especially pertinent to ongoing maintenance of a behavior. Unfortunately, support during the early phases of the DCCT was not assessed. Other research, however, indicates that nondirective support may be more advantageous in ongoing adjustment and management, whereas directive support may be more advantageous in more acute situations. Along these lines, it may be that directive support and the Resource Model are more applicable to initial mastery of a demanding regimen, such as that in the DCCT, but that nondirective support and the Commodity Model are more pertinent to long-term maintenance of skills once learned.

CODA

The economic concept of substitutability integrates and clarifies diverse issues in health and behavior. Central to this integration is the principle that a preference for one behavior, be it consuming dietary fat or smoking cigarettes, is highly dependent on the context of other behaviors available, their costs, and their reinforcers. Thus, even a strong preference for dietary fat was readily alterable by the availability and favorable pricing of an alternative food choice. In a parallel manner, addiction to smoking may be alterable not by changing the addiction per se, but by offering attractive, available alternatives.

The broad utility of the concept of substitutability also is reflected in this chapter's spanning human and animal studies, and observations ranging from the highly precise characterization of choices varying as a function of the VR schedules to the descriptive epidemiology of widowhood. This breadth of observations, all of which incorporate the concept of substitutability, also makes an important point about behavioral economics. The relations it unveils are not limited to pairs of similar commodities such as variously flavored liquids. Rather, the relations may extend, albeit with perhaps less quantifiable precision, to interpersonal and contextual influences on individual choice behavior.

By expanding the domain of substitutability, we run the risk of oversimplifying it so that, by applying it so broadly, it says almost nothing. Understandably, the basic concept is not remote from common sense. Recall George Bernard Shaw's quip in response to a question about how he was enjoying his considerably advanced age: "Considering the alternatives. . . ." Yet, the basic message of substitutability often fails to emerge in policies and programs designed to ameliorate the problems to which even common sense might link it. The just say no approach, for example, treats harmful behavior as if it had no context. Such an oversimplified approach conceives of the problem as existing only within the individual and ignores the social context that can be so powerful in altering or maintaining the harmful behavior. Treatment programs continue to stress insight into personal bases for harmful behaviors, or self-management skills for controlling those behaviors, or empowerment to encourage the individual's confidence in forgoing them, but fail to emphasize the development of pleasing, healthy, available alternatives. Thus, the status of the behavioral economic concept of substitutability might be summarized as widely applicable, widely understandable, but all too narrowly appreciated and applied.

ACKNOWLEDGMENTS

Preparation of this chapter was facilitated by grant MH55308 from the National Institute of Mental Health and by NIH grants DK20579, DK48400, CA6863301, and ES08711.

REFERENCES

Ackroff, K., Vigorito, M., & Sclafani, A. (1990). Fat appetite in rats: The response of infant and adult rats to nutritive and non-nutritive oil emulsions. *Appetite, 15,* 171–188.

Ainsworth, M. D. S., & Bowlby, J. (1991). An ethological approach to personality development. *American Psychologist, 46,* 333–341.

Allison, J. (1983). *Behavioral economics.* New York: Praeger.

Baron, R. S., Cutrona, C. E., Russell, D. W., Hicklin, D., & Lubaroff, D. M. (1990). Social support and immune function among spouses of cancer patients. *Journal of Personality and Social Psychology, 59,* 344–352.

Bickel, W. K., DeGrandpre, R. J., & Higgins, S. T. (1995). The behavioral economics of concurrent drug reinforcers: A review and reanalysis of drug self-administration research. *Psychopharmacology, 118,* 250–259.

Bickel, W. K., Hughes, J. R., DeGrandpre, R. J., Higgins, S. T., & Rizzuto, P. (1992). Behavioral economics of drug self-administration: IV. The effects of response requirement on the consumption of and interaction between concurrently available coffee and cigarettes. *Psychopharmacology, 107,* 211–216.

Bowlby, J. (1988). *A secure base.* New York: Basic Books.

Brugha, T. S., Bebbington, P. E., MacCarthy, B., Sturt, E., Wykes, T., & Potter, J. (1990). Gender, social support and recovery from depressive disorders: A prospective clinical study. *Psychological Medicine, 20,* 147–156.

Carlisle, H. J., & Stellar, E. (1969). Caloric regulation and food preference in normal, hyperphagic, and aphagic rats. *Journal of Comparative and Physiological Psychology, 69,* 107–114.

Cohen, S., Doyle, W. J., Skoner, D. P., Rabin, B. S., & Gwaltney, J. M. (1997). Social ties and susceptibility to the common cold. *Journal of the American Medical Association, 277,* 1940–1944.

Cohen, S., & Hoberman, H. M. (1983). Positive events and social support as buffers of life change stress. *Journal of Applied Social Psychology, 13,* 99–125.

Cohen, S., & Syme, S. L. (1985). *Social support and health.* New York: Academic Press.

Coppotelli, H. C., & Orleans, C. T. (1985). Partner support and other determinants of smoking maintenance among women. *Journal of Consulting and Clinical Psychology, 53,* 455–460.

Cramer, D. W., Welch, W. R., Hutchison, G. B., Willett, W., & Scully, R. E. (1984). Dietary animal fat in relation to ovarian cancer risk. *Obstetrics & Gynecology, 63,* 833–838.

Cutrona, C., Russell, D., & Rose, J. (1986). Social support and adaptation to stress by the elderly. *Psychology and Aging, 1,* 47–54.

Davis, K., Heins, J., & Fisher, E. B., Jr. (1997, June). *Types of social support deemed important by participants in the DCCT.* Paper presented at the annual meeting of the American Diabetes Association, Boston.

Diabetes Control and Complications Trial Research Group. (1993). The effect of intensive treatment of diabetes on the develoment and progression of long-term complications in insulin-dependent diabetes mellitus. *New England Journal of Medicine, 329,* 977–986.

Drewnowski, A. (1992a). Nutritional perspectives on biobehavioral models of dietary change. In *Proceedings: Promoting dietary change in communities: Applying existing models of dietary change to population-based interventions* (pp. 96–109). Seattle, WA: Fred Hutchinson Cancer Research Center.

Drewnowski, A. (1992b). Sensory properties of fats and fat replacements. *Nutrition Reviews, 50,* 17–20.

Eisinger, R. A. (1971). Psychosocial predictors of smoking recidivism. *Journal of Health and Social Behavior, 12,* 355–362.

Etringer, B. D., Gregory, V. R., & Lando, H. A. (1984). Influence of group cohesion on the behavioral treatment of smoking. *Journal of Consulting and Clinical Psychology, 52,* 1080–1086.

Eysenck, H. J. (1980). *The causes and effects of smoking.* Beverly Hills, CA: Sage.

Fisher, E. B., Jr. (1986). A skeptical perspective: The importance of behavior and environment. In K. A. Holroyd & T. L. Creer (Eds.), *Self-management of chronic disease: Handbook of clinical interventions and research* (pp. 541–565). New York: Academic Press.

Fisher, E. B., Jr. (1996). A behavioral-economic perspective on the influence of social support on cigarette smoking. In L. Green & J. H. Kagel (Eds.), *Advances in behavioral economics: Vol. 3. Substance use and abuse* (pp. 207–236). Norwood, NJ: Ablex.

Fisher, E. B., Jr. (1997). Two approaches to social support in smoking cessation: Commodity Model and Nondirective Support. *Addictive Behaviors, 22,* 819–833.

Fisher, E. B., Jr., La Greca, A. M., Greco, P., Arfken, C., & Schneiderman, N. (1997). Directive and Nondirective support in diabetes management. *International Journal of Behavioral Medicine, 4,* 131–144.

Fisher, E. B., Jr., Lichtenstein, E., & Haire-Joshu, D. (1993). Multiple determinants of tobacco use and cessation. In C. T. Orleans & J. D. Slade (Eds.), *Nicotine addiction: Principles and management* (pp. 59–88). New York: Oxford University Press.

Fisher, E. B., Jr., Rehberg, H. R., Beaupre, P. M., Hughes, C. R., Levitt-Gilmour, T., Davis, J. R., & DiLorenzo, T. M. (1991, November). *Gender differences in response to social support in smoking cessation.* Paper presented at the annual meeting of the Association for the Advancement of Behavior Therapy, New York.

Freed, D. E., & Green, L. (1998). A behavioral economic analysis of fat appetite in rats. *Appetite, 31,* 333–349.

Garfield, S. L. (1983). *Clinical psychology.* New York: Aldine.

Gonzalez-Requejo, A., Sanchez-Bayle, M., Baeza, J., Arnaiz, P., Vila, S., Asensio, J., & Ruiz-Jarabo, C. (1995). Relations between nutrient intake and serum lipid and apolipoprotein levels. *Journal of Pediatrics, 127,* 53–57.

Green, L., & Freed, D. E. (1993). The substitutability of reinforcers. *Journal of the Experimental Analysis of Behavior, 60,* 141–158.

Green, L., & Kagel, J. H. (Eds.). (1996). *Advances in behavioral economics: Vol. 3. Substance use and abuse.* Norwood, NJ: Ablex.

Green, L., & Rachlin, H. (1991). Economic substitutability of electrical brain stimulation, food, and water. *Journal of the Experimental Analysis of Behavior, 55,* 133–143.

Griffiths, R. R., Bigelow, G. E., & Liebson, I. (1976). Facilitation of human tobacco self-administration by ethanol: A behavioral analysis. *Journal of the Experimental Analysis of Behavior, 25,* 279–292.

Hamilton, C. L. (1964). Rat's preference for high fat diets. *Journal of Comparative and Physiological Psychology, 58,* 459–460.

Harber, K. D., & Pennebaker, J. W. (1992). Overcoming traumatic memories. In S. A. Christianson (Ed.), *The handbook of emotion and memory: Research and theory* (pp. 359–387). Hillsdale, NJ: Lawrence Erlbaum Associates.

Harlow, H. F. (1958). The nature of love. *American Psychologist, 13,* 673–685.

Harlow, H. F., & Harlow, M. K. (1965). The affectional systems. In A. M. Schrier, H. F. Harlow, & F. Stollnitz (Eds.), *Behavior of non-human primates* (Vol. 2, pp. 287–334). New York: Academic Press.

Harlow, H. F., & Zimmerman, R. R. (1959). Affectional responses in the infant monkey. *Science, 130,* 421–432.

Helzlsouer, K. J., Alberg, A. J., Norkus, E. P., Morris, J. S., Hoffman, S. C., & Comstock, G. W. (1996). Prospective study of serum micronutrients and ovarian cancer. *Journal of the National Cancer Institute, 88,* 32–37.

Henderson, S. (1981). Social relationships, adversity and neurosis: An analysis of prospective observations. *British Journal of Psychiatry, 138,* 391–398.

Henningfield, J., & Nemeth-Coslett, R. (1988). Nicotine dependence-interface between tobacco and tobacco-related disease. *Chest, 98,* 385–395.

House, J. S., Landis, K. R., & Umberson, D. (1988). Social relationships and health. *Science, 241,* 540–544.

Hursh, S. R. (1978). The economics of daily consumption controlling food- and water-reinforced responding. *Journal of the Experimental Analysis of Behavior, 29,* 475–491.

Hursh, S. R. (1991). Behavioral economics of drug self-administration and drug abuse policy. *Journal of the Experimental Analysis of Behavior, 56,* 377–393.

Hursh, S. R., & Bauman, R. A. (1987). The behavioral analysis of demand. In L. Green & J. H. Kagel (Eds.), *Advances in behavioral economics* (Vol. 1, pp. 117–165). Norwood, NJ: Ablex.

Kagel, J. H., Battalio, R. C., & Green, L. (1995). *Economic choice theory: An experimental analysis of animal behavior.* New York: Cambridge University Press.

Kohut, H. (1977). *The restoration of the self.* New York: International Universities Press.

Krug-Porzelius, L., Houston, C. A., Smith, M., Arfken, C. L., & Fisher, E. B., Jr. (1994). Comparison of a behavioral weight loss treatment and a binge eating weight loss treatment. *Behavior Therapy, 26,* 119–134.

Lappalainen, R., & Epstein, L. H. (1990). A behavioral economics analysis of food choice in humans. *Appetite, 14,* 81–93.

Lichtenstein, E., Glasgow, R. E., & Abrams, D. B. (1986). Social support in smoking cessation: In search of effective interventions. *Behavior Therapy, 17,* 607–619.

Marlatt, G. A., & Gordon, J. R. (Eds.). (1985). *Relapse prevention: Maintenance strategies in the treatment of addictive behaviors.* New York: Guilford.

Marshall, W. R., Epstein, L. H., & Green, S. B. (1980). Coffee drinking and cigarette smoking: I. Coffee, caffeine, and cigarette smoking behavior. *Addictive Behaviors, 5,* 389–394.

Mata, P., Garrido, J. A., Ordovas, J. M., Blazquez, E., Alvarez-Sala, L. A., Rubio, J. J., Alonso, R., & de Oya, M. (1992). Effect of dietary monounsaturated fatty acids on plasma lipoproteins and apolipoproteins in women. *American Journal of Clinical Nutrition, 56,* 77–83.

Mela, D. J., & Marshall, R. J. (1992). Sensory properties and perceptions of fats. In D. J. Mela (Ed.), *Dietary fats: Determinants of preference, selection and consumption* (pp. 43–57). London: Elsevier.

Mermelstein, R., Cohen, S., Lichtenstein, E., Baer, J. S., & Kamarck, T. (1986). Social support and smoking cessation programs. *Journal of Consulting and Clinical Psychology, 54,* 447–453.

Morgan, G. D., Ashenberg, Z. S., & Fisher, E. B., Jr. (1988). Abstinence from smoking and the social environment. *Journal of Consulting and Clinical Psychology, 56,* 298–301.

Orleans, C. T., Schoenbach, V. J., Wagner, E. H., Quade, D., Salmon, M. A., Pearson, D. C., Fiedler, J., Porter, C. Q., & Kaplan, B. H. (1991). Self-help quit smoking interventions: Effects of self-help materials, social support instructions, and telephone counseling. *Journal of Consulting and Clinical Psychology, 59,* 429–448.

Pennebaker, J. (1989). Confession, inhibition and disease. In L. Berkowitz (Ed.), *Advances in experimental social psychology* (pp. 211–244), New York: Academic Press.

Rachlin, H., Green, L., Kagel, J. H., & Battalio, R. C. (1976). Economic demand theory and psychological studies of choice. In G. H. Bower (Ed.), *The psychology of learning and motivation* (Vol. 10, pp. 129–154). New York: Academic Press.

Rachlin, H., & Krasnoff, J. (1983). Eating and drinking: An economic analysis. *Journal of the Experimental Analysis of Behavior, 39,* 385–404.

Risch, H. A., Jain, M., Marrett, L. D., & Howe, G. R. (1994). Dietary fat intake and risk of epithelial ovarian cancer. *Journal of the National Cancer Institute, 86,* 1409–1415.

Rogers, C. R. (1957). The necessary and sufficient conditions of therapeutic personality change. *Journal of Consulting Psychology, 21,* 95–103.

Schachter, S. (1959). *Psychology of affiliation.* Stanford, CA: Stanford University Press.

Smith, C. E., Fernengel, K., Holcroft, C., Gerald, K., & Marien, L. (1994). Meta-analysis of the associations between social support and health outcomes. *Annals of Behavioral Medicine, 16,* 352–362.

Smith, J. A., & Epstein, L. H. (1991). Behavioral economic analysis of food choice in obese children. *Appetite, 17,* 91–95.

U.S. Department of Health and Human Services. (1988). *The health consequences of smoking: Nicotine addiction. A report of the Surgeon General* (DHHS Publication No. 88–8406). Washington, DC: U.S. Government Printing Office.

Villar, J., Farnot, U., Barros, F., Victora, C., Langer, A., & Belizan, J. M. (1992). A randomized trial of psychosocial support during high-risk pregnancies. *New England Journal of Medicine, 327,* 1266–1271.

Vuchinich, R. E., & Tucker, J. A. (1988). Contributions from behavioral theories of choice to an analysis of alcohol abuse. *Journal of Abnormal Psychology, 97,* 181–195.

Vuchinich, R. E., & Tucker, J. A. (1996). The molar context of alcohol abuse. In L. Green & J. H. Kagel (Eds.), *Advances in behavioral economics: Vol. 3. Substance use and abuse* (pp. 133–162). Norwood, NJ: Ablex.

Waldron, I., & Lye, D. (1989). Family roles and smoking. *American Journal of Preventive Medicine, 5,* 136–141.

Wiseman, M. J. (1992). Present and past trends in dietary fat consumption. In D. J. Mela (Ed.), *Dietary fats: Determinants of preference, selection and consumption* (pp. 1–8). London: Elsevier.

CHAPTER SIX

The Lonely Addict

Howard Rachlin

State University of New York at Stony Brook

This chapter describes and discusses *relative addiction theory*. Relative addiction theory is part of behavioral economics in that it relies on processes of behavioral allocation, such as melioration (Herrnstein & Vaughan, 1980) and economic maximization (Rachlin, Battalio, Kagel, & Green, 1981), rather than on internal physiological or cognitive mechanisms. The main assertion of relative addiction theory is that social support—the benefit obtained from social activity—is crucial to the behavioral processes that lead to addiction. Groups such as Alcoholics Anonymous and Gamblers Anonymous that stress social support generally believe it to be ancillary to the operation of some more fundamental process (physiological, cognitive, behavioral, or spiritual). Relative addiction theory, on the other hand, places social support and its lack at the center of the addiction process. It says that addicts are addicts *because* they are lonely. Distinctive properties of social support—the way it contributes to present and future utility—may act along with substance consumption to cause addiction. However, before discussing how social activity and substance consumption interact to cause addiction, it is necessary to specify the operative behavioral dynamics.

LOCAL AND OVERALL UTILITY

In calculating utility, economic theory assumes first that a consumer's time horizon is infinite. When a choice is made, all known consequences, no matter how far in the future they may be, are assumed to be taken into

145

account. But then, consequences are assumed to be less powerful, the further in the future they are; reinforcers and punishers are discounted by delay. Animals, including humans, are said to be "impulsive" when they steeply discount future consequences, and "self-controlled" when they weigh future consequences heavily (Rachlin, 1974). The science of microeconomics (Becker, 1996) attempts to describe individual behavior, including the behavior of addicts, by specifying utility and discount functions and calculating their maxima. Behavioral economics (Rachlin et al., 1981) is concerned with emperical determination of these functions.[1]

Calculation of utility may be simplified by abandoning the assumption that organisms discount all future consequences by some mathematical function of their delay. Instead, delayed events are categorized in only two ways: *local* events, which are given full weight (i.e., which are not discounted) and *nonlocal* (distant) events, which are given no weight at all (i.e., which are completely discounted). Each choice alternative has its own local utility. Choice of the alternative with the highest local utility is called *melioration* (Herrnstein & Vaughan, 1980). Melioration is thus a form of maximization: maximization of local utility. Whether an animal is considered to be impulsive or self-controlled, then, depends on whether the line separating local from nonlocal events is drawn in the near or distant future. For example, a person who drinks without regard to the next day's hangover would be maximizing utility within the local temporal boundary of the present. A person who drinks (presumably more moderately) with regard to the possibility of a hangover the next day would be maximizing utility within a local temporal boundary beyond the following morning. Heyman (1996) argued that the boundary line separating local from nonlocal events may vary over wide ranges and be brought under stimulus control, thereby explaining how humans and nonhumans may be impulsive in one situation and self-controlled in another.

This chapter henceforth adopts the language of melioration, distinguishing between *local utility* and *overall utility* (i.e., local plus nonlocal utility). It is important to realize, however, that this usage is undertaken for the sake of explanatory convenience and mathematical simplicity, not because melioration is correct and economic maximization is incorrect. Melioration and maximization are not two competing theories but are instead two alternative modes of explanation—two languages (Rachlin, Green, & Tormey, 1988; Rachlin & Laibson, 1997). Any choice behavior that can be explained by melioration (choice of the highest undiscounted local utility) also can be explained by maximization (choice of the highest discounted overall utility) and vice versa—the two languages are mutually translatable.

---

[1]A version of relative addiction theory based on economic maximization is presented in Rachlin (1997).

In the standard operant concurrent-chain choice situation, for example, an animal chooses not between individual reinforcers but between stimulus-defined "situations" (deVilliers, 1977). Within a situation, the animal may be exposed to a reinforcement contingency for a period of time. Local utility is a function of all reinforcement parameters (e.g., rate, amount, delay) and response parameters (e.g., number, force, duration) during exposure to a stimulus-defined situation. In other words, local utility is a "net" rather than a "gross" amount: It is value minus cost. Although, in the operant laboratory, the response parameters are usually negligible relative to the reinforcement parameters, in the real-life situations to which laboratory results are applied, response parameters are not negligible. In life, rewards have their nonnegligible costs. Local utility, therefore, may vary through increases or decreases of reinforcer value or reinforcer cost. If the price of cigarettes goes up, the local utility of smoking goes down. Moreover, amount per unit may increase or decrease, as when candy bars cost the same but increase or (more often) decrease in size or when cereal manufacturers put less or more air and more or less cereal into the same-sized, same-priced box.

Negative Effects of Present Consumption on Future Local Utility

Present consumption of a given commodity may affect the future local utility of that commodity or of other commodities. For example, if you eat a steak dinner now, you probably will spoil your appetite for a steak dinner an hour from now but increase your appetite for a sweet dessert. If you eat too much or eat too fast, you might have heartburn or indigestion later that evening. If you eat too much, you might gain a little excess weight further along the road. The deleterious effect of present consumption on future activity is especially strong for activities normally considered to be addictive (Green & Kagel, 1996). Drinking alcohol, beyond a certain point, deteriorates health, social relationships, job performance, and almost all other activities, including the pleasure obtained from drinking itself. These reductions in future value have the same effect on future local utility as increases in future cost.

The body may develop resistance (*opponent processes*) to strong or unusual substances such as alcohol; this resistance may become conditioned to stimuli that signal consumption of those substances (S. Siegel, 1976; Solomon, 1980). The opponent processes, in turn, reduce the net utility of a fixed amount of the commodity, requiring more to achieve the same effect—just as, with less cereal per box, more boxes would be have to be bought to satisfy the same appetite. The signals that trigger opponent processes may be external or peripheral: the room in which the alcohol is drunk; the bottle; the glasses; the color, taste, and smell of the drink. But signals also may be quite central: If low levels of alcohol in the blood usually signal higher levels to come, the low levels may trigger the body's protective opponent processes, thereby reducing the effect (the pleasure as well as the harm) of those large levels. Even the casual drinker or smoker experiences some reduced effect with continued use. For the alcoholic, the three-pack-a-day smoker, or the heroin addict, this "tolerance" effect is magnified. Addicts regularly consume amounts of opiates that would kill nonaddicts. Some of this difference may be attributable not to tolerance for the positive effects of the drug but to tolerance for its harmful side effects. But tolerance of aversive side effects cannot counteract the sharply diminishing marginal utility of addictive substances. The alcoholic would be a happy person if the net utility derived from a quart of whisky were 32 times that derived from an ounce. But the alcoholic is not a happy person.

To borrow an economist's terminology (Becker, 1996), *tolerance* is the negative effect of a person's "stock" of a substance (X) on utility. Stock increases with consumption and decreases over time. As an alcoholic drinks more and more, for example, stock of drinking increases and the utility of future drinking decreases. But as time passes without drinking (as the alcoholic "dries out"), stock of drinking decreases and the utility of future drinking increases. Line B–C of Fig. 6.1a illustrates this effect. For simplicity, the effect is assumed to be linear. The horizontal axis indicates a subject's overall distribution of time at X and Y. Exclusive choice of X is represented at the left. Exclusive choice of Y is represented at the right. In the center, a subject is distributing half of the time to X and half to Y. As more and more of the addictive commodity is consumed, stock of X increases and stock of Y decreases; as more and time is spent on other activities, stock of Y increases and stock of X decreases. In other words, the consumer is supposed to move slowly to the right in Fig. 6.1a as the addictive commodity is consumed, and slowly to the left as the addictive commodity is not consumed. Movement to the right decreases local utility of X; movement to the left increases local utility of X. The negative effect of present consumption on future local utility is called *price habituation* (Rachlin, 1997).

Positive Effects of Present Consumption on Future Local Utility

Some activities have an effect on future utility opposite to that of the addictive activities discussed previously: The more the activity is performed, the greater its future local utility. In general, these activities involve learning of skills. Utility of skiing, tennis, golf, and other recreational sports tends to increase as more and more time is spent acquiring the skills necessary to enjoy and master them. Playing chess, reading classical literature, and listening to serious music are other examples. The more time spent in these pursuits, the

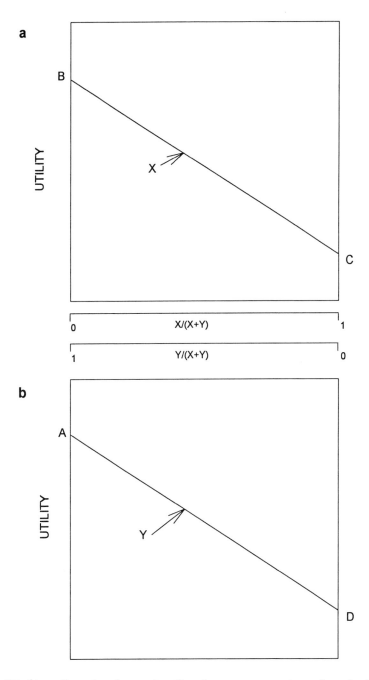

FIG. 6.1. a. Illustration of a negative effect of present consumption on future local utility. The more the commodity (X) is consumed relative to its alternatives (Y), the less the utility of further consumption. b. Illustration of a positive effect of present consumption on future local utility. The more the commodity (Y) is consumed relative to its alternatives (X), the greater is the utility of further consumption.

cheaper they become (the more cereal and less air in the box).[2] Just as an
increase in the frequency of such activities tends to increase local utility, so
a decrease in frequency tends to decrease local utility. The adolescent who
spends large proportions of time reading poetry or playing the violin, who
then out of necessity takes a time-consuming job or engages in time-consuming studies, will find poetry or violin playing not as enjoyable (more
expensive) when, later in life, time becomes available to take them up again.

A crucial assumption of relative addiction theory is that obtaining social
support by means of social activity is such a skill. Although in our society,
in most cases, parents and community provide free social support to children,
childhood is also a learning period for highly complex social skills (Brazelton,
Koslowski, & Main, 1974). The more one engages in social activity, the
greater its local utility becomes, either through enhancement of the activity
itself or through reduction of its cost in terms of time, effort, or money
required to obtain a unit of increased value. Correspondingly, the less one
engages in social activity, the less its local utility becomes, either through a
decrease in enjoyment of the activity itself or an increase in its cost. Line
A–D of Fig. 6.1b illustrates this effect. In Fig. 6.1b, Y stands for social activity
and X stands for all other activities. As a person spends more and more
time in social activity (going from right to left in the diagram), stock of social
activity builds up. As a person spends less and less time in social activity
(moving from left to right), stock depletes. The positive effect of present
consumption on future local utility illustrated in Fig. 6.1b is called *price
sensitization* (Rachlin, 1997).

THE PRIMROSE PATH

Relative addiction theory depends on the existence of a reciprocal relationship between X (an addictive activity) and Y (social activity) such as that
implied by Figs. 6.1a and 6.1b. In Fig. 6.1a, Y is the context of X; in Fig.
6.1b, X is the context of Y. As X increases, Y decreases; as Y increases, X
decreases. If addictive activity and social activity comprised the universe of
all available activities, the reciprocal relation implied by Fig. 6.1 would
follow. But, of course, many activities other than social and addictive ones
are almost always available to all animals. Another condition that would
result in a reciprocal relation between activities is economic substitutability

---

[2]Even addictive activities involve skill acquisition at low levels. Many addictions are "acquired
tastes." The first cigarette burns your throat, the first beer tastes bitter. The solid line of Fig.
6.1a should have been drawn with a slight downward dip at the leftmost edge. The intent of
Fig. 6.1a, however, is not to reflect variations in any particular set of addictions but to show
dominant or overall trends.

(Rachlin & Burkhard, 1978). Consider, for example, the economic substitutes, Coke and Pepsi. There is a market for cola drinks that, it can be assumed, remains fairly constant. It can also be assumed that there is a negligible taste difference between the two brands. Then relative consumption will depend on price, advertising effectiveness, shelf location, and so forth. Assuming constancy of the cola market, and absence of other competing brands, when consumption of Coke goes up, consumption of Pepsi would go down, and vice versa. Coke and Pepsi would be substitutable for each other but not for other commodities. These two commodities would in a sense be competing in their own arena, walled off from others. A central assumption of relative addiction theory is that addictive activities and social activities are walled off in this way—they are at least moderately substitutable for each other but not for any third activity. According to relative addiction theory, when the extrinsic price of social activity increases (e.g., by the death of a spouse or close friend), addictive activity may substitute to some extent for diminished social activity.

When two commodities are substitutable for each other but not substitutable for anything else, economists call this property *separability* (Becker, 1976). If this assumption were true in the case of addictive and social activities, the two classes of activity would vary inversely, as Fig. 6.1 implies. Indeed, recent evidence (summarized by Rachlin, 1997) points to an inverse relation between social activity and addictive activity. Decreases in social support often are accompanied by increases in addiction, and programs to reduce addiction work better when social support is present and worse when it is absent (Fisher, 1996, with cigarettes; Schuster et al., 1995, with cocaine; Vuchinich & Tucker, 1996, with alcohol). Moreover, several experiments with rats have found that social isolation increases consumption of addictive substances (Roske, Baeger, Frenzel, & Oehme, 1994, with alcohol; Wolffgramm, 1990, with ethanol; Wolffgramm & Heyne, 1995, with ethanol and an opiate).

The crucial difference between Coke versus Pepsi and addictive versus social activity is that cola consumption, if it affects future local utilities of Coke and Pepsi, affects them in the same way. But consumption of addictive substances affects future local utility oppositely from the way social activity affects future local utility. As argued previously, addictive activity reduces future local utility, whereas social activity increases future local utility.

Figure 6.2 combines Figs. 6.1a and 6.1b. In Fig. 6.2a, the local utility of social activity (Y) is higher than that of addictive activity (X). The dashed line running from A (100% Y) to C (100% X) represents overall utility. As in Fig. 6.1, the horizontal axis indicates a subject's overall distribution of time at X and Y. At the left (exclusive choice of social activity), overall utility equals the local utility of social activity. At the right (exclusive choice of addictive activity), overall utility equals the local utility of addictive activity.

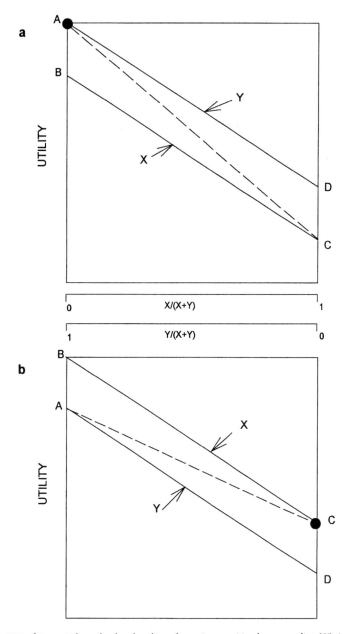

FIG. 6.2. a. When the local utility of a price-sensitized commodity (Y) is consistently greater than that of a price-habituated commodity (X), consumption allocation to the highest local utility stabilizes at 100% to the price-sensitized commodity (the heavy dot). b. When the local utility of a price-habituated commodity (X) is consistently greater than that of a price-sensitized commodity (Y), consumption allocation stabilizes at 100% to the price-habituated commodity. Given that addictive consumption is usually price-habituated, this illustrates conditions of addiction. The dashed line represents overall utility at various (long-run) consumption allocations.

In the center, a subject is distributing half of the time to X and half to Y; therefore, overall utility is halfway between the local utilities of X and Y. As a subject chooses one or the other alternative more frequently, overall utility is weighted proportionally. There is no conflict between local and overall utility in the conditions illustrated in Fig. 6.2a. The point of highest local utility (A) is the same as the point of highest overall utility. A meliorating subject would choose the alternative with highest local utility (social activity—Y) and keep choosing it, coming to rest at point A (the heavy dot).

In Fig. 6.2b, however, the local utility of addictive activity (X) is higher than that of social activity (Y). The conditions illustrated in Fig. 6.2b create a conflict between maximization of local and overall utility. A meliorating subject always would choose the activity with highest local utility (addictive activity—X) and keep choosing it. But repeated choices of X have two effects: (a) they directly reduce future local utility of X; and (b) they imply rejection of the other alternative, Y, thereby indirectly reducing future local utility of Y, as well. Repeated choices of the highest local utility (addictive activity—X) thus bring the subject to rest at point C, the very lowest overall utility. If the extrinsic price of social support suddenly increased, the economic conditions would change from those in Fig. 6.2a to those in Fig. 6.2b. The subject's choice allocation would then go from A in Fig. 6.2a to B in Fig. 6.2b and then gradually to C in Fig. 6.2b—from no consumption to some consumption to addiction. Herrnstein and Prelec (1992) called this "the primrose path."

Stable and Bistable Conditions

Figure 6.2 illustrates conditions where lines $A–D$ and $B–C$ are parallel—where price habituation occurs at the same rate as price sensitization. But these two processes need not correspond in this way. Figure 6.3a illustrates the condition where line $B–C$ (price habituation) is steeper than line $A–D$ (price sensitization). This is called *relative price-habituation* (Rachlin, 1997). With relative price-habituation, increases in addictive activity still decrease the local utility of both addictive and social activity, but the local utility of addictive activity decreases at a faster rate than that of social activity. Eventually, the local utility of social activity may be higher than that of addictive activity; lines $A–D$ and $B–C$ may cross, as in Fig. 6.3a, providing a point of stability at the intersection. This state of affairs may well be the case for most people with respect to most addictive activities. However, for some people, increases in some addictive activities may have a larger (indirect) effect on the future utility of social activity than the direct effect on the future utility of the addictive activity itself; that is, line $A–D$ (price sensitization) may be steeper than line $B–C$ (price habituation). This is called *relative price-sensitization* and is shown in Fig. 6.3b. When the lines cross, a bistable condition results at the two extreme points. If the initial relative

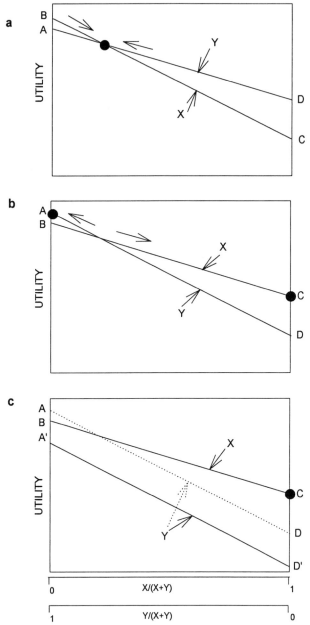

FIG. 6.3. a. Condition of relative price-habituation. Consumption allocation to the highest local utility stabilizes at the intersection of the two lines (the point where local utilities of X and Y are equal). b. Condition of relative price-sensitization. Consumption allocation stabilizes at one or another end point (100% to X or Y) depending on initial conditions. c. If the relative price of the price-sensitized commodity Y increases, consumption allocation stabilizes at only one point, 100% to X (addiction). Return to the conditions of Fig. 6.3b would leave addiction in place.

rate $[X/(X + Y)]$ is to the left of the intersection point, behavior will come to rest at point A, no addictive activity and all social activity ($X = 0$; $Y = 1$). If the initial relative rate is to the right of the intersection point, behavior will come to rest at point C, all addictive activity and no social activity ($X = 1$; $Y = 0$). Thus, the conditions of relative price-sensitization do not doom a person to addiction. However, as Fig. 6.3c illustrates, if the extrinsic price of social activity should suddenly increase (dropping local utility from A–D to A'–D'), a primrose path would be created with only one stable point—at C, complete addiction.[3]

The following scenario would then characterize the progress of addiction according to relative addiction theory. A person begins at point A of Fig. 6.3b as a socially active nonaddict. Occasional addictive activity such as social drinking (drinking for the purpose of enhancing social support) is quite safe because narrow excursions from point A still would be to the left of the intersection point, where the local utility of social activity is higher than that of addictive activity. As soon as the extrinsic pressure to engage in addictive activity (such as the contingency of social support on social drinking) ceases, behavior would drift back to point A. But should such extrinsic pressure persist (e.g., in an environment where social pressure to drink is continuous and intense), social contingencies could push the person up to and across the intersection point of Fig. 6.3b; melioration (choice of the highest local utility) would then bring behavior all the way to point C. This is one path by which addiction may progress. It may well be the main path for young people.

Another path, illustrated in Fig. 6.3c, would involve an increase in the price (hence, a decrease in the local utility) of social activity. This could come about through the death of a spouse or close friend or through being transferred to a job in another city (a scenario more likely as one grows older). In Fig. 6.3c, there is only one stable state—point C, complete addiction. Even if the conditions of Fig. 6.3b were restored (remarriage, making new friends, etc.) point C would remain a stable state. There, contingencies may well act against addictive activity; in most neighborhoods, addiction is socially condemned.[4] But the difference in the local utilities of addictive and

---

[3]The force bringing a person's choices along the path from A' to B to C may be augmented by a kind of intertemporal complementarity called *adjacent complementarity* by Becker (1996). If the degree of reinforcement (irrespective of its valence) were weighted very highly, a person at A' might (rationally but not necessarily consciously) embark on a path from A' to C. The person might prefer the wide variance of utility in the area between C and D' to the narrow variance in the area between A' and B and therefore start to consume X at A' (building up stock) as a sort of investment in a future position at the other end, the high variance end, of the primrose path. See Rachlin (1997) for a more extended discussion of adjacent complementarity.

[4]Although in some it may well not be. In Richard Price's (1993) fictional ghetto neighborhood, in *Clockers,* addiction and dope dealing are the normal ways of life. American middle-class values are portrayed as rare and indeed maladaptive in that environment.

social activities may be too extreme by then (point C may be too far above point D) for contingencies to reverse.

Pseudo Social Support

It often is observed that addicts engage in addictive activity only in the company of certain friends (usually fellow addicts) and never see these friends without engaging in addictive activity. It may seem as if this socialization produces a degree of social support that complements rather than substitutes for addictive activity. However, addictive consumption is highly conditionable. Particular environmental stimuli easily become discriminative signals for consumption (as well as for internal opponent processes), just as TV watching may become a signal for eating for many. A particular group of people, like a particular room or a particular mode of drug taking, may come to serve as such a signal. When this is added to the fact that the substance being consumed may be more easily available among fellow addicts, the observed "social activity" of addicts becomes explicable. But this social activity is not a source of social support in the sense that a family or community is. The opium addict does not go to the opium den for the social support (if any) to be found there.

POSITIVE AND NEGATIVE REINFORCEMENT

The primrose path of Fig. 6.2b is reproduced in Fig. 6.4. The dashed line represents overall utility and separates regions of positive and negative reinforcement. At point A, for example, allocation is 100% to social activity, and overall utility equals the local utility of social activity. But point B is higher in local utility than point A. Switching from social to addictive activity at point A is, therefore, a case of positive reinforcement (Premack, 1965). At point C, on the other hand, allocation is 100% to addictive activity, and overall utility equals the local utility of addictive activity. But point D is lower in local utility than point C. Switching from addictive to social activity at point C would be a case of punishment, whereas switching from social to addictive activity (from D to C) would be a case of negative reinforcement. Colloquially, for a nonaddict, addictive activity is pleasurable, whereas, for an addict, addictive activity merely avoids pain. Between these extremes, addictive activity involves some mixture of positive and negative reinforcement, as indicated in Fig. 6.4 by the portion of the parallelogram, A–B–C–D above and below the dashed line.

Suppose that a person has become an addict and is at point C in Fig. 6.4. There are now two motives for quitting—for taking the "straight and narrow" path from C to D to A. One motive is to increase overall utility; the other is to exchange negative for positive reinforcement. The latter is a

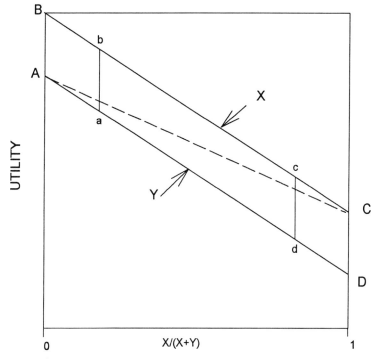

FIG. 6.4. Same as Fig. 6.2b. The dashed line represents overall utility. The area above the dashed line (triangle *A–B–C*), where local utility is above overall utility, represents positive reinforcement. The area below the dashed line (triangle *A–C–D*), where local utility is below overall utility, represents negative reinforcement. Switching from social to addictive activity at the right vertical line (going from *d* to *c*) is negatively reinforced. Switching from social to addictive activity at the left vertical line (going from *a* to *b*) is positively reinforced.

very powerful force in human behavior that, according to Skinner (1971), is tantamount to exchanging slavery for freedom (the literature of addiction is, in fact, full of references to addiction as slavery). Moreover, whereas overall utility is an abstract, temporally extended state, positive reinforcement is a discrete event, albeit from the viewpoint of the addict at *C*, a future event. The dominant motive for quitting then may well be to effect this exchange. However, because it is not socially approved, this motive may go unverbalized and even unrealized by addicts themselves.[5]

As the course of addiction progresses from *A* to *C*, the proportion of positive reinforcement (the space between lines *A–C* and *B–C* in Fig. 6.4)

---

[5]Addicts often voluntarily commit themselves to a detoxification center and also smuggle in the addictive substance. The difference between self-knowledge and self-ignorance would then lie in whether they smuggle in the substance at the time of or after the original commitment.

steadily diminishes, thereby increasing the addict's motive to turn back. At point c, for example, the path $c-d-A$ may be embarked on. But as this path is pursued, the proportion of positive reinforcement that would be obtained by defecting from it and engaging in addictive behavior steadily increases. At point a, for example, positive reinforcement is predominant. Thus a person might cycle around the path $a-b-c-d$, between relatively moderate and relatively high levels of addictive consumption, as positive and negative reinforcement exerted their immediate and long-term effects. Such shuttling (between abstinence and relapse) is notoriously common among addicts (Marlatt & Gordon, 1980).

CONTROLLING ADDICTION

Note again that, except at the two extremes, overall utility, represented by the dashed line in Fig. 6.4, is an abstract, temporally extended state. Utility, at any given moment, is always local—by definition. A point on the dashed line represents the proportion of addictive and social activities (the upper and lower solid lines) within some global boundary significantly wider than the boundary that defines local rates. In a typical concurrent-chain operant conditioning experiment with pigeons, for example, the local utilities would be given by rates of reinforcement in each of the terminal links, whereas the overall rate of reinforcement would be the combined reinforcement rate over the entire experimental session. In Herrnstein and Prelec's (1992) extension of this model to human addiction, local utilities would be given by immediate costs and values of, for example, a night of drinking and a night at home with your family; global utility would be given by the average cost and value over a month or a year of such nights. Aside from the vast discrepancy of temporal scale, the main difference between choice by pigeons in concurrent-chain experiments and choice by humans in everyday life is that future concurrent-chain terminal link conditions are typically independent of present choices, whereas in human life, present addictive or social activity may (as previously discussed) have strong negative or positive effects on future local utility, hence on current overall utility.

Nevertheless, some concurrent-chain experiments have varied future local reinforcement rate explicitly as a function of present choice. Perhaps the most instructive of these experiments pits a fixed-ratio schedule against a progressive-ratio schedule (Wanchisen, Tatham, & Hineline, 1992). The fixed-ratio alternative always remains constant, that is, a brief access to food is contingent on a fixed number of responses (the *cost*). The progressive-ratio alternative starts out with a cost much lower than that of the fixed-ratio alternative, but current choices of either alternative explicitly affect the future cost in the progressive-ratio alternative. Each choice of the progressive ratio increases the next progressive-ratio cost, whereas each choice of the fixed ratio sets the next progressive-ratio cost back to its initial (very low) number of responses. Simply interpreted, melioration (choice of the alternative with the highest local utility) predicts that the progressive-ratio alternative will be chosen until its cost grows to exceed that of the fixed-ratio alternative. Then, the fixed-ratio alternative will be chosen once, setting the progressive-ratio cost back to its initial low value, whereupon the progressive-ratio alternative again will be chosen. But this behavior would fail to maximize overall utility because it fails to take into account the effect of current choice on future local utility. Current choice of the fixed-ratio alternative not only yields some net local utility but also has a positive effect on future local utility, by reducing future cost of the progressive-ratio alternative. To maximize overall utility, the fixed-ratio alternative should be chosen not when its cost is exceeded by that of the progressive ratio but well before that point.

To see this, imagine that a Coke costs $1 (i.e., fixed), whereas a Pepsi initially costs 25 cents but increases in price by 25 cents every time one is purchased (i.e., progressive). Moreover, every time you buy a Coke, the price of the next Pepsi resets to 25 cents. A meliorating consumer would buy four Pepsis, the last of which would cost $1, and then switch to Coke, and then repeat the cycle. The average cost would be 70 cents per can [(.25 + .50 + .75 + 1.00 + 1.00)/5]. Switching one can earlier, however, yields a lower average cost of 63 cents per can [(.25 + .50 + .75 + 1.00)/4]. Switching two cans earlier yields a still lower average cost of 58 cents per can [(.25 + .50 + 1.00)/3]. This last sequence would maximize overall utility by minimizing cost per can. (Switching three cans earlier, alternating between Coke and Pepsi, would raise the cost to 63 cents per can [(.25 + 1.00)/2].)

In tests of concurrent fixed-ratio versus progressive-ratio schedules, animals (rats, pigeons, and people) do not meliorate, that is, they switch from the progressive to the fixed alternative well before the point of equality, much closer to the point where overall utility is maximized (and overall cost is minimized). According to Herrnstein (1991), such apparent deviations from melioration are due to *restructuring*, that is, the boundary line dividing local from overall utility is drawn further and further in the future and past. In the case of progressive-ratio schedules, local reinforcement rate is determined not on the basis of a single exposure to the fixed or progressive alternative, but on the basis of a sequence of exposures. In the Coke versus Pepsi illustration, a person could restructure alternatives from individual cans to individual strings of cans of Pepsi followed by a Coke. Local utilities would then be given by the figures in brackets (see previous equations) rather than by individual cans. Melioration would consist of choice of the lowest-costing string. Overall utility would then have to be defined in still wider terms—the effects of cola consumption versus other foods on future health, perhaps.

From this perspective, local and overall utilities of behavior are relative positions on a continuum with abstract, temporally extended patterns of acts on one end and particular, brief individual responses on the other. Just as any pattern, no matter how wide, can be conceived of as part of some still wider pattern, so any act, no matter how narrow, may be conceived of as composed of still narrower acts (Rachlin, 1995). Restructuring would consist of incorporation of more and more context into local utility. In terms of Figs. 6.2b and 6.4, restructuring would bridge over the solid lines and present choices as various positions on the dashed line. If choices were framed in this way, it would be easy to choose the alternative of highest utility. The question for self-control is how to engender restructuring.

Rachlin (1995) argued that restructuring occurs when behavior is organized into temporal patterns. E. Siegel and Rachlin (1996) found that pigeons chose a larger, delayed food delivery over a smaller, sooner food delivery (thus maximizing a relatively widely defined local utility) when the choice response was preceded by a string of prior responses, but they chose the smaller, sooner food delivery (thus maximizing a relatively narrowly defined local utility) when the choice response was isolated. E. Siegel and Rachlin explained this reversal in terms of response patterning. The initial string of responses, plus the choice response, plus the delay period, plus the larger reinforcer formed a pattern. Once formed, the pattern could be chosen as a unit over the initial string of responses, plus the choice response, plus the smaller reinforcer. Without the initial string of responses, the choice responses and reinforcers formed narrower patterns, where the delay to the larger reinforcer could play a dominant role in determining relative utility.

Kudadjie-Gyamfi and Rachlin (1996) found similar results with human participants. Participants earned points convertible to money by pressing buttons. Each press on button X earned a point delayed by x seconds; each press on button Y earned a point delayed by y seconds. The session ended when $x + y$ reached a fixed value; thus, the less the delay on any given trial, the more money participants could earn over the session. The duration of x was always less than that of y, but as $X/(X + Y)$ increased, both x and y increased together. This created the contingencies illustrated in Fig. 6.2b. Choices of X increased local rate of point acquisition at the expense of overall rate, whereas choices of Y had the reverse effect. The purpose of the experiment was to investigate the patterning of choices on behavior with these contingencies. One group of participants made successive choices at fixed 10-second intervals. Another group made choices in patterns of three rapid choices followed by 30-second intervals. The patterned-choice group pressed *Y*, the button that maximized overall rate, significantly more frequently than did the fixed-interval choice group.

Heyman and Tanz (1995) studied a conflict, with pigeon subjects, much like that illustrated in Fig. 6.2b. One alternative response tended to increase local utility and decrease overall utility, whereas the other did the reverse. Signals could be provided that indicated when overall utility was increasing and when it was decreasing. These signals essentially particularized and localized overall utility, which otherwise was abstract and temporally extended. When the signals were absent, the pigeons tended to choose the alternative that maximized local utility (thereby minimizing overall utility). When the signals were present, however, the pigeons were able to choose the alternative that maximized overall utility. Heyman (1996) drew an analogy between these results and a corresponding ease or difficulty in controlling addictive behavior in everyday life. For example, many American soldiers became addicted to heroin in Vietnam. Yet, when they came home, despite withdrawal symptoms and drug availability, the vast majority stopped taking the drug. According to Heyman (1996), in Vietnam there were no signals to indicate the decreases in global utility contingent on addictive behavior, whereas at home there were signals everywhere relating addictive behavior to ill health, joblessness, and social rejection. These signals enabled the veterans to restructure their behavior into wider patterns. As indicated previously, when behavior is structured in wider patterns, local utility is defined more widely (the boundary between local and overall utility is further in the future and more context is incorporated into local utility). Melioration then approaches maximization of global utility.

Without denying the relevance of such signals, relative addiction theory would focus on the conditions of social support in Vietnam and later at home. Although intense social relationships undoubtedly are formed in combat conditions, by their very nature they must be brief and frequently terminated by transfer or casualty. The risk of loss would discount the value of social relationships made under combat conditions. Heroin, on the other hand, would be a relatively reliable friend. The cheapness of heroin and other drugs relative to social support in Vietnam is exactly the condition that relative addiction theory predicts would produce addiction. A further determinant of addiction, according to relative addiction theory, is the relative steepness of the slopes of the price-habituation and price-sensitization lines. The greater the degree of relative price-sensitization (accompanied by a relatively low price for addictive activity), the more likely addiction would be. The rapidity with which social relationships are formed and lost in combat might well cause the price-sensitization line to be very steep, whereas, back home, social relationships would at least initially be cheap and, once formed, less risky. In any case, relative addiction theory predicts that veterans' difficulty of social adjustment to civilian life should be strongly negatively correlated with their ease of recovery from addiction. This was, in fact, the case. For example, in a study of Vietnam drug users, Robins (1974) reported that of the soldiers who had been addicted to narcotics in Vietnam and continued their use of narcotics after discharge, 42% (of those who were married) became divorced during the 8 to 12 months between discharge and the time of the study. The corresponding figure for those who discontinued narcotic use after discharge was 7%. As Robins wrote, "Drug users in the post-Vietnam period, and particularly narcotics users, carried a heavy burden of poor social adjustment" (p. 74). It is not clear whether the poor social adjustment was the cause of the continued narcotics use or vice versa. But, according to the relative addiction model, social maladjustment and addiction are so intertwined that the causal direction would be difficult or impossible to discover.

In summary, the crucial assumptions of relative addiction theory are as follows:

1. An inverse relation (based on economic substitutability) exists between addictive consumption and social support.
2. Present addictive consumption adversely affects the local utility of future addictive consumption.
3. Present abstinence from social activity adversely affects the local utility of future social support.

The strength of an addictive tendency has been shown to depend on interactions between these three relationships. Evidence exists for all three, and for their interaction, but this evidence is so far not conclusive.

Even if we assume that future evidence will support relative addiction theory, the primrose path to addiction that it postulates would be neither unavoidable nor inescapable. Various external forces such as extrinsic prices, contingencies between addictive behavior and social support, discriminative stimulus effects, classical conditioning effects, preference for positive versus negative reinforcement and, most importantly, restructuring through creation and destruction of behavior patterns, may modify the ease of taking the primrose path to addiction as well as the difficulty of taking the straight and narrow path back from it.

ACKNOWLEDGMENTS

The preparation of this manuscript was supported by grants from the National Institute of Mental Health and the National Institute on Drug Abuse. Correspondence should be addressed to Howard Rachlin, Psychology Department, State University of New York, Stony Brook, NY 11794–2500.

REFERENCES

Becker, G. S. (1976). *The economic approach to human behavior.* Chicago: University of Chicago Press.

Becker, G. S. (1996). *Accounting for tastes.* Cambridge, MA: Harvard University Press.

Brazelton, T. B., Koslowski, B., & Main, M. (1974). The origins of reciprocity: The early mother–infant interaction. In M. Lewis & L. Rosenblum (Eds.), *The effect of the infant on its caregiver* (pp. 49–76). New York: Wiley.

deVilliers, P. A. (1977). Choice in concurrent schedules and a quantitative formulation of the law of effect. In W. K. Honig & J. E. R. Staddon (Eds.), *Handbook of operant behavior* (pp. 233–287). Englewood Cliffs, NJ: Prentice-Hall.

Fisher, E. B., Jr. (1996). A behavioral-economic perspective on the influence of social support on cigarette smoking. In L. Green & J. H. Kagel (Eds.), *Advances in behavioral economics: Volume 3. Substance use and abuse* (pp. 207–236). Norwood, NJ: Ablex.

Green, L., & Kagel, J. H. (1996). *Advances in behavioral economics: Volume 3. Substance use and abuse.* Norwood, NJ: Ablex.

Herrnstein, R. J. (1991). Experiments on stable suboptimality in individual behavior. *American Economic Review, 81,* 360–364.

Herrnstein, R. J., & Prelec, D. (1992). A theory of addiction. In G. Loewenstein & J. Elster (Eds.), *Choice over time* (pp. 331–360). New York: Russell Sage Foundation.

Herrnstein, R. J., & Vaughan, W., Jr. (1980). Melioration and behavioral allocation. In J. E. R. Staddon (Ed.), *Limits to action: The allocation of individual behavior* (pp. 143–176). New York: Academic Press.

Heyman, G. M. (1996). Resolving the contradictions of addiction. *Behavioral and Brain Sciences, 19,* 561–610.

Heyman, G. M., & Tanz, L. (1995). How to teach a pigeon to maximize overall reinforcement rate. *Journal of the Experimental Analysis of Behavior, 64,* 277–298.

Kudadjie-Gyamfi, E., & Rachlin, H. (1996). Temporal patterning in choice among delayed outcomes. *Organizational Behavior and Human Decision Processes, 65,* 61–67.

Marlatt, G. A., & Gordon, J. R. (1980). Determinants of relapse: Implications for the maintenance of behavior change. In P. O. Davidson & S. M. Davidson (Eds.), *Behavioral medicine: Changing health lifestyles* (pp. 410–452). New York: Brunner/Mazel.

Premack, D. (1965). Reinforcement theory. In D. Levine (Ed.), *Nebraska Symposium on motivation* (Vol. XIII, pp. 123–179). Lincoln: University of Nebraska Press.

Price, R. (1993). *Clockers.* New York: Avon.

Rachlin, H. (1974). Self-control. *Behaviorism, 2,* 94–107.

Rachlin, H. (1995). Self-control: Beyond commitment. *Behavioral and Brain Sciences, 18,* 109–159.

Rachlin, H. (1997). Four teleological theories of addiction. *Psychonomic Bulletin & Review, 4,* 462–473.

Rachlin, H., Battalio, R., Kagel, J., and Green, L. (1981). Maximization theory in behavioral psychology. *Behavioral and Brain Sciences, 4,* 371–417.

Rachlin, H., & Burkhard, B. (1978). The temporal triangle: Substitution in instrumental conditioning. *Psychological Review, 85,* 22–48.

Rachlin, H., Green, L., & Tormey, B. (1988). Is there a decisive test between matching and maximizing? *Journal of the Experimental Analysis of Behavior, 50,* 113–123.

Rachlin, H., & Laibson, D. I. (1997). Introduction to Part III. In R. J. Herrnstein (Ed.), *The matching law: Papers in psychology and economics* (pp. 189–193). Cambridge, MA: Harvard University Press.

Robins, L. N. (1974). *The Vietnam drug user returns* (Special Action Office Monograph, Series A, No. 2). Washington, DC: U.S. Government Printing Office.

Roske, I., Baeger, I., Frenzel, R., & Oehme, P. (1994). Does a relationship exist between the quality of stress and the motivation to ingest alcohol? *Alcohol, 11,* 113–124.

Schuster, C. R., Silverman, K., Harrell, S., Brooner, R., Cone, E., & Preston, K. (1995, May). *ASP as a predictor of treatment outcome in a contingency management program for cocaine abusers.* Poster session presented at the annual meeting of the American College of Neuro-psychopharmacology, San Juan, Puerto Rico.

Siegel, E., & Rachlin, H. (1996). Soft commitment: Self-control achieved by response persistence. *Journal of the Experimental Analysis of Behavior, 64,* 117–128.

Siegel, S. (1976). Morphine analgesic tolerance: Its situation specificity supports a Pavlovian conditioning model. *Science, 193,* 323–325.

Skinner, B. F. (1971). *Beyond freedom and dignity.* New York: Knopf.

Solomon, R. L. (1980). The opponent-process theory of acquired motivation. *American Psychologist, 35,* 691–712.

Vuchinich, R. E., & Tucker, J. (1996). The molar context of alcohol abuse. In L. Green & J. H. Kagel (Eds.), *Advances in behavioral economics: Volume 3. Substance use and abuse* (pp. 138–162). Norwood, NJ: Ablex.

Wanchisen, B. A., Tatham, T. A., & Hineline, P. N. (1992). Human choice in "counterintuitive" situations: Fixed- versus progressive-ratio schedules. *Journal of the Experimental Analysis of Behavior, 58,* 67–86.

Wolffgramm, J. (1990). Free choice ethanol intake of laboratory rats under different social conditions. *Psychopharmacology, 101,* 233–239.

Wolffgramm, J., & Heyne, A. (1995). From controlled drug intake to loss of control: The irreversible development of drug addiction in the rat. *Behavioural Brain Research, 70,* 77–94.

PART FOUR

HEALTH BEHAVIOR AS INTERTEMPORAL CHOICE

CHAPTER SEVEN

Self-Control and Health Behavior

A. W. Logue
Baruch College, City University of New York

The media bombard us with descriptions of how we should behave in order to become or remain healthy. Magazines, television reports, and newspapers all tell us about how we can avoid cancer and infectious disease, protect ourselves from accidents, and cure our addictions. Yet, despite this knowledge, many people routinely engage in unhealthy behaviors. For example, even though it is firmly established that cigarette smoking contributes significantly to lung cancer and heart disease, and there are warnings everywhere, including on cigarette packages, approximately 60 million Americans still use tobacco (Holloway, 1991).

This chapter describes a model of self-control, originally developed in the laboratory, that can help us to understand, predict, and possibly modify healthy and unhealthy behaviors. The chapter begins with a description of the model and related basic laboratory findings. Then it applies this model to different types of health behaviors. The overall goal of the chapter is to show how laboratory research can provide new ways of conceptualizing health behaviors, ways that may assist us in promoting good health.

BACKGROUND

Definitions

Self-control can be defined as choice of a more delayed, but ultimately more valued, outcome over a less delayed, but less valued, outcome. *Impulsiveness* can be defined as the opposite (Fig. 7.1). Such choices also have been

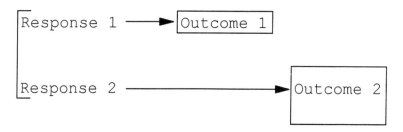

FIG. 7.1. Choice between a less delayed, smaller outcome and a more de-layed, larger outcome (i.e., impulsive and self-control choices). A bracket indicates that a choice is available between the two responses. The length of the line between a response and its outcome indicates the amount of time after the response that the outcome occurs. The size of the outcome box indicates the size of an outcome.

expressed as those between larger, more delayed reinforcers (or rewards) and smaller, less delayed reinforcers (or rewards; Ainslie, 1974; Logue, 1988; Rachlin & Green, 1972). For example, if someone chooses to smoke, that person is choosing the immediate positive stimuli associated with smoking instead of a long, healthy life. Therefore, smoking can be defined as impulsiveness, and not smoking can be defined as self-control.

Several factors should be considered when defining a choice as self-control or impulsiveness. First, the choice must be between two outcomes that differ both in terms of their ultimate values and their delays. Second, these definitions do not presume that self-control is always optimal (maximizing total obtained positive outcome). If impulsive choices result in outcomes being received at a higher rate, the optimal choice may be impulsiveness (Logue, 1995; Logue, King, Chavarro, & Volpe, 1990). The definitions of self-control and impulsiveness refer only to the outcome of a single choice, not to the overall outcome of repeated choices. Finally, because these definitions involve larger and smaller reinforcers, and longer and shorter delays, choices are defined as self-control and impulsiveness only relative to other available choices.

These definitions are operational ones that describe specific types of observable events, thus enabling laboratory investigation. However, they may not apply to all of the types of behaviors commonly described as self-control and impulsiveness outside of the operant conditioning laboratory. For many people, using these terms adds implications about concepts such as willpower that researchers may not intend. Nevertheless, the terms self-control and impulsiveness should be retained because they are concise and clear. In addition, through their use in our culture, these definitions sometimes both help to suggest ideas for experiments and help to clarify the connection between laboratory research and the world outside of the laboratory (Logue, 1995).

Self-control and impulsiveness are defined here in terms of positive outcomes (Fig. 7.2a). They also can be defined in terms of negative outcomes (aversive stimuli or punishers, Fig. 7.2b). In that case, impulsiveness is a choice of a relatively large negative outcome that is more delayed over a relatively small negative outcome that is less delayed, and self-control is the opposite. Any outcome can be stated in either negative or positive terms. Again using cigarette smoking as an example, the self-control choice of not smoking could be stated either as resulting in a healthy life later (a delayed, large, positive outcome) or in not experiencing the positive stimuli of smoking now (an immediate, small, negative outcome). The impulsive choice of smoking could be stated as resulting in the positive stimuli of smoking now (an immediate, small, positive outcome) or in an unhealthy life later (a delayed, large, negative outcome). Most experiments on self-control are

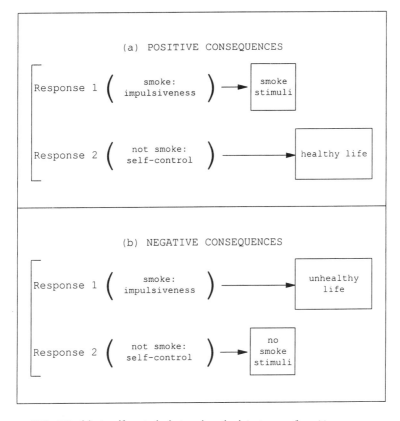

FIG. 7.2. (a) A self-control choice described in terms of positive consequences: smoke stimuli (the impulsive alternative) and a healthy life (the self-control alternative). (b) A self-control choice described in terms of negative consequences: an unhealthy life (the impulsive alternative) and absence of smoke stimuli (the self-control alternative).

stated as choices between positive outcomes (e.g., a choice between a small amount of food available now versus a larger amount of food available later; Logue, 1995). However, a few experiments have been conducted in which the choices were stated as negative outcomes. For example, Deluty (1978) gave rats a choice between a short-duration, less delayed shock (self-control) and a long-duration, more delayed shock (impulsiveness). Some of this chapter's examples of self-control and impulsiveness are most easily described in terms of positive outcomes, and others in terms of negative outcomes. In addition, examples sometimes are simplified for ease of illustration; various qualifying conditions that might affect choice are not always described. However, many of these sorts of qualifying conditions are described in detail in the chapter's section entitled "Factors Related to Self-Control."

Although research on self-control can help us to understand how and why humans do and do not show self-control, this research does not by itself tell us when humans should show self-control. In many aspects of our culture, self-control is considered "good" and impulsiveness "bad" (Brownell, 1991). However, these moral designations are not a direct function of the scientific analysis of self-control and impulsiveness. Even if we decided that the appropriate choice was the one that maximized total received reinforcement, sometimes that outcome will result from a self-control choice, and sometimes from an impulsive choice. Thus, it is more useful to try to understand self-control and impulsiveness with regard to their causes and consequences than to label them as inherently good and bad behaviors.

Evolution and Self-Control

Consideration of how self-control and impulsiveness ultimately may or may not benefit the animal that exhibits them can help us understand how these behaviors may have evolved. Self-control and impulsive choices involve choosing between alternatives that differ in terms of their delay, as well as their size. The longer an event is delayed, the less likely it is that that event will occur. For example, some of the unhealthy consequences of cigarette smoking take a long time to occur. Before those unhealthy effects occur, many things could happen, such as the person could die in a car accident. Therefore, assuming all else is equal, people will maximize their receipt of positive outcomes and minimize their receipt of negative outcomes if they prefer less delayed over more delayed positive outcomes, and more delayed over less delayed negative outcomes. Such preferences have been demonstrated repeatedly in the laboratory using both human and nonhuman subjects (see, e.g., Ainslie & Herrnstein, 1981; Schwarz, Schrager, & Lyons, 1983). These experiments demonstrate that humans and other animals discount (in other words, value less) delayed events.

Humans and other animals may have evolved the tendency to discount delayed events. Humans used to live in an environment more similar to that of other animals, one in which future food sources and, in fact, any future events, are highly unpredictable (Kagel, Green, & Caraco, 1986). Death from disease and accidents was prevalent, and access to food sources was not reliable. Even when hunter–gatherer societies began to settle in particular locations and to engage in agriculture, natural disasters of various sorts could and often did wipe out a crop. Although these people learned how to store food and to trade, they still frequently lived on the edge of starvation (Harlan, 1975). For all of these reasons, life expectancy was short (Cohen, 1987). In these kinds of early human environments, a particular delayed event was not very likely to occur, and, thus, waiting for such events was not very likely to result in any benefit (Kagel et al., 1986). In other words, in an environment in which future events are uncertain, impulsiveness, not self-control, is likely to maximize overall benefits. For example, if, as a result of frequent plagues, individuals are unlikely to live to the completion or even the beginning of their reproductive years, those individuals would have little reason to show self-control with regard to sexual behavior and pregnancy; sexual behavior resulting in pregnancy should be engaged in at every op-portunity. Therefore, during humans' long evolutionary history, people who tended to value delayed outcomes less than immediate outcomes were prob-ably more likely to survive in at least some situations. This means that genes that contributed to impulsiveness probably increased an individual's inclu-sive fitness—the survival of that individual's biological relatives, who are the most likely carriers of that individual's genes (Barash, 1977)—resulting in an increased proportion of future animals possessing genes that tended in some way to contribute to this delayed outcome discounting. For all of these reasons, it is likely that humans and other animals possess genes for delayed outcome discounting.

Discounting and impulsiveness differ according to the situation and the species (Lejeune & Wearden, 1991; Real, 1991; Richelle & Lejeune, 1984; Timberlake, Gawley, & Lucas, 1987), and at least some of these differences may have an evolutionary basis. For example, in laboratory experimental sessions, when food rewards are used, hungry humans tend to be less impulsive than are pigeons (Tobin & Logue, 1994). This species difference may be related to the fact that, in nature, because of their high metabolic rates, pigeons need to forage continually, whereas humans, with much lower metabolic rates, can eat in discrete meals. As another example, hungry hu-mans participating in laboratory experiments tend to be more impulsive for food reinforcers than for points exchangeable for money. For a hungry animal, there is some advantage to obtaining food as quickly as possible, even at the expense of later food, so as to maintain sufficient energy for essential tasks (Forzano & Logue, 1994; Kirk & Logue, 1997).

The environment of the majority of the people in the United States is currently quite different from that of hunter–gatherer or early agricultural societies. First, for most people today, food of some sort is always available. Even if someone has no money for food, our culture has instituted food-stamp programs and soup kitchens. Second, our expected life span is considerably longer than that of evolving humans. Many diseases have been eradicated or are usually curable. At the same time, the chances of someone dying from a flood or a wild animal attack are quite small. Most people can expect to live long, relatively healthy lives. Third, in our current environment, we have formalized the rules by which people must live; we have created laws along with ways in which those laws are enforced (tax collectors, police officers, district attorneys, etc.). Through printed and audiovisual media, as well as by word of mouth, there is extensive communication regarding the existence of these laws and the consequences for breaking them. Fourth, we simply have more knowledge now about the probability of the occur-rence of certain future events, such as particular kinds of weather, demo-graphic trends, and the usable life of a machine. Finally, even when someone does not know for sure what the consequences for a particular action might be, that person may be able to influence events to ensure that a particular outcome occurs. That also might have been true during, for example, hunter–gatherer times, but only if the person could expect to live long enough to exert the necessary and desirable influence—not as likely then as now. Together, these characteristics of our current environment indicate that the consequences for certain behaviors are often (although certainly not always) quite specific and quite certain.

Given that many future events in our current environment are now highly predictable, discounting of those events can be unadaptive (Ainslie, 1992). Discounting of delayed events that are virtually certain to occur can result in choices that are not the best overall strategy. Thus, evolution may have resulted in a mismatch between how we behave and our current environ-ment. People persist in behaving as if many events almost certain to occur are unlikely or nonexistent, and therefore engage in unadaptive impulsive-ness (such as cigarette smoking despite the long-term health risks).

Quantitative Model

A quantitative framework based on the generalized matching law (Baum, 1974) has been used to describe and predict self-control and impulsive behavior as defined in this chapter. According to this model:

$$\frac{B_1}{B_2} = k\left(\frac{A_1}{A_2}\right)^{S_A}\left(\frac{D_2}{D_1}\right)^{S_D}, \tag{1}$$

in which B_i, A_i, and D_i represent the number of choices, the size, and the delay of a particular outcome i, respectively; k represents response bias (if

$k > 1$, there is a bias for outcome 1, and if $k < 1$, there is a bias for outcome 2); and s_A and s_D represent the sensitivity of the subject's behavior to changes in the relative amount and the relative delay of the outcomes, respectively (Logue, Rodriguez, Peña-Correal, & Mauro, 1984). According to Equation 1, the greater the amount of an outcome, the more that outcome is chosen. However, the greater the delay of an outcome, the less that outcome is chosen. In other words, as delay increases, the less a subject values an outcome; delay discounts the value of an outcome. The variable s_D expresses the rate at which that discounting occurs. If s_D is very large, changes in the delay ratio result in even larger changes in the behavior ratio. If s_D is very small, changes in delay have very little effect on behavior.

Figure 7.3 depicts, in accordance with Equation 1, the hypothetical effects of delay on outcome value. In each panel, the two vertical lines show the value of two outcomes at the points in time at which they are received. The curves show how the values of those outcomes are lower at earlier points in time, when there are delays to receipt of the outcomes. Under some conditions, including those in panel a of Fig. 7.3, these curves (hyperbolas) can cross. As a result, in panel a, at point x the larger, more delayed outcome has greater value, and at point y, the smaller, less delayed outcome has greater value. In other words, panel a predicts that self-control will be shown at point x and impulsiveness will be shown at point y. This predicted preference reversal accords well with the preference reversals seen both inside and outside of the laboratory (Ainslie & Haslam, 1992; Green, Fisher, Perlow,

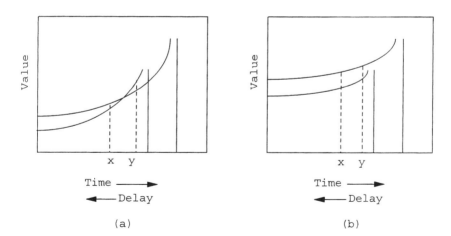

FIG. 7.3. Hypothetical gradients of the value of two positive outcomes as a function of time—a larger, more delayed outcome and a smaller, less delayed outcome. The letters x and y indicate two possible points at which choices between the two outcomes might be made. In the right panel, the gradients are more shallow than in the left panel so that there is no longer a point at which the two gradients cross and self-control is always shown.

& Sherman, 1981). For example, someone may not express a preference to smoke if there are no cigarettes nearby but may express a preference to smoke when in a room where cigarettes are prominently displayed. Panel b shows what can happen when the value of s_D is decreased: The curves are more shallow and there is no longer a crossover point. Now self-control will be shown at both points x and y. Thus, Equation 1 and Fig. 7.3 can help explain the fact that, as discussed subsequently, manipulations that result in less delay discounting of the larger, more delayed outcome (such as manipulations that make time seem to pass faster) also increase self-control.

Variables Related to Self-Control

Researchers have shown that many different variables are related to the demonstration of self-control and impulsiveness. This section describes some of these variables, including methods for changing self-control. For ease of presentation, they are divided into two groups: variables that concern characteristics of an available outcome, and variables that concern characteristics of the person who is choosing between self-control and impulsiveness.

Characteristics of an Outcome. At least three characteristics of an outcome affect whether someone will show self-control: outcome delay, outcome size, and outcome contingencies. The effects of each of these three characteristics are discussed in the following paragraphs.

As explained previously, outcome delay appears to discount the value of an outcome. Impulsiveness occurs when delay discounts the value of a larger outcome to the degree that it is less than that of a smaller, less delayed outcome (Logue, 1995). Therefore, changes in the perceived relative delays of the reinforcers can affect self-control. For example, if someone knew that smoking a cigarette today would result in lung cancer tomorrow, that person probably would be less likely to smoke than if the lung cancer would not appear for 20 years. Making the perceived relative delays of the two alternatives appear more similar should result in greater choice of the larger outcome and vice versa.

A large number of experiments have manipulated the physical values of the relative delays of the two outcomes in a variety of ways. As expected, greater relative delay to the larger outcome results in less self-control (Green et al., 1981; W. Mischel & Grusec, 1967). Other manipulations exist that, although they do not change the physical values of the relative outcome delays, may change the perceived values of the relative outcome delays, and thus also change self-control. For example, preexposure to outcome delays either increases or decreases self-control, depending on the relative lengths of the preexposed delays and the delays within the self-control choice (Eisenberger & Masterson, 1987; Grosch & Neuringer, 1981). One particular kind of delay preexposure involves a fading procedure. In this procedure, subjects first are given a choice between equally delayed large and small outcomes. Then the delay to the small outcome is very gradually decreased (faded) until eventually the subject is choosing between a larger, more delayed outcome and a smaller, immediate outcome. Both pigeons and impulsive children exposed to this procedure subsequently have shown increased self-control (Logue et al., 1984; Mazur & Logue, 1978; Schweitzer & Sulzer-Azaroff, 1988).

One of the most commonly used methods for increasing self-control through manipulation of outcome delays involves manipulation of the perceived speed of the passage of time. If time is perceived as passing very quickly, then the perceived delay to the larger outcome will be shorter, and self-control should increase. The opposite also should occur. It has been postulated that people will be less impulsive if their attention is directed in such a way or they are distracted so that they do not think about the tempting situation, because in such cases time may seem to pass more quickly (Ainslie & Haslam, 1992). In support of this hypothesis, during the delay to the larger outcome, doing enjoyable activities, being instructed to think enjoyable thoughts, or having present some stimuli that previously have been associated with rewards, all increase self-control (Grosch & Neuringer, 1981; W. Mischel & Ebbesen, 1970; W. Mischel, Ebbesen, & Zeiss, 1972). One of the best ways for a subject to ensure maintenance of his or her self-control while waiting for the larger outcome is for the subject to remove completely any attention to the larger outcome's delay period by falling asleep (W. Mischel & Ebbesen, 1970). Time then seems to pass very quickly. Consistent with these results, instructing children not to attend to the outcomes increases self-control (W. Mischel & Patterson, 1976; Patterson & Mischel, 1976). More specifically, Walter Mischel and his colleagues have shown in repeated experiments with children that if a child is told to think, or reports thinking, about the consummatory, motivational properties of outcomes (what Mischel calls "hot thoughts"), self-control decreases. However, if someone is told to think, or reports thinking, about the nonconsummatory, nonmotivational properties of outcomes (what Mischel calls "cool thoughts"), self-control increases (W. Mischel, Shoda, & Rodriguez, 1989). In a typical experiment, Mischel gives children a choice between one pretzel available now and three pretzels available if the child does not ring a bell until after a waiting period. Instructing the child to think about the taste of the pretzels and how crunchy they are decreases self-control. However, instructing the child to think about the shape and color of the pretzels increases self-control (W. Mischel & Baker, 1975).

Whether someone shows self-control is also a function of the sizes of the available outcomes. Simply making the relative size of the larger, more delayed outcome even larger will increase self-control. This can be done by increasing the physical or perceived size of the larger outcome, decreasing the physical or perceived size of the smaller outcome, or a combination of these strategies. Several experiments have demonstrated the success of such techniques using both pigeons and humans (Fantino, 1966; Grusec, 1968; Herzberger & Dweck, 1978). In one experiment, human participants were more likely to choose an alternative requiring more work (the self-control alternative) if that alterative yielded a reward of increased size (Blakely, Starin, & Poling, 1988). Outside the laboratory, an example of how self-control might be increased through decreasing the size of the less delayed reinforcer would be for smokers to meliorate nicotine withdrawal symptoms through the use of nicotine patches or gum.

One particular technique may help people to increase self-control by increasing their awareness of the existence of the larger, more delayed outcome. This technique involves teaching people how to think about self-control situations in terms of cost–benefit rules. People are taught to analyze a choice situation in terms of all of the possible costs and benefits associated with each possible choice, including what opportunities may be lost through making a particular choice (a type of cost). They are also taught to weigh carefully the relative net value of each outcome before making a decision. This technique does appear to increase choices of the alternative that provides the most benefit in the long term (Larrick, Morgan, & Nisbett, 1990).

A final way that the relative size of the self-control outcome may be increased is to combine that outcome with another positive or negative outcome. This increases or decreases, respectively, the net value of the self-control alternative. One way to do this is by delivering reward or punishment each time the self-control choice is made (Karniol & Miller, 1981; Little & Kendall, 1979). For example, someone can give an ex-smoker praise each time the ex-smoker turns down an offered cigarette. Self-reward and self-punishment also can be used (Kanfer, 1971; O'Leary & Dubey, 1979). In self-reward, someone engages in a pleasurable activity (a reward) whenever that person has engaged in another specified activity. In self-punishment, an unpleasurable activity (a punisher) is used instead of the reward. However, given that self-reward and self-punishment are not always manifested by changes in external behavior, it is not always possible to know when self-reward and self-punishment are occurring or what influences them.

Outcome contingencies, the relations between responses and outcomes, also can affect whether self-control is shown. Someone can be aware of the existence of outcomes with specific delays and sizes but be unaware of what responses will or will not result in those outcomes. Certain response contingencies and the perceived presence of those contingencies can affect self-control.

People learn about the consequences for the choices in a self-control paradigm by making the responses and receiving the consequences, or by watching or speaking with other people who are involved in a similar choice or who have some knowledge about such a choice (Kendall, 1982; Kendall & Zupan, 1981). *Modeling*—watching someone else make a self-control choice and benefit by that choice—can help to emphasize the availability of the larger, more delayed outcome (Bandura & Mischel, 1965; LaVoie, Anderson, Fraze, & Johnson, 1981). Modeling also may make the perceived time to the delayed outcome seem shorter. The precise mechanism by which modeling increases self-control is not yet known. *Monitoring*—keeping careful track of one's own responses and the ensuing consequences, perhaps by some formal means such as keeping a list or drawing a graph—may assist in the recognition and memory of behavioral consequences and thus assist self-control (W. Mischel, 1990; Rachlin, 1974). Participants' self-statements also appear to influence the participants' perceptions of the response–outcome contingencies. Participants who make statements during the waiting periods reminding themselves of what will happen if they wait, or of what they have to do to receive the larger reinforcer, are more likely to show self-control (Bentall & Lowe, 1987; Kendall, 1977; Meichenbaum & Goodman, 1971). Self-statements may increase self-control by providing stimuli ("reminders") associated with the response–outcome contingency. Similar stimuli can be provided to nonhuman subjects. When colored lights are present during delay periods, with the precise color used being identical to the color of the choice button that has been pecked, pigeons show more self-control than when such delay lights are not used (Logue & Mazur, 1981). Complex language behavior is apparently not necessary for stimuli to function as reminders of the response–outcome contingencies and for self-control to be increased.

One specific outcome contingency that can affect self-control concerns whether the subject has the option to change his or her choice while waiting for the larger, more delayed outcome. In laboratory research, pigeons are less likely to end up actually receiving the larger, more delayed outcome if such a choice change is available (Logue & Peña-Correal, 1984). Subjects in this situation have essentially many repeated choices between an immediate, smaller outcome and a delayed, larger outcome before they receive the delayed, larger outcome. Therefore, in this situation, the pigeons have more opportunities to be impulsive.

A related type of contingency that also can affect self-control is a precommitment contingency (Ainslie, 1975; Rachlin, 1974; see Fig. 7.4). With this type of contingency, an individual makes a (precommitment) response that prevents a subsequent impulsive choice. For example, an ex-smoker who thinks that he would relapse and smoke at a party could ask a friend to promise to go with him to the party and to forcibly remove any cigarettes from the ex-smoker's hands. Laboratory research has shown that both human and nonhuman subjects can precommit, although there seem to be large individual differences (Rachlin & Green, 1972; Solnick, Kannenberg, Ecker-

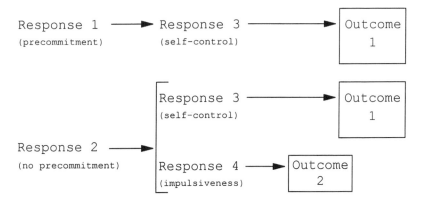

FIG. 7.4. Diagram of precommitment (Response 1) and no precommitment (Response 2) choice alternatives.

man, & Waller, 1980). According to the model used to generate Fig. 7.3, precommitment responses can be made at any point to the left of the crossover point. Precommitment strategies are an extremely useful general self-control technique widely recognized in the popular culture.

Characteristics of an Individual. Even given the same choices, some people show self-control and others are impulsive. For example, much evidence suggests that, in general, self-control appears to increase as children age and become adults (Kopp, 1982; W. Mischel et al., 1989). Many different traits and abilities exist that may be responsible for the increase in self-control that is generally seen as children age, and that also may be partly or wholly responsible for the differences in self-control that are often seen among adults.

For example, individual differences in time perception sometimes are related to self-control. The ability to discriminate time intervals appears to improve with age and to be associated with increased self-control (W. Mischel & Metzner, 1962). In one experiment, boys who would work for a delayed, valuable outcome without any immediate benefit for doing so tended to estimate time more accurately (Levine & Spivak, 1959).

Several different lines of research suggest that self-control is positively related to a variety of measures of intellectual abilities such as those measured by the Peabody Picture Vocabulary Test, SAT scores, and tests of expressive language behavior (Funder & Block, 1989; Golden, Montare, & Bridger, 1977; W. Mischel & Metzner, 1962; Rodriguez, Mischel, & Shoda, 1989). However, the data directly examining the role of language ability in self-control in children are mixed. Some studies have found that language capacity or vocabulary are positively related to self-control (Kopp, 1982; Vaughn, Kopp, Krakow, Johnson, & Schwartz, 1986), but others have not

(Kopp, 1982; Logue, Forzano, & Ackerman, 1996; Maitland, 1967). It is possible that what assists self-control is the ability to make certain kinds of verbalizations during delay periods, not language ability in general.

The learning of general strategies for increasing self-control also can contribute to the development of individual differences in self-control. Around age 5 or 6, children begin to learn what sorts of behaviors will make it easier to wait for a larger, more delayed outcome. For example, they learn that distracting themselves (such as by singing a song, playing a game, or falling asleep) or instructing themselves (such as by repeating to themselves that waiting will result in the larger reward) can help in the demonstration of self-control. In addition, somewhere between the third and sixth grades, children are able to report that thinking abstractly about the rewards and the task (such as thoughts about the shape of the rewards) rather than about the consummatory properties of the rewards (such as their taste) also will help in their demonstrating self-control (H. N. Mischel & Mischel, 1983; W. Mischel et al., 1989). Apparently, as people age, they develop abilities or learn strategies that assist them in decreasing or removing the effects of discounting of delayed outcomes. These age-related traits and abilities may differ in degree among adults, and so also may be responsible for some of the differences in self-control seen among adults.

Gender differences also can contribute to individual differences in self-control. Studies using a variety of self-control paradigms have shown repeatedly that girls tend to demonstrate more self-control than do boys (Kanfer & Zich, 1974; Logue & Chavarro, 1992; Maccoby & Jacklin, 1974; Sonuga-Barke, Lea, & Webley, 1989; Trommsdorff & Schmidt-Rinke, 1980). It is not clear what is responsible for these gender differences. The differences in language ability between boys and girls are too small to explain their differences in self-control (Hyde & Linn, 1988; Jacklin, 1989). In adults, gender differences in self-control have not been demonstrated (Feingold, 1994).

Development of self-control also may differ among people depending on the culture in which they are raised. In the United States, there appear to be strong cultural tendencies for both self-control and impulsiveness. On the one hand, self-control and resistance to temptation have been part of America's Judeo-Christian heritage. However, this early emphasis on self-control may be dissipating, as exemplified by the decrease in the rate of personal savings (Eisenberger, 1989). In contrast, many people consider the Japanese culture to be virtually synonymous with self-control, stressing consensus and cooperation and deemphasizing individual gratification (Christopher, 1983). However, just as in the United States, there is concern that self-control in Japan is decreasing, as exemplified by a recent decrease in the rate of personal savings (Nasar, 1991). Thus, although the Japanese and American cultures sometimes have appeared to be significantly different with respect to self-control, the differences between them may be decreasing.

APPLICATION TO SPECIFIC HEALTH BEHAVIORS

Many of our behaviors can affect the probability that we will become ill or injured at a future time. There are two ways of considering such behaviors, consistent with the positive and negative definitions of self-control outlined in Fig. 7.2. First, in situations in which someone has the opportunity to engage in a behavior (such as overeating) that provides some immediate positive stimuli but is likely to have negative long-term consequences, that person has a choice between not engaging in the behavior in order to be healthy later (self-control) or engaging in the behavior in order to receive the immediate positive stimuli (impulsiveness). Second, in situations in which someone has the opportunity to engage in a behavior (such as going to the dentist) that provides some immediate negative stimuli but is likely to have positive long-term consequences, that person has a choice between engaging in the behavior in order to be healthy later (self-control) or not engaging in the behavior in order not to receive the immediate negative stimuli (impulsiveness). The basic research on self-control described in the preceding sections can help us to understand why people do and do not engage in health-related behaviors described in either of these two ways. This research also can help to suggest ways that those behaviors may be increased or decreased. This section describes some of these possible linkages between basic research on self-control and health behavior. More specifically, this section discusses, in turn, the following health-related topics: eating, cancer, drug abuse, depression and suicide, and other health problems and accidents.

In considering health behaviors, it is useful to remember that delayed events are less likely to occur. Therefore, it is not surprising that people sometimes give as their reason for engaging in unhealthy behaviors the fact that those behaviors will not definitely result in illness. For example, it is not uncommon to hear cigarette smokers state that they do not need to stop smoking because they have relatives who lived to a very old age while smoking heavily. Not everyone who engages in unhealthy behaviors becomes ill. Laboratory research has demonstrated clearly that decreases in outcome probability decrease outcome value, just as do increases in outcome delay (see, e.g., King & Logue, 1992). There has been discussion in the research literature as to whether the decrease in outcome value resulting from increased outcome delay or decreased outcome probability represents two processes or one process (see, e.g., Rachlin, Logue, Gibbon, & Frankel, 1986). There is some laboratory research that supports the view that there is one process, that outcome delay is functionally equivalent to outcome probability (see, e.g., Rachlin, Castrogiovanni, & Cross, 1987). Thus, in the following sections, when people are faced with choices in which one of the two alternatives is a behavior that would increase the probability of developing an illness 10 years later, this may be equivalent to a behavior that definitely would cause that illness 30 years later. Even in the latter case, the person will not necessarily become ill. Before the 30 years are up, the person could die in an accident, or a cure for the illness could be found.

Eating

Several problems associated with eating—overeating, anorexia nervosa, and bulimia nervosa—can be seen as self-control problems (Lowe & Eldredge, 1993). In all of these cases, a person engages in a behavior that results in that person receiving some relatively immediate positive outcome but in the long run is not beneficial to the person's health.

For example, overeating can result in some immediate positive stimuli, including the taste, smell, and texture of the food. However, when extreme obesity results, there is a significant increase in the probability of someone developing a variety of health problems, including hypertension, diabetes, cancer, and heart attack (Simopoulos, 1987). Therefore, overeating can be described as impulsive behavior.

Overeating can be classified in two general types: overeating of all types of foods and overeating of specific types of food. Both types have several different causes as well as several different possible treatments. For example, overeating of all types of food can be caused by having a large number of adipose (fat) cells in the body. People are hungry if their fat cells are not full of fat (LeMagnen, 1985). The number of fat cells that a person has is significantly determined by that person's genes, and may increase if the person gains weight, but can never decrease (Björntorp, 1987; Sjöström, 1978). Impulsive overeating of all types of food also can be caused by exposure to stimuli that have been associated with food. Such a person is said to be *externally responsive*—encountering these stimuli increases the person's insulin level that, in turn, increases the person's hunger level and the tendency for any food consumed to be stored as fat (Rodin, 1985; Weingarten, 1983). Food variety also can increase overeating because, when a variety of foods is eaten, sensory-specific satiety effects are decreased; people and other animals satiate sooner when consuming a limited set of gustatory and olfactory stimuli (Clifton, Burton, & Sharp, 1987; Rolls et al., 1981). Finally, for restrained eaters (people who do not ordinarily eat all that they wish), a belief that alcohol has been consumed also can result in overeating of all types of food (Polivy & Herman, 1976).

Overeating of specific types of food can be due to our genetic predispositions to prefer sweet foods, salty foods, and foods that are high in calories (such as fatty foods). Such preferences would have been adaptive in the environment in which we evolved, an environment in which food supplies were often variable and inadequate. Now, however, most people in the United States have easy access to large amounts of sweet, salty, and fatty foods (including those that provide few nutrients other than calories and salt), and so we tend to overeat those foods (Logue, 1991; Simopoulos, 1987).

These different causes of impulsive overeating suggest a number of different treatments (Epstein, 1990). For example, precommitment procedures can be used to ensure that a person avoids stimuli that have been associated with food, meals containing a lot of different foods, alcohol consumption when food is present, sweet foods, salty foods, high-fat foods, or simply too many opportunities to eat. A specific instance of precommitment might involve taking only a limited amount of money when going grocery shopping. Then, unless the person is able to persuade someone at the store to provide a loan, it will be impossible for that person to buy large amounts of food. Practically speaking, of course, using precommitment procedures to avoid all of these different types of tempting situations is extremely difficult. A combination of different types of treatments, including pharmacotherapy and surgery, may be necessary to decrease overeating.

In contrast to overeating, the eating disorders of anorexia nervosa and bulimia nervosa involve people trying to absorb as few calories as possible, either by eating very little or by eating a great deal but purging the calories. Although such a person may feel that she or he is following an optimal strategy, just about everyone else views people suffering from these two disorders as engaging in behaviors that are not the best strategy over the long run. Therefore, treating either disorder might be facilitated by making the long-term detrimental effects of these disorders seem closer in time. For example, perhaps speaking with people who have encountered some of the health problems caused by anorexia nervosa might be a useful part of treatment. At the same time, it might be helpful to try to decrease the value of being thin for a female anorexic or bulimic by taking steps to convince her that, despite the media's depiction of attractive women as being extremely thin, people do not find her standard of thinness to be attractive. However, these treatment suggestions certainly will be insufficient by themselves. Anorexia nervosa and bulimia nervosa are notoriously difficult to treat and require a combination of treatments. For example, for bulimia nervosa, which is often associated with depression, antidepressants can play an important role in decreasing binging and purging (Agras, 1987; Hudson, Pope, & Jonas, 1984; Walsh et al., 1982).

In one type of situation, eating is the optimal response but is defined as impulsiveness. This occurs when someone is extremely food-deprived and has a choice between a small amount of food now and a larger amount of food later. In such a situation, an animal can starve while waiting for access to a large food source. Therefore, in these situations, choosing the smaller, less delayed outcome is optimal (Logue, 1995). Consistent with this analysis, human participants in the laboratory show less self-control for food reinforcers when they are more hungry (Kirk & Logue, 1997). This example illustrates again that self-control is not always the optimal choice.

Finally, the relations between eating and diabetes illustrate several ways that self-control and impulsiveness can affect health. Diabetics secrete inadequate amounts of the hormone insulin. Insulin assists the body in metabolizing blood glucose. Therefore, diabetics' blood glucose levels are often too high, which can cause a variety of adverse effects, including death (Guyton, 1969). In the past 20 years, the number of people in the United States with diabetes has significantly increased ("Lipogenesis," 1991). One reason for this increase is the increase in obesity in the United States. In the past 10 years, the percentage of adults in the United States who are obese has increased from 25% to 33% (Albu et al., 1997). Obesity can contribute to insulin resistance and hyperinsulemia and thus diabetes (Haffner, 1995). This explains why, if obese diabetics lose weight, the diabetes often improves ("Lipogenesis," 1991). Furthermore, there is some evidence that eating certain foods, such as carbohydrates that have a slow rate of digestion and absorption (Holt & Miller, 1995), can improve blood glucose control. Thus, diabetics sometimes need to experience only certain kinds or amounts of immediate, positive food stimuli in order to be healthy later. (Similarly, people with high cholesterol or hypertension need to eat certain foods and avoid others in order not to have a heart attack or stroke later.) Given humans' tendencies to consume excessive amounts of sweet, salty, and high-caloric food, and the fact that many diseases such as diabetes often have few, if any, currently debilitating symptoms, it can be very difficult for anyone to show self-control and to maintain the sort of diet required in these cases. A precommitment strategy such as making available only healthy foods can help to ensure that impulsiveness does not occur. Treatment for diabetics also may include unpleasant blood monitoring and taking insulin shots or pills. Contingency contracting, another example of a precommitment strategy, can be helpful in obtaining patient adherence to treatment programs, although the patients need to be sufficiently motivated and intelligent to use this self-control technique (Morgan & Littell, 1988). In contingency contracting, someone signs a contract agreeing that if that person behaves in a certain way, certain consequences will ensue.

Drug Abuse

People abuse many different kinds of drugs, such as alcohol, amphetamines, caffeine, cocaine, marijuana, and nicotine. In all of these cases, being exposed to these drugs frequently results in some short-term pleasure (such as the removal of any withdrawal effects) as well as some long-term harm to health (Ray & Ksir, 1993). Furthermore, there is evidence that, in some cases, taking drugs such as alcohol and cocaine can increase impulsiveness in other situations (Evenden & Ryan, 1996; Fromme, Katz, & D'Amico, 1997; Logue et al., 1992; Steele & Josephs, 1990). Thus, drug abuse can both be an example of impulsiveness and can itself cause impulsiveness (Logue, 1995; Madden, Petry, Badger, & Bickel, 1997; Poulos, Le, & Parker, 1995).

Many successful methods for decreasing drug abuse exist that derive from a variety of perspectives. This section considers some possible treatments for drug abuse that are suggested by considering drug abuse within a self-control framework (see also Higgins, 1997). From this perspective, one obvious way to decrease drug abuse is to decrease the relatively immediate rewards that result from taking a drug. For example, if the drug is an addictive one, it may be possible to eliminate the drug-taking reward of removal of craving and withdrawal symptoms by the use of some appropriate medication (Holloway, 1991; Ray & Ksir, 1993). Alternatively, the immediate positive value of taking an abused drug also can be decreased by following exposure to the drug with some immediate negative consequences. This is the principle behind the use of the medication Antabuse to treat alcohol abuse. If someone has taken Antabuse and then consumes alcohol, the Antabuse causes a profound physical reaction including "nausea, vomiting, tachycardia, marked drop in blood pressure, and other symptoms of massive autonomic arousal" (Litman & Topham, 1983, p. 172). Another method for decreasing the relatively immediate positive consequences that can follow use of an abused drug is to increase the value of other rewards present at the same time, thus making the rewards for drug taking seem relatively smaller (Higgins, Bickel, & Hughes, 1994). Precommitment, such as by the use of contingency contracts, is another obvious method of treating impulsive drug abuse, one that is used by the majority of methadone maintenance clinics. Drug abusers sign such contracts when drugs are not currently available. The drug abusers agree that if they abuse drugs, they will receive certain negative consequences, and if they do not abuse drugs, they will receive certain positive consequences (see, e.g., Calsyn, Saxon, & Barndt, 1991; Higgins, Budney, et al., 1994; Higgins et al., 1995; Nolimal & Crowley, 1990). Finally, another way to decrease impulsive drug abuse is to increase the value of the more delayed, larger rewards that result from not taking the drugs—either by directly increasing the value of those rewards or by making the delays to those rewards seem shorter. An example of how this could be done would be to show pregnant women movies clearly demonstrating how the blood supply in an umbilical cord is severely decreased if the mother consumes even a single drink of 100-proof whiskey (Altura et al., 1983).

Depression and Suicide

The American Psychiatric Association's *Diagnostic and Statistical Manual of Mental Disorders* (1994) describes the symptoms of a major depressive episode as including "diminished ability to think or concentrate . . . current thoughts of death . . . suicidal ideation . . . diminished interest or pleasure . . . easily distracted . . . memory difficulties" (pp. 322, 327). These symptoms of depression could be associated with impulsiveness. Given that depressed people have less ability to feel pleasure, then large, delayed rewards might not seem so large to them. Similarly, because of their inability to concentrate and the ease with which they are distracted by immediate stimuli, depressed people might have difficulty waiting for a delayed reward. Furthermore, when the main function of suicide is to avoid short-term aversive stimuli, suicide can be seen as impulsiveness. The possible connection between depression and impulsiveness is bolstered by results from experiments with children showing that children are more likely to show self-control when they are in a positive mood (Moore, Mischel, & Zeiss, 1976; Schwarz & Pollack, 1977). In addition, people who are depressed and suicidal often have low levels of serotonin (Leutwyler, 1997), and serotonin has been shown to be influential in delay tolerance and self-control (Bizot, Thiébot, Le Bihan, Soubrié, & Simon, 1988; Mann & Stanley, 1986; Soubrié, 1986; Thiébot, Le Bihan, Soubrié, & Simon, 1985).

All of this research suggests that it may be possible to decrease depression and suicidal behavior by making delayed, large rewards seem closer. This could be accomplished by having people suffering from depression and suicidal tendencies speak with recovered depressives to hear about the rewarding aspects of life that can follow depression. Support groups can be helpful in this regard. Pharmacological treatments, such as the use of the medication Prozac, which enhances serotonin functioning, also may be useful.

Other Health Problems and Accidents

Impulsiveness also plays a role in someone developing cancer. We now know about a number of different behaviors that can increase the probability of cancer. For example, smoking cigarettes, exposing your skin to the sun, and eating a low-fiber diet all can help to increase the probability of various types of cancer. All of these behaviors involve receiving some immediate stimuli that many people find very rewarding (such as the stimuli involved in smoking cigarettes, feeling the warmth of the sun and getting a tan, and eating large amounts of low-fiber food). Thus, engaging in these behaviors can be described as impulsiveness. In contrast, not engaging in these behaviors (i.e., engaging in cancer prevention) can be described as self-control. Experiencing cancer treatments also can be seen as involving self-control. Similar to going to the dentist, being treated for cancer frequently involves being exposed to relatively immediate aversive stimuli. Both chemotherapy and radiation can cause nausea (Bernstein & Webster, 1985; Smith, Blumsack, & Bilek, 1985), and surgery can be debilitating, with a painful recovery period. However, in the long term, the result of experiencing such treatments is an increased probability of cancer remission or cure.

There are many other situations in which people engage in many other types of behaviors so as to obtain some immediate satisfaction, but at the expense of their long-term health. Thus, these are impulsive behaviors. Some examples are engaging in unprotected sexual activity (which can result in unwanted pregnancy and sexually transmitted diseases), constantly watching television in addition to a sedentary job (so that there is insufficient exercise to maintain health), not going to the doctor when a suspicious symptom occurs (so that minor medical problems become major), not taking your car for regular inspections (possibly resulting in a dangerous vehicle), and not taking the time to "babyproof" your home when you have a very young child (so that the child may be injured). In all of these cases, the consequence of a long, healthy life may be very delayed and not at all certain, and therefore the (discounted) value of a long, healthy life may be very small when choices are being made between healthy and nonhealthy behaviors. The self-control techniques described previously for avoiding, treating, or managing various types of specific health problems can be adapted for these other cases, as well. Use of precommitment techniques, ways of making the delay to the larger outcome seem relatively shorter or the amount of the larger outcome seem relatively larger, are just some examples of strategies that can be used to increase self-control.

SUMMARY AND CONCLUSIONS

This chapter has shown how a self-control analysis can be useful in understanding choices involving healthy behaviors—behaviors that are likely to result in long-term good health. Once healthy behaviors are conceived of as self-control—choice of more delayed outcomes that are ultimately of more value over less delayed outcomes that are of less value—it is easy to see why it is so difficult for many people to engage in these behaviors. The consequence of a long, healthy life may be very delayed and therefore its (discounted) value may be quite small when choices must be made. In addition, the relation between a behavior and a subsequent illness or injury may be somewhat uncertain, which also discounts the value of the consequence of a long, healthy life. We can use a variety of self-control techniques to increase choices of healthy behaviors, and these techniques can be adapted so as to be most effective in particular health-related situations. The concept of self-control can help guide us to longer and healthier lives.

ACKNOWLEDGMENTS

Correspondence concerning this chapter should be addressed to the author at Weissman School of Arts and Sciences, 17 Lexington Avenue - A 1621,

Baruch College, New York, New York 10010. Electronic mail: alexandra_ logue@baruch.cuny.edu.

REFERENCES

Agras, W. S. (1987). *Eating disorders: Management of obesity, bulimia, and anorexia nervosa.* Elmsford, NY: Pergamon.

Ainslie, G. W. (1974). Impulse control in pigeons. *Journal of the Experimental Analysis of Behavior, 21,* 485–489.

Ainslie, G. (1975). Specious reward: A behavioral theory of impulsiveness and impulse control. *Psychological Bulletin, 82,* 463–496.

Ainslie, G. (1992). *Picoeconomics: The strategic interaction of successive motivational states within the person.* Cambridge, England: Cambridge University Press.

Ainslie, G., & Haslam, N. (1992). Self-control. In G. Loewenstein & J. Elster (Eds.), *Choice over time* (pp. 177–209). New York: Russell Sage Foundation.

Ainslie, G., & Herrnstein, R. J. (1981). Preference reversal and delayed reinforcement. *Animal Learning & Behavior, 9,* 476–482.

Albu, J., Allison, D., Boozer, C. N., Heymsfield, S., Kissileff, H., Kretser, A., Krumhar, K., Leibel, R., Nonas, C., Pi-Sunyer, X., VanItallie, T., & Wedral, E. (1997). Obesity solutions: Report of a meeting. *Nutrition Reviews, 55,* 150–156.

Altura, B. M., Altura, B. T., Carella, A., Chatterjee, M., Halevy, S., & Tejani, N. (1983). Alcohol produces spasms of human umbilical blood vessels: Relationship to fetal alcohol syndrome (FAS). *European Journal of Pharmacology, 86,* 311–312.

American Psychiatric Association. (1994). *Diagnostic and statistical manual of mental disorders* (4th ed.). Washington, DC: Author.

Bandura, A., & Mischel, W. (1965). Modification of self-imposed delay of reward through exposure to live and symbolic models. *Journal of Personality and Social Psychology, 2,* 698–705.

Barash, D. P. (1977). *Sociobiology and behavior.* New York: Elsevier.

Baum, W. M. (1974). On two types of deviation from the matching law: Bias and undermatching. *Journal of the Experimental Analysis of Behavior, 22,* 231–242.

Bentall, R. P., & Lowe, C. F. (1987). The role of verbal behavior in human learning: III. Instructional effects in children. *Journal of the Experimental Analysis of Behavior, 47,* 177–190.

Bernstein, I. L., & Webster, M. M. (1985). Learned food aversions: A consequence of cancer chemotherapy. In T. G. Burish, S. M. Levy, & B. F. Meyerowitz (Eds.), *Cancer, nutrition, and eating behavior* (pp. 103–116). Hillsdale, NJ: Lawrence Erlbaum Associates.

Bizot, J. C., Thiébot, M. H., Le Bihan, C., Soubrié, P., & Simon, P. (1988). Effects of imipramine-like drugs and serotonin uptake blockers on delay of reward in rats. Possible implication in the behavioral mechanism of action of antidepressants. *Journal of Pharmacology and Experimental Therapeutics, 246,* 1144–1151.

Björntorp, P. (1987). Fat cell distribution and metabolism. In R. J. Wurtman & J. J. Wurtman (Eds.), *Human obesity* (pp. 66–72). New York: New York Academy of Sciences.

Blakely, E., Starin, S., & Poling, A. (1988). Human performance under sequences of fixed-ratio schedules: Effects of ratio size and magnitude of reinforcement. *Psychological Record, 38,* 111–119.

Brownell, K. D. (1991). Dieting and the search for the perfect body: Where physiology and culture collide. *Behavior Therapy, 22,* 1–12.

Calsyn, D. A., Saxon, A. J., & Barndt, D. C. (1991). Urine screening practices in methadone maintenance clinics: A survey of how the results are used. *Journal of Nervous and Mental Disease, 179*, 222–227.

Christopher, R. C. (1983). *The Japanese mind.* New York: Fawcett Columbine.

Clifton, P. G., Burton, M. J., & Sharp, C. (1987). Rapid loss of stimulus-specific satiety after consumption of a second food. *Appetite, 9*, 149–156.

Cohen, M. N. (1987). The significance of long-term changes in human diet and food economy. In M. Harris & E. B. Ross (Eds.), *Food and evolution: Toward a theory of human food habits* (pp. 261–283). Philadelphia: Temple University Press.

Deluty, M. Z. (1978). Self-control and impulsiveness involving aversive events. *Journal of Experimental Psychology: Animal Behavior Processes, 4*, 250–266.

Eisenberger, R. (1989). *Blue Monday: The loss of the work ethic in America.* New York: Paragon House.

Eisenberger, R., & Masterson, F. A. (1987). Effects of prior learning and current motivation on self-control. In J. A. Nevin & H. Rachlin (Eds.), *Quantitative analyses of behavior: Vol. 5. The effects of delay and of intervening events on reinforcement value* (pp. 267–282). Hillsdale, NJ: Lawrence Erlbaum Associates.

Epstein, L. H. (1990). Behavioral treatment of obesity. In E. M. Stricker (Ed.), *Handbook of behavioral neurobiology: Vol. 10. Neurobiology of food and fluid intake* (pp. 61–73). New York: Plenum.

Evenden, J. L., & Ryan, C. N. (1996). The pharmacology of impulsive behaviour in rats: The effects of drugs on response choice with varying delays of reinforcement. *Psychopharmacology, 128*, 161–170.

Fantino, E. (1966). Immediate reward followed by extinction vs. later reward without extinction. *Psychonomic Science, 6*, 233–234.

Feingold, A. (1994). Gender differences in personality: A meta-analysis. *Psychological Bulletin, 116*, 429–456.

Forzano, L. B., & Logue, A. W. (1994). Self-control in adult humans: Comparison of qualitatively different reinforcers. *Learning and Motivation, 25*, 65–82.

Fromme, K., Katz, E., & D'Amico, E. (1997). Effects of alcohol intoxication on the perceived consequences of risk taking. *Experimental and Clinical Psychopharmacology, 5*, 14–23.

Funder, D. C., & Block, J. (1989). The role of ego-control, ego-resiliency, and IQ in delay of gratification in adolescence. *Journal of Personality and Social Psychology, 57*, 1041–1050.

Golden, M., Montare, A., & Bridger, W. (1977). Verbal control of delay behavior in two-year-old boys as a function of social class. *Child Development, 48*, 1107–1111.

Green, L., Fisher, E. B., Perlow, S., & Sherman, L. (1981). Preference reversal and self control: Choice as a function of reward amount and delay. *Behaviour Analysis Letters, 1*, 43–51.

Grosch, J., & Neuringer, A. (1981). Self-control in pigeons under the Mischel paradigm. *Journal of the Experimental Analysis of Behavior, 35*, 3–21.

Grusec, J. E. (1968). Waiting for rewards and punishments: Effects of reinforcement value on choice. *Journal of Personality and Social Psychology, 9*, 85–89.

Guyton, A. C. (1969). *Functions of the human body* (3rd ed.). Philadelphia: Saunders.

Haffner, S. M. (1995). Are there people who do not need to lose weight: The role of body fat distribution and implications from diabetes research. In D. B. Allison & F. X. Pi-Sunyer (Eds.), *Obesity treatment: Establishing goals, improving outcomes, and reviewing the research agenda* (pp. 65–69). New York: Plenum.

Harlan, J. R. (1975). *Crops & man.* Madison, WI: American Society of Agronomy.

Herzberger, S. D., & Dweck, C. S. (1978). Attraction and delay of gratification. *Journal of Personality, 46*, 214–227.

Higgins, S. T. (1997). Applying learning and conditioning theory to the treatment of alcohol and cocaine abuse. In B. A. Johnson & J. D. Roache (Eds.), *Drug addiction and its treatment* (pp. 367–385). Philadelphia: Lippincott.

Higgins, S. T., Bickel, W. K., & Hughes, J. R. (1994). Influence of an alternative reinforcer of human cocaine self-administration. *Life Sciences, 55,* 179–187.

Higgins, S. T., Budney, A. J., Bickel, W. K., Badger, G. J., Foerg, F. E., & Ogden, D. (1995). Outpatient behavioral treatment for cocaine dependence: One-year outcome. *Experimental and Clinical Psychopharmacology, 3,* 205–212.

Higgins, S. T., Budney, A. J., Bickel, W. K., Foerg, F. E., Donham, R., & Badger, G. J. (1994). Incentives improve outcome in outpatient behavioral treatment of cocaine dependence. *Archives of General Psychiatry, 51,* 568–576.

Holloway, M. (1991, March). R_x for addiction. *Scientific American, 264*(3), 94–103.

Holt, S. H. A., & Miller, J. B. (1995). Increased insulin responses to ingested foods are associated with lessened satiety. *Appetite, 24,* 43–54.

Hudson, J. I., Pope, H. G., & Jonas, J. M. (1984). Treatment of bulimia with antidepressants: Theoretical considerations and clinical findings. In A. J. Stunkard & E. Stellar (Eds.), *Eating and its disorders* (pp. 259–273). New York: Raven.

Hyde, J. S., & Linn, M. C. (1988). Gender differences in verbal ability: A meta-analysis. *Psychological Bulletin, 104,* 53–69.

Jacklin, C. N. (1989). Female and male: Issues of gender. *American Psychologist, 44,* 127–133.

Kagel, J. H., Green, L., & Caraco, T. (1986). When foragers discount the future: Constraint or adaptation? *Animal Behaviour, 34,* 271–283.

Kanfer, F. H. (1971). The maintenance of behavior by self-generated stimuli and reinforcement. In A. Jacobs & L. Sachs (Eds.), *The psychology of private events* (pp. 39–59). New York: Academic Press.

Kanfer, F. H., & Zich, J. (1974). Self-control training: The effects of external control on children's resistance to temptation. *Developmental Psychology, 10,* 108–115.

Karniol, R., & Miller, D. T. (1981). The development of self-control in children. In S. S. Brehm, S. M. Kassin, & F. X. Gibbons (Eds.), *Developmental social psychology: Theory and research* (pp. 32–50). New York: Oxford University Press.

Kendall, P. C. (1977). On the efficacious use of verbal self-instructional procedures with children. *Cognitive Therapy and Research, 1,* 331–341.

Kendall, P. C. (1982). Individual versus group cognitive–behavioral self-control training: 1-year follow-up. *Behavior Therapy, 13,* 241–247.

Kendall, P. C., & Zupan, B. A. (1981). Individual versus group application of cognitive–behavioral self-control procedures with children. *Behavior Therapy, 12,* 344–359.

King, G. R., & Logue, A. W. (1992). Choice in a self-control paradigm: Effects of uncertainty. *Behavioural Processes, 26,* 143–154.

Kirk, J. M., & Logue, A. W. (1997). Effects of deprivation level on humans' self-control for food reinforcers. *Appetite, 28,* 215–226.

Kopp, C. B. (1982). Antecedents of self-regulation: A developmental perspective. *Developmental Psychology, 18,* 199–214.

Larrick, R. P., Morgan, J. N., & Nisbett, R. E. (1990). Teaching the use of cost–benefit reasoning in everyday life. *Psychological Science, 1,* 362–370.

LaVoie, J. C., Anderson, K., Fraze, B., & Johnson, K. (1981). Modeling, tuition, and sanction effects on self-control at different ages. *Journal of Experimental Child Psychology, 31,* 446–455.

Lejeune, H., & Wearden, J. H. (1991). The comparative psychology of fixed-interval responding: Some quantitative analyses. *Learning and Motivation, 22,* 84–111.

LeMagnen, J. (1985). *Hunger.* New York: Cambridge University Press.

Leutwyler, K. (1997, March). Suicide prevention. *Scientific American, 276*(3), 18, 20.

Levine, M., & Spivak, G. (1959). Incentive, time conception and self control in a group of emotionally disturbed boys. *Journal of Clinical Psychology, 15,* 110–113.

Lipogenesis in diabetes and obesity. (1991). *Nutrition Reviews, 49,* 255–257.

Litman, G. K., & Topham, A. (1983). Outcome studies on techniques in alcoholism treatment. In M. Galanter (Ed.), *Recent developments in alcoholism* (pp. 167–194). New York: Plenum.

Little, V. L., & Kendall, P. C. (1979). Cognitive–behavioral interventions with delinquents: Problem solving, role-taking, and self-control. In P. C. Kendall & S. D. Hollon (Eds.), *Cognitive-behavioral interventions* (pp. 81–115). New York: Academic Press.

Logue, A. W. (1988). Research on self-control: An integrating framework. *Behavioral and Brain Sciences, 11,* 665–709.

Logue, A. W. (1991). *The psychology of eating and drinking: An introduction* (2nd ed.). San Francisco: Freeman.

Logue, A. W. (1995). *Self-control: Waiting until tomorrow for what you want today.* Englewood Cliffs, NJ: Prentice-Hall.

Logue, A. W., & Chavarro, A. (1992). Self-control and impulsiveness in preschool children. *Psychological Record, 42,* 189–204.

Logue, A. W., Forzano, L. B., & Ackerman, K. T. (1996). Self-control in children: Age, preference for reinforcer amount and delay, and language ability. *Learning and Motivation, 27,* 260–277.

Logue, A. W., King, G. R., Chavarro, A., & Volpe, J. S. (1990). Matching and maximizing in a self-control paradigm using human subjects. *Learning and Motivation, 21,* 340–368.

Logue, A. W., & Mazur, J. E. (1981). Maintenance of self-control acquired through a fading procedure: Follow-up on Mazur and Logue (1978). *Behaviour Analysis Letters, 1,* 131–137.

Logue, A. W., & Peña-Correal, T. E. (1984). Responding during reinforcement delay in a self-control paradigm. *Journal of the Experimental Analysis of Behavior, 41,* 267–277.

Logue, A. W., Rodriguez, M. L., Peña-Correal, T. E., & Mauro, B. C. (1984). Choice in a self-control paradigm: Quantification of experience-based differences. *Journal of the Experimental Analysis of Behavior, 41,* 53–67.

Logue, A. W., Tobin, H., Chelonis, J. J., Wang, R. Y., Geary, N., & Schachter, S. (1992). Cocaine decreases self-control in rats: A preliminary report. *Psychopharmacology, 109,* 245–247.

Lowe, M. R., & Eldredge, K. L. (1993). The role of impulsiveness in normal and disordered eating. In W. G. McCown, J. L. Johnson, & M. B. Shure (Ed.), *The impulsive client* (pp. 185–224). Washington, DC: American Psychological Association.

Maccoby, E. E., & Jacklin, C. N. (1974). *The psychology of sex differences.* Stanford, CA: Stanford University Press.

Madden, G. J., Petry, N. M., Badger, G. J., & Bickel, W. K. (1997). Impulsive and self-control choices in opioid-dependent patients and non-drug-using control participants: Drug and monetary rewards. *Experimental and Clinical Psychopharmacology, 5,* 256–262.

Maitland, S. D. P. (1967). Time perspective, frustration-failure and delay of gratification in middle-class and lower-class children from organized and disorganized families. *Dissertation Abstracts, 27,* 3676B.

Mann, J. J., & Stanley, M. (1986). *Psychobiology of suicidal behavior.* New York: New York Academy of Sciences.

Mazur, J. E., & Logue, A. W. (1978). Choice in a "self-control" paradigm: Effects of a fading procedure. *Journal of the Experimental Analysis of Behavior, 30,* 11–17.

Meichenbaum, D. H., & Goodman, J. (1971). Training impulsive children to talk to themselves. *Journal of Abnormal Psychology, 77,* 115–126.

Mischel, H. N., & Mischel, W. (1983). The development of children's knowledge of self-control strategies. *Child Development, 54,* 603–619.

Mischel, W. (1990). Personality dispositions revisited and revised: A view after three decades. In L. A. Pervin (Ed.), *Handbook of personality: Theory and research* (pp. 111–134). New York: Guilford.

Mischel, W., & Baker, N. (1975). Cognitive appraisals and transformations in delay behavior. *Journal of Personality and Social Psychology, 31,* 254–261.

Mischel, W., & Ebbesen, E. B. (1970). Attention in delay of gratification. *Journal of Personality and Social Psychology, 16,* 329–337.

Mischel, W., Ebbesen, E. B., & Zeiss, A. R. (1972). Cognitive and attentional mechanisms in delay of gratification. *Journal of Personality and Social Psychology, 21,* 204–218.

Mischel, W., & Grusec, J. (1967). Waiting for rewards and punishments: Effects of time and probability on choice. *Journal of Personality and Social Psychology, 5,* 24–31.

Mischel, W., & Metzner, R. (1962). Preference for delayed reward as a function of age, intelligence, and length of delay interval. *Journal of Abnormal and Social Psychology, 64,* 425–431.

Mischel, W., & Patterson, C. J. (1976). Substantive and structural elements of effective plans for self-control. *Journal of Personality and Social Psychology, 34,* 942–950.

Mischel, W., Shoda, Y., & Rodriguez, M. L. (1989). Delay of gratification in children. *Science, 244,* 933–938.

Moore, B., Mischel, W., & Zeiss, A. (1976). Comparative effects of the reward stimulus and its cognitive representation in voluntary delay. *Journal of Personality and Social Psychology, 34,* 419–424.

Morgan, B. S., & Littell, D. H. (1988). A closer look at teaching and contingency contracting with Type II diabetes. *Patient and Education and Counseling, 12,* 145–158.

Nasar, S. (1991, September 24). Baby boomers fail as born-again savers. *The New York Times,* pp. A1, D5.

Nolimal, D., & Crowley, T. J. (1990). Difficulties in a clinical application of methadone-dose contingency contracting. *Journal of Substance Abuse Treatment, 7,* 219–224.

O'Leary, S. G., & Dubey, D. R. (1979). Applications of self-control procedures by children: A review. *Journal of Applied Behavior Analysis, 12,* 449–465.

Patterson, C. J., & Mischel, W. (1976). Effects of temptation-inhibiting and task-facilitating plans on self-control. *Journal of Personality and Social Psychology, 33,* 209–217.

Polivy, J., & Herman, C. P. (1976). Effects of alcohol on eating behavior: Influence of mood and perceived intoxication. *Journal of Abnormal Psychology, 85,* 601–606.

Poulos, C. X., Le, A. D., & Parker, J. L. (1995). Impulsivity predicts individual susceptibility to high levels of alcohol self-administration. *Behavioural Pharmacology, 6,* 810–814.

Rachlin, H. (1974). Self-control. *Behaviorism, 2,* 94–107.

Rachlin, H., Castrogiovanni, A., & Cross, D. (1987). Probability and delay in commitment. *Journal of the Experimental Analysis of Behavior, 48,* 347–353.

Rachlin, H., & Green, L. (1972). Commitment, choice and self-control. *Journal of the Experimental Analysis of Behavior, 17,* 15–22.

Rachlin, H., Logue, A. W., Gibbon, J., & Frankel, M. (1986). Cognition and behavior in studies of choice. *Psychological Review, 93,* 33–45.

Ray, O., & Ksir, C. (1993). *Drugs, society, & human behavior.* St. Louis, MO: Mosby.

Real, L. A. (1991). Animal choice behavior and the evolution of cognitive architecture. *Science, 253,* 980–986.

Richelle, M., & Lejeune, H. (1984). Timing competence and timing performance: A cross-species approach. In J. Gibbon & L. Allan (Eds.), *Timing and time perception* (pp. 254–268). New York: New York Academy of Sciences.

Rodin, J. (1985). Insulin levels, hunger, and food intake: An example of feedback loops in body weight regulation. *Health Psychology, 4,* 1–24.

Rodriguez, M. L., Mischel, W., & Shoda, Y. (1989). Cognitive person variables in the delay of gratification of older children at risk. *Journal of Personality and Social Psychology, 57,* 358–367.

Rolls, B. J., Rowe, E. A., Rolls, E. T., Kingston, B., Megson, A., & Gunary, R. (1981). Variety in a meal enhances food intake in man. *Physiology and Behavior, 26,* 215–221.

Schwarz, J. C., & Pollack, P. R. (1977). Affect and delay of gratification. *Journal of Research in Personality, 11,* 147–164.

Schwarz, J. C., Schrager, J. B., & Lyons, A. E. (1983). Delay of gratification by preschoolers: Evidence for the validity of the choice paradigm. *Child Development, 54,* 620–625.

Schweitzer, J. B., & Sulzer-Azaroff, B. (1988). Self-control: Teaching tolerance for delay in impulsive children. *Journal of the Experimental Analysis of Behavior, 50,* 173–186.

Simopoulos, A. P. (1987). Characteristics of obesity: An overview. In R. J. Wurtman & J. J. Wurtman (Eds.), *Human obesity* (pp. 4–13). New York: New York Academy of Sciences.

Sjöström, L. (1978). The contribution of fat cells to the determination of body weight. In A. J. Stunkard (Ed.), *Symposium on obesity: Basic mechanisms and treatments* (pp. 493–521). Philadelphia: Saunders.

Smith, J. C., Blumsack, J. T., & Bilek, F. S. (1985). Radiation-induced taste aversions in rats and humans. In T. G. Burish, S. M. Levy, & B. F. Meyerowitz (Eds.), *Cancer, nutrition, and eating behavior* (pp. 77–101). Hillsdale, NJ: Lawrence Erlbaum Associates.

Solnick, J. V., Kannenberg, C. H., Eckerman, D. A., & Waller, M. B. (1980). An experimental analysis of impulsivity and impulse control in humans. *Learning and Motivation, 11,* 61–77.

Sonuga-Barke, E. J. S., Lea, S. E. G., & Webley, P. (1989). Children's choice: Sensitivity to changes in reinforcer density. *Journal of the Experimental Analysis of Behavior, 51,* 185–197.

Soubrié, P. (1986). Reconciling the role of central serotonin neurons in human and animal behavior. *Behavioral and Brain Sciences, 9,* 319–364.

Steele, C. M., & Josephs, R. A. (1990). Alcohol myopia: Its prized and dangerous effects. *American Psychologist, 45,* 921–933.

Thiébot, M.-H., Le Bihan, C., Soubrié, P., & Simon, P. (1985). Benzodiazepines reduce the tolerance to reward delay in rats. *Psychopharmacology, 86,* 147–152.

Timberlake, W., Gawley, D. J., & Lucas, G. A. (1987). Time horizons in rats foraging for food in temporally separated patches. *Journal of Experimental Psychology: Animal Behavior Processes, 13,* 302–309.

Tobin, H., & Logue, A. W. (1994). Self-control across species (*Columba livia, Homo sapiens,* and *Rattus norvegicus*). *Journal of Comparative Psychology, 108,* 126–133.

Trommsdorff, G., & Schmidt-Rinke, M. (1980). Individual situational characteristics as determinants of delay of gratification. *Archiv für Psychologie, 133,* 263–275.

Vaughn, B. E., Kopp, C. B., Krakow, J. B., Johnson, K., & Schwartz, S. S. (1986). Process analyses of the behavior of very young children in delay tasks. *Developmental Psychology, 22,* 752–759.

Walsh, B. T., Stewart, J. W., Wright, L., Harrison, W., Roose, S. P., & Glassman, A. H. (1982). Treatment of bulimia with monoamine oxidase inhibitors. *American Journal of Psychiatry, 139,* 1629–1630.

Weingarten, H. P. (1983). Conditioned cues elicit feeding in sated rats: A role for learning in meal initiation. *Science, 220,* 431–433.

CHAPTER EIGHT

Temporal Changes in the
Value of Objects of Choice:
Discounting, Behavior Patterns,
and Health Behavior

Cathy A. Simpson
Rudy E. Vuchinich
Auburn University

People often behave paradoxically: They do things they later wish they had not done, and they fail to do things they later wish they had. This temporal inconsistency is readily apparent in health-related behavior. People resolve to quit or curtail behaviors with negative health consequences (e.g., smoking and other substance use, overeating, etc.), only to return to excessive consumption at some later time. Similarly, they resolve to initiate new patterns of behavior with positive health consequences (e.g., regular exercise, low-fat diets, etc.), only to fail quickly to adhere to their resolutions.

Preferences expressed in words and action at any time may be assumed to be an accurate reflection of current desires, but short- and long-term preferences often oppose each other. Simply put, preferences change over time. A temporally extended future, to which long-term preferences regarding health behavior typically relate (e.g., "I want to be in better physical condition," or "I want to drink less"), is temporally distant, abstract, and uncertain. Meanwhile, behaviors with negative health consequences typically relate to the tangible rewards of the temporally circumscribed present (e.g., "I don't want to exercise and miss that TV program," or "One more beer now isn't going to hurt me"). Both healthy and unhealthy behavior patterns involve a succession of many individual choices. According to verbal reports, most individuals prefer the long-term benefits of good health over the many smaller but immediate rewards with which healthy behavior patterns compete, such as lack of exercise, poor diet, or substance abuse. However, given temporal changes in the value of objects of choice, and the corresponding changes in preferences, behavior patterns that promote long-term health frequently lose the competition with more immediately rewarding choice options. Apparently, this does not occur because good health has little long-term value, but instead because long-term health is not relatively valuable enough at the time of choice.

The point of this chapter is that temporal changes in the value of objects of choice probably are critical controlling variables of behavioral allocation patterns that have health consequences. The chapter has two main purposes. First, behavioral economic research and theory on the manner in which the temporal distribution of events effects their relative value are explored. Second, implications of these findings for understanding health behavior and health behavior change are discussed.

HEALTH AS AN OBJECT OF CHOICE

A behavioral economic perspective views health as a commodity that is an object of choice (Fuchs, 1987, 1993). As such, the acquisition and maintenance of health are largely under an individual's control. Although variability in uncontrollable circumstances (e.g., genetic characteristics, toxin exposure, accidents) have important effects on health, by and large health is conceived as a commodity similar to other commodities the acquisition of which requires allocation of resources on the part of the consumer (Fuchs, 1993; Gafni, 1995; Grossman, 1972). Critical to this perspective is the assumption that the value of any health-related choice option is relative to the context in which it is available, that is, the value of any health-related choice option partly will depend on both the availability of alternative objects of choice and any delays between choice and receipt of the chosen option.

Health-related choices involve trade-offs, whether implicit or explicit, between health status and other, more immediately valuable, objects of choice. Such exchanges are often implicit and involve diffuse contingencies, the outcomes of which are temporally distant from the choices that produced them. For example, mortality statistics indicate that the life expectancy exchange rate for smoking one cigarette is approximately 8 minutes, whereas a low-fat diet provides about 6 years' greater life expectancy than a high-fat diet (Chapman & Johnson, 1995). A study by Chapman and Johnson supports the idea that individuals are able to evaluate such exchanges when the contingencies involved are made explicit. Participants in that study made (hypothetical) trades between duration of life expectancy and immediately available consumer rewards. In general, the amount of life expectancy the participants traded for immediate rewards was directly related to the monetary value they had assigned to the rewards. For example, on average, participants were willing to trade about 28 days of life expectancy for ownership of a mountain cabin, 5 days of life expectancy for a year's supply of beer, and 14 minutes of life expectancy for a used automobile. These results are consistent with the notion that health is a commodity of malleable value, and that the relative attractiveness of long-term health rewards decreases as the relative attractiveness of competing immediately available alternatives increases.

DISCRETE EVENTS AS THE OBJECTS OF CHOICE

Both healthy and unhealthy behaviors have immediate and delayed, and positive and negative, consequences, and understanding how the value of those consequences changes over time is critical for understanding the allocation of behavior with health consequences. Given the centrality of the temporal dimension, health behavior can be usefully regarded as an intertemporal choice—a choice between smaller sooner rewards (SSRs) and larger later rewards (LLRs), and between smaller sooner costs (SSCs) and larger later costs (LLCs). In the context of health behavior, choice of the SSRs (e.g., substance use, fatty foods) leads to LLCs (e.g., poor health), whereas choice of the LLRs (good health) entails SSCs (foregoing the SSRs). In this section, we discuss how the value of discrete, future events changes with the passage of time. A later section of the chapter considers how value is affected when temporally extended behavior patterns rather than discrete events are the units of analysis.

Temporal Discounting of Discrete Events

Discounting of Delayed Rewards. In general, future rewards are less valuable than present rewards. For example, given a choice between $10 now and $20 next year, most people would opt for the former even though it is only one half the amount of the latter. This is the case because the present value of a future reward is discounted by its delay. Two types of discount functions that attempt to describe how value changes with delay have received the most research attention: (a) exponential,

$$V = Ae^{-kD},$$ (1)

which is common in the economic literature (Becker & Murphy, 1988; cf. Kagel, Battalio, & Green, 1995); and (b) hyperbolic,

$$V = A/(1 + kD),$$ (2)

which is common in the psychological literature (e.g., Ainslie, 1974, 1975, 1992; Mazur, 1987; Myerson & Green, 1995; Rachlin, Raineri, & Cross, 1991).

In both equations, V, A, D, and k represent the present value of a delayed reward, the amount of the delayed reward, the delay until receipt of the reward, and the discounting parameter, respectively. In both equations, the present value of a future reward varies inversely with the discount parameter (k).

A crucial difference between the exponential and hyperbolic functions is that, in the former, equal increments in delay produce constant proportional decrements in reward value, whereas in the latter, equal increments in delay produce larger decrements in value at short delays than at long delays. This difference is critical because it leads to markedly different predictions about the relative value of the SSR and the LLR over time (e.g., Ainslie, 1975; Rachlin et al., 1991; Vuchinich & Simpson, 1998), which leads to different predictions regarding behavioral allocation in intertemporal choice situations relevant to health behavior. These predictions are shown schematically in Fig. 8.1, in which the taller and shorter bars represent the LLR and SSR, respectively, and the curves represent their value during the times before reward receipt. The top and bottom panels in Fig. 8.1 show exponential and hyperbolic discounting, respectively; the curves were drawn according to Equations 1 and 2, respectively.

As the top panel in Fig. 8.1 shows, exponential discounting predicts that whichever reward has the higher value when delays are relatively long also will have the higher value when delays are relatively short. An exponential discounter might prefer the SSR over the LLR or vice versa, depending on the degree of discounting, but preference between the two would never be inconsistent at different points in time. In contrast, as the bottom panel of Fig. 8.1 shows, hyperbolic discounting predicts that preference between the SSR and the LLR depends on the temporal locus of the choice, that is, in the bottom panel, the SSR is preferred after about Time 5, even though prior to that time the LLR was preferred. Studies that have directly compared the hyperbolic and exponential discount functions for both real and hypothetical rewards have found unanimously the hyperbolic function to provide a superior description of change in reward value over time (Kirby, 1997; Kirby & Marakovic, 1995; Myerson & Green, 1995; Rachlin et al., 1991; Vuchinich & Simpson, 1998).

Virtually everyone has experienced the kinds of preference reversals that result from hyperbolic discounting of future rewards. For example, assume that a college student has an important test on Monday, and there is a football game and associated parties on the preceding Saturday afternoon and evening. On the Tuesday prior to the game, parties, and the test, the student prefers the large reward of doing well on the test and getting a good grade (the LLR), so he decides to study all weekend and to forego the athletic festivities (the SSR). As time passes, however, the hyperbolic discount function specifies that the value of the SSR and the LLR will change at

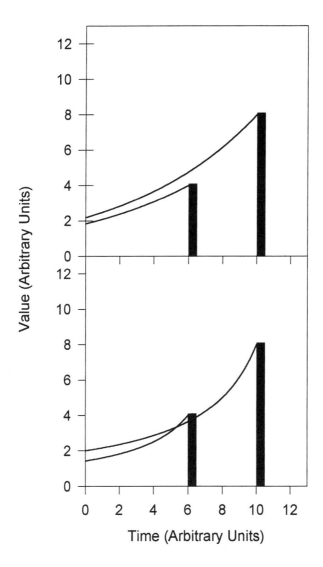

FIG. 8.1. Both panels show an intertemporal choice between a smaller and larger reward available at Time 6 and Time 10, respectively. The curves to the left of the rewards are delay discount functions that represent reward value during the times before they are available; the reward with the highest value curve at the time of choice will be preferred. The upper and lower panels show exponential and hyperbolic discount functions, respectively. The exponential and hyperbolic discount functions were generated from Equation 1 and Equation 2, respectively.

different rates. A common result of such differential changes in value is that when Saturday arrives, the student's preference has reversed and he decides to attend the game and parties rather than study for the test.

Discounting of Delayed Costs. Although research on discounting of discrete events has focused primarily on changes in reward value over time, individuals are also sensitive to both the timing and the magnitude of any costs associated with a choice (Benzion, Rapoport, & Yagil, 1989; Shelly, 1993; Stevenson, 1993; Thaler, 1981). Just as discounting decreases the present value of future rewards, rendering them less attractive as they are delayed, time also has a discounting effect on the present (negative) value of costs. Thus, as costs are delayed, their negative value is discounted and they become subjectively less aversive and, therefore, less unattractive (Benzion et al., 1989; Stevenson, 1993).

Figure 8.2 shows an intertemporal choice between an SSC and an LLC. As in Fig. 8.1, the top and bottom panels of Fig. 8.2 show the changes in value as specified by the exponential and hyperbolic discount functions, respectively. In exactly the same fashion as in the case of rewards, the exponential function predicts consistent preferences between the SSC and the LLC over time, whereas the hyperbolic function predicts a reversal of preference over time. In the bottom panel of Fig. 8.2, the SSC initially is the less aversive and would be preferred, but as its receipt becomes imminent, preference reverses and the LLC becomes less aversive and preferred.

Preliminary research on delayed costs indicates that, like rewards, they too are discounted according to a hyperbolic function, as in Fig. 8.2b (Murphy, Vuchinich, & Simpson, 1998). Moreover, studies have shown that losses are discounted to a lesser degree than are comparable amount rewards, that is, given equivalent changes in the delay of a reward and a cost of comparable amounts, the negative value of the cost will change less than the positive value of the reward (e.g., Benzion et al., 1989).

A common example of choosing between immediate and delayed costs occurs when deciding whether to go to the dentist (Rachlin, 1974). Going to the dentist is hardly pleasant, but the costs associated with dental visits are small relative to the long-term costs of poor dental care and hygiene. Thus, the choice is between seeing the dentist and incurring a little pain and monetary costs now (the SSC) or not seeing the dentist and incurring a lot of pain and monetary costs later (the SSC). According to Fig. 8.2b, at times distant from both a dental visit and later dental problems, the smaller cost of visiting the dentist is preferred. Thus, the individual will make a dental appointment. As the time of the appointment approaches, however, the values of the SSC and the LLC change at different rates. Immediately before the appointment, seeing the dentist becomes more aversive than the later dental problems, and the appointment may be canceled.

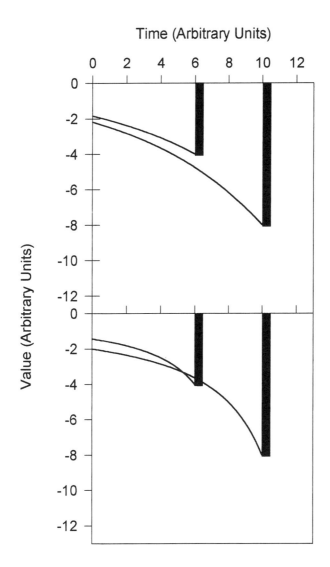

FIG. 8.2. Both panels show an intertemporal choice between a smaller and larger cost that will be incurred at Time 6 and Time 10, respectively. The curves to the left of the rewards are delay discount functions that represent negative values during the times before the costs occur; the cost with the highest value curve at the time of choice will be preferred. The upper and lower panels show exponential and hyperbolic discount functions, respectively. The exponential and hyperbolic discount functions were generated from Equation 1 and Equation 2, respectively.

Discounting of Health Status

The literature summarized in the previous section did not directly address temporal changes in the value of health. Nevertheless, the findings appear to have some generality in that orderly relations also have been shown between temporal variables and the value individuals assign to hypothetical health outcomes (Chapman, 1996b; Chapman & Elstein, 1995; MacKeigan, Larson, Drugalis, Bootman, & Burns, 1993; Redelmeir & Heller, 1993; Rose & Weeks, 1988). In a series of studies, Chapman and colleagues (Chapman, 1996b; Chapman & Elstein, 1995) compared individuals' discounting of (hypothetical) delayed monetary and health outcomes. For monetary outcomes, participants were presented with money amounts that were available immediately and were asked to specify an equally attractive money amount that was available after a specified delay. For health outcomes, participants were presented with a scenario that described an unpleasant but not life-threatening illness and an effective treatment that would return them to full health immediately for a short duration of time. They then were asked to equate the value, in terms of health duration, of a treatment offering longer duration health benefits but that were only available after a specified delay. Consistent with research on temporal changes in the value of money and other commodities, the value of health outcomes decreased as delay increased, and health losses generally were discounted to a lesser degree than were health gains. Moreover, health discounting was greater per unit of time at short delays than at long delays (Chapman, 1996b; Chapman & Elstein, 1995), which is consistent with a hyperbolic discounting function. Furthermore, these studies found that, after amounts (or durations) of the delayed monetary and health rewards were equated in value, discounting was significantly greater for health than for monetary outcomes; that is, per unit of delay time, the value of health rewards decreased more than the value of monetary rewards with which they were compared. Such differences in the degree to which the value of different commodities are discounted has been shown in comparisons between money and other consumer commodities (Madden, Petry, Badger, & Bickel, 1997; Raineri & Rachlin, 1993).

The relevance of these studies for health behavior and health behavior change does not lie in the specific preferences of individuals for smaller sooner or larger later durations of health. With the possible exception of medical treatments for catastrophic illness or injury, few realistic choices would involve such explicit intertemporal exchanges. The relevance of the work instead lies in the systematic demonstration that, at least in hypothetical scenarios, the same variables that have been shown consistently to influence the value of both real and hypothetical monetary and commodity objects of choice appear to exert a similar influence on the value that individuals assign to objects of choice involving health. Thus, such findings provide

initial support for the utility of extending behavioral economic conceptuali-
zations, which have been applied fruitfully to analyses of specific unhealthy
behaviors (e.g., DeGrandpre & Bickel, 1996; Vuchinich & Tucker, 1988), to
an analysis of health behavior more generally.

Relations Between Temporal Discounting and Health Behaviors

Unlike most commodities (e.g., food or automobiles) that are mass-produced
and then traded on an open market, health is largely self-produced through
the lifestyle choices of the individual (Fuchs, 1993). This raises the possibility
that the value of health may vary more among individuals than does the
value of money and other commodities that have greater external constraints
controlling their intertemporal value (e.g., market fluctuations, competition;
Fuchs, 1987, 1993). Moreover, given that health typically refers to the future,
differences between individuals in the degree to which they discount health
and other valuable but delayed commodities may be important for understanding the intertemporal dynamics of health as a more or less valued
object of choice within natural environments typically rich in competing
unhealthy alternatives.

As noted previously, behavioral economics generally has viewed health
behavior as an intertemporal choice between SSRs and LLRs. This framework
makes the clear prediction that consumption of SSRs will be directly related
to the degree of temporal discounting. The choice dynamics underlying this
prediction are illustrated in Fig. 8.3. Both panels of Fig. 8.3 show an SSR
and LLR intertemporal choice with relatively low (top panel) and relatively
high (bottom panel) hyperbolic temporal discounting. In both cases, at times
distant from either reward (e.g., Time 1) the LLR is preferred, and preference
reverses as delay to the rewards decreases. Importantly, with higher temporal
discounting (bottom panel), preference reverses from the LLR to the SSR
much earlier than with lower temporal discounting (top panel). Thus, individuals with relatively greater degrees of temporal discounting would spend
more time preferring the SSR, which should lead to more consumption of
substances with negative health consequences.

Several studies have found relations between measures of temporal discounting derived from laboratory procedures and a variety of behaviors in
the natural environment with negative health consequences. For example,
in a laboratory study involving choices between different amounts of (hypothetical) money available after different delays, Vuchinich and Simpson
(1998) found that heavy social drinkers and problem drinkers discounted
the value of money to a greater degree than did light social drinkers, with
problem drinkers showing the highest temporal discounting. Similar relations
have been reported between temporal discounting and opiate abuse (Mad-

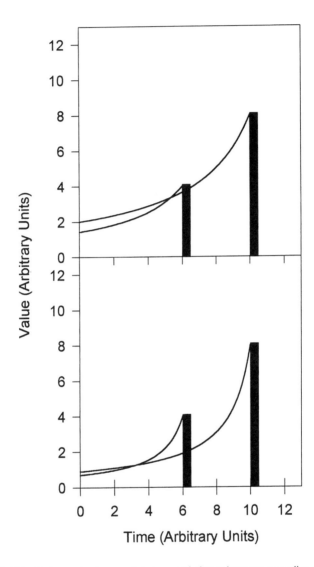

FIG. 8.3. Both panels show an intertemporal choice between a smaller and larger reward available at Time 6 and Time 10, respectively. The curves to the left of the rewards are delay discount functions that represent reward value during the times before they are available; the reward with the highest value curve at the time of choice will be preferred. The upper and lower panels show relatively lower and higher degrees of hyperbolic discounting, respectively. The discount functions were generated from Equation 2.

den et al., 1997); smoking (Fuchs, 1982); diet and exercise (Chapman & Winquist, 1996); and risky sexual behavior (Farr, Vuchinich, & Simpson, 1998).

It is important to note that these studies were correlational and therefore cannot distinguish the temporal priority of the higher discounting or the behavior patterns with long-term negative health consequences (Vuchinich & Simpson, 1998), which is an important issue for future research. Nevertheless, the generality of the same basic discounting–behavior relation across several different domains indicates that individual differences in temporal discounting is an important variable for understanding development and change in behavior with health consequences.

Temporal Discounting in an Analysis of Health Behavior

Although some (but certainly not all) of the research summarized to this point of the chapter is preliminary, several generalizations seem warranted. First, the value of discrete delayed rewards and costs are discounted according to a hyperbolic function. Because such discounting produces preference reversals in intertemporal choice situations, the hyperbolic function can account for the temporal inconsistencies in preference that are a ubiquitous feature of health behavior. Second, the value of delayed costs is discounted less than the value of delayed rewards. Third, the value of delayed health outcomes seems to be discounted to a greater degree than that of other consumer commodities (e.g., money). Finally, behavior patterns with long-term negative health consequences seem to be correlated with greater degrees of temporal discounting.

An example may illustrate the implications of these generalizations for an analysis of health behavior. Consider an individual who decides to initiate an aerobic exercise program that will improve long-term health (LLR). The best time for her to exercise is at 7 p.m., when she had regularly been watching TV (SSR). The temporal discounting literature summarized previously indicates that preference for these objects of choice (health and TV) will reverse with the passage of time, that is, the LLR would be relatively more valuable and therefore preferred at a choice point some temporal distance (e.g., 9 a.m.) from the availability of the SSR. However, as the availability of the SSR becomes imminent (e.g., 6:45 p.m.), its value rapidly increases, according to the hyperbolic function, and would supersede the value of the LLR. This would lead to a reversal of preference between the SSR and the LLR, and the individual would watch TV instead of exercising at 7 p.m., contrary to her earlier plans.

In addition to the hyperbolic discounting function, which specifies the general preference reversal pattern, two of the other variables discussed previously could have an important effect on the likelihood that this individual would follow through with her intention to begin an exercise program. First, if the value of health outcomes is discounted to a greater degree than other commodities, then the point of preference reversal in an intertemporal choice related to health would occur earlier in the temporal sequence than it might for a similar intertemporal choice involving commodities unrelated to health (e.g., money). Second, given that the would-be exerciser has not already established this pattern of behavior with long-term health benefits, it may well be that her behavior is governed by a degree of temporal discounting that is greater than that of other individuals in the population. If so, then this higher discounting would move the point of preference reversal earlier in the sequence than it might be for other individuals. To the extent that either or both of these considerations are relevant to this example, they would decrease the likelihood that this individual would initiate and maintain a regular pattern of exercise.

Finally, the temporal discounting literature indicates that the relative distribution of both rewards and costs associated with a given discrete choice are important determinants of the overall value of the objects of choice (Chapman, 1996b; Loewenstein & Prelec, 1992). This point may be especially important in understanding the dynamics involved in health behavior, which involves SSCs and LLCs as well as SSRs and LLRs. Thus, in an intertemporal choice related to health, both objects of choice involve both a positive and a negative outcome. In our example, choosing the SSR (watching TV and not exercising) incurs the LLC of poorer health, whereas choosing the LLR (exercising and not watching TV) incurs the SSC of forgoing the TV program. The negative outcomes associated with the latter option also may include any costs more specific to the acquisition of the LLR itself (e.g., muscle soreness associated with initiating an exercise regimen). Given that losses are involved and that their negative value may be discounted less than the positive value of any gains, their aversiveness as the availability of the SSR approaches may be disproportionately high relative to the long-term gains associated with the choice. Thus, any intertemporal choice that necessitates earlier losses in exchange for later gains likely will be viewed as very unattractive (e.g., Loewenstein & Prelec, 1992; Shelly, 1993). Such considerations would reduce further the likelihood that the individual in our example would initiate and maintain the exercise program.

Given these choice dynamics derived from hyperbolic temporal discounting, the most obvious way to increase the probability of forgoing the SSR and exercising would be to introduce some sort of external commitment device (Ainslie, 1975; Rachlin, 1974; see also Logue, chap. 7, this volume). Commitment in this context refers to emitting a response early enough in the temporal sequence of an SSR–LLR choice (such as at Time 2 in Fig. 8.3) that constrains or cancels the later availability of the SSR. Thus, some action is taken (the commitment) while the LLR is preferred that prevents the later reversal of preference from the LLR to the SSR, which increases the likelihood of forgoing the SSR and of obtaining the LLR. Such external commitment has been demonstrated in animal subjects with proper arrangement of contingencies (Ainslie, 1974; Rachlin & Green, 1972) and is a readily available technique for increasing self-control in humans.

TEMPORALLY EXTENDED BEHAVIOR PATTERNS AS THE OBJECTS OF CHOICE

Limitations of Discrete Events as the Objects of Choice

As reflected in the foregoing material, most of the behavioral economic literature on intertemporal choice and temporal discounting has characterized the objects of choice (i.e., SSRs and LLRs) as discrete, unitary events with particular temporal loci of occurrence. This representation has produced extremely useful laboratory preparations (e.g., Rachlin & Green, 1972; Rachlin et al., 1991) for studying these phenomena, as well as the commitment devices just mentioned that have been useful in clinical applications. However, several authors recently have noted that, although it is reasonable to conceive of most SSRs as discrete, tangible events that occur at particular points in time, most natural LLRs do not occur as such punctuated events (Gafni, 1995; Kudadjie-Gyamfi & Rachlin, 1996; Rachlin, 1995; Vuchinich & Tucker, 1996, 1998). Instead, the important "LLRs" in natural human environments (e.g., "career success," "marital stability," "health") are more accurately characterized as abstractions that comprise many smaller rewards that occur over an extended temporal interval in a complex but coherent pattern. For example, consider an individual choosing between the SSRs associated with heroin use and the LLR of career success. Even if the individual forgoes all discrete instances of heroin consumption, the LLR of career success will not suddenly appear in its entirety on some specific date in the future. Rather, as more behavior is devoted toward the LLR of career success (e.g., prompt and competent work performance), and less behavior is devoted to competing alternatives that are detrimental to the accrual of career success (e.g., heroin use), more of the LLR's smaller component units may be accrued over an extended temporal interval (e.g., improved performance ratings, seniority, raises, and valued relationships with coworkers).

Moreover, for several reasons, external commitment devices do not seem to provide a sufficient explanation for the development and maintenance of behavior patterns in the natural environment that are consistent with long-term preferences (Rachlin, 1995). Indeed, there are many naturalistic examples of external commitment (cf. Ainslie, 1975; Rachlin, 1995). Nevertheless, behavioral studies in natural environments indicate that, even when faced with numerous, immediately available temptations, many individuals maintain extended patterns of behavior that serve long-term interests without apparent reliance on external environmental constraints based on prior commitments (e.g., Sobell, Cunningham, & Sobell, 1996; Stall & Bernacki, 1986). Also, in natural environments, complete reliance on external commitment poses some problems. Removal of the external restraint may lead to an immediate return to the previous impulsive behavior, external commitment devices do not adapt well to the changing conditions of complex human environments, and most natural settings offer many opportunities to abandon external commitment devices if preference reverses (Rachlin, 1995). Finally, in most natural environments, many different SSRs with long-term negative health consequences become available at different temporal points and in different environmental contexts. This suggests that, to be effective, external commitment devices would have to be implemented against the temptations of a wide variety of SSRs, rather than for only one or two. Given these limitations, it seems unlikely that all, or even most, natural behavior patterns that reflect long-term preferences are developed and maintained through external commitment.

Particular Acts and Patterns of Acts

These considerations led Rachlin (1995) to propose an alternative view of choice situations that can produce inconsistencies in preferences over time. He hypothesized that the temporal inconsistencies often found between individuals' preferences at different points in time (heretofore conceived as a discrete choice between an SSR and an LLR) are more accurately characterized as incongruities between discrete acts that reflect short-term preferences and more temporally extended patterns of acts that reflect long-term preferences. According to this view, realizing long-term preferences entails temporally extended patterns of behavior, but such patterns may be difficult to develop and maintain because the pattern's particular component acts may be relatively less valuable than alternative particular acts that are inconsistent with the pattern.

These relations are illustrated in Fig. 8.4 (adapted from Rachlin, 1995). Act X and Act Y in Fig. 8.4 may be considered either as discrete, particular events or as single components of one of two different temporally extended patterns of behavior (Pattern A or Pattern B). When considered as particular acts in a discrete choice, Act Y has greater value that Act X. On the other hand, when considered as single components of wider patterns, Pattern A (which includes Act X) has greater value than Pattern B (which includes Act Y). Thus, patterns of behavior that are high in value over long temporal intervals may be comprised of single component acts that individually are

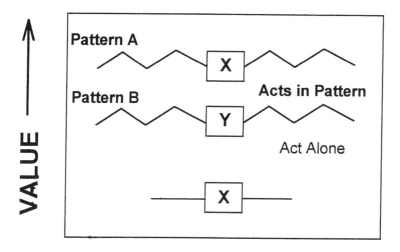

FIG. 8.4. The figure represents the relative value of discrete acts (X and Y) and the relative value of temporally extended patterns of behavior (A and B) that contain Acts X and Y as components. Value is shown on the ordinate, and time is shown on the abscissa. In a discrete choice between the two acts, Act Y has higher relative value than Act X. However, over an extended temporal interval, the behavior pattern composed of repeated choices of Act X (Pattern A) has higher relative value than the pattern composed of repeated choices of Act Y (Pattern B). Adapted from "Self-Control: Beyond Commitment," by H. Rachlin, 1995, *Behavioral and Brain Sciences, 18,* pp. 109–159. Copyright © 1995 by Cambridge University Press. Adapted with permission.

quite low in value relative to alternative acts. Conversely, patterns of behavior that are low in value over long temporal intervals may be comprised of single component acts that individually are quite high in value relative to alternative acts.

For example, suppose that the long-term higher-valued Pattern A in Fig. 8.4 represents behavior that promotes cardiovascular health, and that some of the particular acts (X) that constitute that pattern involve adherence to a low-fat, low-cholesterol diet. The long-term lower-valued Pattern B would then represent a high-fat, high-cholesterol diet, with its individual acts (Y) involving discrete episodes of fatty food consumption. In a discrete choice between Act X and Act Y, the value of consuming a double bacon cheeseburger with french fries (Act Y) may be quite high relative to the value of consuming yogurt and a salad with fat-free dressing (Act X). However, over an extended temporal interval, adherence to a healthy diet (Pattern A) almost certainly would be preferred to the fatty diet (Pattern B) and the increased health risks it creates. Thus, if the objects of choice are perceived as temporally extended patterns of behavior (A and B), then Pattern A likely would be preferred because it has greater value over an extended temporal horizon. On the other hand, if the objects of choice are perceived as individual acts (X and Y), then Act Y likely would be preferred because it has more value in the temporally circumscribed present. The degree of temporal extension with which the objects of choice are perceived, therefore, may be critically important in the allocation of behavior with health consequences. Rachlin (1995) suggested that most naturally occurring patterns of behavior with positive consequences, like Pattern A in Fig. 8.4, likely are developed by organizing behavior into temporally wider patterns that reflect long-term rather than immediate preferences, instead of through external commitment devices.

The Value of Behavior Patterns

Employing patterns of acts, rather than particular acts, as the units of analysis is a recent development in the literature and has not been well researched. But there is some empirical evidence relevant to the possible value of behavior patterns. Rachlin and colleagues showed in laboratory experiments, with both humans (Kudadjie-Gyamfi & Rachlin, 1996) and animals (Siegel & Rachlin, 1995), that if conditions are established that generate cohesive patterns in subjects' behavior, then their behavioral allocation is more consistent with long-term preferences. Rachlin (1995; Siegel & Rachlin, 1995) labeled this sort of behavioral patterning "soft commitment," which, unlike strict, external commitment, does not prevent access to the SSR. Nevertheless, the behavior patterns that constitute soft commitment apparently facilitate choices that produce greater long-term value. Rachlin (1995) argued that there is an inherent cost associated with the interruption of cohesive patterns of behavior, and that these costs subtract from the value of competing SSR alternatives, making them less attractive.

There also is some empirical evidence relevant to the value of patterns of events relative to discrete events. Several studies have shown that if future events are part of a temporally extended sequence or pattern, then their value is greater than if they are independent events in separate, discrete choices (Chapman, 1996a; Chapman & Winquist, 1996; Frank, 1992; Loewenstein & Prelec, 1992, 1993; Ross & Simonson, 1991; Stevenson, 1993). Chapman (1996a), for example, found that participants preferred increasing over decreasing (hypothetical) salary plans over several years, even though the total money amount in each plan was constant. Similar preferences for increasing over decreasing sequences of outcomes, with the sum of the value of each sequence's components held constant, have been reported for the commodities of health (Chapman & Winquist, 1996); college funding programs (Stevenson, 1993); and the quality of meals in restaurants (Loewenstein & Prelec, 1991).

Such findings are interesting, because they are contrary to what would be predicted if the values of the outcome sequences that are the objects of choice are computed as the sum of the discounted values of the elements in each sequence. For example, assume that four rewards, with amounts of 10, 20, 30, and 40 (arbitrary) units, are going to occur in either an increasing or a decreasing sequence at delays of one, two, three, and four (arbitrary) temporal units, respectively. Using Equation 2 with $k = 1.00$, the discounted values of the components of the increasing sequence (10, 20, 30, and 40) would be 5.00, 6.67, 7.50, and 8.00 units, respectively, which sums to 27.17 units. The discounted values of the individual rewards in the decreasing sequence (40, 30, 20, and 10) would be 20.00, 10.00, 5.00, and 2.00 units, respectively, which sums to 37.00 units. Even though the decreasing sequence yields a greater sum of the discounted values of the individual rewards, these studies consistently have found that the increasing sequence is preferred when the objects of choice are temporally extended sequences of outcomes. Thus, preferences tend to be more future-oriented when the objects of choice are multicomponent sequences, the value of which accrues over extended time frames. On the other hand, when given a choice between two discrete outcomes, preferences tend to be more present-oriented or impulsive.

It is possible that at least some of the value of health is due to a similar, sequential accrual over time. That is, both health and money are intermediate commodities (e.g., Fuchs, 1993), in that they apparently have value only in relation to the other commodities to which they allow access. Although money (and commensurate assets, such as stocks, bonds, and certificates of deposit) is essential in modern society, monetary assets have no particular value in and of themselves. Instead, the value of monetary assets presumably derives from the nonmonetary commodities for which they can be traded. Whereas the reward access provided by monetary assets may be straightforward and simple, as in the purchase of a meal, it also may be multicomponent, sequential, and complex. For example, an upper middle-class income provides access to high-quality housing, food, and education. The provision of these initial commodities would then also make possible access to many other tangible and nontangible rewards, such as prestige, a safe environment, and opportunities to participate in exclusive social groups. In turn, these may allow access to still other immediately valuable goods and services.

The reward access that "good health" provides would seem to be conceptually similar to that of money, in that it allows access to other more tangible activities. For example, having health generally means having the ability to perform observable physical and behavioral functions (e.g., mobility, endurance), and some amount of health is necessary for social interactions, job performance, and other valuable life activities. Consistent with this view, examinations of the value of health within medical care contexts indicate that health is most appropriately modeled along several dimensions, in which overall level of health represents an integration of level of functioning across a variety of life areas (e.g., social, occupational) to which health allows access (Kaplan, 1982; Keeler & Kane, 1982). Such studies also have demonstrated that the value individuals assign to a specific state of health is a function of the more immediate, tangible benefits to which it provides access. For example, Bush, Chen, and Patrick (1973) found that improvements in functional capacity accounted for over half of the variance in participants' rating of the desirability of length of time in different health states.

IMPLICATIONS FOR HEALTH BEHAVIOR CHANGE

The behavioral economic literature summarized in this chapter is in the process of developing a cohesive account of the temporal dynamics of change in the value of objects of choice. Although many issues remain unresolved, this literature has several implications for health behavior modification. First, for several reasons, interventions aimed at decreasing behavior with negative health consequences (e.g., substance abuse) should attempt to minimize the costs, generally conceived, associated with the behavior change. The temporal distribution of positive and negative outcomes, including the extent of the interval over which such outcomes are considered, are important determinants of the relative value of objects of choice. Unhealthy behaviors, although less valuable than healthy behaviors over extended temporal intervals, provide significant immediate rewards. Despite their long-term negative consequences, curtailing the consumption of SSRs that damage health is a significant cost in the economy of the individuals' behavioral allocation patterns. Moreover, any positive effects of decreasing such behavior are unlikely to occur immediately, so the present value of these future effects will be significantly discounted. Research on temporal discounting of rewards and costs strongly suggests that if the natural short-term rewards associated with behavior change are relatively small, then the costs associated with behavior change or the rewards associated with continuing the unhealthy behavior pattern need not be large in order to make behavior change unattractive (e.g., Christensen-Szalanski & Northcraft, 1985; Marlatt, Tucker, Donovan, & Vuchinich, 1997).

Most traditional treatments for substance abuse require the client to abstain from substance use without providing commensurate short-term benefits to offset this loss. Considered in the context of the material in this chapter, the unattractive temporal distribution of costs and benefits provided by such behavior change strategies is consistent with the low rate of treatment entry typically found for such behavior problems (e.g., Gallup, 1974; Hartnoll, 1992; Stall & Bernacki, 1986; Tucker & Gladsjo, 1993), as well as the poor posttreatment maintenance of treatment gains (Miller & Hester, 1986; Stark, 1992). An alternative approach would be to attempt to increase the relative value of initially dispreferred healthy behaviors through minimization of the total costs, both implicit and explicit, and the addition of treatment-related rewards. Furthermore, it would not appear to be necessary, at least initially, that these additional rewards be directly related in any way to health, only that they control behaviors that are necessary for its accrual. A recent example of such an alternative strategy is voucher-based treatments for substance abuse (e.g., Higgins et al., 1995), in which clients are directly reinforced for abstinence.

Second, it would be beneficial to develop a better understanding of the valued nonhealth rewards to which health behavior maintenance and good health potentially allow access. Interventions that focus relatively less attention on increasing health and relatively more attention on increasing access to the immediately valuable, tangible activities and rewards to which optimal health allows access potentially will provide the most powerful and lasting interventions. A fundamental principle of behavioral economics is that behavioral allocation is determined by the molar, economic context comprised of alternative rewards and costs, and by the temporal distribution of outcomes. Thus, modifying a particular behavior may be accomplished by modifying the economic context so that alternative behaviors become more attractive (e.g., DeGrandpre & Bickel, 1996; Vuchinich & Tucker, 1988).

Research conducted to date has pointed to some important areas to be developed in the future. First, the relations between individuals' degree of temporal discounting and their engagement in behavior with negative long-term consequences suggests that discounting is an important variable in the development and maintenance of such behavior patterns. Thus, understanding the genesis of degrees of discounting and how discounting may be modified may lead to substantial changes in health behavior.

Second, the concepts associated with viewing temporally extended patterns of behavior, rather than discrete events, as the objects of choice (e.g., the act–pattern distinction, the inherent value of extended patterns, the costs of pattern interruption) are relatively new, are not at this time well supported empirically, and have raised a number of contentious issues (see the commentaries associated with Rachlin, 1995). The conceptual and empirical questions raised by this perspective will be important topics for future research. The Skinnerian tradition of behavior analysis has had a critical influence on the development of behavioral economics. In this tradition, responses and reinforcers are clearly separable conceptual classes. An analysis based on temporally extended patterns of behavior, however, would combine responses and reinforcers as components of the same conceptual class of an economic package. As noted by Rachlin (1995):

A rat's lever press may be said to rewarded extrinsically when the rat eats the food pellet, but a more precise picture of the process may be obtained by considering the pattern: pressing-plus-eating as intrinsically more valuable than not-pressing-plus-not-eating. . . . Thus, eating may be an extrinsic reward when considered separately from the lever press on which it is contingent, or an intrinsic reward when considered together with the lever press as part of the pattern. (p. 121)

Considering health behavior in the natural environment in this manner modifies what is important for us to understand. Instead of being concerned with how particular acts are reinforced by particular consequences, we should be concerned with how acts and consequences develop into extended patterns with more or less intrinsic value and then attempt to facilitate those patterns that maximize the latter.

ACKNOWLEDGMENTS

Preparation of this chapter was supported in part by predoctoral National Research Service Award No. F31 DA05837–01 from the National Institute on Drug Abuse and by grant No. R01 AA08972 from the National Institute on Alcohol Abuse and Alcoholism.

REFERENCES

Ainslie, G. (1974). Impulse control in pigeons. *Journal of the Experimental Analysis of Behavior, 21,* 485–489.

Ainslie, G. (1975). Specious reward: A behavioral theory of impulsiveness and impulse control. *Psychological Bulletin, 82,* 463–509.

Ainslie, G. (1992). *Picoeconomics: The strategic interaction of successive motivational states within the person.* Cambridge, England: Cambridge University Press.

Becker, G. S., & Murphy, K. M. (1988). A theory of rational addiction. *Journal of Political Economy, 96,* 675–700.

Benzion, U., Rapoport, A., & Yagil, J. (1989). Discount rates inferred from decisions: An experimental study. *Management Science, 35,* 270–284.

Bush, J. W., Chen, M. M., & Patrick, D. L. (1973). Health status index in cost-effectiveness of PKU programs. In R. L. Berg (Ed.), *Health status indexes* (pp. 172–194). Chicago: Hospital Research and Education Trust.

Chapman, G. B. (1996a). Expectations and preferences for sequences of health and money. *Organizational Behavior and Human Decision Processes, 67,* 59–75.

Chapman, G. B. (1996b). Temporal discounting and utility for health and money. *Journal of Experimental Psychology: Learning, Memory, and Cognition, 22,* 771–791.

Chapman, G. B., & Elstein, A. S. (1995). Valuing the future: Temporal discounting of health and money. *Journal of Medical Decision Making, 15,* 373–386.

Chapman, G. B., & Johnson, E. J. (1995). Preference reversals in monetary and life expectancy evaluations. *Organizational Behavior and Human Decision Processes, 62,* 300–317.

Chapman, G. B., & Winquist, J. (1996, August). *Framing affects choice in realistic decisions.* Poster session presented at the meeting of the International Society for Medical Decision Making, Turin, Italy.

Christensen-Szalanski, J. J. J., & Northcraft, G. B. (1985). Patient compliance behavior: The effects of time on patients' values of treatment regimens. *Social Science Medicine, 21,* 263–273.

DeGrandpre, R. J., & Bickel, W. K. (1996). Drug dependence as consumer demand. In L. Green & J. H. Kagel (Eds.), *Advances in behavioral economics: Vol. 3. Substance use and abuse* (pp. 1–36). Norwood, NJ: Ablex.

Farr, C. A., Vuchinich, R. E., & Simpson, C. A. (1998, May). *Delayed reward discounting in sexual risk-takers and non-risk-takers.* Poster session presented at the meeting of the Association for Behavior Analysis, Orlando, FL.

Frank, R. (1992). Frames of reference and the intertemporal wage profile. In G. Lowenstein & J. Elster (Eds.), *Choice over time* (pp. 265–284). New York: Russel Sage Foundation.

Fuchs, V. R. (1982). Time preference and health: An exploratory study. In V. R. Fuchs (Ed.), *Economic aspects of health* (pp. 93–120). Chicago: University of Chicago Press.

Fuchs, V. R. (1987). *The health economy.* Chicago: University of Chicago Press.

Fuchs, V. R. (1993). *The future of health policy.* Chicago: University of Chicago Press.

Gafni, A. (1995). Time in health: Can we measure individuals' pure time preference? *Medical Decision Making, 15,* 31–37.

Gallup, G. (1974). *Public puffs on after 10 years of warnings* (Gallup opinion index, Report No. 108, pp. 20–21). Princeton, NJ: Gallup Organization.

Grossman, M. (1972). *The demand for health.* New York: National Bureau of Economic Research.

Hartnoll, R. (1992). Research and the help-seeking process. *British Journal of Addiction, 87,* 429–437.

Higgins, S. T., Budney, A. J., Bickel, W. K., Badger, G. J., Foerg, F. E., & Ogden, D. (1995). Outpatient behavioral treatment for cocaine dependence: One year outcome. *Experimental and Clinical Psychopharmacology, 3,* 205–212.

Kagel, J. H., Battalio, R. C., & Green, L. (1995). *Economic choice theory: An experimental analysis of animal behavior.* Cambridge, England: Cambridge University Press.

Kaplan, R. M. (1982). Human preference measurement for health decisions and the evaluation of long-term care. In R. L. Kane & R. A. Kane (Eds.), *Values and long-term care* (pp. 157–185). Lexington, MA: Heath.

Keeler, E., & Kane, R. (1982). What is special about long-term care? In R. L. Kane & R. A. Kane (Eds.), *Values and long-term care* (pp. 85–100). Lexington, MA: Heath.

Kirby, K. N. (1997). Bidding on the future: Evidence against normative discounting of delayed rewards. *Journal of Experimental Psychology: General, 126,* 54–70.

Kirby, K. N., & Marakovic, N. N. (1995). Modeling myopic decisions: Evidence for hyperbolic delay-discounting with subjects and amounts. *Organizational Behavior and Human Decision Processes, 64,* 22–30.

Kudadjie-Gyamfi, E., & Rachlin, H. (1996). Temporal patterning in choice among delayed outcomes. *Organizational Behavior and Human Decision Processes, 65,* 61–70

Loewenstein, G. F., & Prelec, D. (1991). Negative time preference. *American Economic Review: Papers and Proceedings, 81,* 347–352.

Loewenstein, G. F., & Prelec, D. (1992). Anomalies in intertemporal choice: Evidence and an interpretation. *Quarterly Journal of Economics, 107,* 573–597.

Loewenstein, G., & Prelec, D. (1993). Preferences for sequences of outcomes. *Psychological Review, 100,* 91–108.

MacKeigan, L. D., Larson, L. N., Drugalis, J. R., Bootman, J. L., & Burns, L. R. (1993). Time preference for health gains versus health losses. *PharmacoEconomics, 3,* 374–386.

Madden, G. J., Petry, N. M., Badger, G. J., & Bickel, W. K. (1997). Impulsive and self-controlled choices in opioid-dependent patients and non-drug-using control participants: Drug and monetary rewards. *Experimental and Clinical Psychopharmacology, 5,* 256–263.

Marlatt, G. A., Tucker, J. A., Donovan, D. M., & Vuchinich, R. E. (1997). Help-seeking by substance abusers: The role of harm reduction and behavioral economic approaches to facilitate treatment entry and retention. In L. S. Onken, J. D. Blaine, & J. J. Boren (Eds.), *Beyond the therapeutic alliance: Keeping the drug dependent individual in treatment* (NIDA Research Monograph No. 165, pp. 44–84). Rockville, MD: National Institute on Drug Abuse.

Mazur, J. (1987). An adjusting procedure for studying delayed reinforcement. In M. Commons, J. Mazur, J. A. Nevin, & H. Rachlin (Eds.), *Quantitative analysis of behavior: Vol. 5. The effect of delay and of intervening events on reinforcement value* (pp. 55–73). Hillsdale, NJ: Lawrence Erlbaum Associates.

Miller, W. R., & Hester, R. K. (1986). The effectiveness of alcoholism treatment: What research reveals. In W. R. Miller & R. K. Hester (Eds.), *Treating addictive behaviors: Processes of change* (pp. 121–174). New York: Plenum.

Murphy, J. G., Vuchinich, R. E., & Simpson, C. A. (1998, May). *Delayed reward and cost discounting among college students.* Poster session presented at the annual meeting of the Association for Behavior Analysis, Orlando, FL.

Myerson, J., & Green, L. (1995). Discounting of delayed rewards: Models of individual choice. *Journal of the Experimental Analysis of Behavior, 64,* 263–276.

Rachlin, H. (1974). Self-control. *Behaviorism, 2,* 94–107.

Rachlin, H. (1995). Self-control: Beyond commitment. *Behavioral and Brain Sciences, 18,* 109–159.

Rachlin, H., & Green, L. (1972). Commitment, choice, and self-control. *Journal of the Experimental Analysis of Behavior, 17,* 15–22.

Rachlin, H., Raineri, A., & Cross, D. (1991). Subjective probability and delay. *Journal of the Experimental Analysis of Behavior, 55,* 233–244.

Raineri, A., & Rachlin, H. (1993). The effect of temporal constraints on the value of money and other commodities. *Journal of Behavioral Decision Making, 6,* 77–94.

Redelmeir, D. A., & Heller, D. N. (1993). Time preference in medical decision making and cost-effectiveness analysis. *Medical Decision Making, 13,* 212–217.

Rose, D. N., & Weeks, M. G. (1988). Individuals' discounting of future monetary gains and health states [Abstract]. *Medical Decision Making, 8,* 334.

Ross, W. T., & Simonson, I. (1991). Evaluations of pairs of experiences: A preference for happy endings. *Journal of Behavioral Decision Making, 4,* 273–282.

Shelly, M. K. (1993). Outcome signs, question frames, and discount rates. *Management Science, 39,* 806–815.

Siegel, E., & Rachlin, H. (1995). Soft commitment: Self-control achieved by behavioral persistence. *Journal of the Experimental Analysis of Behavior, 64,* 117–128.

Sobell, L., Cunningham, J., & Sobell, M. (1996). Recovery from alcohol problems with and without treatment: Prevalence in population studies. *American Journal of Public Health, 86,* 966–972.

Stall, R., & Bernacki, P. (1986). Spontaneous remission from the problematic use of substances: An indicative model derived from a comparative analysis of opiate, tobacco, and food/obesity literatures. *International Journal of the Addictions, 21,* 1–23.

Stark, M. J. (1992). Dropping out of substance abuse treatment: A clinically-oriented review. *Clinical Psychology Review, 12,* 93–116.

Stevenson, M. K. (1993). Decision making with long-term consequences: Temporal discounting for single and multiple outcomes in the future. *Journal of Experimental Psychology: General, 122,* 3–22.

Thaler, R. H. (1981). Some empirical evidence on dynamic inconsistency. *Economics Letters, 8,* 201–207.

Tucker, J. A., & Gladsjo, J. A. (1993). Help-seeking and recovery by problem drinkers: Characteristics of drinkers who attended Alcoholics Anonymous or formal treatment or who recovered without assistance. *Addictive Behaviors, 18,* 259–262.

Vuchinich, R. E., & Simpson, C. A. (1998). Hyperbolic temporal discounting in heavy and light social drinkers. *Journal of Experimental and Clinical Psychopharmacology, 6,* 292–305.

Vuchinich, R. E., & Tucker, J. A. (1988). Contributions from behavioral theories of choice to an analysis of alcohol abuse. *Journal of Abnormal Psychology, 97,* 181–195.

Vuchinich, R. E., & Tucker, J. A. (1996). Alcoholic relapse, life events, and behavioral theories of choice: A prospective analysis. *Experimental and Clinical Psychopharmacology, 4,* 19–28.

Vuchinich, R. E., & Tucker, J. A. (1998). Choice, behavioral economics, and addictive behavior patterns. In W. R. Miller & N. Heather (Eds.), *Treating addictive behaviors: Processes of change* (2nd ed., pp. 93–104). New York: Plenum.

PART FIVE

SPECIFIC HEALTH BEHAVIORS: HELP-SEEKING, SMOKING, EATING, EXERCISE, AND GAMBLING

CHAPTER NINE

Waiting to See the Doctor:
The Role of Time Constraints
in the Utilization of Health
and Behavioral Health Services

Jalie A. Tucker
John W. Davison
Auburn University

Access to health care in the United States involves longstanding inequities rooted in socioeconomic class (Institute of Medicine [IOM], 1993; Mechanic, 1994), and the recent emergence of the managed care industry as the dominant form of health insurance has raised new concerns about access, even among the insured. A majority of Americans now are covered by managed care plans and thus are subject to an array of demand-limiting tactics aimed at controlling health care utilization and costs. The ascendance of for-profit managed care organizations (MCOs) in the health care market has occurred in part because the United States has been unwilling to formulate explicit rationing policies to distribute limited health care resources across the population. The U.S. health care system, with its eclectic mix of private and public payers and providers, has no explicit rationing policy, but has a de facto one based on ability to pay and, to a lesser extent, on geographic variations in access to care. For example, the uninsured who are ineligible for Medicaid (e.g., the working poor) exemplify the operation of implicit rationing based on insurance coverage (Feldman, 1994). Among the insured, another form of rationing occurs when MCOs deny or delay approval of reimbursement for treatment, and the decision rules that govern such actions remain ambiguous at best and suspect at worst. Inequity in the national distribution of health care professionals and provider organizations, which favor urban over rural areas, is another form of rationing.

Attempts at explicit rationing have repeatedly failed in the United States. National health insurance has been entertained and abandoned several times this century, the most recent being the 1993–1994 national health care reform initiative. A root issue lay in difficulties in getting the diverse stakeholder groups (e.g., physicians, consumer groups, the insurance industry, state and federal governments, and employer purchasers of health plans) to agree on an affordable package of basic benefits that would be guaranteed to all Americans. This problem also was apparent in Oregon's recent initial failure in its attempt to ration health care to its Medicaid recipients (see the Summer 1991 issue of *Health Affairs* for discussion). The Oregon experience further highlighted the difficulty of maintaining rationing policies in light of a common human tendency, termed the *rule of rescue,* to help individuals with extreme and costly needs, even though that help reduced the group's resources and thus could harm others over the long run.

In contrast to the United States, western European and other British Commonwealth countries (e.g., Canada) consider health care a right, not a privilege, and provide some form of universal coverage but ration its distribution primarily through the use of time costs for less urgent, elective care. When monetary costs to consumers are minimal or nonexistent, time costs function to reduce and regulate demand. As discussed by Feldman (1994), people who wait for services in these queues eventually will be served, if they do not drop out by purchasing care privately, resolving the problem without treatment, or dying. Explicit rationing based on time costs is quite different from the implicit rationing that occurs in the United States, where no assurance exists that people who are forced to wait will ever receive services.[1]

The recent prospect in the United States of passing a national health plan sparked interest in the role of time costs on health services utilization, but this quickly diminished after the initiative failed. For several reasons, we contend that the study of time-related variables should be pursued. First, studying their role in health care utilization provides a "natural laboratory" to investigate relations of conceptual interest in basic and behavioral economics in an arena with great applied and economic significance. Second, delays in health care likely will become more common as administrative inefficiencies increase due to continued growth in the percentage of the U.S. population covered by managed care plans. Third, if regulations are passed that allow for greater consumer choice in health care and close off certain demand management tactics now used by MCOs, they may impose time costs more systematically as a way to limit utilization and costs. Fourth, delays in health care can have significant economic consequences. Consumers may lose wages while waiting, employers may experience lowered productivity and profits while sick workers wait for treatment, and physician caseloads and income may be affected by changes in the speed with which services are delivered.

---

[1]A notable exception in the United States is the organ transplant waiting list system.

Finally, and most important for individual consumers, delays in care can have serious health consequences. Although much of today's debate about health care access centers on managed care tactics to reduce "excessive" demand, it remains painfully clear that the need for care in many areas outstrips the use of services and that delays can be costly, both in terms of money and human life and suffering (IOM, 1993). In addition to generalized impediments posed by a lack of insurance or income, underutilization or delayed utilization of services is a serious problem with respect to several prevalent health and behavioral health disorders. For example, fewer than 25% of persons with mental health or substance abuse problems seek help for these stigmatized behavioral health problems (Mechanic, Schlesinger, & McAlpine, 1995; Regier et al., 1993). In the case of intravenous drug abusers, who have a heightened personal risk of HIV infection and for spreading it to others, making drug treatment more accessible and with minimal delays is an important component of an overall AIDS prevention strategy (National Institutes of Health, 1997). As another example, successful clinical management of heart attacks with "clot buster" drugs that minimize heart tissue damage requires patients to present for treatment as soon as possible, but delays of several hours or more after an attack are the norm (Ell et al., 1994). Finally, delays in seeking medical care among women who find breast lumps launched empirical inquiry several decades ago into understanding impediments to medical help-seeking and epitomize the complex issues involved in seeking earlier versus later treatment for a life-threatening disease with a physically mutilating treatment (Foster et al., 1978).

As these examples suggest, for different health and behavioral health problems, there probably is an optimal configuration of time and monetary costs of care that promotes utilization patterns that are appropriately responsive to the health needs of consumers and that satisfies the economic interests of providers, MCOs, employer purchasers of health plans, and the government. This kind of information would support "rational rationing" that allows for treatment on demand for problems that merit it, with more tightly constrained access and longer waits for care for problems that do not. Such an approach is consistent with the IOM (1993) definition of access as "the timely use of personal health services to achieve the best possible health outcome" (p. 4).

This chapter focuses on how time-related variables influence utilization patterns for health and behavioral health (i.e., mental health and substance abuse) problems. We first describe how the utilization or help-seeking process has been conceptualized and investigated by medical sociologists, health economists, and clinicians, with emphasis on time-related variables. The major findings are then reformulated in terms of a behavioral economic model that emphasizes the temporal dimension of utilization patterns and is attentive to the major variable classes emphasized in the other relevant literatures. Then, research is reviewed on the role of initial appointment delays, travel time, and office waiting time in help-seeking behaviors. This work indicates that time-related variables influence utilization patterns and, relative to certain other variable classes with known effects on utilization (e.g., patient socioeconomic status), they often are more changeable, including as part of the health care system.

PERSPECTIVES ON THE USE OF HEALTH AND BEHAVIORAL HEALTH SERVICES

In addition to its roots in the oncology area, the scientific study of help-seeking patterns can be tied historically to the same values and forces that propelled the social movement of the 1960s and the passage of Medicare and Medicaid in 1965. The original concern, which remains timely today, was on reducing barriers to health care, especially among underserved demographic groups such as minorities, children, and the poor. Medical sociology burgeoned during this period and offered a perspective on help-seeking that remains present and viable today. Starting with the cutbacks in social programs initiated during the Reagan administration and continuing to the present, this perspective was eclipsed by a health economic perspective on demand for health care. The latter approach dominated the 1993–1994 health care reform debate and has added tremendous knowledge about economic and organizational variables that influence demand for care. However, the knowledge contributed by these two largely empirical traditions remains poorly integrated, and neither has connected much with a third, older clinical perspective on help-seeking that can be traced back to the early psycho-analysts. How each perspective views the help-seeking process is summarized next.

The Sociologic Viewpoint: Help-Seeking as a Dynamic Social Process

Sociological analyses of help-seeking have been guided by two related models. The first is Aday and Andersen's (1974; cf. Andersen, 1995) model of health services use, which proposed that utilization is determined by predisposing characteristics (demographics, social structure, and health beliefs); enabling resources (personal, family, and community resources); and need (both perceived and evaluated). Income, health insurance, access to care, and waiting time arc viewed as measures of enabling resources. Later revisions of the model added factors related to the health care system, consumer satisfaction, and health outcomes (Andersen, 1995).

The second model is the health belief model proposed by Rosenstock (1966) and modified by Becker and Maiman (1975), which was more broadly conceived to explain a range of health-related behaviors, including but not limited to medical help-seeking. It includes many of the same variables, but stresses that whether individuals engage in health behaviors will be the outcome of a dynamic process based on their beliefs about the severity of the health problem, their perceived susceptibility to it, treatment efficacy and costs, cues to action, and the value placed on health. Several other accounts of health behavior (see DiMatteo & DiNicola, 1982), such as Ajzen and Fishbein's (1977) theory of reasoned action and Janis and Mann's (1977) conflict theory, expanded on select variables included in the earlier models, usually in the direction of further emphasizing attitudes, beliefs, and cognitive decision-making processes. Common themes running throughout the accounts are that preferences for care are changeable over time; are not rooted in static personal attributes; and depend on the mix of costs and benefits, however represented, of action versus inaction.

Although specific variables included in the models have been only modestly successful in predicting utilization and other health behavior patterns (see reviews by Harrison, Mullen, & Green, 1992; Mechanic, 1979), they have served well as frameworks for research. Research conducted in this tradition has revealed some important generalities (summarized by Mechanic, 1983; Rosenstock & Kirscht, 1979) suggesting that help-seeking is largely a social process, not one driven primarily by physical health status. Individuals typically seek help when the functional consequences of health or behavioral health problems interfere with their day-to-day activities and responsibilities, and they do so in ways that are influenced by their family and social networks (Zola, 1973). Two persons can have similar health problems, but the one who is experiencing greater dysfunction will be more likely to seek help and will do so in ways that are responsive to social norms about such matters. Demographic variables are only modest predictors of help-seeking and probably reflect these social contextual processes to some degree, as well as constraints on health care access related to income and insurance coverage. Thus, research from the medical sociology tradition points to the importance of social contextual factors in patterns of care seeking and away from an account based on static individual characteristics or measures of health and disease states.

The Economic Viewpoint: Health Care Consumption as a Normal Good

The tremendous growth in the availability of health services, insurance, and providers since World War II resulted in an apparent economic anomaly: As the health care supply rose, so did its price, creating practical concerns about runaway medical inflation and its contribution to the budget deficit, and theoretical concerns among economists about whether health care was a "normal" good whose consumption could be described by the law of supply and demand. Several decades of research (summarized by Morrisey, 1992) has shown that the health care market can be understood from the perspective of neoclassical economic theory when the distorting effects of health insurance on demand for care are taken into account; that is, insurance coverage increases demand by protecting consumers from paying the full price of care, and, as out-of-pocket prices to consumers increase, demand decreases, but generally not as steeply as would be expected in the absence of insurance. Furthermore, as was found in the medical sociology research, demand for health care is not well predicted by measures of physical health status and is more related to changes in the price of care, once the effects of insurance are taken into account (Newhouse, 1978).

Importantly, demand for some medical services (e.g., dental and mental health care) has been found to be more "price sensitive" than demand for other services (e.g., hospital-based medical care, emergency care for children), which means that when out-of-pocket prices rise, demand for the former services decreases proportionately more than demand for the latter (Morrisey, 1992; Newhouse and the Insurance Experiment Group, 1993). Changes in demand for ambulatory medical care as a function of price lie in between the previous examples. The responsiveness of consumption of a given commodity to changes in its price is termed its *own-price elasticity of demand,* which is the ratio of the percentage change in consumption over the percentage change in price (see chapters 1 and 2, this volume, for further discussion). Commodities with ratios larger or smaller in absolute value than 1.0 (unity) have relatively elastic and inelastic demand, respectively. Although elasticities vary as a function of the type of health service, demand for health services generally tends to fall toward the inelastic end of the own-price elasticity continuum.

Monetary price is only one of several components that comprise the full price of health care. Time costs are another component and include the opportunity costs of time, which refer to costs resulting from not engaging in whatever activity would be pursued if time were not allocated to health care. Other components of the full price of care include direct costs of using health care (e.g., for travel) and, when care is delayed, costs that result from untreated health problems. The influence of these costs on utilization patterns has been less well studied compared to the effects of monetary price, but the limited research has yielded several preliminary generalizations.

First, relative to money and tangible goods, time is a less fungible commodity, meaning that it is not as easily substitutable (Leclerc, Schmitt, & Dube, 1995). Once time is "spent," it cannot be recovered as one might recover a monetary loss or replace a tangible good. Probably because of this difference, in hypothetical choice situations, individuals tend to be more risk-averse or risk-neutral about potential time losses compared to potential monetary losses, where they tend to be more risk-seeking (Leclerc et al., 1995). Second, the relative influence of time costs on demand for health care often increases as monetary costs decrease (e.g., Acton, 1973a, 1973b), as would be the case under universal health insurance and why time costs can be used as a rationing mechanism. Third, individuals with higher opportunity costs of time (e.g., the employed, those with higher incomes) tend to be more sensitive to time costs and will pay higher monetary prices for reduced time prices (e.g., House, 1981; Whitney, Milgrom, Conrad, Fiset, & O'Hara, 1997). Fourth, individuals vary in the extent to which they discount or devalue future outcomes and thus will vary in their willingness to wait for delayed health services, even if services are free (Cullis & Jones, 1986; cf. chap. 8, this volume). Some persons with relatively shorter "time horizons" and the means to do so will forgo waiting for free or subsidized care and will defect to the private market and pay full prices for health services.

Time costs also can be considered from the perspective of health care providers (House, 1981; Whitney et al., 1997). Providers who wish to maximize their production function and income do not want an empty waiting room and thus have incentives to maintain a waiting list with respect to both appointment and office waiting times. However, accepting too many patients and chronically overscheduling them can create time costs of sufficient magnitude to reduce patient demand for services. As discussed in a subsequent section, such delays have detrimental effects on utilization.

In summary, the own-price elasticity analyses that have dominated health economic research have shown that demand for health care changes as the price of care changes and that health care functions as a normal good. Scant attention has been paid, however, to *cross-price elasticity relations,* that is, how demand for different kinds of care varies when prices of alternative commodities change (see chapters 1 and 2, this volume). These relations are important for two reasons. First, health care increasingly is being delivered in large organizations, and information on how changes in the availability and cost of a subset of services may change demand for other services is essential to maximize profits at the organizational level.[2] Second, as discussed in a subsequent section, the demonstrated influence on utilization

---

[2]A current example concerns the medical offset benefits of including health and behavioral health services in comprehensive health plans (reviewed by Fiedler & Wight, 1989; Mumford, Schlesinger, Glass, Patrick, & Cuerdon, 1984). The inclusion of behavioral health services often reduces the utilization and costs of more expensive medical services, sometimes to the point that they more than pay for themselves. Offset effects tend to be greatest among covered groups who have serious medical problems and mild to moderate behavioral health problems, and when both types of care are managed within a single health care organization or plan that can reap the full net economic returns.

patterns of social variables that are largely external to the health care system may be conceptualized as bearing a cross-price elasticity relation with demand for health care.

The Clinical Viewpoint: Treatment-Seeking as a Measure of Patient Motivation

The large-sample, group-level of analysis preferred by medical sociologists and health economists is useful for addressing public health and health policy issues, but is less informative at the level of clinical service delivery between health care providers and patients. A third view of help-seeking developed from the perspective of the practicing clinician predates these more empirical initiatives and has its roots in psychoanalytic notions about motivation for behavior change. Although mental health providers understandably have embraced this viewpoint more thoroughly than other medical specialties, the shared clinical realities of patient care and the role of patient behavior in clinical management have assured some dissemination of the viewpoint throughout the health care system.

In classic psychoanalytic psychotherapy, the ideal patient seeks treatment voluntarily in response to psychic distress that emanates from ego-dystonic intrapsychic conflicts. Such patients are viewed as intrinsically motivated and are contrasted with those who enter treatment because of external pressures, negative consequences, or other forms of coercion. Extrinsically motivated patients are considered poor psychotherapy candidates and likely to terminate prematurely because they lack the anxiety necessary to motivate change and seek treatment for external reasons that could change and dissipate. Hence, the circumstances surrounding treatment entry (e.g., self-referred or coerced) took on considerable prognostic significance, and how persistent patients were in seeking treatment and their willingness to wait for it came to be viewed as a measure of intrinsic motivation for change, which generally was conceptualized as a stable personality trait. Some psychotherapists imposed waits on potential patients as a way to screen out the extrinsically motivated, thereby reserving limited treatment resources for those thought most likely to benefit (Robin, 1976). Conversely, patients who were offered treatment and who did not attend or comply were variously viewed as unmotivated, in denial, impulsive, antisocial, externalizing, and untreatable until they accepted the need for help (Hyslop & Kershaw, 1981; Kirk & Frank, 1976; cf. Miller, 1985).

As discussed by Miller (1985) and others (e.g., Pringle, 1982; Marlatt, Tucker, Donovan, & Vuchinich, 1997), this perspective contains circular assumptions about the role of intrinsic motivation in help-seeking and behavior change; that is, only intrinsically motivated persons will seek help and change, and those who do not are not intrinsically motivated. The perspective also trivializes the demonstrated effects of environmental contingencies on behavior change initiatives and decisions to seek help (e.g., Marlatt et al., 1997; Matarazzo, Weiss, Herd, Miller, & Weiss, 1984), in favor of an account based on an internal trait that, at best, may be difficult to measure and manipulate and, at worst, may be a fictional construct.

Research on treatment entry and compliance generally has failed to support the traditional clinical view of motivation. In the substance abuse treatment field, for example, treatment often is sought to address problems of living that result from substance abuse (e.g., marital, job, or health problems) and, to the extent that "motivation" must be inferred, it almost certainly emanates from these problems of living, and successful treatment must help to resolve them (Marlatt et al., 1997). Moreover, coercion is a common element in substance abuse treatment entry (e.g., employer or court-ordered treatment) and, contrary to traditional views, research that compared treatment participation and outcomes among coerced and voluntary clients found similar outcomes across groups and reduced attrition among coerced clients (reviewed by De Leon, 1988; Stitzer & McCaul, 1987; Weisner, 1990). As another example, an extensive body of research on compliance with medical regimens (e.g., DiMatteo & DiNicola, 1982; Epstein & Cluss, 1982; Haynes, Taylor, & Sackett, 1979; Meichenbaum & Turk, 1987) has similarly pointed away from an account based on stable patient characteristics in favor of one that emphasizes the complexity of medical regimens and their functional consequences as primary determinants of compliance.

In summary, key predictions of the clinical perspective have not been well supported, but, like many perspectives that emerged from practice rather than from research processes, its influence persists in ways that often go unrecognized and are difficult to dispel. For example, recent efforts to develop interventions to increase treatment entry and retention (e.g., for substance abuse treatment or HIV testing) continue to emphasize the manipulation of psychological constructs such as readiness to change, self-efficacy, and perceived susceptibility (for examples, see Miller & Rollnick, 1991; Onken, Blaine, & Boren, 1997). Although these efforts reject older views of motivation as a personality trait, they continue the clinical tradition of internalizing the relevant controlling variables and thus may overlook changeable features of the health care delivery system and the surrounding social contexts that impede help-seeking, as suggested by the medical sociology and health economic research. Some of the latter variables, such as time costs and delays to see the doctor, may exert more influence on utilization patterns than many of the psychological variables emphasized in the clinical literature, and they may be more amenable to constructive manipulation.

REFORMULATING THE HELP-SEEKING PROCESS
AS INTERTEMPORAL CHOICE: POTENTIAL
CONTRIBUTIONS FROM BEHAVIORAL ECONOMICS

As the preceding summaries suggest, a comprehensive understanding of the help-seeking process almost certainly will be interdisciplinary, and a framework is needed within which the contributions of the relevant disciplines can be organized. The health care access model of Aday and Andersen (1974) has been employed in this fashion, but it does not easily assimilate the health economic data and does not represent well the dynamic nature of the help-seeking process within the social environmental contexts in which it occurs. The health economic perspective is comprehensive, flexible, and conceptually rich, but its empirical translations to date have not extended far beyond the study of own-price elasticity relations, and its ability to accommodate representations of behavior patterns and environmental constraints in terms other than money is uncertain. Neither perspective can be readily applied to the behavior of individuals in clinical situations, which remains a key area of application. A framework is needed that can assimilate the analytic perspective of health economics with the social contextual and behavioral variables demonstrated as influential in the social science literatures and that can represent the temporal dynamics of help-seeking patterns through time at both the group and individual levels of analysis.

Although in the incipient stages of application to health services utilization, behavioral economics appears to have potential for providing this kind of interdisciplinary organizational umbrella and for directing attention toward key variables suggested by the relevant disciplines. As discussed throughout this book, behavioral economics merges the conceptual framework of consumer demand theory in microeconomics with the concepts and methods of behavioral psychology to explain choice behavior in contexts that vary with respect to the range of available commodities and the constraints that exist on access to them. Consistent with economic theory, behavioral studies of choice conducted with a range of species and reinforcers have demonstrated robustly that preference for a given commodity depends on two variable classes: (a) the direct constraints (e.g., in terms of price, delay, or response requirement) on access to the commodity of interest, and (b) what other commodities are included in the available set and the constraints on access to them. In general, preference for a given commodity varies inversely with constraints on access to it and directly with constraints on access to the alternatives.

An important corollary of these relationships concerns the role of delay in patterns of choice over time among commodities that are available at different times and under different constraints. Three findings merit mention (see chapters 7 and 8, this volume, for further discussion). First, future rewards are discounted: Commodities available in the future are less highly valued than ones available now, even if they otherwise have the same tangible value or psychological characteristics. Second, individuals discount future commodities at different rates for reasons that are not wholly explicated, but vary to some degree with their age, income levels, and past reinforcement history. Third, when individuals make choices between rewards of different value that are available after variable delays, which commodity they choose will depend on when they make their choice in relation to the availability of the commodities.

For example, in a simple mutually exclusive choice between a smaller sooner reward (SSR) and a larger later reward (LLR), preference will vary as a function of the delay to receipt of each reward according to a hyperbolic discounting function, which has been empirically supported in laboratory studies of choice (e.g., Ainslie, 1992). A key feature of hyperbolic discounting is that preference between the LLR and SSR will reverse simply with the passage of time. If the choice is made sufficiently far ahead of the availability of the SSR, the LLR will be preferred, but as receipt of the SSR becomes imminent, preference will reverse in favor of the SSR. Although this example describes the SSR and LLR as discrete events, that simplification is unnecessary, and each reward can be viewed as a series of smaller rewards that are distributed over time, but that sum to a different overall collective value that is obtained after a relatively shorter or longer delay.

Choosing whether to seek health care involves a similar series of events with variable costs and benefits that result from either action or inaction and that are distributed in time with variable probabilities of occurrence. The behavioral economic framework suggests that, at a particular point in time, the choice of whether to seek care will depend on the aggregated and discounted costs and benefits in two broad categories: (a) those related to direct constraints that exist on access to health care and the direct benefits received from care; and (b) those related to the consequences of the choice for access to other valued life-health activities, both short and longer term. Variables in the first class include the monetary and time costs of seeking medical care, which are the focal interest of health economics; structural and geographic impediments to care (e.g., distance to facilities, transportation difficulties, lack of childcare), which are included along with cost variables as enabling factors in Aday and Andersen's (1974) model; and direct effects of care on health and behavioral health status, which can include positive or negative outcomes, or a mixture of both, with different associated probabilities of occurrence. Overall, the probability of seeking care should be inversely related to the constraints on access and positively related to the potential direct benefits of care. For example, easily obtained, effective treatments should have higher utilization rates, whereas treatments of lesser effectiveness and greater costs (including costs related to time, money, pain, and suffering) should have lower utilization rates.

Variables in the second class include both immediate and delayed consequences of seeking or forgoing care on access to valued life-health activities in areas such as work, intimate and social relations, physical and mental activities, and independent functioning and mobility. In general, help-seeking should increase to the extent that doing so increases the probability of receipt of rewards in valued areas of functioning. The effects of action or inaction can be either direct or mediated through one's health or behavioral health state. Examples of direct effects include social network or employer reactions to treatment entry, which can be favorable, negative, or a mixture of both, and are among the social contextual variables emphasized in the medical sociology research. Examples of mediated effects are outcomes made possible, or whose probability of occurrence is increased, by maintaining a given health state or health behavior pattern. As noted by Grossman (1972), good health can be viewed as an intermediate state, rather than an end in itself, that supports engagement in other valued activities because of the time and resources it frees up to pursue their consumption. As applied to the time costs of seeking health care, this perspective suggests that individuals are making an exchange of the relatively nonfungible commodity of their time for a health-related intervention that will increase their probability of obtaining certain life-health rewards whose receipt often, but not necessarily, is contingent upon the intermediate commodity of "health."

The two variable domains suggested as important by behavioral economics, direct constraints on health care access and constraints on access to other valued life-health activities, subsume and organize the variable classes emphasized in the health economic and medical sociology literatures. The framework is functional and temporal in organization, not structural, as in Aday and Andersen's (1974) model of health care access. The approach shares the conceptual richness of health economics, provides a meaningful way to study social contextual variables within that general framework, and offers an established approach to representing environment–behavior relations through time. The latter feature is essential for clinical applications concerned with the behavior of individual patients and is a unique advantage of behavioral economics.

In applying the perspective to health services utilization, the effects on help-seeking of direct constraints on health care access involve simpler relations that are more easily operationalized and measured compared to the effects of changing constraints in valued areas of life-health functioning that bear contingent relations with health and help-seeking. Evaluating evidence for the former relations thus seems an appropriate starting point in applying the behavioral economic model to health care utilization, and it is a focus shared with health economics, with its emphasis on own-price elasticity relations. If *behavioral* evidence is found to support the predicted inverse relation between help-seeking and direct constraints on access, as found in the health economic literature using monetary indices of health care costs and utilization, then the model can be expanded to conceptualize and investigate the effects on utilization of changing constraints in other areas of life-health functioning. This suggested course of development follows the development of the behavioral economic literature on drug self-administration, where the study of direct constraints on drug access largely preceded the study of the effects of alternative reinforcers on drug-taking (see reviews by Carroll, 1993; DeGrandpre, Bickel, Hughes, & Higgins, 1992; Vuchinich & Tucker, 1988).

In the remainder of the chapter, the hypothesized inverse relation between help-seeking and constraints on health care access is evaluated by reviewing research on the relation between utilization and delays in receiving health care (including appointment and office waiting time) and the travel time or distance required to obtain care. In addition to having conceptual relevance to the health and behavioral economic perspectives, such time-related variables pose impediments to potential patients and can reduce the productivity of providers if they decrease utilization. Understanding the behavioral processes involved and the extent to which patients will absorb different time constraints on access has implications for developing interventions to promote appropriate patterns of help-seeking.

RELATION OF APPOINTMENT DELAYS
TO INITIAL TREATMENT ENTRY

The research reviewed in this section is limited to experimental and correlational studies that assessed the role of delay in keeping initial appointments for health, mental health, or substance abuse services. Studies of return appointments were excluded because they are influenced by participants' immediate interactions with the health care system and thus provide less definitive information about the effects of delay on appointment keeping. The latter research is pertinent to understanding compliance patterns once treatment has been initiated, which is a topic that has been extensively reviewed (e.g., Baekeland & Lundwall, 1975; Deyo & Inui, 1980; Epstein & Cluss, 1982; Garfield, 1986; Macharia, Leon, Rowe, Stephenson, & Haynes, 1992; Oppenheim, Bergman, & English, 1979; Stark, 1992; Wierzbicki & Pekarick, 1993), but it cannot address why some individuals delay or avoid initiating care.

Studies were further selected for review if they included a quantifiable measure of appointment-keeping behavior, usually the percentage of patients who did and did not attend scheduled initial appointments, over two or more delay intervals, at least one of which involved delays of 30 or fewer days, which is a common clinical standard. Studies that included very long

(> 6 months) or indeterminate delays were excluded (e.g., Patch, Fisch, Levine, McKenna, & Raynes, 1973) because they are subject to alternative explanation based on events that occurred during the lengthy waiting period (e.g., some patients died). Also excluded were health economic studies that reported aggregated measures of utilization in relation to time costs, usually converted into monetary equivalents, if they did not also report on appointment-keeping behavior patterns (e.g., Whitney et al., 1997). Studies that interviewed appointment no-shows concerning the reasons why (e.g., Noonan, 1973) or that intervened to increase attendance (e.g., Mejta, Bokos, Mickenberg, Maslar, & Senay, 1997; Shepard & Moseley, 1976; Yancovitz et al., 1991; cf. Higgins & Budney, 1997) were excluded if they did not report behavioral data on attendance patterns as a function of delay.

Table 9.1 summarizes the 5 medical, 15 substance abuse, and 7 mental health studies that met the inclusion criteria. The studies are grouped according to whether they involved random assignment to delay conditions because it is important to determine if the predicted inverse relation between delay and appointment-keeping was observed when scheduling was not subject to patient and provider selection processes. There may be an understandable tendency, for example, to schedule urgent cases quickly and to allow less urgent cases to wait, a pattern that might bias measures of association and produce different results when randomization was and was not included.

This potential concern generally proved to be unfounded. Similar results were observed across the experimental and descriptive studies and, with few exceptions, they supported the predicted inverse relation between delay and appointment-keeping. Although fewer in number, all of the experimental studies supported the relation. The handful of descriptive studies that did not variously involved unusually long appointment delays (e.g., Gates & Colborn, 1976), showed evidence of scheduling selection processes that may have contributed to the negative results (Orne & Boswell, 1991), or combined initial and return appointment data in the analyses (Alpert, 1964).

Most studies reported data of sufficient detail to support a summary inspection of initial attendance rates as a function of increasing delays up to 35 days, which is presented in Fig. 9.1. The ordinate shows the percentage of appointments kept as reported in the studies, whereas many of the abscissa values reflecting the delay in days are the mean or midpoint of delay categories that spanned more than 1 day. A few studies included an open-ended category for the longest delay investigated (e.g., > 30 days), and these indeterminate values are not included in the figure. Thus, there are more data points for the shorter delays, both for this reason and also because most studies focused on delays of 3 weeks or less. With these qualifications, the figure provides additional evidence for decreased appointment-keeping as a function of increased delays. The correlation across studies of −.464 sug-

TABLE 9.1

Studies of the Relation of Initial Appointment Delay to Rates of Treatment Entry and Other Indices of Treatment Engagement

Experimental Research

Study	Type of Service	Sample (N)	Design	Findings
Health services				
Benjamin-Bauman, Reiss, & Bailey (1984)	Gynecologic exam in a family-planning clinic	337 and 192 females in Studies 1 and 2, respectively	Study 1: random assignment to waits of 1 or 3 weeks. Study 2: random assignment to waits of 1 day or 2 weeks.	Shorter waits produced significantly higher show rates in both studies. Across studies, show rates were similar for next-day and 1-week appointments, and both were higher than for appointments delayed 2 or 3 weeks.
Substance abuse services				
Chafetz, Blane, & Hill (1970)	Outpatient alcohol clinic	200 males referred from a general hospital ED	Random assignment to a "treatment catalyst" intervention (rapid ED processing, same-day alcohol treatment entry typical) or to a usual processing condition with 4–6-week delays to receipt of an alcohol therapist.	Treatment catalyst intervention produced significantly higher treatment entry and retention rates.
Festinger, Lamb, Kirby, & Marlowe (1996)	Outpatient cocaine treatment	78 (38.5% female)	Random assignment to next-day appointment or one delayed 2–7 days.	Significantly higher show rate in shorter waiting condition; no group difference in treatment retention.
Maddux (1993)	Outpatient methadone maintenance clinics	638 (both genders; ratio unspecified)	4 retention interventions, one involving random assignment to rapid or delayed admission, introduced sequentially during a 1-year study period.	Treatment entry within 1 day vs. after a 2-week delay resulted in 95% and 75% participation, respectively.[1]

(Continued)

233

TABLE 9.1
(Continued)

Experimental Research

Study	Type of Service	Sample (N)	Design	Findings
Stark, Campbell, & Brinkerhoff (1990)	Outpatient drug treatment	117 (48.0% female); cocaine and amphetamine abuse most common	2 × 2 design manipulated waiting time (seen immediately or within a mean of 9.7 days) and presence or absence of encouragement to attend.	Significantly higher show rate in no-delay condition, but few clients in any condition remained in treatment at 30 days. Verbal encouragement had no effect.
Mental health services				
Folkins, Hersch, & Dahlen (1980)	CMHC outpatient mental health services	150 (gender unspecified)	Random assignment to 1 of 3 delay conditions (≤ 3, 6–8, or 16–19 days).	Significant decrease in show rates with increasing delays.
Grieves (1973)	CMHC outpatient mental health services	351 males and females (ratio unspecified)	Random assignment to appointment within 2 or 10 days.	Marginally significantly higher show rate in shorter waiting condition ($p < .10$).
Robin (1976)	Outpatient psychiatric services	234 (50.4% female)	Random assignment to appointment within 7 days or, on average, within 12 weeks (range = 6–18 weeks).	Significantly higher show rate in shorter waiting condition. No evidence of increased use of other medical services during the delay.

Descriptive Research

Study	Type of Service	Sample (N)	Design	Findings
Health services				
Alpert (1964)	Outpatient pediatric services in an urban children's hospital	1,588 (gender unspecified)	2-month study period; full sample retrospective chart review; subset of families interviewed who did and did not keep appointments delayed 6 weeks (52% were initial visits; 48% returns).	Show rate unrelated to appointment or office waiting time or to medical problem seriousness. Study limited by data for initial and return appointments being combined, lengthy delays for all appointments, and lengthy in-office waits (> 3 hours for 25% of sample).

Study	Setting	Sample	Design	Findings
Finnerty, Shaw, & Himmelsbach (1973)	Community hypertension screening and clinic referral	953 (gender unspecified)	8-month prospective study; 1–2 week delay for clinic appointment reduced to 1–2 days midway through study.	When delay decreased, clinic no-show rate decreased from 50% to < 5%.
Gates & Colborn (1976)	Urban neighborhood health center	272 males and females (ratio unspecified)	5-month prospective study; appointment delays ranged from 3–21 weeks.	Appointment delay unrelated to show rate; all delay intervals longer than in most studies with positive findings.
Substance abuse services				
Addenbrooke & Rathod (1990)	Detoxification and outpatient drug treatment	130 (35% female)	1-year prospective study with a median delay of 7 days; comparison data obtained from an outpatient psychiatric clinic with a median delay of 39 days.	Significant negative association between delay and show rates, but length of delay confounded with patient population; no relation between initial delay and treatment retention; older alcoholics and physician referrals retained longer.
Donovan, Rosengren, Downey, Cox, & Sloan (1997)	State-funded inpatient and outpatient drug treatment	654 (31.5% female)	Random assignment to an "attrition pre-vention" intervention or to usual care while waiting for treatment.	No significant effect of intervention on treatment entry rates; no-shows, especially for inpatient/residential care, waited longer than did attenders.
Fehr, Weinstein, Sterling, & Gottheil (1991)	Outpatient cocaine treatment	520 (both genders; ratio unspecified)	8-month prospective study; 44% and 94% of appointments occurred within 2 and 6 days, respectively.	Significant decrease in attendance as a function of delay (from 60% to 30% for 1- and 6-day delays, respectively) and distance from clinic; lower show rate if court-referred; gender unrelated.

(Continued)

TABLE 9.1
(Continued)

Descriptive Research

Study	Type of Service	Sample (N)	Design	Findings
Festinger, Lamb, Kountz, Kirby, & Marlowe (1995)	Outpatient cocaine treatment	235 (32% female)	7-month retrospective study; demographic, drug use, referral source, and waiting time variables used to predict treatment entry.	Shorter delays and absence of alcohol problems predicted entry. Most precipitous drop in show rate occurred from the first to second 24 hours of waiting (from 83 to 57% attendance).
Gallant, Bishop, Stoy, Faulkner, & Paternostro (1966)	Outpatient alcohol treatment	569 males	9-month retrospective study; show rates for 3 delay intervals compared (< 2, 2–6, or > 7 days).	Increased delays significantly associated with decreased attendance.
Hyslop & Kershaw (1981)	Alcohol treatment	100 (81% male)	4-month prospective study; subset of no-shows interviewed concerning why.	When delay reduced from a mean of 25 days to ≤ 7 days, show rate increased from 53 to 70%. Age and referral source unrelated to attendance.
Leigh, Ogborne, & Cleland (1984)	Outpatient alcohol treatment	172 (23.3% female)	9-month prospective study; role of delay in show rates assessed for first three visits (intake, assessment, and first therapy session).	Appointments delayed < 15 days resulted in higher show rates for all visits. No-shows for therapy session tended to be younger, use illicit drugs, have lower MAST scores, more alcohol-related convictions, and no dependents at home.
Mayer (1972)	Outpatient alcohol treatment	747 (gender unspecified)	4-year prospective study; evaluated role of delay and participant legal status in attendance.	Inverse relation between delay and attendance. Legal referrals had relatively higher and lower show rates compared to the rest of the sample if the delay was < 4 days or > 3 weeks, respectively. Initial appointment delays similarly affected treatment retention patterns.

Mayer, Needham, & Myerson (1965)	Outpatient alcohol treatment clinic at an urban general hospital	193 (71% male)	12-month prospective study; show rates for three delay intervals compared (< 4, 5–21, or ≥ 22 days).	Significant inverse relation between delay and attendance. Treatment entry rates were higher among attenders if initial waits were > 5 days; this likely reflects selection biases in who received quicker intake appointments (e.g., women, the unemployed, legal referrals).
Raynes & Warren (1971)	Outpatient psychiatric clinic at an urban general hospital	738 (67.0% female)	1-year study; orientation of data collection unclear; delay data available for only 52% of sample and aggregated in 5-day increments.	Show rates were similar across the first 15 days (about two thirds attended) and then decreased with increasing delays to 25% attendance by days 31–35, the final interval assessed.
Wanberg & Jones (1973)	Comprehensive alcohol treatment	257 (17% female)	18-week study period; time orientation unclear; show rates compared for 3 delays (≤ 4, 5–8, and ≥ 9 days).	Significantly lower show rate for delays ≥ 9 days compared to two shorter delays, which did not differ. Higher show rate among physician- than among self-referrals. SES unrelated to attendance.
Mental health services Carpenter, Morrow, Del Gaudio, & Ritzler (1981)	Outpatient psychiatric clinic at a university teaching hospital	1,106 (63% female)	12-month prospective study, with telephone follow-ups of 30% of no-shows; usual appointment delay of about 2 weeks.	Relative to no-shows, treatment entrants waited less, gave clearer reasons for seeking help, and were physician-referred. Appointment delay and no longer needing help cited by no-shows as reasons for nonattendance. Entry status unrelated to demographics or geographic distance.

(Continued)

237

TABLE 9.1
(Continued)

Descriptive Research

Study	Type of Service	Sample (N)	Design	Findings
Korner (1964)	CMHC outpatient mental health services	210 (gender unspecified)	Uncontrolled prospective study; time frame unclear; during study, delays of > 3 months reduced to ≤ 1 week.	No-show rate decreased from 30% to 10% when delay shortened.
Miyake, Chemtob, & Torigoe (1985)	VA day-treatment mental health program	198 (98.5% male)	Prospective study; 8-month baseline and 28-month intervention with mean delays of 5.4 and 1.7 days.	Significantly higher show rate in shorter waiting condition.
Orne & Boswell (1991)	CMHC outpatient mental health services	531 (both genders; ratio unspecified)	12-month study; orientation of data collection unclear.	Attendance decreased with increasing delays up to 9 days, then increased at delays ≥ 10 days. Pattern attributed to time-slot selection processes: Clients in crisis tended to be seen quicker while in need; with somewhat longer waits, crises subsided along with attendance. Clients with chronic, stable problems had the longest delays but remained motivated to attend.
Wolkon (1972)	Mental health services in 3 outpatient clinics	379 (gender unspecified)	Variable retrospective study periods across clinics; delays of 0–1 days, ≤ about 1 week, or ≥ 1 week compared.	Significant negative association between delay and attendance; greatest decrease in attendance occurred after about 1 week.

Note. ED = emergency department; CMHC = community mental health center; MAST = Michigan Alcoholism Screening Test; SES = socioeconomic status; VA = Veterans Administration.
[1]Findings for Maddux (1993) as reported in Mejta, Bokos, Mickenberg, Maslar, and Senay (1997).

gests that the delay variable accounted for more than 20% of the variance in initial attendance patterns. The correlation for the substance abuse studies alone was similar ($r = -.396$). There were too few medical and mental health studies to compute separate correlations for each category, but visual inspection of Fig. 9.1 does not suggest that the relation differed substantially across the different kinds of services.

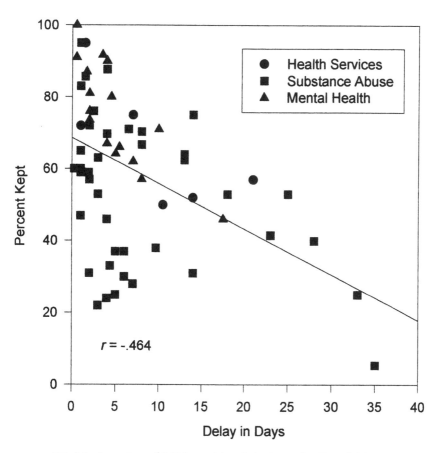

FIG. 9.1. Percentage of initial appointments kept as a function of delay to appointment. Data are from studies presented in Table 9.1 for utilization of medical care, substance abuse, and mental health services. The x axis is delay in days, and the y axis is the percent of participants with scheduled appointments who kept them. The slope of the line reflects the correlation between delay and attendance computed across studies.

Obviously, until parametric experiments are conducted that manipulate the delay interval over a range of durations, it cannot be concluded that the relation between the two variables is linear across the entire range, but the observed association suggests the utility of such research. Several studies that included three or more delay intervals of relatively shorter duration (e.g., Benjamin-Bauman, Reiss, & Bailey, 1984; Festinger, Lamb, Kountz, Kirby, & Marlowe, 1995; Folkins, Hersch, & Dahlen, 1980; Gallant, Bishop, Stoy, Faulkner, & Paternostro, 1966) suggested that the relation may be negatively accelerating over the first week or so, especially during the first few days of waiting, with the downward slope of the curve quickly becoming less steep after 2 or more weeks of waiting. Determining the shape of the relation has both conceptual and practical significance. Conceptually, determining if the relation is better described by an exponential or hyperbolic function would have relevance to a debate in the economic and behavioral economic literatures about the nature of discounting of future rewards (see chap. 8, this volume). Practically, determining the form and parameters of the relation would support empirically based decisions about critical intervals within which it is important to schedule initial appointments in order to achieve target levels of attendance.

A subset of studies reported other findings pertinent to issues raised by one or more of the major perspectives on health services utilization. First, with one exception (Mayer, Needham, & Myerson, 1965), studies that assessed treatment retention rates among those participants who attended an initial appointment did not suggest that participants who were seen rapidly were more likely to drop out, as would be predicted by the clinical perspective if longer waits served to screen out extrinsically motivated individuals. Three studies found no difference in retention as a function of initial appointment delay (Addenbrooke & Rathod, 1990; Festinger, Lamb, Kirby, & Marlowe, 1996; Stark, Campbell, & Brinkerhoff, 1990), and one study (Chafetz, Blane, & Hill, 1970) found that retention rates were higher when the delay to treatment entry was shorter. Woody, O'Hare, Mintz, and O'Brien (1975) also reported improved retention with shorter delays to methadone treatment entry among heroin addicts, although they did not examine how delays influenced rates of initial entry. These findings, which come mainly from the substance abuse field, fail to suggest that rapid treatment entry wastes resources on unmotivated clients. Rather, extended delays appear to discourage receipt of services by individuals in need.

Second, studies that examined treatment entry rates as a function of referral source did not support the conventional clinical wisdom that self-referred clients are more likely to keep initial appointments, nor were demographic characteristics consistently related to attendance patterns (e.g., Addenbrooke & Rathod, 1990; Carpenter, Morrow, Del Gaudio, & Ritzler, 1981; Hyslop & Kershaw, 1981; Mayer, 1972; Wanberg & Jones, 1973). When differences were noted, they favored higher show rates among persons referred by physicians (but not from the emergency room) and lower show rates among younger adults. Ethnic status, income, personality characteristics, and legal involvement were not studied systematically enough to draw inferences. With few exceptions (e.g., Donovan, Rosengren, Downey, Cox, & Sloan, 1997), gender differences, which were widely assessed, were not observed.

Third, studies that investigated the reasons participants gave for not keeping appointments (e.g., Carpenter et al., 1981; Hyslop & Kershaw, 1981; cf. Noonan, 1973) found that no-shows tended to have given less clear reasons why they needed help compared to those who attended and found that a subset of no-shows cited appointment delays and no longer needing help as reasons for nonattendance. The latter pattern probably reflects the fact that some health and behavioral health problems are self-limiting in the absence of treatment, and such cases were a small but reliable percentage of these study samples. This pattern fails to suggest that rapid entry results in much waste of treatment resources on persons who otherwise would resolve their problem without it.

Finally, studies that involved psychologically oriented interventions designed to promote treatment entry and that also measured or manipulated initial appointment delays (e.g., Chafetz et al., 1970; Donovan et al., 1997; Stark et al., 1990) generally found stronger support for the role of delay in attendance rates compared to the effects of the interventions. For example, Donovan et al. found that an "attrition prevention" intervention that provided modest therapeutic and tangible support to drug abusers who were waiting for state-sponsored treatment did not increase the probability of treatment entry compared to a usual care condition. However, the mean waiting time before a treatment slot became available was shorter for participants who entered treatment compared to those who did not, and this difference was especially pronounced for clients who were offered inpatient or residential care. Stark et al. similarly found no effect of a verbal intervention that encouraged treatment entry on attendance rates, but found that attendance was higher with shorter delays. More research is needed to ascertain the relative contribution of these variable classes, but the findings suggest that studies of the effectiveness of motivational and other psychosocial interventions to promote treatment entry and retention routinely need to measure, if not manipulate, how long clients have to wait for services.

In summary, the research supported the inverse relation between delay and treatment entry predicted by the conceptual framework shared by behavioral and health economics. Delays to treatment entry had a more consistent relation with attendance rates compared to several variables highlighted by the clinical perspective, which further questions a trait perspective on motivation for treatment. The shape and parameters of the relation between delay and attendance remain to be determined in parametric experiments and will be important for developing applications to alter treatment entry and retention patterns.

RELATION OF TRAVEL TIME TO UTILIZATION

Travel time is another time-related, direct constraint on access to services with which utilization should vary inversely, unless there are other features of the choice context that outweigh the effects of such a direct constraint. Acting in accordance with the National Health Planning and Resources Development Act of 1974, the U.S. Department of Health, Education, and Welfare (1978) set a 30-minute travel time standard for access to hospital care in rural areas. However, this standard has not been uniformly met (Newacheck, Hughes, & Stoddard, 1996), the law that guided its establishment has since been superseded by legislation that omitted it, and travel time to hospital and other types of care remains variable. This section reviews studies that evaluated the predicted relation between utilization and travel requirements, as measured by time or distance.[3] As in the review of research on appointment delays, it is limited to studies that included quantitative measures of utilization behavior. Studies that described travel patterns to care or that measured patient preferences and hypothetical choices were excluded if these variables were not linked to utilization behavior. In contrast to the review of delay effects, which was limited to studies of initial help-seeking, the review of travel time research included studies that involved both initial and return appointments; the time costs of travel presumably are not changed by interactions with the health care system, as they potentially are with respect to scheduling and complying with return appointments. Finally, the review was limited to studies conducted in developed countries (the vast majority in the United States), because the context of choice in developing countries can be highly variable along dimensions known to influence utilization. Nevertheless, studies conducted in a range of poor, developing countries generally showed that travel time was inversely related to health care utilization (e.g., Hodgkin, 1996; Hotchkiss, 1998; Tuladhar, 1987; Vissandjee, Barlow, & Fraser, 1997).

Table 9.2 summarizes the 34 studies that met the inclusion criteria and includes 3 dental, 9 behavioral health, 13 outpatient or ambulatory medical, 5 maternal and child health, and 4 hospital-based medical care studies. None

---

[3]Because the functional effects of distance will vary with modes of transportation, time is considered a more accurate measure of the opportunity costs of care. Although a comparison of travel time to travel distance has led to different conclusions regarding accessibility in some studies (Shannon & Bashshur, 1973), both types of studies were included in this review, as this distinction did not substantively alter the pattern of results or conclusions.

TABLE 9.2
Studies of the Relation of Travel Time and Distance to the Utilization of Health and Behavioral Health Services

Study	Type of Service	Sample (N)	Design	Findings
Dental care				
Conrad, Grembowski, & Milgrom (1987)	Insured dental care	4,178 families	Influences on probability of any use, expenditures on and volume of basic and specific services assessed in 1980 household mail survey with Pennsylvania Blue Shield families.	For any dental use, significant negative elasticities were found for travel ($-.03$) and office waiting ($-.09$) time; they also were significant and negative for basic expenditures ($-.06$ and $-.17$, respectively). Money price elasticities ranged from $-.01$ to $-.27$.
Grytten (1991)	Dental services in Norway	7,506 (48% male) in 1975; 7,318 (47% male) in 1985; 443 in 1987 (50.8% male)	Dental utilization and travel times assessed in interviews using a national sample conducted in 1975 and 1985; office waiting assessed in 1987 using a smaller county sample.	Significant inverse relation between travel time and utilization in 1975, but not in 1985. More dentists, greater urbanization, and increased mobility cited as possible reasons for change. Office waits > 15 minutes reduced demand in 1987 assessment.
Holtmann & Olsen (1976)	Dental services	923 households	Dental utilization and travel time for 1971–1972 assessed in household interviews conducted in a 5-county area in New York and Pennsylvania.	Travel time and office waiting time were significant predictors of utilization in regression analyses, especially when individual "taste" variables regarding dental care were omitted. Travel time elasticities ranged from $-.08$ to $-.12$. Office waiting elasticities ranged from $-.20$ to $-.26$ and exceeded monetary price elasticities.

(Continued)

TABLE 9.2
(Continued)

Study	Type of Service	Sample (N)	Design	Findings
Substance abuse				
Fortney, Booth, Blow, Bunn, & Cook (1995)	Aftercare following inpatient alcohol treatment	4,621 male veterans (33 treatment programs)	Chart review of aftercare attendance for 30 days after discharge from VA alcohol dependent treatment programs.	Significant inverse relation between travel distance and aftercare participation; relation especially pronounced for elderly and rural veterans.
Greenfield, Brady, Besteman, & De Smet (1996)	Mobile methadone maintenance treatment	399 (67% male)	Treatment retention of mobile service recipients compared to retention at 6 fixed-site methadone programs (N = 1,588) in Baltimore.	Mobile patients retained significantly longer (*Mdn* = 15.5 months) than fixed-site patients who did (3.9) and did not (6.3) live in the zip code served by the mobile unit. Mobile program reduced patient travel time and costs.
Mattson & Del Boca (1998)	Outpatient alcohol treatment (Project MATCH)	1,726 (76% male)	Predictors of treatment compliance investigated using data from a clinical trial of three interventions that did not result in different drinking outcomes.	Travel time and delay to initial treatment session were among the significant predictors of treatment session attendance; both were inversely related to attendance.
Mental health				
Breakey & Kaminsky (1982)	Outpatient mental health services	249 (gender unspecified)	Psychiatric outpatient enrollment at Johns Hopkins for 1977 compared with map distance traveled.	Significant inverse relation between enrollment and distance traveled. Race, income, and social disadvantage did not mediate the relationship.
Hoening & Ragg (1966)	Outpatient psychiatric care	300 (55% male)	Comparison of distance traveled for care at the Manchester (England)	Distance traveled did not differ across groups; however, 84.4% of the sample lived < 9 miles away.

244

Study	Service type	Sample	Method	Results
			Royal Infirmary by 150 psychiatric patients who kept initial appointments and 150 neurological patients who did not.	
Marcus, Olfson, Fortney, & Ryan (1997)	General mental health services	14,430 outpatients (gender ratio unspecified)	Chart review of utilization and patient travel in 1994; assessed for all mental health clinics combined and for 12 specialty clinics (e.g., for schizophrenia, tic disorders).	Patients traveled farther for specialty care ($M = 13.6$ miles) than for care at all clinics combined ($M = 8.4$).
Person (1962)	Inpatient mental health services	N unspecified; hospital served 13 counties in Pennsylvania	Using U.S. census data for 1950 and hospital records for 1948–1952, annual first admissions per 100,000 related to distance between patient residences and the hospital.	Admissions and distance from hospital inversely related. Admission rates in closest zone similar for urban and rural areas; in outlying zones, rates higher in urban than in rural areas.
Stern (1977)	Mental health services at state hospitals and CMHCs	N unspecified; providers served multiple catchment areas in North Carolina	Chart review of admission rates and distance between patient residences and provider sites; time frame of study unspecified.	Significant inverse relation between admissions and distance; relation stronger for hospital than for outpatient services.
White (1986)	Mental health services at CHMCs	224 (57% female)	Utilization and treatment duration for selected months in 1984 were related to client characteristics and distance traveled.	Travel distance was a significant predictor of utilization in regression analyses. Travel elasticities were $-.27$ for rate and $-.37$ for intensity of use.

(Continued)

TABLE 9.2
(Continued)

Study	Type of Service	Sample (N)	Design	Findings
Outpatient medical care				
Acton (1973a)	Ambulatory and inpatient care	5,000 (45% male)	Household surveys, conducted in Brooklyn, New York in 1968 in two low-income neighborhoods, assessed demand for medical care in public and private facilities.	Time-price elasticities of demand for health care exceeded money-price elasticities; the former ranged from –.60 to –1.00 for public outpatient care and from –.25 and –.34 for private outpatient care. Longer office waits reduced demand more at public than private facilities (respective elasticities = –.12 and –.05).
Acton (1973b)	Ambulatory and inpatient care	2,600 (39% male)	Users of municipal hospital outpatient departments in New York City in 1965 surveyed about their health care during the past year.	When medical care was free, demand was significantly and inversely related to time price, as measured by travel distance.
Cunningham & Cornelius (1995)	Ambulatory health care	3,699 Native Americans and Alaskans (48% male)	Use of health care by this sample, as assessed by the National Medical Expenditure Survey in 1987, compared with data for non-Native U.S. residents living in nonmetropolitan areas.	Relative to the comparison group, travel time was significantly higher and health care utilization was significantly lower among Native Americans.
Hays, Kearns, & Moran (1990)	GP services	417 (47% male)	Survey of 168 households in Grisborne, New Zealand concerning utilization of GP services during the past year.	Utilization and travel distance in this urban area unrelated. Nevertheless, less mobile respondents were twice as likely to use the nearest GP compared to private car travelers.

Hershey, Luft, & Gianaris (1975)	Ambulatory and hospital care	1,010 (48% female)	Household interviews in 1972 assessed use and number of physician visits, checkups, and hospital stays during the past year.	Travel time positively related to a combination variable reflecting physician visits and hospital stays, which suggested that longer travel may extend hospital stays to facilitate follow-up care.
Kreher, Hickner, Ruffin, & Lin (1995)	Mammography screening for breast cancer	416 females	Mammography frequency during the past 4 years assessed by questionnaire among rural women over age 40 who visited a family physician for any reason.	Mammography utilization unrelated to travel time or distance. However, the sample may have been biased; it included women who elected to see a doctor, and a very high percentage (88%) had had at least one screening.
Krishan, Drummond, Naessens, Nobrega, & Smoldt (1985)	Ambulatory care	12,583 (52% male) in 1975; 13,959 (53% male) in 1980	1-year retrospective questionnaire survey of physician contacts before and after new rural family practice facility opened in Zumbrota, Minnesota.	Utilization increased among residents closest to the new facility, but most maintained established patterns of care and continued to travel long distances.
Miners, Greene, Salber, & Scheffler (1978)	Ambulatory care	704 rural households (gender unspecified)	Health status and utilization patterns of residents in northern Durham County, North Carolina assessed during 5 home visits in 1973–1975.	Travel time had a greater impact on demand than monetary price and was the main determinant of demand in Caucasian households. Elasticities were −.33 for travel time, −.15 for monetary price, and −.07 for office waiting time.
Okada & Sparer (1976)	Ambulatory care	14,622 households (gender unspecified)	Interviews conducted during 1968–1971 assessed residents' usual source of and travel time to care in 10 U.S. urban areas.	In 7 of 10 areas, persons with longer travel times (> 20 min) made fewer physician visits per year.

(Continued)

TABLE 9.2
(Continued)

Study	Type of Service	Sample (N)	Design	Findings
Okada & Wan (1980)	Ambulatory, hospital, and dental care	8,296 in 1969–1971; 7,595 in 1975 (gender unspecified)	Survey assessment of health services use before (1969–1971) and after (1975) 5 new CHCs opened in California, Missouri, Georgia, South Carolina, and Massachusetts.	New CHCs associated with decreased travel time and increased medical and dental care utilization.
Simon & Smith (1973)	University of Rochester student health services	485 visits before and 297 visits after a change in location	Retrospective chart review of utilization of services over a 9-month period that surrounded the move.	After the move, mean travel time increased from 5–10 min to 20 min and utilization decreased, but the change was significant only for respiratory problems.
Solis, Marks, Garcia, & Shelton (1990)	Preventive health services (dental, physical, eye, and breast exams, Pap smears)	4,811 Hispanic Americans (57% female) in 7 states	Use of preventive services and access to care assessed using data for 1982–1984 from the Hispanic Health and Nutrition Examination Survey.	Travel distance to a health care facility unrelated to utilization among all subgroups except Puerto Ricans, who were receiving relatively higher levels of government-subsidized care.
Yesalis, Wallace, Burmeister, & Fisher (1980)	General medical care in a CHC	829 (49% male)	Household interviews before (1972) and after (1977) a CHC opened in rural Iowa assessed utilization and access to care during the prior year.	After the CHC opened, travel time decreased significantly, and the number of participants who reported > 1 annual physician visit increased from 64.3% to 76.2%.

Maternal and child health care

Bronstein & Morrisey (1992)	Hospital childbirth services	1,331 in 1983; 1,168 in 1988 (100% female)	Hospital discharge data for April 1983 and 1988 used to identify predictors of rural pregnant women's decisions to bypass the nearest hospital for obstetric care elsewhere.	40% of women in 1983 and 45% in 1988 bypassed the nearest rural hospital; 41% in 1983 and 68% in 1988 traveled to metropolitan hospitals, many with neonatal units. Bypassing occurred more frequently when travel time to the nearest hospital was relatively long.
Coffey (1983)	Comprehensive female medical care	960 females	1-year (1977) retrospective interview on choice of provider, entry demand, and physician visits from the Women's Community Health Care Survey.	Total time price (travel, waiting, and treatment time) had a small inverse relation with the probability of using medical care (elasticity = −.09). Time price of alternative activities were included in the model and held constant.
Hilker (1978)	ED services	652 children (gender unspecified)	Parents who brought their child to the ED at Akron, Ohio's Children's Hospital during 2 months in 1977 completed a questionnaire that assessed travel time and physician availability and contact for nonurgent care.	61% of parents who used the ED for nonurgent care lived < 15 min away; 80% had a local physician for their child, but only 38% had tried to contact the physician before coming to the ED.
McDonald & Coburn (1988)	Prenatal care	1,904 females	Stratified random sample of mothers who gave birth between February–August 1983 surveyed by mail concerning prenatal care.	Greater travel time associated with delayed initiation of prenatal care after the first trimester and a lower ratio of actual to prescribed prenatal check-ups.

(Continued)

TABLE 9.2
(Continued)

Study	Type of Service	Sample (N)	Design	Findings
Studnicki (1975)	Hospital childbirth services	16,080 women who had live births	Birth registry data for 1969 from 16 Baltimore hospitals used to assess percent of births at the nearest hospital and extra travel time needed to reach the hospital used.	Distance to hospital unrelated to utilization; only 25% of live births occurred at the nearest hospital. Race and financial issues influenced hospital choice.
Inpatient medical care				
Adams, Houchens, Wright, & Robbins (1991)	Hospital choice	12,266 discharged patients (gender unspecified)	1986 HCFA data on Medicare patients used to assess travel patterns to hospitals in rural Minnesota and eastern North and South Dakota.	Sixty percent chose the nearest hospital, and increased distance deterred choice of an alternative. Odds of hospital choice were nearly proportional to the inverse logarithm of patient travel distance.
Cohen & Lee (1985)	Hospital choice	130,876 patient records	Hospital discharge data from 14 acute-care general hospitals in Rhode Island (RI) related to	Travel time was the most heavily weighted factor in hospital choice and was more influential on choices for adults than for children.

Author (Year)	Topic	Data/Methods	Findings
Goodman, Fisher, Stukel, & Chang (1997)	Hospitalization	2.1 million adults (52% female); 3.5 million children (49% female) travel time data collected by the RI Statewide Planning Agency. Cross-sectional regression analysis of hospitalization rates for 72 service areas in Maine, New Hampshire, and Vermont.	Living further away from a hospital reduced medical hospitalization rates, but this trend diminished for serious "low variation" conditions like strokes, heart attacks, and cancer surgery. Findings suggested underutilization by distant residents and overutilization by proximal residents.
Ozminkowski, Friedman, & Taylor (1993)	Heart and liver transplantation	272 heart (19% female) and 200 liver (56% female) transplant patients. Discharge data from the Hospital Cost and Utilization Project that covered > 500 hospitals used to assess the relation between patient residences and probability of receiving a transplant during 1986–1987	Probability of receiving a transplant unrelated to the distance patients would have had to travel for the surgery.

Note. VA = Veterans Administration; CMHC = community mental health center; GP = general practitioner; CHC = community health center; ED = emergency department; HCFA = Health Care Financing Administration.

of the studies was an experiment and, unless otherwise noted, the research was conducted in the United States. The great majority of studies (73.5%) showed a significant inverse relation between travel time or distance and a measure of utilization, and some studies in all categories of care yielded significant results. As shown in Table 9.2, only a few studies reported time price elasticities (Acton, 1973a; Conrad, Grembowski, & Milgrom, 1987; Holtmann & Olsen, 1976; Miners, Greene, Salber, & Scheffler, 1978; White, 1986). These varied from −.031 for insured dental services (Conrad et al., 1987) to −1.00 for ambulatory medical care in the public sector (Acton, 1973a), with most being in the −.25 to −.40 range.

The results showed that, like the generalized effects of appointment delays on utilization, greater travel requirements reduced utilization across a range of health and behavioral health services. Nevertheless, with the exception of Hoening and Ragg (1966), the predicted inverse relation between travel time and utilization was uniformly significant among studies of dental and behavioral health care, which constitute the more elastic end of the demand continuum with respect to monetary price, whereas the remaining studies with negative or contradictory findings (Bronstein & Morrisey, 1992; Hays, Kearns, & Moran, 1990; Kreher, Hickner, Ruffin, & Lin, 1995; Krishan, Drummond, Naessens, Nobrega, & Smoldt, 1985; Ozminkowski, Friedman, & Taylor, 1993; Solis, Marks, Garcia, & Shelton, 1990; Studnicki, 1975) were distributed over the three categories of medical care.

With one exception, however, there was no easily discernible pattern with respect to the kinds of medical care investigated in studies that did or did not yield significant results. The exception was studies of hospital obstetric care during childbirth (Bronstein & Morrisey, 1992; Studnicki, 1975), which failed to show an inverse relation between travel time or distance and utilization. As discussed by Bronstein and Morrisey, the observed trend for women in more rural areas to bypass local hospitals in favor of urban hospitals appeared to reflect the availability of specialized care, such as neonatal intensive care units, in the latter but not in the former settings. This result is not surprising conceptually, if it can be assumed that the relative reward value curve associated with access to specialized services outweighs the costs associated with greater travel or other direct costs, which is a pattern that would be expected for highly valued health outcomes such as childbirth or care of serious, life-threatening health problems that can best be treated in tertiary medical centers. In a related vein, Ozminkowski et al. (1993) found that patterns of liver and heart transplantation were unrelated to the distance that patients lived from a specialized transplant center.

Another variable that appears to affect the strength of association between travel time and utilization is provider density, which tends to covary directly with population density, distance to facilities, and availability of transportation. Travel time was found to be less influential in urban areas that had many providers concentrated in a relatively small geographic area and to be more influential in rural areas that had fewer providers and entailed more variability in travel time, distance, and the availability of transportation (e.g., Breakey & Kaminsky, 1982; Grytten, 1991; Hays et al., 1990; Studnicki, 1975). For example, in a longitudinal study of dental care utilization in Norway (Grytten, 1991), travel time was inversely related to utilization in 1975, but not in 1985, a pattern that was attributed to the growth in providers and increased urbanization and automobile travel that took place during the decade between assessments. Moreover, the more dense an urban area, the greater the competition among hospitals and other health care providers for patients, which typically introduces a complex array of interacting economic forces that would be expected to further obscure the effects of travel time (cf. Morrill, Earickson, & Rees, 1970).

Some evidence also suggested that, in urban areas with many care options, easy access in the form of minimal distance to facilities may promote substitution of services and lead to higher costs in some instances. Hilker (1978), for example, found that most parents who brought their child to an emergency department (ED) for nonurgent care lived within 15 min of the facility and that 80% of them had a physician in the area, but only 38% had attempted to contact their doctor before using the ED. Similarly, in a comparison of hospitalization rates in three New England states as a function of the seriousness of the health problem (Goodman, Fisher, Stukel, & Chang, 1997), the closer that patients resided to a hospital, the more likely they were to receive inpatient care for less serious problems that could be treated on an outpatient basis. Distance did not influence hospitalizations for serious problems like strokes, heart attacks, and cancer.

Finally, as noted previously, the relative influence of time costs on demand for care has been found to increase with decreasing monetary costs of care (Acton, 1973a, 1973b; Conrad et al., 1987; Miners et al., 1978). For example, in low-income neighborhoods in New York City, time prices exerted more effect on medical care utilization than did monetary price (Acton, 1973a), and when medical care was free, utilization was inversely related to travel distance (Acton, 1973b). Similarly, using a rural sample with low out-of-pocket monetary costs, Miners et al. found that travel time had a greater impact on demand for primary care than did monetary price and, using an insured sample with low monetary price elasticities, Conrad et al. found that travel time elasticities were negatively related to demand for dental services.

Taken together, this research indicates that, with some notable qualifications, travel time or distance is inversely related to demand for health and behavioral health services. The relation tends to be stronger when the monetary cost of care is a relatively smaller proportion of the total cost. The relation tends to be attenuated in urban compared to rural areas, where the restricted range of travel time and distance appears to do little to deter utilization, but where the easy access and minimal time costs afforded by multiple providers may stimulate costly substitutions among ambulatory and hospital-based care. Rural residents appear to be more sensitive to travel costs except for services that have a high value or require specialized care that is available only at distant locations.

RELATIONSHIP OF OFFICE WAITING TIME
TO UTILIZATION

Six studies included in Table 9.1 (Alpert, 1964) or Table 9.2 (Acton, 1973a; Conrad et al., 1987; Grytten, 1991; Holtmann & Olsen, 1976; Miners et al., 1978) also investigated the relation between office waiting time and utilization. Several other studies reported findings relevant to office waiting time, but did not meet all criteria for inclusion in either table (e.g., House, 1981; Sisk et al., 1996; Wolinski & Marder, 1983). Of the six studies included in the tables, all three dental care studies found significant negative elasticities between office waiting time and demand (Conrad et al., 1987; Grytten, 1991; Holtmann & Olsen, 1976), the two studies of outpatient medical care found negative but nonsignificant elasticities (Acton, 1973a; Miners et al., 1978), and the one pediatric care study found no association between office waiting time and appointment-keeping (Alpert, 1964). The small number of studies precludes firm conclusions, but the pattern of results suggests that office waiting time reduces demand relatively more for health services that also are more sensitive to changes in monetary price (e.g., dental care).

The research is too limited to permit clear inferences about the relative influence on demand of office waiting time in relation to other time costs. Simultaneous analyses of appointment delays and office waiting times (Whitney et al., 1997; Wolinski & Marder, 1983) revealed them to be distinct variables associated with different medical, provider, and patient characteristics. For example, physician age was positively correlated with appointment delays but negatively correlated with office waiting times for medical care (Wolinski & Marder, 1983), and appointment delays and office waiting times for dental care were negatively correlated with each other (Whitney et al., 1997). Furthermore, demand for care at public outpatient facilities had an office waiting time elasticity twice that of care at private physician offices (Acton, 1973a). In relation to travel time, Conrad et al. (1987), who studied dental care utilization with an insured sample, reported greater elasticities for office waiting time than for travel time, whereas Acton (1973a), who studied health care utilization with a lower income, urban sample, reported greater elasticities for travel time than for office waiting time.

It is clearer from studies of dental care that higher monetary prices are associated with reduced office waits, but not with shorter appointment delays, and that patients will pay higher monetary prices to avoid long office waits (House, 1981; Whitney et al., 1997). This differential is consistent with the observation cited previously that individuals appear to be more risk-averse with respect to uncertain time- than monetary-cost outcomes, perhaps due to the nonfungible nature of time (LeClerc et al., 1995). The unpredictability of office waits may contribute to the disutility of the experience, and patient satisfaction has been found to decrease with increasing waiting duration (e.g., Kurata, Watanabe, McBride, & Kawai, 1994; Sisk et al., 1996). For example, compared to conventional Medicaid patients, Medicaid managed care enrollees had significantly shorter appointment and office waiting times, and these differences translated into higher satisfaction ratings with providers in managed care plans (Sisk et al., 1996). Similarly, in a comparison of U.S. and Japanese hospital services, U.S. patients reported greater satisfaction, a finding attributed to the lack of an appointment scheduling system in Japan (Kurata et al., 1994). Procedures successfully used to reduce office waiting time or patient dissatisfaction with waits include (a) providing patients with information on how long they must wait (Hui & Zhou, 1996), (b) using problem-based rather than time-based scheduling (Callahan & Redmon, 1987), and (c) using computer systems to track patients and to simulate medical care delivery operations to identify sources of delay and other impediments to care (e.g., Benussi, Matthews, Daris, Crevatin, & Nedoclan, 1990; Saunders, Makens, & Leblanc, 1989).

In summary, although less well researched, office waiting time, like appointment delays and travel time, was found in several studies to be inversely related to utilization, especially use of dental services. Although all three variable classes are inversely related to utilization, long office waits appear to have greater detrimental effects on patient satisfaction, and patients will pay higher monetary costs to reduce office waiting time.

DISCUSSION

The literature reviewed provides strong support for the predicted inverse relation between utilization and appointment delays, travel time, and office waiting time. Across a range of health and behavioral health services, utilization decreased as these time-related direct constraints on access increased. This pattern supports a central hypothesis derived from the conceptual framework shared by health and behavioral economics and was obtained from studies that included quantifiable measures of help-seeking behavior.

Time-related variables, however, have had a much more central place in behavioral economics than in health economics. Except for a brief focus on time costs during the period leading up to the national health care reform debate, the health economic literature has focused much more on the effects of monetary price on demand and has tended to convert time costs to monetary equivalents for study (e.g., Goldman & Grossman, 1978; Phelps, 1975). This empirical simplification is deemed necessary to represent the value of time, which varies across individuals, but, conceptually, it trivializes the fact that, unlike money, time resources are always finite, bounded by death, and are irreplaceable once spent. Furthermore, by pursuing the study of time-related variables as monetary equivalents, the temporal dynamics of choice behavior are lost as a conceptual or empirical focus. The behavioral economic perspective gives the study of behavior patterns through time primary emphasis in its theory and methods, generally treats money as a secondary reinforcer, and has established empirically that relative time allocation to activities in the available set is a viable measure of preference or value (e.g., Baum, 1973; Rachlin, Kagel, & Battalio, 1980). Time allocation patterns reveal preference structures, and their conversion to other metrics like money is not required, although preferences obviously can be studied as patterns of monetary allocation as well.

These variable emphases really are more differences in degree than differences in kind. Nevertheless, the findings of this review argue for greater emphasis on time-related variables in theory and research on demand for health and behavioral health care. Understanding the temporal dynamics of utilization patterns is especially important for applications where the goal is to alter rates and patterns of utilization, including in explicit health care rationing schemes.

Another area of variable emphasis in behavioral and health economic perspectives concerns the relative emphasis placed on studying own-price versus cross-price elasticity relations. As noted previously, studying direct constraints on the commodity of interest usually is easier because potential substitutes or complements often are unknown, and it is an appropriate starting point for empirical inquiry, as exemplified by this review. Nevertheless, health economists have tended to remain focused on how demand for health care varies as its own money price changes, whereas behavioral economists have been more attentive to how choice for one commodity is affected by the availability of alternatives and by the constraints that exist on access to all commodities in the available set. Direct constraints on access often have powerful effects in reducing demand, but it remains the case that these own-price elasticity relations can be modified, sometimes quite substantially, by the presence of complements or substitutes that are available under conditions of variable constraint (Vuchinich, 1997). Coffey (1983) discussed this issue as it applies to relations between the money and time price of health care and concluded that some of the inconsistencies in the research on time costs occurred because the time cross-prices of alternative activities had not been considered and were variable across studies. In particular, to the extent that time prices of nonhealth activities are not constant, ". . . the time [own] price elasticity is underestimated" (Coffey, 1983, p. 409).

This issue has several implications for future work on the present topic. First, the demonstrated reduction in utilization as a function of time-related constraints on access supports an expansion of inquiry into how demand for health care varies with changes in the constraints on access to valued activities in other areas of functioning. Second, the medical sociology literature clearly suggests that this expansion should start in the domain of social contextual variables and in other areas of functioning (e.g., work) that are essential components of day-to-day behavior patterns (cf. chapters 5 and 6, this volume). This literature suggests that preserving or regaining access to valued rewards in these areas may bear substantial cross-price elasticity relations with health care utilization that, in some cases, may overshadow the effects of direct constraints on access. In this regard, the studies reviewed that did not find the predicted inverse relation between travel time and utilization involved health services with a highly valued outcome (successful childbirth) or entailed specialized treatment of life-threatening illnesses that was available only at distant locations. Third, the effects of social and other nonhealth variables on utilization patterns should be most apparent when the direct constraints on health care access are constant and, as suggested by Coffey (1983), the converse should hold with respect to detecting the effects of direct constraints on health care access. As a practical matter for future research, this suggests that studies of the role of social contextual variables on utilization would be most informative when the money and time costs of treatment are held relatively constant.

In conclusion, behavioral economics organizes the variable classes highlighted in the medical sociology and health economic literatures in a functional and temporally extended framework that is both simplifying and powerful. The research evidence concerning the effects of time-related constraints in reducing utilization supports an expansion of inquiry into how social and other nonhealth-related functional variables affect utilization patterns, thus integrating the social and price variables emphasized in these heretofore distinct literatures. This type of analysis has proven useful as an organizing framework for basic and applied research on alcohol and drug abuse. Extending it to the study of health care utilization builds on the contributions of these other disciplines and offers an established approach to studying environment–behavior relations through time. The latter feature is unique to behavioral economics and one that has utility for guiding clinical applications.

ACKNOWLEDGMENTS

Manuscript preparation was supported in part by grants #R01 AA08972 and K02 AA00209 from the National Institute on Alcohol Abuse and Alcoholism.

REFERENCES

Acton, J. P. (1973a). *Demand for health care among the urban poor, with special emphasis on the role of time* (R–1151–OEO/NYC). New York: New York City Rand Institute.

Acton, J. P. (1973b). *Demand for health care when time prices vary more than money prices* (R–1189–OEO/NYC). New York: New York City Rand Institute.

Adams, E. K., Houchens, R., Wright, G. E., & Robbins, J. (1991). Predicting hospital choice for rural Medicare beneficiaries: The role of severity of illness. *Health Services Research, 26,* 583–612.

Aday, L. A., & Andersen, R. M. (1974). A framework for the study of access to medical care. *Health Services Research, 9,* 208–220.

Addenbrooke, W. M., & Rathod, N. H. (1990). Relationship between waiting time and retention in treatment amongst substance abusers. *Drug and Alcohol Dependence, 26,* 255–264.

Ainslie, G. (1992). *Picoeconomics: The strategic interaction of successive motivational states within the person.* Cambridge, England: Cambridge University Press.

Ajzen, I., & Fishbein, M. (1977). Attitude–behavior relations: A theoretical analysis and review of empirical research. *Psychological Bulletin, 84,* 888–918.

Alpert, J. J. (1964). Broken appointments. *Pediatrics, 34,* 127–132.

Andersen, R. M. (1995). Revisiting the behavioral model and access to medical care: Does it matter? *Journal of Health and Social Behavior, 36,* 1–10.

Baekeland, F., & Lundwall, L. (1975). Dropping out of treatment: A critical review. *Psychological Bulletin, 82,* 738–783.

Baum, W. M. (1973). The correlation based law of effect. *Journal of the Experimental Analysis of Behavior, 20,* 137–153.

Becker, M. H., & Maiman, L. A. (1975). Sociobehavioral determinants of compliance with health and medical care recommendations. *Medical Care, 13,* 10–14.

Benjamin-Bauman, J., Reiss, M. L., & Bailey, J. S. (1984). Increasing appointment keeping by reducing the call-appointment interval. *Journal of Applied Behavior Analysis, 17,* 295–301.

Benussi, G., Matthews, L., Daris, F., Crevatin, E., & Nedoclan, G. (1990). Improving patient flow in ambulatory care through computerized evaluation techniques. *Revue de Epidemiologie et de Sante Publique, 38,* 221–226.

Breakey, W. R., & Kaminsky, M. J. (1982). An assessment of Jarvis' law in an urban catchment area. *Hospital & Community Psychiatry, 33,* 661–663.

Bronstein, J. M., & Morrisey, M. A. (1992). Bypassing rural hospitals for obstetrics care. *Journal of Health Politics, Policy and Law, 16,* 87–118.

Callahan, N. M., & Redmon, W. K. (1987). Effects of problem-based scheduling on patient waiting and staff utilization of time in a pediatric clinic. *Journal of Applied Behavior Analysis, 20,* 193–199.

Carpenter, P. J., Morrow, G. R., Del Gaudio, A. C., & Ritzler, B. A. (1981). Who keeps the first outpatient appointment? *American Journal of Psychiatry, 138,* 102–105.

Carroll, M. E. (1993). The economic context of drug and non-drug reinforcers affects acquisition and maintenance of drug-reinforced behavior and withdrawal effects. *Drug and Alcohol Dependence, 33,* 201–210.

Chafetz, M. E., Blane, H. T., & Hill, M. J. (Eds.). (1970). *Frontiers of alcoholism.* New York: Science House.

Coffey, R. M. (1983). The effect of time price on the demand for medical care services. *Journal of Human Resources, 18,* 407–424.

Cohen, M. A., & Lee, H. L. (1985). The determinants of spatial distribution of hospital utilization in a region. *Medical Care, 23,* 27–38.

Conrad, D. A., Grembowski, D., & Milgrom, P. (1987). Dental care demand: Insurance effects and plan design. *Health Services Research, 22,* 341–367.

Cullis, J. G., & Jones, P. R. (1986). Rationing by waiting lists: An implication. *American Economic Review, 81,* 297–301.

Cunningham, P. J., & Cornelius, L. J. (1995). Access to ambulatory care for American Indians and Alaska Natives: The relative importance of personal and community resources. *Social Science & Medicine, 40,* 393–407.

DeGrandpre, R. J., Bickel, W. K., Hughes, J. R., & Higgins, S. T. (1992). Behavioral economics of drug self-administration: III. A reanalysis of nicotine regulation hypothesis. *Psychopharmacology, 108,* 1–10.

De Leon, G. (1988). Legal pressure in therapeutic communities. *Journal of Drug Issues, 18,* 625–640.

Deyo, R. A., & Inui, T. S. (1980). Dropouts and broken appointments: A literature review and agenda for future research. *Medical Care, 18,* 1146–1157.

DiMatteo, M. R., & DiNicola, D. D. (1982). *Achieving patient compliance: The psychology of the medical practitioner's role.* New York: Pergamon.

Donovan, D. M., Rosengren, D. B., Downey, L. M., Cox, G., & Sloan, K. (1997, November). *Motivational interventions to enhance treatment entry among treatment seeking drug abusers.* Paper presented at the annual meeting of the Association for the Advancement of Behavior Therapy, Miami, FL.

Ell, K., Haywood, L. J., Sobel, E., deGuzman, M., Blumfield, D., & Ning, J.-P. (1994). Acute chest pain in African Americans: Factors in the delay in seeking emergency care. *American Journal of Public Health, 84,* 965–970.

Epstein, L. H., & Cluss, P. A. (1982). A behavioral medicine perspective on adherence to long-term medical regimens. *Journal of Consulting and Clinical Psychology, 50,* 950–971.

Fehr, B. J., Weinstein, S., Sterling, R. C., & Gottheil, E. (1991). "As soon as possible": An initial treatment engagement strategy. *Substance Abuse, 12,* 183–189.

Feldman, R. (1994). The cost of rationing medical care by insurance coverage and by waiting. *Health Economics, 3,* 361–372.

Festinger, D. S., Lamb, R. J., Kirby, K. C., & Marlowe, D. B. (1996). The accelerated intake: A method for increasing initial attendance to outpatient cocaine treatment. *Journal of Applied Behavior Analysis, 29,* 387–389.

Festinger, D. S., Lamb, R. J., Kountz, M. R., Kirby, K. C., & Marlowe, D. (1995). Pretreatment dropout as a function of treatment delay and client variables. *Addictive Behaviors, 20,* 111–115.

Fiedler, J. L., & Wight, J. B. (1989). *The medical offset effect and pubic health policy.* New York: Praeger.

Finnerty, F. A., Shaw, L. W., & Himmelsbach, C. K. (1973). Hypertension in the inner city: II. Detection and follow-up. *Circulation, 47,* 76–78.

Folkins, C., Hersch, P., & Dahlen, D. (1980). Waiting time and no-show rate in a Community Mental Health Center. *American Journal of Community Psychology, 8,* 121–123.

Fortney, J. C., Booth, B. M., Blow, F. C., Bunn, J. Y., & Cook, C. A. L. (1995). The effects of travel barriers and age on the utilization of alcoholism treatment aftercare. *American Journal of Drug & Alcohol Abuse, 21,* 391–406.

Foster, R. S., Lang, S. P., Costanza, M. C., Worden, J. K., Haines, C. R., & Yates, J. W. (1978). Breast self-examination practices and breast-cancer stage. *New England Journal of Medicine, 299,* 265–270.

Gallant, D. M., Bishop, M. P., Stoy, B., Faulkner, M. A., & Paternostro, L. (1966). The value of a "first contact" group intake session in an alcoholism outpatient clinic: Statistical confirmation. *Psychosomatics, 7,* 349–352.

Garfield, S. L. (1986). Research on client variables in psychotherapy. In S. L. Garfield & A. E. Bergin (Eds.), *Handbook of psychotherapy and behavior change* (3rd ed., pp. 213–256). New York: Wiley.

Gates, S. J., & Colborn, D. K. (1976). Lowering appointment rates in a neighborhood health center. *Medical Care, 14,* 263–267.

Goldman, F., & Grossman, M. (1978). The demand for pediatric care: An hedonic approach. *Journal of Political Economy, 86,* 259–280.

Goodman, D. C., Fisher, E., Stukel, T. A., & Chang, C. (1997). The distance to community medical care and the likelihood of hospitalization: Is closer always better? *American Journal of Public Health, 87,* 1144–1150.

Greenfield, L., Brady, J. V., Besteman, K. J., & De Smet, A. (1996). Patient retention in mobile and fixed-site methadone maintenance treatment. *Drug & Alcohol Dependence, 42,* 125–131.

Grieves, R. E. (1973). An analysis of service delay and client variables as they relate to mental health center pre-therapy dropout. *Dissertation Abstracts International, 34,* 2126B.

Grossman, M. (1972). *The demand for health: A theoretical and empirical investigation.* New York: National Bureau of Economic Research and Columbia University Press.

Grytten, J. (1991). Effect of time costs on demand for dental services among adults in Norway in 1975 and 1985. *Community Dentistry & Oral Epidemiology, 19,* 190–194.

Harrison, J. A., Mullen, P. D., & Green, L. W. (1992). A meta-analysis of studies of the health belief model with adults. *Health Education Research, 7,* 107–116.

Haynes, R. B., Taylor, D. W., & Sackett, D. L. (Eds.). (1979). *Compliance in health care.* Baltimore: Johns Hopkins University Press.

Hays, S. M., Kearns, R. A., & Moran, W. (1990). Spatial patterns of attendance at general practitioner services. *Social Science & Medicine, 31,* 773–781.

Hershey, J. C., Luft, H. S., & Gianaris, J. M. (1975). Making sense out of utilization data. *Medical Care, 13,* 838–854.

Higgins, S. T., & Budney, A. J. (1997). From the initial clinic contact to aftercare: A brief review of effective strategies for retaining cocaine abusers in treatment. In L. S. Onken, J. D. Blaine, & J. J. Boren (Eds.), *Beyond the therapeutic alliance: Keeping the drug-dependent individual in treatment* (NIDA Research Monograph No. 165, pp. 25–43). Rockville, MD: National Institute of Drug Abuse, National Institutes of Health.

Hilker, T. I. (1978). Nonemergency visits to a pediatric emergency department. *JACEP, 7,* 3–8.

Hodgkin, D. (1996). Household characteristics affecting where mothers deliver in rural Kenya. *Health Economics, 5,* 333–340.

Hoenig, J., & Ragg, N. (1966). The non-attending psychiatric outpatient: An administrative problem. *Medical Care, 4,* 96–100.

Holtmann, A. G., & Olsen, E. O. (1976). The demand for dental care: A study of consumption and household production. *Journal of Human Resources, 11,* 546–560.

Hotchkiss, D. R. (1998). The tradeoff between price and quality of services in the Philippines. *Social Science & Medicine, 46,* 227–242.

House, D. R. (1981). A full-price approach to the dental market: Implications for price determination. *Journal of Health, Policy and Law, 5,* 593–607.

Hui, M., & Zhou, L. (1996). How does waiting time duration information influence consumers' reactions to waiting for services? *Journal of Applied Social Psychology, 26,* 1702–1717.

Hyslop, A., & Kershaw, P. W. (1981). Non-attenders at an alcoholism referral clinic. *Health Bulletin, 39,* 29–42.

Institute of Medicine (1993). *Access to health care in America.* Washington, DC: National Academy Press.

Janis, I. L., & Mann, L. (1977). *Decision making: A psychological analysis of conflict, choice, and commitment.* New York: Free Press.

Kirk, B. A., & Frank, A. C. (1976). Zero interviews. *Journal of Counseling Psychology, 23,* 286–288.

Korner, H. (1964). Abolishing the waiting list in a mental health center. *American Journal of Psychiatry, 120,* 1097–1100.

Kreher, N. E., Hickner, J. M., Ruffin, M. T., & Lin, C. S. (1995). Effect of distance and travel time on rural women's compliance with screening mammography: An UPRNet study. Upper Peninsula Research Network. *Journal of Family Practice, 40,* 143–147.

Krishan, I., Drummond, D. C., Naessens, J. M., Nobrega, F. T., & Smoldt, R. K. (1985). Impact of increased physician supply on use of health services: A longitudinal analysis of rural Minnesota. *Public Health Reports, 100,* 379–386.

Kurata, J. H., Watanabe, Y., McBride, C., & Kawai, K. (1994). A comparative study of patient satisfaction with health care in Japan and the United States. *Social Science & Medicine, 39,* 1069–1076.

Leclerc, F., Schmitt, B. H., & Dube, L. (1995). Waiting time and decision making: Is time like money? *Journal of Consumer Research, 22,* 110–119.

Leigh, G., Ogborne, A. C., & Cleland, P. (1984). Factors associated with patient dropout form an outpatient alcoholism treatment service. *Journal of Studies on Alcohol, 45,* 359–362.

Macharia, W. M., Leon, G., Rowe, B. H., Stephenson, B. J., & Haynes, B. (1992). An overview of interventions to improve compliance with appointment keeping for medical services. *Journal of the American Medical Association, 267,* 1813–1817.

Maddux, J. F. (1993). Improving retention on methadone maintenance. In J. Inciardi, F. Times, & B. Fletcher (Eds.), *Innovative approaches in the treatment of drug abuse: Program models and strategies* (pp. 21–33). Westport, CT: Greenwood.

Marcus, S. C., Olfson, M., Fortney, J. C., & Ryan, N. D. (1997). Travel distance to subspecialty and general mental health services. *Psychiatric Services, 48,* 775.

Marlatt, G. A., Tucker, J. A., Donovan, D. M., & Vuchinich, R. E. (1997). Help-seeking by substance abusers: The role of harm reduction and behavioral-economic approaches to facilitate treatment entry and retention. In L. S. Onken, J. D. Blaine, & J. J. Boren (Eds.), *Beyond the therapeutic alliance: Keeping the drug-dependent individual in treatment* (NIDA Research Monograph No. 165, pp. 44–84). Rockville, MD: National Institute of Drug Abuse, National Institutes of Health.

Matarazzo, J. D., Weiss, S. M., Herd, J. A., Miller, N. E., & Weiss, S. M. (Eds.). (1984). *Behavioral health: A handbook of health enhancement and disease prevention.* New York: Wiley.

Mattson, M. E., & Del Boca, F. K. (1998). Compliance with treatment and follow-up protocols in Project MATCH: Predictors and relationship to outcome. *Alcoholism: Clinical & Experimental Research, 22,* 1328–1339.

Mayer, J. (1972). Initial alcoholism clinic attendance of patients with legal referrals. *Quarterly Journal of Studies on Alcohol, 33,* 814–816.

Mayer, J., Needham, M. A., & Myerson, D. J. (1965). Contact and initial attendance at an alcoholism clinic. *Quarterly Journal of Studies on Alcohol, 26,* 480–485.

McDonald, T. P., & Coburn, A. F. (1988). Predictors of prenatal care utilization. *Social Science & Medicine, 27,* 167–72.

Mechanic, D. (1979). Correlates of physician utilization: Why do major multivariate studies of physician utilization find trivial psychosocial and organizational effects. *Journal of Health and Social Behavior, 20,* 387–396.

Mechanic, D. (1983). The experience and express of distress: The study of illness behavior and medical utilization. In D. Mechanic (Ed.), *Handbook of health, health care, and the health professions* (pp. 591–607). New York: Free Press.

Mechanic, D. (1994). *Inescapable decisions: The imperatives of health reform.* New Brunswick, NJ: Transaction.

Mechanic, D., Schlesinger, M., & McAlpine, D. D. (1995). Management of mental health and substance abuse services: State of the art and early results. *Milbank Quarterly, 73,* 19–55.

Meichenbaum, D., & Turk, D. C. (1987). *Facilitating treatment adherence: A practitioner's guidebook.* New York: Plenum.

Mejta, C. L., Bokos, P. J., Mickenberg, J., Maslar, M. E., & Senay, E. (1997). Improving substance abuse treatment access and retention using a case management approach. *Journal of Drug Issues, 27,* 329–340.

Miller, W. R. (1985). Motivation for treatment: A review with special emphasis on alcoholism. *Psychological Bulletin, 98,* 84–107.

Miller, W. R., & Rollnick, S. (1991). *Motivational interviewing: Preparing people to change addictive behavior.* New York: Guilford.

Miners, L. A., Greene, S. B., Salber, E. J., & Scheffler, R. M. (1978). Demand for medical care in a rural setting: Racial comparisons. *Health Services Research, 13,* 261–275.

Miyake, S. M., Chemtob, C. M., & Torigoe, R. Y. (1985). The effects of decreasing delays in appointments on patients' failure to keep appointments. *International Journal of Partial Hospitalization, 3,* 131–135.

Morrill, R. L., Earickson, R. J., & Rees, P. (1970). Factors influencing distances traveled to hospitals. *Economic Geography, 46,* 161–171.

Morrisey, M. A. (1992). *Price sensitivity in health care: Implications for health care policy.* Washington, DC: National Federation of Independent Business Foundation.

Mumford, E., Schlesinger, H. J., Glass, G. V., Patrick, C., & Cuerdon, T. (1984). A new look at evidence about reduced cost of medical utilization following mental health treatment. *American Journal of Psychiatry, 141,* 1145–1158.

National Health Planning and Resources Development Act of 1974, Pub. L. No. 93–641, § 3, 88 Stat. 2227 (1976).

National Institutes of Health. (1997). Interventions to prevent HIV risk behaviors. *NIH Consensus Statement, 15*(2), 1–41.

Newacheck, P. W., Hughes, D. C., & Stoddard, J. J. (1996). Children's access to primary care: differences by race, income, and insurance status. *Pediatrics, 97,* 26–32.

Newhouse, J. P. (1978). *The economics of medical care: A policy perspective.* Reading, MA: Addison-Wesley.

Newhouse, J. P. & The Insurance Experiment Group. (1993). *Free for all? Lessons from the RAND Health Insurance Experiment.* Cambridge, MA: Harvard University Press.

Noonan, J. R. (1973). A followup of pretherapy dropouts. *Journal of Community Psychology, 1,* 43–44.

Okada, L. M., & Sparer, G. (1976). Access to usual source of care by race and income in ten urban areas. *Journal of Community Health, 1,* 163–74.

Okada, L. M., & Wan, T. T. (1980). Impact of community health centers and Medicaid on the use of health services. *Public Health Reports, 95,* 520–34.

Onken, L. S., Blaine, J. D., & Boren, J. J. (Eds.). (1997). *Beyond the therapeutic alliance: Keeping the drug-dependent individual in treatment* (NIDA Research Monograph No. 165). Rockville, MD: National Institute of Drug Abuse, National Institutes of Health.

Oppenheim, G. L., Bergman, J. J., & English, E. C. (1979). Failed appointments: A review. *Journal of Family Practice, 8,* 789–796.

Orne, D. R., & Boswell, D. (1991). The pre-intake drop-out at a community mental health center. *Community Mental Health Journal, 27,* 375–379.

Ozminkowski, R. J., Friedman, B., & Taylor, Z. (1993). Access to heart and liver transplantation in the late 1980s. *Medical Care, 31,* 1027–1042.

Patch, V. D., Fisch, A., Levine, M. E., McKenna, G. J., & Raynes, A. E. (1973). A mortality study of waiting list patients in the Boston City Hospital methadone maintenance clinic. *Proceedings of the Fifth National Conference on Methadone Treatment* (pp. 523–529). New York: National Association for the Prevention of Addictions to Narcotics.

Person, P. H. (1962). Geographic variation in first admission rates to a state mental hospital. *Public Health Reports, 77,* 719–731.

Phelps, C. E. (1975). Effects of insurance on demand for medical care. In R. Andersen, J. Kravitz, & O. Anderson (Eds.), *Equity in health services: Empirical analyses in social policy* (pp. 105–130). Cambridge, MA: Ballinger.

Pringle, G. H. (1982). Impact of the criminal justice system on the substance abusers seeking professional help. *Journal of Drug Issues, 12,* 275–283.

Rachlin, H., Kagel, J. H., & Battalio, R. C. (1980). Substitutability in time allocation. *Psychological Review, 87,* 355–374.

Raynes, A. E., & Warren, G. (1971). Some characteristics of "drop-outs" at first contact with a psychiatric clinic. *Community Mental Health Journal, 7,* 144–150.

Regier, D. A., Narrow, W. E., Rae, D. S., Manderscheid, R. W., Locke, B. Z., & Goodwin, F. K. (1993). The de facto U.S. mental and addictive disorders service system. *Archives of General Psychiatry, 50,* 85–94.

Robin, A. (1976). Rationing out-patients: A defence of the waiting list. *British Journal of Psychiatry, 128,* 138–141.

Rosenstock, I. M. (1966). Why people use health services. *Milbank Memorial Fund Quarterly, 44,* 94–127.

Rosenstock, I. M., & Kirscht, J. P. (1979). Why people seek health care. In G. C. Stone, F. E. Cohen, & N. E. Adler (Eds.), *Health psychology—A handbook* (pp. 161–188). San Francisco: Jossey-Bass.

Saunders, C. E., Makens, P. K., & Leblanc, L. J. (1989). Modeling emergency department operations using advanced computer simulation systems. *Annals of Emergency Medicine, 18,* 134–140.

Shannon, G. W., & Bashshur, R. L. (1973). Time and distance: The journey for medical care. *International Journal of the Health Services, 3,* 237–244.

Shepard, D. S., & Moseley, T. A. E. (1976). Mailed versus telephoned appointment reminders to reduce broken appointments in a hospital outpatient department. *Medical Care, 14,* 268–269.

Simon, J. L., & Smith, D. B. (1973). Change in location of a student health service: A quasi-experimental evaluation of the effects of distance on utilization. *Medical Care, 11,* 59–67.

Sisk, J. E., Gorman, S. A., Reisinger, A. L., Glied, S. A., DuMouchel, W. H., & Hynes, M. M. (1996). Evaluation of Medicaid managed care: Satisfaction, access, and use. *Journal of the American Medical Association, 276,* 50–55.

Solis, J. M., Marks, G., Garcia, M., & Shelton, D. (1990). Acculturation, access to care, and use of preventive services by Hispanics: Findings from HANES 1982–84. *American Journal of Public Health, 80,* 11–19.

Stark, M. J. (1992). Dropping out of substance abuse treatment: A clinically oriented review. *Clinical Psychology Review, 12,* 93–116.

Stark, M. J., Campbell, B. K., & Brinkerhoff, C. V. (1990). "Hello, may we help you?" A study of attrition prevention at the time of the first phone contact with substance-abusing clients. *American Journal of Drub and Alcohol Abuse, 16,* 67–76.

Stern, M. S. (1977). Factors in the utilization of mental health centers and state hospitals. *Hospital & Community Psychiatry, 28,* 379–381.

Stitzer, M. L., & McCaul, M. E. (1987). Criminal justice interventions with drug and alcohol abusers. In E. K. Morris & C. J. Braukmann (Eds.), *Behavioral approaches to crime and delinquency: A handbook of application, research, and concepts* (pp. 331–360). New York: Plenum.

Studnicki, J. (1975). The minimization of travel effort as a delineating influence for urban hospital service areas. *International Journal of Health Services, 5,* 679–693.

Tuladhar, J. M. (1987). Effect of family planning availability and accessibility on contraceptive use in Nepal. *Studies in Family Planning, 18,* 49–53.

U.S. Department of Health, Education, and Welfare. (1978). *The national guidelines for health planning: Standards regarding the appropriate supply, distribution, and organization of health resources* (DHEW Publication No. HRA 79–645). Washington, DC: U.S. Government Printing Office.

Vissandjee, B., Barlow, R., & Fraser, D. W. (1997). Utilization of health services among rural women in Gujarat, India. *Public Health, 111,* 135–148.

Vuchinich, R. E. (1997). Behavioral economics of drug consumption. In B. A. Johnson & J. D. Roache (Eds.), *Drug addiction and its treatment: Nexus of neuroscience and behavior* (pp. 73–90). Philadephia: Lippincott.

Vuchinich, R. E., & Tucker, J. A. (1988). Contributions from behavioral theories of choice to an analysis of alcohol abuse. *Journal of Abnormal Psychology, 97,* 181–195.

Wanberg, K. W., & Jones, E. (1973). Initial contact and admissions of persons requesting treatment for alcohol problems. *British Journal of Addictions, 68,* 281–285.

Weisner, C. (1990). Coercion in alcohol treatment. In Institute of Medicine (Ed.), *Broadening the base of treatment for alcohol problems* (pp. 579–609). Washington, DC: National Academy Press.

White, S. L. (1986). Travel distance as time price and the demand for mental health services. *Community Mental Health Journal, 22,* 303–313.

Whitney, C. W., Milgrom, P., Conrad, D., Fiset, L., & O'Hara, D. (1997). The relationship between price of services, quality of care, and patient time costs for general dental practice. *Health Services Research, 31,* 773–790.

Wierzbicki, M., & Pekarik, G. (1993). A meta-analysis of psychotherapy dropout. *Professional Psychology: Research and Practice, 24,* 190–195.

Wolinski, F. D., & Marder, W. D. (1983). Waiting to see the doctor: The impact of organizational structure on medical practice. *Medical Care, 21,* 531–542.

Wolkon, G. H. (1972). Crisis theory, the application of treatment, and dependency. *Comprehensive Psychiatry, 13,* 459–464.

Woody, G., O'Hare, K., Mintz, J., & O'Brien, C. (1975). Rapid intake: A method for increasing retention rate of heroin addicts seeking methadone treatment. *Comprehensive Psychiatry, 16,* 165–169.

Yancovitz, S. R., Des Jarlais, D. C., Peyser, N. P., Drew, E., Friedmann, P., Trigg, H. L., & Robinson, J. W. (1991). A randomized trial of an interim methadone maintenance clinic. *American Journal of Public Health, 81,* 1185–1191.

Yesalis, C. E., Wallace, R. B., Burmeister, L. F., & Fisher, W. P. (1980). The effect of a group practice on rural health attitudes and behavior. *Medical Care, 18,* 44–58.

Zola, I. K. (1973). Pathways to the doctor—From person to patient. *Social Science & Medicine, 7,* 677–689.

CHAPTER TEN

Behavioral Economics of Tobacco Smoking

Kenneth A. Perkins
Mary E. Hickcox
James E. Grobe
University of Pittsburgh

Tobacco smoking remains the greatest preventable cause of mortality in the United States, accounting for at least 400,000 annual deaths, as well as 3 million worldwide (Peto et al., 1996). Primary prevention efforts have been instrumental in helping to reduce the prevalence of smoking in the United States from 40% to 25% of adults since the 1950s. However, in the 1990s this trend has flattened, and teenage smoking may be increasing (Giovino, Henningfield, Tomar, Escobedo, & Slade, 1995). Moreover, tobacco use is increasing in developing countries (Peto et al., 1996). Thus, improved interventions to help smokers quit will be needed in order to reduce further health costs due to tobacco.

Using a behavioral economics perspective, we describe factors that promote smoking behavior and smoking cessation interventions that counter these factors, mostly at the individual level but with some discussion of societal influences. After an overview of basic concepts in the behavioral economics of tobacco smoking, historical and individual factors that enhance smoking are presented. In general, the currently low social, behavioral, and economic response cost required to obtain nicotine reinforcement from smoking is the primary factor promoting smoking. The bulk of the chapter reviews various commonly employed interventions for smoking cessation, including behavioral counseling treatments as well as pharmacological strategies. Regardless of the approach, these interventions can be seen as increasing the response cost of smoking or reducing the cost of abstaining from smoking. Viewing interventions within a behavioral economics framework may enable clinical researchers to understand better the relations between smoking and other behaviors and to develop more efficacious interventions.

BASIC CONCEPTS IN BEHAVIORAL ECONOMICS
OF SMOKING

A behavioral economics perspective emphasizes factors that influence the demand curve for consumption (e.g. Bickel & DeGrandpre, 1996), in this case the relationship between the unit price of tobacco and its intake. *Unit price* reflects a reinforcer's behavioral, social, and economic response costs and is most appropriately viewed as a cost–benefit ratio for acquiring a given amount of that reinforcer (Hursh & Winger, 1995). The greater the unit price, the greater the behavior, money, and so forth needed to obtain a unit of the reinforcer. Consistent with a microeconomic model, when price is low, tobacco consumption changes little after an increase in unit price, indicating inelastic demand. However, when price is high, further increases in unit price result in rapid decline in consumption, indicating elastic demand at that point on the demand curve (DeGrandpre, Bickel, Hughes, & Higgins, 1992).

Elasticity of demand is important in understanding factors that can increase consumption and in determining the potential influence of interventions. Factors that can shift the demand curve for tobacco to the right, such that consumption level is maintained despite a substantial increase in unit price (*inelastic demand*), promote greater smoking and may relate to the onset of tobacco dependence. In contrast, factors that shift the demand curve to the left, such that consumption decreases with relatively small increases in unit price (*elastic demand*), may be useful in smoking cessation interventions. These shifts in the demand curve, and corresponding shifts in behavior to obtain smoking, are illustrated in the top panels of Fig. 10.1.

Furthermore, the elasticity of the demand curve for tobacco varies across individuals as a function of their degree of nicotine dependence, as shown in the bottom panels of Fig. 10.1. Smokers are considered dependent on nicotine if they meet the criteria of the fourth edition of the *Diagnostic and Statistical Manual of Mental Disorders* (American Psychiatric Association, 1994) for nicotine dependence, which generally require: a gradual increase in smoking to achieve desired effects (tolerance); occurrence of withdrawal symptoms upon quitting or cutting down; smoking more or for a longer period than intended; persistence of smoking despite a desire to cut down or quit or despite a knowledge of harm from continued use; and spending significant time or giving up significant activities in order to smoke. Eighty percent or more of smokers are considered nicotine-dependent (Giovino et al., 1995), although teens who are just starting to smoke and some adult smokers are nondependent. Some of the criteria for dependence can be seen as characterizing the magnitude of the response cost the smoker is willing to "pay" in order to smoke (persistence of use despite harm, giving up other activities, etc.). The relation between this cost per unit of smoking (*unit price*) and the consumption of smoking is essentially the smoker's demand curve for smoking. Thus, a dependent smoker may require a very large increase in unit price before consumption will decline (relatively inelastic demand). However, a nondependent smoker should require little increase in unit price for tobacco before consumption declines (elastic demand). This difference in demand curves suggests that modest steps may be sufficient to reduce smoking among some segments of the population (e.g. teenagers) but that more vigorous efforts may be necessary to reduce smoking among heavily dependent smokers, those also most likely to suffer the health consequences of smoking. A similar view of demand curves for alcohol as a function of alcohol dependence was presented by Heyman (1996).

Aside from changes in its unit price, smoking demand can be shifted as a function of the availability of alternative reinforcers (Bickel, DeGrandpre, & Higgins, 1995). If the price of an alternative increases, reducing its consumption, and this leads to increased smoking, then smoking and the alternative are considered *substitutes*. For example, cigars and cigarettes are substitutes if cigarette demand increases after a decline in cigar consumption due to an increase in cigar price. By contrast, if smoking decreases as a result of a decrease in the consumption of an alternative reinforcer, smoking and the alternative are considered *complements*. An example here would be a decline in smoking demand after a decline in alcohol consumption due to an increase in alcohol price. No change in smoking as a function of a change in consumption of an alternative reinforcer suggests that smoking and the alternative are independent.

SMOKING ONSET AND MAINTENANCE

In order to appreciate fully smoking cessation interventions, factors that promote the onset and maintenance of tobacco smoking behavior are useful to examine. The unit price of a reinforcer is not an immutable characteristic but varies depending on societal, economic, and behavioral costs or constraints. Moreover, the relation between unit price and consumption—the demand curve—can be shifted to the right or left due to other influences. Unit price and influences on demand curves can and do change over time. The evolution of tobacco products over the past few centuries may represent the best example of how these changes affect populationwide consumption of a reinforcer.

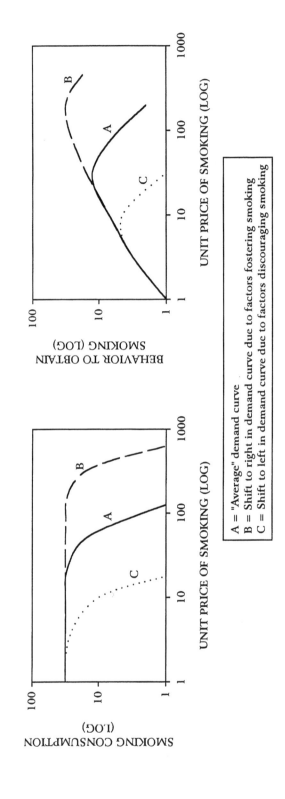

A = "Average" demand curve
B = Shift to right in demand curve due to factors fostering smoking
C = Shift to left in demand curve due to factors discouraging smoking

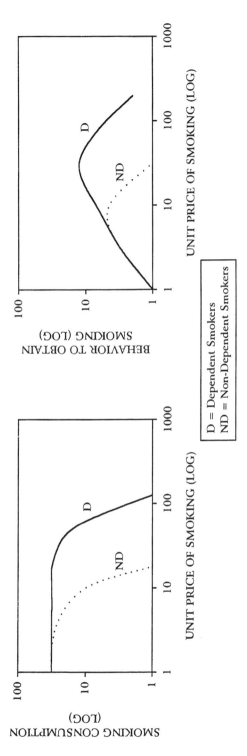

FIG. 10.1. Hypothetical relation between unit price of tobacco and consumption (demand curve) as a function of factors promoting or reducing smoking (top) and in tobacco dependent and nondependent smokers (bottom). Corresponding behavior to obtain smoking in each condition is shown in the right-hand side. The x and y axes are presented on log scales.

Reduction in Unit Price and the Historical Rise
of Tobacco Consumption

Changes in Societal Costs. Although tobacco usually has been legal in most societies and thus free of most societal constraints, some have always opposed tobacco and discouraged its use. Perhaps ironically, sixteenth-century European physicians opposed tobacco use not because they saw it as a risk to health but rather as a benefit—so much so that they feared its use would decrease the need for their services. At the time, tobacco was ground up and rubbed on sores in the hopes of healing them. Because of this belief, tobacco was sold as medicine in Europe. Tobacco use often was discouraged (and occasionally banned) in the 17th and 18th centuries by the rulers of a number of countries, making it difficult to obtain or use and thus keeping the unit price high.

The increase in democracy, along with the governmental benefits of taxing tobacco products, led to an easing of tobacco restrictions (and thus a reduction in its unit price) in Western countries during the nineteenth century (Slaby, 1991). Tobacco smoking became very socially accepted in the twentieth century, to the point where only a minority of men in the United States were nonsmokers by 1950 (Giovino et al., 1995). However, during the 1980s and 1990s, restrictions on its use indoors served to raise the unit price of smoking for most smokers by increasing the behavioral costs required for smoking (e.g. going outside). Similarly, increases in knowledge of its health risks made smoking less appealing, discouraging its use. This effect can be interpreted as reducing the overall reward value of smoking and shifting downward the demand curve for smoking. Nevertheless, cigarette smoking remains legal, inexpensive, and easily obtainable, which almost certainly contributes to its relative inelasticity of demand. Moreover, new tobacco products that generate little smoke are being developed by the industry to reduce some of the fears about the health consequences of smoking and to lessen behavioral costs of indoor smoking restrictions (Kluger, 1996).

Reductions in Economic and Behavioral Costs. Regardless of societal restrictions, tobacco use was somewhat limited before the 20th century, probably because its primary psychoactive ingredient, nicotine, was less readily absorbed via the most common methods of administration at the time—chewing and snuff. Nicotine is absorbed extremely rapidly by smoke inhalation, and tobacco smoking was relatively uncommon until the mid-nineteenth century due to the practical difficulties of having fire to keep pipes lit, the harshness of most tobacco, and the expense of cigarettes and cigars, which were wrapped by hand (Kluger, 1996; Slaby, 1991). Because of the rarity of tobacco smoking, tobacco use produced few adverse health consequences.

In the mid-19th century, several technological advances began to increase the ease and reduce the expense of smoking tobacco, thus greatly reducing its unit price. These advances included (a) invention of the safety match, which could be used as a portable lighting device and which made smoking possible virtually anywhere; (b) development of tobacco "blends" to reduce harshness of smoked tobacco; and (c) the paper rolling machine, which increased cigarette production and greatly reduced the monetary cost (Kluger, 1996). The result of this reduction in the unit price of smoking (along with the creation of modern marketing strategies; Kluger, 1996) was a dramatic increase in cigarette smoking in the first half of this century, from 54 cigarettes per capita (2% of all tobacco consumption) in 1900 to 4,345 cigarettes per capita (more than 80% of all consumption) in 1963 (Giovino et al., 1995; Slaby, 1991). This change in the form, moreso than the amount, of tobacco consumption produced the enormous rise in tobacco-related mortality from cardiovascular and lung diseases and cancers.

The changes in smoking caused by shifts in societal constraints and technology show how use of drugs can be influenced greatly by practical considerations and not just their pharmacology.

Low Unit Price Promotes Individual Smoking Behavior

Nicotine reaches the brain less than 20 seconds after smoke inhalation, perhaps faster even than drug intake by intravenous infusion. This rapidity of nicotine uptake is critical to the reinforcing effects of tobacco smoking (Henningfield & Keenan, 1993). Sensory effects of smoking tobacco (e.g., taste; Rose, Behm, & Levin, 1993) are also virtually immediate. Cigarettes enable smokers easily to alter the intensity with which they inhale tobacco smoke (e.g., number and volume of puffs) and thereby provide smokers with immediate control over their exposure to nicotine and other components of tobacco. These features contrast with most other tobacco products, such as chewing tobacco, and other methods of delivering nicotine, such as by gum or patch, all of which deliver nicotine much more slowly and with generally poorer control by the user over dosing (Henningfield & Keenan, 1993). Even most other drugs (e.g., caffeine, alcohol, powdered cocaine, intravenous heroin, amphetamine) lack this degree of control over the amount and timing of intake. Therefore, the unit price of nicotine reinforcement by cigarette smoking is less than that for all other tobacco products, as well as for most other drugs.

The influence of unit price on tobacco smoking consumption has been more directly examined in laboratory studies of smoking maintenance in dependent smokers. This research clearly shows that decreasing unit price by decreasing the behavior (such as responses on a computer key) required to obtain smoking increases consumption (e.g., Bickel, DeGrandpre, Hughes, & Higgins, 1991; Perkins, Epstein, Grobe, & Fonte, 1994; Perkins, Grobe, & Fonte, 1997). Providing an alternative reinforcer, such as money, shifts the demand curve for smoking to the left, and decreasing the magnitude of this alternative correspondingly increases smoking consumption (DeGrandpre & Bickel, 1995; Perkins et al., 1994). On a more practical note, packaging of cigarettes also makes their use very easy and convenient, keeping the behavioral cost low. Cigarettes usually come 20 to a pack, which is sufficient to meet the daily needs of a typical smoker. Their portability allows smoking to be done in conjunction with other activities (e.g., alcohol use), some of which complement smoking and shift the demand curve up or to the right.

In summary, the very low behavioral, economic, and social costs of reinforcement from smoking tobacco maintain its use among dependent smokers by keeping the unit price of smoking low. Interventions to reduce smoking must focus to some extent on countering this influence.

SMOKING CESSATION INTERVENTIONS

Smoking cessation interventions often focus on reversing factors that promote smoking and can be evaluated within a behavioral economic framework. Although they are rarely described as such, components of these treatments generally strive to increase tobacco's unit price or shift its demand curve down (i.e., less consumption at same unit price) or to the left. Unit price is increased by increasing the costs (behavioral, social, etc.) of smoking or reducing the amount (unit) of reinforcement from smoking. The demand curve also can be shifted to the left by decreasing the costs of abstaining, often by providing alternative reinforcers that substitute for smoking or otherwise attenuate aversive consequences of abstinence (e.g. relieve withdrawal).

Unlike some models for drug use, a behavioral economic model can potentially account for all long-term and acute influences on smoking. As discussed by Vuchinich and Tucker (1996) within the context of alcohol use, a behavioral economic, or choice, model usually takes a *molar* view and accounts for general patterns of drug use based on constraints on its use and availability of other reinforcers. Some others, such as social cognitive models, take a *molecular* view and generally attribute each instance of drug use to acute variations in the state of the user, such as predrug mood (e.g., tension-reduction hypothesis of alcohol intake). However, any increase in drug use due to acute changes in mood or other characteristics of the user can be interpreted within a behavioral economics model if these changes are seen as acutely shifting the demand curve for smoking upward or to the right. This interpretation is separate from, but not mutually exclusive of, the notion that these changes may reduce the availability of alternative reinforcers, leading to an increase in probability of choosing drug use (Vuchinich & Tucker, 1988). Thus, acute changes in the state of the user cannot be viewed as the only influences on drug use but as factors that modulate ongoing patterns of drug use. For example, negative mood or feelings of subjective stress may acutely increase the reinforcing value of smoking and temporarily shift tobacco's demand curve upward or to the right, relative to the demand curve under "average" conditions (see Fig. 10.1, top). Other acute influences on consumption, such as temporary illness (which often decreases smoking) or presence of discriminative stimuli for smoking (e.g., seeing someone else smoke one's preferred brand), also can be seen as momentarily shifting smoking's demand curve. Interventions providing alternative methods of responding to these acute factors can prevent this shift to the right in tobacco's demand curve and perhaps shift it to the left, demonstrating usefulness in cessation efforts.

We first describe, within the context of behavioral economics, the most common components of behavioral smoking cessation programs that focus on increasing the unit price of smoking prior to and during a quit attempt or on shifting the demand curve for smoking to the left. This usually is accomplished by stimulus control techniques and providing alternative reinforcers contingent on abstinence. Factors that may promote smoking by acting as complements are then discussed, along with interventions typically employed to counter their influence on smoking. In addition, alternative reinforcers that may substitute for smoking, shifting the demand curve for smoking to the left, are outlined. Pharmacological interventions for smoking cessation are discussed in a subsequent section.

Stimulus Control Techniques

Preparing to Quit. Several components of behavioral smoking cessation interventions involve stimulus control. Their basic objective is to reduce the relative reinforcing value of smoking by increasing its behavioral costs, by breaking the association between "cues" for smoking (e.g., after a meal) and smoking behavior, or both. Usually, the smoker determines the precise time and amount of tobacco to be consumed. Humans and nonhuman animals often prefer to have control over reinforcers (Burger, 1992). Having a large degree of control over consumption is analogous to having few restrictions on the availability of a reinforcer (i.e., low unit price). Consequently, greater control over administration may lead to increased consumption, and reducing control over reinforcer access may decrease consumption.

For example, smokers preparing to quit are often instructed to keep their cigarettes in a relatively inconvenient location (e.g., in their car). In this way, substantial and purposeful behavior is required to obtain a cigarette, as opposed to merely (and sometimes absent-mindedly) pulling one out from a pack in one's pocket and lighting up. Smokers are also often instructed to smoke only in one location, partly to narrow the environmental stimuli associated with smoking but also to require an added behavioral cost for smoking (i.e., moving to that location). The response cost for smoking at work locations has increased for virtually all smokers over the past few decades because of indoor smoking restrictions. The limited research on the impact of smoking restrictions is unclear, but these restrictions may reduce exposure (e.g., Brigham, Gross, Stitzer, & Felch, 1994) and make subsequent quit attempts more likely. Similarly, heavy smokers are instructed to not buy cartons but purchase individual packs in the days or weeks prior to their quit day, so that they will have to go to the store each time they want to open a new pack. This added behavioral requirement may delay the start of smoking a new pack and reduce smoking frequency.

A similar example of stimulus-control techniques involves control over the timing, rather than the location, of tobacco consumption prior to quitting. One study found that instructing smokers to smoke only at scheduled times of the day rather than ad lib may increase success of subsequently quitting (Cinciripini et al., 1995). Participants were assigned randomly to one of four treatment groups varying by instructions regarding their smoking prior to making a quit attempt: (a) decrease overall consumption and smoke only at instructed times ("scheduled reduction"), (b) decrease consumption but otherwise smoke ad lib ("nonscheduled reduction"), (c) do not change consumption but smoke only at instructed times ("scheduled nonreduction"), and (d) do not change consumption and smoke ad lib ("nonscheduled nonreduction"). In addition to experiencing less tobacco withdrawal, those in the scheduled reduction group had greater 1-year tobacco abstinence (44%) compared to the other treatment groups (18%, 32%, and 22% for nonscheduled reduction, scheduled nonreduction, and nonscheduled nonreduction, respectively). Such results point to the power of relatively simple behavioral interventions in changing tobacco consumption and treating tobacco dependence.

After Quitting. Upon quitting, smokers typically are instructed to get rid of all cigarettes from their home, car, office, and so forth (Lando, 1993). Because of the ease with which cigarettes can be smoked (low unit price), ready access could lead quickly to a lapse (smoking of a cigarette after having quit). Having no cigarettes readily available, on the other hand, would require the ex-smoker to engage in significant behavior in order to obtain cigarettes (e.g., driving to the store to purchase a pack). This extensive effort and the time required to perform it may discourage the ex-smoker from resuming smoking when exposed to transient (and frequent) urges to smoke. In the face of more significant and infrequent stimuli promoting relapse (e.g., stress), which can be seen as acutely shifting the demand curve for smoking to the right, ex-smokers typically are taught to engage in alternative coping behaviors to manage these situations. Presence of cigarettes would decrease the chances of these alternative behaviors being executed, whereas absence of available cigarettes would give the ex-smoker an opportunity to engage in this coping and reconsider the choice of smoking a cigarette.

Finally, another strategy involving a direct increase in the unit price of smoking is to make contingency contracts with ex-smokers, requiring them to pay a relatively large amount of money if they relapse to smoking after a quit attempt (Lando, 1993). Variations include earmarking the money for an organization despised by the ex-smoker or requiring the ex-smoker to perform some type of undesirable activity (e.g., scrub toilets for spouse) rather than paying money.

Direct Reduction in Smoking Reinforcement

Other strategies seek more directly to reduce the magnitude of reinforcement from each cigarette, thereby also increasing the unit price of smoking prior to quitting. A smoking cessation aid consisting of attachable plastic filters (e.g., Waterpik™) impedes the ventilation through a cigarette, reducing nicotine exposure or requiring the smoker to inhale more intensely in order to obtain nicotine. Smokers are supposed to use filters that are progressively more obstructive over the days and weeks prior to quitting. One objective of this product is to make it so difficult to obtain nicotine reinforcement from smoking cigarettes that it is no longer "worth" the effort. A few outcome studies found support for modest efficacy (Lando, 1993). A similar tactic that has been used more widely is "brand-switching," or instructing smokers to switch to brands with progressively lower nicotine yields over the weeks prior to quitting. The rationale of this advice is to reduce the amount of nicotine reinforcement per smoking episode or require greater intensity of smoking (i.e., increase in unit price) in order to obtain the same degree of nicotine reinforcement as that obtained from their previous brands (Lando, 1993). Research shows that lowering nicotine dose reduces responding for nicotine (Rose & Corrigall, 1997), and some have suggested that tobacco dependence could be greatly reduced throughout the United States if the nicotine content of cigarettes was reduced gradually (Benowitz & Henningfield, 1994). However, increasing intensity of smoking, or *behavioral compensation,* is relatively easy and does little to reduce nicotine exposure except at brands with the very lowest yields (below 0.2 mg). Thus, as discussed by DeGrandpre et al. (1992), the demand curve for tobacco is very inelastic across decreases in nicotine yield, and only tobacco with extremely low yields (very high unit price) will decrease consumption in most dependent smokers.

Self-Reward for Smoking Abstinence

An alternative to increasing the unit price of smoking by raising the response cost for smoking or decreasing reinforcement from smoking is to increase the value of not smoking. Laboratory studies show that smoking consumption decreases when the magnitude of a mutually exclusive monetary alternative reinforcer is increased (e.g., Perkins et al., 1994). Thus, providing contingent alternative rewards can shift the demand curve for smoking down or to the left.

A variant on contingency contracting is to provide a reward contingent on maintaining abstinence rather than to collect a penalty contingent on relapse. Contingent rewards for abstinence is a strategy with a long history in the field of drug abuse treatment (e.g., Hunt & Azrin, 1973). These rewards can be either self-rewards or rewards provided by some external entity (such as a formal treatment program). For example, participants often are instructed to save the money that would have been spent on cigarettes and use it toward the purchase of a reward. This procedure has two primary functions: (a) drawing attention to the money spent on smoking should lead to a questioning of the value of smoking in relation to the monetary cost, and (b) provision of an abstinence-contingent reward should decrease the aversive consequences of not smoking in terms of overall reinforcement. Participants are encouraged to use the money for "luxury" items that frequently are not obtained due to cost, such as going to a movie or purchasing jewelry. These contingent rewards are not necessarily economic substitutes for smoking, but those that also can be functional substitutes for smoking might be most clinically effective (Green & Freed, 1993). Use of contingent rewards in smoking cessation may be best illustrated in treatment programs built upon worksite competitions offering rewards such as money and lottery prizes for groups with the greatest proportion of abstinent members. These rewards appear to increase participation in smoking cessation treatments and reduce smoking levels (see Matson, Lee, & Hopp, 1993).

There are clear limitations to interventions involving rewards contingent upon smoking abstinence. The success of these programs depends on reliable assessment of use. Because self-report is often unreliable, biological verification of abstinence through carbon monoxide (CO) or from plasma or salivary cotinine (a nicotine metabolite) is needed. However, continuous verification is still difficult due to limitations in the frequency of contact with participants and the amount of time that these substances can be detected in the body. It is also important that the reinforcement be delivered as close to testing as possible because delay reduces the value of a reinforcer. Substitute reinforcers that can be successfully implemented by the smoker alone would be most helpful, but participants can easily "cheat." The contingency contract may be more reliable when an outside entity is providing the reward. In addition, a reward from an outside entity is more truly an additional reward, compared with spending one's own money for a reward. Duration of treatment effects are also a concern. As with any treatment program, positive results gained from the contingent reinforcement may be lost when the treatment and rewards are discontinued. For example, Stitzer and

Bigelow (1985) demonstrated that smokers would reduce their smoking as much as necessary to earn contingent monetary rewards but returned to regular smoking when the rewards were removed. Lack of generalization of these contingencies to the smoker's environment is often a limitation in maintaining smoking cessation over time. Clearer contingencies between smoking behavior and such relevant costs as health and life insurance premiums could serve to reinforce long-term smoking cessation (see also Bickel & Marsch, chap. 13, this volume).

Social Support for Abstinence

Many social circumstances influence smoking and other drug use. One interpretation of this influence is in terms of social modeling, for example, adolescents learn to smoke because they observe and copy the behavior of peers and family members. However, it is also possible to interpret this phenomenon in behavioral economic terms: Smoking may be a complement to social interactions (i.e., socializing may shift tobacco's demand curve up). Socializing may make smoking more enjoyable through the bond of performing a common behavior, sharing cigarettes, matches, and so forth. Smoking also may make socializing more enjoyable (i.e., *symmetric complementarity*) by increasing attention and relaxation.

On the other hand, social deprivation also may increase smoking consumption. According to behavioral economics, the *reinforcement environment* (e.g., number and accessibility of alternative reinforcers) affects the value of each individual reinforcer (Green & Freed, 1993). If few other reinforcers are available in the environment (e.g., little social contact), then smoking may be more likely to occur because it is easily available as a means to increase overall reinforcement. Smoking may not necessarily be an economic substitute for these missing reinforcers (although see Rachlin, chap. 6, this volume) but may simply be more valuable because of the reinforcement-deprived environment. Animal research supports this concept, as rats that were raised or housed in social isolation tend to consume higher amounts of drugs or alcohol than do those raised in nonstressed, socially enriched (e.g. other rats, toys, running wheels) environments (e.g., Hadaway, Alexander, Coambs, & Beyerstein, 1979). Relatedly, people who experience losses, such as the loss of a spouse, are likely to experience a drop in reinforcement and may increase their intake of cigarettes and other drugs (e.g., Zisook, Shuchter, & Mulvihill, 1990).

Behavioral counseling for smoking cessation often makes use of social support to promote abstinence. Contingency contracting, discussed previously, necessarily involves a social environment supportive of quitting smoking. As with monetary reward contingent on abstinence, social reinforcement contingent on abstinence (e.g., praise) can shift the demand curve for smoking downward or to the left. Perhaps not surprisingly, high levels of social support are associated with better longer term abstinence (Mermelstein, Cohen, Lichtenstein, Baer, & Kamarck, 1986). As with all reinforcers, social support should be more effective when it is stronger and more easily accessible. The success of support groups such as Alcoholics Anonymous (AA) may rely to some degree on providing this kind of reinforcement. Groups such as AA provide a large network of support, and assign to each individual a sponsor—at least one person whom they can contact at any time to receive immediate support and reinforcement. Conversely, negative social interactions resulting from abstaining from smoking (social nonsupport for quitting) can be detrimental to abstinence by increasing the social costs for quitting, among other ways (Glasgow, Klesges, & O'Neill, 1986). Because smoking and certain social environments may be complements, those environments should be avoided by individuals trying to quit smoking. This approach presents a number of problems, however, in that formerly enjoyed activities may be eliminated and relationships with friends who smoke may be compromised. The result may be a drop in social reinforcement, necessitating supplementation with alternative social reinforcement that encourages, or is at least compatible with, not smoking.

In addition, social support has some functional similarities to cigarette smoking that may increase its viability as a substitute for smoking, which also could explain a shift to the left in the demand curve for smoking. Positive social support can be reinforcing by inducing relaxation, relieving stress, relieving boredom, increasing positive feelings, helping to concentrate, and so forth—all reasons that some smokers have endorsed for smoking (e.g., Linn & Stein, 1985).

Substitutes for Smoking in Coping With Stress

Smokers often report, and some research has shown, that they smoke in order to relieve stress or tension and that they relapse or are unable to quit because of stress (e.g., Shiffman, Paty, Gnys, Kassel, & Hickcox, 1996). Stress, therefore, can increase the reinforcing value of smoking and shift tobacco's demand curve up or to the right. Treatment providers often recommend activities that could provide similar direct effects of smoking during stress, such as relaxation techniques, and that may be functional substitutes for smoking. For example, if relaxation techniques are used to reduce stress, smoking may be less valuable and consequently less likely to occur. Few research studies specifically have evaluated the effectiveness of relaxation techniques for smoking cessation, but Wynd (1992) isolated the effect of relaxation training on smoking cessation and showed that it was more effective than a standard treatment.

Although empirical support is lacking, the rationale for the use of relaxation in smoking cessation is clear. Relaxation techniques include visual imagery, deep breathing, and muscle relaxation. If similarity of function is important for substitutability, the viability of relaxation exercises as a substitute can be seen easily. As with smoking, these techniques are readily available and can be performed on demand and at a low behavioral cost. They are relatively fast-acting, and the deep breathing action may be quite similar to the breathing actions of smoking. Practice of relaxation techniques also may improve cognitive task performance for anxious individuals (e.g., Straughan & Dufort, 1969). Meditation training is similar to relaxation training and may similarly substitute for smoking during a quit attempt. Some drug users report that they find substances of abuse to be less enjoyable after initiating meditation (Aron & Aron, 1983).

Sensory Substitutes

As discussed later, nicotine replacement therapies are more efficacious than placebo (see Hughes, 1996). However, the fact that they are not 100% effective suggests that there may be reinforcing aspects of smoking that are not replaced by other sources of nicotine. Substitutability is a continuum, and nicotine replacement therapies may be only partial substitutes.

The behavioral and sensory aspects of smoking also appear to be important to the reinforcing value of smoking (Rose et al., 1993). Other reinforcers that are similar to smoking in these aspects may be able to function as substitutes for smoking, shifting the demand curve for smoking down or to the left. Indeed, smoking cessation programs often recommend plastic straws, cinnamon sticks, plastic cigarettes, and so forth to hold, suck, and manipulate as is usually done with cigarettes. Though their use can be interpreted as behavioral distractions that are relatively incompatible with smoking, they also can be interpreted in behavioral economic terms as acting as substitutes for the reinforcement derived from the sensory or behavioral aspects of smoking. Some of these aspects of smoking may be independently reinforcing or conditioned reinforcers due to repeated association with the reinforcement from the nicotine in cigarettes (Rose & Levin, 1991). Either way, providing easily attainable substitutes for these aspects of smoking may reduce the demand for smoking. Little research has been done on the effectiveness of these substitutes, but one recent study found reduced cigarette craving and withdrawal during brief abstinence in smokers given access to chewing gum (Cohen, Collins, & Britt, 1997).

Rose and colleagues have done extensive work examining the specific sensory aspects of smoking that smokers find reinforcing. They have identified a variety of sensations that smokers find desirable and that can reduce craving for cigarettes and smoking behavior (Behm, Schur, Levin, Tashkin, & Rose, 1993). In particular, the sensory effects of smoking in the back of the throat, labeled the tracheal "scratch," are desired by most smokers. Stimulation of this area of the throat by means of citric acid and other aerosol sprays may reduce craving for cigarettes (Levin, Rose, & Behm, 1990) and provide relief from stress (Levin, Rose, Behm, & Caskey, 1991). In fact, subjective "satisfaction" with these substitutes appears to be correlated with degree of intensity of throat sensation. Similarly, vapor from black pepper extract reduces craving and alleviates negative affect and anxiety (Rose & Behm, 1994). Flavor of a cigarette substitute also may provide satisfaction and craving reduction (Levin, Behm & Rose, 1990).

Reinforcement due to sensory effects also has been demonstrated in participants smoking a low-nicotine, but high "smoking sensation," aerosol (Rose et al., 1993). If given low-nicotine cigarettes, which increase the unit price of smoking, smokers typically puff harder so that they receive their usual dose of nicotine (DeGrandpre et al., 1992). However, participants in Rose et al. (1993) did not perform compensatory puffing with these high smoking sensation aerosols, suggesting that the subjects were satisfied by the sensory similarities. Thus, sensory substitutes may be able to reduce smoking behavior, at least acutely. In addition, local anesthesia of the respiratory airway has been shown to attenuate the reduction in craving normally produced by smoking a cigarette, presumably because of a reduction in reinforcing sensory effects (Rose, Tashkin, Ertle, Zinser, & Lafer, 1985).

Although long-term clinical efficacy of sensory substitutes has not been examined, one clinical trial assessed the efficacy of a hand-held inhaler that delivered a citric-acid aerosol spray that added smoke "flavor" on smoking cessation over 19 days (Behm et al. 1993). Smokers trying to quit were provided with free counseling and use of either the citric acid aerosol or a placebo. Those identified as heavy smokers (based on pre-quit CO) remained abstinent longer if given the citric acid aerosol, although there was no difference among light smokers. Given that nonnicotine cigarettes have been unsuccessful in the marketplace (Jaffe, 1990), devices that only mimic sensory aspects of smoking without the pharmacological actions (i.e., nicotine) may not be useful except during initial withdrawal during the 1st week or so after quitting. Nevertheless, further research in this area may result in low-cost, safe adjuncts to enhance initial cessation.

Alternative Reinforcers: Food

As noted, a key concept in behavioral economics is that the reinforcing value of a reinforcer is not an intrinsic property but varies depending on the availability of alternative reinforcers. Thus, a behavioral economics perspective is particularly useful in characterizing the relation between tobacco intake and other commodities, such as food and other drugs.

One of the best examples of the relation between availability of one reinforcer and consumption of another comes from research showing the influence of food intake and food deprivation on drug consumption. Animal studies show that lack of availability of food can alter drug-seeking behavior by decreasing the elasticity of demand and increasing the relative value of the drug (e.g., Carroll, Gilberto, & May, 1991; see also Carroll & Carroll, chap. 3, this volume). Control procedures verify that these results are not explained by general increases in activity, increases in liquid intake, pharmacokinetic changes, caloric replacement, drug effects on metabolism and feeding behavior, or taste preferences of drugs. Although evidence is not completely clear, these effects do not appear to be due primarily to weight reduction per se but to reduced reinforcement from food. For example, some studies show rapid alterations in drug intake with acute changes in food availability that are too brief to result in substantial changes in weight (e.g., Kanarek & Marks-Kaufman, 1988).

This relation clearly extends to the influence of food deprivation on nicotine reinforcement. In one of the first studies of nicotine self-administration in rats, Lang, Latiff, McQueen, and Singer (1977) found that rats did not self-administer nicotine more than saline solution when at free-feeding weight (100% of expected), suggesting that nicotine was not at all reinforcing in that condition. However, these rats increased nicotine self-administration sevenfold with little change in saline intake when their weights were reduced to 80% of free-feeding weight, demonstrating a dramatic increase in nicotine reinforcement and suggesting an upward shift in the demand curve for nicotine. Food deprivation also has been shown to increase nicotine self-administration in some primates (de la Garza & Johanson, 1987). The reverse relation, the effect of nicotine intake on decreasing food consumption, is also very clear but is more difficult to interpret because of the likely direct pharmacological actions of nicotine on hunger, satiety, and food taste hedonics (Perkins, 1992).

A similar relation between food and smoking also has been seen in human studies. During a World War II semistarvation study, 36 healthy male volunteers were subjected to 6 months on a low-calorie diet, which resulted in a 24% decrease in body weight and an increase in consumption of tobacco products, chewing gum, coffee, and tea (Franklin, Schiele, Brozek, & Keys, 1948). Thus, long-term deprivation of food may shift upward the demand curve for many other available reinforcers, only some of which are drugs. In a more recent study, levels of cotinine, the major metabolite of nicotine, increased by nearly 50% in obese female smokers after 6 months of weight-loss treatment that produced a 20% decline in weight (Niaura, Clark, Raciti, Pera, & Abrams, 1992). Extending the animal research to humans even further, Cheskin et al. (1995) found that relatively brief (6 days) food deprivation slightly but significantly increased CO and cigarette smoking behavior among smokers in a restricted environment, indicating that decreased availability of food reinforcement and not weight reduction per se was responsible.

These observations have important implications for smoking cessation treatment. For example, Perkins, Epstein, Sexton, and Pastor (1990) demonstrated that women who stopped smoking for 1 week showed an increase in consumption of sweets. This increase was then reversed when smoking was purposefully resumed the following week (none of these subjects wanted to quit permanently), suggesting that sweets may be able to substitute for smoking during a cessation attempt. An implication of this relation is that attempting to deprive oneself of alternative food reinforcers after quitting smoking, perhaps in an attempt to prevent expected weight gain, may impair one's ability to remain abstinent from smoking. Supporting this possibility, some studies have found that dieting specifically to prevent weight gain during a smoking cessation attempt may decrease, rather than increase, the chances of remaining abstinent (Perkins, 1994). Similarly, Hall, Ginsberg, and Jones (1986) reported that relapse at 1 year postquit could be predicted by weight gain during the first 6 months postquit; those who gained the least weight during the first 6 months were more likely to relapse between 6 months and 1 year. Although food intake was not assessed, those gaining the least may have been attempting to restrict intake (i.e., experiencing some food deprivation), thus increasing the reinforcing value of resuming smoking. In this situation, food may act as a substitute for smoking reinforcement, although food also may help relieve dysphoric effects associated with quitting smoking (see Perkins, Levine, Marcus, & Shiffman, 1997).

Because relapse to smoking may arise from reduced food reinforcement, long-term smoking abstinence may be enhanced by increasing such reinforcement. Supporting this potential treatment direction, Yung, Gordis, and Holt (1983) concluded that relapse back to alcohol use after treatment was reduced in those with a greater increase in sugar and carbohydrate intake. More relevant to smoking cessation is a study by West, Hajek, and Burrows (1990), who found that providing smokers with simple dextrose (sugar) tablets reduced subjective craving for cigarettes during a quit attempt more than placebo tablets. A recent follow-up study found that 4-week smoking cessation rates were 13% higher ($p < 0.01$, one-tailed) in those given dextrose as opposed to placebo tablets to supplement behavioral cessation counseling (West & Willis, 1998). Notably, there was no group difference in weight gain. The link to animal research showing that access to sweetened solutions reduces drug intake is clear (see Carroll & Carroll, chap. 3, this volume).

Exercise

There is little research examining the relation between smoking and other health behaviors that may act as complements or substitutes. However, the inverse relation between smoking and physical activity (e.g., Marks et al.,

1991; Perkins et al., 1993) has gained recent attention. Because most adults do not find exercise reinforcing, as evidenced by the low incidence of regular exercise behavior and poor long-term adherence with exercise prescriptions (Dubbert, 1992), this relation is probably more accurately described as one of complementarity between smoking and sedentariness. It is also more accurately viewed as a chronic relation, involving association between typical long-term patterns of behavior, rather than as an acute relation between two momentary behaviors (see also Simpson & Vuchinich, chap. 8, this volume). Smoking is associated with a variety of other chronic behaviors that increase risk to health, some of which may be explainable in terms of complementarity with smoking (e.g., higher dietary fat intake; Perkins, 1992).

Because of the inverse relation between smoking and exercise, some smoking cessation programs have included exercise as part of the intervention. One study of 281 woman smokers found 1-year abstinence rates of 11.9% and 5.4% for exercise and control treatments, respectively ($p = 0.05$), added to standard cessation counseling (Marcus et al., 1999). Outcome at each follow-up point revealed a 2-fold better abstinence rate for exercise versus control groups, similar to that observed for nicotine replacement versus placebo (Hughes, 1996). A potential limitation to the widespread usefulness of exercise to smoking cessation may be the low adherence to exercise programs by all adults, smokers or not.

Alternative Reinforcers: Other Drugs

Another major example of complementarity between smoking and other reinforcers involves other drug use. Consumption of a number of other drugs is related directly to smoking (complementary), and smoking cessation interventions must emphasize reduction or elimination of these drugs. (The special case of nicotine replacement as a substitute for smoking within the context of treatment is discussed in the section on pharmacological treatments.)

There are a number of reports suggesting that consumption of certain drugs may be associated with increases in consumption of tobacco, or more specifically an upward or right-ward shift in tobacco's demand curve. In their reanalysis of data from prior studies, Bickel et al. (1995) found that alcohol and heroin each have a complementary relationship with tobacco consumption. As the unit price of these drugs is increased, consumption of these drugs decreases and consumption of cigarettes also declines, indicating complementarity. Many other studies show a positive association between alcohol dependence and tobacco dependence, such that the amount of tobacco consumed is correlated with amount of alcohol consumed (e.g., Batel, Pessione, Maitre, & Rueff, 1995). Similarly, intake of alcohol acutely increases smoking consumption (see Shiffman & Balabanis, 1995). Smoking rate also increased with increasing dose of methadone in one study, as number of cigarettes per day was significantly higher during weeks when the daily dose was 80 mg than during weeks when the dose was 50 mg (Schmitz, Grabowski, & Rhoads, 1994). Finally, smoking also may have complementary relations with stimulant drugs, such as cocaine (Budney, Higgins, Hughes, & Bickel, 1993).

In contrast, the association of tobacco with marijuana and caffeine is less clear. Some laboratory studies have shown that tobacco and coffee consumption may have a weak complementary relation (Bickel, Hughes, De-Grandpre, Higgins, & Rizzuto, 1992), but manipulation of caffeine intake did not affect tobacco consumption in one naturalistic study (Lane & Rose, 1995). Smoking marijuana has been shown in one inpatient study to decrease cigarette smoking more than placebo (Kelly, Foltin, Rose, Fischman, & Brady, 1990), suggesting substitutability, but little other research has been done.

Aside from this last study on marijuana, research to date generally has failed to find any drug other than nicotine that can clearly substitute for tobacco, indicating that tobacco is either complementary or independent of other drug use. This observation implies that deprivation from other drugs generally will not have adverse effects on smoking cessation attempts. The apparent complementarity of smoking with alcohol and opiates suggests that use of these drugs during smoking cessation may put the individual at increased risk for relapse. Whereas opiate use during a smoking cessation attempt has not been systematically examined, alcohol use is well known to be a risk factor for smoking relapse (see Shiffman & Balabanis, 1995). Treatment guidelines for smoking cessation often suggest that smokers attempting to quit avoid alcohol use. However, it is unclear if these recommendations should be applied to all drugs and under all circumstances.

In looking at the reverse relation, the influence of smoking on other drug use, quitting smoking may not necessarily put a person at risk for resumption of other drug intake in those who have abstained from other drug use successfully (e.g., Martin et al., 1997). If tobacco use is complementary with this other drug use, then quitting smoking actually may enhance success in maintaining abstinence from other drug use. On the other hand, these relations between smoking and other drug use may be asymmetrical. For example, although alcohol clearly increases smoking behavior, it is not clear that smoking acutely increases alcohol consumption (Shiffman & Balabanis, 1995). To complicate matters further, the substitutability of reinforcers is not fixed across situations (Green & Freed, 1993). Given the increasing prevalence of other drug dependence among smokers, further research on the relation between smoking and other drug use is warranted.

PHARMACOLOGICAL INTERVENTIONS

From a behavioral economics perspective, pharmacological interventions influence smoking cessation by mechanisms that may be similar at the molar level to those of behavioral interventions. The primary goals for both treatment approaches are to increase the unit price for smoking and lower tobacco's demand curve or shift it to the left, thereby increasing its elasticity of demand (Bickel & DeGrandpre, 1996).

The most widely used pharmacological approach to smoking cessation involves the use of nicotine replacement (e.g., gum, patch, nasal spray). The goal is to provide nicotine in an alternative form that is safer and less dependence-producing than smoking while still serving as a viable substitute for tobacco consumption. By giving the smoker a substitutable reinforcer, the demand curve for tobacco should be shifted to the left, increasing its elasticity (Bickel et al., 1995). Unfortunately, there has not been a direct test of the effects of nicotine replacement on the demand curves for tobacco consumption. However, nicotine replacement clearly enhances success of smoking cessation (e.g., Hughes, 1996). Furthermore, administration of rapid forms of nicotine replacement (nasal spray, intravenous) has been shown to decrease cigarette smoking behavior acutely among smokers not trying to quit (e.g., Perkins, Grobe, Stiller, Fonte, & Goettler, 1992), suggesting substitutability between smoking and some forms of nicotine replacement.

Besides providing a direct substitute for tobacco use, nicotine replacement may influence the demand for tobacco through other mechanisms. In particular, nicotine replacement is thought to reduce severity of withdrawal symptoms experienced during initial cessation of tobacco use. Because the experience of withdrawal can be viewed as a psychological "cost" of quitting, nicotine replacement may reduce this cost and increase the likelihood of maintaining tobacco abstinence. Conversely, because smoking can reverse withdrawal, this withdrawal relief may serve to enhance reinforcement from smoking, shifting its demand curve to the right. Providing withdrawal relief through nicotine replacement may prevent this enhanced reinforcement from smoking and, thus, prevent a shift to the right in tobacco's demand curve.

Although nicotine replacement strategies can facilitate smoking abstinence, long-term success has generally remained below 35% (Hughes, 1996). Newer approaches attempt to match more closely the characteristics of tobacco reinforcement. For example, nicotine nasal spray delivers nicotine more rapidly in a way closer to that of smoking than other nicotine replacement methods (Schneider, Lunell, Olmstead, & Fagerstrom, 1996). As such, one would think that it might serve as a better substitute for smoking than gum or patch, but results of clinical trials suggest it is, at best, only comparable to gum and patch (e.g., Schneider et al., 1995). Other novel delivery methods, such as vapor inhalers, are no more efficacious. The less than ideal success of nicotine replacement methods may lie in the fact that these methods are not as reinforcing as tobacco smoking and thus do not serve as effective substitutes. On the other hand, it may be difficult to develop nicotine delivery devices that fully substitute for smoking but have substantially less health risk, as evidenced by the concerns regarding new "heated tobacco" products introduced by the tobacco industry (e.g., Premier brand; Kluger, 1996). Alternatively, there are other costs associated with these novel nicotine delivery methods, such as aversive side effects (e.g., irritation with nasal spray).

Several other nonnicotine medications have been examined as potential aids to smoking cessation. One promising medication is mecamylamine, a noncompetitive nicotine antagonist that blocks subjective effects of tobacco smoking (Rose, Behm, Westman, Levin, Stein, Lane, et al., 1994). After extended exposure (e.g., days), smokers often reduce their smoking behavior to low levels because of the absence of nicotine reinforcement (Rose, Behm, Westman, Levin, Stein, & Ripka, 1994). Mecamylamine can thus be seen as lowering tobacco's demand curve.

Most other medications being examined for treatment in smoking cessation are not known to directly affect nicotine reinforcement. Rather, these focus on relieving various aversive effects of tobacco withdrawal that may occur in some smokers (Jarvik & Henningfield, 1993). Examples include buspirone to attenuate increases in anxiety that may accompany a quit attempt and bupropion, clonidine, or other antidepressant medications to reduce increases in negative affect or reduce the likelihood of a depressive episode after quitting in smokers with a past history of depression. As noted previously with nicotine replacement, these medications may be seen as reducing the psychological costs, in terms of aversive mood effects, of a quit attempt, or they may prevent a shift to the right in tobacco's demand curve due to enhanced reinforcing effects of smoking in relieving these aversive mood effects of abstinence.

Finally, it is important to recognize that quitting smoking often entails financial costs for purchase of nicotine patches or gum or for smoking cessation counseling. In this respect, smokers are faced with a choice between continuing to smoke, which involves a modest financial cost, or making a quit attempt, which can involve a larger financial cost. Nicotine replacement typically costs at least $3 per day, more than the cost of a pack of cigarettes. (The total cost for nicotine gum and patch treatment was previously higher, because a doctor's visit was required to obtain a prescription for the medication.) Coupled with costs for cessation counseling, it is easy to see why the financial costs for quitting can weigh against a smoker's decision to quit. Reimbursement by health care providers for these costs would remove this financial response cost to cessation, thereby making smoking cessation more attractive (Kaplan, Orleans, Perkins, & Pierce, 1995). This is, unfortunately, rarely done, a particularly surprising observation given the huge benefits of smoking cessation in terms of cost per year of life saved (Kaplan et al., 1995).

CONCLUSIONS

Cigarette smoking initiation and maintenance are enhanced by its very low behavioral, economic, and social costs, and thus its low unit price. The demand curve for smoking often is raised or shifted to the right by factors that complement its use, such as social contact with other smokers and intake of other drugs, including alcohol, opiates, and some stimulants. Even though they are usually not described in this way, smoking cessation interventions often focus on increasing the unit price of smoking both before (e.g., stimulus control) and after quitting (e.g., contingency contracting) and shifting the demand curve for tobacco down or to the left by reducing exposure to complementary factors, among other ways. Interventions also emphasize finding substitutes for smoking, which lower the tobacco demand curve, such as alternative methods to reduce stress and use of commodities that provide some of the sensory effects of smoking. Although food has not been clearly demonstrated to substitute for smoking, a decrease in food intake after quitting smoking may impair chances of remaining abstinent, whereas increasing intake of sweet substances may increase abstinence. Similarly, nicotine replacement may modestly substitute for smoking, but it more likely decreases the psychological costs of abstinence by attenuating tobacco withdrawal. Other pharmacotherapies also decrease the psychological costs of abstaining (e.g., bupropion relief of negative mood) or lower the demand curve for smoking by directly reducing nicotine reinforcement (mecamylamine blockade of nicotine).

Careful consideration of factors that alter the demand curve for smoking—its unit price and availability of complements and substitutes—may lead to more comprehensive and effective behavioral and pharmacological interventions for smoking cessation. In particular, the continued low unit price of smoking and lack of adequate substitutes for smoking are primary obstacles to maintaining abstinence in ex-smokers. Because of the inelasticity of demand for smoking, increasing the unit price of smoking sufficiently to produce a drop in consumption may be difficult as long as it remains a legal product, particularly for dependent smokers. Use of substantial, generalizable, and long-term rewards contingent on abstinence (e.g., systematic decrease in health insurance payments) essentially can provide an alternative reinforcer that will shift the demand curve for tobacco to the left, discouraging smoking. Development of effective substitutes for smoking, which also would shift tobacco's demand curve to the left, may be the most important and most challenging task due to the difficulty of creating products that provide the same magnitude of reinforcement as quickly and cheaply as smoking but without its health risk.

All of these interventions should be examined within a behavioral economics framework in order to determine their full implications for smoking. For example, the influence of each strategy on tobacco's demand curve (i.e., changes in elasticity) needs to be carefully evaluated within the context of available complementary reinforcers, which themselves can increase tobacco consumption, rather than in isolation. The impact of these strategies on smoking behavior across subgroups of smokers (teens, heavily dependent, etc.) also should be assessed, because a particular strategy could shift the demand curve of one group to the left but leave that of another group unchanged or even shifted to the right. In addition, given the likelihood that single approaches are unlikely to have a substantial effect in all smokers, the influence of various combinations of interventions on the demand curve for smoking should be investigated (Bickel & DeGrandpre, 1996). In this way, the optimum set of interventions to reduce smoking in the broad population of smokers can be determined.

ACKNOWLEDGMENTS

Preparation of this chapter was supported by National Institute on Drug Abuse grants DA04174 and DA05807. James E. Grobe also was supported by National Heart, Lung, and Blood Institute predoctoral training grant HL-07560 and by a Mellon predoctoral fellowship.

REFERENCES

American Psychiatric Association. (1994). *Diagnostic and statistical manual of mental disorders* (4th ed.). Washington, DC: Author.

Aron, E. N., & Aron, A. (1983). The patterns of reduction of drug and alcohol use among Transcendental Meditation participants. *Bulletin of the Society of Psychologists in Addictive Behaviors, 2,* 8–33.

Batel, P., Pessione, F., Maitre, C., & Rueff, B. (1995). Relationship between alcohol and tobacco dependencies among alcoholics who smoke. *Addiction, 90,* 977–980.

Behm, F. M., Schur, C., Levin, E. D., Tashkin, D. P., & Rose, J. E. (1993). Clinical evaluation of a citric acid inhaler for smoking cessation. *Drug and Alcohol Dependence, 31,* 131–138.

Benowitz, N., & Henningfield, J. E. (1994). Establishing a nicotine threshold for addiction. *New England Journal of Medicine, 331,* 123–125.

Bickel, W. K., & DeGrandpre, R. J. (1996). Modeling drug abuse policy in the behavioral economics laboratory. In L. Green & J. H. Kagel (Eds.), *Advances in behavioral economics: Vol 3. Substance use and abuse* (pp. 69–95). Norwood, NJ: Ablex.

Bickel, W. K., DeGrandpre, R. J., & Higgins, S. T. (1995). The behavioral economics of concurrent drug reinforcers: A review and reanalysis of drug self-administration research. *Psychopharmacology, 107,* 211–216.

Bickel, W. K., DeGrandpre, R. J., Hughes, J. R., & Higgins, S. T. (1991). Behavioral economics of drug self-administration: II. A unit-price analysis of cigarette smoking. *Journal of the Experimental Analysis of Behavior, 55,* 145–154.

Bickel, W. K., Hughes, J. R., DeGrandpre, R. J., Higgins, S. T., & Rizzuto, P. (1992). Behavioral economics of drug self-administration: IV. The effects of response requirement on the consumption of and interaction between concurrently available coffee and cigarettes. *Psychopharmacology, 107,* 211–216.

Brigham, J., Gross, J., Stitzer, M. L., & Felch, L. J. (1994). Effects of a restricted work-site smoking policy on employees who smoke. *American Journal of Public Health, 84,* 773–778.

Budney, A. J., Higgins, W. K., Hughes, J. R., & Bickel, W. K. (1993). Nicotine and caffeine use in cocaine-dependent individuals. *Journal of Substance Abuse, 5,* 117–130.

Burger, J. M. (1992). *Desire for control: Personality, social, and clinical perspectives.* New York: Plenum.

Carroll, M. E., Gilberto, C. G., & May, S. A. (1991). Modifying drug-reinforced behavior by altering the economic conditions of the drug and a nondrug reinforcer. *Journal of the Experimental Analysis of Behavior, 56,* 361–376.

Cheskin, L. J., Wiersema, L., Hess, J., Goldsborough, D., Tayback, M., Henningfield, J. E., & Gorelick, D. A. (1995). Caloric restriction increases nicotine consumption in cigarette smokers. In L. S. Harris (Ed.), *Problems of drug dependence 1994* (NIDA Research Monograph No. 153). Washington, DC: U.S. Government Printing Office.

Cinciripini, P. M., Lapitsky, L., Seay, S., Wallfisch, A., Kitchens, K., & Van Vunakis, H. (1995). The effects of smoking schedules on cessation outcome: Can we improve on common methods of gradual and abrupt nicotine withdrawal? *Journal of Consulting and Clinical Psychology, 63,* 388–399.

Cohen, L. M., Collins, F. L., & Britt, D. M. (1997). The effect of chewing gum on tobacco withdrawal. *Addictive Behaviors, 22,* 769–773.

DeGrandpre, R. J., & Bickel, W. K. (1995). Human drug self-administration in a medium of exchange. *Experimental and Clinical Psychopharmacology, 3,* 349–357.

DeGrandpre, R. J., Bickel, W. K., Hughes, J. R., & Higgins, S. T. (1992). Behavioral economics of drug self-administration: III. A reanalysis of the nicotine regulation hypothesis. *Psychopharmacology, 108,* 1–10.

de la Garza, R., & Johanson, C. E. (1987). The effects of food deprivation on the self-administration of psychoactive drugs. *Drug and Alcohol Dependence, 19,* 17–27.

Dubbert, P. M. (1992). Exercise in behavioral medicine. *Journal of Consulting and Clinical Psychology, 60,* 613–618.

Franklin, J. C., Schiele, B. C., Brozek, J., & Keys, A. (1948). Observations on human behavior in experimental semistarvation and rehabilitation. *Journal of Clinical Psychology, 4,* 28–45.

Giovino G. A., Henningfield, J. E., Tomar, S. L., Escobedo, L. G., & Slade, J. (1995). Epidemiology of tobacco use and dependence. *Epidemiologic Reviews, 17,* 48–65.

Glasgow, R. E., Klesges, R. C., & O'Neill, H. K. (1986). Programming social support for smoking modification: An extension and replication. *Addictive Behaviors, 11,* 453–457.

Green, L., & Freed, D. E. (1993). The substitutability of reinforcers. *Journal of the Experimental Analysis of Behavior, 60,* 141–158.

Hadaway, P. F., Alexander, B. K., Coambs, R. B., & Beyerstein, B. (1979). The effect of housing and gender on preference for morphine-sucrose solutions in rats. *Psychopharmacology, 66,* 87–91.

Hall, S. M., Ginsberg, D., & Jones, R. T. (1986). Smoking cessation and weight gain. *Journal of Consulting and Clinical Psychology, 54,* 342–346.

Henningfield, J. E., & Keenan, R. (1993). Nicotine delivery kinetics and abuse liability. *Journal of Consulting and Clinical Psychology, 61,* 743–750.

Heyman, G. M. (1996). Elasticity of demand for alcohol in humans and rats. In L. Green & J. H. Kagel (Eds.), *Advances in behavioral economics: Vol 3. Substance use and abuse* (pp. 107–132). Norwood, NJ: Ablex.

Hughes, J. R. (1996). Pharmacotherapy of nicotine dependence. In C. R. Schuster & M. J. Kuhar (Eds.), *Pharmacological aspects of drug dependence* (pp. 599–626). New York: Springer-Verlag.

Hunt, G., & Azrin, N. (1973). A community reinforcement approach to alcoholism. *Behaviour Research and Therapy, 11,* 91–104.

Hursh, S. R., & Winger, G. (1995). Normalized demand for drugs and other reinforcers. *Journal of the Experimental Analysis of Behavior, 64,* 373–384.

Jaffe, J. H. (1990). Tobacco smoking and nicotine dependence. In S. Wonnacott, M. A. H. Russell, & I. P. Stolerman (Eds.), *Nicotine psychopharmacology: Molecular, cellular, and behavioural aspects* (pp. 1–37). New York: Oxford University Press.

Jarvik, M. E., & Henningfield, J. E. (1993). Pharmacological adjuncts for the treatment of tobacco dependence. In C. T. Orleans & J. Slade (Eds.), *Nicotine addiction: Principles and management* (pp. 245–261). New York: Oxford University Press.

Kanarek, R. B., & Marks-Kaufman, R. (1988). Dietary modulation of oral amphetamine intake in rats. *Physiology & Behavior, 44,* 501–505.

Kaplan, R. M., Orleans, C. T., Perkins, K. A., & Pierce, J. P. (1995). Marshaling the evidence for greater regulation and control of tobacco products: A call for action. *Annals of Behavioral Medicine, 17,* 3–14.

Kelly, T. H., Foltin, R. W., Rose, A. J., Fischman, M. W., & Brady, J. V. (1990). Smoked marijuana effects on tobacco cigarette smoking behavior. *Journal of Pharmacology & Experimental Therapeutics, 252,* 934–944.

Kluger, R. (1996). *Ashes to ashes.* New York: Knopf.

Lando, H. A. (1993). Formal quit smoking treatments. In C. T. Orleans & J. Slade (Eds.), *Nicotine addiction: Principles and management* (pp. 221–244). New York: Oxford University Press.

Lane, J. D., & Rose, J. E. (1995). Effects of daily caffeine intake on smoking behavior in the natural environment. *Experimental and Clinical Psychopharmacology, 3,* 49–55.

Lang, W. J., Latiff, A. A., McQueen, A., & Singer, G. (1977). Self adminstration of nicotine with and without a food delivery schedule. *Pharmacology, Biochemistry & Behavior, 7,* 65–70.

Levin, E. D., Behm, F. M., & Rose, J. E. (1990). The use of flavor in cigarette substitutes. *Drug and Alcohol Dependence, 26,* 155–160.

Levin, E. D., Rose, J. E., & Behm, F. (1990). Development of a citric acid aerosol as a smoking cessation aid. *Drug and Alcohol Dependence, 25,* 273–279.

Levin, E. D., Rose, J. E., Behm, F., & Caskey, N. (1991). The effects of smoking related sensory cues on psychological stress. *Pharmacology, Biochemistry, & Behavior, 39,* 265–268.

Linn, M. W., & Stein, S. (1985). Reasons for smoking among extremely heavy smokers. *Addictive Behaviors, 10,* 197–201.

Marcus, B. H., Albrecht, A. E., King, T. K., Paris, A. F., Pinto, B. M., Roberts, M., Niaura, R. S., & Abrams, D. B. (1999). The efficacy of exercise as an aid for smoking cessation in women: a randomized controlled trial. *Archives of Internal Medicine, 159,* 1229–1234.

Marks, B. L., Perkins, K. A., Metz, K. F., Epstein, L. H., Robertson, R. J., Goss, F. L., & Sexton, J. E. (1991). Effects of smoking status on content of caloric intake and energy expenditure. *International Journal of Eating Disorders, 10,* 441–449.

Martin, J. E., Calfas, K. J., Patten, C. A., Polarek, M., Hoffstetter, C. R., Noto, J., & Beach, D. (1997). Prospective evaluation of three smoking interventions in 205 recovering alcoholics: One-year results of project SCRAP-Tobacco. *Journal of Consulting and Clinical Psychology, 65,* 190–194.

Matson, D. M., Lee, J. W., & Hopp, J. W. (1993). The impact of incentives and competitions on participation and quit rates in worksite smoking cessation programs. *American Journal of Health Promotion, 7,* 270–280.

Mermelstein, R., Cohen, S., Lichtenstein, E., Baer, J. S., & Kamarck, T. (1986). Social support and smoking cessation and maintenance. *Journal of Consulting and Clinical Psychology, 54,* 447–453.

Niaura, R., Clark, M. M., Raciti, M. A., Pera, V., & Abrams, D. B. (1992). Increased saliva cotinine concentrations in smokers during rapid weight loss. *Journal of Consulting & Clinical Psychology, 60,* 985–987.

Perkins, K. A. (1992). Effects of tobacco smoking on caloric intake. *British Journal of Addiction, 87,* 193–205.

Perkins, K. A. (1994). Issues in the prevention of weight gain after smoking cessation. *Annals of Behavioral Medicine, 16,* 46–52.

Perkins, K. A., Epstein, L. H., Grobe, J. E., & Fonte, C. (1994). Tobacco abstinence, smoking cues, and the reinforcing value of smoking. *Pharmacology, Biochemistry, & Behavior, 47,* 107–112.

Perkins, K. A., Epstein, L. H., Sexton, J. E., & Pastor, S. (1990). Effects of smoking cessation on consumption of alcohol and sweet, high-fat foods. *Journal of Substance Abuse, 2,* 287–297.

Perkins, K. A., Grobe, J. E., & Fonte, C. (1997). The influence of acute smoking exposure on the subsequent reinforcing value of smoking. *Experimental and Clinical Psychopharmacology, 5,* 277–285.

Perkins, K. A., Grobe, J. E., Stiller, R. L., Fonte, C., & Goettler, J. E. (1992). Nasal spray nicotine replacement suppresses cigarette smoking desire and behavior. *Clinical Pharmacology & Therapeutics, 52,* 627–634.

Perkins, K. A., Levine, M., Marcus, M. D., & Shiffman, S. (1997). Addressing women's concerns about weight gain due to smoking cessation. *Journal of Substance Abuse Treatment, 14,* 173–182.

Perkins, K. A., Rohay, J., Meilahn, E. N., Wing, R. R., Matthews, K. A., & Kuller, L. H. (1993). Diet, alcohol intake, and physical activity as a function of smoking status in middle-aged women. *Health Psychology, 12,* 410–415.

Peto, R., Lopez, A. D., Boreham, J., Thun, M., Heath, C., & Doll, R. (1996). Mortality from smoking worldwide. *British Medical Bulletin, 52,* 12–21.

Rose, J. E., & Behm, F. M. (1994). Inhalation of vapors from black pepper extract reduces smoking withdrawal symptoms. *Drug and Alcohol Dependence, 34,* 225–229.

Rose, J. E., Behm, F. M., & Levin, E. D. (1993). Role of nicotine dose and sensory cues in the regulation of smoke intake. *Pharmacology Biochemistry and Behavior, 44,* 891–900.

Rose, J. E., Behm, F. M., Westman, E. C., Levin, E. D., Stein, R. M., Lane, J. D., & Ripka, G. V. (1994). Combined effects of nicotine and mecamylamine in attenuating smoking satisfaction. *Experimental and Clinical Psychopharmacology, 2,* 328–344.

Rose, J. E., Behm, F. M., Westman, E. C., Levin, E. D., Stein, R. M., & Ripka, G. V. (1994). Mecamylamine combined with nicotine skin patch facilitates smoking cessation beyond nicotine patch treatment alone. *Clinical Pharmacology and Therapeutics, 56,* 86–99.

Rose, J. E., & Corrigall, W. A. (1997). Nicotine self-administration in animals and humans: Similarities and differences. *Psychopharmacology, 130,* 28–40.

Rose, J. E., & Levin, E. D. (1991). Inter-relationships between conditioned and primary reinforcement in the maintenance of cigarette smoking. *British Journal of Addiction, 86,* 605–609.

Rose, J. E., Tashkin, D. P., Ertle, A., Zinser, M. C., & Lafer, R. (1985). Sensory blockade of smoking satisfaction. *Pharmacology Biochemistry & Behavior, 23,* 289–293.

Schmitz, J. M., Grabowski, J., & Rhoads, H. (1994). The effects of high and low doses of methadone on cigarette smoking. *Drug and Alcohol Dependence, 34,* 237–242.

Schneider, N., Lunell, E., Olmstead, R. E., & Fagerstrom, K. (1996). Clinical pharmacokinetics of nasal nicotine delivery. *Clinical Pharmacokinetics, 31,* 65–80.

Schneider, N., Olmstead, R., Mody, F. V., Doan, K., Franzon, M., Jarvik, M. E., & Steinberg, C. (1995). Efficacy of a nicotine nasal spray in smoking cessation: A placebo-controlled, double-blind trial. *Addiction, 90,* 1671–1682.

Slaby, A. E. (1991). Acaytl's curse. In J. A. Cocores (Ed.), *The clinical management of nicotine dependence* (pp. 3–27). New York: Springer-Verlag.

Shiffman, S., & Balabanis, M. (1995). Associations between tobacco and alcohol. In J. Fertig & J. Allen (Eds.), *Alcohol and tobacco: From basic science to clinical practice* (NIAAA Monograph No. 30, pp. 17–36). Washington, DC: U.S. Government Printing Office.

Shiffman, S., Paty, J., Gnys, M., Kassel, J., & Hickcox, M. (1996). First lapses to smoking: Within-subjects analysis of real-time reports. *Journal of Consulting and Clinical Psychology, 64,* 366–379.

Stitzer, M. L., & Bigelow, G. E. (1985). Contingent reinforcement for reduced breath carbon monoxide levels: Target-specific effects on cigarette smoking. *Addictive Behaviors, 10,* 345–349.

Straughan, J., & Dufort, W. H. (1969). Task difficulty, relaxation, and anxiety level during verbal learning and recall. *Journal of Abnormal Psychology, 74,* 621–624.

Vuchinch, R. E., & Tucker, J. A. (1988). Contributions from behavioral theories of choice to an analysis of alcohol abuse. *Journal of Abnormal Psychology, 97,* 181–195.

Vuchinich, R. E., & Tucker, J. A. (1996). The molar context of alcohol abuse. In L. Green & J. H. Kagel (Eds.), *Advances in behavioral economics: Vol 3. Substance use and abuse* (pp. 133–162). Norwood, NJ: Ablex.

West, R. J., Hajek, P., & Burrows, S. (1990). Effect of glucose tablets on craving for cigarettes. *Psychopharmacology, 101,* 555–559.

West, R. J., & Willis, N. (1998). Double-blind placebo controlled trial of dextrose tablets and nicotine patch in smoking cessation. *Psychopharmacology, 136,* 201–204.

Wynd, C. (1992). Personal power imagery and relaxation techniques used in smoking cessation programs. *American Journal of Health Promotion, 6,* 184–189.

Yung, L., Gordis, E., & Holt, J. (1983). Dietary choices and likelihood of abstinence among alcoholic patients in an outpatient clinic. *Drug and Alcohol Dependence, 12,* 355–362.

Zisook, S., Shuchter, S. R., & Mulvihill, M. (1990). Alcohol, cigarette, and medication use during the first year of widowhood. *Psychiatric Annals, 20,* 318–326.

CHAPTER ELEVEN

Behavioral Economics of Obesity: Food Intake and Energy Expenditure

Leonard H. Epstein
Brian E. Saelens
University at Buffalo

Most people make many choices regarding their eating and exercise behaviors every day. When they awake, they must decide whether to eat breakfast, what to eat, and how much to eat. Then they have to decide whether to walk, bike, or take the car to work. Should they pack walking shoes or exercise clothes, or are they not going to exercise that day? There are multiple decisions regarding eating snacks, meals, and activity plans throughout the day that involve such factors as relative preferences for and access to the alternatives. Behavioral economics provides a comprehensive methodological and conceptual approach to studying choices of what to eat, when to eat, and how much to eat, as well as whether to be active, what type of activity, at what intensity, and for what duration (Epstein, 1995).

Obesity is one of the most relevant applications for behavioral choice theory for eating and activity behaviors. Obesity is a major public health problem, with its prevalence increasing in adults (Kuczmarski, Flegel, Campbell, & Johnson, 1994) and children (Troiano, Flegel, Kuczmarski, Campbell, & Johnson, 1995). Obesity is an energy balance problem, with energy intake exceeding energy expenditure, resulting in weight gain (Epstein, 1995). The behavioral treatment and prevention of obesity involves modifying intake and expenditure behaviors. However, weight control interventions typically have poor long-term efficacy (Brownell & Jeffery, 1987). Behavioral economic studies regarding eating and activity may provide new insights into ways to improve weight control (Epstein, 1995).

The purpose of this chapter is to provide an overview of research on the behavioral economics of food intake and physical activity in humans and to discuss how this information may be helpful in the treatment and prevention of obesity. In this chapter, we briefly review laboratory and clinical research on individual differences in the reinforcing value of food and physical activity, and factors that influence choice of food or physical activity. We primarily focus on research completed in our laboratories but also provide an overview of related research findings. Finally, we provide ideas for new directions in research on the behavioral economics of food intake and physical activity.

INDIVIDUAL DIFFERENCES IN THE CHOICE
OR FOOD OR PHYSICAL ACTIVITY

There are wide individual differences in the reinforcing value of food or physical activity. Some people may find food more reinforcing than alternative activities, which may predispose them to obesity and make it more difficult to modify their eating behaviors compared to people who find food less reinforcing. Likewise, some people may find being sedentary highly reinforcing, which would make them more likely to become sedentary, and obese. They also may find it difficult to develop a regular physical activity habit.

Individual Differences in Food as a Reinforcer

Food has been used as a reinforcer to motivate animals and humans in scores of laboratory and applied studies. There are numerous studies that focus on a behavioral economic analysis of food as a reinforcer (Foltin, 1991, 1992, 1994a, 1994b; Foltin & Fischman, 1990; Forzano & Logue, 1992, 1994; Logue & King, 1991; Nader & Woolverton, 1992a, 1992b), and studies that compare the relative reinforcing value of food versus drug self-administration in animals (Carroll, Lac, & Nygaard, 1989; Nader et al., 1992b) and humans (Bulik & Brinded, 1994; Epstein, Bulik, Perkins, Caggiula & Rodefer, 1991).

Although food is a primary reinforcer and is needed for survival, there are substantial individual differences in the reinforcing value of food (Reiss & Havercamp, 1996). Epidemiological evidence suggests that a large percentage of the U.S. population eats above their physiological requirements for calories for weight maintenance, resulting in an increasing prevalence of obesity (Gortmaker, Dietz, & Cheung, 1990). Eating is an important source of pleasure in many people's lives (Westenhoefer & Pudel, 1993), and it may be difficult for other reinforcers to compete with food. Soon after finishing a meal, many people are planning the next meal, they socialize around meals, read about food, and may have trouble exerting control over their eating. These people seem to live merely to eat. Yet, some people never seem to remember to eat and are more involved in other activities than eating. They seem to eat merely to live.

The powerful reinforcing value of food may explain in part why it is difficult for people to modify their eating behavior, because many of the most palatable and reinforcing foods are high-fat foods that require moderation for health benefits. Individuals with high reinforcing efficacy of eating may more likely choose to engage in eating instead of alternative nonfood activities when choosing among activities and perhaps may be more sensitive or exposed to environments conducive to eating. Individual differences in the reinforcing efficacy of food may be etiologically relevant to obesity. The work required to obtain food reinforcers and the availability of alternative nonfood reinforcers has a large influence on the choice to eat or which foods to eat, but it is unclear whether these factors impact everyone in the same way. Individual differences in the reinforcing value of food may help explain weight status differences and differential responsiveness to weight-control programs.

Saelens and Epstein (1996) examined differences between obese and nonobese women in the reinforcing value of food versus nonfood activities. Participants completed a concurrent-schedules choice task to earn points to be traded for high-fat, high-calorie snack foods, such as ice cream and chocolate bars, or for time to engage in nonfood activities such as playing computer games and watching videos. The choice options had similar response requirements during the first trial of the task, but the cost for food reinforcers was increased across subsequent trials and the cost of nonfood activities remained constant. The choices between obese and nonobese participants were similar when the cost of the reinforcers was the same, but differed when the cost of food reinforcers was increased. As can be seen in Fig. 11.1, nonobese women showed a linear decrease in choice of food or sedentary activities as the cost of food reinforcers was increased. Obese women showed an initial increase in responding for food reinforcers, and they decreased their responding for food reinforcers only after more substantial increases were required to obtain food reinforcers.

Logue (1997) also studied individual differences in reinforcer effectiveness using a self-control paradigm, in which participants have the choice for a smaller immediate reinforcer or a larger, delayed reinforcer. Responding for the larger, delayed reinforcer is described as *self-control*, whereas responding for the smaller, immediate reinforcer is described as *impulsive*. Forzano and Logue (1992, 1994; Logue & King, 1991) found individual differences in self-control with food reinforcers. They reported that impulsiveness in obtaining food reinforcers was positively related to current dieting (Logue & King, 1991) and scores on the hunger scale of the Three-Factor Eating Questionnaire, whereas self-control was related to reinforcer desirability (Forzano

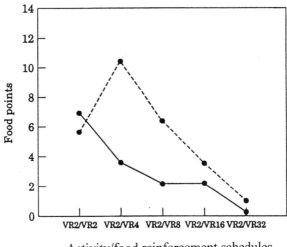

Activity/food reinforcement schedules

FIG. 11.1. The number of food reinforcers earned by obese (- - -) and nonobese (—) women across trials associated with increasing response costs
associated with obtaining food reinforcers. From "Reinforcing Value of Food
in Obese and Non-Obese Women," by B. E. Saelens and L. H. Epstein, 1996,
Appetite, 27, p. 46. Copyright 1996 by Academic Press Limited. Reprinted with
permission.

& Logue, 1992). Logue and her colleagues found little individual variation
in self-control with the use of points in exchange for money (Logue, King,
Chavarro, & Volpe, 1990), which suggests that people may have more problems with self-control over food than some nonfood reinforcers.

Glover and Hanley (1993) examined the reinforcing efficacy of eating in
a setting with alternative activities among adults with Prader–Willi syndrome,
a disorder characterized by overeating. During a free-choice baseline among
various activities, participants engaged in eating for the majority of the time.
In subsequent sessions, the work required to obtain food was increased.
However, instead of introducing an external response, such as responding
on a concurrent-schedules task to obtain food reinforcers, these investigators
made eating contingent upon another activity already present in the environment (Timberlake & Farmer-Dougan, 1991). This activity functioned as
the currency for obtaining the contingent food items. Other activities not
involved in the contingency were freely available and could be participated
in instead of eating or engaging in the activity associated with obtaining
food. Results showed that participants engaged in the maximum amount of
the instrumental activity to obtain the maximal amount of food that the
contingency allowed. Freely available activities did not substitute at all for
eating among these adults, regardless of the amount of work required to

obtain food. These data show how reinforcing food is for Prader–Willi adults, consistent with the difficulties in modifying their food intake.

Individual Differences in Physical Activity as a Reinforcer

Physical activity is part of a healthy lifestyle that is associated with reduced risk of diseases, such as heart disease and colon cancer (Pate et al., 1995), but approximately 40% of the population remains completely sedentary, and the majority of the U.S. population is not active enough to derive health benefits from their physical activity (Stephens, Jacobs, & White, 1985; U.S. Department of Health and Human Services, 1996). The majority of leisure time, and increasingly more work time, is spent being sedentary. Sedentariness is cross-sectionally and prospectively associated with obesity (Dietz & Gortmaker, 1985; Gortmaker et al., 1996) and is a significant public health problem (U.S. Department of Health and Human Services, 1996).

Some people—unfortunately the minority of the population—engage in physical activity on nearly a daily basis and apparently find exercise very reinforcing. Alternatively, other people find sedentary activities more reinforcing than physical activity. This may be particularly true among obese individuals. Dietz, Gortmaker, and colleagues (Dietz & Gortmaker, 1985; Gortmaker et al., 1996) established a strong prospective link between television watching and obesity after controlling for original weight status, which supports the possibility that the higher reinforcing value of sedentary activities may be causal in development of obesity. The choice to be sedentary instead of physically active may contribute to positive energy balance and weight gain.

Epstein et al. (Epstein, Smith, Vara, & Rodefer, 1991) used a concurrent-schedules choice task to examine whether there are differences between obese and nonobese children in the relative reinforcing value of sedentary versus physical activities. They found that both obese and nonobese children spend the majority of their time being sedentary when given the choice among physical and sedentary activities. As shown in Fig. 11.2, with minor increases in work required to get access to sedentary activities, nonobese children quickly switched to working for more time to be physically active. Moderately obese children switched to working for the more easily obtained physical activities with further increases in the amount of work to obtain sedentary activity time, but very obese children did not switch to physical activities despite large disparities in the work required to obtain access to sedentary versus physical activities. This study suggests that the degree of obesity plays a role in how readily active behaviors replace sedentary behaviors: Individual differences between obese and nonobese children's activity choice were not apparent until the work required to obtain access to

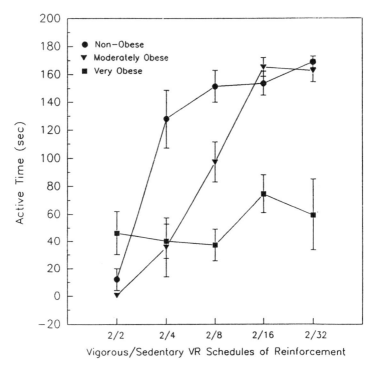

FIG. 11.2. The amount of time earned for physical activity among nonobese, moderately obese, and very obese children across trials associated with increasing response costs associated with obtaining sedentary activity time. From "Behavioral Economic Analysis of Activity Choice in Obese Children," by L. H. Epstein, J. A. Smith, L. S. Vara, and J. S. Rodefer, 1991, *Health Psychology, 10,* p. 312. Copyright 1991 by Lawrence Erlbaum Associates, Inc. Reprinted with permission.

sedentary activities was varied. These results also suggest that environmental factors, such as reinforcer accessibility and response cost to obtain reinforcers, can influence food and activity choice across individuals despite individual differences in the effectiveness of these reinforcers.

FACTORS THAT MODIFY THE CHOICE
OF FOOD AND PHYSICAL ACTIVITY

The relative reinforcing value of food or physical activity can be studied in two ways. First, the relative reinforcing value of these alternatives can be studied in relation to alternatives in different and distinct response classes: nonfood and sedentary alternatives. This choice is relevant to understanding factors that influence eating or not eating, or being physically active or sedentary. Second, choice among food alternatives, or among physically active alternatives, provides information on what a person will choose to eat or what type of physical activity in which they will engage.

Food Versus Nonfood Alternatives

Lappalainen and Epstein (1990) had normal-weight male college students choose between food or money in both food-deprived and nondeprived conditions. When the amount of responding on the computer-controlled concurrent-schedules task needed to obtain food and money was similar, participants in the food-deprived condition chose food, and those in the nondeprived condition chose money. When the amount of responding to earn food was increased, deprived participants switched over to earning money instead of food with increasing effort needed to obtain food. Thus, even when participants were food-deprived, the reinforcing value of food did not compete with money in nonobese participants when the behavioral requirements to obtain food were increased. The nondeprived participants maintained their choice of earning monetary reinforcers as the work required to earn food increased.

Choice Between Food Alternatives

Lappalainen and Epstein (1990) examined the impact of changing the response requirements for food items on food choice. In the first trial of a concurrent-schedules choice task, a highly liked and moderately liked sandwich were equally easy to obtain because both were associated with continuous reinforcement schedules. In subsequent trials, the cost to obtain points to be traded in for the highly liked sandwich was increased, requiring, on average, 32 times more work for the same amount of highly liked sandwich. Alternatively, the cost for the moderately liked sandwich was maintained at a continuous reinforcement schedule throughout all trials. As seen in Fig. 11.3, responding during the first trial was exclusively for the highly liked sandwich. Responding during subsequent trials shifted to the moderately liked sandwich, with increasing cost for obtaining the highly liked sandwich. In fact, responding was almost exclusively for the moderately liked sandwich when the reinforcement schedule for the highly liked sandwich was at the highest response requirements.

Smith and Epstein (1991) compared highly liked high-calorie foods with less-liked low-calorie foods among obese children. They found that obese children initially chose to work for the highly liked high-calorie foods, but chose the less-liked low-calorie foods with increased response requirements to get the highly liked foods. These studies suggest that liking and environmental constraints on foods have an effect on food choice, and that less-liked

300

EPSTEIN AND SAELENS

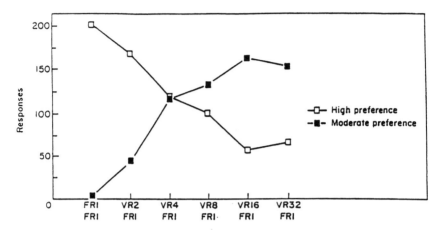

FIG. 11.3. The number of responses for high-preference and moderate-preference sandwiches across trials with increasing response costs associated with obtaining the highly liked sandwich. From "A Behavioral Economics Analysis of Food Choice in Humans," by R. Lappalainen and L. H. Epstein, 1990, *Appetite, 14,* p. 86. Copyright 1990 by Academic Press Limited. Reprinted with permission.

food items can substitute for highly liked food based on the ease of access to the food choices.

Physically Active Versus Sedentary Alternatives

Substitutability among physical and sedentary activities has been explored in the context of examining factors that influence choice between physically active versus sedentary alternatives. For example, the effects of accessibility to exercise and activity facilities are important in determining physical activity levels. Sallis et al. (1990) found in a large population sample that the frequency of physical activity is related to the proximity of physical activity facilities to home. In the environments of most people, there is much greater access to sedentary than to physical activities. Raynor, Coleman, and Epstein (1998) tested the influence of proximity to sedentary and physically active alternatives on choice of sedentary and physically active alternatives. Sedentary male college students were randomly assigned to one of four groups in a 2 × 2 factorial in which physical activities were either near or far and sedentary activities were either near or far. *Near* and *far* were operationalized as immediately accessible (i.e., in the same room) and a 5-minute walk away, respectively. The group in which sedentary activities were far and physical activities were near spent the entire session being physically active. The requirement of walking for 5 min to get access to sedentary activities was enough to shift their choice to physical activity. Alternatively, both groups in which sedentary activities were near spent the majority of time being sedentary.

These data suggest that environmental changes that both increase the proximity and convenience of physical activity and decrease access to sedentary activities likely will increase physical activity. Unfortunately, environments have become saturated with labor-saving and convenient sedentary activities that decrease the need to be physically active. Possibly, such sedentary environments have increased the reinforcing efficacy of sedentary activities or decreased the reinforcing efficacy of physical activity, both of which would contribute to higher rates of sedentary activity and obesity.

Saelens and Epstein (in press) evaluated the substitutability of sedentary activities in 54 sedentary adults. During one baseline session, participants were provided the choice between one physical activity and three sedentary activities, and the amount of time allocated to the sedentary activities were ranked. For the next two sessions, participants were randomized to groups that had to be physically active to gain access to selected sedentary behaviors. The groups were provided access to high-, moderate-, and low-preference sedentary activities contingent on being active, or a noncontingent (free choice) control. Sedentary activities that were not contingent upon being active were freely available. Results showed that participants increased their activity to gain access to high or moderately reinforcing sedentary activities, but not to the low-preference activity or control. Thus, low-preference sedentary behaviors do not substitute for high-preference sedentary activities, and highly valued sedentary activities may compete with physical activity more than lower-valued sedentary activities.

Variations in the liking ratings for physical activity may have little effect on choice for sedentary children when the competing sedentary options are highly liked. Epstein, Smith, et al. (1991) gave children the choice of a highly liked sedentary activity and either a highly liked physical activity or a least-liked physical activity. When the sedentary and physical activity options were equally available in both tasks, the children chose to be sedentary. Children decreased their responding for sedentary activity time with increasing cost for sedentary activity, but the point of switching to physical activity was the same regardless of whether the physical activity option was highly liked or least liked.

Vara and Epstein (1993) examined the effects of number of physically active alternatives or physical activity variety on the choice between physical and sedentary activities among nonobese women. Participants chose to be more sedentary than active when given a choice between physical and sedentary activities, independent of the number of physically active or sedentary alternatives. However, when the choice was between a variety of physical activities versus one physical activity, participants reliably found variety more reinforcing.

The hypothesis that high-preference sedentary behaviors compete with physical activity suggests that reducing access to high-preference sedentary behaviors may increase activity. We found in a series of laboratory studies that reinforcing obese children for decreasing high-preference sedentary activities, such as television watching and video game playing, is associated with increases in physical activity that are similar to the changes that occur when increases in physical activity are reinforced (Epstein, Saelens, Myers, & Vito, 1997; Epstein, Saelens, & O'Brien, 1995). These studies suggest that sedentary activities do not readily substitute for each other. If sedentary activities were completely substitutable, children would simply have replaced all prior time spent in high-preference sedentary activities with time engaged in low-preference sedentary activities. Whereas time spent in low-preference sedentary activity did increase when decreases in high-preference sedentary activity time were reinforced, physical activity increased as well.

The implications of these laboratory studies for treatment outcome in obese children was tested by randomly assigning obese children to groups in which they were reinforced for being more active, reinforced for being less sedentary, or reinforced for the combination of the two (Epstein, Valoski, Vara, McCurley, Wisniewski, Kalarchian, Klein, & Shrager, 1995). All children were provided the same advice regarding dietary changes. Results at 1-year follow-up showed the best results were for the children who were reinforced for reducing sedentary behaviors. Each group showed similar changes in fitness. The improvement in weight control was probably due in part to a shift in allocation of time from sedentary to physically active alternatives, and to a decrease in eating opportunities as time in sedentary behaviors was decreased.

If sedentary behaviors are more reinforcing for some people than being active, perhaps sedentary behaviors can be used to reinforce children for being more active (Timberlake & Farmer-Dougan, 1991). During a baseline session, Saelens and Epstein (1998) provided obese children choice among various sedentary activities and an exercise bike. Children then were assigned randomly to one of two groups. In one group, television activities of video game playing and watching movies on a videocassette recorder were made contingent on riding the exercise bicycle, whereas other sedentary activities of reading and drawing or coloring were freely available. In the other group, all sedentary activities and the exercise bike were freely available, as on the baseline day. This study tested the efficacy of television activities to reinforce physical activity, but allowed for an indirect measure of how well reading and coloring or drawing substitute for television activities, which require riding the exercise bicycle in the contingent group. Findings from this study are presented in Fig. 11.4. Children in the contingent group dramatically increased their physical activity to get access to television activities even though other sedentary activities were freely available. This suggests that television activities can reinforce physical activity, and that television activi-

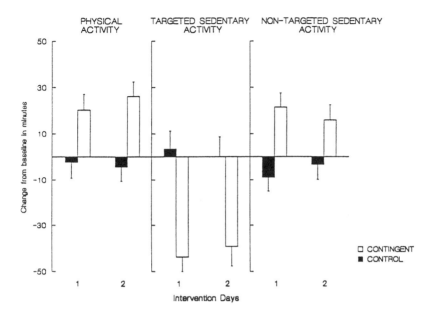

FIG. 11.4. The change (Mean ± SE bars) from baseline in physical activity, targeted sedentary activities, and nontargeted sedentary activities in the Contingent and Control groups during the 1st and 2nd intervention days. From "Behavioral Engineering of Activity Choice in Obese Children," by B. E. Saelens and L. H. Epstein, 1998, *International Journal of Obesity, 22,* pp. 275–277. Copyright by Stockton Press. Reprinted with permission.

ties were not completely substituted for by reading and drawing or coloring, which were the freely available sedentary activities. Our findings point to the importance of considering the impact of sedentary activities and their substitutability on the choice between being physically active or sedentary.

DISCUSSION AND IDEAS FOR FUTURE RESEARCH ON BEHAVIORAL ECONOMICS OF FOOD OR ACTIVITY

Research has only begun to explore human energy balance behaviors within a behavioral economic framework. Preliminary evidence suggests the utility for behavioral economic theory and associated methodologies for investigating choice among eating and activity behaviors. The behavioral economic technique of comparing the reinforcing value of competing activities and manipulating the constraints on or environment of one activity or reinforcer provides valuable information about the reinforcing efficacy of a reinforcer as well as about the substitutability among different activities or reinforcers. The examination of reinforcing efficacy and substitution among energy balance behaviors and the factors that influence these characteristics has implications for obesity development and weight-control interventions. With increased knowledge of the behavioral economics of energy balance behaviors, the field could increase obesity prevention and improve population-based and clinical weight-control interventions to promote more long-term weight-control and health benefits.

Empirical evidence regarding individual differences in the relative reinforcing value of eating versus engaging in nonfood activities (Saelens & Epstein, 1996); food choice (Drewnowski, Brunzell, Sande, Iverius, & Greenwood, 1985; Fisher & Birch, 1995); and activity choice (Epstein, Smith, Vara & Rodefer, 1991) suggests that obese people, in comparison to normal-weight counterparts, find positive energy balance behaviors (i.e., sedentary activity, consumption of high-fat foods) more reinforcing than negative energy balance behaviors (i.e., physical activity). Individual differences in the reinforcing value or efficacy of behaviors may have substantial impact on behavior and behavioral choice (Reiss & Havercamp, 1996), which contribute to energy balance and may affect weight status.

Behavioral economic analyses of physical activity and eating bring into focus the significant impact that environments have upon our behavioral choices. The prevalence of obesity is increasing in the United States as our environments become more conducive to engaging in behaviors associated with poor weight control. Our access to high-fat, high-calorie foods is increasing and work and leisure time are becoming dominated by advances in technology that are making us more sedentary. As a society, we need to consider the negative health impact of these environmental changes and perhaps modify our surroundings to decrease the likelihood of eating and being sedentary. Laboratory findings regarding food as a reinforcer relative to other reinforcers and the effects of varying the response requirements for obtaining reinforcers have relevance for our eating environment. Environmental changes in our society have increased the convenience of obtaining food. Brownell (1997) argued that the United States has created a toxic food environment that has substantially increased access to food within the environment via fast-food restaurants and decreased distance of these restaurants from work, school, and home. Put in a concurrent-schedules context, this change is synonymous with decreasing the response requirements for food without changing the requirements for nonfood reinforcers. This decrease in effort required to obtain food will be accompanied by increases in food consumption and decreases in consumption of nonfood reinforcers (Lappalainen & Epstein, 1990).

Reinforcing Value of Food

Many exciting questions and avenues of inquiry remain. Are there individual differences between obese and nonobese individuals in the relative reinforcing value of certain food items or eating in general? Are these individual differences learned or a result of a genetic predisposition interacting with a specific environment? A better understanding of factors that might increase the reinforcing value of food is needed. The recent growth of interest in the genetics of obesity has led to a search for behavioral phenotypes that may differentiate genotypes. One potential behavior pattern is excessive reinforcing value of food, which may be indicative of a common genetic profile related to dopaminergic activity, believed to mediate reinforcement effects (Robinson & Berridge, 1993; Salamone, 1994). Research already has shown a greater proportion of obese than nonobese people with differences in the A₂ allele of the dopamine gene D_2, and shown that a very large percentage of persons (87%) with a specific constellation of obesity-related behaviors— such as parental obesity, strong preference for carbohydrates, and age of onset—share this genetic profile (Comings, Gade, MacMurray, Muhleman, & Peters, 1996; Cowart, 1981). The inclusion of carbohydrate preference as part of this behavioral constellation is interesting. Sweet preference appears to be genetic, because it can be observed almost from birth (Cowart, 1981), whereas preferences for fat appear at a later age and are learned (Johnson, McPhee, & Birch, 1991; Kern, McPhee, Fisher, Johnson, & Birch, 1993).

The reinforcing value of food also may be influenced by learning. There are many ways in which the reinforcing value of food can be increased. For example, using food as a reward can increase the reinforcing value of food (Birch, Birch, Marlin, & Kramer, 1982; Birch, Marlin, & Rotter, 1984). Using food as a reward is very common and occurs in a wide variety of situations. Although this often is conceptualized as using food to increase instrumental behavior (cleaning a room, getting good grades), food also can be used as a reward if dessert is presented contingent on finishing a meal, or a snack presented after homework is completed. Another way to increase the reinforcing value of food would be to praise children for eating, or finishing all the food on their plate (Birch, Zimmerman, & Hind, 1980). The reinforcing value of food can be increased by providing a rich social environment for eating that increases the positive associations for eating and the motivation to eat.

Additional questions arise with respect to the reinforcing value of food. How reinforcing is food? Can the reinforcing value of food be decreased in those who choose to eat too often or who allocate too much time to food, and too much time to eating? Noncaloric activities that maximally substitute for food or that decrease the reinforcing efficacy of eating have the potential to reduce overall caloric intake and perhaps reduce the reinforcing value of eating. Research should investigate whether individual alternatives to eating can be developed and whether people would prefer to engage in these activities rather than eat.

The relative reinforcing value of food needs to be examined when participants are not food-deprived, because this characterizes the majority of eating episodes. Although the reinforcing value of food generally increases with deprivation, the reinforcing value should be high in a nondeprived state only for those who find food very reinforcing. The role of specific macronutrients (protein, fat, or carbohydrates) or food deprivation and the relative reinforcing value of food may be a very important aspect of eating regulation. Food or relative macronutrient deprivation is central to most approaches to modification of eating. If the goal is to increase intake of more healthy foods, then it is common to limit access to the less-healthy but perhaps more reinforcing and satisfying foods. For example, if the goal is to increase fruit and vegetable intake, then it is logical to remove potato chips and snack cakes from the cupboard and increase storage of apples and carrots. This facilitates increased intake of apples and carrots and reduced intake of Ho-Ho's and Moon Pies. However, at the same time, it produces a relative deprivation of Ho-Ho's and Moon Pies, which may inadvertently cause an increase in the reinforcing value of Ho-Ho's and Moon Pies. In addition, all diets involve a reduction in food intake or reduction in intake of specific types of foods. This reduced access to specific foods may increase the reinforcing value of these foods, creating a tension in changing dietary intake between the foods to be eaten in greater quantities versus those to be consumed in decreasing quantities (Fisher & Birch, in press). Perhaps individual differences in the reinforcing value of food due to deprivation may provide a predictor of how easy it will be to change eating habits. Some people will respond to food deprivation with a shift to other sources of enjoyment, but those who find food very reinforcing, or who have a reduced number of alternatives that are reinforcing, may respond to food deprivation with a greatly enhanced desire to eat.

Reinforcing Value of Physical Activity

There is also the need to better understand individual differences in the reinforcing value of physical activity. There is evidence that fitness (Bouchard, Dionne, Simoneau, & Boulay, 1992; Prud'homme, Bouchard, LeBlanc, Landry, & Fontaine, 1984) and the response to exercise programs may have a strong genetic component (Prud'homme et al., 1984). There is no work, to our knowledge, evaluating genetic contributions to the reinforcing value of physical activity. Differences in the reinforcing value of physical activity may be influenced by learning. The concordance of activity levels within families suggests that parents who are active are arranging an environment in which children can be active, and probably reinforcing and supporting high activity levels. Research is needed to understand better how to make activities more reinforcing for those individuals who are very sedentary. Could using physical activity as a reward, or pairing physical activity with pleasant associations, increase the reinforcing value of physical activity? As deprivation increases the reinforcing value of food, can deprivation increase the reinforcing value of being active? According to the disequilibrium theory of reinforcement (Timberlake & Farmer-Dougan, 1991), reducing physical activity below baseline levels would result in an increase in the reinforcing value of activity. Can brief shifts in reinforcing value be used to produce more permanent shifts in the level and reinforcing value of activity? John Martin, an experienced exercise researcher (Martin & Dubbert, 1982), indicated that in a program with sedentary "couch potatoes," he informed them they could not begin the activity program until they were carefully trained in skills necessary for being active, such as taking heart rate, knowing about perceived exertion, and so forth. These sedentary participants were prevented from exercising in the program for several weeks, so that by the time they were allowed to be active, they were impatient to begin and primed to exercise.

When access to sedentary behaviors is reduced, participants are deprived of the opportunity to engage in these activities, which may result in an increase in the reinforcing value of these alternatives. The manner in which sedentary behaviors are limited may be important in determining whether high-preference sedentary behaviors become more or less reinforcing. Epstein et al. (1997) compared groups in which children were reinforced for being less sedentary, punished for being sedentary, having sedentary activities restricted by removal from the environment, and a no contingency control. Children in the reinforcement and punishment group showed the largest increases in activity, whereas only the reinforcement group showed a decrease in liking of sedentary behaviors after the intervention. The restriction group showed an increase in liking for targeted sedentary behaviors, supporting the idea that the manner in which competing sedentary behaviors are reduced is critical to the activity choice.

Substitutability of Food or Activity Reinforcers

Substitutability among foods, between eating and nonfood activitivies, and between physical and sedentary activities, requires further investigation. Are there characteristics of food items that make foods more or less substitutable for each other (Green, 1997)? For example, do foods that are similar in taste or palatability substitute for each other more readily than foods that are similar in calories? Are macronutrients important to consider in which food items substitute for each other? Are there other food characteristics that make them more or less substitutable for each other? Based on genetic or learning history, are some people more responsive to chocolate, or to different combinations of fat with sweet taste (ice cream, chocolate, pastry, cookies, etc.), or fat with a salty taste (chips, Doritos, etc.)? A particularly important question to be addressed is the influence of macronutrient substitutes or replacements on the reinforcing value of food. Substitutes for sugar have been available for some time, and there are new substitutes for fat that soon will be available. Do these substitutes alter the reinforcing value of the usual foods with sugar or fat? If there are no differences in the reinforcing value of these foods, will people be able to substitute them for the higher calorie version, without increasing volume of food, which may help to reduce body weight or reduce fat intake. On the other hand, if the goal is to improve nutritional content of the diet, substituting a low-nutrient dense food for another low-nutrient dense food, albeit with less sugar or fat, will not shift food preferences or the reinforcing value of that food. The better alternative may be to increase access of more nutrient dense foods rather than shift to sugar or fat replacements.

We have made considerable progress in understanding the substitutability of sedentary and active behaviors, as well as substitutability within classes of sedentary behaviors. People will shift from being sedentary to being active if the cost of being sedentary increases (Epstein, Smith, et al., 1991), and people will not choose sedentary behaviors if access to them is reduced (Raynor et al., 1998). Sedentary activities can be very reinforcing for sedentary persons, as the types (Epstein et al., 1991) or variety (Vara & Epstein, 1993) of physical activities used as alternatives to being sedentary have not increased activity when compared to highly liked and -preferred sedentary behaviors. However, there are differences in the reinforcing value of sedentary behaviors (Saelens & Epstein, 1997), with the implication that choice of being physically active or sedentary may depend in part on the characteristics of the sedentary behaviors that compete with being active as well as characteristics of the physically active alternatives.

This chapter examined behavioral economics of food and physical activity separately. Although they usually are studied as independent classes of behaviors, they can be related. Physical activity can influence eating. Certain sedentary behaviors such as television watching may act as a complement to stimulate eating (Dietz & Gortmaker, 1985), and reducing these behaviors can reduce caloric intake (Epstein, Valoski, et al., 1995). Exercise has reliable effects on food intake in animals, but human research has shown inconsistent effects of exercise (Pi-Sunyer, 1987). Food consumption also may act as a compliment to physical activity. The fat and carbohydrate composition of the diet can have an effect on the amount of physical activity, with the amount of fat in the diet negatively related to the amount of activity (Bandini, Schoeller, & Dietz, 1994). Certainly eating too much food during a meal can reduce the immediate postmeal activity level.

Behavioral economic research provides a conceptual and methodological framework to understand factors that influence food selection and consumption and types and amount of physical activity. Additional laboratory research is needed to identify new ways to utilize this information to influence choice of healthy versus unhealthy behaviors and to translate this basic research into meaningful interventions to prevent and treat obesity.

ACKNOWLEDGMENTS

Appreciation is expressed to John Martin for comments on an earlier version of this chapter. The research presented in this chapter was supported in part by NIH grants HD 25997, HD 20829, and HD 34284 awarded to the first author.

REFERENCES

Bandini, L. G., Schoeller, D. A., & Dietz, W. H. (1994). Metabolic differences in response to a high-fat vs. a high-carbohydrate diet. *Obesity Research, 2,* 348–354.

Birch, L. L., Birch, D., Marlin, D. W., & Kramer, L. (1982). Effects of instrumental consumption on children's food preference. *Appetite, 3,* 125–134.

Birch, L. L., Marlin, D. W., & Rotter, J. (1984). Eating as the "means" activity in a contingency: Effects on young children's food preference. *Child Development, 55,* 431–439.

Birch, L. L., Zimmerman, S. I., & Hind, H. (1980). The influence of social affective context on the formation of children's food preferences. *Child Development, 51,* 856–861.

Bouchard, C., Dionne, F. T., Simoneau, J.-A., & Boulay, M. R. (1992). Genetics of aerobic and anaerobic performances. *Exercise and Sports Science Reviews, 20,* 27–58.

Brownell, K. D. (1997). *A toxic environment for obesity.* Paper presented to the NIDDK Task Force on the Prevention and Treatment of Obesity. Bethesda, MD.

Brownell, K. D., & Jeffery, R. W. (1987). Improving long-term weight loss: Pushing the limits of treatment. *Behavior Therapy, 18,* 353–374.

Bulik, C. M., & Brinded, E. C. (1994). The effect of food deprivation on the reinforcing value of food and smoking in bulimic and control women. *Physiology and Behavior, 55,* 665–672.

Carroll, M. E., Lac, S. T., & Nygaard, S. L. (1989). A concurrently available nondrug reinforcer prevents the acquisition or decrease the maintenance of cocaine-reinforced behavior. *Psychopharmacology, 97,* 23–29.

Comings, D. E., Gade, R., MacMurray, J. P., Muhleman, D., & Peters, W. R. (1996). Genetic variants of the human obesity (OB) gene: Association with body mass index in young women, psychiatric symptoms, and interaction with the dopamine D_2 receptor (DRDz) gene. *Molecular Psychiatry, 1,* 325–335.

Cowart, B. (1981). Development of taste perception in humans: Sensitivity and preference throughout the lifespan. *Psychological Bulletin, 90,* 43–73.

Dietz, W. H., & Gortmaker, S. L. (1985). Do we fatten our children at the television set? Obesity and television viewing in children and adolescents. *Pediatrics, 75,* 807–812.

Drewnowski, A., Brunzell, J. D., Sande, K., Iverius, P. H., & Greenwood, M. R. C. (1985). Sweet tooth reconsidered: Taste responsiveness in human obesity. *Physiology and Behavior, 35,* 617–622.

Epstein, L. H. (1995). Application of behavioral economic principles to treatment of childhood obesity. In D. B. Allison & F. X. Pi-Sunyer (Eds.), *Obesity treatment: Establishing goals, improving outcomes and reviewing the research agenda* (pp. 113–119). New York: Plenum.

Epstein, L. H., Bulik, C. M., Perkins, K. A., Caggiula, A. R., & Rodefer, J. (1991). Behavioral economic analysis of smoking: Money and food as alternatives. *Pharmacology, Biochemistry and Behavior, 38,* 715–721.

Epstein, L. H., Saelens, B. E., Myers, M. D., & Vito, D. (1997). The effects of decreasing sedentary behaviors on activity choice in obese children. *Health Psychology, 16,* 107–113.

Epstein, L. H., Saelens, B. E., & O'Brien, J. G. (1995). Effects of reinforcing increases in active behavior versus decreases in sedentary behavior for obese children. *International Journal of Behavioral Medicine, 2,* 41–50.

Epstein, L. H., Smith, J. A., Vara, L. S., & Rodefer, J. S. (1991). Behavioral economic analysis of activity choice in obese children. *Health Psychology, 10,* 311–316.

Epstein, L. H., Valoski, A. M., Vara, L. S., McCurley, J., Wisniewski, L., Kalarchian, M. A., Klein, K. R., & Shrager, L. R. (1995). Effects of decreasing sedentary behavior and increasing activity on weight change in obese children. *Health Psychology, 14,* 109–115.

Fisher, J. O., & Birch, L. L. (1995). Fat preferences and fat consumption of 3-to 5-year-old children are related to parental adiposity. *Journal of the American Dietetic Association, 95,* 759–764.

Fisher, J. O., & Birch, L. L. (in press). Restricting access to foods and children's eating. *Appetite.*

Foltin, R. W. (1991). An economic analysis of "demand" for food in baboons. *Journal of the Experimental Analysis of Behavior, 56,* 445–454.

Foltin, R. W. (1992). Economic analysis of the effects of caloric alternatives and reinforcer magnitude on "demand" for food in baboons. *Appetite, 19,* 255–271.

Foltin, R. W. (1994a). Are food and self-administered drugs interchangeable in baboons? *Appetite, 23,* 194

Foltin, R. W. (1994b). Does package size matter? A unit-price analysis of "demand" for food in baboons. *Journal of the Experimental Analysis of Behavior, 62,* 293–306.

Foltin, R. W., & Fischman, M. W. (1990). Effects of caloric manipulations on food intake in baboons. *Appetite, 15,* 135–149.

Forzano, L. B., & Logue, A. W. (1992). Predictors of adult humans' self-control and impulsiveness for food reinforcers. *Appetite, 19,* 33–47.

Forzano, L. B., & Logue, A. W. (1994). Self-control in adult humans: Comparison of qualitatively different reinforcers. *Learning and Motivation, 25,* 65–82.

Glover, D. A., & Hanley, G. L. (1993). Choice in a multi-response environment: Testing response substitution for an inelastic behavior. *Learning and Motivation, 24,* 433–457.

Gortmaker, S. L., Dietz, W. H., & Cheung, L. W. Y. (1990). Inactivity, diet, and the fattening of America. *Journal of the American Dietetic Association, 90,* 1247–1255.

Gortmaker, S. L., Must, A., Sobol, A. M., Peterson, K., Colditz, G. A., & Dietz, W. H. (1996). Television watching as a cause of increasing obesity among children in the United States, 1986–1990. *Archives of Pediatric and Adolescent Medicine, 150,* 356–362.

Green, L. & Fisher, E. B. (1997). Economic substitutability: Some implications for health behavior. In W. K. Bickel & R. E. Vuchinich (Eds.), *Reframing health behavior change with behavioral economics.* Mahwah, NJ: Lawrence Erlbaum Associates.

Johnson, S. L., McPhee, L., & Birch, L. L. (1991). Conditioned preferences: Young children prefer flavors associated with high dietary fat. *Physiology and Behavior, 50,* 1245–1251.

Kern, D. L., McPhee, L., Fisher, J., Johnson, S. L., & Birch, L. L. (1993). The postingestive consequences of fat condition preferences for flavors associated with high dietary fat. *Physiology and Behavior, 54,* 71–76.

Kuczmarski, R. J., Flegal, K. M., Campbell, S. M., & Johnson, C. L. (1994). Increasing prevalence of overweight among US adults. *Journal of the American Medical Association, 272,* 205–211.

Lappalainen, R., & Epstein, L. H. (1990). A behavioral economics analysis of food choice in humans. *Appetite, 14,* 81–93.

Logue, A. W. (1997). Self-control and health behavior. In W. K. Bickel & R. E. Vuchinich (Eds.), *Reframing health behavior change with behavioral economics.* Mahwah, NJ: Lawrence Erlbaum Associates.

Logue, A. W., & King, G. R. (1991). Self-control and impulsiveness in adult humans when food is a reinforcer. *Appetite, 17,* 105–120.

Logue, A. W., King, G. R., Chavarro, A., & Volpe, J. S. (1990). Matching and maximizing in a self-control paradigm using human subjects. *Learning and Motivation, 21,* 340–368.

Martin, J. E., & Dubbert, P. M. (1982). Exercise applications and promotion in behavioral medicine: Current status and future directions. *Journal of Consulting and Clinical Psychology, 50,* 1004–1017.

Nader, M. A., & Woolverton, W. L. (1992a). Choice between cocaine and food by rhesus monkeys: Effects of conditions of food availability. *Behavioural Pharmacology, 3,* 635–638.

Nader, M. A., & Woolverton, W. L. (1992b). Effects of increasing response requirement on choice between cocaine and food in rhesus monkeys. *Psychopharmacology, 108,* 295–300.

Pate, R. R., Pratt, M., Blair, S. N., Haskell, W. L., Macera, C. A., Bouchard, C., Buchner, D., Ettinger, W., Heath, G. W., King, A. C., Kriska, A., Leon, A. S., Marcus, B. H., Morris, J., Paffenbarger, R. S., Patrick, K., Pollock, M. L., Rippe, J. M., Sallis, J. F., & Wilmore, J. H. (1995). Physical activity and public health: A recommendation from the Centers for Disease Control and Prevention and the American College of Sports Medicine. *Journal of the American Medical Association, 273,* 402–407.

Pi-Sunyer, F. X. (1987). Exercise effects on calorie intake. *Annals of the New York Academy of Sciences, 499,* 94–103.

Prud'homme, D., Bouchard, C., LeBlanc, C., Landry, F., & Fontaine, E. (1984). Sensitivity of maximal aerobic power to training is genotype-dependent. *Medicine and Science in Sports and Exercise, 16,* 489–493.

Raynor, D. A., Coleman, K. J., & Epstein, L. H. (1998). Effects of proximity on the choice to be physically active or sedentary. *Research Quarterly for Exercise and Sport, 99,* 103.

Reiss, S., & Havercamp, S. (1996). The sensitivity theory of motivation: Implications for psychopathology. *Behaviour Research and Therapy, 34,* 621–632.

Robinson, T. E., & Berridge, K. C. (1993). The neural basis of drug craving: An incentive-sensitization theory of addiction. *Brain Research Reviews, 18,* 247–291.

Saelens, B. E., & Epstein, L. H. (1996). The reinforcing value of food in obese and non-obese women. *Appetite, 27,* 41–50.

Saelens, B. E., & Epstein, L. H. (in press). High rate sedentary activities reinforce physical activity in sedentary individuals. *Health Psychology.*

Saelens, B. E., & Epstein, L. H. (1998). Behavioral engineering of activity choice in obese children. *International Journal of Obesity, 22,* 275–277.

Salamone, J. D. (1994). The involvement of nucleus accumbens dopamine in appetitive and aversive motivation. *Behavioural Brain Research, 61,* 117–133.

Sallis, J. F., Hovell, M. F., Hofstetter, C. R., Elder, J. P., Hackley, M., Caspersen, C. J., & Powell, K. E. (1990). Distance between homes and exercise facilities related to frequency of exercise among San Diego residents. *Public Health Reports, 105,* 179–185.

Smith, J. A., & Epstein, L. H. (1991). Behavioral economic analysis of food choice in obese children. *Appetite, 17,* 91–95.

Stephens, T., Jacobs, D. R., & White, C. C. (1985). A descriptive epidemiology of leisure-time physical activity. *Public Health Reports, 100,* 147–158.

Timberlake, W., & Farmer-Dougan, V. A. (1991). Reinforcement in applied settings: Figuring out ahead of time what will work. *Psychological Bulletin, 110,* 379–391.

Troiano, R. P., Flegal, K. M., Kuczmarski, R. J., Campbell, S. M., & Johnson, C. L. (1995). Overweight prevalence and trends for children and adolescents: The National Health and Nutrition Examination Surveys, 1963 to 1991. *Archives of Pediatric and Adolescent Medicine, 149,* 1085–1091.

U.S. Department of Health and Human Services. (1996). *Physical activity and health: A report of the surgeon general.* Atlanta, GA: Author, Centers for Disease Control and Prevention, National Center for Chronic Disease Prevention and Health Promotion.

Vara, L. S., & Epstein, L. H. (1993). Laboratory assessment of choice between exercise or sedentary behaviors. *Research Quarterly for Exercise and Sport, 64,* 356–360.

Westenhoefer, J., & Pudel, V. (1993). Pleasure from food: Importance for food choice and consequences of deliberate restriction. *Appetite, 20,* 246–249.

CHAPTER TWELVE

Gambling in Socioeconomic Perspective

Patrick M. Ghezzi
University of Nevada

Charles A. Lyons
Eastern Oregon University

Mark R. Dixon
University of Nevada

Ah, I have a premonition—I can't miss! . . . why am I such an irresponsible infant? Can't I see that I am a doomed man? But why can't I come back to life? All I have to do is be calculating and patient once, and I'll make it! I have to hold out for just one hour, and then my whole life will be different.

—Fyodor Dostoyevsky, *The Gambler*

Gambling long has been a favorite national pastime, but lately it has become a national obsession. Casino gambling was limited in 1988 to Nevada and Atlantic City, New Jersey; today, there are 27 states (and the District of Columbia) and three territories that have legalized, through statutes or tribal contracts, casino gambling. At present, 48 of the 50 states (Hawaii and Utah are exceptions) sanction some form of intra- or interstate gambling, including parimutuel wagering on horses and dogs, charity betting, lotteries, bingo, cards, sports, pull-tabs, and scratch tickets. Hundreds of "virtual casinos" and other sites are available on the Internet, and for those who can't leave home without it, gambling is now available on international airline flights.

Our contribution to this volume examines gambling phenomena from a socioeconomic perspective, that is to say, we treat gambling at the aggregate or group level, focusing primarily on buyers and sellers interacting in and with an economic environment. The buyers are the gambling public, and the sellers are the state-sponsored, publicly owned, and privately held entities that offer legal games—the gaming industry. At the center of the interactions between the two are heretofore unexplored questions regarding what it is that is sold in the gaming marketplace and what it is about the marketplace that the public finds so alluring. In that context, we discuss research conducted in the natural gambling environment, highlighting factors that not only influence the public's demand for certain games, but that also reveal variables that would appear to affect the play of individual gamblers. We conclude with a short discussion of public policy development as it pertains to the treatment and prevention of problem and pathological gambling.

We begin with the impact of gambling, calling attention to the major issues that gambling presents to the public and to the institutions that serve and protect its welfare.

THE IMPACT OF GAMBLING

The most apparent and available data on gambling's impact are financial. What the facts and figures reveal is that legalized gambling is a wildly profitable enterprise, generating more revenue than movies, spectator sports, theme parks, cruise ships, and recorded music combined (Doyle, 1997). Annual gross revenues from the sale, distribution, regulation, and taxation of state-sponsored games add up to hundreds of billions of dollars, adding enormous amounts of money to city, state, and tribal governments that look to gambling as the solution to economic hardship. Publicly held corporations, private businesses, charities, and political groups also are experiencing unprecedented wealth: Corporations and businesses post annual profits in the billions; charities reap millions in low-stakes, "Las Vegas Night" donations; and political parties and candidates at all levels of government are finding that the gaming industry is eager to contribute generously to campaigns, platforms, and special interests.

Given the rapid infusion in recent years of extraordinary amounts of money into the economy, progaming politicians and business persons in particular are eager to point to the positive cash flows and other benefits of legalized gambling. Raising state and local revenues without increasing personal taxes, increasing employment, and developing a lucrative tourist industry top the list of what proponents argue are the economic benefits of gaming (Lombardo, 1995). Opponents disagree, claiming instead that revenue, employment, and tourism actually are the economic victims of widespread legalized gambling (Grinols, 1995; Thompson, 1994). Unfortunately, there are insufficient data available to support either point of view firmly.

At the center of disputes over the impact of legalized gambling are a host of unanswered questions regarding the effects that it has on the public and the institutions that serve and protect its welfare. Demographic data show moderate increases over the last decade in several key social indicators (e.g., crime, bankruptcy, psychopathology), raising the alarming possibility that the nation's law enforcement, legal, correctional, and mental health institutions soon will be unable to marshall the resources necessary to remedy or contain the social consequences of gambling (Mapes, 1997). As might be expected given the magnitude of the stakes involved, partisan rhetoric, unsubstantiated speculation, and suspicious and inconclusive research findings dominate the discussion (Grinols, 1995). Indeed, resolving disagreement on the issues is the mission of the National Gambling Impact Study. Commissioned in 1996 by the U.S. House of Representatives, the study examines the economic and social impact of gambling, the influence of the gaming industry's political contributions, gambling-related crime, and off-shore Internet gambling.

Pathological Gambling

There is a core belief that the increase in legalized gambling over the past decade is responsible for increases in the number of problem and pathological gamblers, and, further, that the consequences of excessive gambling are socially burdensome and personally destructive. The basis for this belief comes from various surveys that suggest that roughly two thirds of U.S. adults have participated in some form of gambling, with lifetime incidence reaching 94% in Britain and 92% in Australia (Blaszczynski & McConaghy, 1989). The belief is strengthened from the observation that as greater numbers of people participate in gambling, more gamblers experience difficulty controlling their level of play (Volberg, 1994). Rising estimates of the prevalence of pathological gambling appear to bear this out: Conservative estimates range from 1% to 3% in the population (American Psychiatric Association, 1994), up from a 1974 estimate of less than 1% (Ladouceur, Boisvert, Pepin, Loranger, & Sylvain, 1994). Additional research suggests that pathological gamblers incur significant debt (Lesieur & Rosenthal, 1991); are routinely beset by legal problems (Politzer, Morrow, & Leavey, 1985); and tend to commit income-generating crimes ranging from robbery and mugging to embezzlement and fraud (Blaszczynski & McConaghy, 1994; Brown, 1987). Adding a disproportionately high suicide rate (Phillips, Wetly, & Smith, 1997) to the mix creates an unsettling portrait of the effects that gambling can have on people and the communities in which they live. Ironically, as problem and pathological gamblers reportedly are responsible for roughly 25% of gambling proceeds in legal games (Las Vegas Convention and Visitors Authority, 1996), a situation is created in which the state profits from excessive play and yet is obligated to provide treatment and prevention programs to deal with the social and personal consequences attendant to such play.

There is a growing concern over pathological gambling and the types of public services that are available to help people with gambling and gambling-related problems (Volberg, Dickerson, Ladouceur, & Abbott, 1996). The issues are as complex and contentious as any in the study of gambling's impact. For example, in the treatment domain, there is widespread disagreement about the detection, causes, and development of the condition, and there is no empirically validated therapeutic approach (Legg England & Götestam, 1991). A major difficulty is that many other comorbid conditions are frequently found with pathological gambling, including substance abuse, depression, obsessive–compulsive disorder, and attention-deficit–hyperactivity disorder (DeCaria et al., 1996), leading to confusion regarding diagnosis, metastasis, and treatment. As Dickerson (1989) noted, the result has been a "piecemeal development of the literature" (p. 164) with few controlled studies available for scrutiny by the scientific community.

As in the historical development of research on substance abuse, the volume and sophistication of studies on pathological gambling will almost certainly rise in response to a growing demand, for example, for systematic data on the conditions that encourage and discourage excessive play. One also can anticipate confrontation between biomedical, cognitive, and behavioral researchers over how best to conceptualize pathological gambling (see, e.g., Herrnstein & Prelec, 1992; Leshner, 1997) and what kind of prevention and treatment procedures are most effective.

The issues that we touch on in our brief discussion of the impact of gambling lead to two conclusions: (a) What is sorely needed are more and better designed studies aimed at unraveling the myriad factors involved at all levels of legalized gambling. Although lacking in profundity, this conclusion nonetheless is based upon a thorough reading of the professional and popular literature on the topic. Indeed, our prediction is that the National Gambling Impact Study will reach the same conclusion in its 1999 report, and, further, that the commission will recommend allocating funds for research that is broad in scope, precise and unbiased in interpretation, and, above all, materially beneficial to those persons and organizations that are obligated to serve and protect the public's welfare. (b) Among the studies that are most needed are those that lead not only to understanding the factors that encourage and sustain the public's interest in gambling but also to identifying the variables affecting the behavior of the individual gambler. Both types of studies are relevant to matters regarding the development, treatment, and prevention of problem and pathological gambling.

In socioeconomic perspective, ascertaining what the commodity is that the gaming industry is selling to the public and how it is that so many people are attracted to it is a necessary first step toward identifying the factors that encourage and sustain the public's demand for gambling. We explore these issues next.

THE ATTRACTION OF GAMBLING: THREE VIEWS

One impression given by the financial facts and figures on gambling is that business and government have formed a partnership of sorts, creating a gigantic industry that takes advantage of its peccant customers by coaxing enormous profits from them. The multibillion dollar partnerships between government and the alcohol and tobacco companies are older and more familiar examples of this view and serve as poignant reminders that economic gain can overcome the myriad political and social risks involved in such ventures. A more provocative example is legalized prostitution in Nevada, where business and government have joined forces for many years to control and prosper from the brothel industry. Seen in the light of these examples, gaming has the look of yet another legalized vice industry that must be heavily regulated and subjected to the same extreme "sin taxes" as any other unsavory enterprise.

The "legalized vice" view of gambling is essentially moralistic and thus would suggest that the public is attracted to gambling for hedonic reasons. Shameless "thrill seeking" comes to mind, whereby an intemperate public is attracted to gambling both by the enjoyment of its disinhibiting affects and by its elements of excitement and risk (Wolfgang, 1989). Indeed, this view historically has dominated discussions of gamblers as moral degenerates and gaming as an evil enterprise (Collins, 1996).

Shedding the old-fashioned "vice industry" image, the gaming establishment has adopted the position that it is part of the entertainment industry, seeing itself in the same business as movies, spectator sports, theme parks, and cruise ships. Bringing legitimacy and respectability to an industry that long has suffered from corruption, scandal, and public outrage appears in part to be behind the multibillion move in Las Vegas and elsewhere to offer the public an assortment of family-oriented events and activities alongside the standard fare of coin-operated machines and table games. Video arcades, movie theaters, museums, amusement rides, ice cream shops, shopping malls, and spectacular pyrotechnic and special effects displays, common to many "Disney-style" resorts, are now common to many large hotel-casinos. That this exciting, all-ages atmosphere of wholesome, innocent fun will have the effect of adding legitimacy and respectability to casino gambling is uncertain. What is certain is that people are being drawn in unprecedented numbers to gaming resorts under the auspices of the diverse entertainment that is provided and in the process are allocating increasing amounts of their disposable income to gambling (Ladouceur et al., 1994).

We know of no other form of "entertainment" that entertains its customers in quite the same way as gambling. Part of what we mean by this is that the gambling public understands that the chances of winning are extremely low, which is to say that losing almost always is the consequence of playing. Of course, the gaming industry does not simply take a gambler's money with no return, but achieves the same effect with some games, notably coin-operated machines, both by returning part of the customer's money on an intermittent basis and by deliberate or accidental "near-wins." This is, of course, Skinner's account of gambling as behavior maintained by variable-ratio reinforcement (see Knapp, 1976). Although the relevance of this account is beyond dispute, it is somewhat limited, for example, in explaining differences among individuals' attraction to gambling in general and their preference for certain games in particular (for an extended discussion of Skinner's analysis and views on gambling, see Knapp, 1998).

How is the gaming industry able to sustain a large and profitable economic base despite the losses that nearly all of its patrons incur? The answer seems to center on the emphasis that the industry places on entertainment. That is, given the view forged by the gaming industry and increasingly accepted by the public that gambling is harmless entertainment, the commercially destructive impact of the public eventually losing interest in gambling as a consequence of highly unfavorable odds may be averted. This point is well-illustrated by the common observation that most recreational gamblers are indifferent to either the prospect or the reality of losing money. After all, it's "only entertainment," the cost of which is insignificant compared to the amount of money that can be won.

As rational as it seems to assume that people like to be entertained and that because gambling is entertainment it is therefore that feature of gambling that attracts the public to it, there is an alternative account that is worth examining. It begins with a hypothesis put forth by Rachlin, Battalio, Kagel, and Green (1981): The ideal economic state of affairs for most people is one where relatively little or no work or cost is required to produce an immediate and relatively large monetary gain. Opportunities to achieve this state generally are limited to three circumstances: inheritance, investments, and gambling. Of these, the opportunity that is by far the most widely available, involves the least effort or cost, and that has the potential to produce significant monetary gain with little or no delay is gambling.

With that in mind, it is important to note that people with modest financial means contribute a greater proportion of their disposable income toward gambling than do those with larger incomes (Abbott & Cramer, 1993; Devlin & Peppard, 1996). For that group in particular (although by no means restricted to it), the allure of gambling may be the opportunity it presents to pursue the ideal economic state: Acquire a large sum of money without delay and without having to pay or work indefinitely or in piecemeal fashion for it. Capitalizing on this motive, the gaming industry obliges the general public not only by selling the opportunity to achieve the ideal state, but also by actively promoting itself as the principal means for accomplishing it.

This characterization of the attraction of gambling does not necessarily remove it from the ranks of entertainment, but it does establish parallels with other activities, notably the buying and selling of stocks and bonds. Investing presumably differs from lottery, poker, and coin-operated machine play along important dimensions, and yet what is common to both is the opportunity, as the saying goes among investors, "not to work for your money, but to have your money work for you." That same motive seems to characterize gambling.

One of the outstanding socioeconomic differences between gambling and investing is who can afford to "play the game" and thus have the opportunity to win at it. Reports abound on how the investment industry is experiencing phenomenal growth. It turns out that the principal contributors to that growth, according to demographic data (Lifestyle Market Analyst, 1997), are upper level annual income people. These are the people who can most afford to pay the price in terms of putting forth the time, money, and acumen necessary to realize what is for them a meaningful return, and who also have the luxury of the long term to claim it. Those who can least afford the price of a meaningful investment opportunity must look for other, more affordable opportunities that yield money quickly and in amounts that can make a difference in their short-term circumstances of living. Seen in this light, the gambling industry provides a hybrid investment opportunity that is particularly attractive to, if not ideally suited for, people with relatively scarce financial and other resources who are looking to achieve the ideal economic state: Acquire a relatively large sum of money without delay and without having to work or otherwise pay substantially for it.

Part of the appeal of assuming that the gaming industry markets opportunity is that certain behavioral, economic, and behavioral economic principles and concepts may be brought to bear on a host of gambling phenomena. As a preface to that discussion, however, we take a moment to elaborate upon a few additional assumptions that underlie a socioeconomic perspective on gambling.

GAMBLING IN THE NATURAL ENVIRONMENT

The importance of conducting gambling research in the natural gaming environment cannot be overstated. Certainly there are no laboratory methodologies for large-scale gambling studies of the sort described later in this chapter, nor is it feasible to conduct small-scale laboratory analogues wherein actual gamblers are betting real money under authentic gambling conditions. This assumption is critical of most research on gambling in which college students typically are asked to respond to hypothetical gambling situations with hypothetical wagers or to wagers involving relatively small amounts of money (e.g., Rachlin, Raineri, & Cross, 1991). As important as controlled laboratory studies may be to understanding, for example, the strategies that individual gamblers follow when faced with choosing between probabilistic alternatives (Rachlin et al., 1991), we take the position that it is equally important to study gambling phenomena in the natural gaming environment. That is, in short, where opportunity exists on a scale that matters. There are drawbacks to conducting gambling research in the natural gaming environment, however. The difficulty in obtaining data from state agencies and private businesses, the impossibility of experimentally altering or controlling the conditions of play, and the prohibitions against studying the behavior of individual gamblers currently top the list. Overcoming these obstacles can be achieved, for example, by capitalizing on the occasional manipulations made by state gaming commissions in the structure of certain games, as Lyons and Ghezzi (1995) have shown, by assuring casino operators that the data routinely collected by them will be used only for the sake of scientific knowledge (a hard sell, but well worth the effort; see Steinagle, 1995), and by assuming that factors governing play at the group level also may be operative at the level of the individual.

The assumption that data obtained at the group level are relevant to the behavior of individuals requires some explanation. *Behavior*, in the technical sense of the term (Skinner, 1938), is a property of an individual biological organism. Because a group is neither an individual nor a biological organism, it would be a dreadful mistake to assume that a group behaves as an individual does or to obtain measures at the group level and then automatically interpret them as relevant at the level of the behaving individual. Recognizing the interpretive problems that are created by moving from one level of analyses to another (Johnston & Pennypacker, 1993), we nevertheless believe that it is worthwhile to examine gambling at the group level not only for socioeconomic purposes but also for evidence of the independent variables that influence the behavior of individual gamblers.

We next turn to a fairly lengthy examination of how the state-sponsored gaming industry structures different games and how that structure affects public demand for the opportunities that the games present. For the most part, the data that we discuss represent aggregate dollars wagered on lotteries by large numbers of people gambling in the natural environment in different states. We also discuss demand for games other than lotteries within the same milieu, focusing primarily on the popularity of video poker. We end this section by speculating on the role that verbal events play in affecting the propensity to gamble.

STATE-SPONSORED GAMING

Lotteries

As states began introducing public games over the past two decades, lotteries were often the first to appear. These games typically involve large cumulative jackpots that can be claimed by picking a series of numbers matching those randomly drawn from several million possibilities. The monetary cost of play is very low—$1 usually purchases one or two entries for jackpots ranging into several million dollars—and odds of claiming the jackpot generally exceed 1 in 5 million. Lyons and Ghezzi (1995) compared demand for such games in two western states of similar population (Arizona and Oregon), both of which introduced state lotteries in the mid-1980s. What emerged from that comparison were two variables—*game availability* and *jackpot size*—that contributed greatly to public demand for lottery play. A third variable, *odds of winning*, did not have an appreciable impact on demand. We discuss each variable in turn, speculating on the behavioral, economic, and behavioral economic principles and concepts relevant to their effects.

Game Availability. As Fig. 12.1 shows, increased game availability, in the sense of more frequent draws, was related to higher weekly participation in Arizona and Oregon. When these states moved from weekly (Saturday) drawings to semiweekly (Wednesday and Saturday) drawings, total demand for lottery tickets increased. The differences between weekly and semiweekly sales in the two states were unrelated to the size of the jackpot (see subsequent discussion) on those days or to any other variables available for analysis.

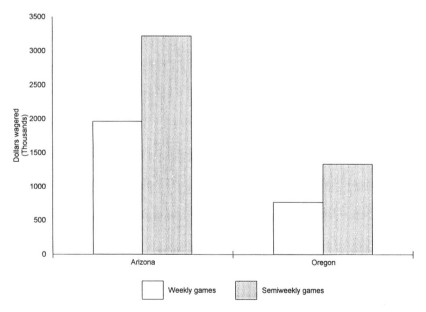

FIG. 12.1. Average weekly lottery wagers for the 35-week periods before and after game frequency was increased from weekly (Saturday) to semiweekly (Wednesday and Saturday) in the Arizona and Oregon lotteries.

More frequent draws represent an increase in the number of opportunities to play and thus to receive feedback on the outcome of a wager, that is, more frequent draws may be viewed as representing a decrease in the temporal delay between purchasing a ticket and later discovering whether it contains any winning numbers. Temporal delay may be the key to understanding the effects of game availability in lottery play: Given a choice between two consumable and equally likely outcomes that differ only in terms of the length of time to one or the other outcome, humans and nonhumans alike will select the alternative that involves the shortest of the two delays (Fantino, Preston, & Dunn, 1993). An important assumption in this case would be that there is a reinforcing function in humans for information concerning the outcomes in question, namely, winning or losing lottery numbers (cf. Perone & Baron, 1980). In other words, "good news" and "bad news" both may sustain lottery play. This concept gains added support from the observation that the vast majority of people who play the lottery never win and yet continue to play time after time.

Jackpot Size. Figure 12.2 illustrates that as jackpot levels increased in either state, wagering also increased. This rather dramatic and orderly affect also has been observed with lotteries in Israel (Shapira & Venezia, 1992).

The drawing power of large prizes seems reasonable from a variety of economic concepts and behavioral principles. Reinforcer size is related to response strength, suggesting that larger jackpots enhance the subjective value of the opportunity to win, thus encouraging heavier play. It also may be the case that the behavioral unit of gambling is a relatively long string of plays culminating in a win (Rachlin, 1990). On this perspective, winning a large jackpot would more than eliminate losses from a long string of negative bets, and larger jackpots would counteract longer losing strings. In more economic terms, a larger jackpot available for the same ticket price increases the expected utility (EU) of a ticket. Because the EU of a lottery wager equals the odds of winning multiplied by the jackpot value, larger jackpots at some point yield an expected utility above the price of a ticket. However, out of a total of 1,063 lottery drawings held during the first 7 years in Arizona and Oregon, the EU exceeded the price of a $1 ticket in less than 14% of games.

The strong relation between jackpot size and ticket sales is bidirectional: Increased betting produces larger jackpots, and larger jackpots drive more betting (Lyons & Ghezzi, 1995). This interdependency may be weakened, however, by the practice in some states of establishing a minimum jackpot size (see subsequent discussion), by announcing estimated jackpot size for an upcoming drawing (providing a sort of "reference point" for players who choose to participate or not), and by televised scenes of people standing in long lines to play lotteries that have reached super-jackpot size ($60 million and over).

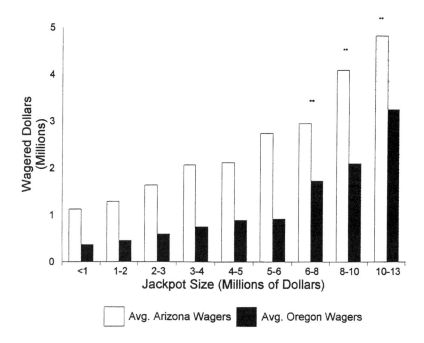

FIG. 12.2. Average wagers as a function of various jackpot levels in Oregon and Arizona. The jackpot bin size was expanded due to limited observations. From "Wagering on a Large Scale: Relationships Between Public Gambling and Game Manipulations in Two State Lotteries," by C. A. Lyons and P. M. Ghezzi, 1995, *Journal of Applied Behavior Analysis, 28*, p. 127. Copyright © 1995 by the Society for the Experimental Analysis of Behavior, Inc. Reprinted with permission.

An additional observation is that demand for large jackpots declines over time. Figure 12.3 and Fig. 12.4 show that in both Arizona and Oregon, jackpots of $1 million drew greater participation than did those same jackpots a few years later. In other words, $1 million jackpots lost drawing power over time.

Because of inflationary economic pressures, the federal government continually reassesses the value of the dollar and expresses this decline in purchasing value in terms of the Consumer Price Index (CPI). One might expect that the value of a $1 million jackpot would decline in real terms, becoming less attractive to players. However, the cost of play declines at the same rate (leaving no change in the EU of the prize), so this strictly economic accounting would not predict a decline in demand. From a behavioral view, demand may have lessened for $1 million games as those games became more common, because repeated presentations diminished the value of the opportunity to win and led to "habituation" of players'

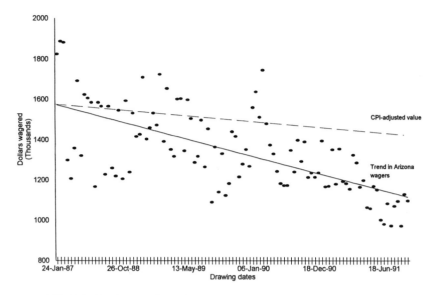

FIG. 12.3. Total wagers for each occasion in which jackpot size was $1 million during the first 540 games in the Arizona lottery. The dashed line represents the decline in the Consumer Price Index-adjusted value of a $1 million jackpot relative to its first occurrence in the game.

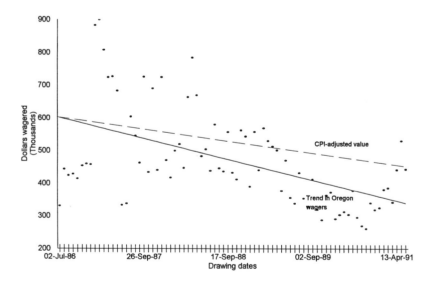

FIG. 12.4. Total wagers for each occasion in which jackpot size was $1 million during the first 522 games in the Oregon lottery. The dashed line represents the decline in the Consumer Price Index-adjusted value of a $1 million jackpot relative to its first occurrence in the game.

hedonic response to the potential prize. It is also true that as more drawings are held, more players experience longer negative strings of gambles (cf. Rachlin, 1990). As an experienced player may judge winning as a distant temporal event, more distant outcomes may be psychologically devalued. This temporal discounting of value is predicted by both economic and psychological analyses, although the predictions differ in terms of whether the discounting is exponential or hyperbolic (Fantino et al., 1993; Herrnstein, 1990).

Odds Manipulations. Wagering in Oregon and Arizona appeared to be unrelated to changes in the odds of winning as a consequence of structural changes in the games, which reduced the odds of winning by more than two thirds (Lyons & Ghezzi, 1995). It could be that individual players either do not accurately calculate the expected utility of a ticket in the formal economic sense (as declining with worsening odds of winning); that they simply do not discriminate changes in the odds of winning in games that begin with an infinitesimal chance of success; or that players do make the discrimination, but odds of winning is not an important variable in controlling lottery play.

Gaming Milieu

Oregon, like most other states, offers public games in the context of a gaming milieu, that is, since the state began offering games in 1985, several gaming products have been added to maintain public interest and increase revenue. Oregon began by offering instant "scratch-it" tickets in early 1985, then later that year added the Megabucks lottery. Breakopens were introduced in 1987, SportsAction in 1989, Keno in 1991, and video poker and Powerball lottery in 1992 (see Table 12.1). Because games were added gradually, the public data allow comparison of the relative demand for these games.

In the early years of Oregon's gambling business, the Instant Scratch-off game (available first) quickly lost standing to the Megabucks lottery, which dominated the field of games by 1988 (see Fig. 12.5). Several aspects of these games are worth noting. Scratch-its were widely available in grocery stores (as were lottery tickets), and costs to play were low in all games. Both Scratch-it and Breakopen games provided players with immediate feedback about winning, whereas Daily 4 winning numbers were posted once each day and Megabucks winning numbers once per week. Odds of winning a prize were much higher in the immediate games; the lowest odds were characteristic of Megabucks (1 in over 3 million claiming the jackpot). However, prize sizes were much higher in Megabucks than in any other game, with jackpots sometimes exceeding $1 million.

TABLE 12.1
Characteristics of Oregon State Games Introduced 1985 Through 1992

Game	Odds of Winning	Frequency	Cost	Maximum Payout	Task
Breakopens	1 in 6.5	Continuous	50 cents	$100	Match 3 symbols (random draw)
Daily 4	1 in 36	Daily	$1 to $5	$1,500 to $7,500	Match 2–4 numbers (random draw)
Keno	1 in 4 to 1 in 16	Every 5 min	$1	$100,000	Match 1–10 numbers (random draw)
Megabucks	From 1 in 328 (with kicker, 1 in 20)	Semiweekly	$1 (two picks), plus $1 for kicker	Minimum jackpot is $1 million	Match 4 to 6 numbers (random draw)
Scratch-its	1 in 3.5	Continuous	$1	$1,000/week for 20 years	Match 3 or 4 symbols (random draw)
Video Poker	1 in 2.2	Continuous	$1 (four game credits)	$1,200	Match winning hands (discard and replace, wildcards)

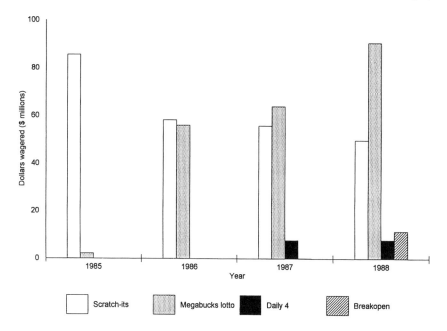

FIG. 12.5. Total annual wagers in Oregon games during the first 4 years of the Oregon lottery.

The importance of game availability and prize size in the lottery data suggests that these variables could affect preference between games as well. The Scratch-it game is continuously available; one could buy any number of tickets, at any time, and play repeatedly, discovering immediately if a game ticket is a winner. In fact, several revenue-enhancing modifications were made in the Scratch-it game between 1989 and 1992. Tickets that once were redeemable only at certain times and locations were made redeemable at the point of purchase. In addition, bingo was added to the Scratch-it options, and larger prize sizes (but with a higher monetary cost of play) were introduced, allowing occasional large winners to receive awards of $1,000 per week for 20 years. By 1992, demand for Scratch-it games exceeded that of Megabucks tickets.

Players also preferred the game of Keno to Megabucks by 1992. In comparison to the lottery, Keno games are more available (a new game is held every 5 minutes), outcomes are announced immediately (they are displayed on TV terminals), and jackpots are moderately large (typically around $100,000).

As Fig. 12.6 shows, demand for video poker grew steadily through 1995 but began declining over the same months in which five Native American tribes opened legal casinos in Oregon that competed with state games. In fact, the onset of competition from Indian casinos is associated with slower

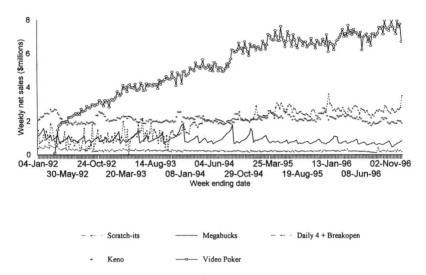

FIG. 12.6.   Weekly wagering in Oregon games since the introduction of video poker, 1992–1996.

growth for all Oregon games (see Fig. 12.6). Competition among games has tightened recently in Oregon, suggesting that the public has become "satiated" with gambling opportunies. In an ironic bailout for public gaming, the 1997 Oregon legislative session approved funding to support Oregon's parimutuel betting industry (greyhound and horse racing), which has experienced declining income as a result of video poker and casino gambling.

As more competing casinos come online in and around Oregon (as of mid-1997, there were seven in Oregon), it is probable that demand will continue to shift from state games in favor of casinos, which offer a greater variety of games, including blackjack, roulette, craps, and slot machines, and which offer nongaming entertainments, as mentioned previously. Where many games are available to players, slot machines ordinarily draw the greatest participation (cf. Fisher & Griffiths, 1995). For example, Nevada's more than 177,000 slot machines accounted for about 63% of the state's gaming revenues in 1997 (Nevada State Gaming Control Board, 1997). What is most conspicuous about slot machines in Nevada is their low cost of participation, that is, they are inexpensive to play (quarter and progressive nickel machines predominate); demand little in terms of skill (a handle pull or button press is all that is required); and are readily available (casinos devote the majority of their floor space to the machines and they are present in virtually every mini-mart, supermarket, cafe, and gas station throughout the state).

Data reported by Steinagle (1995) suggest how low cost—in this case, the expenditure of time—operates in generating casino slot machine revenue. Steinagle obtained a strong positive correlation between length of play and winning or losing, with short play (15 minutes or less) almost always losing and long play (45 minutes or more) almost always winning. Of the 165 casino players studied by Steinagle, 75% played a machine for a short period of time (and almost always lost money). To the extent that noncasino slot machine play also is equally brief, as might be expected, for example, when people take a moment to drop their change into a machine after grocery shopping, low cost operates in favor of the gaming industry by encouraging brief (and frequent) periods of what ordinarily amounts to losing play.

Video Poker

Figure 12.6 shows that video poker quickly became the preferred game in Oregon in 1992. Indeed, by 1997, the game accounted for nearly 50% of all gaming revenues, bringing in roughly $350 million in public funds.

Video poker allows several variations on 5-card draw, played with a single card deck. Payoffs are relatively small but frequent, and price per game is minimal—one dollar buys four games, and winning hands return anywhere from 25 cents to several thousand dollars. Because the player can opt to discard and replace cards to improve a hand, the outcome of the game can be influenced by the player's actions.

Public data demonstrate that demand for video poker is influenced by increasing game availability, which in this case translates to increasing the supply of machines and modifying them to accept larger denominations of cash. As Oregon increased the number of installed terminals from 2,137 in April 1992 to 6,970 in March 1995, average earnings per machine increased about 263%, from $282 to $1,022. Earnings rose further when machines that once accepted $1 and $5 bills were adapted in 1994 also to accept $10 and $20 bills. With that change in 1994, average earnings per machine increased another 20% within a 3-week period.

Figure 12.6 suggests that demand for video poker neither drew sales from, or substituted for, other Oregon games. Rather, the increase in sales represents a substantial influx of new money into the gaming marketplace. What accounts for the increased demand for this product? In Oregon, video poker is available only in establishments licensed to sell alcohol, thus enforcing the regulation limiting participants to age 21 and over. It might be possible to find evidence of complementarity between alcohol consumption and game availability, such that consumption of one influences consumption of the other. However, several other games, including Keno, Scratch-its, and Breakopens are also available at most taverns. Video poker does not pay large jackpots; rather, players win relatively small amounts frequently, with the odds of holding a winning hand (which most often returns only the cost of play) as low as 1 in 2.2. Games are available on demand, and feedback about outcome is immediate, but these characteristics are shared by several other games. It is, as mentioned previously, the only game that allows players to improve a hand by opting to replace cards during the draw, thereby influencing the outcome of the gamble.

Illusion of Control. The opportunity to influence the outcome in video poker is somewhat illusory, however. Even the best strategy for holding certain cards while discarding others will never allow a player to "beat" the machine over the long term. However, objectivity is seldom a gambler's strong suit. Research shows that when players are led to believe that they can control the outcome of a wager, they will bet more money and will play for higher stakes relative to when no "control" is given, despite the fact that the outcome is actually entirely random (Presson & Denassi, 1996). This so-called "illusion of control" (Koehler, Gibbs, & Hogarth, 1994) also can overcome the effects of other independent variables, for example, immediacy of feedback and obvious improvements in the odds of winning. When Preston, Meyer, and Lyons (1997) gave college students (playing draw poker and wagering extra credit points in a laboratory setting) the choice between immediate feedback about the outcome of a gamble or the option of using replacement cards to gain some control over the outcome, they preferred control over immediacy. Furthermore, Dixon, Hayes, and Ebbs (1998) found that when college students, wagering in the laboratory for class points on a computerized game of roulette, were given the opportunity to select better odds or their own personal numbers, they preferred their own numbers. Preference for self-selected numbers over better odds persisted even under conditions where students had to forfeit part of their earnings in order to self-select.

That gamblers often behave in ways that suggest they believe that they are in control of an outcome when in fact they are not has not escaped the attention of the gaming industry. Roulette is a prime example: The last 22 numbers selected are continuously displayed in many casinos on a reader board in full view of the players and spectators. Some players might opt to select their own numbers for personal reasons (e.g., birthdate, age, etc.), whereas for others the numbers displayed may gain control over wagering in that some may choose those numbers that either have or have not been previously selected ("hot" and "cold" numbers, respectively). The fact is that those numbers, as with those that are self-selected, have absolutely no bearing on the outcome of future spins of the wheel.

The Role of Verbal Events

It is a trite observation to note that gambling occurs only in verbal humans. What this means, however, is that verbal events undoubtedly play a significant role in governing play. Illusion of control phenomena, familiar gamblers' fallacies, and the idiosyncratic practices of many players all may be construed as examples of the impact that verbal behavior has in gambling. In recognition of this, incipient attempts at determining the precise role of verbal behavior are now under way. For example, laboratory studies on the effects of rules on roulette play (Dixon, Hayes, & Hernandez, 1998) have shown that undergraduate participants play longer and bet more money when given inaccurate rules regarding play ("Roulette is a winning game, so place your bets at 8:1") relative to those who are given accurate rules ("Roulette is a losing game, so place your bets at even money").

A broader sense in which verbal events affect gambling invokes the behavioral concept of establishing operations (Michael, 1982). To elaborate, manipulations in variables such as game availability, prize size, illusions of control, and rules all may be construed as motivative variables that augment the subjective value of the opportunity to pursue an ideal economic state: Acquire a substantial amount of money without delay and without expenditures of time, judgment, or skill. Increasing game availability makes it easy to pursue this at little cost to the gambler. When coupled with increasing the magnitude of the potential prize, leading gamblers to believe that they have control over the outcome of a chance event, and promoting sundry rules that govern more or riskier play heightens motivation to gamble and thus increases the probability that an individual will do so. A telling example of the effect is media advertising. For instance, lottery commercials routinely pair catchy phrases (e.g., "You can't win if you don't play") and enticing images of a secure, carefree lifestyle as a consequence of winning a substantial amount of money. The influence seems to be motivational: The stimuli verbally establish the opportunity to win money as more valued for the moment, creating a state of "reinforcibility" that augments the effects of the aforementioned variables (cf. Hayes, Zettle, & Rosenfarb, 1989). By the same token, when lottery jackpots stagnate at some level or when alternative games are available, value is attenuated and motivation declines, the net result being to lower the probability that an individual will play the lottery.

The bulk of our contribution up to this point has centered mainly on large-scale lottery research performed in the natural gaming environment. Lottery gambling, by itself and within a gaming milieu wherein demand for video poker reigns supreme, has served as the platform for advancing a variety of behavioral, economic, and behavioral economic concepts and principles useful to understanding the interplay of variables attendant to large numbers of players and perhaps, as well, to the play of individual gamblers.

Consistent with the view expressed previously that researchers must focus on the larger issue of how their efforts can benefit the public's welfare, we next turn to public policy development as it pertains to preventing and treating problem and pathological gambling.

PUBLIC POLICY DEVELOPMENT

Governments, publicly owned corporations, and private businesses continue both to expand legalized gambling and to encourage the public to avail themselves of the enticing financial opportunity that the gaming industry sells. It is widely recognized that this is not a benign commodity, and for this reason the research community has an obligation to inform the public about the impact that gambling is having at all levels of society. At this stage in the evolution of gaming research, however, it is far too early to say just what that impact is or will be in the coming years. For example, at the economic level, it is still not clear whether the infusion of gaming revenues into state and local coffers creates or sustains prosperity in communities that feature gambling. At the societal level, questions remain regarding the prevalence of problem and pathological gambling, whether the gaming industry encourages addiction, whether regulatory agencies or legislative bodies need to intervene on the public's behalf, and whether there are sufficient resources to deal with the myriad consequences of pathological gambling. At the psychological level, the issues range from identifying and manipulating the independent variables that control excessive gambling behavior to devising programs that treat and prevent problem and pathological play.

That the widespread availability of gambling contributes directly to an increase in the prevalence of gambling-related problems is axiomatic (Volberg, 1994). In public health terms, there are basically two avenues available to contain these problems: rigorously control gambling through regulatory or legislative means, or accommodate the problems by providing restrictions to discourage excessive gambling and by funding programs that prevent the spread of pathological gambling. The first avenue is problematic in that it pits government against the gaming industry in a costly legal battle over when, where, how, and with whom the industry conducts its business. The second avenue not only is much more palatable to the gaming industry but is also compatible with the moderate view that prevalence studies, although flawed (Culleton, 1989; Lesieur, 1994), suggest that the vast majority of gamblers do not have a problem controlling their level of play (Walker & Dickerson, 1996). It might be a mistake, therefore, to curtail the recreational play of the majority of gamblers in response to the problems experienced by a small percentage of the gambling public. Apropos of that view, the strategy has been to interfere as little as possible with individual freedom while at the same time providing prevention and treatment services.

Prevention

The good news is that programs designed to prevent problem and pathological gambling are available in the United States and abroad (Volberg et al., 1996). Several states have legislated that a proportion of gambling revenues be set aside for education, prevention, and treatment. Some states have used those funds to established councils on pathological gambling, and some states maintain a telephone hot line whereby people may speak with a counselor who specializes in preventing and treating problem and pathological gambling. Gambling counselors are employed in increasing numbers in community mental health agencies and in the private sector, and provisions are now in place to certify these counselors through the National Gambling Counselors Certification Board and the American Academy of Health Care Providers in the Addictive Disorders.

The bad news is that funds for gambling prevention programs represent a fraction of the amount spent by government and business to promote gambling. Furthermore, research to date has revealed little in terms of usable information for either predicting who is "at risk" for becoming a pathological gambler or for designing prevention programs. The programs that do exist unfortunately appear as a grab bag of information and education activities whose effectiveness has not been adequately documented with valid, reliable, and socially meaningful outcome measures.

The substance abuse and protected sex literature suggests that centers for the study of pathological gambling are best positioned to undertake the research that is needed to design and evaluate prevention programs. Community-based prevention programs that are grounded in prevalence research designed to identify groups of people who are in danger for becoming or remaining problem or pathological gamblers probably will be the most successful and cost-effective. White, middle-aged, poorly educated men would be the primary targets, followed by women, young adults, and minorities, specifically Native Americans (Ladouceur et al., 1994; Volberg, 1994). Because problem and pathological gamblers are a heterogeneous lot (Volberg & Steadman, 1988), prevention programs would have to be tailored to the unique features of each targeted group. A prudent course of action would be to reach out to those groups (a) to educate the members about the perils of gambling before problems arise (e.g., financial loss, marital and family discord, lowered job performance); (b) to teach people to recognize behaviors that predict or constitute pathological play (e.g., preoccupation with gambling, steadily increasing the size of bets, chasing losses); (c) to instruct people how to participate in and enjoy leisure and other pleasurable or reinforcing activities that do not involve gambling and that may serve as a substitute for it (e.g., competitive sports, community volunteer work, hobbies); and (d) to teach self-control as a means to avoid destructive behaviors (e.g., monitoring and limiting betting, setting aside money not to be gambled, distancing oneself from the people, places, and other stimuli associated with gambling). Public funds would be available only to programs that are prepared to document socially meaningful behavior change.

Nevada is always the bellwether state for gaming policy, and its lawmakers are considering limiting the growth of excessive gambling and gambling-related problems by restricting the availability of video poker and slot machines to casinos. Proponents defend this move on two well-founded assumptions (Fisher & Griffiths, 1995): (a) The widespread availability of the machines contributes to the spread of problem and pathological gambling, and (b) People who experience difficulty in controlling their level of play favor coin-operated machines over other gambling activities. Small-businesspeople who depend on revenues from coin-operated machines naturally oppose a ban or phase-out of the machines from noncasino locations, warning that they will form a coalition to defeat any such restrictions on their ability to earn a living. An interesting twist on this issue—and one that illustrates what policymakers and helping professionals are up against—is that the patrons of noncasino venues also are opposed to restricting coin-operated machines. Many of these people are "neighborhood gamblers" who limit their play to local supermarkets, convenience stores, and the like. According to unofficial reports, these people are among the most at-risk group for becoming or remaining pathological gamblers and thus would constitute an additional target for preventative and treatment services (Stearns, 1998)

Treatment

Reminiscent of the early studies on alcohol, drugs, and other abused substances, treatment for pathological gambling ordinarily is based on traditional 12-step programs (Founded in 1957, Gamblers Anonymous uses a 12-step program based on that of Alcoholics Anonymous.) Traditional approaches, unfortunately, appear to be relatively ineffective, with high drop-out rates and 1-year abstinence rates as low as 8% (DeCaria et al., 1996). Case studies have reported successful results from inpatient dependency treatment, counseling, psychoanalysis, paradoxical intention, aversion therapy, couples and family therapy, relaxation training, systematic desensitization, covert sensitization, rational emotive therapy, and cognitive restructuring approaches (Blaszczynski & Silove, 1995; Dickerson, 1989; Knapp & Lech, 1987). Pharmacotherapy efforts aimed at inhibiting the biochemical processes in the brain that are held responsible for pathological gambling (cf. Leshner, 1997) have included lithium carbonate and serotonin selective reuptake blockers (DeCaria et al., 1996).

In a notable break from tradition, Sylvain, Ladouceur, and Boisvert (1997) recently reported the results of one of the few attempts at controlled study of treatment for compulsive gamblers. Using a combination of "cognitive correction," problem-solving training, social skills training, and relapse prevention components in a treatment package, Sylvain and her colleagues found that of the 14 compulsive gamblers treated, 8 had maintained improvement after 12 months.

Research of the sort reported by Sylvain et al. (1997) should encourage other researchers to work toward developing an empirically validated course of treatment for problem and pathological gamblers. As that work progresses, we would caution researchers not to expend limited resources at this time on studies that compare the relative effectiveness of two or more procedures for changing behavior in some overall or general sense or in relation to a broad range of circumstances, that is, rather than pursuing questions regarding "Which treatment is better?" a more productive way to proceed would be, first, to focus on the variables necessary to produce a maximally effective change in behavior, and second, to examine how those variables can most practically be arranged and in turn applied to individual cases (cf. Johnston, 1988).

As in the provision of services for any clinical problem that threatens individual well-being and the public's welfare, effective treatments must be disseminated to persons who actually work with problem and pathological gamblers. Among the most significant challenges that face public policy-makers in that regard will be to overcome ignorance of, or resistance to, behavior science as a means for developing and evaluating treatments, and to provide training for people educated with respect to the value of behavior science to implement and monitor interventions properly. Ultimately, that is where differences are made in the lives of those individuals and their families whose lives are disrupted by gambling.

In closing, we tend to agree with Skinner (1980; see also Knapp, 1998) that gambling "commits a person to repetitious, stultifying behavior" (p. 82) that is, at best, unproductive and, at worst, counterproductive for a society whose members, in alarming numbers, are so engaged. A society is not strengthened when its members stand to prosper from doing little else than picking lottery numbers or dropping coins into a slot machine. A society is strengthened when its members participate in activities that support science, technology, literature, and the arts; that build self-control as a means to counteract impetuous behavior; and that make productive work more enjoyable and financially rewarding.

REFERENCES

Abbott, D. A., & Cramer, S. L. (1993). Gambling attitudes and participation: A midwestern survey. *Journal of Gambling Studies, 9,* 247–263.

American Psychiatric Association. (1994). *Diagnostic and statistical manual of mental disorders* (4th ed.). Washington, DC: Author.

Blaszczynski, A. P., & McConaghy, N. (1989). The medical model of pathological gambling: Current shortcomings. *Journal of Gambling Behavior, 5,* 42–52.

Blaszcynski, A. P., & McConaghy, N. (1994). Criminal offenses in Gamblers Anonymous and hospital treated pathological gamblers. *Journal of Gambling Studies, 10,* 99–127.

Blaszczynski, A. P., & Silove, D. (1995). Cognitive and behavioral therapies for pathological gamblers. *Journal of Gambling Studies, 11,* 195–220.

Brown, R. I. (1987). Pathological gambling and associated patterns of crime: Comparisons with alcohol and other drug additions. *Journal of Gambling Behavior, 3,* 98–114.

Collins, A. F. (1996). The pathological gambler and the government of gambling. *History of the Human Sciences, 9,* 69–100.

Culleton, R. P. (1989). The prevalence rates of pathological gambling: A look at methods. *Journal of Gambling Behavior, 5,* 22–41.

DeCaria, C. M., Hollander, E., Grossman, R., Wong, C. M., Masovich, S. A., & Cherkasky, S. (1996). Diagnosis, neurobiology, and treatment of pathological gambling. *Journal of Clinical Psychiatry, 57,* 80–84.

Devlin, A. S., & Peppard, D. M. (1996). Casino use by college students. *Psychological Reports, 78,* 899–906.

Dickerson, M. (1989). Gambling: Dependence without a drug. *International Review of Psychiatry, 1,* 157–172.

Dixon, M., Hayes, L. J., & Ebbs, R. (1998). Engaging in illusionary control during repeated risk-taking. *Psychological Reports, 48,* 481–509.

Dixon, M. R., Hayes, L. J., Hernandez, M. (May, 1998). *Self-rules, accurate rules, and inaccurate rules: Gambling as a verbally maintained behavior.* Paper presented at the meeting of the Association of Behavior Analysis, Orlando, FL.

Dostoyevsky, F. (1945). *The short novels of Dostoyevsky.* New York: The Dial Press.

Doyle, M. W. (1997). *Gambling: Does it benefit society?* [Videotape]. Princeton, NJ: Films for the Humanities and Sciences.

Fantino, E., Preston, R. A., & Dunn, R. (1993). Delay reduction: Current status. *Journal of the Experimental Analysis of Behavior, 60,* 159–169.

Fisher, S., & Griffiths, M. (1995). Current trends in slot machine play: Research and policy issues. *Journal of Gambling Studies, 11,* 239–247.

Grinols, E. L. (1995). Gambling as economic policy: Enumerating why losses exceed gains. *Illinois Business Review, 52,* 6–12.

Hayes, S. C., Zettle, R. D., & Rosenfarb, I. (1989). Rule-following. In S. C. Hayes (Ed.), *Rule-governed behavior: Cognition, contingencies, and instructional control* (pp. 191–220). New York: Plenum.

Herrnstein, R. J. (1990). Rational choice theory: Necessary but not sufficient. *American Psychologist, 45,* 356–367.

Herrnstein, R. J., & Prelec, D. (1992). A theory of addiction. In G. Loewenstein & J. Elster (Eds.), *Choice over time* (pp. 331–361). New York: Russell Sage.

Johnston, J. M. (1988). Strategic and tactical limits of comparison studies. *The Behavior Analyst, 11,* 1–9.

Johnston, J. M., & Pennypacker, H. S. (1993). *Strategies and tactics of behavioral research* (2nd ed.). Hillsdale, NJ: Lawrence Erlbaum Associates.

Knapp, T. J. (1976). A functional analysis of gambling behavior. In W. R. Eddington (Ed.), *Gambling and society: Interdisciplinary studies on the subject of gambling.* Springfield, IL: Thomas.

Knapp, T. J. (1998). Behaviorism and public policy: B. F. Skinner's views on gambling. *Behavior and Social Issues, 7,* 129–139.

Knapp, T. J., & Lech, B. C. (1987). Pathological gambling: A review with recommendations. *Advances in Behaviour Research and Therapy, 9,* 21–49.

Koehler, J. J., Gibbs, B. J., & Hogarth, R. M. (1994). Shattering the illusion of control: Multi-shot versus single-shot gambles. *Journal of Behavioral Decision Making, 7,* 183–191.

Ladouceur, R., Boisvert, J., Pepin, M., Loranger, M., & Sylvain, C. (1994). Social costs of pathological gambling. *Journal of Gambling Studies, 10,* 399–409.

Las Vegas Convention and Visitors Authority. (1996). *Facts about Las Vegas.* Las Vegas, NV: Author.

Legg England, S., & Götestam, K. G. (1991). The nature and treatment of excessive gambling. *Acta Psychiatrica Scandinavica, 84,* 113–120.

Leshner, A. I. (1997). Addiction is a brain disease, and it matters. *Science, 278,* 45–47.

Lesieur, H. R. (1994). Epidemiological surveys of pathological gambling: Critique and suggestions for modification. *Journal of Gambling Studies, 10,* 385–398.

Lesieur, H. R., & Rosenthal, R. J. (1991). Pathological gambling: A review of the literature (prepared for the American Psychological Association Task Force on DSM–IV Committee on Disorders of Impulse Control Not Elsewhere Classified). *Journal of Gambling Studies, 7,* 5–40.

The Lifestyle Market Analyst. (1997). Des Plaines, IL: SRDS.

Lombardo, J. (1995). Betting on gambling: Maryland rolls dice as states turn to casinos to boost revenues. *Washington Business Journal, 13,* 1–2.

Lyons, C. A., & Ghezzi, P. M. (1995). Wagering on a large scale: Relationships between public gambling and game manipulations in two state lotteries. *Journal of Applied Behavior Analysis, 28,* 127–137.

Mapes, J. (1997, March 9). Gambling on addiction. *The Sunday Oregonian,* pp. A1, A16–A17.

Michael, J. (1982). Distinguishing between discriminative and motivational functions of stimuli. *Journal of the Experimental Analysis of Behavior, 37,* 149–155.

Nevada State Gaming Control Board. (1997). *Gaming revenue report* (Vol. 4). Carson City, NV: Author.

Perone, M., & Baron, A. (1980). Reinforcement of human observing behavior by a stimulus correlated with extinction or increased effort. *Journal of the Experimental Analysis of Behavior, 34,* 239–261.

Phillips, D. P., Welty, W. R., & Smith, M. M. (1997). Elevated suicide levels associated with legalized gambling. *Suicide and Life-Threatening Behavior, 27,* 373–378.

Politzer, R. M., Morrow, J. S., & Leavey, S. B. (1985). Report on the cost benefit/effectiveness of treatments at the Johns Hopkins Center for Pathological Gambling. *Journal of Gambling Behavior, 2,* 131–142.

Presson, P. K., & Denassi, V. A. (1996). Illusion of control: A meta-analytic review. *Journal of Social Behavior and Personality, 11,* 493–510.

Preston, R. E., Meyer, J. J., & Lyons, C. A. (1997, May). *Preferences for control and immediacy in wagering among college students.* Poster session presented at the meeting of the Association for Behavior Analysis, Chicago.

Rachlin, H. (1990). Why do people gamble and keep gambling despite heavy losses? *Psychological Science, 1,* 294–297.

Rachlin, H., Battalio, R., Kagel, J., & Green, L. (1981). Maximization theory in behavioral psychology. *Behavioral and Brain Sciences, 4,* 371–388.

Rachlin, H., Raineri, A., & Cross, D. (1991). Subjective probability and delay. *Journal of the Experimental Analysis of Behavior, 55,* 233–244.

Shapira, Z., & Venezia, I. (1992). Size and frequency of prizes as determinants of the demand for lotteries. *Organizational Behavior and Human Decision Processes, 52,* 307–318.

Skinner, B. F. (1938). *The behavior of organisms.* New York: Appleton-Century-Crofts.

Skinner, B. F. (1980). *Notebooks.* Englewood Cliffs, NJ: Prentice-Hall.

Stearns, J. (1998, March 1). The great slot debate. *Reno Gazette-Journal,* pp. 1E, 6E.

Steinagle, R. (1995). *A descriptive analysis of slot machine play.* Unpublished master's thesis, University of Nevada, Reno.

Sylvain, C., Ladouceur, R., & Boisvert, J. (1997). Cognitive and behavioral treatment of pathological gambling: A controlled study. *Journal of Consulting and Clinical Psychology, 65,* 727–732.

Thompson, W. N. (1994). The states bet on legalized gambling. In D. Stille (Ed.), *1994 World Book Year Book* (pp. 38–46). Yonkers, NY: World Book.

Volberg, R. A. (1994). The prevalence and demographics of pathological gamblers: Implications for public health. *American Journal of Public Health, 84,* 237–241.

Volberg, R. A., Dickerson, M. G., Ladouceur, R., & Abbott, M. W. (1996). Prevalence studies and the development of services for problem gamblers and their families. *Journal of Gambling Studies, 12,* 215–231.

Volberg, R. A., & Steadman, H. J. (1988). Refining prevalence estimates of pathological gambling. *American Journal of Psychiatry, 145,* 502–505.

Walker, M. B., & Dickerson, M. G. (1996). The prevalence of problem and pathological gambling: A critical analysis. *Journal of Gambling Studies, 12,* 233–249.

Wolfgang, A. K. (1989). Gambling as a function of gender and sensation seeking. *Journal of Gambling Behavior, 4,* 71–77.

PART SIX

THE CULTURAL CONTEXT
OF HEALTH BEHAVIOR

CHAPTER THIRTEEN

The Tyranny of Small Decisions: Origins, Outcomes, and Proposed Solutions

Warren K. Bickel
Lisa A. Marsch
University of Vermont

It occurs frequently, I believe, that a person is faced with a choice between a present and future satisfaction or dissatisfaction and that he [sic] decides in favor of lesser present pleasure even though he knows perfectly well, and is even explicitly aware at the moment he makes his choice, that the future disadvantage is the greater and that therefore his well-being, on the whole, <u>suffers by reason of his choice</u> . . . How often does each of us "give into weakness" and allow himself to be swept along into acquiescence or action which he knows immediately he is going to regret on the morrow.

> —Böhm-Bawerk (1889/1970, p. 269, underscore added)

"Suffers by reason of his choice" is a powerful phrase describing a behavioral pattern in which an individual opts to engage in behavior that is desirable at the present time, but is less than desirable and perhaps even harmful at some future point in time. This type of behavior (variously termed as *impulsive, myopic, self-defeating, short-sighted,* or a *self-control failure*) has been the focus of several chapters in this book and is central to this one. Of course, many individuals, on occasion, may suffer by reason of their choice in many different arenas of their lives. Our concern here is not with these occasional choices but rather the persistent and continued choices that cause an individual to suffer time and time again. In a sense, individuals who engage in such patterns of behavior are victimized by their choices. This persistent behavioral pattern is what we are interested in and what we refer to as the *tyranny of small decisions.* This term was first coined by the economist Alfred Kahn (1966), who used it to describe market conditions in which consumer choice, when made as isolated acts of consumption, ultimately may lead to outcomes that consumers would not prefer and would decidedly not choose if the consequences of those individual acts of consumption were viewed as a whole.

In this chapter, we have modified Kahn's (1966) view and employ the term the tyranny of small decisions to refer to situations in which an individual can be victimized by the narrowness of the temporal context in which he or she exercises choice. The value of the term is threefold. First, use of the word "tyranny" suggests a behavioral pattern that occurs more than just occasionally. Second, the tyranny of small decisions specifies not only the behavior (choice) but also its consequence (negative outcomes). Third, this phrase, as we use it in this discussion, suggests the reason for the behavior, namely, that one makes "small decisions" or fails to base his or her present choice upon future events adequately. Nevertheless, this phrase alone does not provide an adequate explanation, because it does not answer the question: Why is the future not adequately taken into account?

In this chapter, we address this issue by forwarding an argument that having a shortened or extended temporal view is a consequence of our environment, most generally, and our culture, in particular. In so doing, we use the terms *temporal view* or *temporal horizon* to refer to the degree to which one's behavior is under the control of temporally proximate events. For example, a short temporal horizon refers to a description of short-sighted behavior or an insensitivity to long-run consequences. Thus, not unlike the frequently employed concept of "reinforcement," we use the terms temporal view or temporal horizon as hypothetical constructs or descriptors of empirical relations, and not as separate entities unto themselves (Mac Corquodale & Meehl, 1951).

We further argue in this chapter that there are a variety of circumstances in our contemporary culture that select for shortened temporal horizons, and that shortened temporal horizons may render individuals at risk for a variety of psychological disorders. Finally, we suggest interventions, including public policy interventions, that may encourage the development of an extended temporal horizon and perhaps render individuals less vulnerable to the tyranny of small decisions. To begin this discussion, we address research-derived factors that affect temporal horizons and considerations of the future consequences of behavior. These factors serve as an organizing framework for the remainder of the chapter.

BEHAVIORAL ECONOMIC PRINCIPLES
THAT AFFECT TEMPORAL HORIZON

Two research-derived principles that have great generality and applicability to issues of selecting immediate or deferred reinforcers are (a) the availability of reinforcers, and (b) the availability of competing reinforcers (e.g., Bickel,

DeGrandpre, & Higgins, 1993; Vuchinich & Tucker, 1988). These principles are derived from substantial research in the fields of behavioral analysis and behavioral pharmacology as well as from specific research domains within those general fields, including behavioral economics and the behavior analysis of choice.

Principle 1: Availability of Reinforcers

The first of these principles specifies that the availability of a reinforcer or commodity determines its consumption (Bickel & DeGrandpre, 1996; Vuchinich & Tucker, 1988). More specifically, this principle states simply that selection of a particular commodity or reinforcer covaries with reinforcer availability. For our purposes, the *availability* of a commodity is defined as the extent to which a commodity can be acquired or bought. Factors influencing availability include the price or response cost necessary to obtain the commodity, the ease of access to obtain the commodity, and the consequences of obtaining or using the commodity. More specifically, availability can be decreased by (a) decreasing the amount or magnitude of the reinforcer, (b) increasing the effort or the number of responses required to obtain that reinforcer, (c) decreasing the probability of obtaining the reinforcer (its predictability), (d) delaying the delivery of the reinforcer, and (e) increasing sanctions against or decreasing benefits of consumption. The studies supporting this empirical generalization have been reviewed elsewhere and are not repeated here (for a review, see Bickel & DeGrandpre, 1996; Ferster & Skinner, 1957; Griffiths, Bigelow, & Henningfield, 1980; Vuchinich & Tucker, 1988).

Principle 2: Competing Reinforcement

The second of these principles, the availability of competing reinforcers, stems largely from the research on choice, in which the responses or amount of time allocated to obtain one reinforcer is a function of the availability of an alternative reinforcer. Specifically, responses allocated to one reinforcer decrease as the availability of a competing reinforcer increases (Bickel & DeGrandpre, 1996; Herrnstein, 1970; Vuchinich & Tucker, 1988). Such alternative reinforcers are broadly conceived of here as those that compete with a reinforcer of interest either by functioning as a substitute or by requiring use of resources that otherwise would be allocated to the initial reinforcer. Importantly, competing reinforcers must be readily available for them to compete effectively with another reinforcer. For example, if one must wait a long amount of time to obtain a competing reinforcer, then the probability that such a reinforcer will compete successfully with another more immediate reinforcer would be low. Again, numerous studies have supported this empirical generalization, and a review of such information is not repeated here (see Bickel & DeGrandpre, 1996; Carroll, 1993; Herrnstein, Rachlin, Laibson, 1997; Vuchinich & Tucker, 1988).

The Two Principles and the Selection of Immediate or Deferred Commodities

These two principles—the availability of reinforcers and the availability of competing reinforcers—have systematic effects on the selection of immediate or deferred reinforcers. Indeed, all five factors that influence availability (outlined previously) and that are subsumed under these principles are the same factors that affect the selection of a delayed or immediately available commodity. The effect of each factor is reviewed in turn.

Selection of Immediate Commodities

Delay. In general, when two commodities or reinforcers of equal magnitude are available at the same response cost, but one is delayed relative to the other, the most immediate reinforcer generally will be selected by both humans and nonhumans (e.g., Chung, 1965). This choice occurs because the immediate reinforcer is more readily available than the delayed reinforcer and thus is functionally a less costly choice. In behavioral economics, the value of the delayed reinforcer is considered to be discounted as a function of the delay, such that the greater the delay, the more the discounting. This sort of discounting is intuitive, in that, for example, very few individuals would select $1,000 deferred by 2 years over an option of receiving the same amount of money immediately. This factor of delay to reinforcement exerts a constant effect on the selection of an immediate versus delayed reinforcer and thus interacts with the effects of the four remaining factors (e.g., Lowenstein & Elster, 1992).

Selection of Delayed Commodities

Magnitude. Decreasing the magnitude of an immediate reinforcer or sufficiently increasing the magnitude of a deferred reinforcer tends to result in selection of the delayed reward. Imagine a choice between $1,000 now and $1,000 in 2 years. Typically, the more immediate reward would be selected. Now, consider the choice when the magnitude of the immediate reinforcer is reduced to $250, but the delayed reinforcer magnitude is unchanged. In that instance, the delayed reward clearly would be selected in most cases. Indeed, a large variety of studies have demonstrated that decreasing the magnitude of the immediate reinforcer will result in selection of a delayed reinforcer (Herrnstein et al., 1997; Kirby & Marakovic, 1996).

Effort or Cost. Second, increasing the price or cost of the immediate reinforcer, thereby rendering it less available, also should result in choice of a deferred reinforcer. Let us reconsider the choice between $1,000 now and $1,000 in 2 years. Now, consider that to be able to select the earlier option, one must provide prior payment of $250, whereas the delayed option required prior payment of $25. Again, the delayed reinforcer would tend to be selected. Although not frequently studied, empirical research supports the role of price in changing choice between immediate and delayed consequences (e.g., Eisenberger & Adornetto, 1986; Eisenberger, Weier, Masterson, & Theis, 1989).

Predictability. Third, changing the probability of delivery of a commodity or reinforcer can result in a deferred choice. Again, consider if one were presented with a choice between $1,000 now or $1,000 in 2 years, but the immediate choice, if selected, would be delivered with only a probability of 0.5 (i.e., on average, the immediate option would be delivered half of the times it was selected). In this example, the immediate choice is risky or scarce; thus, the more probable, less risky, or more abundant choice will tend to be selected (e.g., Rachlin, 1995). In many circumstances, however, the delayed choice is the one that is often more probabilistic or unpredictable. This phenomenon may be the source of the old adage "A bird in the hand is worth two in the bush." Nonetheless, as we review later, circumstances can render the immediate choice less probable and engender selection of a delayed commodity.

Sanctions or Contingencies. Fourth, imposing sanctions or providing inducements may result in selection of a delayed commodity or reinforcer. Again, consider the choice between $1,000 now or $1,000 later. Now, consider a situation in which the immediate choice results in a $250 fine (sanction), selection of a delayed reward results in receipt of an additional $250 (inducement), or both. In these circumstances, the selection of the delayed commodity is more likely. Indeed, contingency management procedures that are used in drug abuse treatment could be interpreted as a means of imposing sanctions on drug use or offering inducements for long periods of drug abstinence (e.g., Higgins et al., 1994). That is, in general, drug-dependent users have a choice to use drugs or to select a drug-free lifestyle, which is composed of a long series of choices with delayed benefits. Providing contingency management procedures to drug users creates a situation in which drug use results in the loss of a reinforcer or commodity (e.g., the ability to purchase recreational items), whereas selection of drug abstinence results in delivery of the long-term benefits associated with abstinence. Of course, for these sanctions and inducements to be effective, contingencies alone are insufficient; rather, surveillance of compliance with contingencies is necessary (Solnick, Kannenberg, Eckerman, & Waller, 1980).

SMALL DECISIONS: ORIGINS, DECLINE, AND RESURGENCE

And that series of inventions by which man [sic] from age to age has remade his environment is a different kind of evolution—not biological, but cultural evolution.

—J. Bronowski (1974, pp. 19–20)

The origin of the tyranny of small decisions begins, but does not end, with our genetic endowment. Humans, as complex organisms, possess a genetic history that pervades all of what we do. That genetic history, although being all-pervasive, is far from being all-encompassing. Our genetics are not all-encompassing, ironically, because of what is perhaps our most important genetic capability—the ability to learn. As the noted evolutionary biologist Ernst Mayr (1988), stated, the behaviors of organisms are "either entirely laid down in the DNA of the genotype (closed programs) or constituted in such a way that they can incorporate additional information (open programs) . . . , acquired through learning, conditioning, or other experiences" (p. 49). Clearly, a large number of nonhuman organisms can incorporate new information acquired through learning. Humans, however, also can acquire information via a variety of symbolic representations that developed cumulatively in our culture. This cumulative development of knowledge may include the development of temporal horizon.

The question is to what extent our temporal horizon results from our biology or from our cumulative knowledge acquired through cultural development. One way to examine this is to explore the extent to which there is evidence of cross-species generality in temporal horizon. Whatever is in common between humans and nonhumans is most likely a function of shared genetic history. Whatever is different may, in turn, either reflect nonshared genetic history or be due to our cumulative development of knowledge. When the behavior of nonhumans (e.g., pigeons and rats) is measured in such a way that discounting of delayed rewards can be measured precisely, the shape of the resulting curves is hyperbolic. *Hyperbolic discounting* refers to the devaluation of delayed rewards proportional to their delay (Ainslie, 1992; Rachlin, 1995). Said another way, for each unit of time that constitutes the delay to delivery, the reward's present value decreases by an increasingly smaller proportion (Kirby, 1997). Nonhuman organisms also generally exhibit a very short temporal horizon; that is, future events are discounted radically. When the discounting of adult normal humans is measured in a similar fashion, discounting is also hyperbolic, demonstrating cross-species continuity (Green, Fry, & Myerson, 1994; Mazur, 1995, 1997). However, the degree of discounting by adult humans is considerably less than that observed in nonhuman animals.

These results suggest that the form of discounting (i.e., hyperbolic), which is similar cross-species, may be tied closely to our biology; however, attempts to explain the cross-species discontinuity in the degree of discounting include at least two possibilities. One possibility is that the relatively limited discounting observed in humans is a function of genetic endowment and that in the process of human biological evolution, the future came to be discounted less (i.e., a longer temporal horizon developed). An alternative possibility is that humans were temporally myopic in the beginning of their phylogenetic history; however, as a result of their ability to acquire knowledge across generations cumulatively, humans may have learned to have longer temporal views. Such changes must have been in response to environmental changes (discussed subsequently) and incorporated into cultural practices. From this perspective, temporal horizon reflects the process of socialization in our culture. Although nonhuman animal behavior undoubtedly can be similarly altered by environmental changes, animals, unlike humans, do not learn via the same specific process of enculturation that involves the use of symbolic representations, including temporal horizon. If this view is correct, then humans have the capability either to radically discount the future or not, depending on the contingencies of the culture. Of course, these two possibilities regarding whether limited discounting by humans is genetically or culturally based may represent polar extremes of a continuum, and the answer may lie somewhere in between. In either case, our biology clearly can support long or short temporal horizons.

Nonetheless, as we review the evidence, our knowledge favors the view that the development of an extended temporal horizon is largely learned from our culture, and, therefore, our culture, over time, may constrict or expand considerations of the future depending upon the prevailing contingencies. Once incorporated, these changes in temporal horizon may influence successive generations raised in that culture. In reviewing evidence in support of this argument, we examine several important developments in the history of humans that led to the adoption of different time horizons, as well as conditions that led to those changes. Identifying the conditions that led to those cultural changes may inform any efforts that seek to alter temporal horizon. We should note, however, that this historical analysis will not be able to call upon specific empirical measures of temporal horizon. As such, our analysis is an inference, and certainly other alternative inferences are possible. However, our analysis is consistent with the historical facts, and these historical changes seem consistent with the behavioral economic principles, outlined previously, that modulate temporal perspective.

The Beginning and Its End

Now this is not the end. It is not even the beginning of the end. But it is, perhaps, the end of the beginning.
—Sir Winston Spencer Churchill (1942, as cited in James, 1974, p. 6693)

When did humans begin to think about more than the next meal? When did they begin to plan for the future? When did tomorrow begin to matter today? In geological time, tomorrow began to matter just yesterday.

Prior to the time when considerations of the future were evident, humans were hunter–gatherers and were so for a long while. Hunter–gathering was the sole form of economic enterprise for all but the last 0.16% of the time of our human lineage on this planet (e.g., R. B. Lee & Devore, 1968). Humans diverged from other animals approximately 7 million years ago, with modern humans diverging from homo erectus about 500,000 years ago. Throughout this history, until approximately 13,000 years ago, all humans and proto-humans exclusively fed themselves by gathering wild plants and hunting wild animals (Diamond, 1997). Many evolutionary psychologists assume that the genetic bases for many of our behaviors (e.g., parent–child relationships) were developed in this hunter–gatherer phase of humankind's existence (Pinker, 1997).

Hunting and gathering is largely an event-based opportunistic activity, in which hunters take action when a herd of animals is located, or gathering occurs when nuts, grains, or berries are ripe (Harlan, 1992). Actions in this mode are opportunistic responses to the circumstances that present themselves. Evidence suggests that hunting skills of early humans were directed to easy-to-kill, nondangerous animals (Diamond, 1997). Also, early humans consumed a limited range of vegetable foods. Only in the relatively recent prehistory were smaller game, fish, and a broader array of vegetable foods increasingly exploited. Thus, hunting and gathering is consistent with a shortened temporal horizon because, in general, food obtained in this way was immediately and easily available without substantial delay.

All this changed 13,000 years ago when a new technology developed. This new technology changed the economic activity of humans and, in turn, began the change of many human activities from an event-based to a time-based mode. This new technology was agriculture. With the advent of agriculture, concerns moved from seeking food or obtaining food when it was available to planning for tomorrow by planting seeds today. Agriculture eliminated the social system based on roving bands of humans and permitted permanent settlements with larger numbers of individuals. Larger populations resulted from the simple fact that farmers and herders could feed 10 to 100 more individuals per acre of land than could be done from hunting and gathering (Diamond, 1997). These permanent settlements are what later permitted the development of specialized skills, governments, technology, and other advances of civilization.

The magnitude of change in temporal perspective associated with the advent of agriculture is wonderfully illustrated by a more recent example with Navajo Native Americans. The Navajos have had an extensive and relatively recent history as hunter–gatherers. Early efforts to promote range control and soil conservation among the Navajos were thwarted by the Navajo's view of time (Givens, 1977), that is, the Navajos had no view of time that would lead them to act on the basis of an expected future. The Navajos' sense of time was only in the here and now, and, therefore, they refused to participate in the proposed future-oriented program. Indeed, for the Navajos, "There is so little reality to the future that a promise of future benefits is not worth thinking about" (Lauer, 1970, p. 113).

What conditions led to the development of agriculture and a more extended view of the future? Making this transition seems nonintuitive at first blush. Hunter–gathering was not a labor-intensive activity. Studies of contemporary hunter–gatherers suggest that they spend only about 2.4 days per week hunting and gathering (R. B. Lee, 1968, 1979). Moreover, a hunter–gathering lifestyle appeared to be healthy. Medical studies indicate that hunter–gatherers were lean, but there is no evidence of nutritional deficiencies, and they were generally in good health (Cashdan, 1989; Truswell & Hansen, 1976). In constrast, farming is a labor-intensive activity. Moreover, studies comparing the health of hunter–gatherers and early farmers indicate that farmers had shorter lives, suffered from more infection, had more chronic malnutrition, and experienced greater growth-disrupting stress (Cohen, 1977). This makes the question even more intriguing: What events resulted in a shift away from the Eden-like world of hunter–gatherers to the difficult, short, and hardworking lives of the agriculturist, a change that required not only consideration of today, but also concerns about tomorrow?

Four factors have been identified that promoted the transition to agriculture (Diamond, 1997) and, we argue, to a longer temporal perspective. Although evidence supports each of these factors, they are controversial in part, because one or more of them may not have played a decisive role in all parts of the world. Nonetheless, these factors are important for understanding the transition to agriculture.

The first factor was the decreased availability of wild food (Diamond, 1997). The food rewards of hunter–gatherers decreased as the resources upon which they depended became increasingly scarce. Considerable evidence confirms this analysis. For example, Polynesian settlers began to intensify food production when numerous, easily hunted species became extinct. Also, evidence suggests that a decline in the abundance of wild gazelles in the fertile crescent was a reason for the increase in animal domestication. Thus, the costs of hunter–gathering functionally increased.

The second factor was the increased availability of domesticable wild plants, which, in turn, favored farming (Diamond, 1997). Climate changes at the end of the Pleistocene era expanded the habitats of wild cereals in certain regions of the world. These cereals permitted a considerable harvest to be obtained in a relatively short time. The increased availability of domesticable wild plants functionally decreased the costs of agriculture.

The third factor was the cumulative development of technologies (Diamond, 1997). Humans exhibit a form of Lamarckian cultural evolution in which, as a result of their open systems, they learn and pass on knowledge by teaching it to their young. Subsequent innovations are added and passed on to others. In particular, the development of technologies for collecting, processing, and storing wild foods supported the transition to agriculture. The sickle, the mortar and pestle, and the process of roasting grain to prevent sprouting during storage were all innovations that were important antecedents of widespread agriculture. Food storage technologies clearly show evidence of increasing concerns about the future and illustrate the cumulative development that led to increasing consideration about the future during this shift to an agricultural system.

The fourth factor refers to a self-reinforcing relationship between food production and population density (Diamond, 1997). As food production increased, populations grew, thus providing more labor for increased production. Moreover, as population densities increased, returning to a hunter–gathering lifestyle became a less viable alternative, as hunter–gathering alone was likely insufficient to support large groups of individuals. As populations of farmers increased, they were better able to displace hunter–gatherers by their sheer number and by the technological advantages they were developing. As a consequence, nearby hunter–gatherers either were displaced or survived by adopting the new technology. Thus, once agriculture was adopted, the cost of returning to hunter–gathering was high.

This analysis suggests that a consideration of long-term outcomes or, in other words, the development of a long temporal horizon results from the decreased availability of resources supporting short temporal horizons and increased availability of resources supporting long temporal horizons. Of course, these changes did not all occur simultaneously; however, over time, these factors likely interacted in various ways to exert increasing influence over humankind. One way to conceptualize this change associated with agriculture is to suggest that thinking of the future does not come naturally to us unless it is the most attractive option (e.g., less costly) relative to the other options.

We should note another important technological advance that resulted from agriculture, namely, the advent of writing (Diamond, 1997; Senner, 1991). The purpose of writing is to make a record today that will impact what we do later. Writing permitted the transmission of more knowledge, with greater accuracy, and in greater quantity and detail, than any other form of communication. Indeed, these factors, along with our contemporary methods of transmitting information, are the foundation of the current information revolution. All societies that developed or adopted writing had institutions that were complex and centralized within socially stratified societies. (Note that hunter–gatherer societies, to our present knowledge, never developed or adopted written language.) For example, writing was independently developed in Egypt and Mesopotamia by 3000 BC, in China by 1300 BC and by Mexican Indians by 600 BC (Diamond, 1997). Not all such societies adopted writing, but all adopters or developers of writing did have these complex socially stratified systems (Diamond, 1997).

Time's Cycle and Time's Arrow

Times arrow and time's cycle is, if you will, a "great" dichotomy because each of its poles capture, by its essence, a theme so central to intellectual (and practical) life that western people who hope to understand history must wrestle intimately with both.

—S. J. Gould (1987, pp. 15–16)

The cycle of time suggests changelessness and continuity. The arrow of time suggests change and forward movement. In our contemporary culture, we primarily view time as an arrow flying by, or as moving forward. Change is largely accepted as a constant in our culture. But this view has not always been prevalent, and, before it, a circular view of time predominated. When did this change in perspective begin and what factors led to this change? To answer this question, we must start at the beginning of antiquity.

In antiquity, circular views of time were widespread. For example, the Egyptians regarded time as a succession of recurring phases (circa 1500 BC). For them, the past was not regarded as receding, and the world was essentially static and unchanging. Such a view is evident in their approach to chronology. Time was marked by the years of a pharaoh's reign. With the ascension of each new pharaoh, time was reset (Whitrow, 1989).

Although in ancient Greece a greater diversity of views was evident, a circular view was prevalent. One example of this diversity was the view that the Mycenaean period (1200 BC), which resulted in the epics of Homer, was a Golden Age and that society had progressively declined from this ideal state (Whitrow, 1989). In contrast, Heraclitus (circa 500 BC) viewed change as a fundamental character of nature and is known for his aphorism "You never step in the same river twice." From 500 BC forward, however, there was generally little belief in the progress of the future. As Whitrow noted, "The typical Greek tended to be backward looking, since the future appeared to him to be the domain of total uncertainty, his only guide to it being delusive expectation" (p. 46). For example, Aristotle believed that knowledge obtained in the arts and sciences was discovered and lost many time in the cycles of time. Similarly, Imperial Rome was focused primarily on the past and the present, not the future. The Romans objected to change and were often suspicious of novelty.

This view of time largely changed with the advent and popoularization of Christianity. Christianity directed attention to the future and ushered in what serves as our contemporary view of time, that is, central to Christianity was the notion that one worked for the future today. This view of time resulted from the perspectives that were prevalent in ancient Israel and Judaism. Instead of adopting a circular view of time, the Jews believed in a linear concept of time and a belief that was based on their view that history and the future were the gradual revelation of God's purpose (Whitrow, 1989). Christianity continued that view and elaborated on it. Christians believed that individuals can be changed, saved, and enter the kingdom of God in the future.

The growth of Christianity from an obscure marginal sect to a dominant religious force in the Western world was a remarkable feat (Stark, 1997). In AD 40, estimates suggest that there were approximately 1,000 Christians, composing 0.0017% of the world's population. By AD 350, the number of Christians swelled to 33,882,000, or 56% of the world's population, a growth rate of approximately 40% per decade. Let us consider the factors and circumstances that led to the acceptance of Christianity along with its new temporal view.

Although the conditions that led to Chistianity's wide adoption can be debated, at least three factors appear to have played important roles (Stark, 1997). The first factor entailed locating to a region of the world where the views of Christianity, including its temporal view, could thrive. This action also permitted the next two factors to operate. Specifically, these factors resulted from the relative benefits of Christianity to its followers as compared to paganism. All of these factors are interrelated and self-reinforcing and suggest that this new view was adopted due the relative benefits of Christianity over its alternatives.

First, Christianity mainly drew converts from the religiously inactive and discontented (Stark, 1997). Christianity rose during the first and second centuries AD in the central and eastern Mediterranean region, where a large number of new religious ideas were generated. These various religious movements were unstable, continuously changing and reassembling in new forms. As such, the challenge for Christianity was not only to survive but also to retain its identity. The insights and view of religion and religious life attributed to Jesus and Christianity had appeal, but some aspects of these insights also were adopted by others promoting their own religious movement, including Judaism. Consequently, those branches of Christianity that remained in Jerusalem could not remain sufficiently differentiated from Judaism and eventually incorporated back into that view. Christianity thus thrived, not by staying in Jerusalem where many other competing religions were operating, but by being directed at areas populated by pagans and Diaspora Jews (Jews who were more worldly and had incorporated aspects of Greek and Roman culture). Among these individuals, Christianity was better able to develop a following.

Second, Christians engaged in actions during traumatic times that promoted Christianity in a variety of ways (Stark, 1997). During the first several centuries AD, epidemics raged throughout the Roman Empire. During these epidemics, pagans isolated those who were ill, and, thus, the sufferers were left alone and not cared for by their pagan families, friends, or neighbors (McNeil, 1976). For those who were ill, these actions or, rather, inactions, hastened the effect of the contagion. Such inactions were a result of the pagans' religious beliefs that the pagan gods did not punish ethical violations (like failing to help the sick) and imposed no ethical demand. Moreover, the pagan priests could not offer salvation, because, according to their religion, there was no escape from mortality, no life after death, and no heaven. By contrast, Christianity required ethical behavior in order to enter the kingdom of God. Thus, the Christians cared for the ill and provided water and food when the sick could not take care of themselves. Although taking care of others sometimes involved risking one's own life, the Christians, by their acts of sacrifice, secured eternal life after death, a temporally distal reward for their efforts.

Importantly, by taking care of the ill, the Christians likely had a profound effect on mortality. The simple act of providing food and water for those too weak to care for themselves may have substantially reduced mortality. Stark (1997) suggested that such action had four effects: (a) Taking care of the ill (who were most often, but not exclusively, Christians) decreased mortality by two thirds and, thus, the proportion of the population that was Christian increased because more Christians survived; (b) the observance of the reduced mortality rate of Christians by the pagans was viewed as miraculous and prompted further conversion of the pagans; (c) many converts to Christianity were obtained because the pagan survivors were able to find a comforting religious explanation for the deaths of loved ones (i.e., they went to the kingdom of God); and (d) the bonds between many pagans may have been diminished by the high death rates among the pagans, and with the Christian acceptance of strangers and pagans, more pagans may have been converted to Christianity.

The third factor that led to the adoption of Christianity involved a variety of other benefits associated with this belief system (Stark, 1997). These benefits included those related to the practice of religion, such as a life after death, as well as material benefits. For example, converting to Christianity provided a social net: Just as Christians were expected to aid the less fortunate, they expected to receive such a benefit during difficult times as well. These practices certainly led to feelings of security and predictability among Christians. Other material benefits accrued when Constantine the Great embraced Christianity in AD 312. Constantine may have embraced Christianity as an astute political response to the growing numbers of Christians, and the most notable of his actions was the conveyance of favors, powers, and immunities to the Christians (Johnson, 1976; Peters, 1970; Stark, 1997). These benefits included promoting Christians over pagans, allowing Christian soldiers not to work on Sundays, and exempting churches from taxation. These and many other inducements continued to swell the number of converts. Altogether, these benefits of Christianity were decisive in establishing Christianity as a major religion and permitting its longer temporal view to become the model for our contemporary Western culture.

Modern Times

Time present and time past
Are both perhaps present in time future,
And time future contained in time past.
—T. S. Eliot (*Collected Poems*, 1930, p. 213)

In the previous sections, we examined two apparent watershed moments in the shaping of our view of time—the transition from hunter–gathering to agriculture and from paganism to Christianity. Both required the development of a more extended temporal view that did not come naturally to humans, but occurred because the more extended time frame was the more attractive option compared to the alternatives, that is, as previously discussed, these changes occurred because the former system (e.g., hunting and gathering) was no longer as viable as the system that replaced it (e.g., agriculture). If both systems had been viable, the transitions (e.g., to agriculture) may never have occurred (e.g., assuming the availability of game and crops, hunting and gathering would have been the least costly option).

In contrast, in modern times, numerous factors may encourage myopic temporal perspectives, or the tyranny of small decisions. We now review several primary influential factors affecting the temporal horizon of the majority of individuals in modern society, including our contemporary culture of consumerism and reduced civic participation, as well as factors affecting specific groups of individuals in modern society, such as increased economic deterioration and destabilization and increased isolation from "mediating structures," including family, neighborhood, and religion. These factors, we argue, are shortening our collective temporal horizon and rendering humankind closer, in terms of our temporal horizon, to our hunter–gatherer an-

TABLE 13.1
Summary of Temporal Horizon in Modern Society

Factors Promoting Short Temporal Horizon in Modern Society	Related Behavioral Principles
Cultural factors	
Culture of immediate gratification–leisure	High availability of low-cost reinforcers; low effort needed to obtain reinforcer; immediate reinforcement (little delay)
Economic deterioration and destabilization	Unpredictable environments–reinforcers
Community factors	
Erosion of civic–community bonds	Lack of behavioral surveillance with contingencies; high availability of low-cost reinforcers
Erosion of religious or moral training	Lack of behavioral surveillance with contingencies
Family–individual factors	
Erosion of the nuclear family	Lack of behavioral surveillance with contingencies; unpredictable environments–reinforcers

cestors. A summary of the factors that we suggest are promoting a short temporal horizon in modern society, along with their related behavioral principles, is provided in Table 13.1.

Leisure Society

I sometimes think that the present-day descendants [of those] who conquered the wilderness are being conquered by a wilderness of leisure. Our constant cry is to make things easy.
—Mrs. Mina Miller Edison (aka Mrs. Thomas Edison; in Coman & Weir, 1925, p. 17)

In modern times, the main focus of many business enterprises is to make consumption and purchase of entertainment and other amusements easier and more immediate. The evidence suggests that this contemporary culture of consumerism is encouraging myopic temporal perspectives. The primary force that is driving these changes began as a consequence of other forces, and it still exerts and extends its influence today. That primary force is leisure.

Leisure, as we know it today, was a consequence of the industrial revolution. Prior to the industrialization of America (circa 1870), and particularly in agricultural and artisan settings, leisure was seemlessly woven into the fabric of life. As O'Malley (1990) noted:

Preindustrial societies enjoyed less of a distinction between "work" and "rest."
. . . They intermingled constantly in the course of living. A wise and diligent
farmer, finishing one task, went straight to work on another, and even at rest,
the farmer remained a farmer; there was relatively little sense of "time off."
(p. 257)

As such, individuals prior to the late 1800s purchased fewer leisure goods
and services, and made their own music and toys (Butsch, 1990). Moreover,
Victorian culture was a strong, but not ubiquitous, force in American society
during this time. Victorian ideals "taught people to work hard, to postpone
gratification, to repress themselves sexually, and to improve themselves and
to be sober, conscientious and even compulsive" (Howe, 1976, p. 17)—indeed, to have extended temporal horizons.

Industrialization led to the growing spread of clocks and watches into all
aspects of life, particularly work. Factory work became synonymous with
the time clock. Thus, factory work resulted in a clear demarcation between
work and leisure. A growing number of wage earners enjoyed a new kind
of free time, and with that free time began the commercialization of leisure
(Rosenzweig, 1983). Movies, phonographs, and saloons were all innovations
that filled leisure time. These leisure activities became tempting, and even
Victorians began to throw off their suspicions of pleasurable indulgence. As
O'Malley (1990) noted, "By the late nineteenth century, to a far greater extent
than before, conspicuous self-gratification had become the credo of the
successful and the envy of the urban middle class" (p. 258). This movement
avidly sought for the replacement of a restrictive culture with one characterized by increased permissiveness and relativism. Thus, sanctions against
impulsive behavior or short temporal horizons were dramatically lessened
in this new permissive culture.

This cultural change also demanded the attention and money of the
populace. The new niche for leisure in the affairs of humans became a
marketplace for all sorts of commodities and activities. Indeed, such leisure,
with its immediately available commodities, may have shortened temporal
horizons, and this change was evidenced in our monetary budgets. The
proportion of income that was spent on items other than food, clothing,
and shelter increased from 10% to 25% from 1875 to the 1930s in working-
class families. By the 1980s, 40% of income was allocated to "goods intensive"
recreation (Horowitz, 1985). Not surprisingly, recent longitudinal studies of
rates of saving confirm that there has been a major and apparently permanent
decline in saving in modern times in 23 Western countries that comprise
60% of the world's output (Maital & Maital, 1994). A decrease in savings is
certainly suggestive of a shortened temporal horizon. Perhaps there can be
no better example or marker of leisure, its consequences, and its effects on
temporal horizon than the unique case of television.

The Special Case of Television

The television set, the electronic organizing principle of living room furniture, then shows them what life should be. Through its commercials it teaches them it is better to relate to things through possession, than to people through sharing. It demonstrates that self-gratification is preferable to self-sacrifice. It educates them in impatience, programming them to expect the resolution of all problems in an hour or less. . . . Servant of now, television deifies the secular moment even as it desanctifies the vow.
— Stephen Bertman (*Hyperculture*, 1998, p. 70)

Most of our leisure activities require the purchase of a commodity such as toys, radios, videocassette recorders, movie tickets, and alcohol. Buying, as a type of leisure activity, is evidenced by the existence of thousands of malls across America. To compete in this burgeoning entertainment industry requires that the recreational commodity's price not be excessive and that enjoyment be immediately available. The commodity that best characterizes the approach to leisure, and that has certainly been the most successful, is television. Although TV sets were expensive when they were introduced, their price decreased over time. Importantly, a TV, once purchased, as J. P. Robinson and Godbey (1997) noted

is readily available in the home, immediately accessible and at low cost, and may be meaningfully consumed in increments of one hour, a half hour, or less. It can be used by people who are tired, illiterate, have a disability, or want to do something else at the same time. It is usable across almost the entire life cycle. (p. 131)

The success of TV as a leisure commodity is demonstrated by the speed of its diffusion. In 1950, TV was in barely 10% of American homes. By 1959, television was in 90% of the homes (Putnam, 1995b). Television viewing consumes 4 hours per day in the lives of average Americans in time-budget analyses. In children, TV consumes between 20 and 40 hours per week on average. The average high school graduate likely will have spent about 15,000 to 18,000 hours in front of a TV, but only 12,000 hours in school (Strasburger, 1992). Next to sleeping, TV occupies the greatest amount of time during childhood (Dietz & Strasburger, 1991). Importantly, each succeeding generation of TV viewers tends to watch 5% to 8% more TV than their immediate predecessor (Putnam, 1995a). Not surprisingly, given the time devoted to this activity, TV has been related to many changes in our society.

Civic participation has been declining in our culture (Putnam, 1995a, 1995b). For example, membership records of diverse organization such as the Elk's club, the PTA, the League of Women Voters, the Red Cross, labor unions, and even bowling leagues declined 25% to 50% over the last two to three decades. Socializing and visiting is down by 25% since 1965. Participation in politics is down 39%, and working for a political party is down 56%. Overall, there is less trust in others, as well. In trying to understand and explain this trend, Putnam (1995b) looked at generational effects. He concluded that individuals born from 1910 to 1940 were substantially more engaged in community affairs and were more trusting than succeeding generations. Moreover, each generation that has reached adulthood since the 1940s has been less engaged in its community than its immediate predecessors.

After exploring a large number of possible reasons for these observed trends, including divorce, economic hard times, and suburbanization, Putnam (1995b) concluded that television and other aspects of the electronic revolution were the forces behind this loss of civic participation. Television, because of its immediate availability and lower cost, competes with civic participation, which simply requires more effort and has gratifying consequences that are more delayed than those offered by TV. Given that there is only so much leisure time per day, the greater amount of time spent on TV necessarily leaves less time to spend in civic participation. As Hirsch (1976) noted, fellowship is the opportunity cost of TV consumption, that is, when there is TV and other goods to consume during our leisure, the cost of socializing increases. Watching TV comes at the expense of talking or meeting with neighbors. Indeed, most studies report a negative correlation between hours of TV viewing and community involvement (Putnam, 1995b).

The decrease in the civic bonds that individuals have with their community and with their neighbors because of TV's monopoly of time may produce some self-reinforcing effects. Consider that, as these bonds are eroded, individuals may be less concerned about what others will say or do about their actions. This, in turn, may lead to greater insensitivity to the concerns of others. This lack of concern about neighbors may foster further TV viewing or other such individualistic behaviors.

This extensive contact with the television also may decrease temporal horizon directly. For example, although some conflicting studies exist, empirical research has shown that children watching violent TV shows display increased aggression and impulsivity (Liebert & Baron, 1972). Although no valid controlled studies exist in which populations exposed to television were compared to populations not exposed to television, epidemiological research has further supported the link between TV watching and increased violence. For example, after television was introduced in Canada and the United States, homicide rates in these countries doubled; at the same time, in South Africa, where television did not exist at the time, homicide rates remained stable. It is interesting to note that the increased rates of homicide were observed about 10 to 15 years after the introduction of television. As homicide is primarily an adult activity, this delayed increase in homicide rates may have been a result of the children of the "television generation" growing up and then being able to affect the homicide rate (Centerwall, 1989). In another study, the effect of television was investigated in a community in Canada (known as "Notel" in the study) that was previously unexposed to television (due to difficulties with signal reception in the community) and that then acquired television (in 1973). A cohort of 45 first and second graders in this community was compared to similar cohorts in two control communities (who had television) in the context of a double-blind research design for a period of 2 years to assess the effects of the introduction of television. Results indicated that, although rates of physical aggression did not change significantly in the two control communities, rates of physical aggression among children in Notel significantly increased by 160%. In addition, after the introduction of television, the children in Notel considerably reduced their participation in social activities, developed fluent reading skills more slowly, and demonstrated reductions in their creativity scores. Importantly, after television was introduced, adults in the community were shown to decrease their task persistence (e.g., they reduced the amount of time they spent working to solve a problem; Centerwall, 1989; Williams, 1986).

The popularization of the remote control devices, in combination with expanding number of channels, has led to a generation of TV viewers that media analysts refer to as "grazers," although we might prefer the term "foragers" (Keyes, 1991). Interestingly, recent studies indicate that these viewers change stations as often as 22 times per min. Thus, these foragers tend to watch a TV show until a commercial is played, at which point they tend to switch to another station. Finally, TV shows promote the notion of the "quick fix," where problems can be overcome within half an hour. (J. P. Robinson & Godbey, 1997).

The commercialization of leisure (and the availability of TV as a marker of leisure), may lead to small or short-sighted decisions. If this is true, then in the same way that civic participation decreased across successive generations, we should expect to find evidence that more and more individuals are engaging in the tyranny of small decisions.

The Culture of Poverty

The culture of poverty is not just a matter of deprivation or disorganization, a term signifying the absence of something. It is a culture in the traditional anthropological sense in that it provides human beings with a design for living, with a ready-made set of solutions for human problems, and so serves a significant adaptive function. . . . Wherever it occurs, its practitioners exhibit remarkable similarity in the structure of their families, in interpersonal relations, in spending habits, in their value systems and in their orientation in time.

—O. Lewis (*Scientific American*, 1966, p. 19)

In the previous section, we reviewed evidence suggesting that contemporary consumerism and leisure promote short temporal horizons, or the tyranny of small decisions, in the majority of individuals in modern society. In this section, we review two additional factors in modern society that generally affect specific groups of individuals and that may promote a myopic temporal perspective that is manifested in the form of "deviant," short-sighted behavior. In so doing, we discuss how environments characterized (a) by economic deterioration and destabilization, with a high prevalence of environmental risk and uncertainty; and (b) by isolation from "mediating structures" such as family, neighborhood, and religion (or low rates of behavioral surveillance), are also those environments in which criminal, drug use, and other short-sighted behaviors are prevalent. In addition, we discuss how those enviroments in which these factors are most prevalent are also those contexts in which such short-sighted behavior (which is often termed as "deviant" by society) is also disproportionally represented. Although each of these various factors that influence such behavior are discussed in turn, we recognize that these and other influential factors do not function independently but rather interact in dynamic and complex ways.

In addition, we suggest that such environments, in which the factors that select for short temporal horizon and socially deviant behavior are disproportionately represented, have increased in modern times, that is, the rapidly expanding capitalism in modern society undoubtedly has promoted a changing relation between social structures and social agents. Those environments in modern society that promote short-sighted "deviant" behavior tend also to be the contexts in which individuals are alienated from many of the social and economic resources of such a capitalistic society and live in "contagious urban decay" (R. Wallace, Thompson Fullilove, & Wallace, 1992).

In discussing this "culture of poverty," we are not suggesting that economic poverty per se causes short-sighted behavior (e.g., drug use or criminal behavior). Rather, as Lewis (1966) suggested, the culture of poverty represents a culture of instability, criminality, violence, and deprivation—indeed, a culture that fails to promote consideration of the future consequences of behavior. For example, it is unlikely that unemployment directly causes crime; rather, a culture in which criminal behavior seems to be natural or normal and more desirable than employment may promote criminal behavior (Himmelfarb, 1995).

Economic Deterioration and Destabilization

If [one] is oppressed by a sense of futility, where can he get it but from the culture around him, a culture that is more powerful in the concreteness and immediacy of its lessons than the shadowy glimpses and the idealized verbalizations of the achievability of a better life?
—Chein, Gerard, Lee, & Rosenfeld (*The Road to H,* 1964, p. 79)

Congruent with our previous discussion, as the occurrence of a desired, future outcome of a behavior becomes more risky or uncertain, the cost of engaging in behaviors that lead to such unpredictable outcomes is increased. Thus, behavior that leads to such unpredictable future outcomes may be replaced by behavior that yields more immediate, predictable outcomes. For example, environments characterized by economic deterioration and destabilization, in which the future outcomes of one's behavior are typically characterized by risk and uncertainty, may select for short-sighted behavior. In many inner-city environments, where community instability and decay (e.g., poverty and violence) are endemic to everyday life (e.g., Greene, 1996), behaving in a way to shape one's future may seem a fruitless endeavor for individuals who may not expect that they will experience the future. Rather, in such a situation, the most adaptive strategy may be to consider only the immediate consequences of a behavior (Strathman, Boninger, Gleicher, & Baker, 1994). Indeed, experimental research has demonstrated that behaviors that lead to unpredictable future outcomes may be replaced by behaviors that yield more immediate predictable outcomes (e.g., Christensen, Parker, Silberberg, & Hursh, 1988; King & Logue, 1992; Navarick, 1987). Although individuals may differentially experience the consequences of such environments (Javier, Herron & Yanos, 1995), in general, individuals who grow up in an environment that is permeated by unpredictability and risk may grow up to believe that the world is an unpredictable place and thus may engage in more present-oriented rather than future-oriented behavior. In contrast, those who grow up in a more predictable environment may be more future-oriented and engage in less risky behavior (Hill, Ross, & Low, 1997).

Indeed, the prevalence of substance abuse, criminal, and many other types of risk behavior is highest in urban and low SES residential environments (e.g., Crum, Lillie-Blanton, & Anthony, 1996; Harrell & Peterson, 1992). For example, economic deterioration and poverty in urban environments have been strongly associated ($r = .89$) with higher rates of narcotic use (Richman, 1977). In addition, the greater the neighborhood poverty, the greater the rate of juvenile substance users (Chein et al., 1964; Smart, Adlaf, & Walsh, 1994) and the greater the risk of adult antisocial behavior, including alcohol and drug abuse, by antisocial youth (Robins & Ratcliff, 1979). Moreover, in a meta-analysis of predictors of homicide, resource deprivation or poverty has been shown to be the strongest predictor of high homicide rates (Land, McCall, & Cohen, 1990). In addition, a significant association has been demonstrated between degree of neighborhood disadvantage and exposure to drugs, such that, for example, youth living in the most disadvantaged neighborhoods are estimated to be 5.6 times more likely to have been offered cocaine relative to those in advantaged neighborhoods (Crum et al., 1996). Furthermore, a strong correlation ($r = .88$) has been reported between the average life expectancy of individuals in an urban environment and their neighborhood homicide rate, with those individuals with the shortest life expectancy also living in places where homicide rates are highest (Wilson & Daly, 1997). In addition, teenage pregnancy is highest among those in low SES, urban environments, where individuals also experience poorer and more uncertain health and higher age-specific mortality rates than do individuals in nonurban or higher SES contexts (Geronimus, 1987, 1996). Finally, environmental stressors, such as the destruction and disempowerment of communities, deterioration of schools, and collapse of public health, have been shown to similarly promote short-sighted behavior (Baumeister, Heatherton, & Tice, 1994; R. Wallace et al., 1992).

Furthermore, the relation between community destabilization–social disintegration and short temporal horizon may be self-reinforcing, that is, myopic behavior that results from environmental stability or uncertainty may, in turn, directly affect subsequent community decay or destabilization, leading to even more short-sighted (e.g., deviant) behavior:

> Indeed, an almost overwhelmingly large amount of the mental and public health literature, in addition to the criminology literature, implies significant disruption of individual and collective social and physical structure can have the most dire and indirect impacts on a broad range of pathological outcomes. (R. Wallace et al., 1992)

The "Mediating Structures" of Family, Neighborhood and Religion

Having made the most valiant attempts to "objectify" the problem of poverty, to see it as the product of impersonal economic and social forces, we are discovering that the economic and social aspects of that problem are inseparable from the moral and personal ones.
—G. Himmelfarb (*The De-moralization of Society*, 1995, p. 242)

The effect of environmental instability on temporal horizon may also be manifested in other elements of one's environment, including one's personal, domestic or community networks, including parents, family, and neighborhood (e.g., Chisholm, 1996). For example, attachment to caregivers has been demonstrated to be an important factor in the development of an extended future time perspective, with greater parental or caretaker attachment and support related to a more positive future outlook (Melges, 1982; Trommsdorff, Lamm, & Schmidt, 1978). In addition, parents and neighborhoods may provide "behavioral surveillance with contingencies" or "countervailing influences" to deviant behavior, such as drug use and criminal behavior by, for example, teaching delayed gratification to a child, exercising immediate punishment for the deviant behavior or by providing alternative sources of reinforcement to a child (Chilcoat & Johanson, 1998; Gottfredson & Hirschi, 1990; Loeber & Dishion, 1984). For example, one study reported that fathers of nondelinquent youth were twice as likely to be attached to their sons, concerned about their sons' welfare, and approximately one fifth as likely to be hostile toward their sons relative to fathers of delinquent youth (Glueck & Glueck, 1950). In another study, children whose parents supervised how they spent their time and ensured that their children met their home- and school-related responsibilities were much less likely to engage later in criminal activity relative to those whose parents did not monitor their children's behavior (McCord, 1979). Indeed, the lack of monitoring by parents of their children's behavior has been shown to be one of the strongest predictors of juvenile delinquency (Patterson & Stouthamer-Loeber, 1984). Nevertheless, urban environments that are characterized by poverty and instability are strongly associated with parenting behaviors that include failing to reward children for desired behaviors as well as lower parental interest in, and responsiveness to, children's socioemotional needs (McLoyd, 1990; Zayas, 1995). In addition, both low levels of attachment to one's neighborhood, as well as neighborhoods that fail to effectively place sanctions on the behavior of its members, are associated with high rates of deviant behavior, including criminal and drug-using behavior (e.g., Hawkins, Catalano, & Miller, 1992).

Moreover, religious or moral training within a family or community may promote long temporal horizons and self-controlled behavior, whereas isolation from such moral training may promote short temporal horizons (e.g., Stark, 1987). For example, as previously discussed in the chapter, the shift from a pagan to Christian society during the first several centuries AD was accompanied by a shift to a linear concept of time in which individuals considered the implications of their current behavior on future outcomes (e.g., entering the Kingdom of God). In addition, a recent epidemiological study found that youth who prayed, read the Bible, attended church activities at least two times per week, and attended revival crusades were approximately one fifth as likely to have initiated drug use relative to those who did not engage in such behavior (Johanson, Duffy, & Anthony, 1996). Moreover, a protective effect of church affiliation or "religiosity" has been found, whereby youth who responded highest on Christian commitment were significantly less likely to have been offered or to have used illicit drugs (Cook, Goddard, & Westall, 1997). Also, urban youth who are involved in church activities (e.g., contributing money to the church, attending church services) have been shown to be more likely to express an intolerant attitude toward drug use relative to those youth who are not involved in such activities (Gary & Berry, 1984). In addition, another study demonstrated that approximately twice as many nondelinquent youth attended church regularly (e.g., one time per week) compared to delinquent youth (Glueck & Glueck, 1950). Finally, a review of the crime rates in 13 industrial nations revealed that more religious countries with higher rates of church attendance and church membership had lower crime rates than did less religious countries (Ellis &

Peterson, 1996). Nevertheless, although religiosity has been shown to function as a buffer to engaging in short-sighted behaviors, its effects do not function in isolation but rather often interact with those of other mediating structures (e.g., Benda & Corwyn, 1997). For example, youth are at a relatively lower risk for substance use if they regularly attend both church and school than if they engage in only one or the other behavior (Zimmerman & Maton, 1992).

Unfortunately, such beneficial effects of religiosity or moral training on temporal horizon may not be realized in inner-city urban contexts, as there is evidence to suggest that individuals in such settings are more isolated from the buffering effects of religion relative to those in rural settings. For example, one study reported, based on data from the Gallup Unchurched American Study, that African Americans residing in urban areas are more likely to be "unchurched" (where being *churched* is defined as being a member of a church that one has attended in the past 6 months) relative to those in nonurban settings (Nelsen, 1988). In addition, adolescents in urban settings have been shown to have significantly lower moral reasoning ability relative to their peers who live in rural settings (Sahoo, 1985). Furthermore, considerable evidence suggests that modern society has been accompanied by a general moral decline. For example, the illegitimacy ratio rose in the United States from 3% in 1920, to 5% in 1960, to 11% in 1970, to more than 18% by 1980, and to more than 30% by 1991. This trend also has been observed in other industrialized nations, although the United States has the highest rate of teenage illegitimacy among all industrialized nations (Himmelfarb, 1995).

In general, urban settings where drug use and other short-sighted behaviors are most prevalent typically are characterized by the *culture of poverty*, which Lewis (1996) described as a culture identified by large numbers of disrupted families, poor parental attachment, high rates of unemployment, economic deterioration, poor health, and high mortality rates (Crum et al., 1996; Currie, 1993; Duncan, Duncan, Biglan, & Ary, 1998). The profound effect of the various values and practices of a family and neighborhood becomes clearer when considering studies comparing persons who have lived in disadvantaged environments for long periods of time to those who have lived there for shorter time periods. For example, Chein et al. (1964) found that adolescents who recently had moved to New York City from Puerto Rico or the rural South had significantly lower rates of drug dependence than did those who had lived for a longer period of time in the urban setting of New York City. Chein et al. (1966) concluded that the cohesive families of the immigrants shielded them from the "prevailing atmosphere of degenerated personal relationships" in the inner-city environment (p. 138). Furthermore, second-generation residents born in New York City from families who migrated to the city were more likely to use drugs than were first-generation residents who had been born elsewhere (Kleinman & Lukoff, 1978). In another similar study, conducted by Velez and Ungemack (1989), Puerto Ricans who migrated to New York City were, on average, twice as likely to abuse drugs as were those remaining in Puerto Rico. In addition, the longer an immigrant had lived in New York City, the more likely she or he was to have used illicit drugs. Indeed, these urban immigrants were

> locked into neighborhoods where most people could expect only low-level jobs and moderate to severe poverty, stripped of the protective values and institutions that have sustained earlier generations in their rural origins, increasingly buffeted by family disruption and demoralized by a world-view that emphasized the bleak and predatory character of social life. (Currie, 1993)

We propose that the effect of migration on increasing myopic, deviant behavior (e.g., drug use) resulted from the prevailing conditions of the new, urban culture relative to that of the more rural culture from which these individuals migrated; that is, those individuals raised in the rural South grew up in a more agrarian, time-based culture (in which behavior is generally intended to influence future outcomes), rather than an urban, event-based culture (in which behavior typically represents an opportunistic response to circumstances that present themselves). Thus, first-generation residents who were raised in a rural, time-based culture were more protected from the effects of the urban, event-based culture promoting immediate gratification, unlike second-generation residents, who grew up in the urban culture. In addition, those individuals raised in the rural culture typically had greater social and economic support, unlike those who generally had weak ties to their extended families after migrating to the inner city. Indeed, rapid migration has been shown to weaken bonds between individuals and their community, resulting in a loss of community control over behavior and increases in a variety of social pathologies (South, 1987).

EVIDENCE FOR INCREASING TRENDS IN SHORT TEMPORAL HORIZONS POST-INDUSTRIALIZATION AND MODERNIZATION

Self-regulation failure is the major social pathology of the present time.
—Baumeister et al. (*Losing Control*, 1994, p. 3)

Thus far, we have suggested that short temporal horizon is a descriptor of various short-sighted behaviors, including drug use and criminal behavior. In addition, we have suggested that various factors that promote short temporal horizon have increased in modern society, including (a) the commercialization of leisure or promotion of immediate gratification, (b) being raised in an environment characterized by instability, and (c) isolation from family, neighborhood, and religion. If these assumptions are accurate, then we also should observe increases in societal problems or rates of short-sighted, deviant behavior in modern times. In this section, we provide evidence demonstrating that a variety of disorders (including drug and alcohol use and dependence, depression and other psychiatric disorders, overweight disorders–obesity, and crime) have increased in prevalence in modern society, producing significant problems both at individual and societal levels. We propose that the increase in these disorders stems from the same underlying phenomena, namely, from cultural changes accompanying modernity that promote short temporal horizons. Thus, individuals with short temporal horizons may engage in a variety of behaviors that produce immediate gratification and discount the future consequences of the behavior.

General Comment

In this section, we review trends over time for a variety of disorders that indicate that these disorders have increased in prevalence or incidence in recent times. We propose that the increased occurrence of these disorders is related to a common source: the short temporal horizons produced by the conditions of modern society. We recognize, however, that the cultural changes accompanying modern society represent a dynamic system of interacting factors, and that it is probable that numerous and diverse social and economic changes have interacted in complex ways to contribute to these trends (e.g., the rate of diagnoses of these disorders by clinicians also may have increased in modern times, thereby contributing to the observed increase in their prevalence). We further propose that the effects of societal conditions on promoting temporal perspective are not unidirectional; rather, short temporal horizons also may perpetuate the societal conditions that give rise to them, thereby promoting the maintenance of such conditions (a self-reinforcing process).

Furthermore, we are aware of the cautions that one must recognize when interpreting longitudinal data. For example, Gould (1996) cautioned against interpreting longitudinal data as indicative of a change over time (e.g., a change in modal score of a normal distribution over time) without first ensuring that the data do not simply represent increased variability over time (e.g., increases in the tail-ends or periphery of a normal distribution). For example, one may argue that the increased rates of drug use that we have observed in the recent past may reflect simply the increased availability of drugs in recent times. We propose that although availability is likely a contributing factor to increased drug use, the increased prevalence of a variety of disorders during modern times, including drug use, psychiatric disorders, obesity, and crime, suggests the ubiquitous nature of these trends and implicates a common mechanism of action across disorders.

Drug and Alcohol Use and Dependence

One such disorder that has increased over time is drug use and dependence. For example, Warner, Kessler, Hughes, Anthony, and Nelson (1995) assessed the prevalence of drug use and dependence by more than 8,000 individuals, composing four U.S. birth cohorts, using data from the National Comorbidity Study, a structured psychiatric diagnostic interview administered to a nationally representative, noninstitutionalized sample. Four 10-year cohorts were assessed for five different 5-year age intervals (ages 4, 9, 14, 19, and 24), including Cohort I (born 1966–1975), Cohort II (born 1956–1965), Cohort III (born 1946–1955), and Cohort IV (born 1936–1945). Results indicated that Cohort IV (born pre-World War II and modern society) had the lowest prevalence of drug use and lifetime dependence. In addition, each later cohort demonstrated an increase in drug use and dependence, with Cohort I (the cohort born most recently in modern society) having the greatest prevalence of lifetime drug dependence (see Fig. 13.1).

The pattern of drug use prevalence observed in the National Comorbidity Study data was similar to the pattern of incidence of drug use observed in data obtained from the National Household Surveys on Drug Abuse. In this study (Substance Abuse and Mental Health Services Administration, 1996), patterns of drug initiation were compared across ten 20th-century birth cohorts from the noninstitutionalized population at ages 15, 21, and 35. Cohort analyses indicated that World War II was a major turning point in the incidence of drug use. Specifically, individuals born after 1945 differed considerably in the range and diversity of their drug use relative to those born before that time, with birth cohorts born after 1945 having higher percentages of use of every drug, except cigarettes, compared to those born earlier in the 20th century.

The rapid rate of industrialization and modernization in 20th century America has been suggested to have a substantial impact on alcohol as well as drug use and dependence (Bales, 1946; Chafetz, Demone, & Solomon, 1962; Helzer & Canino, 1992). Indeed, total annual consumption of alcohol and alcohol consumption per capita increased from the early twentieth century onward in the United States (Helzer & Canino, 1992), as well as in a variety of other industrialized nations, including Switzerland and Germany (Wittchen & Bronisch, 1992); New Zealand (Well, Bushnell, Joyce, Hornblow, & Oakley-Browne, 1992); Taiwan (Yeh & Hwu, 1992); Korea (C. K. Lee, 1992); and Canada (Bland, Newman, & Orn, 1992). Sociocultural stress (e.g., divorce, single-parent families, unemployment, suicide), technological modernization and changing cultural attitudes toward drinking that accom-

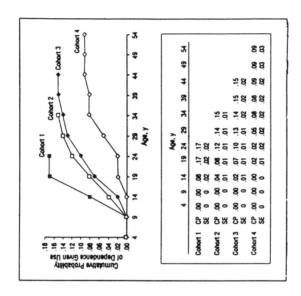

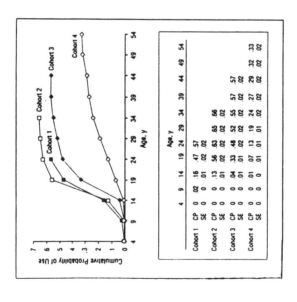

FIG. 13.1. Left panel: Cumulative probability (CP) of drug use, by cohort and age. Right panel: Cumulative probability of drug dependence, given use, by cohort and age. (Cohort I = born 1966–1975; Cohort II = born 1956–1965; Cohort III = born 1946–1955; Cohort IV = born 1936–1945). From "Prevalence and Correlates of Drug Use and Dependence in the United States: Results From the National Comorbidity Study," by L. A. Warner, R. C. Kessler, M. Hughes, J. C. Anthony, and C. B. Nelson, 1995, *Archives of General Psychiatry, 52*, p. 219. Data presented in the figure are in the public domain.

panied industrialization are assumed to have largely contributed to the increased alcohol consumption in these industrialized nations (Bales, 1946; Helzer & Canino, 1992). Indeed, we propose that the mechanism of this effect may be one in which these and other cultural changes associated with modern society may promote a short time horizon, which may be manifested in drug taking behavior, alcohol-taking behavior, or both. That is, as previously discussed, many elements of modern culture promote immediate gratification or seeking immediate rather than delayed rewards. Having a short temporal horizon may function as a premorbid condition for engaging in a variety of short-sighted behaviors, including alcohol or drug use and abuse. Alcohol and other drugs are low-cost, highly reinforcing commodities, which are generally immediately available and often overwhelm the value of alternative reinforcers whose effects are delayed. Thus, those individuals with short temporal perspectives may select the immediate gratification provided by alcohol or drugs without regard to the future negative consequences of engaging in such behavior. Indeed, experimental research with animal models has demonstrated that level of impulsivity predicts magnitude of alcohol self-administration, with higher impulsivity linked to elevated consumption (Poulos, Le, & Parker, 1995).

Depression and Other Psychiatric Disorders

In a manner similar to drugs and alcohol, the incidence and prevalence of major depression have been increasing, whereas age of first onset of depression has been decreasing for successive birth cohorts during this century, with effects most pronounced in cohorts born after 1940. In one study, Burke, Burke, Rae, and Regier (1991) used data from the Epidemiologic Catchment Area Program to conduct an analysis comparing hazard rates and age of onset of major depression and other psychiatric disorders among four birth cohorts (Cohort I was born 1953–1966; Cohort II was born 1937–1952; Cohort III was born 1917–1936; Cohort IV was born before 1917). Results indicated that Cohort I (most recently born) had the highest rates and earliest age of onset of unipolar and bipolar major depression, followed by Cohort II; however, Cohorts III and IV (born before modern society) had very low rates of major depression. In addition, similar patterns of results across cohorts were found on measures of mania and anxiety disorders (including obsessive–compulsive disorders and phobias), with the most recent cohorts exhibiting the highest hazard rates.

The results of this study were replicated by Lewinsohn, Rohde, Seeley, and Fisher (1993), even after controlling for four potential artifacts that may have contributed to the observed effect, namely, current mood state at the time of reporting past depressive episode(s), social desirability response bias, potential effects of subjects' self-labeling their depression on the probability of being diagnosed as depressed, and the time interval between the depressive episode(s) and the interview (see Fig. 13.2). Furthermore, the increased risk for major depression among more recent birth cohorts also has been observed cross-nationally. Specifically, in an international study of more than 39,000 individuals in seven birth cohorts from North America, Puerto Rico, western Europe, the Middle East, Asia, and the Pacific Rim, overall rates of major depression increased over time in all countries, although the magnitude of the increase varied by country (Cross-National Collaborative Group, 1992).

Finally, suicide rates and suicidal behaviors (including suicidal ideas or attempts) have increased significantly in the United States and many European countries in the past century. These increased trends have been observed in children (aged 10–14 years) and adolescents (aged 15–19 years),

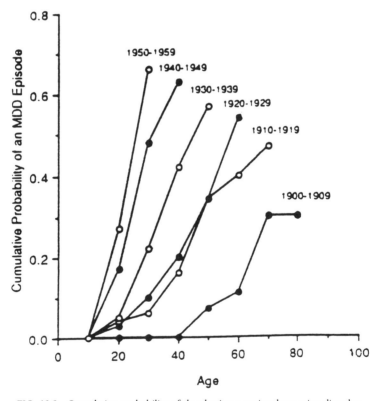

FIG. 13.2. Cumulative probability of developing a major depressive disorder (MDD) episode by birth cohort and age group. From "Age-Cohort Changes in the Lifetime Occurrence of Depression and Other Mental Disorders," by P. M. Lewinsohn, P. Rohde, J. R. Seeley, and S. A. Fischer, 1993, *Journal of Abnormal Psychology, 102*, p. 110. Copyright © 1993 by the American Psychological Association. Reprinted with permission.

as well as adults (e.g., Fombonne, 1995), although a particularly dramatic increase in suicide rates among youths has been observed (Holinger, 1981; Seiden & Freitas, 1980).

These findings have led some researchers to suggest that changing family structure and urbanization may be responsible, at least in part, for these observed trends in depression and other psychiatric disorders (e.g., Klerman & Weissman, 1989). Indeed, life events that tend to precede the onset of depression, including marital instability, unemployment, and other sociocultural stressors (e.g., Lewinsohn, 1974), have increased in prevalence in modern times and likely have contributed to the observed increased rates of depression, a type of short-sighted behavioral pattern. However, in addition, we suggest that such cultural factors also may interact with depressed or other psychiatric symptomatology in a manner that functions to perpetuate depression; that is, once in a depressed state, individuals may be less able to seek support and reinforcement from family, neighborhood, or other mediating structures that may promote an extended temporal horizon and a reduction in depressive symptoms (e.g., Ferster, 1973; Lewinsohn, 1974; Lewinsohn & Alexander, 1990). Indeed, depressed individuals repeatedly have been shown to be passive in nature and have low levels of learned resourcefulness, such that they tend to be reactive to their environment rather than actively manipulating their environment for their long-term good. In addition, depressed individuals often are shown to engage in significantly fewer activities that are positively reinforced and have fewer social skills relative to nondepressed individuals. As a result, depressed individuals often have a "limited, lousy and unchanging view of the world" (Ferster, 1973, p. 862), and are shown to have a considerably short temporal horizon (Neville, 1980).

Overweight/Obesity

Studies have indicated that the prevalence of overweight disorders and obesity also has increased among U.S. adults, children, and adolescents in recent times. Specifically, data collected from the National Health Examination Survey (NHESI; conducted from 1960–1962) and National Health and Nutrition Examination Surveys (NHANES I–III; conducted from 1971–1974, from 1976–1980, and from 1988–1994, respectively) indicate that the prevalence of overweight disorders in adults has increased from 24.3% during the NHESI to 33.3% during the NHANES III. In addition, as seen in Fig. 13.3, the prevalence of Class I, II, and III obesity (differentiated by a measure of obesity, body mass index, or BMI) also has markedly increased from NHES I to NHANES III. Although the prevalence of the more extreme classes of obesity (Classes II and III) is lower than that of the more common type of obesity (Class I), each successive birth cohort of individuals within each class of obesity is shown to have higher prevalence rates than the previous

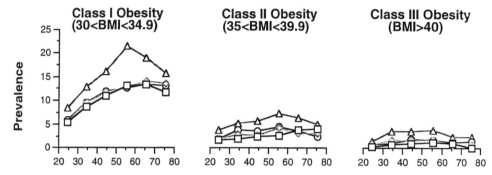

FIG. 13.3. Prevalence of obesity (Classes I–III based on Body Mass Index) by
birth cohort and age group. (Square symbol = data from 1960–1962; diamond
symbol = data from 1971–1974; circle symbol = data from 1976–1980; triangle
symbol = data from 1988–1994). The data used in generating this graph were
obtained from "Overweight and Obesity in the United States: Prevalence and
Trends, 1960–1994," by K. M. Flegal, M. D. Carroll, R. J. Kuczmarski, and C. L.
Johnson, 1998, *International Journal of Obesity, 22,* pp. 39–47.

cohort within each obesity class (Flegal, 1996; Flegal, Carroll, Kuczmarski,
& Johnson, 1998; Kuczmarski, Flegal, Campbell, & Johnson, 1994). Trends
in the prevalence of overweight disorders for children and adolescents, aged
6 to 17, are similar to those of adults (Troiano, Flegal, Kuczmarski, Campbell,
& Johnson, 1995), and no gender or ethnic group differences in the prevalence of overweight disorders or obesity have been found (Flegal et al.,
1998). Like overweight disorders and obesity, the prevalence of bulimic
eating disorders also has increased over time, and a strong cohort effect has
been detected, indicating that the highest lifetime prevalence of bulimia has
been observed among young women in recent years (Bushnell, Wells, Hornblow, Oakley-Browne, & Joyce, 1990).

The increased prevalence of these disorders may be due to a variety of
cultural factors that accompany modern society, including increased access to
low-cost food reinforcers, increased access to high-caloric fatty foods, decreased surveillance of children by parents due in part to changes in parental
work habits, and an increased sedentary lifestyle among Americans (e.g.,
Kuczmarski et al., 1994; Pi-Sunyer, 1994; Troiano et al., 1995). In addition,
television viewing may play an important role in obesity. For example, the
number of hours spent watching television functions as a strong predictor of
obesity, such that prevalence of obesity increases approximately 2% for each
hourly increment in television viewing (Dietz & Gortmaker, 1985). In addition,
children who watched 4 or more hours of television per day had greater body
fat and higher BMIs, whereas children who watched less than 1 hour of
television per day had the lowest BMIs (Andersen, Crespo, Bartlett, Cheskin,
& Pratt, 1998). In addition, excessive television watching has been shown to
be highly correlated with amount of caloric intake (T. N. Robinson & Killen,

1995; Taras, Sallis, Patterson, Nader, & Nelson, 1989). Finally, an obesity treatment study found that reinforcing reductions in sedentary behavior, including television watching, in obese children and their parents, led to greater weight loss than directly reinforcing increased exercise (Epstein et al., 1995). These factors and others that are endemic in modern society may function to promote a shortened temporal horizon and short-sighted behaviors that promote overweight disorders and obesity.

Crime

In general, U.S. crime rates per capita were relatively stable during the late 19th century and early 20th century but have steadily increased during the mid-20th century (J. Q. Wilson & Herrnstein, 1985), although they generally have stabilized or even slightly decreased in the very recent past. Indeed, arrest rates per 100,000 inhabitants increased from 897.1 in 1971 to 1,140.3 in 1995 (Department of Justice, 1996). Moreover, a cohort analysis of trends in violent crime indicated that youth cohorts in the early 1960s displayed substantially higher rates of homicide than previous youth cohorts and tended to maintain these higher rates throughout their lifetime. The most notable cohort increase was shown to occur in cohorts born between 1943 and 1951 (M. D. Smith, 1986). Finally, rates of victimization of many types of violent crimes have increased among young persons (aged 10–25 years) in recent years, and violent juvenile crime arrest rates have progressively increased during the past decade, with dramatically increased violence (including gun use) observed among 10- to 20-year-old youth (e.g., Davis, Rhames, & Kaups, 1997; Rachuba, Stanton, & Howard, 1995).

Such increases in crime rates have been observed in most countries since World War II, despite differences in crime-recording systems across countries and over time. Indeed, crime rates are said to have multiplied by a factor of around five, on average, in most countries (Smith, 1995). As seen in Fig. 13.4, total recorded criminal offenses have increased in numerous countries, except Japan, since the early 1950s.

A decline in respect for conventions, a reduction of social controls (e.g., religious deterioration), the growth of urban centers that often are characterized by social disintegration, unstable and impersonal relationships, a reduced appreciation for the rights and property of others, unemployment, and ineffective childrearing are all factors that accompany modernity (Gottfredson & Hirschi, 1990; Livingston, 1996; Zehr, 1976) and that may interact to promote a short temporal horizon and reduction in self-control. This self-control failure, in turn, may be manifested in the increased criminal behavior that has been observed in modern society (Gottfredson & Hirschi, 1990; Livingston, 1996; J. Q. Wilson & Herrnstein, 1985). Indeed, a cross-cultural analysis of five nations revealed that those nations with the lowest

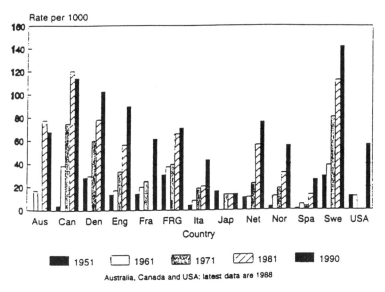

FIG. 13.4. Total recorded criminal offenses, 1951–1990. From "Youth Crime and Conduct Disorders: Trends, Patterns, and Causal Explanations," by D. J. Smith, 1995, in M. Rutter and D. J. Smith (Eds.), *Psychological Disorders in Young People: Time Trends and Their Causes.* Sussex, England: Wiley. Copyright © 1995 by Wiley. Reprinted with permission.

rates of inequality or social stratification also have the lowest rates of violent crimes as opposed to industrialized nations, in which inequality rates were high (Archer & Gartner, 1984). In further support of this argument, Davids, Kidder, and Reich (1962) found that delinquent youth were considerably more present-oriented and less future-oriented than were nondelinquents. Importantly, when conducting the same analysis 15 years later, these researchers found that delinquents were significantly more present-oriented and significantly less willing to delay gratification than were the group of delinquents assessed 15 years before (Davids & Falkof, 1975). In general,

> There is good reason to believe that rising crime rates are accompanied by, and perhaps partially caused by, a shortening of the time horizons of at-risk young persons as well as by an increase in the numbers of such persons. (J. Q. Wilson & Herrnstein, 1985, p. 422).

Indeed, engaging in criminal behavior often provides low-cost, immediate reinforcement, as the rewards from criminal behavior are immediate, whereas any adverse consequences of criminal behavior (e.g., arrests, incarceration) are, at best, considerably delayed, if not nonexistent in many cases.

CLUSTERING OF VARIOUS SHORT-SIGHTED BEHAVIORS

*A large spectrum of deviant behaviors, including early initiation of sexual
activity, early pregnancy, substance use and abuse, and criminal and violent
behavior, are closely intercorrelated . . . and for many communities form a
characteristic nexus . . . they are common responses to shared influences,
particularly social disintegration and disruption of personal, domestic, and
community social networks.*
    —R. Wallace et al. (*Substance Abuse: A Comprehensive Textbook,* 1992, p. 71).

The majority of efforts to address problems of alcohol and drug abuse,
criminal behavior, obesity, depression, and other psychiatric disorders have
tended to focus on treating each of these disorders independently, as if each
represents a unique and distinct problem. Instead, we propose that the
increase in these disorders are all the result of conditions in modern society
that promote short temporal horizons. Indeed, a substantial amount of evidence suggests that these specific types of disordered or short-sighted behaviors do not occur in isolation but rather tend to co-occur. That is, socially
deviant behaviors tend to cluster together to "form a characteristic nexus,"
such that individuals who engage in one deviant behavior tend to follow a
behavioral repertoire or behavioral pattern of engaging in several types of
myopic behavior. As a result, one specific type of deviant behavior may
simply be viewed as part of a constellation of behavioral problems. This
phenomenon has been observed in adolescents, young adults, middle-aged
individuals, as well as older adults (e.g., Achenbach & Edelbrock, 1981;
Achenbach, Howell, Quay, & Conners, 1991; Hill et al., 1997; Neumark-
Sztainer, Story, Dixon, & Murray, 1998).

    One example of this phenomenon is the high correlation that often is
observed between criminal behavior and drug use. In addition, adolescent
delinquent behavior often co-occurs with vandalism, teenage pregnancy,
and alcohol and drug use, whereas most adult criminal behavior co-occurs
with job instability, failed marriages, family violence, alcohol and drug use,
and high mortality rates (e.g., Donovan & Jessor, 1985; Gottfredson & Hirschi,
1990; Livingston, 1996; Lytle & Roski, 1997; Rydelius, 1983). Moreover, adolescent smokers have been shown to have significantly higher rates of watching television, other concurrent drug use, and conduct and academic problems, and also to engage in significantly lower rates of excercise than their
nonsmoking peers (Coogan et al., 1998). Furthermore, various types of drug
use and abuse frequently have been shown to co-occur with depression
and other psychiatric disorders, including personality and conduct disorders
(e.g., Barber et al., 1996; Brown, Lewinsohn, Seeley, & Wagner, 1996; Dulit,
Fyer, Haas, Sullivan, & Frances, 1990; Grant, 1995; Klerman et al., 1996). In
addition, alcohol dependence and impulsive eating, such as binge eating,
have been shown frequently to co-occur, with one study reporting that

approximately 40% of alcoholic women have histories of binge eating (Lacey & Moureli, 1986). Furthermore, individuals with bulimia who engage in high rates of impulsive, self-injurious behavior often also have high rates of depression and a longer duration of illness relative to those who do not engage in such impulsive behavior (Favaro & Santonastaso, 1998). Moreover, many drug abusers engage in a variety of high-risk sexual behaviors, leading to the greater prevalence of sexually transmitted diseases, including HIV, observed in many drug-using populations (e.g., Donoghoe, 1992; Edlin et al., 1994). In addition, problem gambling and substance abuse have been shown to be linked and to have a common association with impulsivity (Vitaro, Ferland, Jacques, & Ladouceur, 1998). Finally, even within a behavioral class, such as drug use or criminal behavior, many individuals use multiple types of drugs and engage in a variety of criminal acts, respectively (e.g., Gottfredson & Hirschi, 1990; Kandel & Yamaguchi, 1993).

Varied research efforts have attempted to identify causal relations among these correlated deviant behaviors; however, little evidence exists to suggest that one such type of deviant behavior causes another (e.g., Akers, 1984). Rather, we propose that the correlation between these various types of "deviant" behavior further supports our argument that these varied behaviors that cluster together may all represent manifestations of a common mechanism of action, namely, a self-control failure. Thus, the short temporal horizons of individuals who engage in deviant behavior may be manifested in a variety of short-sighted behaviors, in which the long-term consequences of the behaviors are discounted in light of the immediate gratification provided by the behaviors. Each specific behavior is not simply an automatic consequence of short temporal horizon; rather, the types of short-sighted behavior in which an individual engages are influenced by the combination of factors (e.g., learning history, family values, availability of drugs) present in one's environment that interact to select for the behavioral pattern.

THE RELATION BETWEEN DEVIANT BEHAVIOR AND SHORT TEMPORAL HORIZONS

Time is both a medium and a perspective. It is a medium through which we live as the future becomes present. As the future becomes present, we become aware of duration and succession. Also, by transcending the present and looking at it from the past or future, we gain perspective on the present. These time processes are fundamental to our construction of reality. If they are disturbed, our view of reality may become distorted.
—F. T. Melges (*Time and the Inner Future*, 1982, p. xxii)

We have proposed that a short temporal perspective gives rise to a variety of disorders. An obvious question at this point is whether individuals who demonstrate a self-control failure and engage in deviant behavior have shorter temporal perspectives. In addressing this question, we provide a brief review of the scientific literature investigating the temporal horizon of populations that are drug- or alcohol-dependent, schizophrenic or psychiatric, or delinquent.

Drug- and Alcohol-Dependent Populations

Substance abusers have been shown to engage consistently in high-risk impulsive behavior without regard to the future or to delayed negative consequences of such behavior, and to discount the subjective value of delayed rewards, more than nondrug users (e.g., Allen, Moeller, Rhoades, & Cherek, 1998). For example, alcohol-dependent individuals have been shown to have a significantly shorter sense of awareness of the future or future time perspective (FTP) relative to matched control individuals, and have been shown to be less coherent in their organization of future events than social drinkers (e.g., Murphy & DeWolfe, 1986). In addition, heavy and problem drinkers have been shown to discount delayed rewards more than light drinkers (Vuchinich & Simpson, 1998), and college students who later became alcohol-dependent have been shown to be more impulsive than their peers (Loper, Kammeier, & Hoffman, 1973).

Opioid-dependent individuals have been shown to have shorter FTPs (Manganiello, 1978; Petry, Bickel, & Arnett, 1998) and engage in more impulsive behavior than matched controls (e.g., Kirby, Petry, & Bickel in press; Madden, Petry, Badger, & Bickel, 1997; Vukov, Baba-Milkic, Lecic, Mijalkovic, & Marinkovic, 1995). In addition, cocaine users have been shown to be significantly more impulsive than alcohol or opioid users (Rosenthal, Edwards, Ackerman, Knott, & Rosenthal, 1990). Finally, preliminary evidence indicates that smokers may discount delayed rewards to a greater extent than nonsmokers (Bickel, Odum, & Madden, in press).

Schizophrenic and Other Psychiatric Populations

Distortions of FTP have been shown to be associated with a variety of psychiatric disorders. For example, schizophrenic individuals have a significantly shorter FTP and are less able to organize future events relative to nonschizophrenic individuals (Murphy & DeWolfe, 1986; Neville, 1980; Neville, Kreisberg, & Kielhofner, 1985; Wallace, 1956). In addition, depressed and suicidal persons have been demonstrated to have an even shorter FTP than schizophrenic individuals (Neville, 1980). Moreover, distortions of temporal perspective (which are unrelated to organic brain disease) have been found to occur significantly more frequently during the active and acute phases of mental illness, and to occur less frequently when individuals' psychiatric illnesses improve (Melges & Fougerousse, 1966; Melges & Freeman, 1977). Indeed, problems with psychological time have been proposed to be not only a manifestation of psychiatric illness but also a contributing mechanism to psychological disorganization (Meerloo, 1966; Melges, 1982).

Delinquent Populations

Several studies have underscored the relation between future time horizon and delinquent behavior, leading some to suggest that an extended FTP may enable one to consider the consequences of his or her action, thereby inhibiting delinquent behavior (e.g., Trommsdorff, 1994). Indeed, as previously discussed, delinquent youth have been shown to have shorter FTPs than nondelinquents (e.g., Davids et al., 1962; Davids & Falkof, 1975; Landau & Center for Studies in Criminology and Criminal Law, 1975). In addition, adolescents with firm identities are more future-oriented than maladjusted adolescents (Cottle & Klineberg, 1974).

Thus, substantial evidence demonstrates a relation between substance abuse, psychiatric disorders, delinquent behavior, and a short future time horizon. The observed relation between short temporal perspective and behavior also may be evidenced in numerous and varied problematic behaviors, including, for example, gambling, excessive spending (as opposed to saving money), and failure to exercise (e.g., Logue, 1995; Steel & Blaszczynski, 1998). In addition, an expanded temporal perspective is systematically related to nondeviant behavior. For example, a significant relation has been reported between achievement-related behavior and extended future time horizon (e.g., Murrell & Mingrone, 1994). Moreover, an extended FTP is associated with more positive health practices, such as safer sexual behavior (Rothspan & Read, 1996; Yarcheski, Mahon, & Yarcheski, 1997).

PROPOSED SOLUTIONS/POLICY IMPLICATIONS

The adoption and maintenance of a cultural practice is a function of its costs and benefits.
                                                              —A. Biglan (1995, p. 108)

The question that confronts us as we approach the end of this chapter is how to produce cultural practices that effectively promote self-control. Indeed, fostering the development and maintenance of self-controlled behavior is a more challenging option, and often a more costly one, than accepting the impulsive behavior that is prevalent in modern society. However, as evidenced by the increasingly high rates of numerous social problems, including drug use, criminal behavior, psychiatric disorders, and a variety of indulgent behaviors that are endemic to modern society, the current cost to society of such pervasive, impulsive (and often deviant) behavior is exceedingly high. Of course, establishing self-controlled behavior would be considerably easier in a world without television and other immediately available distractions, without the immediate gratification evident in the leisure society, and without the chronic economic instability observed in inner-city environments. However, suggestions that we discard all modern-day convenience and return to some idyllic, earlier, and nontechnological time are, of course, not possible. Instead, we need to harness contemporary technology and circumstances in reaching this end.

Solutions, however, are not likely to be unitary or simple, for if they were, they would have been adopted and demonstrated by now. Most likely, efforts will have to be multicomponent and multidimensional. Indeed, efforts must address patterns of short-sighted behavior rather than specific types of impulsive behavior in isolation, because, as has been detailed in this chapter, various short-sighted behaviors are often correlated and may stem from common mechanisms of action. Considerable effort and expense likely will be involved in this process. Among the issues to consider is how specific cultural changes can be imposed that will be self-sustaining and that will interact with other cultural changes, so that self-reinforcing patterns may develop. Indeed, a new cultural niche must be developed and nurtured that promotes an extended temporal horizon and self-controlled behavior. The benefit of implementing such change at a cultural, and, indeed, a policy level, is that, in so doing, multiple risk factors can be targeted across various social contexts and developmental periods and can be maintained more effectively over time. A complete, carefully designed, and thoughtfully developed plan for such a cultural system is beyond the scope of this chapter; however, we outline four suggestions for change that are consistent with the behavioral principles and issues that we have discussed previously in this chapter. We initially propose solutions that may aid in reducing impulsive behaviors in both the general population of the modern leisure society, as well as specific groups that engage in disproportionately high levels of impulsive and often deviant behavior. We then discuss more detailed suggestions for preventing impulsive behavior in these more isolated groups of individuals.

First, in addressing these issues, we must provide incentives to individuals, both children and adults, to receive self-control training, with the goal of establishing new, self-controlled patterns of behavior (cf. Logue, 1995). Without efforts to provide incentives that functionally decrease the cost of attending such training, participation in the training would likely be low. For example, making welfare access contingent on participating in parent-training programs may be a viable option. In addition, developing self-control clubs or ensuring that self-control training is subsumed under some other reinforcing activity (e.g., scouting, martial arts) may represent other possible approaches.

Second, individuals need to be provided with long-term coaching regarding the making of decisions (cf. Nisbett, Fong, Lehman, & Cheng, 1987). In this process, efforts must be made to educate individuals about the consequences of the tyranny of small decisions and to highlight the benefits of accessing large-magnitude delayed rewards relative to accessing many immediate reinforcers. Indeed, such decision-making assistance should consider the short- and long-term consequences of such decisions, with the goal of increasing the cost of maintaining the status quo of impulsive decision making. Finally, once individuals make decisions and experience the consequences of their decisions, the relation between the individuals' choices and their outcomes should be reviewed with the individuals. Such decision-making training may be provided, for example, by community organizations, in educational systems, or via media efforts, such as computer games that require working for long-term goals in order to win.

Experimental research has demonstrated that these two proposals of self-control training and decision-making skills training may be beneficial, as individuals who have a history of experience with delayed rewards tend to have longer temporal horizons, whereas those with a behavioral history of experience with mostly immediate rewards tend to have short temporal horizons or exhibit myopic behavior (e.g., Eisenberger & Adornetto, 1986). In addition, individuals who have a history of rewarded effort have been shown to have high rates of responding that may be channeled into goal-oriented behavior (*learned industriousness*), whereas those who have little experience with receiving rewards for expended effort tend to engage in low rates of responding (*learned laziness*; e.g., Eisenberger, 1992; Eisenberger, Kuhlman, & Cotterell, 1992; Engberg, Hansen, Welker, & Thomas, 1972).

Third, we must provide consistent surveillance with predictable contingencies for engaging in self-controlled choices. Surveillance for long periods of time may be necessary to ensure that individuals are engaging in self-controlled behavior. If such surveillance reveals that self-controlled choices are not being made, then it may be necessary to implement additional contingencies to increase benefits of self-controlled choices. Such surveillance may be provided, for example, by parents, families, neighborhoods, communities, religious organizations, or criminal justice systems.

Finally, in inner-city environments characterized by economic instability, we must provide assistance in resolving environmental instability as well as deprivation from, and unpredictable access to, key reinforcers. Making self-controlled decisions are difficult when one is hungry, or does not have a home, or when the future outcomes of behavior are uncertain or unpredictable. Such assistance may best be provided as one of the incentives of participating in self-control and decision-making skills training.

To implement these last two suggestions, we may, for example, initiate and protect the development and maintenance of mediating structures or countervailing influences to short-sighted behavior, including family, neighborhood, community, and religion, for those individuals who do not have reliable access to such institutions. This may include providing extended support systems beyond the nuclear family, supporting mentoring programs and parental training programs, and fostering climates that support religion and moral training. Such interventions should be initiated with the intention of reducing risk factors predictive of short-sighted behavior and increasing protective factors against such behavior, by both increasing access to behavioral surveillance with contingencies and reducing environmental instability.

This brief list of activities is closely related to the principles we cited previously, and, in the abstract, they may seem difficult to employ. However, to illustrate how these principles could be utilized in real-world settings, we review a program, summarized by Currie (1998), that was developed for impoverished inner-city women who were experiencing their first pregnancy. The majority of individuals in that program were single, and more than one half were supported by welfare. Over a 30-month period, a caseworker affiliated with the program (e.g., a psychologist, nurse, or social worker) completed an average of 28 home visits per participant. The focus of the home visits was multifaceted and included helping the families in securing food and housing and helping the mother in making decisions about school and work. In addition, many of the children of these women also participated in a day-care program managed by individuals in the same program. The curriculum focused on the women's and children's social and emotional development, including how to effectively deal with aggressive behavior. Ten years after initiation of this program, children who participated in the program were shown to be much better adjusted to school than were children in the control group who did not attend the program. The children from the program also showed less predelinquent behavior, such as aggression and acting out. Moreover, the majority of the mothers of the children who participated in the program were self-supporting 10 years later, whereas the circumstances of the majority of mothers in the control group had worsened during this time, and many remained on public assistance. Significantly, even though they had not directly participated in the program themselves, the siblings of the children from the program also demonstrated important gains in areas such as school attendance and performance, emotional status, and overall competence relative to siblings of children in the control group.

In general, this program helped to secure stable resources for program participants effectively, such that once they were secured, the participants were able to focus less on their immediate needs and consider the future outcomes of their behavior. In addition, they were provided with life-skills training and were assisted in problem solving and decision making regarding a variety of life issues. Moreover, the children were provided with skills training in their day care that promoted prosocial behavior. Finally, the home visits by program staff also essentially provided surveillance to ensure that participants were compliant with the program and were engaging in program activities. Such visits also likely provided continued encouragement to participants to comply with the program. As is evidenced from its outcomes, the program was sufficient to change the culture of small decisions in these particular circumstances.

This model is one that may be useful in many inner-city environments, namely, to secure reliable and predictable resources; to provide skills training in which individuals learn the value of engaging in effortful behavior to obtain delayed rewards; to aid in problem solving; and to provide continued contact and surveillance of behavior to ensure that some degree of effective contingencies are maintained (e.g., ranging from approval or disapproval of behavior to more tangible behavioral consequences). Of course, such a proposal will not be easy. In particular, effectively securing reliable resources in the inner city will be challenging and difficult. However, doing so is a necessary component of any effective program designed to promote self-control, as self-controlled behavior cannot be maintained in an environment that fails to support it.

In conclusion, changing our current society and culture to promote self-controlled behavior undoubtedly will be difficult and require a great deal of effort and thoughtfulness. To be more effective in this process, additional systematic research should be conducted in order to understand better the dynamic relations between various impulsive behaviors, as well as effective interventions, at policy, community, and individual levels, designed to prevent impulsive behavior. Indeed, making such cultural changes requires that we must continue to seek to more fully understand the principles that regulate the promotion and maintenance of the tyranny of small decisions in order to prevent it effectively. As Alfred North Whitehead (1929, p. 58) so accurately stated, "The active utilization of well-understood principles is the final possession of wisdom."

ACKNOWLEDGMENTS

Warren K. Bickel and Lisa A. Marsch, Departments of Psychiatry and Psychology.

The authors thank Greg Madden, Rebecca Esch, Tim Shahan, Amy Odum, and Rudy Vuchinich for their useful comments on an earlier version of this chapter.

Correspondence concerning this chapter may be addressed to Warren K. Bickel, Ph.D., University of Vermont, Ira Allen School, 38 Fletcher Place, Burlington, VT 05401-1419. Electronic mail may be sent to warren.bickel@uvm.edu.

REFERENCES

Achenbach, T. M., & Edelbrock, C. S. (1981). Behavioral problems and competencies reported by parents of normal and disturbed children aged four through sixteen. *Monographs of the Society for Research in Child Development, 46*(1), 1–79.

Achenbach, T. M., Howell, C. T., Quay, H. C., & Conners, C. K. (1991). National survey of problems and competencies among four-to-sixteen-year-olds: Parents' reports for normative and clinical samples. *Monographs of the Society for Research in Child Development, 56*(3), 1–106.

Ainslie, G. (1992). *Picoeconomics: The strategic interaction of successive motivational states within the person.* Cambridge, England: Cambridge University Press.

Akers, R. L. (1984). Delinquent behavior, drugs and alcohol: What is the relationship? *Today's Delinquent, 3,* 19–47.

Allen, T. J., Moeller, G., Rhoades, H. M., & Cherek, D. R. (1998). Impulsivity and history of drug dependence. *Drug and Alcohol Dependence, 50,* 137–145.

Andersen, R. F., Crespo, C. J., Bartlett, S. J., Cheskin, L. J., & Pratt, M. (1998). Relationship of physical activity and television watching with body weight and level of fatness among children. *Journal of the American Medical Association, 279,* 938–942.

Archer, D., & Gartner, R. (1984). *Violence and crime in cross-national perspective.* New Haven, CT: Yale University Press.

Bales, R. (1946). Cultural differences in rates of alcoholism. *Quarterly Journal of Studies on Alcohol, 6,* 480–499.

Barber, J. P., Frank, A., Weiss, R. D., Blaine, J., Siqueland, L., Moras, K., Calvo, N., Chittams, J., Mercer, D., & Salloum, I. M. (1996). Prevalence and correlates of personality disorder diagnoses among cocaine dependent outpatients. *Journal of Personality Disorders, 10,* 297–311.

Baumeister, R. F., Heatherton, T. F., & Tice, D. M. (1994). *Losing control: How and why people fail at self-regulation.* New York: Academic Press.

Benda, B. B. & Corwyn, R. F. (1997). Religion and delinquency: The relationship after considering family and peer influences. *Journal for the Scientific Study of Religion, 36,* 81–92.

Bertman, S. (1998). *Hyperculture: The human cost of speed.* New York: Praeger.

Bickel, W. K., & DeGrandpre, R. J. (1996). Psychological science speaks to drug policy: The clinical relevance and policy implications of basic behavioral principles. In W. K. Bickel & R. J. DeGrandpre (Eds.), *Drug policy and human nature* (pp. 31–52). New York: Plenum.

Bickel, W. K., DeGrandpre, R. J., & Higgins, S. T. (1993). Behavioral economics: A novel approach to the study of drug dependence. *Drug and Alcohol Dependence, 33,* 173–192.

Bickel, W. K., Odum, A. L., & Madden, G. J. (in press). Impulsivity and cigarette smoking: Delay discounting in current, never, and ex-smokers. *Psychopharmacology.*

Biglan, A. (1995). Changing cultural practices: A contextualist framework for intervention research. Reno, NV: Context.

Bland, R. C., Newman, S. C., & Orn, H. (1992). Alcohol abuse and dependence in Edmonton, Canada. In J. E. Helzer & G. J. Canino (Eds.), *Alcoholism in North America, Europe, and Asia* (pp. 97–112). New York: Oxford University Press.

Böhm-Bawerk, E. V. (1970). *Capital and interest.* South Holland, IL: Libertarian Press. (Original work published 1889)

Bronowski, J. (1974). *The ascent of man.* Boston: Little, Brown.

Brown, R. A., Lewinsohn, P. M., Seeley, J. R., & Wagner, E. F. (1996). Cigarette smoking, major depression, and other psychiatric disorders among adolescents. *Journal of the American Academy of Child and Adolescent Psychiatry, 35,* 1602–1610.

Burke, K. C., Burke, J. D., Rae, D. S., & Regier, D. A. (1991). Comparing age at onset of major depression and other psychiatric disorders by birth cohorts in five U.S. community populations. *Archives of General Psychiatry, 48,* 789–795.

Bushnell, J. A., Wells, J. E., Hornblow, A. R., Oakley-Browne, M. A., & Joyce, P. (1990). Prevalence of three bulimia syndromes in the general population. *Psychological Medicine, 20,* 671–680.

Butsch, R. (Ed.). (1990). *For fun and profit: The transformation of leisure into consumption.* Philadelphia: Temple University Press.

Carroll, M. E. (1993). The economic context of drug and nondrug reinforcers affects acquisition and maintenance of drug-reinforced behavior and withdrawal effects. *Drug and Alcohol Dependence, 33,* 201–210.

Cashdan, E. (1989). Hunters and gatherers: Economic behavior in bands. In S. Plattner (Ed.), *Economic anthropology* (pp. 21–48). Stanford, CA: Stanford University Press.

Centerwall, B. S. (1989). Exposure to television as a risk factor for violence. *American Journal of Epidemiology, 129,* 643–652.

Chafetz, M. E., Demone, H. W., & Solomon, H. C. (1962). *Alcoholism and society.* New York: Oxford University Press.

Chein, I. (1966). Narcotics use among juveniles. In J. A. O'Donnell & J. C. Ball (Eds.), *Narcotic Addiction,* New York: Harper & Row, pp. 123–141.

Chein, I., Gerard, D. L., Lee, R. S., & Rosenfeld, E. (1964). *The road to H: Narcotics, delinquency, and social policy.* New York: Basic Books.

Chilcoat, H. D., & Johanson, C. E. (1998). Vulnerability to cocaine abuse. In S. T. Higgins & J. L. Katz (Eds.), *Cocaine abuse behavior, pharmacology, and clinical applications.* New York: Academic Press.

Chisholm, J. S. (1996). Evolutionary ecology and attachment organization. *Human Nature, 7,* 1–38.

Christensen, J., Parker, S., Silberberg, A., & Hursh, S. (1988). Trade-offs in choice between risk and delay depend on monetary amounts. *Journal of the Experimental Analysis of Behavior, 69,* 123–139.

Chung, S. H. (1965). Effects of delayed reinforcement in a concurrent situation. *Journal of the Experimental Analysis of Behavior, 8,* 439–444.

Cohen, M. (1977). *The food crisis in prehistory.* New Haven, CT: Yale University Press.

Coman, M., & Weir, H. (1925, August). Home can make or break you: An interview with Mrs. Thomas A. Edison. *Colliers Weekly, 76,* 17.

Coogan, P. F., Adams, M., Geller, A. C., Brooks, D., Miller, D. R., Lew, R. A., & Koh, H. K. (1998). Factors associated with smoking among children and adolescents in Connecticut. *American Journal of Preventive Medicine, 15,* 17–24.

Cook, C. C. H., Goddard, D., & Westall, R. (1997). Knowledge and experience of drug use amongst church affiliated young people. *Drug and Alcohol Dependence, 46,* 9–17.

Cottle, T. J., & Klineberg, S. L. (1974). *The present of things future: Explorations of time in human experience.* New York: Macmillan.

Cross-National Collaborative Group. (1992). The changing rate of major depression. *Journal of the American Medical Association, 268,* 3098–3105.

Crum, R. M., Lillie-Blanton, M., & Anthony, J. (1996). Neighborhood environment and opportunity to use cocaine and other drugs in late childhood and early adolescence. *Drug and Alcohol Dependence, 43,* 155–161.

Currie, E. (1993). *Reckoning: Drugs, cities, and the American future.* New York: Hill & Wang.

Currie, E. (1998). *Crime and punishment in America.* New York: Metropolitan.

Davids, A., & Falkof, B. B. (1975). Juvenile delinquents then and now: Comparison of findings from 1959 and 1974. *Journal of Abnormal Psychology, 84,* 161–164.

Davids, A., Kidder, C., & Reich, M. (1962). Time orientation in male and female juvenile delinquents. *Journal of Abnormal and Social Psychology, 64,* 239–240.

Davis, J. W., Rhames, M. P., & Kaups, K. L. (1997). More guns and younger assailants. *Archives of General Psychiatry, 132,* 1067–1070.

Diamond, J. (1997). *Guns, germs, and steel: The fates of human societies.* New York: Norton.

Dietz, W. H., & Gortmaker, S. L. (1985). Do we fatten our children at the television set? Obesity and television viewing in children and adolescents. *Pediatrics, 75,* 807–812.

Dietz, W. H. & Strasburger, V. C. (1991). Children, adolescents, and television. *Current Problems in Pediatrics, 1,* 8–31.

Donoghoe, M. J. (1992). Sex, HIV, and injecting drug users. *British Journal of Addiction, 87,* 405–416.

Donovan, J. E., & Jessor, R. (1985). Structure of problem behavior in adolescence and young adulthood. *Journal of Consulting and Clinical Psychology, 53,* 890–904.

Dulit, R. A., Fyer, M. R., Haas, G. L., Sullivan, T., & Frances, A. J. (1990). Substance use in borderline personality disorder. *American Journal of Psychiatry, 147,* 1002–1007.

Duncan, S. C., Duncan, T. E., Biglan, A., & Ary, D. (1998). Contributions of the social context to the development of adolescent substance use: A multivariate latent growth modeling approach. *Drug and Alcohol Dependence, 50,* 57–71.

Edlin, B. R., Irwin, K. L., Faruque, S., McCoy, C. B., Word, C., Serrano, Y., Inciardi, J. A., Bowser, B. P., Schilling, R. F., Holmberg, S. D., & The Multicenter Crack Cocaine and HIV Infection Study Team. (1994). Intersecting epidemics: Crack cocaine use and HIV infection among inner-city young adults. *New England Journal of Medicine, 331,* 1422–1427.

Eisenberger, R. (1992). Learned industriousness. *Psychological Review, 99,* 248–267.

Eisenberger, R., & Adornetto, M. (1986). Generalized self-control of delay and effort. *Journal of Personality and Social Psychology, 51,* 1020–1031.

Eisenberger, R., Kuhlman, M., & Cotterell, N. (1992). Effects of social values, effort training, and goal structure on task persistence. *Journal of Research in Personality, 26,* 258–272.

Eisenberger, R., Weier, F., Masterson, F. A., & Theis, L. Y. (1989). Fixed-ratio schedules increase generalized self-control: Preference for large rewards despite high effort or punishment. *Journal of Experimental Psychology: Animal Behavior Processes, 15,* 383–392.

Eliot, T. S. (1930). *Collected Poems, 1909–1935.* New York: Harcourt Brace.

Ellis, L., & Peterson, J. (1996). Crime and religion: An international comparison among thirteen industrial nations. *Personality and Individual Differences, 20,* 761–768.

Engberg, L. A., Hansen, G., Welker, R. L., & Thomas, D. R. (1972). Acquisition of key-pecking via autoshaping as a function of prior experience: "Learned Laziness." *Science, 178,* 1002–1004.

Epstein, L. H., Valoski, A. M., Vara, L. S., McCurley, J., Wisniewski, L., Kalarchian, M. A., Klein, K. R., & Shrager, L. R. (1995). Effects of decreasing sedentary behavior and increasing activity on weight change in obese children. *Health Psychology, 14,* 109–115.

Favaro, A., & Santonastaso, P. (1998). Impulsive and compulsive self-injurious behavior in bulimia nervosa: Prevalence and psychological correlates. *The Journal of Nervous and Mental Disease, 186,* 157–165.

Ferster, C. B. (1973). A functional analysis of depression. *American Psychologist, 28,* 857–870.

Ferster, C. B., & Skinner, B. F. (1957). *Schedules of reinforcement.* Englewood Cliffs, NJ: Prentice-Hall.

Flegal, K. M. (1996). Trends in body weight and overweight in the U.S. population. *Nutrition Reviews, 54,* 97–100.

Flegal, K. M., Carroll, M. D., Kuczmarski, R. J., & Johnson, C. L. (1998). Overweight and obesity in the United States: Prevalence and trends, 1960–1994. *International Journal of Obesity, 22,* 39–47.

Fombonne, E. (1995). Depressive disorders: Time trends and possible explanatory mechanisms. In M. Rutter & D. J. Smith (Eds.), *Psychological disorders in young people: Time trends and their causes.* New York: Wiley.

Gary, L. E., & Berry, G. L. (1984). Some determinants of attitudes toward substance use in an urban ethnic community. *Psychological Reports, 54,* 539–545.

Geronimus, A. T. (1987). On teenage childbearing and neonatal mortality in the United States. *Population and Development Review, 13,* 245–279.

Geronimus, A. T. (1996). What teen mothers know. *Human Nature, 7,* 323–352.

Givens, D. R. (1977). *An analysis of Navajo temporality.* Washington, DC: University Press of America.

Glueck, S., & Glueck, E. (1950). *Unraveling juvenile delinquency.* Cambridge, MA: Harvard University Press.

Gottfredson, M. R., & Hirschi, T. (1990). *A general theory of crime.* Stanford, CA: Stanford University Press.

Gould, S. J. (1987). *Time's arrow, time's cycle.* Cambridge, MA: Harvard University Press.

Gould, S. J. (1996). *Full house: The spread of excellence from Plato to Darwin.* New York: Three Rivers.

Grant, B. F. (1995). Comorbidity between DSM–IV drug use disorders and major depression: Results of a national survey of adults. *Journal of Substance Abuse, 7,* 481–497.

Green, L., Fry, A. F., & Myerson, J. (1994). Discounting of delayed rewards: A life-span comparison. *Psychological Science, 5,* 33–36.

Greene, M. B. (1996). Youth and violence: Trends, principles, and programmatic interventions. In R. J. Apfel & B. Simon (Eds.), *Minefields in their hearts: The mental health of children in war and communal violence* (pp. 128–148). New Haven, CT: Yale University Press.

Griffiths, R. R., Bigelow, G. E., & Henningfield, J. E. (1980). Similarities in animal and human drug-taking behavior. In N. K. Mello (Ed.), *Advances in substance abuse* (Vol. 1, pp. 1–90). Greenwich, CT: JAI.

Harlan, J. (1992). *Crops and man* (2nd ed.). Madison, WI: American Society of Agronomy.

Harrell, A. V., & Peterson, G. E. (1992). *Drugs, crime and social isolation: Barriers to urban opportunity.* Washington, DC: Urban Institute Press.

Hawkins, J. D., Catalano, R. F., Miller, J. Y. (1992). Risk and protective factors for alcohol and other drug problems in adolescence and early adulthood: Implications for substance abuse prevention. *Psychological Bulletin, 112,* 64–105.

Helzer, J. E., & Canino, G. J. (1992). *Alcoholism in North America, Europe, and Asia.* New York: Oxford University Press.

Herrnstein, R. J. (1970). On the law of effect. *Journal of the Experimental Analysis of Behavior, 13,* 243–266.

Herrnstein, R. J., Rachlin, H., & Laibson, D. I. (Eds.). (1997). *The matching law: Papers in psychology and economics.* New York: Harvard University Press.

Higgins, S. T., Budney, A. J., Bickel, W. K., Foerg, F. E., Donham, R., & Badger, G. J. (1994). Incentives improve treatment retention and cocaine abstinence in ambulatory cocaine-dependent patients. *Archives of General Psychiatry, 51,* 568–576.

Hill, E. M., Ross, L. T., & Low, B. S. (1997). The role of future unpredictability in human risk-taking. *Human Nature, 8,* 287–325.

Himmelfarb, G. (1995). *The de-moralization of society: From Victorian virtues to modern values.* London: IEA Health and Welfare Unit.

Hirsch, F. (1976). *Social limits to growth.* Cambridge, MA: Harvard University Press.

Holinger, P. C. (1981). Self-destructiveness among the young: An epidemiological study of violent deaths. *International Journal of Social Psychology, 27,* 277–282.

Horowitz, D. (1985). *The morality of spending: Attitudes toward the consumer society in America, 1875–1940.* Baltimore: Johns Hopkins University Press.

Howe, D. W. (Ed.). (1976). *Victorian America.* University of Pennsylvania Press.

James, R. R. (Ed.). (1974). *Winston S. Churchill: His complete speeches 1897–1963* (Vol VI). New York: Chelsea House.

Javier, R. A., Herron, W. G., & Yanos, P. T. (1995). Urban poverty, ethnicity, and personality development. *Journal of Social Distress and the Homeless, 4,* 219–235.

Johanson, C. E., Duffy, F., & Anthony, J. (1996). Associations between drug use and behavioral repertoire in urban youths. *Addiction, 91,* 523–534.

Johnson, P. (1976). *A history of Christianity.* New York: Atheneum.

Kahn, A. E. (1966). The tyranny of small decisions: Market failures, imperfections, and the limits of economics. *Kyklos, 19,* 23–47.

Kandel, D., & Yamaguchi, K. (1993). From beer to crack: Developmental patterns of drug involvement. *American Journal of Public Health, 83,* 851–855.

Keyes, R. (1991). *Timelock.* New York: HarperCollins.

King, G. R., & Logue, A. W. (1992). Choice in a self-control paradigm: Effects of uncertainty. *Behavioural Processes, 26,* 143–154.

Kirby, K. N. (1997). Bidding on the future: Evidence against normative discounting of delayed rewards. *Journal of Experimental Psychology: General, 126,* 54–70.

Kirby, K. N., & Marakovic, N. N. (1996). Delay-discounting probabilistic rewards: Rates decrease as amounts increase. *Psychonomic Bulletin and Review, 3,* 100–104.

Kirby, K. N., Petry, N. M., & Bickel, W. K. (in press). Heroin addicts discount delayed rewards at higher rates than non-drug using controls. *Journal of Experimental Psychology: General.*

Kleinman, P. H., & Lukoff, I. F. (1978). Ethnic differences in factors related to drug use. *Journal of Health and Social Behavior, 19,* 194–195.

Klerman, G. L., Leon, A. C., Wickramaratne, P., Warshaw, M. G., Mueller, T. I., Weissman, M. M., & Akiskal, H. (1996). The role of drug and alcohol abuse in recent increases in depression in the US. *Psychological Medicine, 26,* 343–351.

Klerman, G. L., & Weissman, M. M. (1989). Increasing rates of depression. *Journal of the American Medical Association, 261,* 2229–2235.

Kuczmarski, R. C., Flegal, K. M., Campbell, S. M., & Johnson, C. L. (1994). Increasing prevalence of overweight among U.S. adults. *Journal of the American Medical Association, 272,* 205–211.

Lacey, J. H., & Moureli, E. (1986). Bulimic alcoholics: Some features of a clinical sub-group. *British Journal of Addiction, 81,* 389–393.

Land, K. C., McCall, P. L., & Cohen, L. E. (1990). Structural covariates of homicide rates: Are there any invariances across time and social space? *American Journal of Sociology, 95,* 922–963.

Landau, S. F., & Center for Studies in Criminology and Criminal Law. (1975). Future time perspective of delinquents and non-delinquents: The effect of institutionalization. *Criminal Justice and Behavior, 2,* 22–36.

Lauer, R. H. (1970). *Social time and social change.* Unpublished doctoral dissertation, Washington University, Saint Louis, MO.

Lee, C. K. (1992). Alcoholism in Korea. In J. E. Helzer & G. J. Canino (Eds.), *Alcoholism in North America, Europe, and Asia* (pp. 247–263). New York: Oxford University Press.

Lee, R. B. (1968). What hunters do for a living, or how to make out on scarce resources. In R. B. Lee & I. DeVore (Eds.), *Man the hunter* (pp. 30–48). Chicago: Aldine-Atherton.

Lee, R. B. (1979). *The !Kung San: Men, women, and work in a foraging society.* Cambridge, England: Cambridge University Press.

Lee, R. B., & DeVore, I. (Eds.). (1968). *Man the hunter.* Chicago: Aldine-Atherton.

Lewinsohn, P. M. (1974). The behavioral study and treatment of depression. In M. Hersen, R. M. Eisler, & P. M. Miller (Eds.), *Progress in behavior modification* (Vol. 1, pp. 19–64). New York: Academic Press.

Lewinsohn, P. M., & Alexander, C. (1990). Learned resourcefulness and depression. In M. Rosenbaum (Ed.), *Learned resourcefulness: On coping skills, self-control, and adaptive behavior.* (Vol. 24, pp. 202–217). New York: Springer.

Lewinsohn, P. M., Rohde, P., Seeley, J. R., & Fisher, S. A. (1993). Age-cohort changes in the lifetime occurrence of depression and other mental disorders. *Journal of Abnormal Psychology, 102,* 110–120.

Lewis, O. (1966, October). The culture of poverty. *Scientific American, 215,* 19–25.

Liebert, R. M., & Baron, R. A. (1972). Short-term effects of televised aggression on children's aggressive behavior. In J. P. Murray, E. A. Rubinstein, & G. A. Comstock (Eds.), *Television and social behavior* (Vol II, pp. 181–201). Rockville, MD: National Institute of Mental Health.

Livingston, J. (1996). *Crime and Criminology* (2nd ed.). Englewood Cliffs, NJ: Prentice-Hall.

Loeber, R., & Dishion, T. J. (1984). Boys who fight at home and school: Family conditions influencing cross-setting consistency. *Journal of Consulting and Clinical Psychology, 52,* 759–768.

Logue, A. W. (1995). *Self-control: Waiting until tomorrow for what you want today.* Englewood Cliffs, NJ: Prentice-Hall.

Loper, R. G., Kammeier, M. L., & Hoffman, H. (1973). MMPI characteristics of college freshman who later became alcoholics. *Journal of Abnormal Psychology, 82,* 159–162.

Lowenstein, G., & Elster, J. (Eds.). (1992). *Choice over time.* New York: Russell Sage Foundation.

Lytle, L. A., & Roski, J. (1997). Unhealthy eating and other risk-taking behavior: Are they related? *Annals of the New York Academy of Science, 817,* 49–65.

Mac Corquodale, K., & Meehl, P. E. (1951). Operational validity of intervening constructs. In M. H. Marx (Ed.), *Psychological theory: Contemporary readings* (pp. 103–111). New York: MacMillan.

Madden, G. J., Petry, N. M., Badger, G. J., & Bickel, W. K. (1997). Impulsive and self-control choices in opioid-dependent patients and non-drug-using control participants: Drug and monetary rewards. *Experimental and Clinical Psychopharmacology, 5,* 256–262.

Maital, S., & Maital S. L. (1994). Is the future what it used to be? A behavioral theory of the decline of saving in the West. *Journal of Socio-Economics, 23,* 1–32.

Manganiello, J. A. (1978). Opiate addiction: A study identifying three systematically related psychological correlates. *International Journal of the Addictions, 13,* 839–847.

Mayr, E. (1988). *Toward a new philosophy of biology: Observations of an evolutionist.* Cambridge, MA: Harvard University Press.

Mazur, J. E. (1995). Conditioned reinforcement and choice with delayed and uncertain primary reinforcers. *Journal of Experimental Analysis of Behavior, 63,* 139–150.

Mazur, J. E. (1997). Choice, delay, probability and conditioned reinforcement. *Animal Learning and Behavior, 25,* 131–147.

McCord, J. (1979). Some child-rearing antecedents of criminal behavior in adult men. *Journal of Personality and Social Psychology, 37,* 1477–1486.

McLoyd, V. C. (1990). The impact of economic hardship on Black families and children: Psychological distress, parenting, and socioemotional development. *Child Development, 61,* 311–346.

McNeil, W. H. (1976). *Plagues and peoples.* Garden City, NY: Doubleday.

Meerloo, J. A. M. (1966). The time sense in psychiatry. In J. T. Fraser (Ed.), *The voices of time: A cooperative survey of man's views of time as expressed by the sciences and by the humanities* (pp. 235–252). New York: Braziller.

Melges, F. T., (1982). *Time and the inner future: A temporal approach to psychiatric disorders.* New York: Wiley.

Melges, F. T., & Fougerousse, C. E. (1966). Time sense, emotions, and acute mental illness. *Journal of Psychiatric Research, 4,* 127–140.

Melges, F. T., & Freeman, A. M. (1977). Temporal disorganization and inner–outer confusion in acute mental illness. *American Journal of Psychiatry, 134,* 874–877.

Murphy, T. J., & DeWolfe, A. S. (1986). Future time perspective in alcoholics, process and reactive schizophrenics, and normals. *International Journal of the Addictions, 20,* 1815–1822.

Murrell, A., & Mingrone, M. (1994). Correlates of temporal perspective. *Perceptual and Motor Skills, 78,* 1331–1334.

Navarick, D. J. (1987). Reinforcement probability and delay as determinants of human impulsiveness. *Psychological Record, 37,* 219–226.

Nelsen, H. M. (1988). Unchurched Black Americans: Patterns of religiosity and affiliation. *Review of Religious Research, 29,* 398–412.

Neumark-Sztainer, D., Story, M., Dixon, L. B., & Murray, D. M. (1998). Adolescents engaging in unhealthy weight control behaviors: Are they at risk for other health-compromising behaviors? *American Journal of Public Health, 88,* 952–955.

Neville, A. (1980). Temporal adaptation: Application with short-term psychiatric patients. *American Journal of Occupational Therapy, 34,* 328–331.

Neville, A., Kreisberg, A., & Kielhofner, G. (1985). Temporal dysfunction in schizophrenia. *Occupational Therapy in Mental Health, 51,* 1–17.

Nisbett, R. E., Fong, G. T., Lehman, D. R., & Cheng, P. W. (1987). Teaching reasoning. *Science, 238,* 625–631.

O'Malley, M. (1990). *Keeping watch: A history of American time.* New York: Viking Penguin.

Patterson, G. R., & Stouthamer-Loeber, M. (1984). The correlation of family management practices and delinquency. *Child Development, 55,* 1299–1307.

Peters, F. E. (1970). *The harvest of Hellenism: A history of the Near East from Alexander the Great to the triumph of Christianity.* New York: Barnes and Noble.

Petry, N. M., Bickel, W. K., & Arnett, M. (1998). Shortened time horizons and insensitivity to future consequences in opioid-dependent individuals. *Addiction, 93,* 729–738.

Pinker, S. (1997). *How the mind works.* New York: Norton.

Pi-Sunyer, F. X. (1994). The fattening of America. *Journal of the American Medical Association, 272,* 238–239.

Poulos, C. X., Le, A. D., & Parker, J. L. (1995). Impulsivity predicts individual susceptibility to high levels of alcohol self-administration. *Behavioural Pharmacology, 6,* 810–814.

Putnam, R. D. (1995a). Bowling alone: America's declining social capital. *Journal of Democracy, 6,* 65–78.

Putnam, R. D. (1995b). Tuning in, tuning out: The strange disappearance of social capital in America. *Political Science & Politics, 28* 664–682.

Rachlin, H. (1995). Self-control: Beyond commitment. *Behavioral and Brain Sciences, 18,* 109–159.

Rachuba, L., Stanton, B., & Howard, D. (1995). Violent crime in the United States. *Archives of Pediatrics and Adolescent Medicine, 149,* 953–960.

Richman, A. (1977). Ecological studies of narcotic addiction. *The epidemiology of drug abuse: Current Issues* (NIDA Research Monograph No. 10, pp. 173–196). Rockville, MD: National Institute on Drug Abuse.

Robins, L. N., & Ratcliff, K. S. (1979). Continuation of antisocial behavior into adulthood. *International Journal of Mental Health, 7,* 96–116.

Robinson, J. P., & Godbey, G. (1997). *Time for life: The surprising ways Americans use their time.* University Park: The Pennsylvania State University Press.

Robinson, T. N., & Killen, J. D. (1995). Ethnic and gender differences in the relationships between television viewing and obesity, physical activity and dietary fat intake. *Journal of Health Education, 26,* 91–98.

Rosenthal, T. L., Edwards, N. B., Ackerman, B. J., Knott, D. H., & Rosenthal, R. H. (1990). Substance abuse patterns reveal contrasting personality traits. *Journal of Substance Abuse, 2,* 255–263.

Rosenzweig, R. (1983). *Eight hours for what we will: Workers and leisure in an industrial city, 1870–1920.* Cambridge, England: Cambridge University Press.

Rothspan, S., & Read, S. J. (1996). Present versus future time perspective and HIV risk among heterosexual college students. *Health Psychology, 15,* 131–134.

Rydelius, P. A. (1983). Alcohol-abusing teenage boys. *Acta Psychiatrica Scandinavica, 68,* 368–380.

Sahoo, M. K. (1985). Moral reasoning of urban and rural high school students. *Perspectives in Psychological Researches, 8,* 6–9.

Seiden, R. H., & Freitas, R. P. (1980). Shifting patterns of deadly violence. *Suicide and Life-Threatening Behavior, 10,* 195–209.

Senner, W. (Ed.). (1991). *The origins of writing.* Lincoln: University of Nebraska Press.

Smart, R. G., Adlaf, E. M., & Walsh, G. W. (1994). Neighbourhood socio-economic factors in relation to student drug use and programs. *Journal of Child and Adolescent Substance Abuse, 3,* 37–46.

Smith, D. J. (1995). Living conditions in the twentieth century. In M. Rutter & D. J. Smith (Eds.), *Psychological disorders in young people: Time trends and their causes* (pp. 194–295). New York: Wiley.

Smith, M. D. (1986). The era of increased violence in the United States: Age, period, or cohort effect? *Sociological Quarterly, 27,* 239–251.

Solnick, J. V., Kannenberg, C. H., Eckerman, D. A., & Waller, M. B. (1980). An experimental analysis of impulsivity and impulse control in humans. *Learning and Motivation, 11,* 61–77.

South, S. J. (1987) Metropolitan migration and social problems. *Social Science Quarterly, 68,* 3–18.

Stark, R. (1987). Religion and deviance: A new look. In J. M. Day & W. S. Laufer (Eds.), *Crime, values, and religion* (pp. 111–120). Norwood, NJ: Ablex.

Stark, R. (1997). *The rise of Christianity.* Princeton, NJ: Princeton University Press.

Steel, Z., & Blaszczynski, A. (1998). Impulsivity, personality disorders and pathological gambling severity. *Addiction, 93,* 895–905.

Strasburger, V. C. (1992). Children, adolescents, and television. *Pediatric Review, 13,* 144–151.

Strathman, A., Boninger, D. S., Gleicher, F., & Baker, S. M. (1994). Constructing the future with present behavior: An individual difference approach. In Z. Zaleski (Ed.), *Psychology of future orientation* (pp. 107–119). Lublin, Poland: Towarzystwo Naukowe.

Substance Abuse and Mental Health Services Administration. (1996). *Trends in the incidence of drug use in the United States, 1919–1992.* Rockville, MD: U.S. Department of Health and Human Services.

Taras, H. L., Sallis, J. F., Patterson, T. L., Nader, P. R., & Nelson, J. A. (1989). Television's influence on children's diet and physical activity. *Journal of Developmental and Behavioral Pediatrics, 10,* 176–180.

Troiano, R. P., Flegal, K. M., Kuczmarski, R. J., Campbell, S. M., & Johnson, C. L. (1995). Overweight prevalence and trends for children and adolescents. *Archives of Pediatric Medicine, 149,* 1085–1091.

Trommsdorff, G. (1994). Future time perspective and control orientation: Social conditions and consequences. In Z. Zaleski (Ed.), *Psychology of future orientation* (pp. 39–62). Lublin, Poland: Towarzystwo Naukowe.

Trommsdorff, G., Lamm, H., & Schmidt, R. (1978). A longitudinal study of adolescents' future orientation (time perspective). *Journal of Youth and Adolescence, 8,* 131–147.

Truswell, A. S., & Hansen, J. (1976). Medical research among the !Kung. In R. B. Lee & I. DeVore (Eds.), *Kalahari hunter gatherers.* Cambridge, MA: Harvard University Press.

U.S. Department of Justice. (1996). *Sourcebook in criminal justice.* Bureau of Justice Statistics.

Velez, C. N., & Ungemack, J. A. (1989). Drug use among Puerto Rican youth: An exploration of generational status differences. *Social Science and Medicine, 29,* 779–787.

Vitaro, F., Ferland, F., Jacques, C., & Ladouceur, R. (1998). Gambling, substance use, and impulsivity during adolescence. *Psychology of Addictive Behaviors, 12,* 185–194.

Vuchinich, R. E., & Simpson, C. A. (1998). Hyperbolic temporal discounting in social drinkers and problem drinkers. *Experimental and Clinical Psychopharmacology, 6,* 292–305.

Vuchinich, R. E., & Tucker, J. A. (1988). Contributions from behavioral theories of choice to an analysis of alcohol abuse. *Journal of Abnormal Psychology, 97,* 181–195.

Vukov, M., Baba-Milkic, N., Lecic, D., Mijalkovic, S., & Marinkovic, J. (1995). Personality dimensions of opiate addicts. *Acta Psychiatrica Scandinavica, 91,* 103–107.

Wallace, M. (1956). Future time perspective in schizophrenia. *Journal of Abnormal Social Psychology, 52,* 240–245.

Wallace, R., Thompson Fullilove, M., & Wallace, D. (1992). Family systems and deurbanization: Implications for substance abuse. In J. H. Lowinson (Ed.), *Substance abuse: A comprehensive textbook* (pp. 944–955). Baltimore: Williams and Wilkins.

Warner, L. A., Kessler, R. C., Hughes, M., Anthony, J. C., & Nelson, C. B. (1995). Prevalence and correlates of drug use and dependence in the United States. *Archives of General Psychiatry, 52,* 219–229.

Wells, J. E., Bushnell, J. A., Joyce, P. R., Hornblow, A. R., & Oakley-Browne, M. A. (1992). Alcohol abuse and dependence in New Zealand. In J. E. Helzer & G. J. Canino (Eds.), *Alcoholism in North America, Europe, and Asia* (pp. 199–214). New York: Oxford University Press.

Whitehead, A. N. (1929). *The aims of education and other essays.* New York: New American Library.

Whitrow, G. J. (1989). *Time in history: Views of time from prehistory to the present day.* New York: Oxford University Press.

Williams, T. M. (Ed.). (1986). *The impact of television: A natural experiment in three communities.* Orlando, FL: Academic Press.

Wilson, J. Q., & Herrnstein, R. J. (1985). *Crime and human nature.* New York: Touchstone.

Wilson, M., & Daly, M. (1997). Life expectancy, economic inequality, homicide, and reproductive timing in Chicago neighbourhoods. *British Medical Journal, 314,* 1271–1274.

Wittchen, H. U., & Bronisch, T. (1992). Alcohol use, abuse, and dependency in West Germany: Lifetime and six month prevalence in the Munich follow-up study. In J. E. Helzer & G. J. Canino (Eds.), *Alcoholism in North America, Europe, and Asia* (pp. 159–181). New York: Oxford University Press.

Yarcheski, A., Mahon, N. E., & Yarcheski, T. J. (1997). Alternate models of positive health practices in adolescents. *Nursing Research, 46,* 85–92.

Yeh, E. K., & Hwu, H. G. (1992). Alcoholism in Taiwan Chinese communities. In J. E. Helzer & G. J. Canino (Eds.), *Alcoholism in North America, Europe, and Asia* (pp. 215–246). New York: Oxford University Press.

Zayas, L. H. (1995). Family functioning and child rearing in an urban environment. *Developmental and Behavioral Pediatrics, 16,* 21–24.

Zehr, H. (1976). *Crime and the development of modern society: Patterns of criminality in nineteenth-century Germany and France.* London: Croom Helm.

Zimmerman, M. A., & Maton, K. I. (1992). Life-style and substance use among male African-American urban adolescents: A cluster analytic approach. *American Journal of Community Psychology, 20,* 121–138.

Author Index

Valenstein, E. S, 71
Valoski, A. M., 302, 308

vanRee, J. M., 66, 71
Vara, L. S., 297, 298, 301, 302, 304, 308
Vaughn, B. E., 178
Vaughan, W., 145, 146
Velez, C. N., 365
Venezia, I., 322
Vigorito, M., 141
Villar, J., 128
deVilliers, P. A., 147
Vissandjee, B., 242
Vitaro, F., 376
Vito, D., 302
Volberg, R. A., 316, 332, 333
Volpe, J. S., 168, 296
Vuchinich, R. E., 16, 63, 79, 138, 151, 196, 198, 201, 203, 205, 210, 211, 226, 231, 256, 272, 283, 343, 344, 377
Vukov, M., 377

W

Wagner, E. F., 375
Waldron, I., 132
Walker, M. B., 332
Wallace, D., 360
Wallace, M., 377
Wallace, R., 360, 362, 375
Wallace, R. B., 248
Waller, M. B., 178, 346
Walsh, B. T., 182
Wanberg, K. W., 237, 240
Wanchisen, B. A., 158
Wan, T. T., 248
Wantanabe, Y., 255
Warner, L. A., 368
Warren, G., 237
Warren-Boulton, F. R., 50
Wasserman, J., 93, 94, 95
Watson, D. S, 27
Wearden, J., H., 171
Webley, P., 179
Webster, M. M., 185

Wechsler, H., 8, 93, 95
Weeks, M. G., 200
Weier, F., 345
Weingarten, H. P., 181
Weinstein, S., 235
Weir, H., 355
Weisner, C., 227
Weiss, R. D., 81
Weiss, S. M., 227
Weissman, M. M., 371
Welch, W. R., 118
Welker, R. L., 380
Wellman, P. J., 75
Wells, J. E., 367, 372
Welty, W. R., 315
West, R. J., 282
Westall, R., 363
Westenhoefer, J., 294
Westman, E. C., 286
White, C. C., 297
White, S. L., 245, 252
Whitehead, A. N., 382
Whitney, C. W., 225, 232, 254, 255
Whitrow, G. J., 351, 352
Wierzbicki, M., 231
Wight, J. B., 225
Wikler, A., 45
Willet, W., 118
Williams, T. M., 359
Willis, N., 282
Wilson, J. Q., 373, 374
Wilson, M., 362
Winkler, J., 93
Winkler, R. C., 4
Winger, G., 31, 33, 34, 35, 36, 266
Winquist, J., 203, 208
Winston, G., 90
Wise, R. A, 75, 76, 81
Wiseman, M. J., 118
Wisnieswski, L., 302
Wittchen, H. U., 367
Wolfgang, A. F., 317
Wolffgramm, J., 151
Wolinski, F. D., 254
Wolkon, G. H., 238
Woods, J. H., 33
Woody, G., 240

Subject Index

A

Addiction, see also Alcohol Abuse, Drug Abuse, Gambling, and Smoking
    economic models, 89–107, 53–56, *see also* Economic models of addiction
    opponent process, 147–148
    Rational Addiction Theory, 89, 92–105
    Relative Addiction Theory, 145–162
        primrose path, 150–156
        reinforcement, 156–158
    and self-control, 183–184
    and temporal horizon, 367–369
    tolerance, 148
    treatment, 45–56
        with agonist therapy, 47–48
        with antagonist therapy, 48–50
        and delayed reward discounting, 17–20
        for gambling, 334–335
        and income, 21–22
        and relative addiction, 158–162
        for smoking, 272–288
Alcohol Abuse, *see also* Addiction
    and alternative reinforcers, 16,50–56
    and delayed reward discounting, 201–203
    and demand, 11–12, 96–100
    economic models of, 96–100
    and myopia, 91
    prevention, 105–107
    Rational Addiction Theory, 92–105
    Relative Addiction Theory, 145–162
    and self-control, 183–184

and substitutability, 139–139
    and temporal horizon, 367–369
    tolerance, 91, 148
    withdrawal, 91–92
Alternative reinforcers, 12–16
    compliments, 14–15, 41, 103, 267
    exercise, 282–283
    food, 282–283, 299
    independents, 14
    for smoking, 280–284
    substitutes, 13–14, 37–43, 103, 267, 278–280
    substitution of nondrug reinforcers and drug self-administration, 68–74
    substitution of nondrug reinforcers and reinstatement of drug self-administration, 79–82
    treatment implications, 16, 50–56

B

Behavioral Economics
    definition, 5–6
        goods, 6
        services, 6
        reinforcer, 6
    and drug abuse, 53–56
    and fat consumption, 118–127
        and substitutes, 119–128
    and food choice, 117–118, 127–128
    and food intake, 293–308
    and health behavior, 27–60, 56, 90–93, 115–141
    and health care utilization, 228–257
    history, 4–6
    and public policy, 53–55
    and smoking, 265–288